PrincetonReview.com

THE BEST 169 LAW SCHOOLS

2014 EDITION

**Eric Owens, Esq., John Owens, Esq.,
Jennifer Adams, Andrea Kornstein,
and The Staff
of The Princeton Review**

*Random House, Inc.
New York*

TPR Education IP Holdings, LLC
111 Speen Street, Suite 550
Framingham, MA 01701
E-mail: editorialsupport@review.com

ISBN: 978-0-8041-2434-8
ISSN: 2161-5764

Senior VP, Publisher: Robert Franek
Production: Best Content Solutions, LLC
Production Editor: Lee Elder
Content Manager: David Soto
Editor: Kristen O'Toole

9 8 7 6 5 4 3 2 1

2014 Edition

Editorial

Robert Franek, VP Test Prep Books, Publisher
Selena Coppock, Senior Editor
Calvin Cato, Editor
Meave Shelton, Editor
Kristen O'Toole, Editor
Alyssa Wolff, Editorial Assistant

Random House Publishing Team
Tom Russell, Publisher
Nicole Benhabib, Publishing Manager
Ellen L. Reed, Production Manager
Alison Stoltzfus, Managing Editor
Erika Pepe, Associate Production Manager
Kristin Lindner, Production Supervisor
Andrea Lau, Designer

ACKNOWLEDGMENTS

Thanks to Laura Braswell and Kristen O'Toole for their support and guidance on this book and to Bob Spruill for his LSAT expertise.

In addition, many thanks should go to David Soto and Stephen Koch for spearheading the law school data collection efforts. Their survey allowed for the completion of a totally cohesive stat-packed guide.

A special thanks must go to our production team: Scott Harris and Lee Elder. Your commitment, flexibility, and attention to detail are always appreciated in both perfect and crunch times.

—Eric Owens

I'd like to send my thanks:

To Eric Owens, my quasi-cousin, who kept me in mind for this project.

To my editors at The Princeton Review, who trusted me (and the other Eric Owens) enough to give me the chance.

To my family and friends, who support me in the things I do.

To the law students who took the time to complete the law student survey.

—John Owens

ABOUT THE AUTHORS

Eric Owens, Esq., attended Cornell College for his undergraduate degree and Loyola University—Chicago for law school. He is now an American diplomat.

John Owens, Esq., earned his undergraduate degree in accountancy at the University of Illinois, Urbana-Champaign. He then matriculated at Loyola University—Chicago School of Law, where he earned his JD. John works in the tax department of a Chicago law firm. He is currently working on a book, which he hopes to finish up this year. In his spare time, John likes to rock.

CONTENTS

PREFACE

Welcome to *The Best 169 Law Schools*, The Princeton Review's truly indispensable guide for anyone thinking about entering the law school fray. This is not simply a reprint of the garden-variety fluff in each law school's admissions booklet. We have attempted to provide a significant amount of essential information from a vast array of sources to give you a complete, accurate, and easily digestible snapshot of the best law schools in the country. Here you'll find a wealth of practical advice on admissions, taking and acing the Law School Admission Test (LSAT), choosing the right school, and doing well once you're there. You'll also find all the information you need on schools' bar exam pass rates, ethnic group and gender breakdown percentages, tuition, average starting salaries of graduates, and much more. For 169 ABA-approved law schools, you'll find descriptive profiles of the student experience based on the opinions of the only true law school experts: current law school students. Indeed, with this handy reference, you should be able to narrow your choices from the few hundred law schools in North America to a handful in no time at all.

Never trust any single source of information too much, though—not even us. Take advantage of all the resources available to you, including friends, family members, the Internet, and your local library. Obviously, the more you explore all the options available to you, the better decision you'll make. We hope you will be happy wherever you end up and that this guide will be helpful in your search to find the best law school for you.

Best of luck!

ALL ABOUT LAW SCHOOL

CHAPTER 1
So You Want to Go to Law School

Congrats! Law school is a tremendous intellectual challenge and an amazing experience. It can be confusing and occasionally traumatic—especially during the crucial first year—but the cryptic ritual of legal education will make you a significantly better thinker, a consummate reader, and a far more mature person over the course of three years.

The application process is rigorous, but it's not impossible. Here's our advice.

WHAT MAKES A COMPETITIVE APPLICANT?
It depends. One of the great things about law schools in the United States is that there are a lot of them, and standards for admission run the gamut from appallingly difficult to not very hard at all.

Let's just say, for example, you have your heart set on Yale Law School, arguably the finest law school in all the land. Let's also say you have stellar academic credentials: a 3.45 GPA and an LSAT score in the 99th percentile. With these heady numbers, you've got a whopping 2 percent chance of getting into Yale, at best. However, with the same 3.45 GPA and LSAT score in the 99th percentile, you are pretty much a lock at legal powerhouses like Duke University School of Law and Boston College Law School. With significantly lower numbers—say, a 3.02 GPA and an LSAT score in the 81st percentile—you stand a mediocre chance of getting into top-flight law schools like Case Western or Indiana. With a little bit of luck, these numbers might land you a spot at George Washington or UCLA.

> ### *Essential Acronyms*
> *LSAC: Law School Admission Council,*
> *headquartered in beautiful Newtown, PA*
> *LSAT: Law School Admission Test*
> *CAS: Credential Assembly Service*
> *ABA: American Bar Association*

This is good news. The even better news is that there are several totally respectable law schools out there that will let you in with a 2.5 GPA and an LSAT of 148 (which is about the 36th percentile). If you end up in the top 10 percent of your class at one of these schools and have even a shred of interviewing skill, you'll get a job that is just as prestigious and pays just as much money as the jobs garnered by Yale grads. Notice the important catch here, however: You *must* graduate in the top 10 percent of your class at so-called "lesser" schools, while almost every Yale Law grad who wants a high-paying job can land one.

Ultimately, there's a law school out there for you. If you want to get into a "top-flight" or "pretty good" school, you're in for some fairly stiff competition. Unfortunately, it doesn't help that the law school admissions process is somewhat formulaic; your LSAT score and your GPA are vastly more important to the process than anything else about you. If your application ends up in the "maybe" pile, your recommendations, your major, the reputation of your college alma mater, a well-written and nongeneric essay, and various other factors will play a larger role in determining your fate.

THE ADMISSIONS INDEX
The first thing most law schools will look at when evaluating your application is your "index." It's a number (which varies from school to school) made up of a weighted combination of your undergraduate GPA and LSAT score. In virtually every case, the LSAT is weighted more heavily than the GPA.

While the process differs from school to school, it is generally the case that your index will put you into one of three piles:

(Probably) Accepted. A select few applicants with high LSAT scores and stellar GPAs are admitted pretty much automatically. If your index is very, very strong compared with the school's median or target number, you're as good as in, unless you are a convicted felon or you wrote your personal statement in crayon.

(Probably) Rejected. If your index is very weak compared with the school's median or target number, you are probably going to be rejected without much ado. When Admissions Officers read weaker applications (yes, at almost every school every application is read) they will be looking for something so outstanding or unique that it makes them willing to take a chance. Factors that can help include ethnic background, where you are from, or very impressive work or life experience. That said, don't hold your breath because not many people in this category are going to make the cut.

Well . . . Maybe. The majority of applicants fall in the middle; their index number is right around the median or target index number. People in this category have decent enough LSAT scores and GPAs for the school, but not high enough for automatic admission. Why do most people fall into this category? For the most part, people apply to schools they think they have at least a shot of getting into based on their grades and LSAT scores; Yale doesn't see very many applicants who got a 140 on the LSAT. What will determine the fate of those whose applications hang in the balance? One thing law schools often look at is the competitiveness of your undergraduate program. On the one hand, someone with a 3.3 GPA in an easy major from a school where everybody graduates with a 3.3 or higher will face an uphill battle. On the other hand, someone with the same GPA in a difficult major from a school that has a reputation for being stingy with A's is in better shape. Admissions Officers will also pore over the rest of your application—personal statement, letters of recommendation, resume, etc.—for reasons to admit you, reject you, or put you on their waiting lists.

ARE YOU MORE THAN YOUR LSAT SCORE?

Aside from LSAT scores and GPAs, what do law schools consider when deciding who's in and who's out? It's the eternal question. On the one hand, we should relieve you hidebound cynics of the notion that they care about nothing else. On the other hand, if you harbor fantasies that a stunning application can overcome truly substandard scores and grades, you should realize that such hopes are unrealistic.

Nonquantitative factors are particularly important at law schools that receive applications from thousands of numerically qualified applicants. A "top ten law school that receives ten or fifteen applications for every spot in its first-year class has no choice but to "look beyond the numbers," as admissions folks are fond of saying. Such a school will almost surely have to turn away hundreds of applicants with near-perfect LSAT scores and college grades, and those applicants who get past the initial cut will be subjected to real scrutiny.

Less competitive schools are just as concerned, in their own way, with "human criteria" as are the Harvards and Stanfords of the world. They are on the lookout for capable people who have relatively unimpressive GPAs and LSAT scores. The importance of the application is greatly magnified for these students, who must demonstrate their probable success in law school in other ways.

CAN PHYSICS MAJORS GO TO LAW SCHOOL?

"What about my major?" is one of the more popular questions we hear when it comes to law school admissions. The conventional answer to this question goes something like, "There is no prescribed, pre-law curriculum, but you should seek a broad and challenging liberal arts education, etc."

Translation: It really doesn't matter what you major in. Obviously, a major in aviation or hotel and restaurant management is not exactly ideal, but please—we beg you!—don't feel restricted to a few majors simply because you want to attend law school. This is especially true if those particular majors do not interest you. Comparative literature? Fine. American studies? Go to town. Physics? No problem whatsoever. You get the idea.

Think about it. Because most would-be law students end up majoring in the *same* few fields (e.g., political science and philosophy), their applications all look the *same* to the folks in law school Admissions Offices. You want to stand out, which is why it is a good idea to major in something *different*. Ultimately, you should major in whatever appeals to you. Of course, if you want to major in political science or philosophy (or you already have), well, that's fine too.

DOES GRAD SCHOOL COUNT?

Your grades in graduate school will not be included in the calculation of your GPA (only the UGPA, the undergraduate grade point average, is reported to the schools) but will be taken into account separately by an Admissions Committee if you make them available. Reporting grad school grades would be to your advantage, particularly if they are better than your college grades. Admissions Committees are likely to take this as a sign of maturation.

ADVICE FOR THE "NONTRADITIONAL" APPLICANT

The term "nontraditional" is, of course, used to describe applicants who are a few years or many years older than run-of-the-mill law school applicants.

In a nutshell, there's no time like the present to start law school. While it's true that most law students are in their early to mid-twenties, if you aren't, don't think for a minute that your age will keep you from getting in and having a great experience. Applicants for full-time and part-time slots at U.S. law schools range in ages from twenty-one to seventy-one and include every age in between. Some of these older applicants always intended to go to law school and simply postponed it to work, travel, or start a family. Other older applicants never seriously considered law school until after they were immersed in other occupations.

Part-time attendance is especially worth checking into if you've been out of college for a few years. Also, dozens of law schools offer evening programs—particularly in urban centers.

Waiting Lists

If a law school puts you on its waiting list, it means you may be admitted depending on how many of the applicants they've already admitted decide to go to another school. Most schools rank students on their waiting list; they'll probably tell you where you stand if you give them a call. Also, note that schools routinely admit students from their waiting lists in late August. If you are on a school's waiting list and you really, really want to go there, keep your options at least partially open. You just might be admitted in the middle of first-year orientation.

MINORITY LAW SCHOOL APPLICANTS

Things are definitely looking up for minority applicants. According to figures published by the American Bar Association's Committee on Legal Education, in 1978 more than 90 percent of the law students in the ABA-approved schools were white. In recent years, however, the number of non-whites enrolled in law school has more than doubled, from about 10 percent to nearly 23 percent. Taking an even longer view, figures have tripled since 1972, when minority enrollment was only 6.6 percent. These days, the American Bar Association and the legal profession in general seem pretty committed to seeking and admitting applicants who are members of historically underrepresented minority groups.

WOMEN IN LAW SCHOOL

During the past decade, the number of female lawyers has grown, and women undeniably have become more visible in the uppermost echelons of the field. According to ABA employment statistics, women comprise a full third of the legal profession, and hold over a quarter of judgeships at the federal and state levels. In the 2011–2012 academic year, women made up 46.7 percent of students enrolled in law school.

Gender discrimination certainly lingers here and there. You might want to check certain statistics for the law schools you are interested in, such as the percentage of women on Law Review and the percentage of female professors who are tenured or on track to be tenured. (According to the ABA statistics on law school faculty and staff, in 2010–2011, women held 30.8 percent of tenured positions and almost half—48 percent—of tenure-track positions.) Also, visit each law school and talk with students and professors about their experiences. Finally, see if the school has published any gender studies about itself. If it has, you should check those out, too.

Engineering and Math Majors Make Great Law Students

A disproportionate number of law students with backgrounds in the so-called "hard sciences" (math, physics, engineering, etc.) earn very high grades in law school, probably because they are trained to think methodically and efficiently about isolated problems (as law students are supposed to do on exams).

YOUR CHANCE OF ACCEPTANCE

Who knows how law schools end up with their reputations? Everything else being equal, you really do want to go a to a well-respected school. It will enhance your employment opportunities tremendously. Remember, whoever you are and whatever your background, your best bet is to select a couple of "reach" schools, a couple of schools at which you've got a good shot at being accepted, and a couple of "safety" schools where you are virtually assured acceptance. Remember also that being realistic about your chances will save you from unnecessary emotional letdowns. Getting in mostly boils down to numbers. Look at the acceptance rates and the average LSATs and GPAs of incoming classes at various schools to assess how you stack up.

CHAPTER 2
CHOOSING A LAW SCHOOL

There are some key things you should consider before randomly selecting schools from around the country or just submitting your application to somebody else's list of the Top 10 law schools.

LOCATION

It's a big deal. If you were born and raised in the state of New Mexico, care deeply about the "Land of Enchantment," wish to practice law there, and want to be the governor someday, then your best bet is to go to the University of New Mexico. A school's reputation is usually greater on its home turf than anywhere else (except for some of the larger-than-life schools, like Harvard and Yale). Also, most law schools tend to teach law that is specific to the statutes of the states in which they are located. Knowledge of the eccentricities of state law will help you immensely three years down the road when it comes time to pass the bar exam. Even further, the Career Services Office at your school will be strongly connected to the local legal industry. As a purely practical matter, it will be much easier to find a job and get to interviews in Boston, for example, if you live there. Still another reason to consider geographical location is the simple fact that you'll put down professional and social roots and get to know many really great people throughout your law school career. Leaving them won't be any fun. Finally, starting with geographic limitations is the easiest way to reduce your number of potential schools dramatically.

SPECIALIZATION

Word has it that specialization is the trend of the future. General practitioners in law are becoming less common, so it makes sense to let future lawyers begin to specialize in school. At certain schools, you may receive your JD with an official emphasis in, say, taxation. Specialization is a particularly big deal at smaller or newer schools whose graduates cannot simply get by on their school's reputation. Just between us, it's kind of hard to specialize in anything at most law schools because every graduate has to take this huge exam—the bar—that tests about a dozen topics. Most of your course selections will (and should) be geared toward passing the bar, which leaves precious few hours for specialization. You'll almost certainly specialize, but it's not something to worry about until you actually look for a job. All of that said, if you already know what kind of law you want to specialize in, you're in good shape. Many schools offer certain specialties because of their locations. If you are very interested in environmental law, you'd be better off going to Vermont Law School or Lewis and Clark's Northwestern School of Law than to Brooklyn Law School. Similarly, if you want to work with children as an attorney, check out Loyola University Chicago's Child Law Center. So look at what you want to do in addition to where you want to do it.

JOINT-DEGREE PROGRAMS

In addition to offering specialized areas of study, many law schools have instituted formal dual-degree programs. These schools, nearly all of which are directly affiliated with a parent institution, offer students the opportunity to pursue a JD while also working toward some other degree. Although the JD/MBA combination is the most popular joint-degree sought, many universities offer a JD program combined with degrees in everything from public policy to public administration to social work. In today's perpetually competitive legal market, dual degrees may make some students more marketable for certain positions. However, don't sign up for a dual-degree program on a whim—they require a serious amount of work and often a serious amount of tuition.

Dean's List

According to a letter signed by just about every dean of every ABA-approved law school in the country, the following are the factors you should consider when choosing a law school:

- Breadth and support of alumni network
- Breadth of curriculum
- Clinical programs
- Collaborative research opportunities with faculty
- Commitment to innovative technology
- Cost
- Externship options
- Faculty accessibility
- Intensity of writing instruction
- Interdisciplinary programs
- International programming
- Law library strengths and services
- Loan repayment assistance for low-income lawyers
- Location
- Part-time enrollment options
- Public interest programs
- Quality of teaching
- Racial and gender diversity within the faculty and student body
- Religious affiliation
- Size of first-year classes
- Skills instruction
- Specialized areas of faculty expertise

YOUR CHANCE OF ACCEPTANCE

Who knows how law schools end up with their reputations? Everything else being equal, you really do want to go a to a well-respected school. It will enhance your employment opportunities tremendously. Remember, whoever you are and whatever your background, your best bet is to select a couple of "reach" schools, a couple of schools at which you've got a good shot at being accepted, and a couple of "safety" schools where you are virtually assured acceptance. Remember also that being realistic about your chances will save you from unnecessary emotional letdowns. Getting in mostly boils down to numbers. Look at the acceptance rates and the average LSATs and GPAs of incoming classes at various schools to assess how you stack up.

The Dreaded Bar Exam

Once you graduate, most states require you to take a bar exam before you can practice law. Some state bar exams are really, really hard; New York's and California's are examples. If you don't want to take a bar exam, consider a law school in beautiful Wisconsin. Anyone who graduates from a state-certified Wisconsin law school does not need to take the state bar exam to practice law in the Badger State, as long as they are approved by the Board of Bar Examiners.

PERSONAL APPEAL

A student at a prominent law school in the Pacific Northwest once described his law school to us as "a combination wood-grain bomb shelter and Ewok village." Another student at a Northeastern law school told us her law school was fine except for its "ski-slope classrooms" and "East German Functionalist" architecture. While the curricula at various law schools are pretty much the same, the weather, the surrounding neighborhoods, the nightlife, and the character of the student populations are startlingly different. An important part of any graduate program is enjoying those moments in life when you're not studying. If you aren't comfortable in the environment you choose, it's likely to be reflected in the quality of work you do and your attitude. Before you make a $10,000 to $130,000 investment in any law school, you really ought to check it out in person. While you are there, talk to students and faculty. Walk around. Kick the tires. *Then* make a decision.

EMPLOYMENT PROSPECTS

Where do alumni work? How much money do they make? What percentage of graduates is employed within nine months of graduation? How many major law firms interview on campus? These are massively important questions, and you owe it to yourself to look into the answers before choosing a school.

YOUR VALUES

It is important that you be honest about defining your criteria for judging law schools. What do you want out of a law school? Clout? A high salary? A hopping social life? To live in a certain city? To avoid being in debt up to your eyeballs? A non-competitive atmosphere? Think about it.

MAKE A LIST

Using these criteria (and others you find relevant), develop a list of prospective schools. Ideally, you'll find this book useful in creating the list. Assign a level to each new school you add (something like *reach*, *good shot*, and *safety*).

At your *reach* schools, the average LSAT scores and GPAs of incoming students should be higher than yours. These are law schools that will probably not accept you based on your numbers alone. In order to get in, you'll need to wow them with everything else (e.g., personal statement, stellar recommendations, work experience).

Did You Know?

According to the people who take the LSAT, the average applicant applies to four or more law schools.

Your *good shot* schools should be the schools you like that accept students with about the same LSAT scores and GPA as yours. Combined with a strong and *cohesive* application, you've got a decent shot at getting into these schools.

At your *safety* schools, the average LSAT scores and GPAs of current students should be below yours. These schools should accept you pretty painlessly if there are no major blemishes on your application (e.g., a serious run-in with the law).

CHAPTER 3
APPLYING TO LAW SCHOOL

Our advice: Start early. The LSAT alone can easily consume eighty or more hours of prep time, and completing a single application form might take as many as thirty hours if you take great care with the essay questions. Don't sabotage your efforts through last-minute sloppiness or by allowing this already-annoying process to become a gigantic burden.

WHEN TO APPLY

Yale Law School's most recent final due date was March 1, but Loyola University—Chicago's School of Law was accepting your application materials up to March 31. There is no regular pattern. However, the longer you wait to apply to a school, regardless of its deadline, the worse your chances of getting into that school may be. No efficient admissions staff is going to wait to receive all the applications before starting to make their selections.

If you're reading this in December and hope to get into a law school for next fall but haven't done anything about it, you're in big trouble. If you've got an LSAT score you are happy with, you're in less trouble. However, your applications will get to the law schools after the optimum time and, let's face it, they may appear a little rushed. The best time to think about applying is early in the year. Methodically take care of one thing at a time, and *finish by December*.

Early Admissions Options. A few schools have Early Admissions options (for instance, New York University's Early Decision deadline is November 15), so you may know by December if you've been accepted. Early Admission is a good idea for a few reasons. It can give you an indication of what your chances are at other schools. It can relieve the stress of waiting until April to see where you'll be spending the next three years of your life. Also, it's better to get wait listed in December than in April (or whenever you would be notified for regular admission); if there is a "tie" among applicants on the waiting list, they'll probably admit whoever applied first. Of course, not every school's Early Admission option is the same (and many schools don't even have one), so do your research. Keep in mind that some Early Admission offers (such as NYU's) are binding. If the decision is binding, you should only apply early if you are certain you want to attend a particular school.

Rolling Admissions. Many law schools evaluate applications and notify applicants of admission decisions continuously over the course of several months (ordinarily from late fall to midsummer). Obviously, if you apply to one of these schools, it is vital that you apply as early as possible because there will be more spots available at the beginning of the process.

Applying Online. Almost all law schools allow applicants to submit applications online. The LSAC online service (LSAC.org) has a searchable database and applications to ABA-approved schools.

LAW SCHOOL ADMISSION COUNCIL: THE LAW SCHOOL APPLICATION SOURCE

In addition to single-handedly creating and administering the LSAT, an organization called the Law School Admissions Council (LSAC) maintains the communication between you and virtually every law school in the United States. It runs the Credential Assembly Service (CAS), which provides information (in a standard format) on applicants to the law schools. They—not you—send your grades, your LSAT score, and plenty of other information about you to the schools. You'll send only your actual applications directly to the law schools themselves. Oh, by the way, the fee for this service is $155 of your hard-earned money plus $21 very time you want CAS to send a report about you to an additional law school.

THE BIG HURDLES IN THE APPLICATION PROCESS: A BRIEF OVERVIEW

Take the LSAT. The Law School Admission Test is a roughly three-and-a-half-hour multiple-choice test used by law schools to help them select candidates. The LSAT is given in February, June, October (or, occasionally, late September), and December of each year. It's divided into five multiple-choice sections and one writing sample. All ABA-approved and most non-ABA-approved law schools in the United States and Canada require an LSAT score from each and every applicant.

Register for CAS. You can register for the Law School Data Assembly Service at the same time you register to take the LSAT; all necessary forms are contained in the *LSAT and CAS Registration Information Book* (hence the name). It can also be done, of course, online.

Get applications from six or seven schools. Why so many? Because it's better to be safe than sorry. As early as July, select a couple of *reach* schools, a couple of schools to which you've got a good shot at being accepted, and a couple of *safety* schools to which you are virtually assured of acceptance. Your safety school—if you were being realistic—will probably accept you pretty quickly. It may take a while to get a final decision from the other schools, but you won't be totally panicked because you'll know your safety school is there for you. If, for whatever reason, your grades or LSAT score is extremely low, you should apply to several safety schools. Most schools won't post online applications until mid-September at the earliest. Still, it is a good idea to familiarize yourself with the previous year's applications as soon as possible, as law schools tend not to radically alter components of their applications from one year to the next.

Write your personal statement. With any luck, you'll only have to write one personal statement. Many, many schools will simply ask you the same basic question: "Why do you want to obtain a law degree?" However, just in case you need to write several personal statements and essays, you need to select your schools fairly early.

Obtain two or three recommendations. Some schools will ask for two recommendations, both of which must be academic. Others want more than two recommendations and want at least one to be from someone who knows you outside traditional academic circles. As part of your CAS file, the LSAC will accept up to three letters of recommendation on your behalf, and they will send them to all the schools to which you apply. This is one of the few redeeming qualities of the LSAC. The last thing the writers of your recommendations are going to want to do is sign, package, and send copies of their letters all over the continent.

Update/create your resume. Most law school applicants ask that you submit a resume. Make sure yours is up to date and suitable for submission to an academic institution. Put your academic credentials and experience first—no matter what they are. This is just a supplement to the rest of the material; it's probably the simplest part of the application process.

Get your academic transcripts sent to CAS. When you subscribe to CAS, you must request that the Registrar at every undergraduate, graduate, and professional school you ever attended send an official transcript to Law Services. Don't even think about sending your own transcripts anywhere; these people don't trust you any farther than they can throw you. *Make these requests in August.* If you're applying Early Decision, start requesting transcripts as early as May. Law schools require complete files before making their decisions, and CAS won't send your information to the law schools without your transcripts. Undergraduate institutions can and will screw up and delay the transcript process—even when you go there personally and pay them to provide your records. Give yourself some time to fix problems should they arise.

Write any necessary addenda. An addendum is a brief explanatory letter written to explain or support a "deficient" portion of your application. If your personal and academic life has been fairly smooth, you won't need to include any addenda with your application. If, however, you were ever on academic probation, arrested, or if you have a low GPA, you may need to write one. Other legitimate addenda topics are a low/discrepant LSAT score, DUI/DWI suspensions, or any time gap in your academic or professional career.

An addendum is absolutely not the place to go off on a rant about the fundamental unfairness of the LSAT or how that evil campus security officer was only out to get you when you got arrested. If, for example, you have taken the LSAT two or three times and simply did not do very well, even after spending time and money preparing with a test prep company or a private tutor, simply tell the Admissions Committee that you worked diligently to achieve a high score. Say you explored all possibilities to help you achieve that goal. Whatever the case, lay out the facts, but let them draw their own conclusions. Be brief and balanced. Be fair. Do not go into unneccessary detail. Explain the problem and state what you did about it. This is no time to whine.

CAS Fees

CAS Basic Fee: $155

CAS Law School Reports: $21 each

A Legal Education: Priceless

Fee Waivers

Taking the LSAT, subscribing to CAS, and applying to law Taking the LSAT, registering for the LSAC's CAS, and applying to law schools at $50 to $100 per application will cost you an arm and a leg (though these costs are but a drop in the bucket compared to the amount of money you are about to spend on your law school education). If you are financially strapped and are accepted into the LSAC fee waiver program, you get to take two LSATs and register for the CAS free of charge. You also get four CAS law school reports and a complimentary copy of the *Official LSAT SuperPrep®*. You can download a Fee Waiver form at www.lsac.org or request to have one sent to you by calling 215-968-1001.

Send in your seat deposit. Once you are accepted at a particular school, that school will ask you to put at least some money down to hold your place in that year's class. A typical fee runs $200 or more. This amount will be credited to your first-term tuition once you actually register for classes.

Do any other stuff. You may find that there are other steps you must take during the law school application process. You may request a fee waiver, for example. Also make sure to get a copy of the LSAC's *LSAT/CAS Registration and Information Book*, which is unquestionably the most useful tool in applying to law school. It has the forms you'll need, a sample LSAT, admissions information, the current Law Forum schedule, and sample application schedules.

LAW SCHOOL APPLICATION CHECKLIST (suitable for framing)	
January	• **Take a practice LSAT.** Do it at a library or wherever you won't be interrupted. Also, take it all at once.
February	• **Investigate LSAT prep courses.** If you don't take one with The Princeton Review, do *something*. Just as with any test, you'll get a higher score on this one if you prepare for it first.
March	• **Obtain an *LSAT/CAS Registration and Information Book*.** The books are generally published in March of each year. You can get one at any law school, by calling the LSAC at 215-968-1001, or by stopping by The Princeton Review office nearest you. You can also download one in a PDF format at www.lsac.org.
April	• **Register for the June LSAT.** • **Begin an LSAT prep course.** At the very, very least, use some books or software.
May	• **Continue your LSAT prep.**
June	• **Take the LSAT.** If you take the test twice, many schools will average them. Your best bet is to take it once, do exceedingly well, and get it out of your hair forever.
July	• **Register for CAS.** • **Research law schools.**
August	• **Obtain law school applications.** You can call or write, but the easiest and cheapest way to get applicationa is via the Internet. This is, of course, only necessary if you plan to send in paper applications. Go to Lsac.org to access and submit online applications. • **Get your undergraduate transcripts sent to LSDAS.** Make sure to contact the registrar at each undergraduate institution you attended.
September	• **Write your personal statements.** Proofread them. Edit them. Edit them again. Have someone else look them over for all the mistakes you missed. • **Update your resume,** or create a resume if you don't have one. • **Get your recommendations in order.** You want your professors to submit recommendations exactly when you send your applications (in October and November).
October	• **Complete and send early decision applications.**
November	• **Complete and send all regular applications.**
December	• **Chill.** • **Buy holiday gifts.** • **Make plans for New Year's.**

CHAPTER 4
THE LSAT

As you may know, we at The Princeton Review are pretty skeptical of most of the standardized tests out there. They make us a lot of money, of course, and we like that, but they are hideously poor indicators of anything besides how well you do on that particular standardized test. They are certainly not intelligence tests. The LSAT is no exception. It is designed to keep you out of law school, not facilitate your entrance into it. For no good reason we can think of, this 125-question test is *the single most important factor in all of law school admissions*, and, at least for the foreseeable future, we're all stuck with it.

Unfortunately, with the possible exception of the MCAT (for medical school), the LSAT is the toughest of all the standardized tests. Only 24 to 26 of the 125 questions have a "correct" answer (Logic Games), as opposed to Arguments and Reading Comprehension, for which you must choose the elusive "best" answer. As ridiculous as they are, the GMAT, GRE, SAT, MCAT, and ACT at least have large chunks of math or science on them. There are verifiably correct answers on these tests, and occasionally you even have to know something to get the right answers. *Only the LSAT requires almost no specific knowledge of anything whatsoever, which is precisely what makes it so difficult.* The only infallible way to study for the LSAT is to study the LSAT itself. The good news is that *anybody* can get significantly better at the LSAT by working diligently at it. In fact, your score will increase exponentially directly in proportion to the amount of time and work you put into preparing for it.

HOW IMPORTANT IS THE LSAT?

The LSAT figures very prominently in your law school application, especially if you've been out of school for a few years. Some law schools won't even look at your application unless you achieve a certain score on your LSAT. Most top law schools average multiple LSAT scores, so you should aim to take it only once. By the way, each score you receive is valid for five years after you take the test.

LSAT STRUCTURE

Section Type	Sections	Qustions Per Section	Time Per Section
Logical Reasoning (Arguments)	2	24–26 2 sections, about 25 questions each	35 minute sections
Analytical Reasoning (Games)	1	22–24	35 minutes
Reading Comprehension	1	27–28	35 minutes
Experimental	1	22–28	35 minutes
Writing Sample	1	1	35 minutes

Each test has approximately 99 to 102 questions. Neither the Experimental section nor the Writing Sample counts toward your score. The multiple-choice sections may be given in any order, but the Writing Sample is always administered last. The Experimental section can be any of the three types of multiple-choice sections and is used by the test writers to test out new questions on your time and at your expense.

The Writing Sample is not scored, and unlikely to be read by anyone other than you. However, the law schools to which you apply will receive a copy of your writing sample, so you should definitely do it. A blank page would stand out like a sore thumb, and you wouldn't want the Admissions Office to think you were some kind of revolutionary.

WHAT'S ON THE LSAT, EXACTLY?

We asked the experts in the LSAT Course Division of The Princeton Review for the lowdown on the various sections of the LSAT. Here's what they had to say.

Analytical Reasoning: If you've ever worked logic problems in puzzle books, then you're already somewhat familiar with the Analytical Reasoning section of the LSAT. The situations behind these problems—often called "games" or "logic games"—are common ones: deciding in what order to interview candidates, or assigning employees to teams, or arranging dinner guests around a table. The arrangement of "players" in these games is governed by a set of rules you must follow in answering the questions. Each Analytical Reasoning section is made up of four games, with five to seven questions each. Questions may ask you to find out what *must* be true under the rules or what *could* be true under the rules; they may add a new condition that applies to just that question; or they may ask you to count the number of possible arrangements under the stated conditions. These questions are difficult mostly because of the time constraints under which they must be worked; very few test-takers find themselves able to complete twenty-four questions on this section in the time allotted.

Logical Reasoning: Because there are two scored sections of them, Logical Reasoning questions on the LSAT are the most important to your score. Each Logical Reasoning—sometimes called "arguments"—question is made up of a short paragraph, often written to make a persuasive point. These small arguments are usually written to contain a flaw—some error of reasoning or unwarranted assumption that you must identify to answer the question successfully. Questions may ask you to draw conclusions from the stated information, to weaken or strengthen the argument, to identify its underlying assumptions, or to identify its logical structure or method. There are most often a total of fifty or fifty-one argument questions between the two sections—roughly half of the scored questions on the LSAT.

As of June 2007 a modification, called Comparative Reading, appears as one of the four sets in the LSAT Reading Comprehension section. In general, Comparative Reading questions are similar to traditional Reading Comprehension questions, except that Comparative Reading questions are based on two shorter passages that together are roughly the same length as one Reading Comprehension passage. A few of the questions that follow a Comparative Reading passage pair might concern only one of the two passages, but most questions will be about both passages and how they relate to each other. Also, since June 2007, test-takers no longer are randomly assigned one of two different kinds of writing prompt—decision or argument—for the writing sample. All test-takers will be assigned a decision prompt. The Writing Sample will continue to be unscored.

We strongly recommend that you prep for this test. Although we provide the best prep for the LSAT, you certainly don't have to take The Princeton Review's course (or buy our book, *Cracking the LSAT*, or sign up for our awesome distance learning course), as much as we would obviously like it. There are plenty of books, software products, courses, and tutors out there. The people who make the LSAT will gleefully sell you plenty of practice tests as well. The key is to find the best program for you. Your first step should be taking a free full-length practice LSAT given under realistic testing conditions (we offer them across the country), so you can gauge where you stand and how much you need to improve your LSAT score. Whatever your course of action, however, make sure you remain committed to it, so you can be as prepared as possible when you take the actual test.

WHEN SHOULD YOU TAKE THE LSAT?

Here is a quick summary of test dates along with some factors to consider for each.

JUNE

The June administration is the only time the test is given on a Monday afternoon. If you have trouble functioning at the ordinary 8:00 A.M. start time, June may be a good option. Furthermore, taking the LSAT in June frees up your summer and fall to research schools and complete applications. However, if you are still in college, you'll have to balance LSAT preparation with academic course work and, in some cases, final exams. Check your exam schedules before deciding on a June LSAT test date.

OCTOBER/SEPTEMBER

The October test date (which is sometimes in late September) will allow you to prepare for the LSAT during the summer. This is an attractive option if you are a college student with some free time on your hands. Once you've taken the LSAT, you can spend the remainder of the fall completing your applications.

DECEMBER

December is the last LSAT administration that most competitive law schools will accept. If disaster strikes and you get a flat tire on test day, you may end up waiting another year to begin law school. December test-takers also must balance their time between preparing for the LSAT and completing law school applications. Doing so can make for a hectic fall, especially if you're still in college. You should also remember that, while a law school may accept December LSAT scores, taking the test in December could affect your chances of admission. Many law schools use a rolling admissions system, which means that they begin making admissions decisions as early as mid-October and continue to do so until the application deadline. Applying late in this cycle could mean that fewer spots are available. Check with your potential law schools to find out their specific policies.

FEBRUARY

If you want to begin law school in the following fall, the February LSAT will be too late for most law schools. However, if you don't plan to begin law school until the next academic year, you can give yourself a head start on the entire admissions process by taking the LSAT in February, spending your summer researching schools, and devoting your fall to completing applications. As you chart your own timeline, keep in mind that the LSAT is administered four times a year—in February, June, October, and December. Visit www.lsac.org for specifics about dates, deadlines, and local testing centers.

HOW IS THE LSAT SCORED?

LSAT scores currently range from 120 to 180. Why that range? We have no idea. The table on page 16 indicates the percentile rating of the corresponding LSAT scores between 141 and 180. This varies slightly from test to test.

Your raw score (the number of questions you answer correctly) doesn't always produce the same scaled score as previous LSATs. What actually happens is that your raw score is compared with that of everyone else who took the test on the same date you did. The LSAC looks at the scales from every other LSAT given in the past three years and "normalizes" the current scale so that it doesn't deviate widely from those scaled scores in the past.

LSAT Score	Percent Below	LSAT Score	Percent Below
180	99.9	160	80.4
179	99.9	159	77.6
178	99.9	158	74.6
177	99.8	157	70.9
176	99.6	156	67.4
175	99.4	155	63.9
174	99.2	154	59.7
173	99.0	153	55.6
172	98.6	152	52.2
171	98.0	151	48.1
170	97.4	150	44.3
169	96.7	149	40.3
168	95.9	148	36.3
167	94.6	147	33.0
166	93.2	146	29.5
165	92.0	145	26.1
164	90.0	144	22.9
163	88.1	143	20.5
162	85.9	142	17.8
161	83.4	141	15.2

A GOOD LSAT SCORE

A good score on the LSAT is the score that gets you into the law school you want to attend. Remember that a large part of the admissions game is the formula of your UGPA (undergraduate grade point average) multiplied by your LSAT score. Chances are, you are at a point in life where your UGPA is pretty much fixed (if you're reading this early in your college career, start getting very good grades pronto), so the only piece of the formula you can have an impact on is your LSAT score. We cannot emphasize enough the notion that you must prepare for this test.

A LITTLE IMPROVEMENT GOES A LONG WAY

A student who scores a 154 is in the 62nd percentile of all LSAT-takers. If that student's score was 161, however, that same student would jump to the 85th percentile. Depending upon your score, a seven-point improvement can increase your ranking by more than twenty-five percentile points.

COMPETITIVE LSAT SCORES AROUND THE UNITED STATES

The range of LSAT scores from the 25th to 75th percentile of incoming full-time students at U.S. law schools is pretty broad. Here is a sampling.

Law School	Score 25 to 75 percentile
Widener University, School of Law, Harrisburg	148–152
Gonzaga University, School of Law	153–157
Rutgers University-Newark, School of Law	155–160
University of Pittsburgh, School of Law	157–161
University of Arizona, College of Law	158–163
Temple University, James E. Beasley School of Law	158–163
University of Florida, Levin College of Law	160–164
University of Tennessee, College of Law	156–162
Case Western Reserve University, School of Law	153–160
University of Alabama, School of Law	158–167
Southern Methodist University, School of Law	158–166
Loyola University Chicago, School of Law	158–163
University of San Diego, School of Law	158–162
Emory University, School of Law	159–166
The College of William & Mary, Law School	161–167
George Washington University, Law School	162–168
University of California-Berkeley, School of Law	162–170
Georgetown University, Law Center	167–171
Stanford University, School of Law	167–172
University of Chicago, Law School	167–172
Yale University, Yale Law School	170–177

PREPARING FOR THE LSAT

No matter who you are—whether you graduated *magna cum laude* from Cornell University or you're on academic probation at Cornell College—the first thing you need to do is order a recent LSAT. One comes free with every *Official LSAT Registration Booklet*. Once you get the test, take it, but not casually over the course of two weeks. Bribe someone to be your proctor. Have them administer the test to you under strict time conditions. Follow the test booklet instructions exactly, and do it right. Your goal is to simulate an actual testing experience as much as possible. When you finish, score the test honestly. Don't give yourself a few extra points because "you'll do better on test day." The score on this practice test will provide a baseline for mapping your test preparation strategy.

If your practice LSAT score is already at a point where you've got a very high-percentage shot of getting accepted to the law school of your choice, chances are you don't need much preparation. Order a half dozen or so of the most recent LSATs from LSAC and work through them over the course of a few months, making sure you understand why you are making specific mistakes. If your college or university offers a free or very cheap prep course, consider taking it to get more tips on the test. Many of these courses are taught by pre-law advisors who will speak very intelligently about the test and are committed to helping you get the best score you can.

If, after you take a practice LSAT, your score is not what you want or need it to be, you are definitely not alone. Many academically strong candidates go into the LSAT cold because they assume that the LSAT is no more difficult than or about the same as their college courses. Frankly, many students are surprised at how poorly they do the first time they take a dry run. Think about it this way: It's better to be surprised sitting at home with a practice test than while taking the test for real.

If you've taken a practice LSAT under exam conditions and it's, say, ten or fifteen points below where you want it to be, you should probably consult an expert. Ask around. Assess your financial situation. Talk to other people who have improved their LSAT scores and duplicate their strategies.

Whatever you decide to do, make sure you are practicing with real LSAT questions and you take full-length practice tests under realistic testing conditions—again and again and again.

SOME ESSENTIAL, DOWN-AND-DIRTY LSAT TIPS

Slow down. Way down. The slower you go, the better you'll do. It's that simple. Any function you perform, from basic motor skills to complex intellectual problems, will be affected by the rate at which you perform that function. This goes for everything from cleaning fish to taking the LSAT. You can get twenty-five questions wrong and still get a scaled score of 160, which is a very good score (it's in the 84th percentile). You can get at least six questions wrong per section or, even better, you can ignore the two or three most convoluted questions per section, *still* get a few more questions wrong, and you'll get an excellent overall score. Your best strategy is to find the particular working speed at which you will get the most questions correct.

There is no penalty for guessing. If you don't have time to finish the exam, it's imperative that you leave yourself at least thirty seconds at the end of each section in which to grab free points by bubbling in some answer to every question before time is called. Pick a letter of the day—like B—don't bubble in randomly. If you guess totally randomly, you might get every single guess right. Of course, you may also get struck by lightning in the middle of the test. The odds are about the same. *You are far more likely to miss every question if you guess without a plan.* However, if you stick with the same letter each time you guess, you will definitely be right once in a while. It's a conservative approach, but it is also your best bet for guaranteed points, which is what you want. By guessing the same letter pretty much every time as time runs out, you can pick up anywhere from two to four raw points per section. Be careful about waiting until the very last second to start filling in randomly, though, because proctors occasionally cheat students out of the last few seconds of a section.

Use process of elimination all the time. This is absolutely huge. On 75 percent of the LSAT (all the Logical Reasoning and Reading Comprehension questions), you are *not* looking for the *right* answer, only the *best* answer. It says so right there in the instructions. Eliminating even one answer choice increases your chances of getting the question right by 20 to 25 percent. If you can cross off two or three answer choices, you are really in business. Also, very rarely will you find an answer choice that is flawless on the LSAT. Instead, you'll find four answer choices that are definitely wrong and one that is the least of five evils. You should constantly look for reasons to get rid of answer choices so you can eliminate them. This strategy will increase your odds of getting the question right, and you'll be a happier and more successful standardized test-taker. We swear.

Attack! Attack! Attack! Read the test with an antagonistic, critical eye; look for holes and gaps in the reasoning of arguments and in the answer choices. Many LSAT questions revolve around what is wrong with a particular line of reasoning. The more adept you become at identifying what is wrong with a problem before going to the answer choices, the more successful you'll be.

Write all over your test booklet. Actively engage the exam, and put your thoughts on paper. Circle words. *Physically cross out wrong answer choices you have eliminated.* Draw complete and exact diagrams for the logic games. Use the diagrams you draw.

Do the questions in whatever order you wish. Just because a logic game question is first doesn't mean you should do it first. There is *no order of difficulty* on the LSAT—unlike some other standardized tests—so you should hunt down and destroy those questions at which you are personally best. If you are doing a Reading Comprehension question, for example, or tackling an argument, and you don't know what the hell is going on, then cross off whatever you can, guess, and move on. If you have no idea how to solve a particular logic game, don't focus your energy there. Find a game you can do and milk it for points. Your mission is to gain points wherever you can. By the way, if a particular section is really throwing you, it's probably because it is the dastardly Experimental section (which is often kind of sloppy and, thankfully, does not count toward your score).

CHAPTER 5
WRITING A GREAT PERSONAL STATEMENT

There is no way to avoid writing the dreaded personal statement. You'll probably need to write only one personal statement, and it will probably address the most commonly asked question: "Why do you want to obtain a law degree?" This question, in one form or another, appears on virtually every law school application and often represents your only opportunity to string more than two sentences together. Besides your grades and your LSAT score, it is the most important part of your law school application. Your answer should be about two pages long, and it should amount to something significantly more profound than "A six-figure salary really appeals to me," or "I watch *Law & Order* every night."

Unlike your application to undergraduate programs, the personal statement on a law school application is not the time to discuss what your trip to Europe meant to you, describe your wacky chemistry teacher, or try your hand at verse. It's a fine line. While you want to stand out, you definitely don't want to be *overly* creative here. You want to be unique, but you don't want to come across as a weirdo or a loose cannon. You want to present yourself as intelligent, professional, mature, persuasive, and concise because these are the qualities law schools seek in applicants.

THE BASICS
Here are the essentials of writing essays and personal statements.

Find your own unique angle. The admissions people read tons of really boring essays about "how great I am" and how "I think there should be justice for everyone." If you must explain why you want to obtain a law degree, strive to find an angle that is interesting and unique to you. If what you write *isn't* interesting to you, we promise that it won't be remotely interesting to an Admissions Officer. Also, in addition to being more effective, an interesting essay will be far more enjoyable to write.

In general, avoid generalities. Again, Admissions Officers have to read an unbelievable number of boring essays. You will find it harder to be boring if you write about particulars. It's the details that stick in a reader's mind.

Good writing is easily understood. You want to get your point across, not bury it in words. Don't talk in circles. Your prose should be clear and direct. If an Admissions Officer has to struggle to figure out what you are trying to say, you'll be in trouble. Also, legal writing courses make up a significant part of most law school curricula; if you can show that you have good writing skills, you have a serious edge.

Buy and read *The Elements of Style* **by William Strunk Jr. and E. B. White.** We can't recommend it enough. In fact, we're surprised you don't have it already. This little book is a required investment for any writer (and, believe us, you'll be doing plenty of writing as a law student and a practicing attorney). You will refer to it forever, and if you do what it says, your writing will definitely improve.

Have three or four people read your personal statement and critique it. If your personal statement contains misspellings and grammatical errors, Admissions Officers will conclude not only that you don't know how to write but also that you aren't shrewd enough to get help. What's worse, the more time you spend with a piece of your own writing, the less likely you are to spot any errors. You get tunnel vision. Ask friends, boyfriends, girlfriends, professors, brothers, sisters—somebody—to read your essay and comment on it. Use a computer with a spellchecker. *Be especially careful about punctuation!* Another tip: Read your personal statement aloud to yourself or someone else. You will catch mistakes and awkward phrases that would have gotten past you otherwise because they sounded correct in your head.

Don't repeat information from other parts of your application. It's a waste of time and space.

Stick to the length that is requested. It's only common courtesy.

Maintain the proper tone. Your essay should be memorable, without being outrageous and easy to read, without being too formal or sloppy. When in doubt, err on the formal side.

Being funny is much harder than you think. An applicant who can make an Admissions Officer laugh never gets lost in the shuffle. The clever part of the personal statement is passed around and read aloud. Everyone smiles and the Admissions Staff can't bear to toss your application into the "reject" pile. But beware! Most people think they're funny, but only a few are able to pull it off in this context. Obviously, stay away from one-liners, limericks, and anything remotely off-color.

WHY DO YOU WANT TO GO TO LAW SCHOOL?

Writing about yourself often proves to be surprisingly difficult. It's certainly no cakewalk explaining who you are and why you want to go to law school, and presenting your lifetime of experiences in a mere two pages. On the bright side, the personal statement is the only element of your application over which you have total control. It's a tremendous opportunity to make a great first impression as long as you avoid the urge to communicate your entire genetic blueprint. Your goal should be much more modest.

DON'T GET CARRIED AWAY

Although some law schools set no limit on the length of the personal statement, you shouldn't take their bait. You can be certain that your statement will be at least glanced at in its entirety, but Admissions Officers are human, and their massive workload at admissions time has an understandable impact on their attention spans. You should limit yourself to two or three typed, double-spaced pages. Does this make your job any easier? Not at all. In fact, practical constraints on the length of your essay demand a higher degree of efficiency and precision. A two-page limit allows for absolutely no fluff.

MAKE YOURSELF STAND OUT

We know you know this, but you will be competing against thousands of well-qualified applicants for admission to just about any law school. Consequently, your primary task in writing your application is to separate yourself from the crowd. Particularly if you are applying directly from college or if you have been out of school for a very short time, you must do your best to ensure that the Admissions Committee cannot categorize you too broadly. Admissions Committees will see innumerable applications from bright twenty-two-year-olds with good grades. Your essay presents an opportunity to put those grades in context, to define and differentiate yourself.

WHAT MAKES A GOOD PERSONAL STATEMENT?

Like any good writing, your law school application should be clear, concise, and candid. The first two of these attributes, clarity and conciseness, are usually the result of a lot of reading, rereading, and rewriting. Without question, repeated critical revision by yourself and others is the surest way to trim and tune your prose. The third quality, candor, is the product of proper motivation. Honesty cannot be superimposed after the fact; your writing must be candid from the outset.

In writing your personal statement for law school applications, pay particularly close attention to the way your essay is structured and the fundamental message it communicates. Admissions Committees will read your essay two ways: as a product of your handiwork and as a product of your mind. Don't underestimate the importance of either perspective. A well-crafted essay will impress any Admissions Officer, but if it does not illuminate, you will not be remembered. You will not stand out. Conversely, a thoughtful essay that offers true insight will stand out unmistakably, but if it is not readable, it will not receive serious consideration.

THINGS TO AVOID IN YOUR PERSONAL STATEMENT

"MY LSAT SCORE ISN'T GREAT, BUT I'M JUST NOT A GOOD TEST-TAKER."

If you have a low LSAT score, avoid directly discussing it like the plague in your personal statement. Law school is a test-rich environment. In fact, grades in most law-school courses are determined by a single exam at the semester's end, and as a law student, you'll spend your Novembers and Aprils in a study carrel, completely removed from society. Saying that you are not good at tests will do little to convince an Admissions Committee that you've got the ability to succeed in law school once accepted.

Consider also that a low LSAT score speaks for itself—all too eloquently. It doesn't need you to speak for it too. The LSAT may be a flawed test, but don't go arguing the merits of the test to Admissions Officers, because ordinarily it is the primary factor they use to make admissions decisions. We feel for you, but you'd be barking up the wrong tree. The attitude of most law school Admissions Departments is that while the LSAT may be imperfect, it is equally imperfect for all applicants. Apart from extraordinary claims of serious illness on test day, few explanations for poor performance on the LSAT will mean much to the people who read your application.

About the only situation in which a discussion of your LSAT score is necessary is if you have two (or more) LSAT scores and one is significantly better than another. If you did much better in your second sitting than in your first, or vice versa, a brief explanation couldn't hurt. However, your explanation may mean little to the committee, which may have its own hard-and-fast rules for interpreting multiple LSAT scores. Even in this scenario, however, you should avoid bringing up the LSAT in the personal statement. *Save it for an addendum.*

The obvious and preferable alternative to an explicit discussion of a weak LSAT score would be to focus on what you *are* good at. If you really are bad at standardized tests, you must be better at something else, or you wouldn't have gotten as far as you have. If you think you are a marvelous researcher, say so. If you are a wonderful writer, show it. Let your essay implicitly draw attention away from your weak points by focusing on your strengths. There is no way to convince an Admissions Committee that they should overlook your LSAT score. You may, however, present compelling reasons for them to look beyond it.

"MY COLLEGE GRADES WEREN'T THAT HIGH, BUT . . ."

This issue is a bit more complicated than the low LSAT score. Law school Admissions Committees will be more willing to listen to your interpretation of your college performance but only within limits. Keep in mind that law schools require official transcripts for a reason. Members of the Admissions Committee will be aware of your academic credentials before ever getting to your essay. As with low LSAT scores, your safest course of action is to *explain low grades in addendum.*

If your grades are unimpressive, you should offer the Admissions Committee something else by which to judge your abilities. Again, the best argument for looking past your college grades is evidence of achievement in another area, whether in your LSAT score, your extracurricular activities, your overcoming economic hardship as an undergraduate, or your career accomplishments.

"I'VE ALWAYS WANTED TO BE A LAWYER."

Sure you have. Many applicants seem to feel the need to point out that they really, really want to become attorneys. You will do yourself a great service by avoiding such throwaway lines. They'll do nothing for your essay but water it down. Do not convince yourself in a moment of desperation that claiming to have known that the law was your calling since age six (when—let's be honest—you really wanted to be a firefighter) will somehow move your application to the top of the pile. The Admissions Committee is not interested in how much you want to practice law. They want to know *why*.

"I WANT TO BECOME A LAWYER TO FIGHT INJUSTICE."

No matter how deeply you feel about battling social inequity, between us, writing it down makes you sound like a superhero on a soapbox. Moreover, though some people really do want to fight injustice, way down in the cockles of their hearts, most applicants are motivated to attend law school by less altruistic desires. Among the nearly one million practicing lawyers in the United States, there are relatively few who actually earn a living defending the indigent or protecting civil rights. Tremendously dedicated attorneys who work for peanuts and take charity cases are few and far between. We're not saying you don't want to be one of them; we're merely saying that people in law school admissions won't *believe* you want to be one of them. They'll take your professed altruistic ambitions (and those of the hundreds of other personal statements identical to yours) with a (huge) grain of salt.

If you can, in good conscience, say that you are committed to a career in the public interest, show the committee something tangible on your application and in your essay that will allow them to see your statements as more than mere assertions. If however, you cannot show that you are already a veteran in the good fight, don't claim to be. Law school Admissions Committees certainly do not regard the legal profession as a saints versus sinners proposition, and neither should you. Do not be afraid of appearing morally moderate. If the truth is that you want the guarantee of the relatively good jobs a law degree practically ensures, be forthright. Nothing is as impressive to the reader of a personal statement as the ring of truth, and what's wrong with wanting a good job, anyway?

CHAPTER 6

RECOMMENDATIONS

The law schools to which you apply will require two or three letters of recommendation in support of your application. Some schools will allow you to submit as many letters as you like. Others make it clear that any more than the minimum number of letters of recommendation is unwelcome. If you've ever applied to a private school (or perhaps a small public school) then you know the drill.

Unlike the evaluation forms for some colleges and graduate programs, however, law school recommendation forms tend toward absolute minimalism. All but a few recommendation forms for law school applications ask a single, open-ended question. It usually goes something like, "What information about this applicant is relevant that is not to be found in other sources?" The generic quality of the forms from various law schools may be both a blessing and a curse. On the one hand, it makes it possible for those writing your recommendations to write a single letter that will suffice for all the applications you submit. This convenience will make everybody much happier. On the other hand, if a free-form recommendation is to make a positive impression on an Admissions Committee, it must convey real knowledge about you.

WHOM TO ASK

Your letters of recommendation should come from people who know you well enough to offer a truly informed assessment of your abilities. Think carefully before choosing them to do this favor for you, but, as a general rule, pick respectable people whom you've known for a long time. If the writers of your recommendations know you well and understand the broader experience that has brought you to your decision to attend law school, they will be able to write a letter that is specific enough to do you some good. You also want people who can and are willing to contribute to an integrated, cohesive application.

The application materials from most law schools suggest that your letters should come, whenever possible, from people in academic settings. Some schools want at least two recommendations, both of which must be academic. Others explicitly request that the letters come from someone who has known you in a professional setting, especially if you've been out of school for a while.

HELP YOUR RECOMMENDATION WRITERS HELP YOU

Here, in essence, is the simple secret to great recommendations: Make sure the writers of your recommendations know you, your academic and professional goals, and the overall message you are trying to convey in your application. The best recommendations will fit neatly with the picture you present of yourself in your own essay, even when they make no specific reference to the issues your essay addresses. An effective law school application will present to the Admissions Committee a cohesive picture, not a montage. A great way to point your recommendation writers in the right direction and maximize their abilities to contribute to your overall cause is to provide them with copies of your personal statement. Don't be bashful about amiably communicating a few "talking points" that don't appear in your personal statement, as well.

ACADEMIC REFERENCES

Most applicants will (and should) seek recommendations from current or former professors. The academic environment in law school is extremely rigorous. Admissions Committees will be looking for assurance that you will be able not just to survive but to excel. A strong recommendation from a college professor is a valuable corroboration of your ability to succeed in law school.

You want nothing less than stellar academic recommendations. While a perfunctory, lukewarm recommendation is unlikely to damage your overall application, it will obviously do nothing to bolster it. Your best bet is to choose at least one professor from your major field. An enthusiastic endorsement from such a professor will be taken as a sign that you are an excellent student. Second—and we hope that this goes without saying—you should choose professors who do not immediately associate your name with the letter C.

Helpful Websites

findlaw.com

This site is the mother lode of free information about law, law schools, and legal careers.

ilrg.com

Mother lode honorable mention.

hg.org/students.html

Another honorable mention.

jurist.law.pitt.edu

The University of Pittsburgh School of Law's splendid "Legal News and Research" website offers a wealth of useful information.

Specifics are of particular interest to Admissions Officers when they evaluate your recommendations. If a professor can make *specific* reference to a particular project you completed, or at least make substantive reference to your work in a particular course, the recommendation will be strengthened considerably. Make it your responsibility to enable your professors to provide specifics. Drop hints, or just lay it out for them. You might, for example, make available a paper you wrote for them of which you are particularly proud. Or you might just chat with the professor for a while to jog those dormant memories. You might feel uncomfortable tooting your own horn, but it's for the best. Unless your professors are well enough acquainted with you to be able to offer a very personal assessment of your potential, they will greatly appreciate a tangible reminder of your abilities on which to base their recommendation.

ESCAPING THE WOODWORK

If you managed to get through college without any professors noticing you, it's not the end of the world. Professors are quite talented at writing recommendations for students they barely know. Most consider it part of their job. Even seemingly unapproachable academic titans will usually be happy to dash off a quick letter for a mere student. However, these same obliging professors are masters of a sort of opaque prose style that screams to an Admissions Officer, "I really have no idea what to say about this kid who is, in fact, a near-total stranger to me!" Although an Admissions Committee will not outrightly dismiss such a recommendation, it's really not going to help you much.

REELING IN THE YEARS

Obviously, the longer it has been since you graduated, the tougher it is to obtain academic recommendations. However, if you've held on to your old papers, you may still be able to rekindle an old professor's memory of your genius by sending a decent paper or two along with your request for a recommendation (and, of course, a copy of your personal statement). You want to provide specifics in any way you can.

NON-ACADEMIC REFERENCES

Getting the mayor, a senator, or the CEO of your company to write a recommendation helps only if you have a personal and professional connection with that person. Remember, you want the writers of your recommendations to provide specifics about your actual accomplishments. If you're having trouble finding academic recommendations, choose people from your workplace, from the community, or from any other area of your life that is important to you. If at all possible, talk to your boss or a supervisor from a previous job who knows you well (and, of course, likes you).

SEND A THANK-YOU NOTE

Always a good idea. It should be short and handwritten. Use a blue pen so the recipient knows for sure that your note is no cheap copy. As with any good thank-you note and any good recommendation, mention a specific. (Send a thank-you note if you have an interview at a law school, too.)

CHAPTER 7
REAL-LIFE WORK EXPERIENCE
AND COMMUNITY SERVICE

WORK EXPERIENCE IN COLLEGE

Most law school applications will ask you to list any part-time jobs you held while you were in college and how many hours per week you worked. If you had to (or chose to) work your way through your undergraduate years, this should come as good news. A great number of law schools make it clear that they take your work commitments as a college student into consideration when evaluating your undergraduate GPA.

WORK EXPERIENCE IN REAL LIFE

All law school applications will ask you about your work experience beyond college. They will give you three or four lines on which to list such experience. Some schools will invite you to submit a resume. If you have a very good one, you should really milk this opportunity for all it's worth. Even if you don't have a marvelous resume, these few lines on the application and your resume are the only opportunities you'll have to discuss your post-college experience meaningfully—unless you choose to discuss professional experience in your personal statement as well.

The kind of job you've had is not as important as you might think. What interests the Admissions Committee is what you've made of that job and what it has made of you. Whatever your job was or is, you want to offer credible evidence of your competence. For example, mention in your personal statement your job advancement or any increase in your responsibility. Most important, though, remember your overriding goal of cohesive presentation—you want to show off your professional experience within the context of your decision to attend law school. This does not mean that you need to offer geometric proof of how your experience in the workplace has led you inexorably to a career in law. You need only explain truthfully how this experience influenced you and how it fits nicely into your thinking about law school.

COMMUNITY SERVICE

An overwhelming majority of law schools single out community involvement as one of several influential factors in their admissions decisions. Law schools would like to admit applicants who show a long-standing commitment to something other than their own advancement.

It is certainly understandable that law schools would wish to determine the level of such commitment before admitting an applicant, particularly since so few law students go on to practice public interest law. Be forewarned, however, that nothing—*nothing*—is so obviously bogus as an insincere statement of a commitment to public interest issues. It just reeks. Admissions committees are well aware that very few people take the time out of their lives to become involved significantly in their communities. If you aren't one of them, trying to fake it can only hurt you.

CHAPTER 8

INTERVIEWS

The odds are very good that you will never have to sit through an interview in the law school admissions process. Admissions Offices just aren't very keen on them. They do happen occasionally, however, and if you are faced with one, here are a few tips.

BE PREPARED

Interviews do make impressions. Some students are admitted simply because they had great interviews; less often, students are rejected because they bombed. Being prepared is the smartest thing you can do.

Don't ask questions that are answered in the brochures you got in the mail. You have to read those brochures—at breakfast before the interview would be an ideal time.

If there is a popular conception of the school (e.g., Harvard is overly competitive), don't ask about it. Your interviewer will have been through the same song and dance too many times. While you don't want to seem off the wall by asking bizarre questions, you don't want to sound exactly like every other boring applicant before you.

LOOK GOOD, FEEL GOOD

Wear nice clothes. If you aren't sure what to wear, *ask the Admissions Staff*. Get a respectable haircut. Don't chew gum. Clean your fingernails. Brush your teeth. Wash behind your ears. You can go back to being a slob as soon as they admit you.

DON'T WORRY ABOUT TIME

Students sometimes are told that the sign of a good interview is that it lasts longer than the time allowed for it. Forget about this. Don't worry if your interview lasts exactly as long as the assistant said it would. Don't try to stretch out the end of your interview by suddenly becoming long-winded or asking questions you don't care about.

CHAPTER 9
MONEY MATTERS

Law school is a cash cow for colleges and universities everywhere and, especially at a private school, you are going to be gouged for a pretty obscene wad of cash over the next three years. Take American University Washington College of Law, where tuition is about $44,000 a year. If you are planning to eat, live somewhere, buy books, and (maybe) have health insurance, you are looking at about $67,000 per year. Multiply that by three years of law school and you get $201,000. Now faint. Correct for inflation (USC certainly will), add things like computers and other miscellany, and you can easily spend $208,000 to earn a degree. Assume that you have to borrow every penny of that $201,000. Multiply it by 8 percent through ten years (a common assumption of law school applicants is that they will be able to pay all their debt back in ten years or less). Your monthly payments will be about $3,015.

On the bright side, while law school is certainly an expensive proposition, the financial rewards of practicing can be immensely lucrative. You won't be forced into bankruptcy if you finance it properly. There are tried-and-true ways to reduce your initial costs, finance the costs on the horizon, and manage the debt with which you'll leave school—all without ever having to ask, "Have you been in a serious accident recently?" in a television commercial.

LAW SCHOOL ON THE CHEAP
Private schools aren't the only law schools, and you don't have to come out of law school saddled with tens of thousands of dollars of debt. Many state schools have reputations that equal or surpass some of the top private ones. It might be worth your while to spend a year establishing residency in a state with one or more good public law schools. Here's an idea: Pack up your belongings and move to a cool place like Minneapolis, Seattle, Berkeley, Austin, or Boulder. Spend a year living there. Wait tables, hang out, listen to music, walk the Earth, write the great American novel, and *then* study law.

COMPARISON SHOPPING
Here are the full-time tuition costs at law schools around the country. The two schools listed for each state are randomly paired schools in the same region (one public and one private) and are provided to help you get a feel of what law school costs are going to run you. Those schools that have the same tuition in both columns are private law schools.

Law School	In-State	Out-of-State
Florida State University, College of Law (tuition + fees)	$19,731	$39,743
University of Miami, School of Law	$38,918	$38,918
Indiana University—Bloomington, Maurer School of Law	$28,662	$46,738
University of Notre Dame, Law School	$45,500	$45,500
University of Tennessee, College of Law	$15,168	$31,596
Vanderbilt University, Law School	$46,000	$46,400
The University of Iowa, College of Law	$35,608	$46,056
Drake University, Law School	$35,170	$35,170
Southern University, Law Center	$21,980	$37,180
Tulane University, Law School	$41,500	$41,500
University of California—Los Angeles, School of Law	$47,464	$53,959
University of San Francisco, School of Law	$42,284	$42,284
The University of Texas at Austin, School of Law	$33,162	$49,244
Baylor University, School of Law	$47,334	$47,334
University of Illinois, College of Law	$37,100	$44,520
Northwestern University, School of Law	$53,168	$53,168
University of Oregon, School of Law	$27,054	$34,074
Lewis & Clark College, Law School	$38,180	$38,180

LOAN REPAYMENT ASSISTANCE PROGRAMS

If you are burdened with loans, we've got more bad news. The National Association of Law Placement (NALP) shows that while salaries for law school graduates who land jobs at the big, glamorous firms have skyrocketed in the past few years, salaries of less than $85,000 are more common than salaries of $100,000 to $130,000 for the general run of law school grads. There are, however, a growing number of law schools and other sources willing to pay your loans for you through loan forgiveness programs in return for your commitment to work in public interest law.

While doing a tour of duty in public service law will put off dreams of working at a big firm or becoming the next Mark Geragos, the benefits of these programs are undeniable. Here's how just about all of them work. You commit to working for a qualified public service or public interest job. As long as your gross income does not exceed the prevailing public service salary, the programs will pay off a good percentage of your debt. Eligible loans are typically any educational debt financed through your law school, which really excludes only loan sharks and credit-card debts.

The Skinny on Loan Repayment Assistance Programs
For a comprehensive listing of assistance programs and for other loan-forgiveness information, call Equal Justice Works at 202-466-3686, or look them up online at equaljusticeworks.org..

MAXIMIZE YOUR AID

A simple but oft-forgotten piece of wisdom: If you don't ask, you usually don't get. Be firm when trying to get merit money from your school. Some schools have reserves of cash that go unused. Try simply asking for more financial aid. The better your grades, of course, the more likely schools are to crack open their safe of financial goodies for you. Unfortunately, grants aren't as prevalent for law students as for undergrads. Scholarships are not nearly as widely available either. To get a general idea of availability of aid at a law school, contact the Financial Aid Office.

PARENTAL CONTRIBUTION?!

If you are operating under the assumption that, as a tax-paying grownup who has been out of school for a number of years, you will be recognized as the self-supporting adult you are, you could be in for a surprise. Veterans of financial aid battles will not be surprised to hear that even law school Financial Aid Offices have a difficult time recognizing when apron strings have legitimately been cut. Schools may try to take into account your parents' income in determining your eligibility for financial aid, regardless of your age or tax status. Policies vary widely. Be sure to ask the schools you are considering exactly what their policies are regarding financial independence for the purposes of financial aid.

BORROWING MONEY

It's an amusingly simple process, and several companies are in the business of lending large chunks of cash specifically to law students. Your law school Financial Aid Office can tell you how to reach them. You should explore more than one option and shop around for the lowest fees and rates.

WHO'S ELIGIBLE?

Anyone with reasonably good credit, regardless of financial need, can borrow enough money to finance law school. If you have financial need, you will probably be eligible for some types of financial aid if you meet the following basic qualifications:

- You are a United States citizen or a permanent U.S. resident.

- You are registered for Selective Service if you are a male, or you have the documentation to prove that you are exempt.

- You are not in default on student loans already.

- You don't have a horrendous credit history.

- You haven't been busted for certain drug-related crimes, including possession.

> **Let the Law School Pick Up the Tab for Phone Calls Whenever Possible**
>
> Many schools have free telephone numbers that they don't like to publish in books like this one. If the number we have listed for a particular law school is not an 800 number, it doesn't necessarily mean that you have to pay every time you call the school. Check out the school's website, or ask for the 800 number when you call the first time.

WHAT TYPES OF LOANS ARE AVAILABLE?

There are three basic types of loans: federal, private, and institutional.

Federal

The federal government funds federal loan programs. Federal loans, particularly the Stafford Loan, are usually the first resort for borrowers. Most federal loans are need-based, but some higher-interest loans are available regardless of financial circumstances. Visit studentaid. ed.org for the most comprehensive, up-to-date information.

Private

Private loans are funded by banks, foundations, corporations, and other associations. A number of private loans are targeted to aid particular segments of the population. You may have to do some investigating to identify private loans for which you might qualify. As always, contact your law school's Financial Aid Office to learn more.

Institutional

The amount of loan money available and the method by which it is disbursed vary greatly from one school to another. Private schools, especially those that are older and more established, tend to have larger endowments and can offer more assistance. To find out about the resources available at a particular school, refer to its catalog or contact—you guessed it—the financial aid office.

TABLE OF LOANS			
NAME OF LOAN	**SOURCE**	**ELIGIBILITY**	**MAXIMUM ALLOCATION**
Federal Stafford (Unsubsidized) Student Loan Studentaid.ed.gov/ students/publications/ student_guide/index. html	Federal, administered by school.	Not need-based.	The total Stafford loan limit is $20,500. The maximum aggregate total of Stafford loans is $138,500, including undergraduate loans.
Federal PLUS Loans	Federal, administered by school.	Not need-based.	The maximum allocation is the cost of attendance (including tuition, educational expenses, and reasonable living expenses as determined by the school).
Perkins Loan Contact school for more information.	Federal, administered by school.	Exceptional financial need.	$8,000/year, with aggregate of $60,000. Aggregate amount includes undergraduate loans.

TABLE OF LOANS (Continued)			
REPAYMENT AND DEFFERAL OPTIONS	**INTEREST RATE**	**PROS**	**CONS**
10–30 years to repay. Interest begins to accrue from day loan is disbursed; you can pay the interest or have it capitalized (added to principal). Begin repayment 6 months after graduation.	Fixed, 6.8%.	Not need-based.	Interest is not paid by the government while you're in school.
10 years to repay. Begins 1 year after graduation. Deferrable during residency and under special circumstances.	Fixed, 7.9%.	Fixed, relatively low interest rate.	Very limited availability.
10 years to repay. Begin repayment 9 months after graduation.	Fixed, 5%	Fixed, relatively low interest rate.	Low maximum allocation.

CHAPTER 10
Law School 101

IS IT REALLY THAT BAD?

The first semester of law school has the well-deserved reputation of being among the greatest challenges to your intellect and stamina that you'll ever face. It requires tons and tons of work and, in many ways, it's an exercise in intellectual survival. Just as the gung-ho army recruit must survive boot camp, so, too, must the bright-eyed law student endure the humbling effects of the first year.

Though complex and difficult, the subject matter in first-year law school courses is probably no more inherently difficult than what is taught in other graduate or professional schools. The particular, private terror that is shared by roughly 40,000 1Ls every year stems more from law school's peculiar *style*. The method of instruction unapologetically punishes students who would prefer to learn passively.

THE FIRST-YEAR CURRICULUM
The first-year curriculum in the law school you attend will almost certainly be composed of a combination of the following courses:

TORTS
The word comes from the Middle French for *injury*. The Latin root of the word means *twisted*. Torts are wrongful acts, excluding breaches of contract, over which you can sue people. They include battery, assault, false imprisonment, and intentional infliction of emotional distress. Torts can range from the predictable to the bizarre, from "Dog Bites Man" to "Man Bites Dog" and everything in between. The study of torts mostly involves reading cases to discern the legal rationale behind decisions pertaining to the extent of, and limits on, the civil liability of one party for harm done to another.

CONTRACTS
They may seem fairly self-explanatory, but contractual relationships are varied and complicated, as two semesters of contracts will teach you. Again, through the study of past court cases, you will follow the largely unwritten law governing the system of conditions and obligations a contract represents, as well as the legal remedies available when contracts are breached.

CIVIL PROCEDURE
Civil procedure is the study of how you get things done in civil (as opposed to criminal) court. "Civ Pro" is the study of the often dizzyingly complex rules that govern not only who can sue whom, but also how, when, and where they can do it. This is not merely a study of legal protocol, for issues of process have a significant indirect effect on the substance of the law. Rules of civil procedure govern the conduct of both the courtroom trial and the steps that might precede it: obtaining information (discovery), making your case (pleading), pre-trial motions, and so on.

PROPERTY
You may never own a piece of land, but your life will inevitably and constantly be affected by property laws. Anyone interested in achieving an understanding of broader policy issues will appreciate the significance of this material. Many property courses will emphasize the transfer of property and, to varying degrees, economic analysis of property law.

CRIMINAL LAW
Even if you become a criminal prosecutor or defender, you will probably never run into most of the crimes to which you will be exposed in this course. Can someone who shoots the dead body of a person he believes to be alive be charged with attempted murder? What if they were both on drugs or had really rough childhoods? Also, you'll love the convoluted exam questions in which someone will invariably go on a nutty crime spree.

CONSTITUTIONAL LAW

"Con Law" is the closest thing to a normal class you will take in your first year. It emphasizes issues of government structure (e.g., federal power versus state power) and individual rights (e.g., personal liberties, freedom of expression, property protection). You'll spend a great deal of time studying the limits on the lawmaking power of Congress as well.

LEGAL METHODS

One of the few twentieth-century improvements on the traditional first-year curriculum that has taken hold nearly everywhere, this course travels under various aliases, such as Legal Research and Writing or Elements of the Law. In recent years, increased recognition of the importance of legal writing skills has led more than half of the U.S. law schools to require or offer a writing course after the first year. This class will be your smallest, and possibly your only, refuge from the Socratic Method. Methods courses are often taught by junior faculty and attorneys in need of extra cash and are designed to help you acquire fundamental skills in legal research, analysis, and writing. The methods course may be the least frightening you face, but it can easily consume an enormous amount of time. This is a common lament, particularly at schools where very few credits are awarded for it.

In addition to these course requirements, many law schools require 1Ls to participate in a moot-court exercise. As part of this exercise, students—sometimes working in pairs or even small groups—must prepare briefs and oral arguments for a mock trial (usually appellate). This requirement is often tied in with the methods course so that those briefs and oral arguments will be well researched—and graded.

THE CASE METHOD

In the majority of your law school courses, and probably in all of your first-year courses, your only texts will be things called casebooks. The case method eschews explanation and encourages exploration. In a course that relies entirely on the casebook, you will never come across a printed list of "laws." Instead, you will learn that in many areas of law there is no such thing as a static set of rules, but only a constantly evolving system of principles. You are expected to understand the principles of law—in all of its layers and ambiguities—through a critical examination of a series of cases that were decided according to such principles. You will often feel utterly lost, groping for answers to unarticulated questions. This is not only normal but also intended.

In practical terms, the case method works like this: For every class meeting, you will be assigned a number of cases to read from your casebook, which is a collection of (extremely edited) written judicial decisions in actual court cases. The names won't even have been changed to protect the innocent. The cases are the written judicial opinions rendered in court cases that were decided at the appeals or Supreme Court level. (Written opinions are not generally rendered in lower courts.)

Your casebook will contain no instructions and little to no explanation. Your assignments will be to simply read the cases and be in a position to answer questions based on them. There will be no written homework assignments, just cases, cases, and more cases.

You will write, for your own benefit, summaries—or briefs—of these cases. Briefs are your attempts to summarize the issues and laws around which a particular case revolves. *By briefing, you figure out what the law is.* The idea is that, over the course of a semester, you will try to integrate the content of your case briefs and your notes from in-class lectures, discussions, or dialogues into some kind of cohesive whole.

Tips for Classroom Success

- Be alert. Review material immediately before class so that it is fresh in your memory. Then review your notes from class later the same day and the week's worth of notes at the end of each week.

- Remember that there are few correct answers. The goal of a law school class is generally to analyze, understand, and attempt to resolve issues or problems.

- Learn to state and explain legal rules and principles with accuracy.

- Don't want to focus on minutiae from cases or class discussions; always try to figure out what the law is.

- Accept the ambiguity in legal analysis and class discussion; classes are intended to be thought provoking, perplexing, and difficult.

- No one class session will make or break you. Keep in mind how each class fits within the course overall.

- Write down the law. Don't write down what other students say. Concentrate your notes on the professor's hypotheticals and emphases in class.

- Review the table of contents in the casebook. This is a simple but effective way of keeping yourself in touch with where the class is at any given time.

- If you don't use a laptop, don't sit next to someone who does. The constant tapping on the keys will drive you crazy, and you may get a sense that they are writing down more than you (which is probably not true).

- Don't record classes. There are better uses of your time than to spend hours listening to the comments of students who were just as confused as you were when you first dealt with the material in class.

THE SOCRATIC METHOD

As unfamiliar as the case method will be to most 1Ls, the real source of anxiety is the way in which the professors present it. Socratic instruction entails directed questioning and limited lecturing. Generally, the Socratic professor invites a student to attempt a cogent summary of a case assigned for that day's class. Hopefully, it won't be you (but someday it will be). Regardless of the accuracy and thoroughness of your initial response, the professor then grills you on details overlooked or issues unresolved. Then, the professor will change the facts of the actual case at hand into a hypothetical case that may or may not have demanded a different decision by the court.

The overall goal of the Socratic Method is to forcibly improve your critical reasoning skills. If you are reasonably well prepared, thinking about all these questions will force you beyond the immediately apparent issues in a given case to consider its broader implications. The dialogue between the effective Socratic instructor and the victim of the moment will also force nonparticipating students to question their underlying assumptions of the case under discussion.

WHAT IS CLINICAL LEGAL EDUCATION?

The latest so-called innovation in legal education is ironic in that it's a return to the old emphasis on practical experience. Hands-on training in the practical skills of lawyering now travels under the name "Clinical Legal Education."

HOW IT WORKS

Generally, a clinical course focuses on developing practical lawyering skills. "Clinic" means exactly what you would expect: a working law office where second- and third-year law students counsel clients and serve human beings. (A very limited number of law schools allow first-year students to participate in legal clinics.)

In states that grant upper-level law students a limited right to represent clients in court, students in a law school's clinic might actually follow cases through to their resolution. Some schools have a single on-site clinic that operates something like a general law practice, dealing with cases ranging from petty crime to landlord-tenant disputes. At schools that have dedicated the most resources to their clinical programs, numerous specialized clinics deal with narrowly defined areas of law, such as employment discrimination. The opportunities to participate in such live-action programs, however, are limited.

> *Watch* **The Paper Chase.** *Twice.*
>
> This movie is the only one ever produced about law school that comes close to depicting the real thing. Watch it before you go to orientation. Watch it again on Thanksgiving break, and laugh when you can identify prototypes of your classmates.

OTHER OPTIONS

Clinical legal education is much more expensive than traditional instruction, which means that few law schools can accommodate more than a small percentage of their students in clinical programs. If that's the case, check out external clinical placements and simulated clinical courses. In a clinical externship, you might work with a real firm or public agency several hours a week and meet with a faculty advisor only occasionally. Though students who participate in these programs are unpaid, they will ordinarily receive academic credit. Also, placements are chosen quite carefully to ensure that you don't become a gopher.

There are also simulated clinical courses. In one of these, you'll perform all of the duties that a student in a live-action clinic would, but your clients are imaginary.

CHAPTER 11
HOW TO EXCEL AT ANY LAW SCHOOL

Preparation for law school is something you should take very seriously. Law school will be one of the most interesting and rewarding experiences of your life, but it's also an important and costly investment. Your academic performance in law school will influence your career for years to come. Consider the following facts when thinking about how important it is to prepare for law school:

- For the class of 2015, it is estimated that the average student will incur nearly $211,000 of debt. (Source: Law School Transparency)

- The median income for 2011 law school graduates is $60,000. (Source: National Association for Legal Career Professionals)

> B-pluses put you in the top quarter at most schools and in the top fifth at many.

As you can see, most law students cannot afford to be mediocre. Money isn't everything, but when you're strapped with close to six figures of debt, money concerns will weigh heavily on your career choices. Even if money is not a concern for you, your academic performance in law school will profoundly affect your employment options after graduation and, ultimately, your legal career. Consider these additional facts

- Students who excel in law school may have opportunities to earn up to $135,000 plus bonuses right out of law school.

- Only law students who excel academically have opportunities to obtain prestigious judicial clerkships, teaching positions, and distinguished government jobs.

As you can see, law students who achieve academic success enjoy better career options and have a greater ability to escape the crushing debt of law school. The point is obvious: Your chances of achieving your goals—no matter what you want to do with your career—are far better if you succeed academically.

Now comes the hard part: How do you achieve academic success? You are going to get plenty of advice about how to excel in law school—much of it unsolicited. You certainly don't need any from us. We strongly advise, however, that you pay close attention to what Don Macaulay, the president of Law Preview, has to say about surviving and thriving as a law student. Macaulay, like all the founders of Law Preview, graduated at the top of his law school class and worked at a top law firm before he began developing and administering Law Preview's law school prep course in 1998.

> **Contact Law Preview**
> Law Preview is an intensive week-long seminar designed to help you conquer law school. To learn more, visit www.LawPreview.com.

While there are many resources that claim to provide a recipe for success in law school, Law Preview is the best of the lot. They have retained some of the most talented legal scholars in the country to lecture during their week-long sessions, and they deliver what they promise—a methodology for attacking and conquering the law school experience.

We asked Macaulay a few questions to which we thought prospective law students might like to know the answers:

It is often said that the first year of law school is the most important year. Is this true, and, if so, why?

It is true. Academic success during the first year of law school can advance a successful legal career unlike success in any other year because many of the top legal employers start recruiting so early that your first-year grades are all they will see. Most prestigious law firms hire their permanent attorneys from among the ranks of the firm's "summer associates"—usually second-year law students who work for the firm during the summer between the second and third years of law school. Summer associates are generally hired during the fall semester of the second year, a time when only the first year grades are available. A student who does well during the first year, lands a desirable summer associate position, and then impresses his or her employer, is well on his or her way to a secure legal job regardless of his or her academic performance after the first year.

In addition, first-year grades often bear heavily upon a student's eligibility for law review and other prestigious scholastic activities, including other law journals and moot court. These credentials are considered the most significant signs of law school achievement, often even more than a high grade point average. Many of the top legal employers in the private and the public sectors seek out young lawyers with these credentials, and some employers will not even interview candidates who lack these honors, even after a few years of experience. As a result, a solid performance during the first year of law school can have a serious impact upon your professional opportunities available after graduation.

How does law school differ from what students experienced as undergraduates?

Many students, especially those who enjoyed academic success in college, presume that law school will be a mere continuation of their undergraduate experience, and that, by implementing those skills that brought them success in college, they will enjoy similar success in law school. This couldn't be further from the truth. Once law school begins, students often find themselves thrown into deep water. They are handed an anchor in the form of a casebook (they are told it's a life preserver), and they are expected to sink or swim. While almost nobody sinks in law school anymore, most spend all of their first year just trying to keep their heads above water. In reality, virtually every student who is admitted into law school possesses the intelligence and work ethic needed to graduate. But in spite of having the tools needed to survive the experience, very few possess the know-how to truly excel and make Law Review at their schools.

What makes the law school experience unique is its method of instruction and its system of grading. Most professors rely on the case method as a means for illustrating legal rules and doctrines encountered in a particular area of the law. With the case method, students are asked to read a particular case or, in some instances, several cases, that the professor will use to lead a classroom discussion illustrating a particular rule of law. The assigned readings come from casebooks, which are compilations of cases for each area of law. The cases are usually edited to illustrate distinct legal rules, often with very little commentary or enlightenment by the casebook editor. The casebooks often lack anything more than a general structure, and law professors often contribute little to the limited structure. Students are asked to read and analyze hundreds of cases in a vacuum. Since each assigned case typically builds upon a legal rule illustrated in a previous case, it isn't until the end of the semester or, for some classes, the end of the year, that students begin to form an understanding of how these rules interrelate.

One of the objectives of Law Preview's law school prep course is to help students to understand the big picture before they begin their classes. We hire some of the most talented law professors from around the country to provide previews of the core first-year law school courses: Civil Procedure, Constitutional Law, Contracts, Criminal Law, Property, and Torts. During their lectures, our professors provide students with a roadmap for each subject by discussing the law's development, legal doctrines, and recurring themes and policies that students will encounter throughout the course. By providing entering law students with a conceptual framework for the material they will study, Law Preview eliminates the frustration that most of them will encounter when reading and analyzing case law in a vacuum.

What is the best way to prepare for law school, and when should you start?

When preparing for law school, students should focus on two interrelated tasks: (1) developing a strategy for academic success, and (2) preparing mentally for the awesome task ahead. The primary objective for most law students is to achieve the highest grades possible, and a well-defined strategy for success will help you direct your efforts most efficiently and effectively toward that goal. You must not begin law school equipped solely with some vague notion of hard work. Success requires a concrete plan that includes developing a reliable routine for classroom preparation, a proficient method of outlining, and a calculated strategy for test-taking. The further you progress in law school without such a plan, the more time and energy you will waste struggling through your immense workload without moving discernibly closer to achieving academic success.

You must also become mentally prepared to handle the rigors of law school. Law school can be extremely discouraging because students receive very little feedback during the school year. Classes are usually graded solely based on final exam scores. Midterm exams and graded papers are uncommon, and classroom participation is often the only way for students to ascertain if they understand the material and are employing effective study methods. As a result, a winning attitude is critical to success in law school. Faith in yourself will help you continue to make the personal sacrifices during the first year that you need to make to succeed in law school, even when the rewards are not immediately apparent.

Incoming law students should begin preparing for law school during the summertime prior to first year, and preparation exercises should be aimed at gaining a general understanding of what law school is all about. A solid understanding of what you are expected to learn during the first year will give you the information you need to develop both your strategy for success and the confidence you need to succeed. There are several books on the market that can help in this regard, but those students who are best prepared often attend Law Preview's one-week intensive preparatory course specifically designed to teach beginning law students the strategies for academic success.

What factors contribute to academic success in law school?

Academic success means one thing in law school—exam success. The grades that you receive, particularly during the first year, will be determined almost exclusively by the scores you receive on your final exams. Occasionally, a professor may add a few points for class participation, but that is rare. In most classes, your final exam will consist of a three- or four-hour written examination at the end of the semester or—if the course is two semesters long—at the end of the year. The amount of material you must master for each final exam will simply dwarf that of any undergraduate exam you have ever taken. The hope that you can "cram" a semester's worth of information into a one-week reading period is pure fantasy and one that will surely lead to disappointing grades. The focus of your efforts from day one should be success on your final exams. Don't get bogged down in class preparation or in perfecting a course outline if it will not result in some discernible improvement in your exam performance. All of your efforts should be directed at improving your exam performance in some way. It's as simple as that.

What skills are typically tested on law school exams?

Law school exams usually test three different skills: (1) the ability to accurately identify legal issues, (2) the ability to recall the relevant law with speed, and (3) the ability to apply the law to the facts efficiently and skillfully. The proper approach for developing these skills differs, depending on the substantive area of law in question and whether your exam is open book or closed book.

Identifying legal issues is commonly known as issue spotting. On most of your exams, you will be given complex, hypothetical fact patterns. From the facts you are given, you must identify the particular legal issues that need to be addressed. This is a difficult skill to perfect and can only be developed through practice. The best way to develop issue-spotting skills is by taking practice exams. For each of your classes, during the first half of the semester, you should collect all of the available exams that were given by your professor in the past. Take all of these exams under simulated exam conditions—find an open classroom, get some blue books, time yourself, and take the exams with friends so that you can review them afterward. It is also helpful for you to practice any legal problems you were given during the semester. Issue spotting is an important skill for all lawyers to develop. Lawyers utilize this skill on a daily basis when they listen to their clients' stories and are asked to point out places where legal issues might arise.

The ability to recall the law with speed is also very important and frequently tested. On all of your exams, you will be given a series of legal problems, and for each problem you will usually be required to provide the relevant substantive law and apply it to the facts of the problem. Your ability to recall the law with speed is critical because, in most classes, you will be under time constraints to answer all of the problems. The faster you recall the law, the more problems you will complete and the more time you will have to spend on demonstrating your analytical skills. For courses with closed-book exams, this means straight memorization or the use of memory recall devices, such as mnemonics. Do not be passive about learning the law—repeatedly reviewing your outline is not enough. You must actively learn the law by studying definitions and using memory-assistance devices like flash cards. When you have become exceedingly familiar with your flash cards, rewrite them so as to test your memory in different words. This is particularly critical for courses such as torts and criminal law where you must learn a series of definitions with multiple elements. For courses with open-book exams, this means developing an index for your outline that will enable you to locate the relevant law quickly. Create a cover page for your outline that lists the page number for each substantive subtopic. This will help you get there without any undue delay.

The final skill you need to develop is the ability to apply the law to the facts efficiently and skillfully. On your exams, once you have correctly identified the relevant issue and stated the relevant law, you must engage in a discussion of how the law applies to the facts that have been given. The ability to engage in such a discussion is best developed by taking practice exams. When you are practicing this skill, you should focus on efficiency. Try to focus on the essential facts, and do not engage in irrelevant discussions that will waste your energy and your professor's time.

Books About Doing Well in Law School

Getting to Maybe: How to Excel on Law School Exams, Professors Jeremy Paul and Michael Fischl

This book is excellent! While many books and professors may preach "IRAC"—Issue, Rule, Application, Conclusion—as a way of structuring exam answers, Getting to Maybe rightly points out that such advice does not help students correctly identify legal issues or master the intricacies of legal analysis.

Law School Confidential: A Complete Guide to the Law School Experience (Second Edition), Robert H. Miller, Esq.

Robert H. Miller, a former federal judicial clerk, Law Review editor, and graduate of University of Pennsylvania Law School, covers every aspect of the law school experience in thoughtful detail. Whether you are a college student just starting to think about law school, a student in the midst of law school applications, or someone who has already been admitted, Law School Confidential is a book you should not be without. An extensive new chapter is devoted to an exclusive one-on-one interview with Dean of Admissions Richard Geiger of the Cornell Law School, wherein closely guarded secrets of the increasingly competitive admissions process are discussed openly for the first time anywhere. In another chapter, Miller goes one-on-one with the hiring partners of two prestigious U.S. law firms about how to succeed in the hiring process, and what it takes to make it to partnership.

Any final comments for our audience of aspiring law students?

The study of law is a wonderful and noble pursuit, one that I thoroughly enjoyed. Law school is not easy, however, and proper preparation can give you a firm foundation for success. I invite you to visit our website (LawPreview.com) and contact us with any questions (888-PREP-YOU).

CHAPTER 12
CAREER MATTERS

Okay, it's a long time away, but you really ought to be thinking about your professional career beyond law school from day one, especially if your goal is to practice with a major law firm. What stands between you and a job as an associate, the entry-level position at one of these firms, is a three-stage evaluation: first, a review of your resume, including your grades and work experience; second, an on-campus interview; and last, one or more call-back interviews at the firm's offices. It's a fairly intimidating ordeal, but there are a few ways to reduce the anxiety and enhance your chances of landing a great job.

YOUR RESUMÉ
The first thing recruiters tend to notice after your name is the name of the law school you attend. Tacky, but true. Perhaps the greatest misconception among law students, however, is that hiring decisions are based largely upon your school's prestige. All those rankings perpetuate this myth. To be sure, there are a handful of schools with reputations above all others, and students who excel at these schools are in great demand. But you are equally well situated, if not better off, applying from the top of your class at a strong, less prestigious law school class than from the bottom half of a Top Ten law school class.

FIRST-YEAR GRADES ARE THE WHOLE ENCHILADA
Fair or not, the first year of law school will unduly influence your legal future. It's vital that you hit the ground running because law school grades are *the* critical factor in recruitment. An even harsher reality is that *first-year grades are by far the most critical in the hiring process.* Decisions about who gets which plum summer jobs are generally handed down before students take a single second-year exam. Consequently, you're left with exactly *no* time to adjust to law school life and little chance to improve your transcript if you don't come out on top as a first-year student.

WORK EXPERIENCE
If you're applying to law school right out of college, chances are your most significant work experience has been a summer job. Recruiters don't expect you to have spent these months writing Supreme Court decisions. They are generally satisfied if you show that you have worked diligently and seriously at each opportunity. Students who took a year or more off after college obviously have more opportunities to impress but also more of a burden to demonstrate diligence and seriousness.

Work experience in the legal industry—clerkships and paralegal jobs for instance—can be excellent sources of professional development. They are fairly common positions among job applicants, though, so don't feel you have to pursue one of these routes just to show your commitment to the law. You'll make a better impression by working in an industry in which you would like to specialize (e.g., a prospective securities lawyer summering with an investment bank).

Making Law Review
Every law school has an academic periodical called Law Review, produced and edited by law students. It contains articles about various aspects of law—mostly written by professors. While some schools sponsor more than one Law Review, there is generally one that is more prestigious than all the others. In order to "make" Law Review, you will have to finish the all-important first year at (or very, very near) the top of your class or write an article that will be judged by the existing members of the Law Review. You might have to do both. Making Law Review is probably the easiest way to guarantee yourself a job at a blue-chip firm, working for a judge, or in academia. In all honesty, it is a credential you will proudly carry for the rest of your life.

A Couple Good Books
If you are thinking about law school, here are a few books you might find interesting:

The Princeton Review's Law School Essays That Made a Difference
Check out successful essays written for an assortment of selective schools.

Jeff Deaver, The Complete Law School Companion: How to Excel at America's Most Demanding Post-Graduate Curriculum
This straightforward law school survival guide gives excellent advice on how to brief cases, sample briefs, survive class, and plenty more.

THE INTERVIEWS

There are as many right approaches to an interview as there are interviewers. That observation provides little comfort, of course, especially if you're counting on a good interview to make up for whatever deficiencies there are on your resumé. Think about the purpose of the initial 30-minute interview you are likely to have: it provides a rough sketch of not only your future office personality but also your demeanor under stress. The characteristics you demonstrate and the *impression* you give are more important than anything you say. Composure, confidence, maturity, articulation, and an ability to develop rapport are characteristics recruiters are looking for. Give them what they want.

CHAPTER 13
HOW TO USE THIS BOOK

It's pretty simple.

The first part of this book provides a wealth of indispensable information covering everything you need to know about selecting and getting into the law school of your choice. There is also a great deal about what to expect from law school and how to do well. You name it—taking the LSAT, choosing the best school for you, writing a great personal statement, interviewing, paying for it—it's all in the first part.

The second part is the real meat and potatoes of *The Best 169 Law Schools*. It contains portraits of 169 law schools across the United States and Canada. Each school has one of two possible types of entries. The first type of entry is a two-page descriptive profile. It contains data The Princeton Review has collected directly from law school administrators and textual descriptions of the school we have written based on our surveys of current law students. The second type of entry is a data listing, which includes all the same data that appears in the sidebars of the descriptive profiles but does not have the student survey-driven descriptive paragraphs. For an explanation of why all schools do not appear with descriptive profiles, turn to page 59. As is customary with school guidebooks, all data, with the exception of tuition (which should be for the current year if the school reported it by our deadline), reflects figures for the academic year prior to publication unless otherwise noted on the pages. Since law school demographics vary significantly from one institution to another and some schools report data more thoroughly than others, some entries will not include all the individual data described below.

The third part of the book hosts the "School Says . . ." profiles. The "School Says . . ." profiles give extended descriptions of admissions processes, curricula, internship opportunities, and much more. This is your chance to get even more in-depth information on programs that interest you. These schools have paid us a small fee for the chance to tell you more about themselves, and the editorial responsibility is solely that of the law school. We think you'll find these profiles add lots to your picture of a school.

WHAT'S IN THE PROFILES: DATA
The Heading: The first thing you will see for each profile is (obviously) the school's name. On the facing page, you'll find the school's snail mail address, telephone number, fax number, e-mail address, and website. You can find the name of the Admissions Office contact person in the heading, too.

INSTITUTIONAL INFORMATION
Public/Private: Indicates whether a school is state-supported or funded by private means.

Affiliation: If the school is affiliated with a particular religion, you'll find that information here.

Student/Faculty Ratio: The ratio of law students to full-time faculty.

% Faculty Part-Time: The percentage of faculty who are part-time.

% Faculty Female: The percentage of faculty who are women.

% Faculty Minority: The percentage of people who teach at the law school who are also members of minority groups.

Total Faculty: The total number of faculty members at the law school.

> **Yet Another Good Book**
> Scott Turow, *One L: The Turbulent True Story of a First Year at Harvard Law School*
> This law school primer is equal parts illuminating and harrowing.

SURVEY SAYS

The Survey Says list appears in the sidebar of each law school's two-page descriptive profile, and up to three Survey Says items will appear on each list. As the name suggests, these items communicate results of our law student surveys. There are ten possible Survey Says items, each explained below. Of these ten, the three items that appear are those about which student respondents demonstrated the greatest degree of consensus. Survey Says items represent the agreement among students only at *that particular law school* and are not relative to how students at other law schools feel about that particular Survey Says item.

Liberal students: Students report that their fellow law students lean to the left politically.

Conservative students: Students report that their fellow law students lean to the right politically.

Students love Hometown, State: Students are pleased with the location of their law school.

Good social life: Students report a lively social life at the law school.

Students never sleep: Students report a low average number of hours of sleep each night. Little sleep in law school is often an indication of extra-long hours of study on a daily basis.

Heavy use of Socratic Method: Students report that their professors primarily employ the traditional Socratic Method in the classroom.

Beautiful campus: Students report that their law school campus is practical and beautiful.

Great research resources: Students report that the library, computer databases, and other research tools are good.

Great judicial externship/internship/clerkship opportunities: Students rate these opportunities as excellent.

Diverse opinions in classrooms: Students agree that differing points of view are tolerated in the classroom.

STUDENTS

Enrollment of Law School: The total number of students enrolled in the law school.

% Male/Female: The percentage of full-time students with an X and a Y chromosome and the percentage of students with two X chromosomes, respectively.

% Out-of-state: The percentage of full-time students who are out-of-state.

% Full-time: The percentage of students who attend the school on a full-time basis.

% Minority: The percentage of full-time students who represent underrepresented minority groups.

% International: The percentage of students who hail from foreign soil.

# of Countries Represented: The number of different foreign countries from which the current student body hails.

Average Age of Entering Class: On the whole, how old the 1Ls are.

ACADEMICS

Academic Experience Rating: The quality of the learning environment, on a scale of 60 to 99. The rating incorporates the Admissions Selectivity Rating and the average responses of law students at the school to several questions on our law student survey. In addition to the Admissions Selectivity Rating, factors considered include how students rate the quality of teaching and the accessibility of their professors, the school's research resources, the range of available courses, the balance of legal theory and practical lawyering skills stressed in the curriculum, the tolerance for diverse opinions in the classroom, and how intellectually challenging the course work is. This individual rating places each law school on a continuum for purposes of comparing all law schools within this edition only. If a law school receives a "low" Academic Experience Rating, it doesn't mean that the school provides a bad academic experience for its students. It simply means that the school scored lower than other schools in our computations based on

> **Law School Fun Fact**
>
> The least litigated amendment in the Bill of Rights is the Third Amendment, which prohibits the quartering of soldiers in private homes without consent of the owner.

the criteria outlined above. Because this rating incorporates law student opinion data, only those law schools that appear in the section with the descriptive profiles based on student surveys receive an Academic Experience Rating.

Professors Interesting Rating: Based on law student opinion. We asked law students to rate the quality of teaching at their law schools on a scale from 60 to 99. Because this rating incorporates law student opinion data, only those law schools that appear in the section with the descriptive profiles receive a Professors Interesting Rating.

Professors Accessible Rating: Based on law student opinion. We asked law students to rate how accessible the law faculty members at their schools are on a scale from 60 to 99. Because this rating incorporates law student opinion data, only those law schools that appear in the section with the descriptive profiles receive a Professors Accessible Rating.

Hours of Study Per Day: From our student survey. The average number of hours students at the school report studying each day.

Academic Specialties: Different areas of law and academic programs on which the school prides itself.

Advanced Degrees Offered: Degrees available through the law school and the length of the program.

Combined Degrees Offered: Programs at this school involving the law school and some other college or degree program within the larger university, and how long it will take you to complete the joint program.

Grading System: Scoring system used by the law school. (Appears in the data listings section only.)

Academic Requirements: Most law schools require their students to complete some courses and/or programs that go beyond traditional legal theory, whether to broaden their understanding of and experience with the law or to develop important practical lawyering skills.

    Clinical Program Required? Indicates whether clinical programs are required to complete the core curriculum.

    Clinical Program Description: Programs designed to give students hands-on training and experience in the practice of some area of law. (Appears in the data listings section only.)

    Legal Writing Course Requirement? Tells you whether there is a required course in legal writing.

    Legal Writing Description: A description of any course work, required or optional, designed specifically to develop legal writing skills vital to the practice of law. (Appears in the data listings section only.)

    Legal Methods Course Requirements? Indicates whether there is a mandatory curriculum component to cover legal methods.

    Legal Methods Description: A description of any course work, required or optional, designed specifically to develop the skills vital to legal analysis. (Appears in the data listings section only.)

    Legal Research Course Requirements? If a school requires course work specifically to develop legal research skills, this field will tell you.

    Legal Research Description: A description of any course work, required or optional, designed specifically to develop legal research skills vital to the practice of law. (Appears in the data listings section only.)

    Moot Court Requirement? Indicates whether participation in a moot court program is mandatory.

    Moot Court Description: This will describe any moot court program, mandatory or optional, designed to develop skills in legal research, writing, and oral argument. (Appears in the data listings section only.)

    Public Interest Law Requirement? If a school requires participation on a public interest law project, we'll let you know here.

    Public Interest Law Description: Programs designed to expose students to the public interest law field through clinical work, volunteer opportunities, or specialized course work. (Appears in the data listings section only.)

Academic Journals: This field will list any academic journals offered at the school. (Appears in the data listings section only.)

ADMISSIONS INFORMATION

Admissions Selectivity Rating: How competitive admission is at the law school, on a scale of 60 to 99. Several factors determine this rating, including LSAT scores and the average undergraduate GPA of entering 1L students, the percentage of applicants accepted, and the percentage of accepted applicants who enrolled in the law school. We collect this information through a survey that law school administrators completed for the fall 2012 entering class. This individual rating places each law school on a continuum for purposes of comparing all law schools within this edition only. All law schools that appear in this edition of the guide, whether in the section with the descriptive profiles based on student surveys or in the section with school-reported statistics only, receive an Admissions Selectivity Rating. If a law school has a relatively low Admissions Selectivity Rating, it doesn't necessarily mean that it's easy to gain admission to the law school. (It's not easy to get into any ABA-approved law schools, really.) It simply means that the school scored lower relative to other schools in our computations based on the criteria outlined in the previous page.

# of Applications Received: The number of people who applied to the law school's full-time JD program.

# of Applicants Accepted: The number of people who were admitted to the school's full-time class.

# of Acceptees Attending: The number of those admitted who chose to attend the school full-time.

Average LSAT/LSAT Range: Indicates the average LSAT score of incoming 1Ls, as reported by the school. The range is the 25th to 75th percentiles of 1Ls.

Average Undergrad GPA: It's usually on a 4.0 scale.

Application Fee: How much it costs to apply to the school.

Regular Application Deadline and "Rolling": Many law schools evaluate applications and notify applicants of admission decisions on a continuous, rolling basis over the course of several months (ordinarily from late fall to midsummer). Obviously, if you apply to one of these schools, you want to apply early because there will be more places available at the beginning of the process.

Regular Notification? The official date by or on which a law school will release a decision for an applicant who applied using the regular admission route.

Early Application Program? Whether the law school has an early application program. If you are accepted to an early decision program, you are obligated to attend that law school. If you are accepted under an early action program, you have no obligation to attend. You just get to know earlier whether you got in.

Early Application Deadline: The official date by which the law school must receive your application if you want to be considered for its early application program.

Early Application Notification: The official date on which a law school will release a decision for an applicant who applied using the early application route.

Transfer Students Accepted? Whether transfer students from other schools are considered for admission.

Evening Division Offered? Whether the school offers an evening program in addition to its full-time regular program. Evening division programs are almost always part-time and require four years of study (instead of three) to complete.

Part-time Accepted? Whether part-time students may enroll in the JD program on a basis other than the standard full-time.

CAS Accepted? "Yes" indicates that the school utilizes the Law School Data Assembly Service. *Please note—the organization formerly known as Law School Data Assembly Service is now Credential Assembly Service (CAS).

Applicants Also Look At: The law schools to which applicants to this school also apply. It's important. It's a reliable indicator of the overall academic quality of the applicant pool.

INTERNATIONAL STUDENTS

TOEFL Required/Recommended of International Students? Indicates whether or not international students must take the TOEFL, or Test of English as a Foreign Language, to be admitted to the school.

Minimum TOEFL: Minimum score (paper and computer) an international student must earn on the TOEFL to be admitted.

FINANCIAL FACTS

Annual Tuition (Residents/Nonresidents): What it costs to go to school for an academic year. For state schools, both in-state and out-of-state tuition is listed.

Books and Supplies: Indicates how much students can expect to shell out for textbooks and other assorted supplies during the academic year.

Fees Per Credit (Residents/Nonresidents): That mysterious extra money you are required to pay the law school in addition to tuition and everything else, on a per-credit basis. If in-state and out-of-state students are charged differently, both amounts are listed.

Tuition Per Credit (Residents/Nonresidents): Dollar amount charged per credit hour. For state schools, both in-state and out-of-state amounts are listed when they differ.

Room and Board (On-/Off-campus): This is the school's estimate of what it costs to buy meals and to pay for decent living quarters for the academic year. Where available, on- and off-campus rates are listed.

Financial Aid Application Deadline: The last day on which students can turn in their applications for monetary assistance.

% First-Year Students Receiving Some Sort of Aid: The percentage of new JD students who receive monetary assistance.

% Receiving Some Sort of Aid: The percentage of all the students at the school presently accumulating a staggering debt.

% of Aid That Is Merit-Based: The percentage of aid not based on financial need.

% Receiving Scholarships: The percentage of students at the school who received some sort of "free money" award. This figure can include grants as well.

Average Grant: Average financial aid amount awarded to students that does not have to be paid back. This figure can include scholarships as well.

Average Loan: Average amount of loan dollars accrued by students for the year.

Average Total Aid Package: How much aid each student at the school receives on average for the year.

Average Debt: The amount of debt—or, in legal lingo, arrears—you'll likely be saddled with by the time you graduate.

EMPLOYMENT INFORMATION

Career Rating: How well the law school prepares its students for a successful career in law, on a scale of 60 to 99. The rating incorporates school-reported data and the average responses of law students at the school to a few questions on our law student survey. We ask law schools for the median starting salaries of graduating students, the percentage of graduating students who find employment after graduation, and the percentage of students who pass the bar exam the first time they take it. We ask students about how much the law program encourages practical experience; the opportunities for externships, internships, and clerkships; and how prepared to practice law they will feel after graduating. If a school receives a "low" Career Rating, it doesn't necessarily mean that the career prospects for graduates are bad; it simply means that the school scored lower relative to how other schools scored based on the criteria outlined above. Because this rating incorporates law student opinion data, only those law schools that appear in the section with the descriptive profiles receive a Career Rating.

Rate of Placement (nine months out): Percent of graduates who secured employment within nine months of graduating from law school.

Median Starting Salary: The average amount of money graduates of this law school make the first year out of school.

State for Bar Exam: The state for which most students from the school will take the bar exam.

Pass Rate for First-Time Bar: After three years, the percentage of students who passed the bar exam the first time they took it. It's a crucial statistic. You *don't* want to fail your state's bar.

Employers Who Frequently Hire Grads: Firms where past grads have had success finding jobs.

Prominent Alumni: Those who made it . . . *big*.

Grads Employed by Field: The percentage of students in the most recent graduating class who have obtained jobs in a particular field.

Academia: The percentage of graduates who got jobs at law schools, universities, and think tanks.

Business/Industry: The percentage of graduates who got jobs working in business, corporations, consulting, and so on. These jobs are sometimes law-related and sometimes not.

Government: Uncle Sam needs lawyers like you wouldn't even believe.

Judicial Clerkships: The percentage of graduates who got jobs doing research for judges.

Military: The percentage of lawyers who work to represent the Armed Forces in all kinds of legal matters, like Tom Cruise in *A Few Good Men*.

Private Practice: The percentage of graduates who got jobs in traditional law firms of various sizes or "put out a shingle" for themselves as sole practitioners.

Public Interest: The percentage of (mostly) altruistic graduates who got jobs providing legal assistance to people who couldn't afford it otherwise.

NOTA BENE

If a 60* appears for any of a law school's ratings, it means that the school's administrators did not report by our deadline all of the statistics that rating incorporates.

Please note that we target each law school for resurveying at least every other year, which means we rewrite each law school's descriptive profile at least every other year, too. Student surveys captured via our online survey (http://survey.review.com) are considered current for the purposes of our own rating, rankings, and Survey Says items for two years.

WHAT'S IN THE PROFILES: DESCRIPTIVE TEXT

Academics, Life, and Getting In Sections: The text of the descriptive profiles is broken out into three sections: Academics, Life, and Getting In. The Academics and Life sections of each descriptive profile are driven by the student survey responses collected from current law students at the school, and the quotations sprinkled throughout each of these sections come directly from the written comments students provided us with on their surveys. In the Academics section, we often discuss professors and their teaching methods, the workload, special, clinical programs, the efficiency of the administration, and the helpfulness of the library staff. In the Life section, we often discuss how academically competitive the student body is, how (and if) students separate into cliques, clubs, or organizations students often join, and the amenities of the town in which the school is located. We don't follow a cookie-cutter formula when writing these profiles. Instead we rely on students' responses to the open-ended questions on our student survey and analysis of their aggregate responses to our multiple choice questions to determine each profile's major "theme." The information in the Getting In section is based on the data we collect from law school administrators and our own additional research.

DECODING DEGREES

Many law schools offer joint- or combined-degree programs with other departments (or sometimes even with other schools) that you can earn along with your Juris Doctor. You'll find the abbreviations for these degrees in the individual school profiles, but we thought we would give you a little help in figuring out exactly what they are.

AMBA	Accounting Master of Business		MEM	Master of Environmental Management
BCL	Bachelor of Civil Law		MFA	Master of Fine Arts
DJUR	Doctor of Jurisprudence		MHA	Master of Health Administration
DL	Doctor of Law		MHSA	Master of Health Services Administration
EdD	Doctor of Education		MIA	Master of International Affairs
HRIR	Human Resources and Industrial Relations		MIB	Master of International Business
IMBA	International Master of Business Administration		MIP	Master of Intellectual Property
JD	Juris Doctor		MIR	Master of Industrial Relations
JSD	Doctor of Juridical Science		MILR	Master of Industrial and Labor Relations
JSM	Master of the Science of Law		MJ	Master of Jurisprudence
LLB	Bachelor of Law		MJS	Master of Juridical Study (not a JD)
LLCM	Master of Comparative Law (for international students)		MLIR	Master of Labor and Industrial Relations
LLM	Master of Law		MLIS	Master of Library and Information Sciences
MA	Master of Arts		MLS	Master of Library Science
MAcc	Master of Accounting		MMA	Master of Marine Affairs
MALD	Master of Arts in Law and Diplomacy		MOB	Master of Organizational Behavior
MAM	Master of Arts Management		MPA	Master of Public Administration
MM	Master of Management		MPAFF	Master of Public Affairs
MANM	Master of Nonprofit Management		MPH	Master of Public Health
MAPA	Master of Public Administration		MPP	Master of Public Planning or Master of Public Policy
MAUA	Master of Arts in Urban Affairs		MPPA	Master of Public Policy
MBA	Master of Business Administration		MPPS	Master of Public Policy Sciences
MCJ	Master of Criminal Justice		MPS	Master of Professional Studies in Law
MCL	Master of Comparative Law		MRP	Master of Regional Planning
MCP	Master of Community Planning		MS	Master of Science
MCRP	Master of City and Regional Planning		MSEL	Master of Studies in Environmental Law
MDiv	Master of Divinity		MSES	Master of Science in Environmental Science
ME	Master of Engineering or Master of Education		MSF	Master of Science in Finance
MEd	Master of Education		MSFS	Master of Science in Foreign Service
MED	Master of Environmental Design		MSI	Master of Science in Information

MSIA	Master of Science in Industrial Administration
MSIE	Master of Science in International Economics
MSJ	Master of Science in Journalism
MSPH	Master of Science in Public Health
MSW	Master of Social Welfare or Master of Social Work
MT	Master of Taxation
MTS	Master of Theological Studies
MUP	Master of Urban Planning
MUPD	Master of Urban Planning and Development
MURP	Master of Urban and Regional Planning
PharmD	Doctor of Pharmacy
PhD	Doctor of Philosophy
REES	Russian and Eastern European Studies Certificate
SJD	Doctor of Juridical Science
DVM	Doctor of Veterinary Medicine
MALIR	Master of Arts in Labor and Industrial Relations

LAW SCHOOLS RANKED BY CATEGORY

ABOUT OUR LAW SCHOOL RANKINGS

On the following few pages, you will find eleven top ten lists of ABA-approved law schools ranked according to various metrics. It must be noted, however, that none of these lists purports to rank the law schools by their overall quality. Nor should any combination of the categories we've chosen be construed as representing the raw ingredients for such a ranking. We have made no attempt to gauge the *prestige* of these schools, and we wonder whether we could accurately do so even if we tried. What we have done, however, is presented a number of lists using information from two very large databases—one of statistical information collected from law schools and another of subjective data gathered via our survey of more than 18,000 law students at 169 ABA-approved law schools. We target each law school's student body for resurveying at least every other year. This means that schools' student opinion data is considered current for the book's rankings and descriptive profiles for two years.

Ten of the ranking lists are based partly or wholly on opinions collected through our law student survey. The only schools that may appear in these lists are the 169 ABA-approved law schools from which we were able to collect a sufficient number of student surveys to accurately represent the student experience in our various ratings and descriptive profiles.

One of the rankings, Toughest to Get Into, incorporates *only* admissions statistics reported to us by the law schools. Therefore, any ABA-approved law school appearing in this edition of the guide, whether we collected student surveys from it or not, may appear on this list.

In the 2010 edition of this book, we introduced the Best Classroom Experience list, based on student assessment of professors' teaching abilities, balance of theory and practical skills in the curricula, and tolerance for differing opinions in class discussion.

Under the title of each list is an explanation of the criteria on which the ranking is based. For explanations of many of the individual rankings components, go back to page 46–49.

It's worth repeating: There is no one best law school in America, but there is a best law school for you. By using these rankings in conjunction with the descriptive profiles and data listings of the schools in this book, we hope that you will begin to identify the attributes of a law school that are important to you, as well as the law schools that can best help you to achieve your personal and professional goals.

The schools in each category appear in descending order.

TOUGHEST TO GET INTO
BASED ON THE ADMISSIONS SELECTIVITY RATING (SEE PAGE 47 FOR EXPLANATION)

1. Yale University
2. Harvard Law School
3. Stanford University
4. University of California—Berkeley
5. University of Virginia
6. The University of North Carolina at Chapel Hill
7. Columbia University
8. Duke University
9. University of Pennsylvania
10. The University of Chicago

BEST PROFESSORS
BASED ON STUDENT ASSESSMENT OF PROFESSORS' TEACHING ABILITIES AND ACCESSIBILITY OUTSIDE CLASS

1. Boston University
2. Duke University
3. Stanford University
4. Washington and Lee University
5. Pepperdine University
6. University of Virginia
7. Loyola Marymount University
8. University of Chicago
9. University of St.Thomas
10. Regent University

MOST COMPETITIVE STUDENTS
BASED ON LAW STUDENT ASSESSMENTS OF: THE NUMBER OF HOURS THEY SPEND STUDYING OUTSIDE OF CLASS EACH DAY, THE NUMBER OF HOURS THEY THINK THEIR FELLOW LAW STUDENTS SPEND STUDYING OUTSIDE OF CLASS EACH DAY, THE DEGREE OF COMPETITIVENESS AMONG LAW STUDENTS AT THEIR SCHOOL, AND THE AVERAGE NUMBER OF HOURS THEY SLEEP EACH NIGHT

1. Baylor University
2. Brigham Young University
3. Case Western Reserve University
4. Thomas M. Cooley Law School
5. Whittier College
6. Nova Southeastern University
7. Widener University (PA)
8. Faulkner University
9. University of California—Hastings
10. Syracuse University

BEST CAREER PROSPECTS
BASED ON THE CAREER RATING (SEE PAGE 49 FOR EXPLANATION)

1. Columbia University
2. The University of Chicago
3. University of Pennsylvania
4. Harvard Law School
5. New York University
6. University of California—Berkeley
7. Northwestern University
8. Georgetown University
9. The George Washington University
10. University of Southern California

BEST CLASSROOM EXPERIENCE

BASED ON STUDENT ASSESSMENT OF PROFESSORS' TEACHING ABILITIES, BALANCE OF THEORY AND PRACTICAL SKILLS IN THE CURRICULA, AND TOLERANCE FOR DIFFERING OPINIONS IN CLASS DISCUSSION

1. The University of Chicago
2. Stanford University
3. Duke University
4. University of Virginia
5. Boston University
6. Northwestern University
7. University of Michigan
8. New York University
9. University of Pennsylvania
10. University of California—Berkeley

MOST CONSERVATIVE STUDENTS

BASED ON STUDENT ASSESSMENT OF THE POLITICAL BENT OF THE STUDENT BODY AT LARGE

1. Ave Maria School of Law
2. Regent University
3. Brigham Young University
4. Samford University
5. George Mason University
6. University of Notre Dame
7. Pepperdine University
8. University of Alabama
9. Baylor University
10. Louisiana State University

MOST LIBERAL STUDENTS

BASED ON STUDENT ASSESSMENT OF THE POLITICAL BENT OF THE STUDENT BODY AT LARGE

1. Northeastern University
2. Vermont Law School
3. American University
4. Lewis & Clark College
5. University of Oregon
6. University of San Francisco
7. Brooklyn Law School
8. University of the District of Columbia
9. New York University
10. University of California—Berkeley

BEST ENVIRONMENT FOR MINORITY STUDENTS

BASED ON THE PERCENTAGE OF THE STUDENT BODY THAT IS FROM UNDERREPRESENTED MINORITIES AND STUDENT ASSESSMENT OF WHETHER ALL STUDENTS RECEIVE EQUAL TREATMENT BY FELLOW STUDENTS AND THE FACULTY, REGARDLESS OF ETHNICITY

1. University of Hawaii at Manoa
2. Southern University
3. Florida International University
4. St. Thomas University
5. Whittier College
6. University of California—Davis
7. Loyola Marymount University
8. University of the District of Columbia
9. Stanford University
10. Hofstra University

MOST DIVERSE FACULTY

BASED ON THE PERCENTAGE OF THE LAW SCHOOL FACULTY THAT IS FROM A MINORITY GROUP AND STUDENT ASSESSMENT OF WHETHER THE FACULTY MAKES UP A BROADLY DIVERSE GROUP OF INDIVIDUALS

1. Southern University
2. University of the District of Columbia
3. University of Hawaii at Manoa
4. Florida International University
5. University of New Mexico
6. Drexel University
7. Rutgers, The State University of New Jersey—Newark
8. University of San Francisco
9. University of Miami
10. Seattle University

MOST CHOSEN BY OLDER STUDENTS

BASED ON THE AVERAGE AGE OF ENTRY OF LAW SCHOOL STUDENTS AND STUDENT REPORTS OF HOW MANY YEARS THEY SPENT OUT OF COLLEGE BEFORE ENROLLING IN LAW SCHOOL

1. University of the District of Columbia
2. University of Maine
3. Southern University
4. Phoenix School of Law
5. University of Hawaii at Manoa
6. Lewis & Clark College
7. Touro Law Center
8. Northwestern University
9. Seattle University
10. University of New Mexico

BEST QUALITY OF LIFE

BASED ON STUDENT ASSESSMENT OF: WHETHER THERE IS A STRONG SENSE OF COMMUNITY AT THE SCHOOL, THE LOCATION OF THE LAW SCHOOL, THE QUALITY OF THE SOCIAL LIFE

1. Duke University
2. University of San Francisco
3. University of Virginia
4. University of Oklahoma
5. Vanderbilt University
6. Samford University
7. Northwestern University
8. University of Pennsylvania
9. Chapman University
10. Pepperdine University

LAW SCHOOL DESCRIPTIVE PROFILES

In this section you will find the two page descriptive profile of each of the 169 ABA-approved law schools. As there are currently a total of 200 ABA-approved law schools in the country, there are obviously many law schools not appearing in this section; those schools appear in the following section, Law School Data Listings.

In order for a law school to appear in this section, we had to collect the opinions of a sufficient number of current law students at that school to fairly and responsibly represent the general law student experience there. Our descriptive profiles are driven primarily by (1) comments law students provide in response to open-ended questions on our student survey, and (2) our own statistical analysis of student responses to the many multiple-choice questions on the survey. While many law students complete a survey unsolicited by us at http://survey. review.com, in the vast majority of cases we rely on law school administrators to get the word out about our survey to their students. In an ideal scenario, the law school administration e-mails a Princeton Review–authored e-mail to all law students with an embedded link to our survey website (again, http://survey.review.com). If for some reason there are restrictions that prevent the administration from contacting the entire law student body on behalf of an outside party, they often help us find other ways to notify students that we are seeking their opinions, like advertising in law student publications or posting on law student community websites or electronic mailing lists. In almost all cases, when the administration is cooperative, we are able to collect opinions from a sufficient number of students to produce an accurate descriptive profile and ratings of its law school.

There is a group of law school administrators, however, that doesn't agree with the notion that the opinions of current law students presented in descriptive profile and rankings formats are useful to prospective law school students trying to choose the right schools to apply to and attend. Administrators at the 34 ABA-approved law schools not appearing in this section are a part of this group. They either ignored our multiple attempts to contact them to request their assistance in notifying their students about our survey, or they simply refused to work with us at all. While we would like to be able to write a descriptive profile on each of these 34 schools anyway, we won't do so with minimal law student opinion. So if you are a prospective law school student and would like to read the opinions of current law students about your dream school(s), contact the missing school(s) and communicate this desire to them. (We include contact information in each of the data listings.) If you are a current law student at one of the 34 ABA-approved law schools not profiled in this section, please don't send us angry letters; instead, go to http://survey.review.com, complete a survey about your school, and tell all of your fellow students to do the same. If we collect enough current student opinion on your school in the coming year, we'll include a descriptive profile in the next edition of the guide.

SPECIAL NOTE ON THE TEXT OF EACH DESCRIPTIVE PROFILE

The Academics and Life sections of each descriptive profile are driven by the student opinions collected from current law students at the school, and the quotations sprinkled throughout each of these sections comes directly from the written comments with which students provided us on their surveys. The Getting In section is based on the data we collect from law school administrators and our own additional research. Every law school with a descriptive profile has its students resurveyed and its profile rewritten at least every other year.

SPECIAL NOTE ON THE SIDEBAR STATISTICS

Explanations of what each field of data signifies may be found in the How to Use This Book section, which begins on page 45.

ALBANY LAW SCHOOL

INSTITUTIONAL INFORMATION

Public/private	Private
Affiliation	No Affiliation
Student-faculty ratio	13:1
% faculty part-time	45
% faculty female	56
% faculty underrepresented minority	13
Total faculty	91

SURVEY SAYS...

Great library staff, Abundant externship/internship/clerksip opportunities

STUDENTS

Enrollment of law school	617
% male/female	49/51
% part-time	6
% underrepresented minority	21
Average age of entering class	23

ACADEMICS

Academic Experience Rating	**69**
Profs interesting rating	76
Profs accessible rating	77
Hours of study per day	3.96

Academic Specialties

Civil Procedure, Constitutional, Criminal, Environmental, Government Services, International, Labor, Taxation, Intellectual Property

Advanced Degrees Offered

LLM (must be continuously enrolled and complete 24 credits within 3 years); LLM for International Law Graduates (must be continuously enrolled and complete 24 credits within 3 years); For those on an F1 visa: full-time, 1 year MS in Legal Studies

Combined Degrees Offered

JD, 3 years; JD/MBA, JD/MPA, JD/ MSW, JD/MRP, JD/MPP, 3.5–4 years; LLM 1–3 years; LLM for International Law Graduates, 1 year

Academics

At Albany Law School, the "research facilities and resources are endless, well staffed, and easily accessible." Moreover, one of the greatest aspects of Albany Law is the "wealth of practical experience and internship opportunities." Indeed, "there is no excuse for not having a summer internship, or an academic year internship... There is absolutely no shortage of court, government, and political exposure." As one content student explains, "The connection to New York State government is fantastic and the biggest selling point of the school." And while some students might head to Boston or New York City for internships, many brag that "You can't beat the law-student thrill of being able to walk up to the highest court in New York, the Court of Appeals, and then walk down two blocks to find yourself at the federal Appellate courthouse."

Although students do have great access to internships, etc. a number still express dissatisfaction at the need to "place a greater emphasis on practical application of the law." One frustrated student reveals, "I will have finished a year of contracts without actually looking at a single contract. In a rough job market, the school could really stand to improve on producing great attorneys, instead of great law students. You would think the school would know how to do this by now, considering it's the oldest independent law school in the country." A handful of students also complain that there's "no way to complete a concentration because enough of the specialty courses aren't offered, and the ones that are almost always conflict with bar classes."

Thankfully, for the most part students are fond of their professors. "They are brilliant, work hard, and are easily accessible." As one student happily shares, "There are some incredible, pedigreed professors at this school." And many "are able to take their genius and make it relatable and teachable in the classroom." Another student reveals, "I have had professors that inspire me to learn through their enjoyment of the field, and I've also had teachers that motivate me to learn through fear of being called on." Unfortunately, compliments do not extend to the administration. As another student bemoans, "I attended a public undergraduate institution with 18,000 students that was far more responsive to student needs than the administration of this 750-student private law school. Instead of sending an email to or leaving a message with administrators, instead write down your issues or questions and then light the paper on fire—there is no difference between the two."

Life

The student body is "competitive but friendly" at Albany and "relations among students are generally very strong." "It's not like people hide in books or anything," says a 2L. Another 2L adds, "I would say the crowd nowadays is more on the conservative side politically, but the liberal side socially." A fellow student interjects, "I'm a liberal who constantly feels out of place because I'm not here to pursue a six figure salary... It's rather shocking how conservative the school is considering Albany is a very progressive city."

Nadia Castriota, Assistant Dean and Director of Admissions
80 New Scotland Avenue, Albany, NY 12208
Tel: 518-445-2361 Fax: 518-445-2369
E-Mail: admissions@albanylaw.edu • Website: www.albanylaw.edu

While students are "very busy" there is ample opportunity for socializing "if you make it a priority." Many claim that Albany Law "is like high school" but few complain about a campus where "smallish cliques are the norm," as the social life is "great" and "people are free to interact with multiple cliques, and those groups often get together to form a whole." There are many student organizations to join if one is inclined, though with many students commuting, they're not as popular as some would like.

Albany, as a city, "is pretty dingy and small," many students choose to live outside the city limits and commute (which amounts to only a fifteen-minute drive). Students still often choose to walk around Albany at night," and students and staff definitely do live within walking distance of the campus. "There are several colleges and universities [nearby], and so the police chaperone as necessary." Unlike many law schools, parking is not too much of a problem, even for a city campus. "Commuting to internships (even at rush hour) is never problematic," says a student. Overall, the facilities are "well-maintained and look great," and a nice bonus is that the law school is entirely self-contained, with library access in the main classroom building. "It is much appreciated when you need a quiet place to sit with only an hour in between classes and when it's too cold to want to walk outside to get to another building."

Getting In

Admissions officers at Albany Law School seek academically driven candidates who are intellectually curious. Accepted students in the 25th percentile earned an LSAT score of 151 and a GPA of 3.04. Accepted students in the 75th percentile achieved an LSAT score of 157 and a GPA of 3.54.

Clinical program required	No
Legal writing course requirement	Yes
Legal methods course requirement	Yes
Legal research course requirement	Yes
Moot court requirement	No
Public interest law requirement	No

ADMISSIONS

Selectivity Rating	70
# applications received	1,771
% applicants accepted	63
% acceptees attending	18
Median LSAT	152
LSAT Range (25th to 75th percentile)	149–155
Median undergrad GPA	3.31
Application fee	$70
Regular application deadline	3/1
Transfer students accepted	Yes
Evening division offered	No
Part-time accepted	Yes
CAS accepted	Yes

FINANCIAL FACTS

Annual tuition	$43,248
Books and supplies	$1,000
Fees	$275
Room & Board	$10,400
% first-year students receiving some sort of aid	99
% all students receiving some sort of aid	96
% of aid that is merit based	100
% receiving scholarships	37
Average grant	$19,796
Average loan	$44,383
Average total aid package	$50,518
Average debt	$113,674

EMPLOYMENT INFORMATION

Career Rating	60*
Total 2012 JD Grads	233
% for whom you have useable information	81
# employed full-time	160
# employed part-time	31
# employed bar required	138
# employed JD preferred	31
# employed professional/other	12
# employed non-professional	9
# pursuing advanced degree	4
# unemployed and seeking employment	23
# not seeking employment	9
% grads employed by school	1
State for bar exam	NY
Pass rate for first-time bar	81.5

Prominent Alumni

Thomas Vilsack, Secretary US Agriculture, former Governor of Iowa; Richard D. Parsons, Former Chairman Citibank, former CEO AOL Time Warner; Andrew Cuomo, Governor of New York State.

Grads Employed by Field (%)

Academic (3)
Business/Industry (19)
Government (6)
Judicial Clerkship (4)
Private Practice (43)
Public Interest (4)

AMERICAN UNIVERSITY
WASHINGTON COLLEGE OF LAW

INSTITUTIONAL INFORMATION

Public/private	Private
Student-faculty ratio	11:1
% faculty part-time	43
% faculty female	38
% faculty underrepresented minority	16
Total faculty	410

SURVEY SAYS...

Diverse opinions accepted in class-rooms, Abundant externship/internship/clerkship opportunities, Liberal students

STUDENTS

Enrollment of law school	1,522
% male/female	43/57
% part-time	20
% underrepresented minority	35
% international	1
# of countries represented	53
Average age of entering class	24

ACADEMICS

Academic Experience Rating	87
Profs interesting rating	83
Profs accessible rating	81
Hours of study per day	4.36

Academic Specialties

Commercial, Constitutional, Corporation Securities, Criminal, Environmental, Government Services, Human Rights, International, Labor, Legal History, Property, Taxation, Intellectual Property

Advanced Degrees Offered

LLM, International Legal Studies, 12–18 months; LLM, Law and Government 12 months; LLM, Advocacy 12–18 months; SJD, 3–4 years

Combined Degrees Offered

JD/MA International Affairs, JD/MS Justice, JD/MPA, JD/MPP, all 3.5–4 year programs; LLM/MBA, LLM/MPA, LLM/MPP, 2–3 years

Academics

Boasting some of the country's top international law programs, American University's Washington College of Law takes a student-centered approach in which students internalize material and gain working knowledge of the law. Professors are "less interested in embarrassing students and cold-calling on them, and more interested in helping students work through nuance in legal theory and practice," and there is an "abundance of opportunities for practical, experiential programs." The centers and offices (such as the War Crimes Research Office and the Center for Human Rights and Humanitarian Law) at WCL "provide students with practical experience all without leaving the school."

The atmosphere at WCL is "encouraging and developmentally oriented, while simultaneously being highly rigorous and constantly challenging." The professors are "experts in their fields," "easily accessible," and "do everything they can to help their students find internships and jobs." Every professor has "a true open door policy" and "is willing to provide assistance with class materials and general advice concerning choosing a law as a career." The school offers "a broad array of classes" taught by a list of well-respected legal experts, and there is a great breadth of international exchange and dual-degree programs, including "a rich curriculum of courses" in private and public international law.

A prime location in the nation's capital creates fertile career ground—DC is where "basically every heavy-hitting law firm has an office"—and "the adjunct faculty is essentially composed of partners at these firms." For example, the higher-level electives are taught by "former ambassadors and government employees, all [of whom] teach wonderful courses." "I cannot imagine wanting to be an international lawyer and attending school anywhere else," says a student.

WCL also makes "excellent use" of the resources that K Street and the federal government provides in regards to hiring faculty and providing internship/externship/clinical opportunities. The "great legal writing program" helps to imbue the American law degree with a good deal of cache when starting out, but many say that "the Office of Career and Professional Development could be more accessible and energetic," particularly to those students who are interested in niche areas of the law. The school also has a "growing" business law program, and the American University Business Law Review is the first business-focused journal in DC.

Life

The diversity of the school is second to none; WCL is "packed" with students and staff that "come from all over the world and bring various and insightful points of view," and "you can hear three or four languages easily at any time." The renowned international law and human rights focus means the school is "an excellent venue for important events," and there are "so many activities and incredible speakers every day that it is positively overwhelming." "In less than one year, I have attended lectures by the Swiss Ambassador to the US, was seated next to the Cypriot Ambassador to the US while listening to the Lichtenstein Foreign Minister discuss the ICC, [and] attended a panel discussion with three OAS Ambassadors on the current state of OAS," says a 1L.

AKIRA SHIROMA, ASSISSTANT DEAN OF ADMISSIONS AND FINANCIAL AID
4801 MASSACHUSETTS AVENUE, NW, WASHINGTON, D.C. 20016
TEL: 202-274-4101 FAX: 202-274-4107
E-MAIL: WCLADMIT@WCL.AMERICAN.EDU • WEBSITE: WWW.WCL.AMERICAN.EDU

While it's true that "the facilities are not the prettiest," the planned new building (currently a couple of years out) "will be a tremendous and welcomed change," particularly since the current law school "is not within walking distance of the nearest Metro station." Students are "generally not competitive with each other," this "definitely very liberal school" school as a whole "is very cooperative," with the sharing of outlines and notes a commonplace practice. "The academic environment is nurturing and does not feel nearly as competitive as I thought it would be," says a 1L.

Getting In

Admitted students at the 25th percentile have LSAT scores of 156 and GPAs of about 3.19. Admitted students at the 75th percentile have LSAT scores of 162 and GPAs of 3.58. WCL says that it generally considers your highest score if you take the LSAT more than once.

Clinical program required	No
Legal writing course requirement	Yes
Legal methods course requirement	No
Legal research course requirement	Yes
Moot court requirement	No
Public interest law requirement	No

ADMISSIONS

Selectivity Rating	88
# applications received	5,390
% applicants accepted	33
% acceptees attending	23
Median LSAT	159
LSAT Range (25th to 75th percentile)	156–162
Median undergrad GPA	3.44
Application fee	$70
Regular application deadline	3/1
Early application deadline	1/11
Early application notification	1/25
Transfer students accepted	Yes
Evening division offered	Yes
Part-time accepted	Yes
CAS accepted	Yes

FINANCIAL FACTS

Annual tuition	$45,914
Books and supplies	$8,147
Fees	$889
Room & Board	$15,263
Financial aid application deadline	3/1
% first-year students receiving some sort of aid	83
% all students receiving some sort of aid	87
% of aid that is merit based	10
% receiving scholarships	39
Average grant	$13,504
Average loan	$56,444
Average total aid package	$61,900
Average debt	$153,020

EMPLOYMENT INFORMATION

Career Rating	80
Total 2012 JD Grads	463
% for whom you have useable information	99
% grads employed nine months out	76
Median starting salary	$60,000
# employed full-time	291
# employed part-time	62
# employed bar required	196
# employed JD preferred	120
# employed professional/other	25
# employed non-professional	9
# pursuing advanced degree	17
# unemployed and seeking employment	71
# not seeking employment	17
% grads employed by school	5
State for bar exam	NY, MD, VA, CA, NJ
Pass rate for first-time bar	80.2

Prominent Alumni
Hon. Gerald B. Lee, US Dist Court Judge for the Eastern District of Virginia; Kenneth G. Lore, Partner and Co-Chair of Real Estate Practice Group, Bingham McCutchen; Benjamin R. Jacobs, Managing Partner, The JBG Companies.

Grads Employed by Field (%)
Academic (4)
Business/Industry (16)
Government (14)
Judicial Clerkship (8)
Private Practice (24)
Public Interest (11)

APPALACHIAN SCHOOL OF LAW

Academics

The Appalachian School of Law is a young, private institution, organized in 1994 and given full accreditation from the American Bar Association in 2006. The traditional-looking campus is very beautiful and the library is "new." Wireless Internet access is available and, in recent years, "The technology aspect of the Law School has shown a significant improvement."

Students report that "trial advocacy training," "moot court programs," and other "practical courses" are "first rate" at ASL. The mock trial team "has trounced big names" in national competitions. "The law school's emphasis on practical legal skills has thoroughly prepared me for everyday situations in the general practice of law," says a 3L. "I will graduate and know what to do in a courtroom besides espouse constitutional theory with opposing counsel at lunch." Appalachian also "distinguishes itself from the majority of other law schools by requiring 150 hours of community service." A summer externship is also "required of all first-year students." "The community-service requirement promotes student involvement in law school organizations, benefits the community, and strengthens the reputations of both ASL and the legal profession in general," explains one student. "The summer externship program provides all rising 2Ls with the opportunity to apply the knowledge they gained from first-year classes to real-life situations." There is also a "mandatory alternative dispute resolution requirement," though the school seems keener on this than the students.

The "knowledgeable" and "very approachable" professors here are "down-to-earth people who have a wide variety of legal experience" and "extensive practical and theoretical knowledge of the subjects they teach." Their dedication means that "they are exceptionally concerned with bar passage" and always "available outside of the classroom." "My experience at the Appalachian School of Law has been nothing short of exceptional," confides one student. "The teachers love interacting with the students and are our greatest cheerleaders, mentors, and leaders." "Faculty turnover" has been a problem, though. The "remote location" is "not the most appealing place" for academics to "hang their hats for the long term." However, "The town and area are progressing."

Students tell us that "the greatest strength" of their law school is its "concern and respect for students as individuals." "The administration, faculty, staff, and students have created a community where you can receive an excellent legal education in the midst of the natural beauty of the Appalachian Mountains," explains one student. However, there is a "communication gap between students and administration," meaning that "it often takes days to cut through whatever hidden red tape or underlying ineptness or unwillingness exists." "The administration is very unpredictable" as well. "I realize every new school needs to work out its quirks, but ASL especially needs to do so," gripes one student. Career Services could stand to be "more active," and there seems to be a revolving door regarding deans. "The school appears to promote diversity among our deans with the tenure running about a dean a year," observes a wry 2L.

Life

Grundy is a "small community" located near the convergence of Virginia, Kentucky, and West Virginia. "You can't go to the grocery store without seeing another law student." "The remote location of the school" helps to make "studying [the] number-one priority." One student explains, "There's nothing to do but study in Grundy, so I went from a below-average college student to above average," adds a proud 3L. "I will probably graduate with honors. I'm not so sure that's [because] of the law school itself…[or] the general area."

Town-gown relations are strained. "There is some resentment from locals toward law students and vice versa," most agree. "The rugged, desolate terrain" and "isolation" lead students to say that "Appalachian could benefit from more things to do in Grundy outside of law school activities." Students lament that "there isn't a bar or club in the town" where they could "relieve stress and get a drink." (In fact, there is "no liquor by the drink in the county.") "The three-screen movie theater is the most diversion many will get," says one student. That said, people here take a DIY approach to entertainment and "typically find or make [their] own fun to blow off the steam and stress of law school." "A culture of frugal bacchanalia persists in the form of student-hosted house parties." When cabin fever sets in, students take "sojourns" to the nearest bigger cities, "both of which are over the mountains and about forty-five minutes away."

Not surprisingly, "You definitely develop a sense of family with the law school students and faculty." "The law students are a very tight-knit group," though beware as "gossip flourishes" and "everyone's life is an open book." "With scant few exceptions, the student body is Caucasian." Most students would like to see "diversity promoted" at ALS, feeling that "out in town" "underlying discrimination" exists "based on race, sexual orientation, socioeconomic status, and even geographic origin."

Getting In

Appalachian Law School's admitted students at the 25th percentile have LSAT scores of 146 and GPAs of 2.60. Admitted students at the 75th percentile have LSAT scores of 152 and GPAs of 3.30.

Clinical program required	Yes
Legal writing course requirement	Yes
Legal methods course requirement	Yes
Legal research course requirement	Yes
Moot court requirement	Yes

ADMISSIONS

Selectivity Rating	75
# applications received	990
% applicants accepted	46
% acceptees attending	32
Average LSAT	148
LSAT Range (25th to 75th percentile)	146–152
Average undergrad GPA	2.8
Application fee	$50
Regular application deadline	4/1
Transfer students accepted	Yes
Evening division offered	No
Part-time accepted	No
CAS accepted	Yes

FINANCIAL FACTS

Annual tuition	$19,900
Books and supplies	$2,500
Fees	$250
Room & Board	$12,295
% all students receiving some sort of aid	64
Average grant	$6,468
Average loan	$21,372

EMPLOYMENT INFORMATION

Career Rating	69	Grads Employed by Field (%)
Median starting salary	$45,000	Business/Industry (11)
State for bar exam	VA, TN, KY, NC, WV	Judicial Clerkship (19)
Pass rate for first-time bar	52	Private Practice (69)

ARIZONA STATE UNIVERSITY
SANDRA DAY O'CONNOR COLLEGE OF LAW

INSTITUTIONAL INFORMATION

Public/private	Public
Affiliation	No Affiliation
% faculty part-time	56
% faculty female	33
% faculty underrepresented minority	7
Total faculty	144

SURVEY SAYS...

Diverse opinions accepted in class-rooms, Great research resources

STUDENTS

Enrollment of law school	577
% male/female	59/41
% from out-of-state	29
% underrepresented minority	23
% international	3
# of countries represented	11
Average age of entering class	26

ACADEMICS

Academic Experience Rating	89
Profs interesting rating	82
Profs accessible rating	82
Hours of study per day	4.18

Academic Specialties

Constitutional, Environmental, International, Legal Philosophy, Intellectual Property

Advanced Degrees Offered

LLM in Biotechnology/Genomics; LLM in Tribal Policy, Law and Government; LLM in Global Legal Studies; Customized LLM; MLS Master of Legal Studies

Combined Degrees Offered

JD/MBA; JD/Ph.D. Psychology; JD/Ph.D. Justice & Social Inquiry; JD/MD; Master of Legal Studies/Master of Accountancy; Master of Legal Studies/MBA; Master of Legal Studies/Master of Real Estate Development; Master of Legal Studies/Master of Taxation; Master of Legal Studies/Master of Science in Information Management; Master of Legal Studies/Master of Science in Management.

Academics

The College of Law at Arizona State University is a smaller law school with smaller classes where "you get a lot of personal attention." At the same time, "The range of courses is extensive." The Indian Legal Program here is one of the finest of its kind in the country. Another point of pride is the Center for Law, Science and Innovation, which—not very surprisingly—concentrates on the intersection between law and science. Hands-on opportunities to "get real-world experience in nearly any legal field" are abundant. Eleven clinics allow students "to employ lawyer[ing] skills instead of just talking about it or writing legal memos," and virtually every student who wants to participate in a clinic can participate. There are "almost too many opportunities for externships" with judges, legislative offices, and administrative agencies, observes one awed student. The faculty at ASU is "a wide mix of both hardscrabble, old-school courtroom warriors, and young, innovative minds." There are a lot of adjunct faculty members "who enjoy teaching and who bring real practical experience into the classroom" as well. Most professors are "very accessible and happy to help." "They enjoy getting to know students outside of the classroom." Inside the classroom, "professors use the Socratic Method mostly, but not in a scary way." The focus is "more on teaching relevant materials than playing games with students." "Although the material is sometimes as dry as the Arizona desert, the teachers do a great job [of] keeping the class interesting." "I could not have asked for better professors my first semester," beams a 1L. A few students tell us that the administration is "only concerned with raising ASU's ranking" but the overwhelming sentiment is that with programs like the 3L Bar (taking the AZ bar exam in the 3rd year) and a new building in the works the top brass is "visionary" and "extremely responsive." The law school staff as a whole is "totally" approachable and "wonderful to work with at every level" (though it's a much different story when you are "forced to deal with the red tape of the general university").

Students here have "amazing access" to the Phoenix legal market and Career Services "will bend over back[ward] for you to help you make contacts in the job market." Students also point out that for better or for worse, they are "bombarded with opportunities to meet with practicing attorneys." Opinions concerning the portability of an ASU degree are decidedly split, though. Some students say it's very easy if you want to work in another state upon graduation. "ASU law degrees actually travel quite well and are respected throughout the United States," boasts a confident 1L. Others disagree. "ASU is well-known in Arizona but needs to gain more national prominence," they say. "If you want to work anywhere out of Arizona, the degree doesn't travel well."

Some of ASU's facilities are "old and outdated." Though the school has recently renovated their classrooms and taken down "the paneling from the 1970s," the "well-equipped" law library is "pretty nice," though. It's relatively new and "state-of-the-art in its technology and environment." In addition to four floors of study space, there's an all-night study room that allows students to come as late or early as they please and stay as long as they want. "I have never had a problem finding a quiet place to study," notes a 1L.

SHELLI SOTO, ASSOCIATE DEAN FOR ADMISSIONS AND FINANCIAL AID
1100 S. MCALLISTER AVE., P.O. BOX 877906, TEMPE, AZ 85287-7906
TEL: 480-965-1474 FAX: 480-727-7930
E-MAIL: LAW.ADMISSIONS@ASU.EDU • WEBSITE: WWW.LAW.ASU.EDU

Life

Students describe the academic atmosphere at ASU as "competitive but not overly combative." It's "enough to motivate, but not intolerable." Students are "focused on studies when they need to be," but they "study together, share outlines, and generally help each other." "Courses are tough but the atmosphere is upbeat and actually fun." "The Tempe sunshine makes us friendlier," suggests a 1L. The law school is located on ASU's main campus in a "suburban" part of the fast-growing Phoenix metro area. This "extremely active" law student population is "a mix of students living in Tempe and commuter students." "Students who are married live a little farther away from campus," explains a 3L. "However, most law students only a few years removed from undergrad tend to live very close to campus and are very involved in extracurriculars and other student organizations." Social events are "frequent." "There are opportunities to party, but not the pressure to." "Intramurals are a great way to blow off steam" as well, and if you are an outdoorsy type, "There is always stuff to do" in the vicinity all year round. "Almost always, some club or activity is providing lunch for us," notes a sated 1L. There's "a very stimulating, steady stream of speakers on a variety of legal topics." Also, students can take advantage of all the "opportunities to get involved" on one of the largest public university campuses in the country.

Getting In

The numbers speak for themselves at Arizona State's Sandra Day O'Connor School of Law. Enrolled students at the 25th percentile have an LSAT score of 161 and a GPA of roughly 3.30. Enrolled students at the 75th percentile have an LSAT score of 165 and a GPA of 3.82 or so. If you find yourself somewhere within these two ranges, you've got a fair chance of gaining admission.

Clinical program required	No
Legal writing course requirement	Yes
Legal methods course requirement	Yes
Legal research course requirement	Yes
Moot court requirement	Yes
Public interest law requirement	No

ADMISSIONS

Selectivity Rating	89
# applications received	1,865
% applicants accepted	34
% acceptees attending	24
Average LSAT	162
Median LSAT	163
LSAT Range (25th to 75th percentile)	161–165
Average undergrad GPA	3.55
Median undergrad GPA	3.65
Application fee	$65
Regular application deadline	2/1
Early application deadline	11/15
Transfer students accepted	Yes
Evening division offered	No
Part-time accepted	No
CAS accepted	Yes

FINANCIAL FACTS

Annual tuition (in-state out-of-state)	$25,751/$40,299
Books and supplies	$1,888
Fees	$514
Room & Board	$12,366
Financial aid application deadline	3/1
% first-year students receiving some sort of aid	100
% all students receiving some sort of aid	94
% of aid that is merit based	69
% receiving scholarships	49
Average grant	$11,713
Average loan	$36,225
Average total aid package	$39,397
Average debt	$101,560

EMPLOYMENT INFORMATION

Career Rating	94	
Total 2012 JD Grads	212	
% grads employed nine months out	96	
Median starting salary	$70,000	
% job accepting grads providing useable salary information	33	
# employed full-time	176	
# employed part-time	27	
# employed bar required	164	
# employed JD preferred	27	
# employed professional/other	10	
# employed non-professional	2	
# pursuing advanced degree	7	
# unemployed and seeking employment	0	
# not seeking employment	1	
% grads employed by school	9	
State for bar exam	AZ	
Pass rate for first-time bar	87	

Prominent Alumni
Dan Burk, Founding faculty member at University of California Irvine School of Law; Rebecca Berch, Chief Justice, Arizona State Supreme Court; Barry Silverman, U.S. Court of Appeals for the Ninth Circuit.

Grads Employed by Field (%)
Academic (7)
Business/Industry (18)
Government (11)
Judicial Clerkship (8)
Private Practice (46)
Public Interest (10)

AVE MARIA SCHOOL OF LAW

Academics

As a Catholic school with a strong commitment to its "mission" and "religious foundation," Ave Maria "incorporates the Catholic faith into classes." Many students choose the school for its "conservative" ideology, and some feel that "Ave Maria may be the only school in America where God and American Values are paramount." This Catholic foundation engenders "a very strong community at our school," and also attracts like-minded faculty, who "all come from the tops of their respective fields:" "Because the school is mission-oriented, some very high quality professors have chosen to teach here instead of a more prestigious school." Many students love that Ave Maria has "built an environment conducive to learning how my Catholic faith informs my understanding of the law, without sacrificing the quality study of the black-letter law." Others point out what they miss in the Catholic curriculum; one student wishes the school would directly confront "discussions on "morally repugnant" issues. For example, in family law, I would like to learn about prenuptial agreements but they were glanced over because Catholics don't believe in them."

Students also appreciate Ave Maria's "small size," which "encourages personal accountability, facilitates smooth registration, and increases access to faculty and resources." "There are few enough students that the instructors actually care if I succeed." With an eye on the future, the school offers "courses that prepare the students for real life lawyering," "which focus on practical skills and focuses on students' success on practicing law and not just on theory." Of course, it's "the superb professors with amazing career experience" who foster this academic environment, and students say the "unparalleled" faculty "are extremely approachable and accommodating," "genuinely want you to succeed," and "are interested in your development as a person and a lawyer."

Notably, Ave Maria recently moved from Michigan to its present location in Naples, Florida, and students say the move has resulted in some "disarray" in promoting the school as nationally recognized: "this school needs its faculty and students to push its name on a national scale." There are ways in which the new location works in the school's favor, though; for one, Ave Maria is "the only law school within ninety-plus miles," so "the opportunities for internships are definitely there." The school "is striving to improve the bar passage rate and is making significant progress" after the relocation, partially due to a newly added "bar prep" class; some students believe that more "state specific classes" might also be helpful. Overall, students choose Ave Maria for its "unique educational philosophy that emphasizes the moral foundations of the law, presents insights from the Catholic intellectual tradition, and encourages a broader perspective of the law and its role in society."

MONIQUE McCARTHY, ASSISTANT DEAN FOR ADMISSIONS
1025 COMMONS CIRCLE, NAPLES, FL 34119
TEL: 239-687-5300 FAX: 239-352-2890
E-MAIL: INFO@AVEMARIALAW.EDU • WEBSITE: WWW.AVEMARIALAW.EDU

Life

"The Naples, FL area is a beautiful place to study," students agree, and the "classroom and campus [are] beautiful" as well. Even though breaks in law school can be few and far between, students love that "the beach is always there for a nice relaxing break". However, some students claim that Naples isn't much more than a pretty face: "Naples is small and the law school is small so if you want a life away from law school, it's not easy to do…there aren't a lot of twenty-somethings." That said, students bond together on campus: "Ave Maria School of Law is a small institution, which foster[s] a true sense of community and purpose." The "rigorous" second semester is notoriously devoid of fun, as students go from "six classes to seven classes." As noted above in terms of the school's improving bar passage rates, student reviews of Ave Maria's locational integration are mixed. Some praise its "close proximity to a federal courthouse, creating many internship opportunities," while others feel that "Career Services is in shambles" and "there is much to be done in the Southwest Florida community toward making others aware of the school's successes." Perhaps, as one student diagnoses "The school simply needs time to adjust to a new location," and "The bar passage rate will improve as the faculty and students adjust."

Getting In

Ave Maria seems to be settling into its new location, as reflected in its reports that this year about three-quarters of its students passed the bar on their first try. The median LSAT score for its entering class is 144, meaning that if you haven't got the grades or scores for a better-known school, especially if a Catholic education is high priority for you, Ave Maria may be a very solid choice.

Clinical program required	No
Legal writing course requirement	Yes
Legal methods course requirement	Yes
Legal research course requirement	Yes
Moot court requirement	Yes
Public interest law requirement	No

ADMISSIONS

Selectivity Rating	69
# applications received	1,292
% applicants accepted	57
% acceptees attending	15
Average LSAT	149
Median LSAT	148
LSAT Range (25th to 75th percentile)	144–153
Average undergrad GPA	3.10
Median undergrad GPA	3.1
Application fee	$50
Regular application deadline	7/1
Transfer students accepted	Yes
Evening division offered	No
Part-time accepted	No
CAS accepted	Yes

FINANCIAL FACTS

Annual tuition	$36,490
Books and supplies	$1,500
Fees	$780
Room & Board	$13,131
Financial aid application deadline	6/1
% first-year students receiving some sort of aid	94
% all students receiving some sort of aid	93
% of aid that is merit based	21
% receiving scholarships	47
Average grant	$21,535
Average loan	$41,291
Average total aid package	$58,269
Average debt	$126,485

EMPLOYMENT INFORMATION

Career Rating	70	Grads Employed by Field (%)
Total 2012 JD Grads	166	Academic (2)
% for whom you have useable information	100	Business/Industry (18)
% grads employed nine months out	72	Government (8)
# employed full-time	93	Judicial Clerkship (2)
# employed part-time	20	Private Practice (38)
# employed bar required	65	Public Interest (2)
# employed JD preferred	27	
# employed professional/other	8	
# employed non-professional	12	
# pursuing advanced degree	5	
# unemployed and seeking employment	37	
# not seeking employment	4	
% grads employed by school	1	
State for bar exam	FL, CA, CO, NJ, VA	
Pass rate for first-time bar	68.5	

BAYLOR UNIVERSITY
SCHOOL OF LAW

INSTITUTIONAL INFORMATION

Public/private	Private
Affiliation	Baptist
Student-faculty ratio	13:1
% faculty part-time	35
% faculty female	25
% faculty underrepresented minority	7
Total faculty	51

SURVEY SAYS...

Heavy use of Socratic method, Great research resources, Beautiful campus

STUDENTS

Enrollment of law school	405
% male/female	51/49
% from out-of-state	23
% part-time	0
% underrepresented minority	14
# of countries represented	1
Average age of entering class	23

ACADEMICS

Academic Experience Rating	89
Profs interesting rating	78
Profs accessible rating	82
Hours of study per day	6.20

Academic Specialties

Civil Procedure, Criminal, Intellectual Property

Combined Degrees Offered

JD/MBA, JD/M Taxation, JD/MPPA, all 3.5–4 year programs.

Academics

Baylor University's Sheila & Walter Umphrey Law Center's reputation for being a "tough school" is complemented by its stature as an "excellent school" with "one of the most rigorous [law] courses in the state." Students report that Baylor Law does a good job of preparing them "for the real world by teaching the law, practical lawyering skills, and professionalism." "We learn how to write well, how to research efficiently and effectively, and we most definitely learn how to advocate," says a 1L. "It's the greatest school for future trial lawyers." The "phenomenal" faculty has "a genuine interest in ensuring students know and understand the material," but they "can be tough" and "expect students to be well-prepared for every class." With a reputation as "the Marine Corps of law schools," Baylor students take comfort in the fact that with great effort comes great reward. "Throughout lectures, the professors strike the perfect balance of teaching legal theory and practice," says a 2L. "And this balance must be working as Baylor Law consistently has the highest bar passage rate in the state of Texas and our graduates are ready to practice law the day they graduate." While Baylor's faculty is lauded for its commitment to students, the same can't be said of its administration. Descriptions of the administration range from "disconnected" to "out of touch," with many students reporting that "decisions seem to be made without student input or the students' needs in mind."

Baylor Law places an emphasis on "legal theory and practice" through its "rigorous" Practice Court Program, a course that many feel leaves them "ready to practice law the day they graduate." That said, those uninterested in becoming trial lawyers wouldn't mind seeing it be done away with. "[The school] could end the Practice Court Program as a mandatory requirement and make it optional for only those students who wish to become litigators," says a 2L. A 3L further explains, "You really get a true practical experience from day one, but it's not for everyone. Practice Court is brutal—eighteen hours a day of studying and class, plus you get humiliated and booted out of class if you are called up and can't recall a holding from one of the fifteen to twenty-five cases you were assigned the night before. The weak of heart need not apply."

Students agree that Baylor Law prepares them "to be lawyers better than almost any school in the country," but they find that "it is very difficult to find jobs." Though the career services office "has improved recently," students want to see the school "reestablish its reputation in Texas as a great law school and try to reach a broader market." "No one outside of Texas has heard of us, and no one respects the hard work we do culminating in the third-year Practice Court unless they've already hired a Baylor grad," says a 2L. Luckily, Baylor's "devoted alumni" can go a long way in helping you secure employment after graduation, provided that "you want to live in Texas."

If there's one word that's used to describe Baylor's campus, it's "beautiful." "[We have] the best building of any law school in Texas (and I would venture to say in the country)," says a 2L. "Students can enjoy looking over the water from the library, student lounge, and the back porch off the student lounge," says a 1L. "Additionally, students enjoy close parking in front of the building." The "state-of-the-art" classrooms and facilities are "stellar," "spacious," and "comfortable."

NICOLE NEELEY, ASSISTANT DEAN OF ADMISSIONS
ONE BEAR PLACE #97288, WACO, TX 76798
TEL: 254-710-1911 FAX: 254-710-2316
E-MAIL: NICOLE-NEELEY@BAYLOR.EDU • WEBSITE: LAW.BAYLOR.EDU

Life

With "approximately 420 students," the study body at Baylor Law is "small" and "intelligent." This lends a "close-knit" air to the school, though opinion is divided between the environment being "friendly" and "caring," or "cutthroat." "From Day One, the professors and administration told us that we were all in competition with one another due to the bell curve grading," says a 2L. "It was heavily emphasized, day after day. The competition became extremely cutthroat." Many here find that this pressure "divides" students, with some being "friendly with each other until the first set of grades are released," and others remaining "extremely cooperative" and "down-to-earth." Despite the academic competition, students find "community through suffering." "We all go through the same pain and as a result our bonds with each other are very strong," says a 2L. One point that all students agree on is that "the law school could stand to improve the diversity of its student body and its faculty members."

Perhaps the kindest thing students say about Baylor's location in Waco, Texas, is that the town offers "the perfect place to be engaged in the rigors of law school" (i.e., very few distractions). Students readily admit that despite some "decent bars and things to do" there's "not much going on" in Waco. However, with Dallas and Austin "an hour and a half away," it's "not uncommon for people to quickly flee Waco as soon as a break rolls around." For those who choose to stay on campus, the Student Bar Association "hosts many social and community service opportunities throughout the year, including four intramural sports, Law Prom, four Immunity Days (where students pay money to a designated charity and in return don't get called on in class the next day), an annual blood drive in memory of two alumni, and more."

Getting In

Recently admitted students at Baylor Law at the 25th percentile have LSAT scores of 161 and GPAs in the 3.3 range. Admitted students at the 75th percentile have LSAT scores of 167 and GPAs of roughly 3.75. Minority candidates are strongly encouraged to apply to Baylor Law School and admissions officers may consider minority status as a "plus factor" in the context of the individualized application review.

Clinical program required	Yes
Legal writing course requirement	Yes
Legal methods course requirement	Yes
Legal research course requirement	Yes
Moot court requirement	Yes
Public interest law requirement	No

ADMISSIONS

Selectivity Rating	**95**
# applications received	2,532
% applicants accepted	27
% acceptees attending	9
Average LSAT	163
Median LSAT	162
LSAT Range (25th to 75th percentile)	161–163
Average undergrad GPA	3.69
Median undergrad GPA	3.51
Application fee	$0
Regular application deadline	3/1
Early application deadline	11/1
Early application notification	3/1
Transfer students accepted	Yes
Evening division offered	No
Part-time accepted	No
CAS accepted	Yes

FINANCIAL FACTS

Annual tuition	$47,334
Books and supplies	$1,926
Fees	$2,147
Room & Board (on/off campus)	$11,606/$7,962
Financial aid application deadline	3/1
% first-year students receiving some sort of aid	91
% all students receiving some sort of aid	90
% of aid that is merit based	41
% receiving scholarships	80
Average grant	$27,700
Average loan	$38,456
Average total aid package	$50,628
Average debt	$93,252

EMPLOYMENT INFORMATION

Career Rating	**91**	
Total 2012 JD Grads	164	**Prominent Alumni**
% grads employed nine months out	86	Leon Jaworski, Special Prosecutor for the
Median starting salary	$60,000	Watergate trials; William Sessions, Former
# employed full-time	132	FBI Director.
# employed part-time	6	**Grads Employed by Field (%)**
# employed bar required	122	Academic (2)
# employed JD preferred	11	Business/Industry (14)
# employed professional/other	4	Government (7)
# employed non-professional	0	Judicial Clerkship (2)
# pursuing advanced degree	1	Private Practice (73)
# unemployed and seeking employment	15	Public Interest (2)
# not seeking employment	3	
% grads employed by school	2	
State for bar exam	TX	
Pass rate for first-time bar	94	

BOSTON COLLEGE
LAW SCHOOL

INSTITUTIONAL INFORMATION

Public/private	Private
Affiliation	Jesuit
Student-faculty ratio	13:1
% faculty part-time	46
% faculty female	30
% faculty underrepresented minority	8
Total faculty	112

SURVEY SAYS...
Great research resources, Great library staff

STUDENTS

Enrollment of law school	760
% male/female	53/47
% from out-of-state	75
% part-time	0
% underrepresented minority	21
% international	2
# of countries represented	19
Average age of entering class	24

ACADEMICS

Academic Experience Rating	**91**
Profs interesting rating	85
Profs accessible rating	85
Hours of study per day	3.81

Academic Specialties
Civil Procedure, Commercial, Constitutional, Corporation Securities, Criminal, Environmental, Human Rights, International, Labor, Legal History, Legal Philosophy, Property, Taxation, Intellectual Property

Advanced Degrees Offered
JD, 3 years; LLM, 1 year

Combined Degrees Offered
JD/MBA, 4 years; JD/MSW, 4 years; JD/Med 3 years; JD/MA Philosophy, 3.5 years; JD/MA Environmental law, 3.5 years

Academics

Located at the Newton campus location of Boston College, just west of Brookline, Boston College Law is a "welcoming community" that benefits from strong ties to the surrounding area and judicial system. Academics are "challenging but by no means unmanageable," and a solid writing program and "incredibly motivated" student body contribute to a "very positive" overall experience. Law school "horror stories" are unfounded at Boston College; "everyone here is willing to share notes, [with] very few 'gunners'." Public interest is also "heavily emphasized."

Professors are "supportive and very approachable," and are "available to assist you and provide you with all of the necessary resources." They are "brilliant and incredible teachers" and are "committed to teaching and also helping students beyond classroom." "Our teachers are the best and most approachable group of scholars," says a student. "Even adjuncts are amazing in the classroom."

Though the curriculum can be "pretty broad and theoretical," the first-year Legal Reasoning, Research & Writing course "is the best" and thoroughly prepares students for their future careers. There are "several advanced research courses in specific practice areas," and though the professors expect a lot, "they do their best to make it an atmosphere of learning and not fear." This "unmatched" faculty is clearly intellectual and gifted, and what makes Boston College outstanding is "how all the professors buy into the community of the school." "Everyone feels like they are a part of something and with the campus outside Boston, you also feel like you are in a very unique place that is untouched by frivolous things like rankings."

Some students here admit that the school could stand for "better organization," as the rough waters from recent transitions have "trickled down to all aspects of the school." Luckily, most think that "in the next year or two the school will be back on track." BC's career services also "relies entirely upon alumni and offers little real advice or opportunity for specific organizations or careers/internships outside of those connected with current alumni," says one student. This can hinder those students looking for non-firm jobs, international positions, or those outside of Massachusetts.

However, the close relationships among school, alumni, and the Boston legal community are "the greatest strengths of BC Law." The school possesses more partners in Boston firms than Boston University and Harvard Law. This stems from the fact that more Boston College graduates remain in the area, and "this can be a great assistance to students as they seek to network and find employment, since BC is so well-respected." The school also boasts an excellent library, which staffs "reference librarians every single day until 7:00 P.M., [who are] ... available over the summer, too." In addition, there exist "particularly strong" clinical programs and opportunities for getting practical experience.

Living

"The people are what make BC Law a great place," according to one student. This is a group of about 800 "down to earth, interesting," and "intelligent" people who exist in a "non-competitive atmosphere" in which everyone is "always willing to send you notes." While everyone strives to do their best, "no one cuts each other down and everyone tries to help each other out." "We've really got a sense that we're all in it together," says a student. "With all the stresses of law school, it's nice to be around a group of people who aren't all awful." "Almost everyone I have come across—from fellow students to faculty and administration—has been supportive, dedicated, and deeply interested in the work that they do," says another. "Until finals begin one can—almost—forget that they attend an elite law school (in a good way)."

The "very collegial," "mellow" student body is "friendly and unpretentious," and there is "a real sense of fun and community here"; although, many would like to see more diversity in the student body. Still, "the general ambiance of the school is nice," and everyone here "forms a unique community" where "everyone approaches problems as part of a team," and "students develop strong study groups to form meaningful questions for the faculty."

Facilities are "excellent in the renovated areas, but just adequate in the older parts of the building." Even in the new areas of the campus, "it isn't ideal to be sharing a cafeteria and study space with 18 year-old freshmen during exam time" since the lounge areas are also shared with undergrads. The campus is located "far from public transportation"; getting a parking space in the morning is difficult, and "generally means you will be in the back lot and have to walk up a bunch of stairs with your books."

Getting In

Only about one in five applicants is admitted to BC Law, but the school offers prospective students some nice application options. The admissions process opens in mid-September and runs through March 15th. Applicants are admitted on a rolling basis. One may also reactivate an application submitted in the previous year by submitting a new application form, personal statement, CAS report, and application fee.

Clinical program required	No
Legal writing course requirement	Yes
Legal methods course requirement	Yes
Legal research course requirement	Yes
Moot court requirement	No
Public interest law requirement	No

ADMISSIONS

Selectivity Rating	91
# applications received	4,774
% applicants accepted	29
% acceptees attending	18
Median LSAT	164
LSAT Range (25th to 75th percentile)	161–166
Median undergrad GPA	3.61
Application fee	$75
Regular application deadline	3/31
Regular notification	rolling
Transfer students accepted	Yes
Evening division offered	No
Part-time accepted	No
CAS accepted	Yes

FINANCIAL FACTS

Annual tuition (in-state out-of-state)	$43,170
Books and supplies	$1,300
Fees	$136
Room & Board (on/off campus)	$0/$11,300
Financial aid application deadline	3/15
% first-year students receiving some sort of aid	90
% all students receiving some sort of aid	86
% of aid that is merit based	46
% receiving scholarships	55
Average grant	$19,631
Average loan	$34,617
Average debt	$106,550

EMPLOYMENT INFORMATION

Career Rating	95	Prominent Alumni
Total 2012 JD Grads	260	John Kerry, United States Secretary of
% grads employed nine months out	84	State; Debra Yang, Former United States
Median starting salary	$85,344	Attorney, CA; Daniel Malloy, Governor, CT;
# employed full-time	196	Shannon Miller, Olympic Gold.
# employed part-time	23	**Grads Employed by Field (%)**
# employed bar required	186	Academic (4)
# employed JD preferred	27	Business/Industry (15)
# employed professional/other	4	Government (10)
# employed non-professional	2	Judicial Clerkship (7)
# pursuing advanced degree	4	Military (3)
# unemployed and seeking employment	29	Private Practice (54)
# not seeking employment	6	Public Interest (8)
% grads employed by school	5	
State for bar exam	MA	
Pass rate for first-time bar	91.8	

BOSTON UNIVERSITY
SCHOOL OF LAW

INSTITUTIONAL INFORMATION

Public/private	Private
Affiliation	No Affiliation
% faculty part-time	69
% faculty female	32
% faculty underrepresented minority	8
Total faculty	146

SURVEY SAYS...

Diverse opinions accepted in classrooms, Great library staff

STUDENTS

Enrollment of law school	734
% male/female	49/51
% part-time	0
% underrepresented minority	25
% international	4
# of countries represented	12
Average age of entering class	24

ACADEMICS

Academic Experience Rating	**98**
Profs interesting rating	99
Profs accessible rating	98
Hours of study per day	4.06

Academic Specialties

Corporation Securities, International, Intellectual Property

Advanced Degrees Offered

LLM Taxation; LLM Banking and Financial Law; LLM American Law; LLM Intellectual Property Law; Executive LLM in International Business Law

Combined Degrees Offered

JD/MBA, JD/MBA Sector Management, JD/MA International Relations, JD/MS Mass Communication, JD/MA Preservation Studies, JD/MPH Public Health, JD/MA Philosophy, JD/LLM in Taxation, JD/LLM in Banking and Financial Law; JD/LLM in European law; JD/LLM in Asian Legal Studies; JD/LLM in International and European Business Law

Academics

Among much to praise at BU's seriously competitive law school, students report almost universally that "The dedication of the faculty and administration has to be the greatest strength" of the program. BU was one of the first law schools to admit women and minorities, and continues its commitment to diversity with a stunningly broad range of specialized programs for law students: six concentrations, fourteen dual-degree programs, seventeen study abroad options in both English and foreign languages, and a fleet of clinical programs and externships in the professionally target-rich surrounding city of Boston. In addition, "the school encourages faculty-student interaction through numerous mentorship and social programs." These, obviously, aid job placement for students in Boston and elsewhere, and while there can be a "sometimes uphill battle to receive the initial offers for summer employment," students report that they're equipped to compete with the best: "My classmates and I are consistently considered the top summer interns at our jobs."

Students appreciate BU's practice-oriented curriculum, including "the great moot court opportunities beyond 1L, with 2L moot court competitions and 3L teams." While BU students have sometimes suffered from a reputation, many are eager to counteract this image: "Some of us were admitted to Harvard but chose BU due to its focus on teaching, its small class size, and its generous financial aid."

Few law schools elicit as much praise from students for both the "top notch" professors and the "absolutely wonderful" administration. "Everything runs very smoothly" as a result of the combined efforts of "the administration and professors," who "are extremely friendly, intelligent, and accommodating." While the Career Development Office (CDO) "is still scrambling with the recession/jobs market," it excels at tuning in to students' needs: "I have been impressed by how open they are to feedback—from the Dean down." Similarly, BU's professors, who are at "the top of their field," "love their areas of law, and they love teaching. They go out of their way to be accessible—even offering their home phone numbers." "The one universal complaint at BU law is that the elevators run too slow between classes" and indeed, virtually the only widely panned aspect of the BU law experience is that "the physical facilities are certainly lacking." However, thanks to a recent $18 million donation from alumnus Sumner Redstone, a new building is currently under construction that will house most law school classes beginning in 2014.

Life

While BU's graduates are prepared to compete with the best, they pride themselves on avoiding the typically competitive law student portrait: students say BU has "managed to get together a good group of people who are intelligent and competitive but fun-loving and caring." Another reports, "I came to law school expecting to jump into a shark tank, and have been delightfully surprised by the smart, funny, thoughtful students I have found instead." "The community at BU is very accepting and encourages personal growth," many students agree, without sacrificing the "drive of the students." In addition to the demands of law school, some notable BU lawyers-to-be find the time to participate in Legal Follies, the law school's "regionally (some might say nationally) well-known sketch comedy group": "The fact that some students are willing to practice 15–20 hours a week to put on a great show really speaks to the type of people that attend BU."

While they're smart, BU students also resist being characterized as nerds: "Sure we may be the 'bright' kids, but we're not an excessively nose to the book school." The average age upon entrance is twenty-four, but students are anxious to point out that "the community is by no means monolithic and includes directors of non-profits, former Marines, and students that have never gone to a bar review."

Getting In

Admission to BU's law school is extremely competitive, with a high median LSAT score of 166. Each year, BU Law enrolls a class of students characterized by extraordinary academic achievement and diverse life experiences. Applicants whose first choice is BU Law can apply via the Boston University School of Law Distinguished Scholar Binding Early Decision Programs. Students admitted via the binding early decision process will receive a full-tuition scholarship.

Clinical program required	No
Legal writing course requirement	Yes
Legal methods course requirement	No
Legal research course requirement	Yes
Moot court requirement	Yes
Public interest law requirement	No

ADMISSIONS

Selectivity Rating	95
# applications received	5,971
% applicants accepted	30
% acceptees attending	11
Median LSAT	166
LSAT Range (25th to 75th percentile)	162–167
Median undergrad GPA	3.75
Application fee	$75
Regular application deadline	4/1
Early application deadline	11/15
Early application notification	12/20
Transfer students accepted	Yes
Evening division offered	No
Part-time accepted	No
CAS accepted	Yes

FINANCIAL FACTS

Annual tuition	$43,278
Books and supplies	$5,772
Fees	$890
Room & Board	$12,070
Financial aid application deadline	3/1
% first-year students receiving some sort of aid	88
% all students receiving some sort of aid	98
% of aid that is merit based	37
% receiving scholarships	81
Average grant	$18,293
Average loan	$38,379
Average total aid package	$50,123
Average debt	$110,437

EMPLOYMENT INFORMATION

Career Rating	93	
Total 2012 JD Grads	273	
% for whom you have useable information	98	
% grads employed nine months out	88	
Median starting salary	$135,000	
% job accepting grads providing useable salary information	40	
# employed full-time	200	
# employed part-time	67	
# employed bar required	262	
# employed JD preferred	17	
# employed professional/other	2	
# employed non-professional	1	
# pursuing advanced degree	7	
# unemployed and seeking employment	12	
# not seeking employment	2	
% grads employed by school	14	
State for bar exam	MA, NY, CA, NJ, IL	
Pass rate for first-time bar	91.4	

Prominent Alumni
Judd Gregg, U.S. Senator, New Hampshire; William S. Cohen, Former Secretary of Defense; David Kelley, Executive Producer.

Grads Employed by Field (%)
Academic (1)
Business/Industry (9)
Government (11)
Judicial Clerkship (7)
Private Practice (43)
Public Interest (17)

BRIGHAM YOUNG UNIVERSITY
J. REUBEN CLARK LAW SCHOOL

Academics

Law students at Brigham Young University love the "small class sizes," "superb" academic experience, and the "lowest tuition that you'll find anywhere for a respected law school." Add "great professors" to the mix and you've got the makings of a solid law school experience. "BYU has a great faculty with amazing credentials" (several faculty have moved from top schools and have clerked for the Supreme Court), and "all faculty members are incredibly student-oriented," says a 2L. The school doesn't hedge on the quality of 1L professors either. "The school uses some of its brightest and best faculty to teach first-year classes," explains a 1L. "I have had multiple professors who were previously U.S. Supreme Court clerks as professors in each semester." Professors here are "always open to meeting with students," some going so far as to give out "cell phone numbers in class." "[Professors] take time to attend law school events and make genuine efforts to know students, especially if students are willing to get involved and meet professors halfway," says a 2L. Students find the administration "transparent in its policies and responsive to students' needs and concerns." The administration "doesn't please all the students all the time, of course, but my sense is that the school wants to satisfy its students as well as prospective employers and works hard to do so."

Students are quick to point out that for the "minimal tuition price," the "value of the education" at BYU Law "can't be beat." That said, nearly all agree that a "broader range of courses" is needed. In addition to more classes, many note that they could benefit from "a more robust clinical program." "[BYU Law] places a lot of emphasis on externships— and the externship program is pretty awesome—but we could gain a lot more practical experience with on-campus clinical opportunities," says a 2L. Finally, some students would like a school as religious as BYU to be, well, more religious. "I have only had one professor who legitimately integrated gospel aspects into law teaching, and it was only very briefly," says a 2L. "I know many people wonder if BYU Law School is like Sunday School, but I can say it definitely is not."

Most students believe that BYU is "a 'law firm' school" since "that is where most people end up and that is mostly who comes to campus to interview." "I have sought advice on non-firm careers, and have obtained little useful help from BYU thus far," says a 3L. "Both my summer jobs have come from my own work and connections." Regardless, students appreciate the "helpful" Career Services Office, though they "could do a better job marketing the school and its students to the larger, regional firms outside of Utah." The "networking" and "benefits" of "the J. Reuben Clark Law Society and the alumni" are also a plus for BYU Law job hunters.

The school boasts "Internet connection in all the classrooms," "personal study space" (i.e., everyone has their "own individual desk in the library"), and overall "great" facilities. "The law building itself is a bit dated" (circa 1973), but "They're progressively renovating," says a 1L. The administration has recently built a state-of-the-art moot court room, and all classrooms, carrels, study rooms, and sitting areas in the library have wireless Internet and computer power jacks. Plenty of students find themselves wishing for a "face-lift" for the building and classrooms, but, as one 2L explains, "When I am paying 70 percent less [in tuition] than my colleagues are at peer schools, I guess I cannot complain."

GaeLynn Kuchar, Director of Admissions
340 JRCB, Brigham Young University Law School, Provo, UT 84602
Tel: 801-422-4277 Fax: 801-422-0389
E-Mail: kucharg@law.byu.edu • Website: www.law.byu.edu

Life

When you've got a student body that's "99 percent Mormon and 65 percent married," the social life is, for lack of better words, "quite unique!" "The reason that the students are so hardworking and competitive is that many of the students are married, or are planning on getting married, so their studies and academic success [mean] more than just mere prestige, or even a high salary," says a 3L. "These students understand that others are depending on them to do well" and are "more willing to take responsibility for their time and efforts." The environment is "competitive, but civil." "I know that everyone else is working very hard, and yet I have never felt that other students were 'out to get me,'" says a 2L. As for diversity, it depends on who you ask. For some students, the lack of diversity can be blamed on BYU Law being "very conservative," which "tends to attract more conservative people." On the other hand, some find that their "colleagues are more diverse" than "expected for a Mormon school in the middle of Utah."

Since a "large percentage" of students are "already married," many find the traditional law school "social dynamic" changed "significantly." "People tend [to] get together for game nights and baby showers instead of parties or clubbing," says a 2L. "It feels less like college and more like real life." Also, as BYU has a strict honor code, don't expect to "find a lot of people here to party with." Conversely, some students wish others adhered a little less to the code in question. "I wish more of my classmates would drink themselves out of the running." "As a completely dry campus nobody does anything but study and the competition is extremely fierce," says a 1L. Indeed, most social life revolves around the library. But when students take a break from the books, Salt Lake City and its more varied social scenery is only "forty-five minutes away."

Getting In

Recently admitted students at BYU Law at the 25th percentile have LSAT scores of 160 and GPAs in the 3.52 range. Admitted students at the 75th percentile have LSAT scores of 166 and GPAs of roughly 3.85.

Clinical program required	No
Legal writing course requirement	Yes
Legal methods course requirement	No
Legal research course requirement	Yes
Moot court requirement	Yes
Public interest law requirement	No

ADMISSIONS

Selectivity Rating	96
# applications received	753
% applicants accepted	29
% acceptees attending	64
Median LSAT	162
LSAT Range (25th to 75th percentile)	158–165
Median undergrad GPA	3.75
Application fee	$50
Regular application deadline	3/1
Transfer students accepted	Yes
Evening division offered	No
Part-time accepted	No
CAS accepted	Yes

FINANCIAL FACTS

Annual tuition (in-state out-of-state)	$10,950/$21,900
Books and supplies	$1,724
Room & Board	$11,412
% first-year students receiving some sort of aid	92
% all students receiving some sort of aid	90
% of aid that is merit based	35
% receiving scholarships	42
Average grant	$7,388
Average loan	$25,067
Average total aid package	$24,026
Average debt	$57,080

EMPLOYMENT INFORMATION

Career Rating	94	
Total 2012 JD Grads	147	
% for whom you have useable information	100	
% grads employed nine months out	91	
Median starting salary	$70,750	
% job accepting grads providing useable salary information	32	
# employed full-time	120	
# employed part-time	13	
# employed bar required	107	
# employed JD preferred	24	
# employed professional/other	2	
# employed non-professional	0	
# pursuing advanced degree	1	
# unemployed and seeking employment	7	
# not seeking employment	6	
% grads employed by school	5	

State for bar exam	UT, CA, NV, AZ, TX
Pass rate for first-time bar	94

Prominent Alumni
Mike Lee, US Senator; N. Randy Smith, US Court of Appeals, Ninth Circuit; Jay Bybee, US Court of Appeals, Ninth Circuit.

Grads Employed by Field (%)
Academic (3)
Business/Industry (18)
Government (10)
Judicial Clerkship (16)
Private Practice (37)
Public Interest (2)

BROOKLYN LAW SCHOOL

INSTITUTIONAL INFORMATION

Public/private	Private
Student-faculty ratio	15:1
% faculty part-time	53
% faculty female	39
% faculty underrepresented minority	10
Total faculty	155

SURVEY SAYS...

Abundant externship/internship/clerkship opportunities, Liberal students, Students love Brooklyn, NY

STUDENTS

Enrollment of law school	1,260
% male/female	55/45
% from out-of-state	47
% part-time	21
% underrepresented minority	25
% international	1
# of countries represented	6
Average age of entering class	23

ACADEMICS

Academic Experience Rating	**84**
Profs interesting rating	84
Profs accessible rating	82
Hours of study per day	3.51

Academic Specialties

Civil Procedure, Commercial, Constitutional, Corporation Securities, Criminal, Environmental, Government Services, Human Rights, International, Labor, Legal History, Legal Philosophy, Property, Taxation, Intellectual Property

Advanced Degrees Offered

JD, 2 years full-time (accelerated), 3 years full-time, 4 years part-time; LLM Program for Foreign-Trained Lawyers, 1 year full-time, 1.5–2 years part-time

Combined Degrees Offered

JD/MBA, JD/MS City and Regional Planning, JD/MS Library/ Information Science, JD/M Urban Planning, 4-6 Years

Academics

Located in everyone's favorite borough, Brooklyn Law School offers students a "broad range of classes," "four scholarly journals," and a renowned moot court program. Additionally, BLS maintains four joint-degree programs. These provide a modicum of "flexibility" and grant students the opportunity "to pursue parallel interests and to tailor [their] legal education [to their] particular career goals." Additionally, students are quick to highlight the "fantastic" clinic program. As one third year explains, "It gave me the opportunity to apply legal theory to the real world, and to contribute to the Brooklyn community."

When it comes to their professors, students at Brooklyn Law are quick to heap praise and accolades. As one second year gushes, "The faculty at Brooklyn Law is comprised of some of the best teachers that I have ever had. They are enthusiastic, dedicated, brilliant, and are passionate about teaching." And a grateful third year chimes in, "Our professors our fantastic. We are extremely lucky to have some leaders in their fields." Perhaps even more noteworthy, the faculty here makes it a point to not only "help with coursework but also [offer] career advice and placement." As a relieved fellow third year shares, "I've had professors pull all sorts of strings for me, and I'm not even at the top of the class. I'm very appreciative of their backing and support."

Another aspect of Brooklyn Law that students appreciate is the school's prime location. Indeed, since BLS is near both the Southern and Eastern District Courts of New York "students are able to intern at the federal courts during the school year." Additionally, the school is also a stone's throw from "major New York law firms" and as one grateful third year asserts, "a surprisingly large number of law firms do hire Brooklyn Law students (or at least interview them)." A fellow third year adds (and reiterates), "The location of Brooklyn is top-notch. Several schools in Manhattan compete over the Southern District of New York where Brooklyn has almost free reign over the Eastern District. District Courts, Second Circuit, Bankruptcy Courts, US Attorney, District Attorney, Kings County Courts—are ALL located within a few blocks from the school. This leads first to incredible clinical opportunities, and for many—jobs." A pleased second year sums up, "Brooklyn Law School has a great reputation in the NYC legal market, and the school really encourages internships and real-world experience."

Though students enjoy their academic experience, they are less than enamored with Brooklyn's administration. While some do acknowledge that there are "good individual administrators," they quickly note that the "administration is too departmentalized [with] not enough communication between departments." A less than pleased third year students complains, "The administrators seem to be more concerned with the school's ranking, alumni donations, and number of students who obtain post-graduate clerkships than the actual quality of the school." A fellow third year is more sympathetic stating, "The administration generally seems like it is working hard for the betterment of the school community, although we had some instability due to a dean search that has recently ended."

Henry W. Haverstick III, Dean of Admissions and Financial Aid
250 Joralemon Street, Brooklyn, NY 11201
Tel: 718-780-7906 Fax: 718-780-0395
E-Mail: admitq@brooklaw.edu • Website: www.brooklaw.edu

Life

Diversity "in terms of race, ethnicity, and interests" is "thriving" among the "hardworking and intelligent" students here. You'll probably be able to find whatever scene you are after. There's "frat culture spilling out from students who attended straight from undergrad." There's also a contingent of slightly older people who have taken some time off and have been living in New York for awhile. A lot of people here "already have lives and friends" and "have their own thing going on." At the same time, "There's a great sense of community," especially for students living in campus housing.

Academically, BLS is known for having a tough curve "that is a humbling experience for some 1Ls." Nevertheless, students assure us, "There is a spirit of cooperation and unity that creates a very supportive environment." "Students tend to get along and help each other more than compete." Outside the classroom, the school sponsors "tons of" lectures and "student groups are very active." Students call surrounding Brooklyn Heights "a great neighborhood." "You have more courts within two blocks than you could ever visit, much less intern with." "Shops and restaurants dot tree-lined Montague Street on the way to the Brooklyn Heights Promenade (with the best view of Manhattan)," says a 2L. "The rest of the neighborhood consists of well-kept historic brownstones. It's just a great place to wander around." And of course the Big Apple offers a never-ending array of activities and night-life. As one happy student concludes, "Brooklyn has become the center of the cultural universe and Brooklyn Law School is right in the epicenter. We are located in the greatest city in the world, the capital of Big Law and right near two of the most prestigious federal districts in the nation."

Getting In

Admission into Brooklyn Law is competitive. Accepted students at the 25th percentile have an LSAT score around 160 and a GPA around 3.2. Admitted students at the 75th percentile have an LSAT score around 165 and a GPA around 3.56.

Clinical program required	No
Legal writing course requirement	Yes
Legal methods course requirement	Yes
Legal research course requirement	Yes
Moot court requirement	Yes
Public interest law requirement	No

ADMISSIONS

Selectivity Rating	85
# applications received	3,966
% applicants accepted	40
% acceptees attending	20
Average LSAT	161
Median LSAT	161
LSAT Range (25th to 75th percentile)	158–164
Average undergrad GPA	3.3
Median undergrad GPA	3.33
Application fee	$0
Regular application deadline	
Early application deadline	12/1
Early application notification	12/31
Transfer students accepted	Yes
Evening division offered	Yes
Part-time accepted	Yes
CAS accepted	Yes

FINANCIAL FACTS

Annual tuition	$49,976
Books and supplies	$1,300
Fees	$371
Room & Board	$24,925
% first-year students receiving some sort of aid	92
% all students receiving some sort of aid	89
% of aid that is merit based	35
% receiving scholarships	70
Average grant	$27,875
Average loan	$43,700
Average total aid package	$55,515
Average debt	$105,916

EMPLOYMENT INFORMATION

Career Rating	82	State for bar exam	NY
Total 2012 JD Grads	466	Pass rate for first-time bar	86
% for whom you have useable information	97	**Prominent Alumni**	
% grads employed nine months out	76	David Dinkins, former Mayor, City of New York; Stephen J. Dannhauser, Chairman, Weil Gotshal & Manges LLP; Barry Salzberg, CEO Deloitte & Touche USA LLP.	
Median starting salary	$61,500		
# employed full-time	302		
# employed part-time	22	**Grads Employed by Field (%)**	
# employed bar required	252	Academic (1)	
# employed JD preferred	41	Business/Industry (16)	
# employed professional/other	18	Government (10)	
# employed non-professional	9	Judicial Clerkship (5)	
# pursuing advanced degree	9	Private Practice (33)	
# unemployed and seeking employment	100	Public Interest (6)	
# not seeking employment	10		
% grads employed by school	0		

CAMPBELL UNIVERSITY
NORMAN ADRIAN WIGGINS SCHOOL OF LAW

Academics

Campbell University School of Law is a small, Baptist-affiliated school in North Carolina that offers a Christian perspective on law and boasts a stellar bar-passage rate. Also, small class sizes prevent you from getting lost in a sea of people. The curriculum is decidedly focused on the actual practice of law "instead of relying on theory." The trial and appellate advocacy programs here are some of the most extensive in the country. "A Campbell lawyer can walk into any courtroom and never feel lost," proclaims a 2L. "Campbell is a hard law school," though. "It over-prepares you," suggests a 1L, "so that when you get out, you are not as surprised as most first-year lawyers." Most professors are dyed-in-the-wool believers in the Socratic Method, so you'll be able to breathe easy only if you've read and actually thought about the assignment for that day. "The pressure lets up after your 1L year," but "Course work is extremely rigorous, and the school is not afraid to fail students who perform poorly." Student complaints generally center on the very limited range of available courses. In short, Campbell needs to "offer more electives." Also, the massive number of required courses is "ridiculous."

Despite their hardcore approach, professors at Campbell are generally beloved by students. The faculty is reportedly "dedicated" and "always happy to answer questions." "Professors are very engaged and take time to get to know students individually." "The accessibility of our professors is one of the greatest strengths of Campbell Law," beams a 1L. "Their open-door policy makes it easy to slip in after class to ask a quick question or stay even longer to discuss legal issues." Critics call the top brass "out of touch with reality," but most students say that the administration is "extremely responsive and attentive." "They really strive to make themselves available to the students."

According to many students, the Career Center is "great for the students who utilize it." They say the staff "does an impressive job" and is "much more efficient and effective than at most law schools." Other students charge that this aspect of Campbell Law "is in need of vast improvement." Whatever the case, this school is located "in the heart of the state capital," "a hop, skip, and a jump away from" a bevy of state courts and government buildings. "Externships and internships (though most are unpaid) can easily be had," and there are "hundreds of attorneys within just a few miles" if you're looking to pad your resume with part-time employment. The "vicious" grading curve is "a hindrance in finding a job," and it's tough "to find jobs outside of North Carolina," but most students seem pretty confident about their career prospects.

Students tell us, "Resources and facilities are fantastic" at Campbell. "There could be additional space for individual study," but the shiny, newer building here is "gorgeous" and technologically "state-of-the-art." Another perk is the fact that "active" state court proceedings "reside at Campbell Law" as well, making Campbell one of the few law schools with a functioning court inside its walls.

DEXTER A. SMITH, MED, JD, ASSISTANT DEAN OF ADMISSIONS AND FINANCIAL AID
225 HILLSBOROUGH ST. RALEIGH, NC 27603
TEL: 914-865-5988 FAX: 914-865-5992
E-MAIL: ADMISSIONS@LAW.CAMPBELL.EDU • WEBSITE: WWW.LAW.CAMPBELL.EDU

Life

Students spend a great deal of time together, and the overwhelming sentiment is that there's "a strong community feeling" at Campbell Law. "The size allows you to form close working and personal relationships, not only with your fellow classmates, but also with the professors, deans, and administration," explains a 1L. "You will never be a number at Campbell." "I am able to leave my laptop and purse in the commons area while I attend class," adds a 3L. But some students say there's "no sense of camaraderie at Campbell Law. According to them, many students "go to school, go home, and hang out with a completely unique set of friends."

Opportunities for meaningful participation in extracurricular activities are reportedly plentiful. Social activities are also quite common. Beyond the law school realm, the local area has a lot to offer. In addition to being North Carolina's capital city, Raleigh is the state's second largest city (behind Charlotte). It's also among a rapidly growing city in a geographic region that has burgeoned economically over the past few decades. The metropolitan area here, which encompasses Raleigh, Durham, and Chapel Hill, as well as three huge research universities, offers very adequate amounts of culture and urban energy.

Getting In

Admitted students at the 25th percentile have LSAT scores in the mid 150s and undergraduate grade point averages approaching 3.2. At the 75th percentile, LSAT scores are in the high 150s, and GPAs are close to 3.6.

Clinical program required	No
Legal writing course requirement	Yes
Legal methods course requirement	Yes
Legal research course requirement	Yes
Moot court requirement	Yes
Public interest law requirement	No

ADMISSIONS

Selectivity Rating	79
# applications received	1,103
% applicants accepted	53
% acceptees attending	27
Median LSAT	154
LSAT Range (25th to 75th percentile)	152–157
Median undergrad GPA	3.3
Application fee	$50
Regular application deadline	5/1
Early application deadline	11/15
Early application notification	12/15
Transfer students accepted	Yes
Evening division offered	No
Part-time accepted	No
CAS accepted	Yes

FINANCIAL FACTS

Annual tuition	$33,400
Books and supplies	$2,300
Fees	$510
Room & Board	$8,500
Financial aid application deadline	7/2
% first-year students receiving some sort of aid	100
% all students receiving some sort of aid	96
% of aid that is merit based	52
% receiving scholarships	51

EMPLOYMENT INFORMATION

Career Rating	60*

Prominent Alumni
Elaine Marshall, North Carolina Secretary of State; John Tyson, Judge, North Carolina Court of Appeals; Richard Thigpen, General Counsel, Carolina Panthers NFL Franchise.

CAPITAL UNIVERSITY
LAW SCHOOL

INSTITUTIONAL INFORMATION

Public/private	Private
Affiliation	Lutheran
Student-faculty ratio	23:1
% faculty part-time	36
% faculty female	21
% faculty underrepresented minority	14
Total faculty	29

SURVEY SAYS...

Diverse opinions accepted in class-rooms, Great research resources, Abundant externship/internship/ clerkship opportunities, Students love Columbus, OH

STUDENTS

Enrollment of law school	683
% male/female	54/46
% from out-of-state	27
% part-time	39
% underrepresented minority	9
% international	1
# of countries represented	9
Average age of entering class	25

ACADEMICS

Academic Experience Rating	83
Profs interesting rating	79
Profs accessible rating	81
Hours of study per day	3.58

Academic Specialties
Corporation Securities, Environmental, Government Services, International, Labor, Taxation

Advanced Degrees Offered
LLM in Taxation, 1–6 years; LLM in Business, 1–6 years; LLM in Business & Taxation, 1–6 years; MT, 1-6 years

Combined Degrees Offered
JD/MBA, 3.5–6 years; JD/MSN, 3.5–6 years; JD/MSA, 3.5–4 years; JD/MTS, 4–6 years

Academics

It's a simple fact: Capital University Law School is "an underrated gem." Boasting "one of the highest Bar passage rates in Ohio," a "good practical skills program," "small classes" and "abundant" resources, it's easy to understand how the program attracts so many future JDs. Students greatly benefit from "a strong mandatory legal research and writing program, including a mandatory drafting class for 3Ls." Moreover, beyond the general clinic program, students can take advantage of a fabulous "Foster Youth Advocacy Clinic." Additionally, those prospective students hoping/needing to work while attending law school will be delighted to discover that Capital "offers [that] rare alternative in legal education, a high-quality part-time evening program." Students really appreciate the "opportunity to take courses with people who have work experience gives a unique diversity to course discussions."

Impressively, Capital's faculty is comprised of "scholars who are nationally known in the areas of family, children's, environmental, and regulatory law." Further, a number of professors have "[practical] experience in litigation, negotiation, and public service." Accessibility is another common attribute of Capital's faculty and, typically, they are "more than willing to meet with students out of class when necessary." Students here also find that their professors are "motivated and engaged in the material." Their "love for teaching is infectious" and they continually find ways to be "creative" in the classroom. And, as one sage third-year explains, "the dedicated professors make all the difference."

Students certainly have a difference of opinion when it comes to Capital's administration. As one third-year laments, "The registar's office needs a lot of help." He further elaborates, "[A]lmost every semester I attended Capital, it cancelled classes after I registered. During my fall semester of my last year four out of five of the classes I wanted to take got cancelled. This semester, a class got cancelled abruptly, with over eighty students registered, because of 'unforeseen changes in the professor's personal life.'" However, a second-year argues that the "administration is generally quick to address problems," and a first-year asserts that they "make great efforts to accommodate the needs of [their] students."

Life

Capital is able to foster a "strong student community." This can largely be attributed to the fact that it's "not overly competitive, and the students at the school are all friends." As a knowing third-year tells us, "We share notes, study suggestions, even outlines. I've NEVER seen any underhanded or mean competitive actions." While there tends to be a divide between full-time first-years and part-time students, another third-year informs us that "as soon as you hit 2L year (even as a full-time day student) you almost always have to take a night course or two." He continues, "I can't underscore how valuable this is to class discourse, diversity or students, and networking. CULS also has a number of veterans in the night program, which brings the conversation to a whole different level."

LINDA J. MIHELY, ASSISTANT DEAN OF ADMISSIONS AND FINANCIAL AID
303 E. BROAD STREET, COLUMBUS, OH 43215-3200
TEL: 614-236-6310 FAX: 614-236-6972
E-MAIL: ADMISSIONS@LAW.CAPITAL.EDU • WEBSITE: WWW.LAW.CAPITAL.EDU

Outside the classroom, students benefit from CULS's prime Columbus location. Indeed, the program's great reputation and proximity to the capital virtually guarantees "amazing externship opportunities." A third-year explains, "Varieties of positions are available at the Supreme Court of Ohio, the Legislature, Executive branch, numerous agencies, or lobbying organizations." And, given the "current evolving legal market, public service work continues to be one of the more stable practice areas. [Attending] CULS provides outstanding preparation and networking opportunities." Beyond the legal world, students can take advantage of all the great entertainment options Columbus offers—from the zoo and aquarium to NHL hockey, the symphony, opera and numerous restaurants and cafes.

Getting In

The admissions office at Capital takes a fairly straightforward approach. There's a healthy balance of qualitative and quantitative assessment so expect your undergraduate GPA, test scores, personal statements, recommendations and work history to all be closely vetted and considered. The median GPA for accepted students is 3.16 and the median LSAT score is 150. Therefore, if you're a solid student and a decent test taker you'll likely be considered a competitive applicant.

Clinical program required	No
Legal writing course requirement	Yes
Legal methods course requirement	Yes
Legal research course requirement	Yes
Moot court requirement	No
Public interest law requirement	No

ADMISSIONS

Selectivity Rating	85
# applications received	1,575
% applicants accepted	40
% acceptees attending	41
Average LSAT	153
LSAT Range (25th to 75th percentile)	151–156
Average undergrad GPA	3.21
Application fee	$40
Regular application deadline	
Early application deadline	5/1
Transfer students accepted	Yes
Evening division offered	Yes
Part-time accepted	Yes
CAS accepted	Yes

FINANCIAL FACTS

Annual tuition (in-state out-of-state)	$24,795
Books and supplies	$898
Fees	$0
Room & Board	$10,580
Financial aid application deadline	4/1
% first-year students receiving some sort of aid	94
% all students receiving some sort of aid	93
% of aid that is merit based	40
% receiving scholarships	40
Average grant	$8,000
Average loan	$23,570
Average total aid package	$28,737
Average debt	$70,806

EMPLOYMENT INFORMATION

Career Rating	91
% grads employed nine months out	95
Median starting salary	$59,849
State for bar exam	OH
Pass rate for first-time bar	87

Prominent Alumni
David Tannenbaum, Partner, Fulbright Jaworski—Patent Law; Deborah Pryce, U.S. Congress Woman; Paul McNulty, Deputy Attorney General, U.S. Dept. of Justice.

Grads Employed by Field (%)
Academic (4)
Business/Industry (19)
Government (21)
Judicial Clerkship (3)
Military (1)
Private Practice (46)
Public Interest (6)

CARDOZO SCHOOL OF LAW

INSTITUTIONAL INFORMATION

Public/private	Private
Affiliation	Jewish
Student-faculty ratio	15:1
% faculty part-time	64
% faculty female	39
% faculty underrepresented minority	6
Total faculty	172

SURVEY SAYS...

Diverse opinions accepted in classrooms, Students love New York, NY

STUDENTS

Enrollment of law school	1,139
% male/female	47/53
% from out-of-state	56
% part-time	9
% underrepresented minority	25
% international	6
# of countries represented	17
Average age of entering class	24

ACADEMICS

Academic Experience Rating	86
Profs interesting rating	79
Profs accessible rating	79
Hours of study per day	3.56

Academic Specialties

Commercial, Constitutional, Corporation Securities, Criminal, International, Legal Philosophy, Property, Taxation, Intellectual Property

Advanced Degrees Offered

JD can be obtained in 3 academic years, or 2.5 years; LLM (in Intellectual Property Law, Comparative Legal Thought, Dispute Resolution and Advocacy, or General Studies) can be obtained in 1 year full time; up to 3 years part time.

Combined Degrees Offered

JD/LLM in Intellectual Property Law or JD/LLM in Dispute Resolution and Advocacy can be obtained in 7 semesters; JD/MSW can be obtained in 4 years

Academics

Throughout its brief 36-year existence, Cardozo School of Law continues to brim with the enthusiasm and vigor of a young institution on the rise. At this New York City school, "The faculty, administrators and students are all energized and optimistic. We're willing to try new ideas and new programs in ways that older schools are not." At the heart of the experience, Cardozo's "outstanding" professors "come from a wide variety of backgrounds," and "many of them are just so brilliant that it makes your head want to explode." A current student enthuses, "I'm a 2L and so far I have had class with two professors who clerked for US Supreme Court justices, professors who argued before the Supreme Court, and professors who taught us cases (from our text books) which they actually litigated." As at any school, "There are a few cranky professors who never seem to have their morning coffee"; however, most professors "absolutely love to teach," and "go out of their way to make sure the students are comfortable with the course and the material." While class sizes can be fairly large, "The faculty makes a special effort to get to know all of their students."

Cardozo's first-year core curriculum is undeniably tough, but professors and administrators "appreciate the challenges that the 1L year presents and are very sympathetic to that pressure." Happily, "The only required course after 1L year is Advanced Legal Research," and students tell us that, "The electives, specifically in Intellectual Property, are second to none." Cardozo's curriculum further distinguishes itself through its "dedication to a practical, effective legal education," graduating students who are "prepared to walk into a court room or negotiation." With New York City as a backdrop, "There are so many diverse opportunities for students to get out of the classroom and start practicing law," including a "wide variety of internships, clinics, and externships." A current student elaborates, "Sure, there's law review, moot court, and mock trial, but there's also a dozen clinics that are eager to take on students—not to mention the envied Innocence Project—and then a slew of clubs and advocacy organizations." In addition, "There are a lot of study abroad opportunities that are affordable and really unique," such as trips to places like Haiti or Hong Kong during school vacations.

While some complain that, "the academic experience at Cardozo is unfairly underrated" in national rankings, they are confident that this "hidden gem" remains a robust contender. As it ages, the school's "ideal location, range of externship and field clinic opportunities, and growing alumni network will surely continue to attract the best students." Plus, it has already gained a strong foothold in New York City. In fact, Cardozo is dedicated to helping students navigate the tough local job market, right off the bat: "All 1Ls meet with counselors to discuss their resumes, and plenty of information is provided to help students secure summer jobs." Beyond the Career Services office, Cardozo's "Administration is generally friendly and helpful," though students say registration can be a bit arduous. When it comes to campus resources, "There is no free LEXIS and WestLaw printing," but "the legal collection is fairly extensive and there are lots of computers available to students." While the building is small, students say it is up-to-date, though you may have to study at home on the weekends: "Its Jewish affiliation means that the building closes at sundown on Fridays and is closed all day on Saturday."

DAVID G. MARTINIDEZ, DEAN OF ADMISSIONS
55 FIFTH AVENUE, NEW YORK, NY 10003
TEL: 212-790-0274 FAX: 212-790-0482
E-MAIL: LAWINFO@YU.EDU • WEBSITE: WWW.CARDOZO.YU.EDU

Life

Mirroring the vivid atmosphere of surrounding New York City, the Cardozo campus is bustling with activity. With more than 1,200 students enrolled in the program, the school crams a lot of energy (and people) into the small law school building. For those who want to get involved in the law school community, "Your out-of-class schedule can be quickly and easily filled with fun legal things to do outside the classroom." For example, "There are a variety of journals, lots of student organizations, and tons of presentations and lunches" on campus. A current student declares, "The events are amazing. I have been to so many panel events, networking events, speaker series. There are several every week, and all the speakers are wonderful."

Although Cardozo is affiliated with Yeshiva University, "Admissions does a good job of bringing a very diverse class of students," recruiting a cadre of future lawyers who are "intelligent and motivated without being crazily competitive or mean-spirited towards each other." Here, "You are free to be who you are. Merit is the only quality that can set you apart from other students." By all accounts, the school has a "great community feel," and students make friends easily. Obviously, the school's "location in Greenwich Village" is another major plus of the program, offering all the social events, entertainment, and resources of New York City.

Getting In

Cardozo accepts students three times annually, for the fall, January, and May terms, though prospective students can only apply to the program once per calendar year. In recent years, the incoming full-time class had a median GPA of 3.54 and a median LSAT score of 163; part-timers reported a 3.45 median GPA and a median LSAT score of 159. In recent years, the school has received more than 4,000 applications for fewer than 400 incoming class spots.

Clinical program required	No
Legal writing course requirement	Yes
Legal methods course requirement	Yes
Legal research course requirement	Yes
Moot court requirement	Yes
Public interest law requirement	No

ADMISSIONS

Selectivity Rating	**88**
# applications received	3,859
% applicants accepted	34
% acceptees attending	20
Median LSAT	163
LSAT Range (25th to 75th percentile)	160–166
Median undergrad GPA	3.54
Application fee	$75
Regular application deadline	4/1
Transfer students accepted	Yes
Evening division offered	No
Part-time accepted	Yes
CAS accepted	Yes

FINANCIAL FACTS

Annual tuition (in-state out-of-state)	$49,476
Books and supplies	$6,078
Fees	$570
Room & Board	$18,700
Financial aid application deadline	4/15
% first-year students receiving some sort of aid	84
% all students receiving some sort of aid	83
% of aid that is merit based	35
% receiving scholarships	60
Average grant	$28,968
Average loan	$41,878
Average total aid package	$54,851
Average debt	$120,008

EMPLOYMENT INFORMATION

Career Rating	**84**	
Total 2012 JD Grads	387	
% grads employed nine months out	79	
Median starting salary	$62,025	
# employed full-time	258	
# employed part-time	48	
# employed bar required	258	
# employed JD preferred	26	
# employed professional/other	18	
# employed non-professional	4	
# pursuing advanced degree	12	
# unemployed and seeking employment	37	
# not seeking employment	26	
% grads employed by school	0	
State for bar exam	NY, NJ	
Pass rate for first-time bar	86.7	

Prominent Alumni
Randi Weingarten '83, President, American Federation of Teachers; Hon. Sandra J. Feuerstein '79, Federal Judge, U.S. District Court, Eastern District of NY; David Samson '93, President, Florida Marlins.

Grads Employed by Field (%)
Academic (1)
Business/Industry (18)
Government (11)
Judicial Clerkship (4)
Military (1)
Private Practice (36)
Public Interest (8)

CASE WESTERN RESERVE UNIVERSITY
SCHOOL OF LAW

Academics

Well known for its professional schools and status as a world-class research institution, Case Western Reserve University's School of Law only fortifies the school's reputation. All students follow the school's unique practical legal curriculum, CaseARC, which one student calls "the greatest strength of our school." This integrated skills program brings together legal theory and fundamental practice skills with traditional classroom methods, putting students in the role of a practicing lawyer. Second and third year students have a wide discretion in selecting their courses, and with seven areas of concentration and 10 dual-degree and certificate programs, there are many choices, and there is "not much difficulty in getting into any class you'd like." The law clinic, which allows students to handle a broad range of civil, criminal, health, and business matters "is the greatest experience I've had in law school," according to one student. It "really increases the value of the classroom experience." "Few law schools mandate so many practical courses, and provide so many elective options in various specialty areas."

Beyond the strength of the academics and the great "breadth of its specialty programs and classes," the school has a "highly respected" faculty that "provide a first-rate legal education," though a few students mention their experience is "lacking in one on one attention." All of the professors have at least a decade of experience in practice, and the faculty boasts attorneys with backgrounds from the WTO, World Bank, and corporate law, as well as "national public sector international scholars." Most professors are "excellent teachers who match up well against the best in any of [the] top tier law school[s]," and "lots of them have written the textbooks and know their subjects inside and out." Many have also moved beyond the traditional Socratic method, in order "to find what works for their subject and students."

Aside from faculty, "the staff clearly cares about the school and the students," and "the school's administration is very accessible and knowledgeable." It "learns from its mistakes... if something isn't working, they try to fix it." Research facilities are also "really amazing," especially "the access to international law information through the War Crimes Portal and through all of the database access in the library." "I worked on a journal and the librarians were literally the largest sources of knowledge I've ever encountered," says a student.

Truly, it is the school's curriculum that shines through for students. One student proclaims, "[It] has allowed me to hit the ground running in my legal summer work." Another states, "[It] provides opportunities that I know other schools don't," such as an exchange program with Chinese law schools and "the ability to extern at an international war crimes tribunal for a semester instead of taking classes." "When I was participating in [the international tribunal externship], I had students from Yale, Harvard and Georgetown doing summer internships at the tribunals who were very envious and surprised that we had this opportunity to continue on in the fall for credits." Some do say that the Career Services Office "needs to improve its relationship between the school and the alumni" and "to focus on expanding its influence into legal markets such as New York, Chicago, and Washington, D.C." However, nearly all agree that "Case does a great job of giving students the resources they need to succeed, [and] everything else is (and should be) up to the individual."

ELAINE GREAVES, ASSISTANT DEAN FOR ADMISSIONS
11075 EAST BOULEVARD, CLEVELAND, OH 44106
TEL: 800-756-0036 FAX: 216-368-1042
E-MAIL: LAWADMISSIONS@CASE.EDU • WEBSITE: WWW.LAW.CASE.EDU

Life

As the school is housed in a building "a bit too small for the number of students," a lot of courses "have to be offered at night," which is great for adjuncts and people who work. The students are the best part of the school. Case students "aren't competitive, but rather friendly and helpful, and always looking out for each other." In Cleveland, "you make your own fun," so "it's a great environment to study without getting distracted." "You can have as much of a social life as you want. Some weeks, I go out three or four times a week. Other times not at all," says a student. Cleveland itself "isn't horribly dangerous, but you do have to be careful about where you go."

Case has "more than a fair amount of diversity" in this "very friendly, cohesive community," and "there are many students who represent many different communities," with strong student associations for African Americans, Jewish students, and South Asian students, among others.

Getting In

With little over 200 spots in Case Western Reserve's entering law school class, competition is high. While the selection process is rigorous, it is not rigid. According to the school's website, "We insist upon diversity in our student body because we believe that the entire law school community benefits from it." The admissions committee evaluates applicants holistically, "looking carefully at the candidate's undergraduate grade point average and LSAT score as well as other, non- quantitative factors, such as level and difficulty of undergraduate course work, writing ability, and work experience." The majority of students come from outside of Ohio.

Clinical program required	No
Legal writing course requirement	Yes
Legal methods course requirement	Yes
Legal research course requirement	Yes
Moot court requirement	No
Public interest law requirement	No

ADMISSIONS

Selectivity Rating	80
# applications received	1,503
% applicants accepted	54
% acceptees attending	19
Median LSAT	160
LSAT Range (25th to 75th percentile)	156–161
Median undergrad GPA	3.38
Application fee	$40
Regular application deadline	4/1
Early application deadline	2/1
Transfer students accepted	Yes
Evening division offered	No
Part-time accepted	No
CAS accepted	Yes

FINANCIAL FACTS

Annual tuition	$44,500
Books and supplies	$1,600
Fees	$120
Room & Board	$17,530
Financial aid application deadline	5/1
% first-year students receiving some sort of aid	96
% all students receiving some sort of aid	86
% of aid that is merit based	100
% receiving scholarships	75
Average grant	$20,041
Average loan	$42,744
Average total aid package	$65,960
Average debt	$118,806

EMPLOYMENT INFORMATION

Career Rating	87
Total 2012 JD Grads	172
% grads employed nine months out	86
Median starting salary	$65,000
% job accepting grads providing useable salary information	50
# employed full-time	117
# employed part-time	23
# employed bar required	100
# employed JD preferred	31
# employed professional/other	6
# employed non-professional	3
# pursuing advanced degree	6
# unemployed and seeking employment	21
# not seeking employment	3
State for bar exam	OH, NY, PA, IL, MD
Pass rate for first-time bar	82.6

Prominent Alumni
Barry M. Meyer '67, Chairman and CEO, Warner Bros. Entertainment; Martin Gruenberg '79, Chairman, FDIC; Capricia Marshall '90, Ambassador, U.S. Chief of Protocol.

Grads Employed by Field (%)
Academic (1)
Business/Industry (26)
Government (16)
Judicial Clerkship (4)
Military (1)
Private Practice (39)
Public Interest (12)

THE CATHOLIC UNIVERSITY OF AMERICA
COLUMBUS SCHOOL OF LAW

INSTITUTIONAL INFORMATION

Public/private	Private
Affiliation	Roman Catholic
Student-faculty ratio	16:1
% faculty part-time	65
Total faculty	116

SURVEY SAYS...

Diverse opinions accepted in classrooms, Great research resources, Great library staff, Beautiful campus

STUDENTS

Average age of entering class	26

ACADEMICS

Academic Experience Rating	**84**
Profs interesting rating	79
Profs accessible rating	80
Hours of study per day	3.13

Academic Specialties

Civil Procedure, Corporation Securities, Criminal, International, Labor, Intellectual Property, Communications, Law and Public Policy

Advanced Degrees Offered

JD, three years (full-time) or four years (part-time). LL.M degrees offered in Communications Law, Securities Law, or Comparative and International Law

Combined Degrees Offered

JD/MA programs in accounting, canon law, history, philosophy, psychology, politics, library science, economics, and social work, 3-4 years.

Academics

Catholic University of America's Columbus School of Law combines the professional opportunities and legal resources of Washington, D.C. with the intimate, student-friendly atmosphere of a private law school. Drawing from the surrounding city's large legal community, many CUA professors are "full-time practicing attorneys" with a "deep understanding of their particular field." Here, professors come from "interesting and diverse legal backgrounds," including "younger faculty already making names for themselves in areas like civil procedure, First Amendment conscience protection, and protecting children from sexual abuse." While the school attracts top-notch names, the atmosphere is "warm" and accommodating, with professors described as "intelligent, sympathetic, approachable, and caring." While the JD program is not overly easy, "the emphasis is on creating successful students," with ample support services to promote that goal. For instance, "there is a program for individuals in [the] lower 15 percent of the class with additional lectures, and study technique assistance—they don't let people slip through the cracks." The accommodating culture extends to the administrative offices and staff, too. From financial aid to the program dean, "the administration is very helpful and will address student concerns promptly."

Legal education extends beyond the classroom at CUA, and the administration puts a lot of "emphasis on the school's moot court, arbitration, and trial teams, as well as journals and clinics." Plus, "All of the professors are more than willing and able to help connect students with internships, clerkships, and eventual jobs." Research is also a major component of the academic program, and "the research librarians bend over backwards to help any student who asks." If they cannot find what they need at CUA, the school provides "access to all major research databases as well as catalogs from most major libraries in Washington, D.C. through the interlibrary loan program." When it comes to the job hunt, many would love to see CUA's Career Services department significantly enhanced. A current student details, "While the people working there currently do a very good job, that office needs more funding and larger staff so they can help students learn about and apply for jobs." However, "the connections to government and legislative opportunities" are strong at CUA, and the "very active alumni network" helps students make inroads in D.C.'s legal community. On that note, students point out that the school "focuses primarily on D.C. and government jobs, so if you're a student looking to work elsewhere after graduation, Catholic may not be the best option."

Catholic University of America's religious affiliation is more than just in name alone, and, depending on their own background, students either praise or deride the Catholic influence on their law school education. Prospective students should be aware that, even in strict legal discussion, "You don't get away from that Catholic perspective" at CUA. For example, "The school's connection to the Catholic church prevents student groups from participating in certain activities, and makes some journal-writing topics off limits." Others explain that because of the school's stringent standards, "there can sometimes be trouble in getting outside speakers approved in a timely manner." Excluding religious affiliations, most students are happy to note that the school's Catholic values are wonderfully demonstrated in its "commitment to public service and pro bono" work.

SHANI BUTTS, DIRECTOR OF ADMISSIONS
3600 JOHN MCCORMACK ROAD, NE, WASHINGTON, D.C. 20064
TEL: 202-319-5151 FAX: 202-319-6285
E-MAIL: ADMISSIONS@LAW.EDU • WEBSITE: WWW.LAW.EDU

Life

Described as "a great place to learn and study," CUA offers a comfortable campus environment, which also affords access to the many events, venues, and recreational opportunities in greater Washington, D.C. Within the law school, the "facilities are phenomenal," offering classrooms that are "large, technologically current, and well-kept." Per the school's recommendation, "Every student has a laptop," and there is "wireless internet and power outlets at each desk." When students need a quiet place to concentrate, the "vast and beautiful" law library "is well-lit and expansive; and it has a great view of the Catholic University campus."

Taking a cue from the school's friendly teaching staff, "Students tend to be much more collegial at Catholic compared with the more cutthroat competition you find at other area schools." This student body is a convivial crew who are instilled with the knowledge that "the people in our classes are going to be our colleagues when we are done with school, so everyone is willing to work together if someone needs help." When they are not convening for study groups, CUA students also get together for clubs, association meetings, and school social events. Among other happenings, "The school provides the opportunity for a vast number of happy hours both on and off campus."

Getting In

When evaluating candidates at CUA Law, a prospective student's academic record and performance on the LSAT are the two most important factors in any admissions decision; however, the admissions committee will also consider other elements of an applicant's history, such as previous leadership or professional experience, letters of recommendation, and one's personal statement. Recent students who enrolled had an LSAT range (in the 25th–75th percentile) of 151–160. Incoming students join the program from more than thirty U.S. states and internationally.

Clinical program required	No
Legal writing course requirement	Yes
Legal methods course requirement	Yes
Legal research course requirement	No
Moot court requirement	No
Public interest law requirement	No

ADMISSIONS

Selectivity Rating	85
# applications received	2,991
% applicants accepted	32
Median LSAT	157
LSAT Range (25th to 75th percentile)	151–160
Median undergrad GPA	3.28
Application fee	$65
Regular application deadline	3/16
Early application deadline	11/1
Early application notification	12/15
Transfer students accepted	Yes
Evening division offered	Yes
Part-time accepted	Yes
CAS accepted	Yes

FINANCIAL FACTS

Annual tuition (in-state out-of-state)	$43,080
Books and supplies	$1,500
Fees	$465
Room & Board (off-campus)	$14,600
% first-year students receiving some sort of aid	95
% all students receiving some sort of aid	86
Average grant	$13,033
Average loan	$47,403
Average total aid package	$49,257
Average debt	$142,000

EMPLOYMENT INFORMATION

Career Rating	60*	**Prominent Alumni**	
Total 2012 JD Grads	246	Robert Casey, US Senator, Pennsylvania;	
% for whom you have useable information	98	Michael Bidwill, President, Arizona Cardinals NFL Team; Charlene Barshefsky,	
% grads employed nine months out	81	(former) US Trade Ambassador; Peggy	
# employed full-time	186	Quince, Justice, Florida Supreme Court.	
# employed part-time	13	**Grads Employed by Field (%)**	
# employed bar required	100	Academic (5)	
# employed JD preferred	82	Business/Industry (31)	
# employed professional/other	12	Government (23)	
# employed non-professional	5	Judicial Clerkship (13)	
# pursuing advanced degree	2	Private Practice (26)	
# unemployed and seeking employment	36	Public Interest (5)	
# not seeking employment	5		
State for bar exam	MD, VA, CA, NY, FL		

CHAPMAN UNIVERSITY
SCHOOL OF LAW

Academics

Chapman University School of Law is located "in the heart of Southern California," "just minutes away from the Orange County courts and only thirty-five miles from downtown" Los Angeles. "The law school itself is beautiful." "The facilities are state-of-the-art," "very modern," "grand yet cozy," and generally "amazing." "Classrooms are a dream." Study space is ample. "The research facilities leave students wanting for nothing." "It is a very nice environment in which to spend large amounts of time." It's not just all the bells and whistles that make Chapman great—Chapman offers the academic heft to complement its beautiful facilities. The school boasts two law journals and a unique certificate program in entertainment law. Certificates are also available in tax law, international law, business law, environmental law and land use, and dispute resolution. Moot court and other trial competition teams are perennial powerhouses. There are "numerous clinics that provide valuable experience in a broad range of fields," including a family violence clinic, a meditation clinic, and a constitutional jurisprudence clinic. Students seeking international exposure can study abroad in England. "Chapman also has a very comprehensive bar preparation program that it provides for students at no additional cost" during the spring and summer of their third year. Class sizes tend to be smaller here, which affords "a very intimate feeling, unlike that of a larger school," and students have nothing but praise for their professors. The faculty is brimming with "fun, brilliant" profs who are "challenging but not patronizing." Outside of class, faculty members are reportedly "easily accessible and always open to discussion with students." In class, "they manage to make even subjects like federal income tax exciting." "We have professors that quote popular television shows during class, sing songs about the subject matter, and make witty comments that make us laugh to lighten the mood between the times when they scare us to death with the Socratic method," relates a 1L.

Administratively, complaints are rare. "It's an ongoing 'love-in' between the administration and the students," explains a 2L. "It's like Woodstock, only without the hallucinogenic substances and endless rain." The top brass reportedly provides "overwhelming and unending support" and "really cares about making the school better." "They have tons of money," adds a 3L, "and they spend it pretty effectively." High grades are difficult to achieve on a consistent basis here. Students also point out that Chapman's reputation beyond the immediate area "could improve." "The legal community outside of Orange County doesn't know much about the school," laments a 3L, although "the administration is working hard" to change that, starting with the recent hiring of a new high profile dean with connections throughout the state.

Life

"Chapman has a reputation as being a conservative school," explains a 3L,"but I think that reputation is true only when compared to other schools." Students agree, "Chapman has strong diversity of thought." "Regardless of race, ethnicity, sexual orientation, political views, religious preference, or cultural background, the social fabric of the Chapman community is tightly knit, and no one is viewed as an outsider here." "Being a liberal student, I have not felt uncomfortable in any way," declares another 3L. "Quite the opposite, the school has always fostered an environment of healthy discussion and acceptance of all students." Beyond politics, students here are "witty, darn[ed] smart, and pleasant to be around." The Chapman Law population is comprised of "very social" younger students and older students who "seem to spend more time studying and less time hanging out at school, so that when they have free time, they can spend it with their families." The "relaxed but rigorous" academic atmosphere is "very community-

Tracy Simmons, Assistant Dean of Admissions and Diversity Initiatives
One University Drive, Orange, CA 92866
Tel: 714-628-2500 Fax: 714-628-2501
E-Mail: lawadm@chapman.edu • Website: www.chapman.edu/law

oriented." "Everyone is aware that we're being curved against each other, but that doesn't stop us from helping each other succeed," relates a 2L. "Everyone pushes each other to success." "Law students do compete for grades," though, and there are definitely "competitive undertones." When students have the time or just can't bring themselves to brief another case, "There are plenty of opportunities to steal away" from course work. For one thing, "the weather is always perfect." "There is a club for everyone." "The school is also very successful in bringing in high-level speakers, including judges and well-known academics." "A multitude of dialogues, lectures, and panels "presents various legal issues and different perspectives on those issues. "The school is located in an area with a ton of fun restaurants and bars right down the street" as well.

Getting In

Enrolled students at the 75th percentile have LSAT scores of about 160 and GPAs a little lower than 3.68. Enrolled students at the 25th percentile have LSAT scores of approximately 155 and GPAs a little over 3.21. Also worth noting here is the fact that the admissions staff will look at all of your LSAT scores, not just your best one.

Clinical program required	No
Legal writing course requirement	Yes
Legal methods course requirement	Yes
Legal research course requirement	Yes
Moot court requirement	Yes
Public interest law requirement	No

ADMISSIONS

Selectivity Rating	83
# applications received	2,365
% applicants accepted	42
% acceptees attending	17
Average LSAT	157
Median LSAT	158
LSAT Range (25th to 75th percentile)	154–160
Average undergrad GPA	3.39
Median undergrad GPA	3.37
Application fee	$75
Regular application deadline	4/15
Transfer students accepted	Yes
Evening division offered	No
Part-time accepted	Yes
CAS accepted	Yes

FINANCIAL FACTS

Annual tuition	43,120
Books and supplies	$1,800
Fees	$416
Room & Board	$17,280
Financial aid application deadline	3/2
% first-year students receiving some sort of aid	95
% all students receiving some sort of aid	93
% of aid that is merit based	30
% receiving scholarships	66
Average grant	$25,005
Average loan	$48,214
Average total aid package	$57,334
Average debt	$133,711

EMPLOYMENT INFORMATION

Career Rating	76
Total 2012 JD Grads	178
% for whom you have useable information	100
% grads employed nine months out	69
Median starting salary	$63,173
# employed full-time	102
# employed part-time	21
# employed bar required	76
# employed JD preferred	37
# employed professional/other	4
# employed non-professional	5
# pursuing advanced degree	1
# unemployed and seeking employment	43
# not seeking employment	11
% grads employed by school	2
State for bar exam	CA, NY, OR, IL, AZ
Pass rate for first-time bar	81

Prominent Alumni
Steve Ruden, Partner, Knobbe Martens; Courtney Mason, Associate General Counsel, Phoenix Suns; Jason Rednour, Partner, Paul Hastings.

Grads Employed by Field (%)
Academic (2)
Business/Industry (17)
Government (3)
Military (1)
Private Practice (44)
Public Interest (1)

CHARLESTON SCHOOL OF LAW

Academics

Charleston School of Law is one of the South's premiere legal programs. Armed with a "challenging curriculum" and "emphasis on practical skills," the university has managed to attract "some of the biggest legal influences in the state of South Carolina." Students greatly benefit from studying with professors who have incredibly diverse professional backgrounds including "retired Deans from top law schools, district attorneys, former partners and associates in 'Big Law' firms in large cities, and some of the top local attorneys in South Carolina." Not surprisingly, these professors "do a great job of bringing practical and "real life" issues to the classroom." And while teachers here certainly "keep you on your toes in class with the Socratic method," students can breathe a sigh of relief knowing that they "[won't] belittle you."

In addition to their impressive credentials and towering intellect, it's obvious that professors at Charleston "truly care about their students." Importantly, they "do an excellent job in making themselves available outside of the classroom." A first-year student elaborates, "The faculty employ an open door policy in which students can come to their office hours to get help if they are falling behind or simply to clarify a minor topic. The professors actually get upset if students don't come and take advantage of their openness. They don't try and hide the ball from you and want their students to be the best lawyers they can be."

This friendliness and accessibility also extends to the administration. The deans, who "are a pleasure to work with," really "take the time to get to know the students personally." They "portray a positive attitude at all times and are dedicated to making the school the best it can be." A second-year wholeheartedly supports this notion exclaiming, "A large majority of the administrators know my name and year before I walk through the door, and everyone works hard to cultivate a welcoming and encouraging atmosphere."

Charleston's infrastructure and amenities do leave a little bit to be desired. As a third-year student admonishes, "Facilities need upgrading, for a more professional experience/appearance." A first-year student quickly adds, "The library is small and lacks the print resources of some other law schools." Of course, a more understanding peer counters, "… With today's growing dependency on technology and the increasing availability of online material, I don't find these issues to be a problem. I always have a quiet seat in the library when I go to study and enough room in my classes to comfortably take notes and follow along."

Life

Charleston School of Law prides itself on the fact that it "doesn't have the cut-throat mentality that so many law schools are rumored to [possess]." Indeed, "people generally seem very willing to help one another out, send each other outlines, and review material together." As one relived third-year shares, "It certainly has made the otherwise intimidating culture of law school more of a non-factor so that students can concentrate on studies more." Moreover, "we work hard in Charleston to cultivate an atmosphere of civility and camaraderie within the student body, and I believe that that will continue to be achieved… I am thankful that our student body is helpful, encouraging, and genuinely happy to hear about my success." A classmate concurs adding, "The overall environment is collegiate, cooperative, stimulating, and above all else, welcoming."

These future JDs can also take advantage of "great connections with the Charleston legal community, and surrounding cities." What's more, these lucky students have access to "amazing speakers and potential opportunities for externships, internships, and various other programs." Students also rave about hometown Charleston, a "fantastic," "beautiful" and "historic" city. As a second-year student boasts, "The location is also second to none. I don't know if [there] is a better place to go to law school than in Charleston. With its world class restaurants, bars, history, culture, white sand beaches, and gorgeous weather, Charleston has everything a law student could desire while taking a break from the stress of classes."

Getting In

Charleston's admission committee gives each application a thorough vetting. Both undergraduate GPA and LSAT performance are of primary importance. After all, those are the strongest indicators of law school success. Charleston also gives consideration military service, employment history, community service, leadership experience and extracurricular involvement. The only prerequisite is an undergraduate degree from an accredited university. No pre-law curriculum necessary.

Clinical program required	No
Legal writing course requirement	Yes
Legal methods course requirement	No
Legal research course requirement	Yes
Moot court requirement	No
Public interest law requirement	Yes

ADMISSIONS

Selectivity Rating	73
# applications received	1,649
% applicants accepted	57
% acceptees attending	15
Median LSAT	152
LSAT Range (25th to 75th percentile)	149–155
Median undergrad GPA	3.19
Application fee	$50
Regular application deadline	3/1
Transfer students accepted	Yes
Evening division offered	No
Part-time accepted	Yes
CAS accepted	Yes

FINANCIAL FACTS

Annual tuition	$37,774
Books and supplies	$1,250
Fees	$100
Room & Board	$10,800
Financial aid application deadline	5/15
% first-year students receiving some sort of aid	88
% all students receiving some sort of aid	89
% of aid that is merit based	7
% receiving scholarships	32
Average grant	$7,487
Average loan	$46,290
Average total aid package	$47,773

EMPLOYMENT INFORMATION

Career Rating	**75**	**Grads Employed by Field (%)**
Total 2012 JD Grads	229	Academic (1)
% for whom you have useable information	100	Business/Industry (13)
% grads employed nine months out	74	Government (6)
# employed full-time	157	Judicial Clerkship (8)
# employed part-time	13	Private Practice (42)
# employed bar required	137	Public Interest (3)
# employed JD preferred	14	
# employed professional/other	9	
# employed non-professional	8	
# pursuing advanced degree	9	
# unemployed and seeking employment	42	
# not seeking employment	8	
% grads employed by school	0	
State for bar exam	SC, NC, VA, TN, GA	
Pass rate for first-time bar	74	

City University of New York

School of Law

INSTITUTIONAL INFORMATION

Public/private	Public
Student-faculty ratio	10:1
% faculty part-time	15
% faculty female	64
% faculty underrepresented minority	38
Total faculty	61

SURVEY SAYS...

Great library staff, Liberal students

STUDENTS

Enrollment of law school	428
% male/female	36/64
% from out-of-state	16
% part-time	1
% underrepresented minority	39
% international	1
# of countries represented	39
Average age of entering class	27

ACADEMICS

Academic Experience Rating	**82**
Profs interesting rating	79
Profs accessible rating	89

Academic Specialties

Civil Procedure, Commercial, Constitutional, Criminal, Environmental, Government Services, Human Rights, International, Labor, Property

Advanced Degrees Offered

JD, 3 years, full-time only

Combined Degrees Offered

None

Academics

The incredibly affordable CUNY—Law is "full of school spirit, clinical training, and no page ripping out of library books." Working under the mission "law in the service of human needs," the school is "genuinely committed to the struggle for justice," and tends to attract a different type of law student; unlike a lot of New York law schools, the vast majority of the "dedicated" and "idealistic" students here go on to careers in public interest. This mission creates a law school experience like no other—students are encouraging to one another and help each other to thrive, and everyone involved with the school wishes success on each new class. "Put it this way, I have a number of my professors' cell phone numbers, I call them by their first names, and our janitors come to our graduation because they are proud of us," says a 3L.

The curriculum here provides a well-rounded education of law and case-teaching method, along with policy and legal theory, enabling students to do more progressive work in the legal field. There is no grading curve, classes stress doctrinal work and advocacy, seminars teach practical skills with lawyering, and the research requirements prepare students for internships/careers. Legal clinics offer myriad of practical experience, particularly in the third year. Professors are "diverse, engaged and receptive to students," and many "have amazing histories of advocacy work," with backgrounds in feminist organizing work, gay rights, environmental justice, reproductive rights, and "everything else fun and liberal." There can be a touch of disorganization and bureaucracy in the administration, but it's kept to a minimum, and administrators "can be great if you find them on a good day." CUNY Law recently moved locations to Long Island City, which is within walking distance of seven subway lines, the Long Island Railroad, and many buses, not to mention the Long Island City courthouse. The new LEED Gold certified building now makes the law school one of the greenest law schools in the country. All classrooms are equipped with at least one computer and a SmartBoard for easy note-taking, and outside of the classroom, discussions are continued "on the course websites that each professor dedicate to maintain."

In the end, it's the complete commitment from faculty, staff, and students to the school's mission that wins students over, and the comfortable, supportive environment created when surrounded by people with similar motives. "No one here is trying to be an ambulance chaser or a barracuda or any of the other stereotypes of lawyers. Everyone here is genuinely interested in being a champion for a cause and the cause is people who genuinely need the law on their side," says a proud student.

Life

Most who attend school here have been out of undergrad for quite awhile and have a wide variety of experience working for nonprofit organizations and activist jobs, so they come to school with a clear idea of the type of public interest law they want to practice. This results in an "incredibly collaborative learning environment" and students want to see each other succeed. In fact, they're downright rabid about the fact that competition does not exist at CUNY: "I had computer problems during midterms and finals my first semester, and people were practically throwing their outlines at me so I would do well!" says a student. Since a lot of people commute and there is no out-of-state housing, it "sometimes feels hard to get everyone together," but "small class sizes make it easier to make 'school friends.'" and people "definitely coalesce around local bars to celebrate midterms, finals and anything in between." There are many student clubs and events, even if students are often too exhausted to take part in them.

HELENA QUON, DIRECTOR OF ADMISSIONS
TWO COURT SQUARE, LONG ISLAND CITY, NY 11101-4356
TEL: 718-340-4210 FAX: 718-340-4435
E-MAIL: ADMISSIONS@LAW.CUNY.EDU • WEBSITE: WWW.LAW.CUNY.EDU

Although the school is very liberal in its ideology, when it comes to conversation and debate, "No one is shunned because they aren't of a certain persuasion." This liberalism also translates to action, and "Everything gets heated up, from new listservs, banning Coke products, and scheduling of classes and finals." Still, everyone here gets along really well and is "like a family," but just like in a family, "Any drama is magnified because of the school's small size."

Getting In

CUNY evaluates prospective students based on their demonstrated abilities and intellectual capacity to complete a rigorous legal program, using test scores, previous academic records, and, where applicable, post-college work experience. In addition to these factors, CUNY seeks students who can bring diversity of background and experience to the campus and who express a specific interest in and affinity for the values of the program. Finally, CUNY favors New York residents or students with a particular interest in serving the New York community.

Clinical program required	Yes
Legal writing course requirement	Yes
Legal methods course requirement	Yes
Legal research course requirement	Yes
Moot court requirement	No
Public interest law requirement	Yes

ADMISSIONS

Selectivity Rating	**88**
# applications received	2,076
% applicants accepted	25
% acceptees attending	23
Average LSAT	156
Median LSAT	155
LSAT Range (25th to 75th percentile)	154–159
Average undergrad GPA	3.25
Median undergrad GPA	3.32
Application fee	$60
Regular application deadline	4/15
Regular notification	6/16
Transfer students accepted	Yes
Evening division offered	No
Part-time accepted	No
CAS accepted	Yes

FINANCIAL FACTS

Annual tuition (in-state out-of-state)	$12,090/$20,090
Books and supplies	$1,712
Fees	$312
Room & Board	$18,090
Financial aid application deadline	5/1
% first-year students receiving some sort of aid	97
% all students receiving some sort of aid	89
% of aid that is merit based	17
% receiving scholarships	47
Average grant	$3,373
Average loan	$33,408
Average total aid package	$33,385
Average debt	$79,680

EMPLOYMENT INFORMATION

Career Rating	**76**	**Prominent Alumni**
Total 2012 JD Grads	141	Rita Mella, Manhattan Surrogate Court
% for whom you have useable information	99	Judge; William Massey, Partner at Gladstein, Reif & Meginniss LLP; Kary
% grads employed nine months out	84	Moss, Executive Director, American Civil
Median starting salary	$48,000	Liberties Union.
% job accepting grads providing useable salary information	47	**Grads Employed by Field (%)** Academic (2)
# employed full-time	114	Business/Industry (6)
# employed part-time	4	Government (7)
# employed bar required	83	Judicial Clerkship (6)
# employed JD preferred	30	Military (1)
# employed professional/other	4	Private Practice (25)
# employed non-professional	1	Public Interest (23)
# pursuing advanced degree	0	
# unemployed and seeking employment	22	
# not seeking employment	1	
% grads employed by school	12	
State for bar exam	NY	
Pass rate for first-time bar	69.5	

CLEVELAND STATE UNIVERSITY
CLEVELAND-MARSHALL COLLEGE OF LAW

Academics

Students at Cleveland State University's Cleveland-Marshall College of Law call their school "a diamond in the rough." The focus here is squarely on bar preparation and practical training. "The greatest strengths are the opportunities for real-world experience," says a 3L. There are a half dozen clinics and they cover a wide range of legal areas. Externships with judges, government entities, and public interest groups are "readily available" in Cleveland and the greater metropolitan area. The moot court program is strong. The legal writing program thoroughly emphasizes "advocacy skills." If students run into academic difficulties, they can take advantage of Cleveland-Marshall's academic support programs, which provide group training and one-on-one assistance to help students with their course work. Areas of concentration are available in business law, civil litigation and dispute resolution, criminal law, employment law, health law, and international law. There are five dual-degree programs and three journals. Cleveland-Marshall Law is also quite a bargain, particularly if you are an Ohio resident.

"On average, Marshall professors are knowledgeable, passionate, and approachable," relates a 2L. "I have never been taught something as inherently boring as civil procedure in such an invigorating manner," beams a 1L. Professors are also generally accessible outside the classroom. The "excellent" administration is "extremely open to student interaction and answers questions and concerns promptly." However, "Heading to the main campus to get administrative stuff done can be tedious." Students' biggest academic complaint involves the distribution of grades. The curve here, which permits faculty members to give over 50 percent of all 1Ls a grade of C+ or lower, can be pretty rough.

Cleveland-Marshall Law is located in downtown Cleveland on the main campus of the larger university, which means that part-time work at local firms is easy to come by throughout the year. According to some students, "the facilities could be a little fancier." Most say that the layout of the law school is "not only aesthetically pleasing but functional," though. "The library is great." "The new addition is modern and beautiful," relates a 1L. "It's eye-catching from the street and a great place for students to study or relax between classes."

More than 75 percent of all newly minted graduates take jobs in either private practice or the corporate world. The overwhelming majority of Cleveland-Marshall's alumni practice in Ohio and the school's reputation is very solid throughout the northeastern part of the state. Students rave about Cleveland-Marshall Law's "connection to the Cleveland legal community" as well as "a supportive, active alumni base that extends opportunities to anyone who seeks them."

Life

The part-time program at Cleveland-Marshall is pretty large and "evening and day students do have very different experiences." As you would expect, full-timers are generally younger while part-timers are older and have "more time in the real world" already under their belts. "In my class, we have architects, engineers, law enforcement officials, researchers, bankers, and people with other varying careers," says a part-time 2L. Some part-time students complain that they are "excluded from a lot of school activities and

CHRISTOPHER LUCAK, ASSISTANT DEAN FOR ADMISSION AND FINANCIAL AID
2121 EUCLID AVENUE, LB 138, CLEVELAND, OH 44115-2214
TEL: 866-687-2304 FAX: 216-687-6881
E-MAIL: ADMISSIONS@LAW.CSUOHIO.EDU • WEBSITE: WWW.LAW.CSUOHIO.EDU

classes." Others assert that "the full- and part-timers are treated equally." "I am a full-time 3L who frequently takes night classes due to my part-time work schedule and I haven't noticed a divide between night and day professors' focus on the students," explains one student. "Some of the best professors I have had in law school teach night classes."

Student opinion concerning the academic atmosphere is mixed. Some students flatly call it "competitive." Others, staking something of a middle ground, say that "people are friendly and willing to help, most of the time." Still others describe "a great sense of camaraderie." "Students here help one another better than at any institution I've ever encountered," declares a 3L. Socially, clubs and extracurricular activities are abundant. "The student bar association plans fun socials at least once a month with free food and drinks for students to unwind." "Everyone seems to fall into whatever groups make them happy and things move right along." "Most of the students know one another," explains a 3L. "We have lockers, prom (Barrister's Ball), socials, drama, and tons of drinking." Beyond the law school orbit, Cleveland isn't generally listed among the greatest cities in the United States but there really are a lot of charming neighborhoods and the cost of living is comparatively low.

Getting In

Enrolled students at the 75th percentile at Cleveland-Marshall have LSAT scores around 157 and grade point averages of 3.66. At the 25th percentile, LSAT scores are 153, and GPAs are 3.09.

Clinical program required	No
Legal writing course requirement	Yes
Legal methods course requirement	No
Legal research course requirement	Yes
Moot court requirement	No
Public interest law requirement	No

ADMISSIONS

Selectivity Rating	86
# applications received	1,768
% applicants accepted	35
% acceptees attending	34
Average LSAT	156
LSAT Range (25th to 75th percentile)	153–157
Average undergrad GPA	3.38
Application fee	
Regular application deadline	5/1
Transfer students accepted	Yes
Evening division offered	Yes
Part-time accepted	Yes
CAS accepted	Yes

FINANCIAL FACTS

Annual tuition (in-state out-of-state)	$16,478/$22,608
Books and supplies	$1,400
Fees	$25
Room & Board	$11,000
Financial aid application deadline	5/1
% first-year students receiving some sort of aid	90
% all students receiving some sort of aid	95
% of aid that is merit based	90
% receiving scholarships	40
Average grant	$6,457
Average loan	$24,070
Average total aid package	$24,906
Average debt	$59,458

EMPLOYMENT INFORMATION

		Grads Employed by Field (%)
Career Rating	70	Academic (3)
% grads employed nine months out	90	Business/Industry (24)
Median starting salary	$81,823	Government (12)
State for bar exam	OH, NY, MD, MA, FL	Judicial Clerkship (5)
Prominent Alumni		Military (2)
Tim Russert, the late moderator and Sr.		Private Practice (53)
VP, NBC News; Hon. Louis Stokes, US		Public Interest (3)
House of Representatives, Rtd.; Hon.		
Maureen O'Connor, Justice, Supreme		
Court of Ohio.		

THE COLLEGE OF WILLIAM & MARY
MARSHALL-WYTHE LAW SCHOOL

INSTITUTIONAL INFORMATION

Public/private	Public
Affiliation	No Affiliation
Student-faculty ratio	14:1
% faculty part-time	58
% faculty female	29
% faculty underrepresented minority	9
Total faculty	91

SURVEY SAYS...

Diverse opinions accepted in classrooms, Great research resources, Great library staff

STUDENTS

Enrollment of law school	627
% male/female	51/49
% from out-of-state	65
% part-time	0
% underrepresented minority	20
% international	2
# of countries represented	10
Average age of entering class	24

ACADEMICS

Academic Experience Rating	**94**
Profs interesting rating	88
Profs accessible rating	85
Hours of study per day	4.21

Academic Specialties

Civil Procedure, Commercial, Constitutional, Corporation Securities, Criminal, Environmental, Human Rights, International, Labor, Legal History, Legal Philosophy, Property, Taxation, Intellectual Property

Advanced Degrees Offered

JD, 3 years; LLM in the American Legal System, 1 year

Combined Degrees Offered

JD/Master of Public Policy, 4 years; JD/Master of Business Administration, 4 years; JD/Master of Arts in American Studies, 4 years

Academics

William & Mary is an "excellent" public law school with a long and celebrated history. Since Thomas Jefferson helped found the school in 1779, many great attorneys have passed through its hallways. Today, William & Mary professors continue to be "brilliant experts in their field who, while focused on their research, also really care about students and teaching." "Distinguished and knowledgeable" but rarely intimidating, faculty and staff "facilitate an extremely comfortable, relaxed, non-competitive atmosphere that helps every student excel." Rather than lecture or pontificate, "professors are interested in student opinions and foster debate within the classroom." On the whole, coursework is challenging, and "the curve is naturally difficult because of the quality of the students." Luckily, there are plenty of ways to get extra help. For example, "the TA program the school has in place for all first-year courses is much appreciated by 1Ls," as it offers students the chance to review course material with upperclassmen several times per semester. Equally important, the majority of instructors "are very accessible and are always willing to meet with students outside of class, whether it is to explain a certain concept discussed in class or to give advice on how to break into a certain field of the legal market." Some even enjoy lunching with first-year students.

The JD curriculum begins with core coursework in legal areas like torts, contracts, and criminal law. In the second and third year, students can tailor their education by choosing from more than 100 elective courses. In addition to the regular 1L core, the school has a "Legal Practice" curriculum, which focuses heavily on writing. While Legal Skills was highly "disorganized" at the outset, the administration is currentlyWhile the program was formerly known as "Legal Skills" and was described as highly "disorganized"; it has been overhauled and many students believe "it will be as outstanding as the rest of the classes in the coming years." "As a state-run school with low tuition costs, there are certainly glitches" in the day-to-day running of the school; nevertheless, students believe that William & Mary's deans and administrators have their best interests at heart. When interacting with law students, the "administration is very forthcoming and responds to student issues swiftly."

Thomas Jefferson's original vision was to educate "citizen lawyers," who would contribute to their community and adhere to a high code of ethics. To this day, "the Honor Code is really important" at William & Mary, placing trust in the student body to act responsibly. For example, students take exams without proctors—and even on their own time. What's more, "the sense of civic duty held by the students" creates a sense of shared purpose across the William & Mary community. A student shares, "Every time I have had a question, needed assistance, or wanted to network, I have been met with enthusiasm by administration, professors, older students, library staff, alumni, and even peers."

In terms of job placement, William & Mary maintains a strong reputation in Virginia and the greater Washington, D.C. area, and the school's Career Services department generally "focuses on those markets, as that is where the majority of students would like to end up." However, graduates willing to put in a little extra legwork are able to find placements beyond the capital region. A current student agrees, "Many of my 3L classmates have already secured positions for the fall outside of the Virginia/D.C. area—New York City, Texas, Florida, Delaware. Our students successfully compete for positions in these larger markets."

Faye Shealy, Associate Dean
William & Mary Law School, Office of Admission, P.O. Box 8795, Williamsburg, VA 23187-8795
Tel: 757-221-3785 Fax: 757-221-3261
E-Mail: lawadm@wm.edu • Website: law.wm.edu

Life

There is a "strong sense of community" at William & Mary. Both inside and outside the classroom, "the atmosphere is one of teamwork and collaboration—not grueling competition." In fact, there's such great trust among the student body that no one worries about their classmates cheating or stealing. A student recounts, "I freely leave my laptop, phone, or iPad in the library, even for hours. Nobody would ever bother your stuff, and in fact, many students leave their stuff overnight." On the flip side, the cozy environment and "small class size" means students are deeply involved in each other's lives. A current student jokes, "We call [it] George Wythe High School for a reason. The students tend to love gossip."

Some of the facilities are in need of a facelift (think "poor food selection" and "painted cinder-block walls"), so "the law school is planning a big renovation" over the next few years. Fortunately, one important resource has already gotten the once-over: "The law library is beautiful and was renovated only a few years ago." Located in Williamsburg, Virginia, the College of William & Mary campus is "quiet, peaceful, and beautiful." Though it does not offer a lot of cultural or nightlife options, most say the school is a wonderful place to live, work, and study. A student beams, "Overall, this tiny city, this small school, and these classmates make for an absolutely wonderful experience. I can't express how much I love it here."

Getting In

William & Mary accepts applications for the fall semester on a rolling basis between September 1 and March 1. Decisions are communicated no later than April 1. Admission is competitive with the acceptance rate hovering around 32 percent. In recent years, as many as 6,000 students applied for 210 spots in the incoming class. For the class of 2015, students had a median GPA of 3.74 and a median LSAT score of 164. Close to 50 percent had professional work experience before entering the program.

EMPLOYMENT INFORMATION			
Career Rating	93	# not seeking employment	0
Total 2012 JD Grads	204	% grads employed by school	0
% for whom you have useable		State for bar exam	VA, PA, NJ, NY, MD
information	100	Pass rate for first-time bar	93
% grads employed nine months out	95	**Grads Employed by Field (%)**	
Median starting salary	$60,000	Academic (2)	
% job accepting grads providing		Business/Industry (9)	
useable salary information	64	Government (22)	
# employed full-time	190	Judicial Clerkship (18)	
# employed part-time	3	Military (2)	
# employed bar required	154	Private Practice (30)	
# employed JD preferred	28	Public Interest (12)	
# employed professional/other	11		
# employed non-professional	0		
# pursuing advanced degree	3		
# unemployed and seeking employment	8		

Clinical program required	No
Legal writing	
course requirement	Yes
Legal methods	
course requirement	Yes
Legal research	
course requirement	Yes
Moot court requirement	No
Public interest	
law requirement	No

ADMISSIONS

Selectivity Rating	**93**
# applications received	5,573
% applicants accepted	32
% acceptees attending	11
Average LSAT	163
Median LSAT	164
LSAT Range	
(25th to 75th percentile)	161–166
Average undergrad GPA	3.64
Median undergrad GPA	3.74
Application fee	$50
Regular application deadline	3/1
Regular notification	3/30
Transfer students accepted	Yes
Evening division offered	No
Part-time accepted	No
CAS accepted	Yes

FINANCIAL FACTS

Annual tuition (in-state	
out-of-state)	$22,843/$32,286
Books and supplies	$1,450
Fees	$5,514
Room & Board	
(on/off campus)	$4,957/$5,514
Financial aid application	
deadline	2/15
% first-year students receiving	
some sort of aid	98
% all students receiving	
some sort of aid	93
% of aid that is merit based	68
% receiving scholarships	75
Average grant	$11,345
Average loan	$37,043
Average total aid package	$39,203
Average debt	$94,577

COLUMBIA UNIVERSITY
SCHOOL OF LAW

INSTITUTIONAL INFORMATION

Public/private	Private
% faculty part-time	43
% faculty female	32
% faculty underrepresented minority	15
Total faculty	219

SURVEY SAYS...

Diverse opinions accepted in classrooms, Great research resources, Abundant externship/internship/clerkship opportunities, Students love New York, NY

STUDENTS

Enrollment of law school	1,290
% male/female	54/46
% underrepresented minority	32
% international	11
# of countries represented	45
Average age of entering class	24

ACADEMICS

Academic Experience Rating	95
Profs interesting rating	86
Profs accessible rating	75
Hours of study per day	3.16

Academic Specialties
Civil Procedure, Commercial, Constitutional, Corporation Securities, Criminal, Environmental, Government Services, Human Rights, International, Labor, Legal History, Legal Philosophy, Property, Taxation, Intellectual Property

Advanced Degrees Offered
LLM, 1 year; JSD, 2 semesters in residence and a dissertation.

Combined Degrees Offered
JD/Ph.D.; JD/MA; JD/MBA; JD/MFA (Arts Administration); JD/MS Urban Planning, JD/MS Social Work; JD/MS Journalism; JD/MIA in International Affairs; JD/MPA in Public Administration with Columbia; JD/MPA in Public Affairs with Woodrow Wilson School at Princeton; JD/MPH in Public Health

Academics

Columbia Law School is "a very exciting and dynamic place." The curriculum is very heavy on legal theory "with a dash of practical, just for show," and the "breadth of course offerings" is staggering. There are countless centers and programs specializing in everything from law, media, and the arts to European legal studies to tax policy to gender and sexuality law. "Getting on a journal is remarkably noncompetitive." "Being in New York affords the opportunity to participate in almost any internship you could imagine." Programs in international law and intellectual property law are reportedly excellent. Columbia is also "a corporate lawyer factory" and the "best place in the country for budding transactional lawyers." Public interest law is yet another strong suit here. Students who are involved are "a bit clique-ish" but, if you are in the clique, you'll have access to a wealth of opportunities as well as a tremendously generous loan repayment assistance program.

The "unbelievable," "unmatched" faculty at Columbia is "amazing" "across the board." "Columbia does a good job mixing the young, relatable rising superstars with older, more practiced professors." Virtually all of them "make class interesting," and "they're the number-one reason to come to CLS (besides the prestige, of course)." Professors also "make a huge effort to be approachable" and "are happy to give career-related advice or answer questions." The administration isn't as beloved. Happier students note that there are some "really caring people" on staff. However, the general sentiment seems to be that management is somewhat "disdainful."

When the time comes to find a real job, "employment prospects are unbeatable and the alumni network is extraordinarily strong." Career Services is "very helpful in offering support in a variety of capacities." Columbia boasts a "high placement rate in big law firms" and "the opportunities for working in prestigious government and sought-after public interest positions are unparalleled." "It's Columbia," candidly explains a 2L. "The name buys you a lot." About the only complaint we hear is the contention that "the employment focus is a little too New York–centric."

The facilities here are far from great. "Everything is very modern" and "the building is serviceable and clean, but it is ugly." Classrooms "aren't terribly comfortable," and "They're not as pretty as what you'll find at other Ivy League law schools." "The library is one of the best in the country" as far as the resources on offer are concerned, but its aesthetic "is absolutely hideous," says an appalled 2L.

Life

The population of future lawyers at Columbia is "extremely diverse," generally young, and "quite national." Students describe this place as "a nerd paradise" full of "geniuses" who are "brilliant and accomplished but surprisingly cool." "There are spoiled brats, and awkward types, and public interest people, and friendly people, and inflated egos, and social people," reports a 3L. A few students say there is a "divide between students of different economic and academic" backgrounds. However, many others insist that personal circumstances don't matter at all. "There isn't any sort of conspicuous divide between the student body on socioeconomic or geographic factors until you realize that most of the Ivy kids are terrible at beer pong," quips a 1L.

NKONYE IWEREBON, DEAN OF ADMISSIONS
435 WEST 116TH STREET, BOX A-3, NEW YORK, NY 10027
TEL: 212-854-2670 FAX: 212-854-1109
E-MAIL: ADMISSIONS@LAW.COLUMBIA.EDU • WEBSITE: WWW.LAW.COLUMBIA.EDU

Academically, "There is an atmosphere of [intensity] here." Students are "constantly assessing how they stack up, which feeds into the collective neurosis." Some students assert that the struggle for top grades is pretty brutal. "People in general are not happy to share notes," claims a 2L. "They are, in fact, very secretive about their notes." "Our reputation for gunning, competitive jerks is unfortunately true for about 5 percent of the class," laments a 1L. Other students tell us, "People are extremely generous about sharing their outlines and studying together." "If you miss a class," they say, "your neighbors will e-mail you their notes without you even asking."

Columbia's location in a "safe, relatively quiet" neighborhood on Manhattan's Upper West Side provides few distractions when you are trying to study. When students put down their casebooks, though, they can take advantage of a "vibrant student community." "You'll be happy socially here unless you are a complete tool," promises a 2L. "Everyone is fairly involved in all sorts of organizations." "There are multiple lunch events every day, and there's some sort of lecture or panel or firm event with dinner almost every evening." There are "plenty of students who want to party like it's college," too, and "no shortage of happy hours." Living in the Big Apple is also a massive plus. "It's hard to explain the type of magnetic force this place can be unless you've lived here and worked here," reflects a 1L. "New York City means students can do anything they please (with the free hours they have)."

Getting In

Getting into any Ivy League law school is exceedingly difficult and Columbia is certainly no exception. Entering students at the 25th percentile have LSAT scores of about 170 and undergraduate grade point averages of almost 3.7. At the 75th percentile, LSAT scores are a whopping 175 or so and GPAs are around 3.8.

Clinical program required	No
Legal writing course requirement	Yes
Legal methods course requirement	Yes
Legal research course requirement	Yes
Moot court requirement	Yes
Public interest law requirement	Yes

ADMISSIONS

Selectivity Rating	98
# applications received	6,592
% applicants accepted	18
% acceptees attending	30
Average LSAT	171
Median LSAT	172
LSAT Range (25th to 75th percentile)	170–174
Average undergrad GPA	3.70
Median undergrad GPA	3.71
Application fee	$85
Regular application deadline	2/15
Early application deadline	11/15
Early application notification	1/1
Transfer students accepted	Yes
Evening division offered	No
Part-time accepted	No
CAS accepted	Yes

FINANCIAL FACTS

Annual tuition (in-state out-of-state)	$51,080
Books and supplies	$1,518
Fees	$1,822
Room & Board (on/off campus)	$20,550
Financial aid application deadline	3/1
% first-year students receiving some sort of aid	79
% all students receiving some sort of aid	77
% of aid that is merit based	47
% receiving scholarships	46
Average grant	$15,405
Average loan	$51,200
Average total aid package	$38,405
Average debt	$129,400

EMPLOYMENT INFORMATION

Career Rating	99
Total 2012 JD Grads	456
% for whom you have useable information	99
% grads employed nine months out	99
Median starting salary	$160,000
% job accepting grads providing useable salary information	97
# employed full-time	443
# employed part-time	2
# employed bar required	437
# employed JD preferred	6
# employed professional/other	2
# employed non-professional	0
# pursuing advanced degree	5
# unemployed and seeking employment	1
# not seeking employment	2
State for bar exam	NY, CA, NJ, PA, MD
Pass rate for first-time bar	97.7

Prominent Alumni
Ruth Bader Ginsburg, Justice, U.S. Supreme Court; George Pataki, Governor, New York State; Franklin D. Roosevelt, former President of U.S.

Grads Employed by Field (%)
Academic (1)
Business/Industry (5)
Government (9)
Judicial Clerkship (9)
Private Practice (68)
Public Interest (6)

CORNELL UNIVERSITY
LAW SCHOOL

INSTITUTIONAL INFORMATION

Public/private	Private
Student-faculty ratio	10:1
Total faculty	47

SURVEY SAYS...
Abundant externship/internship/clerkship opportunities, Beautiful campus

STUDENTS

Enrollment of law school	576
% part-time	0
Average age of entering class	23

ACADEMICS

Academic Experience Rating	93
Profs interesting rating	93
Profs accessible rating	80
Hours of study per day	3.98

Academic Specialties
International

Advanced Degrees Offered
JD, 3 years; LLM, 1 year; JD/LLM in International and Comparative Law, 3 years; JD/Maitrise en Driot French Law degree, 4 years; JSD, 2 years; JD/MLLP Master of German and European Law and Legal Practice, 4 years

Combined Degrees Offered
JD/MBA (3 and 4 years), JD/MPA, JD/MA, JD/Ph.D., JD/MRP, JD/MILR

Academics

Cornell University is a small school with a big name. Thanks to this favorable combinati- Cornell University's Law School works hard to keep up its reputation for producing quality lawyers. The law school places a big emphasis on cultivating a diverse student body, from work background and race to hometown. This "great and unique" law school stands out due to its smaller size since there are less than 200 students in each year's class, which means sections consist of about 30-35 students, and "you get a real sense of community being here." Every Wednesday, the school has a student/faculty coffee hour called "The Weekly Perk," where all of the students and professors "can mingle and have some coffee and cookies." The Deans also host a monthly breakfast for the leaders of the student organizations "so they can hear concerns and suggestions from the students themselves." In case it is not clear from all of the food-based collaboration, the "eager to help" administration "works hard to provide as many opportunities as they can, including public interest grants for summer work." Students who want to be involved in the Cornell community have plenty of opportunities, and "faculty take a genuine interest in student's ideas and research goals."

Much of the high tuition at Cornell goes to maintaining the excellence in the faculty. The "rock star" professors here are "amazing" and "truly want every student to succeed and excel." Some say "the ability to take classes with some of the leading professionals and thinkers in a particular area is one of the best aspects of a Cornell Law education." "They are like legal celebrities." Others say that it is "the ease with which graduates can land a big law job in NYC." "Our career services department made the process both painless and simple, and most students had their summer employment locked down by the beginning of Fall 2011," according to one student. The rest of Cornell Law School also "runs like a well-oiled machine." "I have had the opportunity to see my legal writing published in national magazines, and I have been given chances to do things I never thought I could achieve, through the guidance of the staff and faculty at Cornell," says one student.

Students are required to take thirteen credits per semester, leaving many wishing for "more mandatory pass/fail one credit classes," since many students are left "scrambling for that extra credit" in the second semester. Still, the focus on the practical experience is what firms are looking for in this economy, and "the clinical classes give students a chance to apply what they've learned to real world problems." "It's refreshing to have theory classes taught by individuals who also have real-world experience in the field," says one student. "For example, my Public International Law professor helped to draft the new constitution for Kenya and [has a working relationship] with Kofi Annan." One huge benefit of the school's size includes the opportunities to schedule a directed reading or supervised writing. With a directed reading, if a student is interested in taking a course in something that is not currently offered, that student can contact the professor and set up a directed reading or supervised writing to receive credit and study a particular topic.

Though students frequently admit, "Ithaca is a lovely place," they are also keenly aware that "there aren't the same type of part-time externship opportunities that one would find in New York City, Washington, D.C., or even the smaller cities." Luckily, networking opportunities and reputation can help compensate, and "just having 'Cornell' on your resume can open certain doors."

HOPE JAMISON, ASSOCIATE DIRECTOR OF ADMISSIONS
226 MYRON TAYLOR HALL, ITHACA, NY 14853-4901
TEL: 607-255-5141 FAX: 607-255-7193
E-MAIL: JDADMISSIONS@CORNELL.EDU • WEBSITE: WWW.LAWSCHOOL.CORNELL.EDU

Life

"Because we study in a small town, we all know each other well and work together as much as possible," says one student of Ithaca. Of course there are still some gunners and "a few overly type-A individuals," but for the most part Cornell students make up a "tightly knit community that seems to care more about getting through this together rather than a bunch of individuals doing anything to make sure they are the best in the class." The town may not be the best place to live for three years "if you're used to a much more cosmopolitan area," but "many students do visit NYC/Boston on weekends," and the nightlife can be "quite active." Additionally, each semester there are usually two formal events that many students attend, and if you "really put yourself out there by initiating study groups (which double as dinner and drinking groups) or get involved in volunteer activities/sports/religion," then you can have a decent social life.

Though the facilities "are not the most modern," they are "more than adequate" and "it makes up for it in charm." The library is particularly "state-of-the-art." The campus is "beautiful," and students often remark, "We attend school in a castle." This castle is "a very insular community," and a lot of law students don't venture far off of the hill. The student body is understandably "extremely close." "I know the names of the majority of my fellow students in my class year," says one; however, the small population can "create a bubble of stress that can sometimes be hard to overcome."

Getting In

Admission to Cornell is highly competitive. The Admissions Committee weighs all aspects of an applicant's background, including extracurricular and community activities, graduate work, LSAT scores, letters of recommendation, and undergraduate transcripts. Applicants are also encouraged to submit a separate document that details how their ethnic, cultural, or linguistic background will contribute to the diversity of the school community. The median LSAT score for the 2012 entering class was 167 and the median undergraduate GPA was 3.68.

Clinical program required	No
Legal writing course requirement	Yes
Legal methods course requirement	Yes
Legal research course requirement	Yes
Moot court requirement	No
Public interest law requirement	No

ADMISSIONS

Selectivity Rating	92
# applications received	4,091
% applicants accepted	
Median LSAT	167
LSAT Range (25th to 75th percentile)	166–168
Median undergrad GPA	3.68
Application fee	$80
Regular application deadline	2/1
Early application deadline	11/1
Transfer students accepted	Yes
Evening division offered	No
Part-time accepted	No
CAS accepted	Yes

FINANCIAL FACTS

Annual tuition	$57,270
Books and supplies	$1,100
Room & Board	$11,250
Financial aid application deadline	3/15
% first-year students receiving some sort of aid	50

EMPLOYMENT INFORMATION

Career Rating	60*	# not seeking employment	0
Total 2012 JD Grads	190	% grads employed by school	7
% grads employed nine months out	93	State for bar exam	NY
# employed full-time	177	Pass rate for first-time bar	92
# employed part-time	0	**Grads Employed by Field (%)**	
# employed bar required	175	Academic (0)	
# employed JD preferred	0	Business/Industry (2)	
# employed professional/other	2	Government (11)	
# employed non-professional	0	Judicial Clerkship (10)	
# pursuing advanced degree	0	Private Practice (67)	
# unemployed and seeking employment	13	Public Interest (7)	

CREIGHTON UNIVERSITY
SCHOOL OF LAW

INSTITUTIONAL INFORMATION

Public/private	Private
Affiliation	Roman Catholic
Student-faculty ratio	15:1
% faculty part-time	49
% faculty female	27
% faculty underrepresented minority	7
Total faculty	70

SURVEY SAYS...

Diverse opinions accepted in classrooms, Great research resources, Great library staff

STUDENTS

Enrollment of law school	397
% male/female	67/33
% from out-of-state	60
% part-time	3
% underrepresented minority	15
% international	2
# of countries represented	4
Average age of entering class	25

ACADEMICS

Academic Experience Rating	78
Profs interesting rating	84
Profs accessible rating	96
Hours of study per day	3.74

Academic Specialties

Commercial, Corporation Securities, Criminal, International

Combined Degrees Offered

JD/MBA; JD/Master of Arts in International Relations; JD/Master of Science in Government and Leadership; JD/Master of Science in Information Technology Management; JD/Master of Science in Negotiation and Dispute Resolution. These combined degrees can each be completed in three years with summer study.

Academics

Founded in 1878, Creighton is a Jesuit-affiliated university that "will uplift you rather than scare you." The Jesuit tradition is embodied in the School of Law's motto: "educating for service and justice." Creighton looks to produce attorneys that are not only skilled and knowledgeable, but who work to service society at large. The school offers four areas of concentration as well as five joint-degree programs. Supreme Court Justice Thomas even co-teaches a class at Creighton on a bi-annual basis. The school has a "dedicated alumni base." "Located in an economically strong region," Creighton University offers students many opportunities in Omaha, "one of the best business cities in the United States." Students rave about the "networking if you plan to stay in Omaha," although "the Career Development Office is not optimized for students wanting to practice outside Nebraska."

One thing that is important at any law school is the library, and Creighton students rave about the "beautiful," "large and well-equipped" library that is replete "with plenty of available study rooms, computer labs, and private workstations." "The resources available in the library are fantastic," and "the research librarians are always there to help with finding anything and teach you how to find it on your own." If there is a primary complaint about Creighton, it is "Cost. Cost. Cost." "It's quite expensive, especially considering the earning potential in the rural areas of the Midwest," a 3L explains. However, another student says that despite being on "the high end for the cost of tuition," "most people who end up in law firms will be making anywhere from 50k to 80k."

The cost of Creighton is offset by the "awesome professors" without whom "Creighton Law wouldn't be worth it." These "dedicated, knowledgeable, passionate educators," are "all well versed in law and have accomplished backgrounds." "I love my professors!" a 3L declares. "They have very diverse viewpoints and methods of teaching, yet most of them seem very invested in our education." The administration is also "always helpful and friendly." "I cannot imagine needing something that the school does not already offer," one student says. The dean of the law school is "accessible to the entire student body and sees herself as the 'mom' of the school." "The education I receive is tailored to me," a 2L says. "The practical experiences available at Creighton are unreal" at Creighton, including "trial teams [that] are competitive nationally" as well as a Negotiations team "taught by the man who wrote the book on Negotiations competitions—quite literally." Students are very pleased with the school's "open door policy" which encourages students to interact with professors one-on-one. Perhaps most importantly, the professors "provide numerous opportunities to learn about and make connections with potential employers in the Omaha area." Although Creighton is not ranked as highly as many other schools, students say they "have never felt that I was at a disadvantage or less prepared for practical law work than students from more 'prestigious' law schools." One student sums his experience up thusly: "I do not know if I could say enough wonderful things about Creighton Law School and how pleased I have been with my experience here."

ANDREA D. BASHARA, ASSISTANT DEAN
2500 CALIFORNIA PLAZA, OMAHA, NE 68178
TEL: 402-280-2586 FAX: 402-280-3161
E-MAIL: LAWADMIT@CREIGHTON.EDU • WEBSITE: CREIGHTON.EDU/LAW

Life

Being situated in Omaha, the largest city in Nebraska, provides Creighton students with plenty of job and social opportunities. "Everyone is friendly and social" and "tend to skew a little older with much more work experience than I thought coming in." "As far as politics, it appears to me that professors and students alike are right down the middle," a 3L says. The school is "lacking, and visibly so" in racial and cultural diversity though. "I can literally count the number of non-white students," one student says, and another thinks "the school needs more female students/applicants." Students do report that the school is making strides on both fronts. It would be remiss of us not to note the "top ranked basketball team" which is a huge "selling point and attracts high attendance from undergrad and law students."

Getting In

Applicants are required to send two letters of recommendation, a personal statement, resume, and an Credential Assembly Service Report. The entering 2012 class had an average GPA of 3.21 and an average LSAT of 153. The school leans heavily on the LSAT and GPA scores when evaluating applications, so if your scores match up well with those you have a strong shot at getting in.

Clinical program required	No
Legal writing course requirement	Yes
Legal methods course requirement	No
Legal research course requirement	Yes
Moot court requirement	Yes
Public interest law requirement	No

ADMISSIONS

Selectivity Rating	68
# applications received	888
% applicants accepted	67
% acceptees attending	21
Average LSAT	153
Median LSAT	152
LSAT Range (25th to 75th percentile)	150–156
Average undergrad GPA	3.21
Median undergrad GPA	3.24
Application fee	$50
Regular application deadline	5/1
Transfer students accepted	Yes
Evening division offered	No
Part-time accepted	Yes
CAS accepted	Yes

FINANCIAL FACTS

Annual tuition	$31,986
Books and supplies	$1,355
Fees	$1,504
Room & Board	$14,400
Financial aid application deadline	7/1
% first-year students receiving some sort of aid	93
% all students receiving some sort of aid	90
% of aid that is merit based	13
% receiving scholarships	38
Average grant	$13,803
Average loan	$44,141
Average total aid package	$46,718
Average debt	$116,287

EMPLOYMENT INFORMATION

Career Rating	83
Total 2012 JD Grads	165
% for whom you have useable information	98
% grads employed nine months out	83
Median starting salary	$56,000
% job accepting grads providing useable salary information	36
# employed full-time	120
# employed part-time	17
# employed bar required	107
# employed JD preferred	18
# employed professional/other	5
# employed non-professional	7
# pursuing advanced degree	7
# unemployed and seeking employment	15
# not seeking employment	2
% grads employed by school	1
State for bar exam	IA, NE, CO, AZ, MO
Pass rate for first-time bar	85

Prominent Alumni
Michael O. Johanns, United States Senator and former Secretary of Agriculture; Laura Duffy, US Attorney for the Southern District of California; Gary Blackford, CEO of Universal Hospital Services.

Grads Employed by Field (%)
Academic (2)
Business/Industry (18)
Government (15)
Judicial Clerkship (4)
Military (1)
Private Practice (38)
Public Interest (5)

DePaul University
College of Law

INSTITUTIONAL INFORMATION

Public/private	Private
Affiliation	Roman Catholic
Student-faculty ratio	14:1
% faculty part-time	62
% faculty female	41
% faculty underrepresented minority	14
Total faculty	114

SURVEY SAYS...

Diverse opinions accepted in class-rooms, Students love Chicago, IL

STUDENTS

Enrollment of law school	884
% male/female	50/50
% part-time	16
% underrepresented minority	21
Average age of entering class	24

ACADEMICS

Academic Experience Rating	76
Profs interesting rating	78
Profs accessible rating	78
Hours of study per day	4.23

Academic Specialties

Commercial, Corporation Securities, Criminal, Human Rights, International, Labor, Taxation, Intellectual Property

Advanced Degrees Offered

LLM in Health Law, 1–3 years; LLM in Taxation, 1–3 years; LLM in Intellectual Property Law, 1–3 years; LLM in International Law, 1– 3 years

Combined Degrees Offered

JD/MBA, 3–4 years; JD/MS in Public Service Management, 4 years; JD/MA in International Studies, 4 years; JD/MA in International & European Business Law, 4 years; JD/MS in Computer Science, 4 years

Academics

Located in the heart of Chicago near the major courthouses and law offices, DePaul University's College of Law "stresses practical instruction across the board" while enabling its students to get "as much practical experience in the legal community as they can handle while still going to class." "My corporate law, evidence, and tax classes were all centered on learning the law and applying it in future practice," says a grateful 2L. The plethora of practical skills courses that are offered, such as Trial Advocacy and Commercial Arbitration, are also "geared entirely toward teaching students how to employ those skills when they leave the law school." "Through the Field Placement program as well as the legal clinics, I have gained some very useful practical lawyering skills while getting school credit," says a 3L.

With only 240 students in the school's full-time day program, the grading curve can be tough, but this also means that there are "very small classes so each student gets individual attention." "My class only has twelve students and it's very easy to visit office hours for help," says a student. Nearly all of the classes here are also available in the evening. Everyone agrees that the faculty at DePaul is "incredible" and "impressive" in terms of teaching effectiveness and professional experience, with "excellent connections not just in Chicago, but even internationally as well." "I really can't applaud the faculty enough," says a 3L. This "highly approachable, interesting, animated, and even really funny" group of instructors "really care about their classes and the students."

Though some people feel the law school administration is "incredibly receptive," many are on the "very frustrated" side of the fence, feeling that there is "more of an overall student focus" rather than an outreach to individuals. Career services "seems like they always need improvement in helping students—non-law-review students—to get a job." Given the breadth of the school's alumni (which includes three former Chicago mayors), DePaul "definitely opens doors to almost any practice area imaginable" within Chicago, which is "one of the largest legal markets in the country." "Try finding any firm in the greater metropolitan area that doesn't have a DePaul Law grad," challenges a student. Still, Catholic-affiliated DePaul remains a service-oriented school, and for many, "the desire to advocate for the country's less fortunate is stronger than the desire to make money."

Students readily admit that DePaul's classroom facilities are "outdated" and "definitely need to revamp," though "some of the high-tech gadgets do the trick." In addition, the law school is in the middle of a substantial renovation of its facilities, scheduled to wrap up in fall 2011. The library here is more than "complete," with full access to Westlaw and LexisNexis.

MICHAEL S. BURNS, ASSOCIATE DEAN & DIRECTOR OF ADMISSION
25 EAST JACKSON BOULEVARD, CHICAGO, IL 60604
TEL: 312-362-6831 FAX: 312-362-5280
E-MAIL: LAWINFO@DEPAUL.EDU • WEBSITE: WWW.LAW.DEPAUL.EDU

Living

DePaul touts its diversity, which most students feel is up to par with the city that surrounds it. "Everyone has their own background that [they bring] to the experience of school to aid in the workplace after graduation," says a student. The school's small size can lead to some "clique-ish" tendencies, but "anyone who wants an active social life can have one." DePaul's location certainly helps to expand social horizons, as the easy access to non-DePaul activities and people means that "the school is not the normal college bubble." Students "are hard-pressed to not find fun stuff to do, given that we're in a huge city." There is also a "very popular" study abroad program that is given at a substantial discount (per credit hour) to encourage students to attend. Outside of the city's offerings, there are "always events for students to put on and get involved in," and the administration also recently upgraded the registered student organization facilities to allow for the creation of more student organizations.

Though "the school is competitive," there is a real sense of community among students and "a great balance between working very hard during the week and having a social life on the weekends. Everyone is "supportive," though people "are not here to baby you, but help you advance your career in an enjoyable environment." The student body tends to be "extremely liberal politically but very conservative morally."

Getting In

Students admitted for the fall entering class of 2009 at the 25th percentile had an LSAT score of 158 and an average GPA of 3.11, while admitted students at the 75th percentile had an LSAT score of 162 and a GPA of 3.57. Like many law schools, DePaul offers rolling admissions, but first-year students may only be admitted for the fall semester.

Clinical program required	No
Legal writing course requirement	Yes
Legal methods course requirement	No
Legal research course requirement	Yes
Moot court requirement	No
Public interest law requirement	No

ADMISSIONS

Selectivity Rating	73
# applications received	3,666
% applicants accepted	56
% acceptees attending	11
Average LSAT	156
Median LSAT	158
LSAT Range (25th to 75th percentile)	153–160
Average undergrad GPA	3.30
Median undergrad GPA	3.41
Application fee	$0
Regular application deadline	3/1
Transfer students accepted	Yes
Evening division offered	Yes
Part-time accepted	Yes
CAS accepted	Yes

FINANCIAL FACTS

Annual tuition	$43,220
Books and supplies	$1,480
Fees	$312
Room & Board	$13,524
% first-year students receiving some sort of aid	93
% all students receiving some sort of aid	90
% of aid that is merit based	19
% receiving scholarships	66
Average grant	$13,382
Average loan	$40,567
Average total aid package	$44,473
Average debt	$130,197

EMPLOYMENT INFORMATION

Career Rating	82
Total 2012 JD Grads	368
% grads employed nine months out	75
Median starting salary	$62,975
% job accepting grads providing useable salary information	61
# employed full-time	166
# employed part-time	22
# employed bar required	171
# employed JD preferred	63
# employed professional/other	32
# employed non-professional	10
# pursuing advanced degree	2
# unemployed and seeking employment	67
# not seeking employment	4
% grads employed by school	1
State for bar exam	IL, CA, NY, IN, WI
Pass rate for first-time bar	88

Prominent Alumni
Richard M. Daley, Former Mayor, City of Chicago; Mary Dempsey, Commissioner for Chicago Public Library; Frank Clark, President, ComEd.

Grads Employed by Field (%)
Academic (2)
Business/Industry (16)
Government (7)
Judicial Clerkship (2)
Military (1)
Private Practice (42)
Public Interest (4)

DRAKE UNIVERSITY
LAW SCHOOL

INSTITUTIONAL INFORMATION

Public/private	Private
Affiliation	No Affiliation
Student-faculty ratio	13:1
% faculty part-time	30
% faculty female	32
% faculty underrepresented minority	14
Total faculty	50

SURVEY SAYS...

Great research resources, Great library staff, Abundant externship/internship/clerkship opportunities

STUDENTS

Enrollment of law school	409
% male/female	56/44
% from out-of-state	39
% part-time	2
% underrepresented minority	11
# of countries represented	3
Average age of entering class	25

ACADEMICS

Academic Experience Rating	76
Profs interesting rating	80
Profs accessible rating	82
Hours of study per day	3.38

Academic Specialties

Civil Procedure, Commercial, Constitutional, Corporation Securities, Criminal, Environmental, Government Services, Human Rights, International, Labor, Property, Taxation, Intellectual Property

Advanced Degrees Offered

JD, 3 years; LLM, 1 year

Combined Degrees Offered

JD/MBA(6 semesters, 2 summers); JD/MPA(6 semesters, 2 summers); JD/PharmD; JD/MA Political Science(6 semesters, 1 summer); JD/MS Ag. Econ. (6 semesters, 1 summer); JD/MSW; JD/MPH; JD/MHA

Academics

A core of "very approachable, knowledgeable" professors who boast "a lot of real world experience" form the backbone of the no-nonsense, "meat and potato" academics at Drake. "Don't look for cutting edge here," suggests one student. And that's not a bad thing. As another student notes, "given the opportunity to go through the law school admissions process again, knowing what I know now, I would not change anything." The "practical emphasis placed on legal research and writing skills" during your first year sets the groundwork for all that follows, not to mention sets students up for being able to successfully attain a clerkship with area firms. "My academic experience has been great," a 1L boasted. "My 1L professors prepared me for a summer clerkship with one of the larger and most respected firms in Des Moines."

Students indicate the administration can be "hit or miss"—some say they are "fantastic," others that they "are a bit cold and hard to work with"—but even those students with a negative view of the administration have praise for the teaching staff. "They have all had practical careers before teaching, giving each class an added dimension. We're not only learning the theory, but we are learning the law in practice from the numerous examples from our professors." These educators are "open to answering questions" and tend to be "understanding and supportive," a group who are "compassionate and understand that students have lives outside of school and emergencies that may distract us from class."

The facilities receive as much praise as the professors. "The research facilities and resources are great. The library is beautiful and a calm place to study with plenty of tables for 1Ls and carrels for upperclassmen." Even though the facilities are not entirely up to date—some classrooms are on the older side—that will soon change. "The law school is just starting a renovation, so the facilities will be upgraded by the start of next fall." Class scheduling can be an issue for some, and at times it "suffers from a lack of course selection" but "the administration does its best to work with students to make sure they are able to take the classes they want and need."

Life

Located in Des Moines and populated by a relatively diverse student body, those who attend Drake will find no shortage of things to keep them busy. "Drake Law's geographic location and community ties are its greatest strengths," giving students excellent access to top law firms and affording them an opportunity to engage in practical, hands-on learning. "It's almost like a big-small town in that you have the social life, art, and entertainment of a big city, but with the feeling of living in a small town." Opportunities to get involved with your fellow students and/or student organizations abound, as well as opportunities to apply what you are learning to the real world. As one student notes, "I've been on the executive board of one student organization, served on the SBA and Honor Board, been a junior staffer on the Law Review, and worked as both a Legal Research and Writing Teaching Assistant and a Research Assistant."

When it comes to the school itself, "the physical infrastructure of the school needs urgent attention," but future attendees need not worry, as renovations are underway. A few "little things" can be irksome, such as the fact that the school "doesn't have a decent gym," but overall students find life here to be a pleasant but challenging mix of academics and career advancement. "I've met some really awesome people and I feel like I'm getting a very practical legal education that translates well into a firm or public service setting."

Getting In

At the 25th percentile, students recently admitted to Drake Law have LSAT scores of 153 and GPAs in the 3.1 range, while admitted students at the 75th percentile have LSAT scores of 158 and GPAs of roughly 3.6.

Clinical program required	No
Legal writing course requirement	Yes
Legal methods course requirement	Yes
Legal research course requirement	Yes
Moot court requirement	Yes
Public interest law requirement	No

ADMISSIONS

Selectivity Rating	70
# applications received	853
% applicants accepted	66
% acceptees attending	22
Average LSAT	156
Median LSAT	155
LSAT Range (25th to 75th percentile)	152–159
Average undergrad GPA	3.27
Median undergrad GPA	3.3
Application fee	$50
Regular application deadline	
Early application deadline	4/1
Transfer students accepted	Yes
Evening division offered	No
Part-time accepted	Yes
CAS accepted	Yes

FINANCIAL FACTS

Annual tuition	$35,170
Books and supplies	$1,500
Fees	$112
Room & Board	$16,745
Financial aid application deadline	3/1
% first-year students receiving some sort of aid	89
% all students receiving some sort of aid	92
% of aid that is merit based	20
% receiving scholarships	58
Average grant	$18,093
Average loan	$37,978
Average total aid package	$44,814
Average debt	$106,368

EMPLOYMENT INFORMATION

Career Rating	88	
Total 2012 JD Grads	139	
% for whom you have useable information	100	
% grads employed nine months out	90	
Median starting salary	$52,750	
# employed full-time	116	
# employed part-time	9	
# employed bar required	86	
# employed JD preferred	31	
# employed professional/other	7	
# employed non-professional	1	
# pursuing advanced degree	1	
# unemployed and seeking employment	8	
# not seeking employment	5	
% grads employed by school	1	
State for bar exam	IA	
Pass rate for first-time bar	91	

Prominent Alumni
Dwight D. Opperman, CEO, West Publishing Company; Mark Cady, Current Chief Justice of Iowa Supreme Court; Robert Ray, Former Governor.

Grads Employed by Field (%)
Academic (1)
Business/Industry (24)
Government (12)
Judicial Clerkship (7)
Private Practice (40)
Public Interest (6)

DREXEL UNIVERSITY
EARLE MACK SCHOOL OF LAW

Academics

Drexel's brand-new law school was established in 2006, and "As a new school, everything is modern and state of the art." Students name the school's newness as one of its strengths: the professors are passionate and dedicated to making a name for the school, all the facilities are up to date, and the school offers competitive financial aid packages to attract legal talent. "This school may not have the long-standing reputation of many other schools throughout the country, but the fact that it is so new makes the faculty and staff strive to help the students achieve success." The "very accessible" faculty, particularly, impress Drexel's students: Drexel "has the most invested administration and faculty of any of the law schools I considered" because they "went out and recruited some of the best of the best to be members of the faculty." Budding lawyers revere the ethical grounding of the school, too: "The Dean of Students is one of the most amazing people I've ever met and his ethos of honesty, integrity and passion for the law can be found throughout the Administration and the Faculty."

Drexel's graduates feel well-prepared for the job market due to the program's "emphasis on gaining practical experience," and creating ""work-ready" graduates." "Drexel does an excellent job making networking easy." "Gone are the days where employment waits for every single one of those who complete a JD program. With this truth in mind, Drexel Law equips its students to be practicing attorneys before even taking a bar exam." Indeed, "the law school strongly encourages students to co-op for a semester," and requires a measure of pro-bono legal work: "Drexel offers so many experiential learning opportunities through co-op, clinics, fellowships, the pro-bono requirement, and internships/externships." It seems the university has taken seriously its obligation to measure up to older highly-ranked schools, which students notice and appreciate: "Drexel's commitment to building a top-notch law school shows not only in its staffing and funding levels, but in the strong extra-curricular support and skills training they make available to us."

Students also feel that because Drexel's law school isn't old, it hasn't struggled to break free of the values of the old guard in the way that other programs may: "I think the diversity and academic learning environment are this school's strong suit. I briefly attended a highly ranked school and I quickly realized that tolerance and diversity were not as prevalent as I had expected."

ISABEL "ISSA" DISCIULLO, ASSISTANT DEAN FOR ADMISSIONS
3320 MARKET STREET, ROOM 102, PHILADELPHIA, PA 19104
TEL: 215-895-1529 FAX: 215-571-4769
E-MAIL: LAWADMISSIONS@DREXEL.EDU • WEBSITE: WWW.EARLEMACKLAW.DREXEL.EDU

Life

Drexel escapes the shark-tank reputation of many of its competitors in social atmosphere: "The student body is extremely friendly despite the competitive atmosphere that law school creates through its use of the curve." One student credits the university for having "made the process of being in law school relaxed." As the school's roots have grown, so has the social network of the law school: "People hang out all the time. There is a bar right across the school where you can find law students every evening." While some students "do commute from New Jersey or from the suburbs," "many people live a trolley, bus, or train ride away" and find plenty to do socially around the Philadelphia campus, especially in nearby Center City. A common complaint congeals around the fact that the law school's new facilities are still integrating with the rest of the campus: "The library is very nice, however we have to share it with Drexel's undergraduates after 6:00 P.M. on weeknights and all weekend long. The undergrads do not have the same respect for our space that we do." Many students echo that it "would be nice if we did not have to share the library with the undergraduate students at certain hours." Overall, though, Drexel's students credit its "small community" for creating "a great student life here."

Getting In

For the 140 students in Drexel's class of 2015, the median LSAT range was 154–159 and the median GPA range was 3.02–3.60, placing the school among the best, but not quite the best of the best, in American law school rankings. However, Drexel poises itself to compete with financial aid offers: all applicants are automatically reviewed for financial aid candidacy, and 91 percent of the class of 2015 received academic merit scholarships between $2,500 and $32,000 a year.

Clinical program required	No
Legal writing course requirement	Yes
Legal methods course requirement	Yes
Legal research course requirement	Yes
Moot court requirement	No
Public interest law requirement	Yes

ADMISSIONS

Selectivity Rating	83
# applications received	2,178
% applicants accepted	39
% acceptees attending	17
Average LSAT	157
Median LSAT	157
LSAT Range (25th to 75th percentile)	154–159
Average undergrad GPA	3.29
Median undergrad GPA	3.28
Application fee	$0
Regular application deadline	
Transfer students accepted	Yes
Evening division offered	No
Part-time accepted	No
CAS accepted	Yes

FINANCIAL FACTS

Annual tuition	$37,254
Books and supplies	$9,200
Fees	$820
Room & Board	$13,000
Financial aid application deadline	3/1
% first-year students receiving some sort of aid	97
% all students receiving some sort of aid	96
% of aid that is merit based	28
% receiving scholarships	84
Average grant	$18,804
Average loan	$32,655
Average total aid package	$44,445
Average debt	$98,820

EMPLOYMENT INFORMATION

		Grads Employed by Field (%)	
Career Rating	80		
Total 2012 JD Grads	155	Academic (2)	
% grads employed nine months out	77	Business/Industry (18)	
# employed full-time	98	Government (12)	
# employed part-time	22	Judicial Clerkship (10)	
# employed bar required	90	Private Practice (30)	
# employed JD preferred	15	Public Interest (6)	
# employed professional/other	11		
# employed non-professional	4		
# pursuing advanced degree	2		
# unemployed and seeking employment	22		
# not seeking employment	5		
% grads employed by school	2		
State for bar exam	PA, NJ, NY, CA, DE		
Pass rate for first-time bar	80		

DUKE UNIVERSITY
SCHOOL OF LAW

Academics

Though Duke University is nationally recognized for its stellar academic programs, students say it is the intimate atmosphere and emphasis on teaching that distinguishes their law school from other top-ranked institutions. Duke's "ridiculously engaging" professors are "dedicated to both excellent scholarship and excellent teaching." As at any prestigious school, the faculty's "academic reputation is made from publishing"; however, "the professors here want to be professors, [they are] not [here to] just write." That dedication is amply demonstrated in the faculty's incredible accessibility to their students. After class is out, "Professors all maintain an open door policy, and they actually mean it. You can just walk in and talk to them about class, other subjects you're interested in, careers, or where to find the best microbrew in Durham." A current student fondly remembers, "My 1L Con Law professor came to our softball game and had us over to his house for a picnic, and a variety of upper-level professors enjoy bowling with us every week." Enrolling just over 200 first-year students annually, Duke's modest size practically ensures a personal relationship with the faculty: "With even the largest 1L classes topping out around 75, it's easy for professors to know you by name, and it's never hard to spend one-on-one time with professors if you want to."

Despite it's all-around excellence, Duke is surprisingly down-to-earth. A current student details, "What really won me over about Duke was the school philosophy, as voiced by Dean Levi: 'We take scholarship, service, professionalism, and teaching seriously; but we try not to take ourselves too seriously.'" To that end, the Duke culture "promotes a balanced life, instead of letting schoolwork consume you." For example, the school's "responsive administration" encourages students to pursue their personal passions, not just their required coursework. A 2L recounts, "Regarding the administration, they are very open to new ideas and flexible in their approach to the curriculum. One of my friends started a program to aid in Haiti's reconstruction and the school has provided both financial and academic resources." On that note, while "Duke expects initiative from students," students have all of the "tools and opportunities" to reach their goals. Across departments, administrators and staff "are warm, friendly, and always available to help." When it comes to schedule planning, "The academic advising department is fantastic and always available."

Proud of their unique community, "People really rally around Duke, including alumni, and the enthusiasm for the school is infectious." In this context, it is easy for students to make "both personal and professional connections with alumni around the country." When it comes to jobs and internships, "Duke isn't the biggest law school, so it's not going to have the sheer number of alums that Harvard, Columbia, Georgetown, and others have. However, it is the kind of place that inspires loyalty." With that loyalty as an asset, Duke boasts "strong placement in numerous legal markets all over the country," without a strong focus in any one region. Students point out the school's "terrific connections with federal judges" and a "fantastic network in New York," yet feel that students are still placed in other markets across the United States. A current student affirms that, "Regardless of what you want to do (big law, government, non-profit, etc.) or where you want to work, you will find Duke grads who are willing to help you break into that particular field."

As one would expect from a high-ranking school, facilities are excellent at Duke. Within the School of Law, "All the classroom are stuffed to the gills with technology," and "The common area is wide open, with huge windows and comfy chairs."

WILLIAM J. HOYE, ASSOCIATE DEAN FOR ADMISSIONS AND STUDENT AFFAIRS
P.O. BOX 90393, DURHAM, NC 27708-0393
TEL: 919-613-7020 FAX: 919-613-7257
E-MAIL: ADMISSIONS@LAW.DUKE.EDU • WEBSITE: ADMISSIONS.LAW.DUKE.EDU

Throughout the classrooms, "the outlet:student ratio must be around 2:1." Of particular importance to busy law students, "Goodson Library is amazing, homey, and comfortable, and has all the resources you might ever need." Upon using the facilities, "The research librarians and online guides are a great help with writing courses, general research, and journal work."

Life

For a top-tier law school, Duke's atmosphere is decidedly low-key and "collegial." Most students enjoy the social life, noting that Duke is "a small enough school that you can be friends with everyone." Within the law school, "Everyone works hard, but the school is not a scary or stressful place because we also have many opportunities for extracurriculars and fun activities." Students say that, "Between a softball league, well-attended bar reviews, and other DBA-planned parties, there's a lot to do for fun outside of school." According to students, "If you don't have a robust social life at Duke, it's because you've chosen not to." On top of that, having "access to $10 Duke basketball tickets" is a major perk for Blue Devil fans; across the campus, "The camaraderie around March cannot be beat."

Off campus, "Durham is a fun city in the middle of a revitalization," which features "a brand new performing arts center with lots of great concerts and shows coming through (Adele, Wicked), tons of new little independent restaurants, bakeries, breweries, food trucks(!), etc." When struggling to live on a law student's limited budget, "It's worth mentioning that cost of living in Durham is obscenely low." Not to mention, "The weather is SO NICE in Durham—year round." When students need a bit more action (or want to attend a legal conference), the school is "only a few hours away from D.C."

Getting In

Duke Law operates a regular admissions program, as well as early, binding admissions. Candidates are evaluated on the strength and breadth of their undergraduate studies, graduate-level work, and test scores, in addition to leadership experience, background, and perspective. In recent years, the school received more than 6,000 applications for 200 spots. The median GPA for incoming students was 3.75.

Clinical program required	No
Legal writing course requirement	Yes
Legal methods course requirement	Yes
Legal research course requirement	Yes
Moot court requirement	Yes
Public interest law requirement	No

ADMISSIONS

Selectivity Rating	98
# applications received	6,099
% applicants accepted	15
% acceptees attending	23
Median LSAT	170
LSAT Range (25th to 75th percentile)	167–171
Median undergrad GPA	3.75
Application fee	$70
Regular application deadline	2/15
Transfer students accepted	Yes
Evening division offered	No
Part-time accepted	No
CAS accepted	Yes

FINANCIAL FACTS

Annual tuition (in-state out-of-state)	$48,800
Books and supplies	$1,326
Fees	$817
Room & Board	$10,890
Financial aid application deadline	3/15

EMPLOYMENT INFORMATION

Career Rating	92	**Grads Employed by Field (%)**
Total 2012 JD Grads	207	Academic (3)
% grads employed nine months out	95	Business/Industry (6)
State for bar exam	NY, CA, NC, TX, MD	Government (7)
Pass rate for first-time bar	94	Judicial Clerkship (17)
		Private Practice (62)
		Public Interest (6)

EMORY UNIVERSITY
SCHOOL OF LAW

INSTITUTIONAL INFORMATION

Public/private	Private
Affiliation	Methodist
% faculty part-time	55
% faculty female	30
% faculty underrepresented minority	8
Total faculty	150

SURVEY SAYS...

Diverse opinions accepted in classrooms, Great research resources, Students love Atlanta, GA

STUDENTS

Enrollment of law school	812
% male/female	55/45
% from out-of-state	85
% part-time	0
% underrepresented minority	27
% international	4
# of countries represented	22
Average age of entering class	24

ACADEMICS

Academic Experience Rating	**92**
Profs interesting rating	91
Profs accessible rating	82
Hours of study per day	3.53

Academic Specialties

Environmental, Human Rights, International

Advanced Degrees Offered

LLM, 1 year; JM, 1 year; SJD

Combined Degrees Offered

JD/MBA, 4 years; JD/MTS, 4 years; JD/MDIV, 5 years; JD/MPH, 3.5 years; JD/REES, 3 years; JD/Ph.D. Religion, 7 years; JD/MA Judaic Studies, 4 years

Academics

Emory Law is the perfect program for up and coming legal scholars who desire to be simultaneously "challenged...and supported." The school is "extremely welcoming" and very focused on helping students "achieve [their] career goals." Indeed, there are a number of "practice societies...that bring together students, professors, alums, and practicing attorneys throughout the semesters." Many are also quick to highlight the transactional certificate program which offers students the opportunity to "learn how to draft contracts, do due diligence, negotiate with opposing counsel, draft a term sheet [and covers] doctrinal information [in] classes like business associations, corporate tax and mergers and acquisitions."

By and large, the faculty at Emory Law is seen as "phenomenal" and "brilliant." Perhaps more importantly, professors are truly "dedicated to [their] students" and "constantly make themselves available outside of class." Additionally, students happily reveal that, for the most part, professors use a "modified" version of the infamous Socratic Method. While "everyone is still called on and expected to participate, you are more aware of when 'you'll be up.'"

High praise also abounds for the Career Services office. Students are "assigned a particular counselor to guide you through the OCI and overall career process." However, "if you have any questions, it seems as if the entire office wants to help you." An incredulous second-year student supports this notion sharing, "As a transfer student, I feel that this is something that differs significantly from my prior school in that literally the entire office tried their best to get me in contact with practicing attorneys in the specific practice area I am interested in."

Students also speak effusively about Emory Law's "effective" and "really great" administrators. It's evident that they are "genuinely interested in student success" and take great pains to ensure that they are "accessible." A surprised and grateful first-year illustrates, "There [are] casual opportunities for open discussions with all of the Deans on a weekly basis... I know most law schools claim to have 'open door policies' but Emory's policy is more like 'let's grab coffee and chat.' The school reminds me of the private, college preparatory school I attended for high school. Being a student at Emory Law is a remarkable experience."

Life

While the transition to law school can be "difficult," Emory does a fantastic job of helping students ease into legal life. Indeed, the program truly fosters a "fun, engaging and comfortable" atmosphere. Students describe their peers as "very driven, but are very genuinely nice people who enjoy everyone's company." "They say it a thousand times during orientation, but Emory Law really is all about community. Everyone shares outlines, we all study together. Even the gunners are quick to help." A pleasantly surprised first-year elaborates, "2Ls and 3Ls were truly the definition of welcoming. Some of my closest law school friends are in the 2L class. Academically, this is a huge advantage to 1Ls because every upperclassman is excited to help, give advice, send you their outlines from the prior year, and overall assist you in any way they can."

ETHAN ROSENZWEIG, ASSISTANT DEAN FOR ADMISSION
1301 CLIFTON ROAD, ATLANTA, GA 30322-2770
TEL: 404-727-6801 FAX: 404-727-2477
E-MAIL: LAWINFO@LAW.EMORY.EDU • WEBSITE: WWW.LAW.EMORY.EDU

With regards to the social side of life here, we're told that you can "always [count on] a party." Indeed, "Emory Law and Emory grad students in general definitely know how to have a great time." The school itself hosts a number of events including "bar review Thursday, Friday and Saturday nights" which frequently occur in "fun spots throughout the city." Additionally, a content first-year quickly informs us that "as all good law schools should, we have a keg…every Thursday afternoon." Outside of casual drinking, students love partaking in the "Halloween party [and] Harvest Moon Ball" as well as the "Barrister's Ball, a fabulous black-tie gala." Of course, there's much to experience off-campus too. A first-year boasts that hometown Atlanta "is an absolute blast" and it's certainly easy to be "impressed with what the city has to offer." As a fellow student explains, "There are theaters, art museums, art and music festivals, concerts, tons of hiking, and great shopping. You are in law school, but in a picturesque setting 10 minutes from a world class city with something for everyone. I can say without a doubt that Atlanta offers more to do than I will ever have time for in three years."

Getting In

Securing admission to Emory law is definitely a competitive process. The median undergraduate GPA for successful applicants is 3.7 and the median LSAT score is 165. Therefore, strong test scores and solid academic record are imperative. Emory operates on a basis of rolling admissions, so the earlier a candidate applies, the better his/her chances.

Clinical program required	No
Legal writing course requirement	Yes
Legal methods course requirement	Yes
Legal research course requirement	Yes
Moot court requirement	No
Public interest law requirement	No

ADMISSIONS

Selectivity Rating	90
# applications received	3,943
% applicants accepted	31
% acceptees attending	21
Average LSAT	163
Median LSAT	165
LSAT Range (25th to 75th percentile)	161–166
Average undergrad GPA	3.59
Median undergrad GPA	3.7
Application fee	$80
Regular application deadline	3/1
Transfer students accepted	Yes
Evening division offered	No
Part-time accepted	No
CAS accepted	Yes

FINANCIAL FACTS

Annual tuition	$44,600
Books and supplies	$5,696
Fees	$498
Room & Board	$18,602
Financial aid application deadline	3/1
% first-year students receiving some sort of aid	94
% all students receiving some sort of aid	92
% of aid that is merit based	37
% receiving scholarships	79
Average grant	$18,144
Average loan	$34,261
Average total aid package	$48,343
Average debt	$95,797

EMPLOYMENT INFORMATION

Career Rating	96	
Total 2012 JD Grads	225	
% for whom you have useable information	100	
% grads employed nine months out	96	
Median starting salary	$70,000	
% job accepting grads providing useable salary information	69	
# employed full-time	177	
# employed part-time	33	
# employed bar required	186	
# employed JD preferred	18	
# employed professional/other	6	
# employed non-professional	0	
# pursuing advanced degree	3	
# unemployed and seeking employment	6	
# not seeking employment	0	
% grads employed by school	13	
State for bar exam	GA	
Pass rate for first-time bar	94.9	

Prominent Alumni
Hon. Sanford Bishop, U.S. Congressman; Hon. Leah Sears, Former Chief Justice, Georgia Supreme Court; Hon. Sam A. Nunn, U.S. Senator (ret.), CEO Nuclear Threat Initiative.

Grads Employed by Field (%)
Academic (4)
Business/Industry (11)
Government (12)
Judicial Clerkship (11)
Private Practice (49)
Public Interest (12)

FAULKNER UNIVERSITY
THOMAS GOODE JONES SCHOOL OF LAW

INSTITUTIONAL INFORMATION

Public/private	Private
Affiliation	Church of Christ
% faculty part-time	23
% faculty female	19
% faculty underrepresented minority	7
Total faculty	31

SURVEY SAYS...

Heavy use of Socratic method, Diverse opinions accepted in classrooms, Great research resources, Great library staff

STUDENTS

Enrollment of law school	314
# of countries represented	1
Average age of entering class	26

ACADEMICS

Academic Experience Rating	**74**
Profs interesting rating	88
Profs accessible rating	89
Hours of study per day	4.08

Academics

Faulkner University's Jones School of Law in Montgomery, Alabama is "a Church of Christ–affiliated school" with "a non-intimidating environment." According to students here, it's "the best-kept secret in Alabama." The "bar-passage rate is very high;" in fact, students report that Faulkner has had "the highest bar-passage rate in the state of Alabama." "The trial advocacy program is top-notch." "The faculty and administration actually care about you as a person" and "make sure you have practical knowledge for the real world." Many appreciate that professors "treat them like a friend and not a subordinate." Some feel that Jones "could benefit from a broader curriculum." While the "small" campus can mean fewer opportunities, many students find that "the resources of the law school are growing everyday."

The many "very knowledgeable" and "distinguished" professors here "truly are a hidden gem." Their ranks include "some of the most experienced legal minds anywhere." They also "possess a great deal of real-world experience" and "give practical lessons about real-life lawyering." The faculty is pretty big on the "Socratic Method." A student explains that his torts professor "writes everyone's name on a playing card. Before class he draws three cards, and the three people have a roundtable discussion presenting the cases that were assigned. It is by far the most memorable first-year experience." "Small class sizes" "allow for greater participation" and "You are able to get to know your professors better." The intimacy "strongly encourages differing viewpoints and class discussion" as well. Professors here "truly care about your success and take an interest in your life outside of the classroom." "The amount of time each professor is willing to dedicate to each student never fails to impress me," agrees another student. "They genuinely want each student to succeed."

The "professional looking" facilities (featuring "marble and mahogany throughout") are "outstanding." There is also "Internet access throughout the school." "Every classroom is equipped with plenty of electrical outlets," notes one student. Most students would also like to see the library "open later hours."

The well-liked administration here is "always available and extremely helpful" It's worth noting that the Jones School of Law was recently granted full ABA approval, becoming the third accredited law school in Alabama. A significant milestone for the school, it basically means that students can take any bar exam in any state when they graduate just like graduates of all ABA-approved law schools.

Joshua M. Roberts, Director of Admissions
5345 Atlanta Highway, Montgomery, AL 36109
Tel: 334-386-7210 Fax: 334-386-7908
E-Mail: law@faulkner.edu • Website: www.faulkner.edu/law

Life

"There is a definite sense of community" since "Everyone knows everyone," but students insist that "that's a plus." At the same time, "There is a competitive environment, but that's what the real world is like." "We are all in this struggle together, and we help each other to survive," explains a 3L. "This includes saving someone who is drowning in class when briefing a case or forming study groups for exams." Faulkner University is definitively "Christian oriented," and overall, it's "a very conservative campus." The law school is "extremely conservative" as well, but people who aren't on the political right feel welcome here. "Even though I am very liberal and a bit outside the norm, the faculty and staff do not attempt to curtail my individuality," comments a 3L. "I do not hesitate to be vocal in my opinions and viewpoints (both in and out of class) and have never had any repercussions."

Ethnic diversity "leaves a lot to be desired." However, students do say that their peers "come from all strata of society and bring varying perspectives based upon their personal, professional and educational experiences." "There are people that are directly out of college as well as people that have been out of undergrad for fifteen to twenty years," explains one student.

Outside of class, there are "seminars, speakers," and "even school parties," but students feel "There should be a few more social opportunities, especially on the weekends." Many students are active in church. "I play basketball with friends," says an athletic 2L. "We also play flag football and get together for poker and other events to take our minds off school."

Getting In

Admitted students at the 25th percentile have LSAT scores in the high 140s and GPAs of about 2.79. Admitted students at the 75th percentile have LSAT scores in the low 150s and GPAs of 3.28. If you take the LSAT more than once, Faulkner will use your highest score.

Clinical program required	No
Legal writing course requirement	Yes
Legal methods course requirement	Yes
Legal research course requirement	Yes
Moot court requirement	Yes
Public interest law requirement	No

ADMISSIONS

Selectivity Rating	68
# applications received	785
% applicants accepted	62
% acceptees attending	26
Average LSAT	148
Median LSAT	147
LSAT Range (25th to 75th percentile)	145–150
Average undergrad GPA	3.00
Median undergrad GPA	3.05
Application fee	$50
Regular application deadline	6/15
Transfer students accepted	Yes
Evening division offered	No
Part-time accepted	No
CAS accepted	Yes

FINANCIAL FACTS

Annual tuition	$33,000
Books and supplies	$2,400
Fees	$360
Room & Board	$12,000
Financial aid application deadline	7/15
% of aid that is merit based	100
% receiving scholarships	32
Average grant	$16,500
Average debt	$107,330

EMPLOYMENT INFORMATION

Career Rating	72	
Total 2012 JD Grads	104	
% grads employed nine months out	84	
Median starting salary	$45,000	
# employed full-time	76	
# employed part-time	11	
# employed bar required	60	
# employed JD preferred	15	
# employed professional/other	4	
# employed non-professional	8	
# pursuing advanced degree	2	
# unemployed and seeking employment	10	
# not seeking employment	2	
% grads employed by school	0	
State for bar exam	AL, GA, FL, TN, MS	

Prominent Alumni
Greg Allen, Partner of Beasley, Allen, et.al.; Kelli Wise, Associate Justice, Alabama Supreme Court; Ernestine Sapp, Partner of Gray, Langford, Sapp, et.al.

Grads Employed by Field (%)
Academic (4)
Business/Industry (17)
Government (6)
Judicial Clerkship (3)
Private Practice (52)
Public Interest (2)

FLORIDA INTERNATIONAL UNIVERSITY
COLLEGE OF LAW

INSTITUTIONAL INFORMATION

Public/private	Public
Affiliation	No Affiliation
Student-faculty ratio	13:1
% faculty part-time	45
% faculty female	39
% faculty underrepresented minority	40
Total faculty	75

SURVEY SAYS...
Diverse opinions accepted in classrooms, Great research resources, Great library staff, Beautiful campus

STUDENTS

Enrollment of law school	508
% male/female	49/51
% from out-of-state	4
% part-time	32
% underrepresented minority	57
% international	1
# of countries represented	28
Average age of entering class	24

ACADEMICS

Academic Experience Rating	**91**
Profs interesting rating	85
Profs accessible rating	83
Hours of study per day	3.67

Academic Specialties
International, Intellectual Property

Advanced Degrees Offered
LLM for international lawyers; 1 year

Combined Degrees Offered
JD/MSW (Master of Social Work), 4.5 years; JD/MPA (Master of Public Administration), 3.5 years; JD/MIB (Master of International Business), 3.5 years; JD/MSPsych (Master of Science in Psychology), 4 years; JD/MALACS (Master of Latin America and Caribbean Studies), 3.5 years; JD/MBA (Master of Business Administration), 4 years; JD/MSCS (Master of Science in Criminal Justice), 3.5 years; JD/MSES (Master of Environmental Studies), 4 years

Academics

Florida International University College of Law is a relatively new school. It received its full accreditation from the ABA in 2006. It was created to provide opportunities for underrepresented groups and to serve the immediate community. Students come from all over the globe, and most agree it's a great educational experience for the cost—truly "an affordable gem." One student says, "The school has surpassed all of my expectations." The school offers eight clinical programs, giving students the chance to gain experience in the courtroom by representing real cases. In the human rights and immigration clinic, they represent clients in political asylum, as well as other immigration cases. This real-world experience is "something employers are always looking for" and is a part of the "hands-on" experience many students refer to. At FIU, education is practical. Community service is required, as well as a three-semester legal writing program. Professors spend time teaching how to write memos, petitions, appeals, and oral arguments. Students are prepared for the tangible world of legal practice and claim they measure up well against those of other more established institutions, performing highly in both national and international moot courtroom competitions. "FIU compares to the top law schools of the country," one student boasts. Students attribute this to the faculty, who are some of the "most qualified and brilliant professors in the field." "They care about our success." Another thing that sets this program apart from others is the school's "focus on international education." There's an international law requirement in the first year. Most classes devote some time to global issues, respecting "current legal trends and the importance of globalization." "The curriculum is challenging but fair and offers a good variety of electives in the second and third years." However, some students would prefer a chance to specialize in areas such as tax, business, or criminal law. They hope FIU will confer the LLM degree in the future, as well.

Students love the "familial atmosphere" of FIU, claiming "the deans and administrators know most students by name." The class sizes are small, and students say professors honestly appear happy when they drop by their offices. The professors "provide real-world insight," and even the administrative body is "committed" to its students. The career development office assists students with writing resumes and cover letters, as well as prepping them for mock interviews. "The administration does not just 'operate' the school, but understands itself to be partners of the students in their journey through law school." There are many opportunities for internships within Miami. Another perk is the school's proximity to both state and federal courts. In addition to the many Miami firms, Florida's Third District Court of Appeals is situated right behind the campus. Furthermore, "The dean and the professors do everything that they can to bring the legal world to us." The school hosts visiting lecturers from across the country. Some students argue the school's newness might hamper their vocational opportunities beyond state lines, citing its lack of recognition outside of Florida. "Not many employers conduct on-campus interviews here," but "The administration is working hard at facilitating networking and externship and internship opportunities that could lead to jobs down the road." Most students feel confident that FIU's reputation as a law school will grow, claiming, "It has already made excellent progress in its short history."

ALMA O. MIRÓ, DIRECTOR OF ADMISSIONS AND FINANCIAL AID
FIU COLLEGE OF LAW, OFFICE OF ADMISSIONS AND FINANCIAL AID, RDB 1055, MIAMI, FL 33199
TEL: 305-348-8006 FAX: 305-348-2965
E-MAIL: LAWADMIT@FIU.EDU • WEBSITE: LAW.FIU.EDU

Life

Students at FIU are "very down-to-earth, easily approachable, and thoroughly diverse." They challenge each other in a way better characterized as "Olympic spirit" rather than "academic Darwinism." The student body is comprised of people from more than twenty-seven countries, and "There are student organizations for just about every interest you can imagine."

FIU students enjoy a "beautiful" library, "state-of-the-art facilities," and "courtyards decorated with professional and student art." Students say going to law school in a city is fun for the downtimes when you're not studying. Miami, although admittedly difficult for some transplants, is a true multicultural hub with a population of more than two million people. Students also have access to the Everglades National Park, as well as miles of Florida's beaches.

Getting In

The LSAT and GPA are the most important criteria to the admissions committee, followed by letters of recommendation and personal essay. Admitted students in the 25th percentile have GPAs just under 3.3 and LSAT scores in the low 150s. Admitted students in the 75th percentile have GPAs just under 3.8 and LSAT scores in the high 150s. Transfer students are accepted as long as their current institution is accredited by the ABA and they're in the upper-third tier of their first-year class. A maximum of thirty-one hours can be transferred. Last year, 138 out-of-state applicants were accepted, and the average age of the entering class was twenty-four. Roughly one in five students is admitted.

Clinical program required	No
Legal writing course requirement	Yes
Legal methods course requirement	Yes
Legal research course requirement	Yes
Moot court requirement	No
Public interest law requirement	Yes

ADMISSIONS

Selectivity Rating	89
# applications received	2,293
% applicants accepted	23
% acceptees attending	23
Median LSAT	156
LSAT Range (25th to 75th percentile)	151–157
Median undergrad GPA	3.6
Application fee	$20
Regular application deadline	5/1
Transfer students accepted	Yes
Evening division offered	Yes
Part-time accepted	Yes
CAS accepted	Yes

FINANCIAL FACTS

Annual tuition (in-state out-of-state)	$18,463/$32,707
Books and supplies	$3,088
Fees	$377
Room & Board (on/off campus)	$15,710/$22,936
Financial aid application deadline	2/15
% first-year students receiving some sort of aid	98
% all students receiving some sort of aid	92
% of aid that is merit based	4
% receiving scholarships	72
Average grant	$6,946
Average loan	$29,970
Average total aid package	$38,448
Average debt	$85,586

EMPLOYMENT INFORMATION

Career Rating	85	
Total 2012 JD Grads	184	
% grads employed nine months out	87	
# employed full-time	144	
# employed part-time	16	
# employed bar required	127	
# employed JD preferred	30	
# employed professional/other	3	
# employed non-professional	0	
# pursuing advanced degree	3	
# unemployed and seeking employment	5	
# not seeking employment	13	
% grads employed by school	3	
State for bar exam	FL, TX	
Pass rate for first-time bar	89.5	

Prominent Alumni

Carlos Lago, Atty, Greenberg Traurig; Christopher Kokoruda, Atty, Miami-Dade County Attorney's Office; Katie A. Edwards, Member, Florida House of Representatives; Shannon O-Shea, Law Clerk, U.S. Court of Appeals, 11th Circuit; Andrea Canona, Fellow, Dept. of Justice Honors Program.

Grads Employed by Field (%)

Academic (1)
Business/Industry (12)
Government (13)
Judicial Clerkship (2)
Military (1)
Private Practice (54)
Public Interest (3)

FLORIDA STATE UNIVERSITY
COLLEGE OF LAW

INSTITUTIONAL INFORMATION

Public/private	Public
% faculty part-time	30
% faculty female	44
% faculty underrepresented minority	16
Total faculty	84

SURVEY SAYS...

Diverse opinions accepted in class-rooms, Abundant externship/intern-ship/clerkship opportunities, Students love Tallahassee, FL, Good social life

STUDENTS

Enrollment of law school	698
% male/female	59/41
% from out-of-state	12
% part-time	0
% underrepresented minority	21
% international	2
# of countries represented	10
Average age of entering class	24

ACADEMICS

Academic Experience Rating	**93**
Profs interesting rating	92
Profs accessible rating	94
Hours of study per day	2.78

Academic Specialties

Business, Criminal, Environmental, International

Advanced Degrees Offered

JD, minimum 88 Credit Hours to Graduate; LLM in Environmental Law and Policy; LLM in American Law for Foreign Lawyers International Law Certificate Program; Environmental and Land Use Law Certificate Program; Business Law Certificate Program

Combined Degrees Offered

JD/MBA, JD/MS URP, JD/MS IA, JD/MS Economics, JD/MPA, JD/MS SW, JD/MS LIS, JD/MS Family & Child SCI, JD/MS Sports Mgmt, most programs take 4 years to complete

Academics

At FSU, its students report, prepare for a friendly, individualized law school experience at a state school price. Of the faculty and administration, who "all [have] open door policies," students say "I never imagined law professors would be so accessible" and "Any problems or concerns ranging from externships to the temperature of the classrooms someone is always polite and wanting to help." This is undoubtedly because "There is so much conversation between the stellar faculty and the students" and "The administration is fairly transparent and keeps students informed." Students feel connected to their professors: "All of the professors at FSU Law seem to enjoy teaching here, and I believe that says something about the faculty, facilities, and student body."

Looking beyond law school, while "FSU is very much focused on policy and theory rather than on teaching legal-practice skills from day one," "It's clear that the school places great weight on job placement." "The placement office, deans office, and all other staff here to support the students are phenomenal. They are constantly offering small workshops, resume reviews, intimate gatherings with local judges and attorneys, and more."

Students offer high praise for FSU's facilities as well: "The classrooms are freshly renovated and the technology is great." "Our new advocacy center, the previous Florida 1st DCA building, has brought five new courtrooms to the law school as well as conference rooms, new classrooms, and interview rooms. I would put the facilities of FSU law up against any law school." Study space is widely available: "The law library is comfortable and spacious enough to fit all the students without overcrowding during exams" and across campus, facilities are "open 24/7 for students with our ID cards so no matter when we want to study we can." Add "very low" tuition, "great" program availability, "openness toward transfer students," and a "location in a capital city," and it's easy to see why FSU's law students are so satisfied with their choice.

Life

Of all the things to love about FSU Law, its "location in Tallahassee is a great asset. Being in the capital city offers opportunities to law students in multiple different disciplines in the legal profession." Faculty and staff are eager to help students maximize these connections, cultivating local firms to host "events for students who are pursuing study in a particular field...because there are so many local lawyers, there are more networking opportunities than any student can possibly participate in." Students benefit from the university's deep roots in Florida, finding that FSU's "alumni base is also great for reaching out and networking." One student puts it strongly: "FSU Law is located in the capital city, literally within the shadow of the Florida Capitol Building. Being so close to the seat of power in Florida means many opportunities to interact with Supreme Court justices, legislators, and others."

JENNIFER L. KESSINGER, DIRECTOR OF ADMISSIONS AND RECORDS
425 WEST JEFFERSON STREET, TALLAHASSEE, FL 32306-1601
TEL: 850-644-3787 FAX: 850-644-7284
E-MAIL: ADMISSIONS@LAW.FSU.EDU • WEBSITE: WWW.LAW.FSU.EDU

In terms of social culture, "my classmates all seem to get along and there isn't a sense of throat cutting competition." Reports confirm that "The other students are smart and actually nice to each other" and "competition is very low. It's a great combination of hard work and plenty of play." Indeed, "The students here are kind to one another, will email you notes if you are sick, and I've never heard of a book being hidden in the library!" Students register a few complaints about "parking" availability on campus and wishing for "more food options at school," as well as the fact that, as at many large universities "there is often a mismatch between available seats in a class and demand," but as a whole, one student sums it up revealingly: "I think we're one of the nation's best kept secrets."

Getting In

Don't be fooled by FSU's position as a large state university: getting in takes some chops. FSU's median LSAT is 160, its median GPA is 3.54, and a quarter of its students have two or more years of work experience. However, only 19 percent of entering FSU law students are non-Florida residents, suggesting that out-of-state students might be reviewed kindly. FSU Law has a good reputation for being transfer-friendly; all transfer students must be in the top third of their class to be eligible for admission.

Clinical program required	No
Legal writing course requirement	Yes
Legal methods course requirement	Yes
Legal research course requirement	Yes
Moot court requirement	No
Public interest law requirement	Yes

ADMISSIONS

Selectivity Rating	88
# applications received	2,499
% applicants accepted	33
% acceptees attending	23
Median LSAT	160
LSAT Range (25th to 75th percentile)	157–162
Median undergrad GPA	3.54
Application fee	$30
Regular application deadline	4/1
Transfer students accepted	Yes
Evening division offered	No
Part-time accepted	No
CAS accepted	Yes

FINANCIAL FACTS

Annual tuition	$17,210
Books and supplies	$3,000
Fees (in-state out-of-state)	$2,521/$22,533
Room & Board	$10,000
Financial aid application deadline	6/15
% first-year students receiving some sort of aid	86
% all students receiving some sort of aid	88
% of aid that is merit based	22
% receiving scholarships	43
Average grant	$6,799
Average loan	$28,941
Average total aid package	$29,611
Average debt	$83,409

EMPLOYMENT INFORMATION

Career Rating	83
Total 2012 JD Grads	286
% grads employed nine months out	89
Median starting salary	$45,278
# employed full-time	231
# employed part-time	24
# employed bar required	198
# employed JD preferred	50
# employed professional/other	3
# employed non-professional	4
# pursuing advanced degree	9
# unemployed and seeking employment	10
# not seeking employment	9
% grads employed by school	0
State for bar exam	FL, GA, TX, CA, NY
Pass rate for first-time bar	88.3

Prominent Alumni
Mark Williamson, Alston & Bird LLP; Justice Rick Polston, Florida Supreme Court; Jeffrey A. Stoops, President of SBA Communications Corp.

Grads Employed by Field (%)
Academic (3)
Business/Industry (13)
Government (22)
Judicial Clerkship (4)
Military (1)
Private Practice (38)
Public Interest (9)

FORDHAM UNIVERSITY
SCHOOL OF LAW

INSTITUTIONAL INFORMATION

Public/private	Private
Affiliation	Roman Catholic
Student-faculty ratio	14:1
% faculty part-time	69
% faculty female	35
% faculty underrepresented minority	20
Total faculty	280

SURVEY SAYS...

Diverse opinions accepted in classrooms, Abundant externship/internship/clerkship opportunities, Students love New York, NY

STUDENTS

Enrollment of law school	1,427
% male/female	54/46
% from out-of-state	51
% part-time	16
% underrepresented minority	22
% international	3
# of countries represented	13
Average age of entering class	24

ACADEMICS

Academic Experience Rating	**90**
Profs interesting rating	86
Profs accessible rating	76
Hours of study per day	3.39

Academic Specialties

Civil Procedure, Commercial, Constitutional, Corporation Securities, Criminal, Environmental, Government Services, Human Rights, International, Labor, Legal History, Legal Philosophy, Property, Taxation, Intellectual Property

Advanced Degrees Offered

JD, 3 years full-time, 4 years part-time; LLM, 1 year full-time

Combined Degrees Offered

JD/MBA with Fordham Grad School of Business (4 years full-time); JD/MSW with Fordham Grad School of Social Work (4 years full-time). JD/MA in International Political Economy

Academics

Fordham University School of Law "in the heart of New York City" takes "a seriously practical approach" to the study of law, and "The breadth of the programs" here is paralleled at few other places. Students laud the excellent and thorough legal writing program. Fordham Law also does a really good job in taking advantage of its location "through courses involving fieldwork," externships, judicial placements, and various extracurricular events. "A large selection of clinics" includes some very unique opportunities in international law, and Fordham "will fund students' trips abroad to engage in human rights work." There are several more meat-and-potatoes offerings, such as family law, federal litigation, and housing rights as well. As befits its Jesuit heritage, Fordham is also very big on public interest law. "A crackerjack team of public interest minds" is willing and able to help students start service projects or find meaningful ways to make the world a better place.

While a few professors are "awful beyond belief," the faculty is mostly filled with "a cross section of bright and charismatic teachers"—"some of the most brilliant minds currently teaching the law." They're "incredibly candid," "witty," and "engaging in the classroom." The faculty interacts with students "out of the classroom," as well. Sadly, dealing with Fordham's bureaucracy is a wholly different story. The "shaky," "disorganized" administration is generally disliked. "It works out for those of us who cannot get anything in on time," notes an upbeat 1L. "There is no way they would ever notice."

It's a perennial lament among students here that their school is "extremely underrated" and "would be ranked higher" if only New York University and Columbia weren't each a few subway stops away. Fordham Law boasts a "particularly strong" and loyal alumni network, though, and the school is located in "one of the best locations in Manhattan," within walking distance to several of the world's biggest and most revered white-shoe law firms. Students also tell us that Fordham has a reputation for producing "exceptionally hardworking, occasionally pugilistic (figuratively), and bright" lawyers. Average starting salaries are quite comfortable and employment prospects are pretty good if you can manage a solid class rank. "With good enough grades—at least top third of the class—you can snag a big law job if you want," relates a 2L.

The research facilities are great at Fordham, and the librarians are "incredibly helpful," but students have few other good things to say about the accommodations. The "cramped," "crowded," "decrepit," and generally "inadequate" building "feels more like a 1950s fallout shelter than a law school." Luckily, "Its days are numbered." There's a new building in the works, and "The design is striking." The space concerns and depressing architecture of this drab concrete cinderblock "will no longer be an issue" once the new law school building is completed.

STEPHEN BROWN, ASSISTANT DEAN FOR ENROLLMENT SERVICES
33 WEST 60TH STREET, NINTH FLOOR, NEW YORK, NY 10023
TEL: 212-636-6810 FAX: 212-636-7984
E-MAIL: LAWADMISSIONS@LAW.FORDHAM.EDU • WEBSITE: LAW.FORDHAM.EDU

Life

Many students here "are from the so-called tri-state area" (Connecticut, New Jersey, and New York), but there are tons of people from all over the country, as well. Minority enrollment is solid, and the evening program attracts a slew of older students who have professional experience in a variety of fields. The academic environment is "competitive," "but most people work together very well and are friends outside of class." "People still want to get good grades and awesome jobs, but no one is cutting throats to get there," explains a 2L. "There are gunners, of course, but they're lovable gunners."

While many, if not most, students have lives outside of school, "The school has strong esprit de corps." "First-year sections are intimate," and "There is no shortage of interaction and friendship." "Almost every personality type will find a niche here." "It's really a place where you meet lifelong friends and mentors." "Whether you're looking for a new group of close friends, or just nine-to-five friends who will go home to their families and relationships at the end of the day, you'll find people like you at Fordham." "Classy and fun" school-sponsored social activities are plentiful. "There are bar nights every week, kegs in the caf' once a month, and various drinking events throughout the school year." Also, of course, "Fordham's best asset" is its "super nice" (though also super expensive) location in one of the greatest and most exciting cities in the world. There are a million things to do when you take a break from your casebooks.

Getting In

Admitted students at the 25th percentile have LSAT scores in the lower 160s and undergraduate grade point averages just under 3.4. At the 75th percentile, LSAT scores are about 168, and GPAs are a little more than 3.7. If you're a marginal candidate, note that the stats for the evening division are a little lower.

Clinical program required	No
Legal writing course requirement	Yes
Legal methods course requirement	Yes
Legal research course requirement	Yes
Moot court requirement	No
Public interest law requirement	No

ADMISSIONS

Selectivity Rating	91
# applications received	6,516
% applicants accepted	32
% acceptees attending	21
Median LSAT	165
LSAT Range (25th to 75th percentile)	162–166
Median undergrad GPA	3.52
Application fee	$70
Regular application deadline	3/15
Early application deadline	10/15
Early application notification	12/15
Transfer students accepted	Yes
Evening division offered	Yes
Part-time accepted	Yes
CAS accepted	Yes

FINANCIAL FACTS

Annual tuition	$48,900
Books and supplies	$1,772
Fees	$626
Room & Board	$18,960
Financial aid application deadline	4/1
% first-year students receiving some sort of aid	78
% all students receiving some sort of aid	76
% receiving scholarships	39
Average grant	$10,000
Average debt	$134,319

EMPLOYMENT INFORMATION

Career Rating	60*
State for bar exam	NY

George Mason University
School of Law

INSTITUTIONAL INFORMATION

Public/private	Public
Affiliation	No Affiliation
% faculty part-time	75
% faculty female	27
% faculty underrepresented minority	10
Total faculty	157

SURVEY SAYS...

Conservative students, Students love Arlington, VA

STUDENTS

Enrollment of law school	636
% male/female	57/43
% from out-of-state	55
% part-time	31
% underrepresented minority	14
% international	2
Average age of entering class	26

ACADEMICS

Academic Experience Rating	86
Profs interesting rating	81
Profs accessible rating	74
Hours of study per day	3.71

Academic Specialties
Corporation Securities, Criminal, Government Services, International, Legal Philosophy, Taxation, Intellectual Property

Advanced Degrees Offered
LLM—a post-JD degree specializing in (a) Intellectual Property or (b) Law and Economics. More information can be found here: www.law. gmu.edu/admissions/faq_llm.

Combined Degrees Offered
JD/MPP: Information on the JD/MPP can be found at www.law.gmu. edu/academics/llm.html. JD/MA or Ph.D. in Economics: The law school offers credit for certain classes taken by students enrolled in GMU's Master's or Ph.D. program in Economics. More information can be found here: www.law.gmu.edu/academics/regulations

Academics

George Mason University's law students agree that "The professors are brilliant" and "Mason is a hidden gem that prepares students for actual practice better than any other law school out there." However, there's plenty more to say about the school that incites a disagreement typical of students who are being taught to argue for a living. Some contend that "One of the school's strengths is the four-semester legal writing requirement" while some refer disparagingly to "the nightmare of a writing program that the school has instituted." Others synthesize the two arguments: "The students often complain about the [legal writing] program, but most recognize that it is tremendously useful and will help them with future legal opportunities." Students are similarly divided on GMU's pedagogical ethos: some assert that "there is a very good blend of theory and practical knowledge conveyed" in the curricula, while others maintain that "the emphasis on economics in many ways is distracting from understanding the black letter law" or that "This is a patent law heavy school with unequal opportunities for students with social science rather than hard science backgrounds." GMU is stringent about its graduation requirements, leading some students to complain about "too many required courses," yet students also appreciate that "There are many classes available to practice both courtroom advocacy and writing skills, and taking part in these classes has given me invaluable experience for litigation."

In terms of faculty, administration, and other on-campus support, students feel that GMU's "Administration is vested in student outcomes" and that "The staff is unbelievably open to outside discussion and help providing high government contacts and networking." The university's ten-minutes-away proximity to Washington, DC, provides a major asset to job-seeking graduates "with ready access to fabulous internships and other educational opportunities at a public school price." This proximity also creates a culture of working lawyers amongst its faculty: "most of the professors aren't just professors. They're also practicing attorneys or policy specialists who have major influences on their respective fields, and on the development of those fields." Students find the school's facilities "Extremely up to date" and "outstanding," and extol the librarians: "The librarians are perhaps the most wonderful people on campus." There are some complaints about the law school's relationship to the rest of the university: students claim "The law school is like the estranged step-child to the main campus," that they "could use better amenities," and that they sometimes "feel like nothing more than a cash cow to the main campus in Fairfax" due to rising tuition prices in the last few years. That said, Virginia locals appreciate the "in-state tuition rate," which is "relatively cheap."

ALISON PRICE, SR. ASSOCIATE DEAN AND DIRECTOR OF ADMISSIONS
3301 FAIRFAX DRIVE, ARLINGTON, VA 22201
TEL: 703-993-8010 FAX: 703-993-8088
E-MAIL: APRICE1@GMU.EDU • WEBSITE: WWW.LAW.GMU.EDU

Life

Even as they argue about, well, everything, GMU students seem to like each other, reporting that the school's culture has a "down-to-earth personality" and that "George Mason invites very bright and hard working students." "There is a social scene if you want it but most prefer to keep it to the weekends," and students observe a "Great community." They attribute this to the intimacy of the program: "GMU has small class sizes. This leads to more approachable professors and a greater camaraderie between the students. Though it is still competitive, I have not seen any animosity or heard about nefarious acts by students." This supportive social atmosphere is mirrored in the "Safe, well-lit campus," which is "metro accessible" to D.C. and the other surrounding areas. This, as well as the school's wide offering of evening classes, makes GMU a good choice for working or commuting students: "Being an evening student I appreciate the fact that the night courses are taught by the same faculty as the day classes."

GMU hardly conveys that liberals need not apply, but prospectives are well-advised to know that "The school has a noticeable libertarian (not necessarily conservative) bias, but the faculty and students are accepting of other viewpoints and willing to engage in respectful debate." Some attest that "there is no ideological diversity" and that the school could use "more diversity of viewpoints on the faculty," but many others value the school's "conservative perspective deriving from its focus on law and economics." In general, though, GMU's law students feel "camaraderie" in their peer community, and like that GMU is "not a cutthroat environment."

Getting In

Many students feel that GMU's ranking isn't consummate with its quality of education; its high admissions standards underscore this. For the students matriculating in 2012, the median LSAT was 163 and median GPA was 3.70.

Clinical program required	No
Legal writing course requirement	Yes
Legal methods course requirement	No
Legal research course requirement	Yes
Moot court requirement	Yes
Public interest law requirement	No

ADMISSIONS

Selectivity Rating	89
# applications received	3,856
% applicants accepted	28
% acceptees attending	14
Average LSAT	161
Median LSAT	163
LSAT Range (25th to 75th percentile)	158–164
Average undergrad GPA	3.48
Median undergrad GPA	3.7
Application fee	$35
Regular application deadline	4/1
Regular notification	4/15
Early application deadline	12/15
Early application notification	1/31
Transfer students accepted	Yes
Evening division offered	Yes
Part-time accepted	Yes
CAS accepted	Yes

FINANCIAL FACTS

Annual tuition (in-state out-of-state)	$22,047/$36,985
Books and supplies	$1,3,500.00
Fees	$2,576
Room & Board	$16,710
Financial aid application deadline	3/1
% first-year students receiving some sort of aid	76
% all students receiving some sort of aid	78
% of aid that is merit based	5
% receiving scholarships	17
Average grant	$9,604
Average loan	$46,958
Average total aid package	$45,732

EMPLOYMENT INFORMATION

Career Rating	80	**Prominent Alumni**
Total 2012 JD Grads	220	Attorney General Ken Cuccinelli, Attorney
% grads employed nine months out	93	General, Commonwealth of Virginia; The
Median starting salary	$60,000	Hon. Maureen Ohlhausen, Commissioner,
% job accepting grads providing		Federal Trade Commission; The Hon. Scott
useable salary information	66	Clarkson, Ninth Circuit Court of Appeals.
# employed full-time	179	**Grads Employed by Field (%)**
# employed part-time	26	Academic (7)
# employed bar required	122	Business/Industry (16)
# employed JD preferred	70	Government (21)
# employed professional/other	11	Judicial Clerkship (7)
# employed non-professional	1	Military (2)
# pursuing advanced degree	2	Private Practice (39)
# unemployed and seeking employment	8	Public Interest (7)
# not seeking employment	3	
% grads employed by school	12	
State for bar exam	VA, MD, DC, CA, NY	

THE GEORGE WASHINGTON UNIVERSITY
LAW SCHOOL

INSTITUTIONAL INFORMATION

Public/private	Private
Affiliation	No Affiliation
Student-faculty ratio	15:1
% faculty part-time	73
% faculty female	33
% faculty underrepresented minority	11
Total faculty	394

SURVEY SAYS...
Abundant externship/internship/clerkship opportunities, Students love Washington, D.C.

STUDENTS
Average age of entering class	25

ACADEMICS
Academic Experience Rating	90
Profs interesting rating	95
Profs accessible rating	68

Academic Specialties
Civil Procedure, Commercial, Constitutional, Corporation Securities, Criminal, Environmental, Government Services, Human Rights, International, Labor, Legal History, Legal Philosophy, Property, Taxation, Intellectual Property

Advanced Degrees Offered
JD full-time, 3 years; JD part-time, 4 years; Master of Laws, 1–2 years; Doctor of Juridical Science, 3 years

Combined Degrees Offered
JD/MBA; JD/MPA; JD/MA International Affairs; JD/MA History; JD/MA Women's Studies JD/MPH, all can be completed in 4 years with full-time and summer attendance

Academics

The caliber of the "limitless" resources available to a George Washington University law students are outstanding, and the location cannot be beat; its various connections to federal agencies, lobbyists, firms, and judges in the area make it easy to find some area of law that will interest any student, as well as allowing for a wealth of outside placement and internship possibilities. "I have enough room in my schedule to go hear oral arguments at the Supreme Court or the Federal Circuit Court," says a student. "Nearly everyone I know has had the opportunity to intern in the federal or D.C. courts or some federal agency," says another. Even if students aren't happy with the Career Development office (and many outside of the top 15 percent of the class are not), there's the matter of the upstanding reputation with employers. "People that don't get jobs that attend GW either (1) didn't try hard enough to diversify where they were applying (particularly, geographically—people seem to forget there are jobs outside D.C., NY and the coasts), or (2) aren't trying hard enough period," says a 3L. Add to that stellar academics, and this "close knit, high energy" school is definitely on the move, though the price tag can be steep. The somewhat high enrollment means "at times it feels a bit crowded" at GW, but the law school complex is very big, and the school has done a good job of expanding spaces, having recently developed a café for students and enlarging student conference spaces. In addition to the excellent law library, at one's fingertips on any given day there are lectures, panels, and workshops.

The Student Bar Association is one of the best in the nation, which is a reflection of the close relationship between the students and the administration, who "make a clear effort to engage students on the decisions of the law school." GW Law's Dean is a "terrific fundraiser and cheerleader," and even normally teaches a 1L Criminal Law class. The emphasis placed upon professors' teaching abilities is reflected in the inclusion of a student panel on the Faculty Appointments Committee, where students' views as reflected in their reports to the faculty are "given serious consideration during the appointment process." It shows, too, as the professors at GW are first-rate; there are "so many 'musttakes' here that you are guaranteed a great professor (at least by reputation) for each major doctrinal course." Indeed, GW Law professors are well-known locally and nationally, and "it's not unusual to attend a professor's class, and then later see him or her on the television that evening." These superstars are approachable as well, and "you would be hardpressed to go to a student function and not find a friendly face from the faculty and staff enjoying time away from the formal school setting and lending their wisdom and wit to the outside student life." Classes mix theory and practice, placing an emphasis on didactic ability, and "There can be a little tough love involved" if needed. Each lecture "is an experience," and while the Socratic Method is used, it is used "very gently, and tends to create more of an open discussion format than a fear-invoking grilling process." However, students would like to see their torts class expanded to two semesters. The student culture and atmosphere at GW Law rounds out the experience, as "people actually like each other and enjoy a good conversation, whether studying or not."

ANNE M. RICHARD, ASSOCIATE DEAN FOR ADMISSIONS & FINANCIAL AID
700 20TH STREET, NW, WASHINGTON, D.C. 20052
TEL: 202-994-7230 FAX: 202-994-3597
E-MAIL: JDADMIT@LAW.GWU.EDU • WEBSITE: WWW.LAW.GWU.EDU

Life

As a large law school, "There is a group (or clique) for everyone," and while "most law students are naturally type-A," the school is not competitive, possibly because most students have a job when graduating. There is a genuine atmosphere of camaraderie, where "students are colleagues not just in the classroom, but in the outside world as well." Only a few blocks from the National Mall and a short walk to Georgetown and Dupont Circle, GW has the perfect location for the social, career, and academic needs of students. It "is expensive to live here," but "The benefits far outweigh the costs." Students are all business for the most part in the classroom, but "relaxed and laid-back outside of it," and most "tend to be social and well-adjusted." The school is a social paradise, with "beautiful people, [a] 200-student ski trip, weekly special events at local bars, formal dances at luxury hotels, intra-class dating, and every other extracurricular activity necessary for keeping your sanity in law school is provided for in healthy amounts." Despite the more visible liberal element at the school, "liberals and conservatives, atheists, Jews, Mormons, the occasional Evangelical, and kids of all different backgrounds and ethnicities get together and enjoy each others' company on a regular basis." Tons of student groups help bring together the already diverse student body, and a huge percentage attend SBA events like the Halloween party and Barrister's Ball.

Getting In

Admission to George Washington is highly competitive. It's not quite as hard to get in as it is at its crosstown rival, Georgetown, but it's close. You should have an LSAT score at or above the 90th percentile and an A-minus average to be seriously considered.

Clinical program required	No
Legal writing course requirement	Yes
Legal methods course requirement	Yes
Legal research course requirement	Yes
Moot court requirement	No
Public interest law requirement	No

ADMISSIONS

Selectivity Rating	91
# applications received	8,652
% applicants accepted	
Average LSAT	167
LSAT Range (25th to 75th percentile)	162–168
Median undergrad GPA	3.82
Application fee	$80
Regular application deadline	3/1
Early application deadline	1/5
Early application notification	1/30
Transfer students accepted	Yes
Evening division offered	Yes
Part-time accepted	Yes
CAS accepted	Yes

FINANCIAL FACTS

Annual tuition	$40,100
Books and supplies	$1,185
Room & Board	$13,600
% first-year students receiving some sort of aid	85
% all students receiving some sort of aid	87
% of aid that is merit based	48
% receiving scholarships	47
Average grant	$13,000
Average loan	$35,000
Average total aid package	$35,000
Average debt	$107,000

EMPLOYMENT INFORMATION

Career Rating	98	Grads Employed by Field (%)
% grads employed nine months out	95	Academic (7)
Median starting salary	$136,643	Business/Industry (12)
State for bar exam	NY, VA, MD, CA	Government (18)
Pass rate for first-time bar	94	Judicial Clerkship (9)
		Private Practice (43)
		Public Interest (9)

GEORGETOWN UNIVERSITY
LAW CENTER

INSTITUTIONAL INFORMATION

Public/private   Private
Affiliation   Roman Catholic-Jesuit
Student-faculty ratio   11:1
% faculty female   42
% faculty underrepresented
  minority   14
Total faculty   276

SURVEY SAYS...
Great research resources

STUDENTS
Average age of entering class   24

ACADEMICS
Academic Experience Rating   96
Profs interesting rating   89
Profs accessible rating   81
Hours of study per day   3.53

Academic Specialties
Civil Procedure, Commercial,
Constitutional, Corporation
Securities, Criminal, Environmental,
Government Services, Human
Rights, International, Labor, Legal
History, Legal Philosophy, Property,
Taxation, Intellectual Property

Advanced Degrees Offered
SJD; LLM taxation, LLM securities
and financial regulation, LLM international business and economic law,
LLM global health law, LLM global
health law and international institutions, LLM national security law, LLM
individualized program; LLM general
studies and LLM international legal
studies; LLM Advocacy; LLM and
Certificate in Legal English; Certificate
in employee benefits law; Certificate in
estate planning; Certificate in
International Human Rights Law;
Certificate in International Taxation;
Certificate in State and Local Taxation;
Certificate in International Arbitration
and Dispute; Certificate in WTO
Studies; Certificate in Refugees &
Humanitarian Emergencies; and LLM
and Master of International Affairs

Academics

The "prestigious," "ridiculously large," and tangentially Jesuitical Georgetown University Law Center is "a choose-your-own-adventure school" in "a prime downtown D.C. location." "The sheer variety of the offerings is stunning," declares a 2L. "If you are looking to do something, odds are there is a club, or a class, or a journal, or some other event on this campus that is targeted at that." The range of courses is "extremely impressive and covers a broad spectrum of subjects." Georgetown is "a particularly great choice for students looking for opportunities in public interest or government." "Its international focus is without par," and there are several study abroad programs offered. In addition to the orthodox first-year curriculum, you can take an alternative set of 1L courses that emphasize the interconnected impact of government regulation and "concentrates on making law school applicable to the legal world." The clinics "cover a breathtaking array of topics." Internships and externships galore on Capitol Hill and all over D.C. during the academic year give students "a leg up on summer internships and future employment." Another fabulous feature here is the Supreme Court Institute's moot court program. Attorneys who are about to appear before the U.S. Supreme Court routinely practice their oral arguments on Georgetown's campus "in front of professors" in "a perfect, scaled-down replica of the actual Supreme Court (right down to the carpeting)." "It's remarkably educational to see an advocate's dry run" and "then, a week later, actually go watch the same argument" for real.

Some of the "classes are very large [during the] first year" but faculty members are "very accessible" and they generally manage to "turn dull information into lively debate." "The professors make all the reading and writing worthwhile," encourage "diverse points of view, and [take] an interest in students' academic, professional, and personal lives," gushes a 3L. Professors are also "extremely accomplished" and they "bring fantastic experience and knowledge to the classroom." Often, though, "the 'big-name' professors are the worst teachers because they just tell war stories that are irrelevant to the exam, albeit interesting." Some students tell us that the top brass is "hard-working" and "surprisingly accessible for a big school." "They definitely make a very conscious effort to make the school seem smaller," opines a 1L. Others students say that "a ton of red tape" plagues Georgetown. "It seems like nothing is ever done on time," they say, and the registrar is "sloppy and inefficient."

Career Services staffers are "far from uber-helpful life coaches," and "There is a general feeling among the student body that Career Services is more interested in statistics (e.g., how many students went to big firms) than in helping students find paths that will make them happy." An optional first year program titled The Search Before the Search (SBTS) encourages students to reflect on their own strengths and interests while providing insight into the myriad opportunities available to Georgetown law graduates. The Georgetown brand has "an amazing domestic and international presence," though. "A huge range of firms and government agencies" recruits on campus each year. The pool of alumni is colossal. "Georgetown has amazing support for public interest students" as well, including a discrete office tailored to help them "pursue careers and co-curricular options." The biggest chunk of graduates stay in Washington, D.C., or head to New York City or California. About 50 percent go into private practice.

ANDREW P. CORNBLATT, DEAN OF ADMISSIONS
600 NEW JERSEY AVENUE, NW, ROOM 589, WASHINGTON, D.C. 20001
TEL: 202-662-9010 FAX: 202-662-9439
E-MAIL: ADMIS@LAW.GEORGETOWN.EDU • WEBSITE: WWW.LAW.GEORGETOWN.EDU

"The facilities are comfortable and more than adequate" here. Classrooms "are in great condition." The five-story law library is "enjoyable to spend time in and has plenty of nooks and crannies." The law school is located "away from the main campus." But " The proximity to SCOTUS (The Supreme Court), the Capitol, the White House, and the many international institutions in D.C. make for a special experience."

Life

Students at Georgetown Law are "very nice and good-natured, but really busy." Minority representation clocks in at about 28 percent and people come from all over the planet and all manner of backgrounds. "There is truly a diversity of opinions" as well. "When you put together students from many different walks of life," says a 2L, "you're bound to have an eclectic environment which makes the law school experience more tolerable."

Academically, there are "those few students with an exceptionally competitive attitude" but, for the most part, "students share notes, help each other, and actually want to work together." "I would say the level of competition is moderate," estimates a 1L. Outside of class, "Extracurriculars are very popular." "There are plenty of student organizations and there are always more activities on campus than are possible to attend." "Famous speakers" are ubiquitous. Supreme Court justices "pop by all the time," for example. The swanky, "state-of-the-art" fitness center is a "great escape from studying" and it's exclusively for law students. Amenities include a swimming pool, racquetball courts, a full-size basketball court, and whirlpools. You can also take classes in spinning, yoga, dance, boxing, and much else. "A lot of the student body commutes from a good distance to school," but "There is a buzzing social scene, particularly among 1Ls." On the weekends, "Students tend to go en masse to Dupont Circle and other parts of D.C."

Getting In

Overall, students at the 25th percentile have LSAT scores in the high 160s and GPAs just over 3.4. At the 75th percentile, LSAT scores are in the low 170s and GPAs are approximately 3.8. Part-time students have somewhat less intimidating numbers.

Combined Degrees Offered

JD/MBA, JD/MPH, JD/MPP, JD/MSFS, JD/MAAS; JD/MAGES; JD/MALAS, JD/MAREES, JD/MASSP; JD/Ph.D. Government and JD/Ph.D. or MA Philosophy; and JD/LLM taxation, JD/LLM international business and economic law, JD/LLM national security law, and JD/LLM securities and financial regulation.

Clinical program required	No
Legal writing course requirement	Yes
Legal methods course requirement	Yes
Legal research course requirement	Yes
Moot court requirement	No
Public interest law requirement	No

ADMISSIONS

Selectivity Rating	92
# applications received	8,087
% applicants accepted	28
% acceptees attending	25
Median LSAT	169
LSAT Range (25th to 75th percentile)	165–170
Median undergrad GPA	3.72
Application fee	$85
Regular application deadline	3/1
Early application deadline	3/1
Transfer students accepted	Yes
Evening division offered	Yes
Part-time accepted	Yes
CAS accepted	Yes

FINANCIAL FACTS

Annual tuition	$48,835
Books and supplies	$1,120
Room & Board (on/off campus)	$23,545
Financial aid application deadline	3/15
% first-year students receiving some sort of aid	78
% all students receiving some sort of aid	76
% of aid that is merit based	40
% receiving scholarships	37
Average grant	$19,279
Average loan	$51,985
Average total aid package	$60,335
Average debt	$146,169

EMPLOYMENT INFORMATION

Career Rating	98
Total 2012 JD Grads	626
% grads employed nine months out	92
Median starting salary	$160,000
# employed full-time	556
# employed part-time	22
# employed bar required	472
# employed JD preferred	90
# employed professional/other	12
# employed non-professional	2
# pursuing advanced degree	12
# unemployed and seeking employment	29
# not seeking employment	4
% grads employed by school	1
State for bar exam	NY, MD, CA, VA
Pass rate for first-time bar	87.8

Prominent Alumni
Senator George Mitchell (L'61), Partner & Chair Emeritus, DLA Piper; Savannah Guthrie (L'02), TODAY co-host, third hour, and Chief Legal Analyst; Gov. Mitch Daniels (L'79), Governor of Indiana.

Grads Employed by Field (%)
Academic (1)
Business/Industry (5)
Government (14)
Judicial Clerkship (7)
Military (1)
Private Practice (49)
Public Interest (14)

GEORGIA STATE UNIVERSITY
COLLEGE OF LAW

INSTITUTIONAL INFORMATION

Public/private	Public
Affiliation	No Affiliation
Student-faculty ratio	14:1
% faculty part-time	26
% faculty female	45
% faculty underrepresented minority	14
Total faculty	102

SURVEY SAYS...

Diverse opinions accepted in classrooms, Great library staff, Abundant externship/internship/clerkship opportunities

STUDENTS

Enrollment of law school	678
% male/female	55/45
% from out-of-state	15
% part-time	30
% underrepresented minority	20
% international	3
# of countries represented	6
Average age of entering class	27

ACADEMICS

Academic Experience Rating	96
Profs interesting rating	92
Profs accessible rating	81
Hours of study per day	3.32

Academic Specialties

Civil Procedure, Commercial, Corporation Securities, Criminal, Environmental, Human Rights, International, Taxation, Intellectual Property

Combined Degrees Offered

JD/MBA, 4 years; JD/MBA/MHA, 4 years; JD/MPA (Masters in Public Administration), 4 years; JD/MA Philosophy, 4 years: JD/MCRP, 4 years; JD/MHA, 4 years; JD/MSHA, 4 years; JD/MPA (Master of Professional Accounting), 4 years

Academics

According to its students, Georgia State University's College of Law offers "a top-quality law school education without the aggressive environment." Of particular note is the school's "top-notch part-time program full of talented students." "GSU COL offers an incredible value to students—strong academic reputation with a low cost of attendance," says a 2L. "Tuition is unbelievable," adds a 1L. "[With] only about $10,000 a year for a very strong education, you can graduate with minimal debt, enabling you to begin a law career of your choice." The "amazing" professors are "diverse and open-minded." "Impressively, professors believe in the program and voluntarily teach evening classes," says a 2L. "I am challenged every day by brilliant professors who make me think in ways I never thought possible," explains a 1L. Most students find that the administration is "very responsive" and committed to ensuring quality instruction and improving academic instruction." Others students note, "They are always willing to go the extra mile and show concern for the success of their students."

Students appreciate GSU COL's "flexible class hours," particularly those involved in the very popular part-time program. Some feel that, due to this program, there is "a weighting toward evening classes" and that those evening classes are "where the best adjuncts teach." That said, others believe the "emphasis on the part-time program is a bit overstated." "It's available and great, but the full-time day classes are on par with any you will find," says a 3L. Regardless of which program students partake in, the "effective" courses offered are roundly praised. "The health law program is dynamic and first-rate," says a 2L. "Charity Scott is a legend in this city and any future health care attorney would be lucky to take a class with her." "The school is not afraid to try new ideas," adds another 2L. "I've taken 'Law and the Internet,' which is all about legal issues and the online community," says one student, and another tells us, "I'm now in a new non-traditional class that combines Wills, Trusts, Estates, and Taxes, in which the students form their own law firms and actually prepare all of the documents as if in the real-world."

By and large, students are very happy with their decision to attend GSU COL. However, when it comes to the school's Career Services Office, opinions have some believing "they could do a better job." Despite this, "the access to the Atlanta legal community" that GSU's location offers goes a long way in making up for any career office shortcomings. "I have clerked for a year with a Superior Court judge, worked for a professor as a GRA, competed in a National Moot Court competition, become president of numerous societies, and have a job lined up after graduation," says a 3L.

With a prime spot in downtown Atlanta, GSU's location allows students to "walk to the 11th Circuit, Supreme Court, and Northern District of Georgia courthouses." On campus, the law school's buildings aren't quite as appreciated as the university's metropolitan location. "The technology available in the classrooms and libraries [is] high quality, but the classrooms themselves are not," says a 1L. "The current law school is old, and was never meant to be used for anything aside from administrative purposes." However, plans are in place for a new—and "much more aesthetically pleasing"—building. "We are all looking forward to breaking ground on the new law school in 2012, because a new building will give the professors and students more opportunities to show just how amazing the school really is!" says a 2L.

Dr. Cheryl Jester-George, Director of Admissions

P.O. Box 4049, Atlanta, GA 30302-4049

Tel: 404-413-9200 Fax: 404-413-9203

E-Mail: admissions@gsulaw.gsu.edu • Website: law.gsu.edu

Life

Thanks to GSU COL's non-traditional student population, "The school [has] a more diverse student body than most other schools" since "the introduction of older students with more work experience adds a great deal to the classroom experience." While "the part-time (evening) students work well together," among full-time students, "the competition is still severe," though it is "not as cutthroat as it is at other law schools." Students attribute this "to the evening students being older, with full-time jobs." "The younger students tend to be more social with one another," explains a 2L. "The older students, who come from the working world, are almost entirely focused on school." A 3L gives a more specific breakdown: "First year is difficult and competitive. However, the second and third years are much more cooperative and fun. Students begin to help each other out in terms of outlines, readings, etc." Regardless of whether students are part of the part-time or full-time programs, all agree that their "fellow classmates have been the best thing about law school—they're a great bunch of people."

"On the social side, there is a substantial group of part-time students that get together monthly on an ad-hoc basis, purely for social time, usually with spouses or significant others," says a 2L. "I was pleasantly surprised." Others find that the urban campus has a negative effect on socializing. "So many people are spread out all over the city…that no one stays around to socialize after class" says a 1L. "If you just go to class and go home I think you will miss out on the social life," says a 2L. "If you make an effort to meet people then it is easy to make friends."

Getting In

Recently admitted students at Georgia State University College of Law have median GPAs of 3.48 and LSAT scores of 160. Though 90 percent of GSU COL students are in-state residents, the admissions committee "considers each student's credentials regardless of residence."

Clinical program required	No
Legal writing course requirement	Yes
Legal methods course requirement	No
Legal research course requirement	Yes
Moot court requirement	No
Public interest law requirement	No

ADMISSIONS

Selectivity Rating	97
# applications received	2,731
% applicants accepted	16
% acceptees attending	50
Median LSAT	159
LSAT Range (25th to 75th percentile)	158–162
Median undergrad GPA	3.4
Application fee	$50
Regular application deadline	3/15
Transfer students accepted	Yes
Evening division offered	Yes
Part-time accepted	Yes
CAS accepted	Yes

FINANCIAL FACTS

Annual tuition (in-state out-of-state)	$12,528/$32,592
Books and supplies	$2,000
Fees	$1,121
Financial aid application deadline	4/1
% first-year students receiving some sort of aid	81
% all students receiving some sort of aid	78
% of aid that is merit based	12
% receiving scholarships	7
Average grant	$5,051
Average loan	$19,497
Average total aid package	$20,500
Average debt	$39,246

EMPLOYMENT INFORMATION

Career Rating	95	State for bar exam	GA
Total 2012 JD Grads	186	Pass rate for first-time bar	91
% for whom you have useable information	98	**Prominent Alumni**	
% grads employed nine months out	92	Ronald J. Freeman, Founding Partner at Johnson and Freeman; Honorable Cynthia J. Becker, Judge, Superior Court of Georgia, Stone Mountain Judicial Curcuit; Lynne R. O'Brien, Director of Corporate Real Estate, the Coca Cola Company.	
Median starting salary	$73,962		
% job accepting grads providing useable salary information	66		
# employed full-time	157		
# employed part-time	17	**Grads Employed by Field (%)**	
# employed bar required	139	Academic (2)	
# employed JD preferred	22	Business/Industry (22)	
# employed professional/other	12	Government (12)	
# employed non-professional	1	Judicial Clerkship (4)	
# pursuing advanced degree	1	Military (2)	
# unemployed and seeking employment	21	Private Practice (53)	
# not seeking employment	3	Public Interest (6)	
% grads employed by school	0		

GONZAGA UNIVERSITY
SCHOOL OF LAW

INSTITUTIONAL INFORMATION

Public/private	Private
Affiliation	Roman Catholic
Student-faculty ratio	16:1
% faculty part-time	45
% faculty female	40
% faculty underrepresented minority	7
Total faculty	58

SURVEY SAYS...

Great research resources, Great library staff, Beautiful campus

STUDENTS

Enrollment of law school	460
% male/female	54/46
% from out-of-state	59
% part-time	0
% underrepresented minority	11
% international	1
# of countries represented	2
Average age of entering class	26

ACADEMICS

Academic Experience Rating	**68**
Profs interesting rating	78
Profs accessible rating	87
Hours of study per day	3.84

Combined Degrees Offered
JD/MBA, JD/MAcc, JD/MSW, 3–4 years

Academics

"Smaller classes, smaller community, close knit school identity." Much at Gonzaga University, a small Jesuit school in Spokane, Washington, is couched in terms of size, but size does not define the school. With a "very accessible" administration, an "amazing" classroom environment, and "intellectual property professors who are experts in their field," Gonzaga's impact on students is larger than its size would suggest. Perhaps that's because its size affords students a chance to work closely with administrators and instructors alike. "Communication between faculty and students is pretty good," students note, with leadership that is "very accessible and approachable but respectable." The same is said about the "great" professors here. "All seem qualified, engaging, and effective instructors," a group who "come from excellent schools from around the country and have many years of professional experience."

Technology and access to information is paramount at Gonzaga. The "top notch" facilities and "incredibly helpful library assistants" make research a breeze. "There is a concerted effort to familiarize students with every online resource that is available (as well as) with information in more traditional formats." In addition, "the library and staff work very hard to ensure students have access to the most relevant and up to date materials." This works hand-in-hand with the accolades the legal research and writing program receives. This four-semester program, with an optional fifth semester, gives students "an ability to research better than most and have experience drafting multiple legal memorandums, motions to the court, and appellate briefs."

The new required skills labs during 1L year "need drastic improvements," due in part to an inconsistent approach between professors, but this is balanced by the two-year LRW program, "which really helps a student compete for hard to get internships and compete with bigger schools like U.W." The idea is to give students practical, hands-on experience that will allow them to succeed in the real world. The school also has "an excellent mentorship program that they do not force the students to participate in even though it is an excellent opportunity." In addition, "the clinic and externship requirements are great. They require real world experience so you are practice ready when you graduate." Overall, the "wonderful facilities, faculty that cares about the students, and very helpful professional development office" make Gonzaga stand taller than its size would seem to allow.

Life

Comfortable and inviting, the "collegial, friendly, laid back atmosphere" of Gonzaga "is definitely a plus." The "small, close-knit law school environment" fits well with the "modern and pleasant" facilities and "beautiful" building. "They could have made it a little bigger to allow for more extracurricular use and perhaps a relaxation lounge area, but it has been a great place to spend the last three years." In some ways, the easygoing atmosphere is designed to offer balance to the "difficult" classes. As one student notes, "The law school experience is challenging enough without having to deal with difficult people and difficult conditions."

SUSAN LEE, DIRECTOR OF ADMISSIONS
P.O. BOX 3528, 721 N. CINCINNATI STREET, SPOKANE, WA 99220-3528
TEL: 800-793-1710 FAX: 509-313-3697
E-MAIL: ADMISSIONS@LAWSCHOOL.GONZAGA.EDU • WEBSITE: WWW.LAW.GONZAGA.EDU

That said, "there is a glaring lack of diversity at the school." As a Jesuit school, a certain conservative atmosphere comes as no surprise, but some students complain about an "overall sense of intolerance" in some areas. "While I recognize that it is a Jesuit Catholic school," one student said, "this is counter to the school's mission of tolerance and respect for all." Those who do fit into the atmosphere here, though—and most do—find that "students are encouraged to work together and have good relations with each other." Indeed, "it is easy to standout, get personalized attention, and get involved at Gonzaga Law." This kind of camaraderie is welcome, since many students complain that Spokane is a "boring" town. Students must often create their own distractions, which tend to focus on outdoor activities like biking, rock climbing, and more. Thankfully, Glacier National Park, Banff, Seattle, Northern Idaho, and lower British Columbia are all within a few hours, making weekend getaways varied and easily accessible.

Getting In

Among admitted students at the 25th percentile, Gonzaga's students have LSAT scores in the range of 153 and GPAs hovering around 3.0. Meanwhile, admitted students at the 75th percentile have LSAT scores of about 157 and GPAs of roughly 3.6.

Clinical program required	Yes
Legal writing course requirement	Yes
Legal methods course requirement	No
Legal research course requirement	Yes
Moot court requirement	No
Public interest law requirement	Yes

ADMISSIONS

Selectivity Rating	71
# applications received	1,145
% applicants accepted	63
% acceptees attending	18
Average LSAT	155
Median LSAT	155
LSAT Range (25th to 75th percentile)	153–157
Average undergrad GPA	3.26
Median undergrad GPA	3.27
Application fee	$50
Regular application deadline	4/15
Early application deadline	2/1
Transfer students accepted	Yes
Evening division offered	No
Part-time accepted	No
CAS accepted	Yes

FINANCIAL FACTS

Annual tuition	$35,310
Books and supplies	$1,030
Fees	$150
Room & Board	$11,359
Financial aid application deadline	2/1
% first-year students receiving some sort of aid	100
% all students receiving some sort of aid	98
% of aid that is merit based	22
% receiving scholarships	80
Average grant	$13,500
Average loan	$38,573
Average total aid package	$52,073
Average debt	$102,316

EMPLOYMENT INFORMATION

Career Rating	74	**Prominent Alumni**
Total 2012 JD Grads	166	Christine Gregoire, Governor, State of
% grads employed nine months out	81	Washington, former; Barbara Madsen,
Median starting salary	$46,700	Chief Justice, Washington Supreme Court;
# employed full-time	123	Mike McGrath, Chief Justice, Montana
# employed part-time	10	Supreme Court.
# employed bar required	92	**Grads Employed by Field (%)**
# employed JD preferred	30	Academic (2)
# employed professional/other	4	Business/Industry (25)
# employed non-professional	7	Government (7)
# pursuing advanced degree	5	Judicial Clerkship (10)
# unemployed and seeking employment	22	Private Practice (34)
# not seeking employment	4	Public Interest (3)
% grads employed by school	0	
State for bar exam	WA, UT, OR, AZ, CA	
Pass rate for first-time bar	73.9	

HAMLINE UNIVERSITY
SCHOOL OF LAW

INSTITUTIONAL INFORMATION

Public/private	Private
Student-faculty ratio	15:1
% faculty part-time	0
% faculty female	52
% faculty underrepresented minority	12
Total faculty	35

SURVEY SAYS...

Diverse opinions accepted in class-rooms, Great research resources, Great library staff

STUDENTS

Enrollment of law school	536
% male/female	46/54
% part-time	29
% underrepresented minority	10
% international	3
Average age of entering class	28

ACADEMICS

Academic Experience Rating	**72**
Profs interesting rating	81
Profs accessible rating	81
Hours of study per day	4.04

Academic Specialties
Commercial, Criminal, Government Services, International, Labor, Property, Intellectual Property

Advanced Degrees Offered
JD, 3 years; LLM for international lawyers, 1 year; Masters in the Study of Law, 1 year

Combined Degrees Offered
JD/MAPA (Masters of Public Administration), 4 years; JD/MANM (Masters-Nonprofit Mgmt), 4 years; JD/MAOL (Masters of Arts in Organizational Leadership), 4 years; JD/MBA, 4 years; JD/MFA (Master of Fine Arts Creative Writing)

Academics

In addition to the traditional full-time program, the excellent and "extremely under-rated" Hamline University School of Law in Minnesota's Twin Cities offers a unique part-time, four-year weekend program that "truly creates flexibility for people who want to keep their present job." "Hamline takes a practical approach to legal education that has...a regional reputation for creating graduates who are strong legal writers and are ready to work Day One," explains a 2L. "Hamline graduates end up being the attorneys who like getting their hands dirty and who are probably the most realistic and practical of the law school [graduates] in the area." There are eleven clinics and twelve specialized areas of focus on offer. Hamline does health law "exceptionally well," but the crown jewel is the Dispute Resolution Institute, where students learn the art of the deal. Other perks include an Academic Success Program, which offers structured study groups, workshops, and one-on-one tutoring for free. Study abroad options include programs in Hungary, Israel, and Norway. According to many students, "The writing program is also fantastic." Not everyone loves it, though. "It feels really self-taught," grouses a 1L.

Classes at Hamline are usually conducted in "a semi-Socratic atmosphere." "The majority of professors use the Socratic Method or some sort of system that includes calling on unsuspecting students, but not in a bad way," relates a 3L. Students have very few negative comments about the faculty. "The professors are great." They are "outstanding educators who are passionate about their work," and they "provide a diverse range of expertise and experiences." Once class is over, profs are "highly accessible outside of the classroom" and "individual attention" is plentiful if you seek it out. Some students love the top brass as well. "The administration keeps everything running very smoothly," says a 1L, "such that I don't need to waste any of my time untangling messes." "The administration is strongly focused on the law school experience from start to graduation," emphasizing "bar passage, and career development," adds a 2L. Other students complain that management is "unwilling to respond to student problems with course registration or student complaints."

According to students, "The appearance of the law school building is lackluster." "The interior of the building is comfortable but could be updated." "Some new carpet here and there wouldn't be a bad thing." However, "The classrooms are all up-to-date with the latest technology, including plug-ins for your laptop." Opinions regarding Career Services are decidedly mixed. Critics charge that the staff "hardly does anything worthwhile to help students with their job searches or career issues." Other students counter that Career Services is "incredibly helpful, open, and dedicated to helping students find jobs, internships, and develop skills of professionalism," as well as careers after graduation. A strong alumni network also helps in this regard. "Hamline alumni have been very helpful in connecting me with other attorneys and notifying me when they hear of opportunities that [they] know I am interest[ed] in," notes a 2L.

Robin Ingli, Director of Admissions
1536 Hewitt Avenue, St. Paul, MN 55104-1284
Tel: 800-388-3688 Fax: 651-523-3064
E-Mail: lawadm@gw.hamline.edu • Website: www.hamline.edu/law

Life

A "community atmosphere" is pervasive at Hamline, though the student body is really composed of two very different subgroups. The younger students in the full-time day program here are "competitive but not cutthroat." "Generally, the students are friendly toward each other and are willing to help each other out," relates a 2L. "There are a few zealots, but they tend to identify themselves quickly so you know who to avoid." "I am very comfortable providing my classmates with help and frequently receive assistance in return," adds a 1L. Meanwhile, students in the part-time, weekend program say their program has its own "very special, very communal essence." "The weekend program students have a wealth of experience and are extremely welcoming," explains a 1L. "Law school is merely one important component in our lives."

Socially, "There are cliques and 'in' groups," but "common courtesy" and Midwestern affability is ubiquitous. Intramural sports are pretty popular. There are over two dozen clubs and organizations. The location provides plenty of options for culture and nightlife as well. "The campus is within walking distance of several great ethnic restaurants" and bar review on Thursday nights "at different bars in the Twin Cities area" is pretty well attended.

Getting In

Enrolled full-time students at the 25th percentile have LSAT scores of about 148 and GPAs near 3.2. Enrolled students at the 75th percentile have LSAT scores close to around 156 and GPAs near 3.6.

Clinical program required	No
Legal writing course requirement	Yes
Legal methods course requirement	Yes
Legal research course requirement	Yes
Moot court requirement	No
Public interest law requirement	Yes

ADMISSIONS

Selectivity Rating	71
# applications received	966
% applicants accepted	61
% acceptees attending	21
Average LSAT	153
Median LSAT	153
LSAT Range (25th to 75th percentile)	148–156
Average undergrad GPA	3.33
Median undergrad GPA	3.38
Application fee	$35
Regular application deadline	
Transfer students accepted	Yes
Evening division offered	Yes
Part-time accepted	Yes
CAS accepted	Yes

FINANCIAL FACTS

Annual tuition	$36,066
Books and supplies	
Fees	$230
Room & Board (on/off campus)	$12,786/$20,339
Financial aid application deadline	4/1
% first-year students receiving some sort of aid	97
% all students receiving some sort of aid	96
% receiving scholarships	63
Average grant	$19,126
Average loan	$34,337
Average total aid package	$43,933
Average debt	$104,647

EMPLOYMENT INFORMATION

Career Rating	88	Grads Employed by Field (%)	
Total 2012 JD Grads	190	Academic	(2)
% grads employed nine months out	91	Business/Industry	(36)
Median starting salary	$55,000	Government	(8)
# employed full-time	157	Judicial Clerkship	(10)
# employed part-time	14	Military	(1)
# employed bar required	92	Private Practice	(26)
# employed JD preferred	63	Public Interest	(5)
# employed professional/other	10		
# employed non-professional	5		
# pursuing advanced degree	2		
# unemployed and seeking employment	7		
# not seeking employment	5		
% grads employed by school	0		
State for bar exam	MN, WI, IL, NY, CA		
Pass rate for first-time bar	87.7		

HARVARD UNIVERSITY
HARVARD LAW SCHOOL

INSTITUTIONAL INFORMATION

Public/private	Private
Student-faculty ratio	11:1
% faculty female	19
% faculty underrepresented minority	14
Total faculty	108

SURVEY SAYS...

Great research resources, Great library staff, Abundant externship/ internship/clerkship opportunities

STUDENTS

Enrollment of law school	1,727
% male/female	53/47
% part-time	0
% underrepresented minority	32
% international	7
# of countries represented	78
Average age of entering class	24

ACADEMICS

Academic Experience Rating	**94**
Profs interesting rating	79
Profs accessible rating	67
Hours of study per day	3.62

Academic Specialties

Civil Procedure, Commercial, Constitutional, Corporation Securities, Criminal, Environmental, Government Services, Human Rights, International, Labor, Legal History, Legal Philosophy, Property, Taxation, Intellectual Property

Advanced Degrees Offered

LLM (Master of Laws), 1 year; SJD (Doctor of Judicial Science (SJD)— course work, exam, and dissertation.

Combined Degrees Offered

JD/MBA, JD/MPP, JD/MPA/ID, JD/ Ph.D., JD/MPH, JD/MUP, JD/MALD, JD/LLM (with Cambridge University)

Academics

Harvard Law School—perhaps you've heard of it?—is like the land of Oz for aspiring lawyers, where "anything you want exists." Indeed, the school has plenty of funding for student scholarships, interests, and activities, and the opportunities for "public service, research and publication, faculty mentor relationships, editorial, moot court, or legal aid experience, and international study and service options are endless." The "you name it, it's on the menu" mentality is definitely present for most students, and humility can (understandably) be a bit short in supply. "Harvard is Harvard. This is...simply a reinforcing circle of virtue, i.e., you get brilliant professors, amazing students, interesting courses, great opportunities, attracting brilliant professors and amazing students, etc."

The "abundance of resources" available here lends itself to excellent support for public interest law, including a formidable public interest advising group, who "do a lot to build the community." "Though there's a lot of pressure to take a firm job, the counselors at [the public interest office] do a heck of a job fighting back. They'll chase you down in the hall and tell you it's time to start applying for fellowships, clerkships, and jobs," says a student. "When employers start cutting their recruiting classes, the last place they cut is HLS," says another. Everyone agrees that the economy has taken its toll, though—the ice skating rink closed—and "While the Harvard name will open doors, students still have to put in work and make sure that they are putting their best foot forward."

Though each HLS class is hefty in size, it actually creates an "atmosphere of conversation and collaboration." "Because our class is so big, there is always a critical mass for any interest, activity, or cause students want to pursue," says a 2L. "I was a little concerned entering this school that its size would be intimidating or overwhelming, but in fact I've found that its size is one of its greatest strengths," agrees a 1L.

As expected, the courses offered are top-notch, with "a lot of very random options" to diversify the curriculum, though many students wish there was "more emphasis on practical lawyering skills," not to mention an alternative to the "arcane and mysterious" registration system. Though in recent years, a sizeable portion of the faculty has "fled to Washington, D.C., to work on Change," students are "still terribly spoiled to have as many wonderful professors as we do." According to a student, "O[bama] left us a couple of our best profs," and plenty of "superstar" professors remain at Harvard, and "everyone is extremely accomplished and an expert in his/her field." "Not everyone is a natural teacher," but "Most of them are approachable and have interesting insights into the law (and many other areas)." There are also many research assistant and student writing opportunities offered.

The administration is "very flexible and willing to work with students as circumstances arise," and the school "really strives to please students, even in tough economic times." Classroom buildings are "often ugly, but all are nicely equipped and in good condition," research facilities "could not be better," and the library—the largest law library in the world, by the way—is "huge and lovely, with a staggering quantity of books." In other words, don't come to this corner of Boston if you're looking for the entire package of "sunshine, butterflies and architectural triumphs"—"There are reasons to come here; aesthetic bliss is not one of them."

JESSICA SOBAN, ASSISTANT DEAN AND CHIEF ADMISSIONS OFFICER
1515 MASSACHUSETTS AVENUE, CAMBRIDGE, MA 02138
TEL: 617-495-3109
E-MAIL: JDADMISS@LAW.HARVARD.EDU • WEBSITE: WWW.LAW.HARVARD.EDU

Life

There is most definitely "a lot of underlying stress and tension" at HLS, but "It's never about beating your classmates." While Harvard isn't the same cutthroat school of the Paper Chase era, "There are still quite a few gunners"; however, once you hit your second year, "Everyone has relaxed a bit and gotten comfortable with their law school identities."

It's "very easy to find a great group of friends" because people are "generally fun and good-humored (in addition to being extremely smart and accomplished)." There is a Bar Review every week, and "The student government and other organizations host happy hours and other social events." While the size of the school means that students "wouldn't say the school as a whole has a strong general sense of community," it does provide a larger potential pool for friends, and students "are able to find a sense of community by joining various organizations." Be careful—students often "overwhelm themselves with extracurricular activities."

Students tend to be "quite liberal," but "One of the biggest surprises at HLS is how acceptable it is to be a conservative," as students here "tend to be tolerant and accepting of people despite their gender, race, religion, ethnicity, or sexual orientation." "It's very cooperative—there's a definite feeling of 'we're all in this together,'" says a 1L.

Getting In

When students arrive at law school to hear the dean say, "The competition is over. You've won," it's safe to say that getting in wasn't what most would call easy. Admitted students at the 25th percentile have LSAT scores of 171 and GPAs of about 3.78. Admitted students at the 75th percentile have LSAT scores of 176 and GPAs of about 3.96. (Note that Harvard looks at all LSAT scores in their contexts.) The school also aggressively seeks applicants from underrepresented minority groups.

Clinical program required	No
Legal writing course requirement	Yes
Legal methods course requirement	Yes
Legal research course requirement	Yes
Moot court requirement	Yes
Public interest law requirement	Yes

ADMISSIONS

Selectivity Rating	**99**
# applications received	5,388
% applicants accepted	16
% acceptees attending	68
Median LSAT	173
LSAT Range (25th to 75th percentile)	170–175
Median undergrad GPA	3.88
Application fee	$85
Regular application deadline	2/1
Transfer students accepted	Yes
Evening division offered	No
Part-time accepted	No
CAS accepted	Yes

FINANCIAL FACTS

Annual tuition	$49,950
Books and supplies	$3,250
Fees	$3,098
Room & Board	$19,502
% first-year students receiving some sort of aid	72
% all students receiving some sort of aid	83
% of aid that is merit based	0
% receiving scholarships	46
Average grant	$21,559
Average loan	$48,673
Average total aid package	$57,842
Average debt	$124,312

EMPLOYMENT INFORMATION

Career Rating	99	Prominent Alumni
Total 2012 JD Grads	590	Barack H. Obama, President of the United States
% for whom you have useable information	100	**Grads Employed by Field (%)**
% grads employed nine months out	96	Academic (2)
Median starting salary	$160,000	Business/Industry (5)
# employed full-time	563	Government (4)
# employed part-time	5	Judicial Clerkship (22)
# employed bar required	516	Military (1)
# employed JD preferred	43	Private Practice (56)
# employed professional/other	7	Public Interest (7)
# employed non-professional	1	
# pursuing advanced degree	6	
# unemployed and seeking employment	14	
# not seeking employment	1	
% grads employed by school	3	
State for bar exam	NY, MA, PA, MD, CT	
Pass rate for first-time bar	96.9	

HOFSTRA UNIVERSITY
MAURICE A. DEANE SCHOOL OF LAW

INSTITUTIONAL INFORMATION

Public/private	Private
Affiliation	No Affiliation
Student-faculty ratio	15:1
% faculty part-time	39
% faculty female	33
% faculty underrepresented minority	11
Total faculty	95

SURVEY SAYS...
Diverse opinons accepted in classrooms

STUDENTS

Enrollment of law school	975
% male/female	55/45
% part-time	3
% underrepresented minority	36
% international	5
# of countries represented	15
Average age of entering class	24

ACADEMICS

Academic Experience Rating	**68**
Profs interesting rating	76
Profs accessible rating	72
Hours of study per day	3.89

Academic Specialties
Civil Procedure, Commercial, Constitutional, Corporation Securities, Criminal, Environmental, Human Rights, International, Labor, Property, Taxation, Intellectual Property

Advanced Degrees Offered
JD: full-time, 3 years, part-time, 4 years; LLM: full-time, 1 year, part-time, 2 years, in the following areas: Family Law and American Legal Studies (for foreign lawyers)

Combined Degrees Offered
JD/MBA: full-time, 4 years

Academics

There is a "professional, collaborative environment" at Hofstra Law, where the school's students are huge fans of the "outstanding" administration, who, in many cases, "are willing to bend over backwards to accommodate you." "The administration is great because they are very accessible and interested in our success as lawyers and as students," says a 1L. The Career Center here is similarly involved, "not only [in] our futures, but also in helping alumni find new jobs." Right from the first week of class, Hofstra Law is big on helping students to network with attorneys and alumni and putting a realistic perspective on the possibilities out there (Note: The school does rank students within classes.), though a few students do lament the school's rather intense focus on work in the public sector, and far more than a few bemoan the lack of "quality internships." "I've had the opportunity to learn about how much work and how many different areas of law you can practice...now I actually know what I can do with a JD," says a first-year law student. Though not every single person leaves a satisfied customer, the school certainly shows a "desire to improve," and all who go here pretty much generally agree, "If you are proactive and work hard, Hofstra will work hard for you as well."

Its location close to New York City helps the school to attract "some legendary professors at the top of their fields," most of whom are "readily available outside of class, and...seem to genuinely care about the students' success." "Not a single one stands on ceremony," says a student. Most "do not implement harsh variations of the Socratic Method"; they have "real-world experience that they bring to their lectures" and use "practical methods that help students to try [to] learn, rather than simply memorize the material." Hofstra Law's focus on practical and legal writing skills "never ceases to pay off during internships/clerkships." "I thought that Hofstra would not offer the same kind of academic experience as those in the top schools. I was very pleasantly surprised," says a student. "They are constantly trying to...help develop the students into lawyers."

Some bigger picture gripes include that the school recently "terminated the whole night program," and that tuition is not easy on the wallet. "Lower tuition please. I don't have a money tree in my backyard," begs a 1L. Classrooms "are adequate for the purpose they serve"; though the technology is up-to-date (lectures are webcast, Wi-Fi is readily available), the facilities as a whole could use a face-lift. Also, as one weary student puts it, "Not to beat a dead horse, but parking is always an issue."

Life

First-year students have all their classes with the same section, so "there is a sense that we are all getting through together." This instantly creates a nice community for incoming students, who also appreciate their access to 2Ls and 3Ls that "are more than happy to help with information about classes and professors." "There is some small amount of competition, but that is what keeps us on our toes. It shouldn't be frowned upon," says a student. Students are encouraged to work in study groups (and the overwhelming majority do), and "there is a strong desire to help others understand"; students "get lots of support from...fellow law school brothers and sisters." "We actually like one another!" says a 1L.

JOHN CHALMERS, ASSOCIATE DEAN FOR ENROLLMENT MANAGEMENT
108 HOFSTRA UNIVERSITY, HEMPSTEAD, NY 11549
TEL: 516-463-5916 FAX: 516-463-6264
E-MAIL: LAWADMISSIONS@HOFSTRA.EDU • WEBSITE: LAW.HOFSTRA.EDU

While the school's location on the edge of the somewhat tucked-away neighborhood of Hempstead is far from ideal, "Security on campus is very efficient." Long Island is "a little boring," but "there is ample opportunity for social activities," as the law school itself has many different student organizations, "so it's easy to find a group of people you can relate to and who have interest[s] in common with you." Commuting to and from New York City, for school or for fun, is also an option. Law students here do tend to be a bit "stressed out," but the school as a whole still remains a "very friendly environment that the students really enjoy." It is a "laid-back atmosphere, [where students are] serious about work but not competitive."

Getting In

Hofstra Law is not the toughest school to get into, but it's not a cakewalk, either. As with almost every school, there's no set minimum score required for admission here, but the entering class of 2010 had LSAT scores of 156 and a GPA of 3.17 at the 25th percentile, and an LSAT score of 160 and GPA of 3.69 at the 75th percentile.

Clinical program required	No
Legal writing course requirement	Yes
Legal methods course requirement	Yes
Legal research course requirement	Yes
Moot court requirement	No
Public interest law requirement	No

ADMISSIONS

Selectivity Rating	77
# applications received	3,892
% applicants accepted	49
% acceptees attending	17
Average LSAT	157
Median LSAT	157
LSAT Range (25th to 75th percentile)	153–159
Average undergrad GPA	3.23
Median undergrad GPA	3.26
Application fee	$0
Regular application deadline	4/15
Early application deadline	11/15
Early application notification	12/15
Transfer students accepted	Yes
Evening division offered	No
Part-time accepted	Yes
CAS accepted	Yes

FINANCIAL FACTS

Annual tuition	$47,034
Books and supplies	$1,400
Fees	$626
Room & Board (on/off campus)	$15,729/$16,760
Financial aid application deadline	4/1
% first-year students receiving some sort of aid	90
% all students receiving some sort of aid	90
% of aid that is merit based	94
% receiving scholarships	62
Average grant	$16,000
Average loan	$46,220
Average total aid package	$48,000
Average debt	$129,461

EMPLOYMENT INFORMATION

Career Rating	80	
Total 2012 JD Grads	363	
% for whom you have useable information	97	
% grads employed nine months out	78	
Median starting salary	$55,000	
% job accepting grads providing useable salary information	39	
# employed full-time	236	
# employed part-time	46	
# employed bar required	218	
# employed JD preferred	34	
# employed professional/other	20	
# employed non-professional	10	
# pursuing advanced degree	7	
# unemployed and seeking employment	61	
# not seeking employment	2	
% grads employed by school	5	
State for bar exam	NY	
Pass rate for first-time bar	82.1	

Prominent Alumni
Maurice A. Deane, President, Bama Equities, Inc.; Hon. Maryanne Trump Barry, Judge, US Court of Appeals for the Third Circuit; Hon. David A. Paterson, Former Governor of New York; Randy L. Levine, President, New York Yankees.

Grads Employed by Field (%)
Academic (4)
Business/Industry (18)
Government (13)
Judicial Clerkship (4)
Private Practice (56)
Public Interest (5)

ILLINOIS INSTITUTE OF TECHNOLOGY
CHICAGO-KENT COLLEGE OF LAW

INSTITUTIONAL INFORMATION

Public/private	Private
Affiliation	No Affiliation
Student-faculty ratio	11:1
% faculty part-time	62
% faculty female	33
% faculty underrepresented minority	10
Total faculty	185

SURVEY SAYS...
Diverse opinions accepted in classrooms, Great library staff, Students love Chicago, IL

STUDENTS

Enrollment of law school	903
% male/female	53/47
% from out-of-state	46
% part-time	18
% underrepresented minority	21
% international	4
# of countries represented	26
Average age of entering class	25

ACADEMICS

Academic Experience Rating	79
Profs interesting rating	79
Profs accessible rating	76
Hours of study per day	2.77

Academic Specialties
Criminal, Environmental, International, Labor, Intellectual Property

Advanced Degrees Offered
JD, 3 years full-time, 4 years part-time; LLM, 2–8 semesters.

Combined Degrees Offered
JD/MBA, 3.5–5 years; JD/LLM, 4–5 years; JD/MS in Finance, 4–5 years; JD/MPA, 3.5–5 years; JD/MS in Environmental Management & Sustainability, 3.5–5 years; JD/Master of Public Health, 3.5 years

Academics

If you're looking to "feel both challenged and encouraged to learn" rather than "beaten down by the stereotypical combination of sadistic professors and hyper-competitive classmates," then you might want to try the Chicago-Kent College of Law, which works to create a scholarly community under the auspices of a science and engineering heavyweight. Placed "just high enough in the rankings to attract talented students who aren't arrogant, but not too high so that the professors are attracted for research rather than teaching," the school makes it clear up front that the experience "will be competitive," while also stressing "how important it is to not dwell on grades and rank even though they're important."

Known for its "intense" and "well-recognized" legal writing program (one of the few three-year programs in the country), students at Chicago-Kent must endure "several hellish weeks each semester" so they can say, "The memo [I] did in the first three weeks of school is the equivalent of another school's 1L final project." "Every attorney I've worked with in the past three years has commented on the strength of my legal writing skills," boasts one third-year student. Other tough aspects of the school's curriculum include its grading curve, though a more lenient curve has been adopted beginning in fall 2013. Many also cite the Intellectual Property Program and the variety of in-house clinics (in which students work with actual clients for credit) as strengths.

As one would expect judging from its parent institution, Chicago-Kent's "top-notch" classrooms are "enabled with the best educational technology," including myriad outlets, and the entire campus is blanketed with wireless Internet (some even claim the technology "outranks" the institute itself). The comprehensive library provides plenty of study space, and is run by a "knowledgeable" staff that is "willing to assist you with any issues." Chicago-Kent's location in the West Loop "is crucial to practical experience" and "maximizes chances for great externships," though summer jobs "aren't all that easy to come by with the competition of Northwestern, University of Chicago, U of I, and Michigan so close by."

Despite a large contingent of part-time faculty in the upper-level courses, professors at Chicago-Kent are "passionately engaged in the subject matter" and "totally committed to the students as well as to their research." They "work hard to encourage you and support you outside of the classroom" and are particularly good at "treating the students as adults and expecting them to perform at a higher level," according to a first-year student. Though they're not without complaints, most here say that the administration is "very accommodating [of] students' needs" and "are always quick to reply to questions." The general opinion of the Career Services Office is one of mild discontent, and a large number of students wish the school could "expand its ability to place students in the legal workplace nationwide" having noticed that most of the "prestigious" law firms only hire the top 10 percent of Chicago-Kent students. "For some reason, I say we are associated with IIT, and people outside of the legal community think I am going to truck driving school," complains a 3L. Chicago-Kent has implemented a career services policy that matches each student to a specific career counselor to address some of these issues. After three years at Chicago-Kent, one student can safely say, "Students are happy, teachers want to teach, and learning is fun, yet also difficult."

Life

Numerous clubs and organizations "for everything you can imagine" mean that "there is a constant flow of speakers and programs for students to attend that cover all areas of

NICOLE VILCHES, ASSISTANT DEAN FOR ADMISSIONS
565 WEST ADAMS STREET, CHICAGO, IL 60661
TEL: 312-906-5020 FAX: 312-906-5274
E-MAIL: ADMISSIONS@KENTLAW.IIT.EDU • WEBSITE: WWW.KENTLAW.IIT.EDU

the law." After a hard day of classes and legal writing boot camp, students look forward to the Student Bar Association's monthly "Kent Nights," for which the SBA rents out a different downtown bar for a "really great way to get noses out of books and make the student body relax with each other to have a good time." The student body at Chicago-Kent is a friendly bunch, and while there is a "subtle" competitive streak throughout the program years, most agree, "There is definitely a friendly, helpful attitude that prevails among students here," especially between the different sections of 1Ls. "I love being surrounded by individuals who allow me to have intelligent and insightful discussions about current issues or about what we are discussing in classes," says one student. However, a definite divide exists between day and evening students, with evening students complaining that most of the extracurricular activities are "pretty much unavailable to the evening students due to the timing of special events." The administration has attempted to answer these concerns with increased flexibility for scheduling and bringing evening events to Tuesday nights. While it's true that students live scattered all throughout the Chicago area, preventing some from attending certain events, others see it as a plus: "Most students will spend the better part of their day interacting with each other, instead of simply coming to class and then going home," explains a third-year student.

Getting In

Though admissions are on a rolling basis, Chicago-Kent's binding early decision program is somewhat unique in the field of law school admissions. Recently enrolled students at the 25th percentile had an LSAT score of 154 and a GPA of 3.09, while enrolled students at the 75th percentile had an LSAT score of 161 and a GPA of 3.62.

Clinical program required	No
Legal writing course requirement	Yes
Legal methods course requirement	No
Legal research course requirement	Yes
Moot court requirement	Yes
Public interest law requirement	No

ADMISSIONS

Selectivity Rating	77
# applications received	3,199
% applicants accepted	52
% acceptees attending	15
Average LSAT	158
Median LSAT	159
LSAT Range (25th to 75th percentile)	154–161
Average undergrad GPA	3.37
Median undergrad GPA	3.47
Application fee	$0
Regular application deadline	3/15
Regular notification	rolling
Early application deadline	11/1
Early application notification	12/1
Transfer students accepted	Yes
Evening division offered	Yes
Part-time accepted	Yes
CAS accepted	Yes

FINANCIAL FACTS

Annual tuition	$42,900
Books and supplies	$1,636
Fees	$1,190
Room & Board	$14,463
Financial aid application deadline	3/1
% first-year students receiving some sort of aid	95
% all students receiving some sort of aid	92
% of aid that is merit based	29
% receiving scholarships	68
Average grant	$18,135
Average loan	$38,831
Average total aid package	$45,541
Average debt	$112,405

EMPLOYMENT INFORMATION

Career Rating	75	**Prominent Alumni**
Total 2012 JD Grads	282	The Honorable Ilana Diamond Rovner, U.S.
% grads employed nine months out	83	Court of Appeals for the 7th Circuit; The
Median starting salary	$60,900	Honorable Anne Burke, Illinois Supreme
# employed full-time	212	Court; Thomas Demetrio, Partner, Corboy
# employed part-time	22	& Demetrio.
# employed bar required	188	**Grads Employed by Field (%)**
# employed JD preferred	25	Academic (2)
# employed professional/other	21	Business/Industry (16)
# employed non-professional	0	Government (5)
# pursuing advanced degree	4	Judicial Clerkship (3)
# unemployed and seeking employment	25	Private Practice (55)
# not seeking employment	7	Public Interest (2)
% grads employed by school	1	
State for bar exam	IL, CA, NY, TX, FL	
Pass rate for first-time bar		

INDIANA UNIVERSITY
MAURER SCHOOL OF LAW (BLOOMINGTON)

Academics

Students at the Indiana University Maurer School of Law enjoy "first-rate resources and education" at "an excellent value." The law school boasts no fewer than nineteen clinical programs and projects including a community legal clinic, an entrepreneurship law clinic, and an inmate legal assistance project. Externship programs include the Washington Public Interest Program, which allows 3Ls to earn credit for public interest internships with government agencies and nonprofits in Washington, D.C. Students can study in Paris, Florence, Barcelona, Beijing, Auckland, and a host of other international cities, and they can apply for summer internships in India or Brazil through the school's Center on the Global Legal Profession. An unusual 1L course in the legal profession helps students discover their strengths while they explore career options. Several interesting dual-degree programs, including a three-year JD/MBA and a bevy of specialization programs in taxation, international and comparative law, and intellectual property round out IU's "excellent" academic options.

The "extremely knowledgeable and accessible" faculty at IU "is really impressive." "When you go to class, you get the sense that your professors want to be in the class-room, and that makes engaging yourself in the material much easier," says a 2L. "There's a nice balance between professors who try to scare the pants off of you and the ones who really encourage you to take risks and push yourself, even if you turn out to be wrong." Even "boring" professors "really have a lot of important things to say." Outside the classroom, professors "participate in the law school social events" and "will go to great lengths to help students publish, research, and get placed" in jobs.

IU's administration "is genuinely concerned about students as individuals," and its "helpful and nice" Financial Aid Office "is the best in the country." Though in the past students have noted that "Career Services, while improving, has a long way to go," the Office of Career and Professional Development has since created an alternative career series, lunch-with-a-lawyer programs, and two alumni career service committees as well as expanded off campus interviews, hired new staff and hosted alumni-sponsored welcome-to-the-city events in key cities around the country. Many students tell us that the Office of Career and Professional Development "does all it can to assist students in obtaining jobs." "I think they're great," declares a 1L. "They're not going to get a job for you, but they'll do pretty much everything else." "If you are near the top of the class," "You'll have the Indy firms drooling all over you," and you won't have a problem work-ing at "any of the best firms in Chicago" "or even Washington, D.C.".

Everyone here agrees that the campus surrounding the law school is "beautiful." Classrooms once described as "uncomfortable," have been recently renovated. "The entire building has wireless Internet," and "There are electrical outlets at each seat." The gem of IU is the law library, which students claim is "without equal in the world, in part because of its staff." "With large windows that look out on the forest in the middle of campus, it's easy to forget that you're in the middle of a Big Ten school."

Life

IU's Midwestern location helps encourage a collegial attitude that frowns on aggressive competition." Students "simply do not let the abstract, competitive nature of the grading system affect their outward nature or the way they see their classmates." "If there is a more laid-back group of students at any law school in the country, I'd like to see it," chal-lenges a 2L. "Students find their groups and comfort zones relatively quickly." Smaller class sizes "contribute to some minor drama at times," but students "get to know each

FRANK MOTLEY, ASSISTANT DEAN OF ADMISSIONS
211 SOUTH INDIANA AVENUE, BLOOMINGTON, IN 47405-1001
TEL: 812-855-4765 FAX: 812-855-1967
E-MAIL: LAWADMIS@INDIANA.EDU • WEBSITE: WWW.LAW.INDIANA.EDU

other better and have a closer relationship with the faculty." "You can learn as much law as well here as at Harvard or Yale," promises a 3L. "But you will pay less, will see people being nicer to each other, and don't have to live in a grungy New England city."

The law school is "settled into a big university" "far away from the real-world" in "one of the greatest college towns in America." "The school is great for young undergraduates who appreciate a small-town environment." "Moving from a city to the boonies is still taking some getting used to," says one urbanite, "but the school offers some phenomenal cultural opportunities." There are "at least thirty ethnically diverse restaurants within a three-minute walk from the law school." Students here "work hard," but "There is great balance between the social life and the academic life." "The fitness and recreation facilities are superb," and "There are law school teams for intramurals." The Law and Drama Society "puts on a play in the school's moot court room." "The annual Women's Law Caucus Auction" is a big hit, as is an annual basketball game in IU's beloved Assembly Hall, which pits students against professors. Mostly, though, "The social environment is aimed at those who like to go out and party." "We're very social, very involved, and very fun," boasts a 2L. "The school is the focal point around which life spins, but there's always something to do, somewhere to go, someone to talk to." "There are after-hours activities sponsored by the school or a student group almost each week, and if there's nothing going on students will always congregate somewhere to have fun."

Getting In

Admitted students at the 25th percentile have LSAT scores of about 156 and GPAs hovering around 3.39. Admitted students at the 75th percentile have LSAT scores of approximately 165 and GPAs of approximately 3.85.

Clinical program required	No
Legal writing course requirement	Yes
Legal methods course requirement	No
Legal research course requirement	Yes
Moot court requirement	No
Public interest law requirement	No

ADMISSIONS

Selectivity Rating	84
# applications received	2,364
% applicants accepted	46
% acceptees attending	19
Average LSAT	161
Median LSAT	164
LSAT Range (25th to 75th percentile)	156–166
Average undergrad GPA	3.60
Median undergrad GPA	3.8
Application fee	$50
Early application deadline	11/15
Early application notification	12/15
Transfer students accepted	Yes
Evening division offered	No
Part-time accepted	No
CAS accepted	Yes

FINANCIAL FACTS

Annual tuition (in-state out-of-state)	$28,662/$46,738
Books and supplies	$1,800
Fees	$1,283
Room & Board	$13,396
Financial aid application deadline	3/10
% first-year students receiving some sort of aid	93
% all students receiving some sort of aid	93
% of aid that is merit based	46
% receiving scholarships	79
Average grant	$26,547
Average loan	$32,249
Average total aid package	$47,967
Average debt	$112,907

EMPLOYMENT INFORMATION

Career Rating	94
Total 2012 JD Grads	204
% grads employed nine months out	82
Median starting salary	$90,000
# employed full-time	159
# employed part-time	9
# employed bar required	132
# employed JD preferred	26
# employed professional/other	7
# employed non-professional	3
# pursuing advanced degree	3
# unemployed and seeking employment	12
# not seeking employment	12
% grads employed by school	3
State for bar exam	IN, IL, NY
Pass rate for first-time bar	86

Prominent Alumni
Scott Flanders, CEO, Playboy Enterprises; Lee Hamilton, Former Congressman; Kathleen O'Connor-St.Louis, VP & Gen'l Auditor Corp. Tax, Eli Lilly & Co.

Grads Employed by Field (%)
Academic (4)
Business/Industry (16)
Government (11)
Judicial Clerkship (8)
Military (2)
Private Practice (37)
Public Interest (5)

INDIANA UNIVERSITY—INDIANAPOLIS
ROBERT H. McKINNEY SCHOOL OF LAW

INSTITUTIONAL INFORMATION

Public/private	Public
Student-faculty ratio	15:1
% faculty part-time	60
% faculty female	37
% faculty underrepresented minority	10
Total faculty	143

SURVEY SAYS...

Diverse opinions accepted in classrooms, Beautiful campus, Students love Indianapolis, IN

STUDENTS

Enrollment of law school	975
% male/female	55/45
% from out-of-state	17
% part-time	35
% underrepresented minority	16
% international	3
# of countries represented	23
Average age of entering class	26

ACADEMICS

Academic Experience Rating	**83**
Profs interesting rating	80
Profs accessible rating	76
Hours of study per day	3.62

Academic Specialties

Constitutional, Criminal, Government Services, Human Rights, International, Labor, Taxation, Intellectual Property

Advanced Degrees Offered

SJD, LLM, 1 year

Combined Degrees Offered

JD/MPA, 4 years; JD/MBA, 4 years; JD/MHA, 4 years; JD/MPH, 4 years; JD/MPhil, 4 years; JD/MLS 4 years; JD/MSW, 4 years; JD/MD 6 years

Academics

Indiana University Robert H. McKinney School of Law is a relatively large school on an "urban campus" in "a great downtown location." The "lovely," spacious, and "comfortable" facility here is "a beautiful, high-tech place to learn." "Classrooms are modern and large and sport electric outlets at every seat," and "There are many places, such as the reading room, where students can go to study." Several joint-degree programs are available. There are four law reviews, six clinics, and summer study abroad programs in China and Croatia. Opportunities to specialize include intellectual property law and international law as well as a "particularly strong" health law curriculum.

The faculty as a whole is "excellent" and "engaging." They "do their best to make sure the material is as interesting as possible" and "take a very practical tack in their approach to teaching." "The atmosphere at IU Indy is such that, while the work is intense, I've never felt like not wanting to go to class," beams a 2L. "Ever." Outside of class, "Professors are accessible and students are not afraid to approach them for help on a concept or to share a joke." The two-semester legal writing program (with optional third semester) generally receives high marks. Student opinion concerning the administration is mixed. Defenders of it tell us that the top brass is student-friendly and "does a fairly good job." "The administration always tries its best to help us succeed," says a happy 2L. Detractors complain that "the administration has no idea what's going on." One complaint is that registration can be difficult for 2Ls and 3Ls. "Too many classes clumped at the same time make it difficult" to take all the courses you want (or need). A few professors are "not interested in teaching at all."

IU Indy is the lesser known of the two IU law schools (the other one is in Bloomington), but students say that attending the only law school in Indiana's state capital and commercial hub definitely has its perks. The school is close to "all of the large firms" in the city and "within blocks of city, state, and federal government offices, and courthouses." "This enables us to work at some of the state's best and largest firms throughout the school year," explains a 3L. "It also provides us with the opportunity to do externships with all of the state's major courts and organizations." "Being in downtown Indianapolis is excellent for networking opportunities with the legal community," too. Some students applaud the efforts of the "hardworking" staff in the Office of Professional Development to secure career opportunities. Other students are less than thrilled. "They don't help anyone get jobs," gripes a 3L, "and they don't respond to phone calls or e-mails, either." Also, while the school's reputation in the state is very good, "It's an uphill battle to find employment outside of Indiana."

PATRICIA KINNEY, ASSISTANT DEAN FOR ADMISSIONS
530 WEST NEW YORK STREET, INDIANAPOLIS, IN 46202-3225
TEL: 317-274-2459 FAX: 317-278-4780
E-MAIL: LAWADMIT@IUPUI.EDU • WEBSITE: INDYLAW.INDIANA.EDU

Life

Students here describe themselves as "quite friendly." "Animosity is pleasantly absent." "Students generally get along quite well with one another and are collegial in the classroom," relates a 1L. While there's "a decent amount of diversity" and IU Indy is "very welcoming environment to students of all backgrounds," a pretty vast chasm exists between the full-time day students and the part-time evening students. A large percentage of the full-timers come "straight out of undergrad" and "chose to attend Indianapolis for its proximity to firm, corporate, and political experiences." The part-time program constitutes about one-third of the student body, and it's mostly "older, nontraditional" students who already have occupations, families, and their own social lives.

IU Indy is located on the campus of Indiana University—Purdue University Indianapolis (where "parking is absolutely atrocious"). "The school's central location is used to its fullest advantage through symposiums, networking functions, alumni activities, and other gatherings where members of the Indianapolis legal community mingle with students," relates a 2L. Life beyond academics gets mixed reviews. By all accounts, Indianapolis is "a great city" with lots to see and do. Some students tell us that the school provides many social outlets. "There are a lot of activities," and you can "relive high school all over again" "with more drinking." Others give the campus "a mediocre rating for social life." "The problem is that it's a commuter school and people are coming from all over the place." "People do their work and go home." "As a result, there is not a whole lot of socializing."

Getting In

Enrolled full-time students at the 25th percentile at IU Robert H. McKinney School of Law have an average LSAT score of 157 and a GPA of about 3.51. Admissions statistics for part-time students are lower.

Clinical program required	No
Legal writing course requirement	Yes
Legal methods course requirement	Yes
Legal research course requirement	Yes
Moot court requirement	No
Public interest law requirement	No

ADMISSIONS

Selectivity Rating	83
# applications received	1,381
% applicants accepted	47
% acceptees attending	32
Average LSAT	157
Median LSAT	157
LSAT Range (25th to 75th percentile)	154–160
Average undergrad GPA	3.47
Median undergrad GPA	3.5
Application fee	$50
Regular application deadline	3/1
Early application deadline	11/15
Early application notification	12/31
Transfer students accepted	Yes
Evening division offered	Yes
Part-time accepted	Yes
CAS accepted	Yes

FINANCIAL FACTS

Annual tuition (in-state out-of-state)	$21,517/$43,016
Books and supplies	$1,600
Fees	$939
Room & Board	$21,124
Financial aid application deadline	3/10
% first-year students receiving some sort of aid	88
% all students receiving some sort of aid	83
% of aid that is merit based	13
% receiving scholarships	39
Average grant	$5,233
Average loan	$30,850
Average total aid package	$31,439
Average debt	$92,112

EMPLOYMENT INFORMATION

		Grads Employed by Field (%)	
Career Rating	86	Academic	(4)
Total 2012 JD Grads	252	Business/Industry	(23)
% grads employed nine months out	87	Government	(14)
Median starting salary	$60,000	Judicial Clerkship	(5)
State for bar exam	IN, IL	Military	(2)
Pass rate for first-time bar	83	Private Practice	(50)
Prominent Alumni		Public Interest	(3)

Ann Slaughter Andrew, US Ambassador to Costa Rica; John Pistole, Administrator of the Transportation Security Administration; Pamela Carter, President, Cummins Distribution.

THE JOHN MARSHALL LAW SCHOOL

INSTITUTIONAL INFORMATION

Public/private	Private
Affiliation	No Affiliation
% faculty part-time	61
% faculty female	34
% faculty underrepresented minority	13
Total faculty	218

SURVEY SAYS...

Diverse opinions accepted in class-rooms, Great research resources, Students love Chicago, IL

STUDENTS

Enrollment of law school	1,466
% male/female	53/47
% part-time	22
% underrepresented minority	21
Average age of entering class	23

ACADEMICS

Academic Experience Rating	68
Profs interesting rating	76
Profs accessible rating	73
Hours of study per day	3.95

Academic Specialties

Human Rights, International, Taxation, Intellectual Property

Advanced Degrees Offered

LLM Degrees require 24 hours of credit, and approximately 1–3 years to complete. LLM Degrees are offered in: Employee Benefits, Estate Planning, U.S. Legal Studies (for foreign law-yers), Information Technology and Privacy Law, Intellectual Property Law, International Business and Trade Law, Real Estate Law, Tax Law and Trial Advocacy. MS degrees require 24 hours of credit, and approximately 1–3 years to complete. MS degrees are offered in: Employee Benefits, Information Technology and Privacy Law, Intellectual Property Law, Real Estate Law, Tax Law.

Combined Degrees Offered

JD/MBA; JD/MPA; JD/MA; JD/LLM

Clinical program required	No

Academics

The John Marshall Law School is an independent bastion of legal education that offers day and evening programs as well as both fall and spring admission. John Marshall is pretty large as far as law schools go and it "places a huge emphasis on real-world prac-tice." Students report that they are "ready to hit the ground running even as clerks and interns." The "unparalleled" writing program "creates students who can file complaints and briefs immediately, with little or no additional training." The trial advocacy program is "outstanding" as well. "When you graduate from John Marshall, you are ready to work in a courtroom," a 2L says. John Marshall also offers specialized programs and joint JD/LLM programs in a host of areas including employee benefits, information technol-ogy and privacy law, international business and trade law, real estate law, intellectual property law, and tax law. "Students are encouraged to find a specific field of interest and are given every opportunity to become experts" in that field.

"The school's faculty is comprised mostly of professors who have accumulated years of experience," a 2L explains. "Their experiences and knowledge give a true and practical look at the actual practice of law." Students boast that John Marshall's "accessible" faculty is comprised of "the best professors, judges, and lawyers in Chicago." It's also worth noting that the hardcore, old-school Socratic Method is very much alive and well at John Marshall. A few professors are "very hard to comprehend" and "not good teachers," though. Opinion concerning the administration is split. One faction of stu-dents calls management "extremely helpful." "There seems to be a genuine interest in the needs of the students," they say. Other students aren't so happy. "The deans never get anything done," a 3L says.

About 10 percent of each graduating class is able to obtain the really plum jobs at big firms. Most students tell us they are satisfied with their career prospects. "The connec-tions that John Marshall has to the Chicago area are incredible," a 1L says. "It is very easy to connect with other John Marshall alumni, who are very willing to meet with and help you." A 3L adds, "John Marshall has done everything possible to put its graduates in a position of getting a job." Some students aren't as pleased, though. "I have had little help from the staff at the Career Services office," a 2L gripes. "Every time I have asked for assistance, they have merely told me where to look. I really could have figured that out for myself."

John Marshall is located in the middle of Chicago's South Loop "in the heart of the legal community" and "close to all the action." The U.S. District Court for the Northern District of Illinois and the United States Court of Appeals for the 7th Circuit are across the street. The Chicago Bar Association is "right next door." As for the actual law school facilities, "The buildings are old Chicago architectural mainstays," and "They've got charm." John Marshal's student lounge received an award winning renovation and expansion in 2011 to increase the available study space on campus. Students also com-plain that John Marshall is generally "overcrowded." "Elevators are hard to come by," and "It's slightly hard to get around."

Life

The student population at John Marshall is pretty diverse, ethnically and just about every other way. Some students tell us that the academic atmosphere is cordial. "We help each other, share outlines, and study in groups," a 2L says. However, the prevailing opinion seems to be that John Marshall is home to "a very competitive environment, which rewards achievement." "One thing that sets John Marshall apart is that they give people who would otherwise not get to go to law school a chance," a 2L explains. "After first semester things became much more competitive among people in my section," another 2L recalls.

Students here say that it's "very easy to find friends here," and they promise that they are a "very nice, normal bunch." "People are split into those active in school activities, such as trial teams, versus those who choose to work outside of school." "The social aspect really depends on the individual," a 1L says. "Some prefer to get in, do the work, and get out. Others prefer to socialize. There is something for everyone." If you want to get involved, "There are plenty of school-sponsored social events." "We have over fifty student organizations to choose from so that everyone can find their niche," a 3L notes. "Being a joiner at John Marshall is easy and doesn't feel corny like it did in undergrad."

Getting In

Admitted students at the 25th percentile have LSAT scores in the low 150s and GPAs around 3.02. Admitted students at the 75th percentile have LSAT scores in the mid 150s and GPAs in the 3.5 range.

Legal writing course requirement	Yes
Legal methods course requirement	Yes
Legal research course requirement	Yes
Moot court requirement	No
Public interest law requirement	No

ADMISSIONS

Selectivity Rating	71
# applications received	3,003
% applicants accepted	63
% acceptees attending	19
Median LSAT	151
LSAT Range (25th to 75th percentile)	149–155
Median undergrad GPA	3.17
Application fee	
Regular application deadline	3/1
Transfer students accepted	Yes
Evening division offered	Yes
Part-time accepted	Yes
CAS accepted	Yes

FINANCIAL FACTS

Annual tuition	$41,180
Books and supplies	$2,410
Fees	$124
Room & Board	$15,435
Financial aid application deadline	3/29
% first-year students receiving some sort of aid	92
% all students receiving some sort of aid	89
% of aid that is merit based	95
% receiving scholarships	45
Average grant	$12,000
Average loan	$43,204
Average total aid package	$20,500
Average debt	$142,587

EMPLOYMENT INFORMATION

Career Rating	79	**Prominent Alumni**
Total 2012 JD Grads	414	Mark Pedowitz, President of The CW
% grads employed nine months out	78	Network; Bill Daley, former White House
Median starting salary	$53,000	Chief of Staff; Leo Melamed, Chair
# employed full-time	276	Emeritus Chicago Mercantile Exc. and
# employed part-time	45	Globex
# employed bar required	200	**Grads Employed by Field (%)**
# employed JD preferred	86	Academic (1)
# employed professional/other	26	Business/Industry (17)
# employed non-professional	7	Government (14)
# pursuing advanced degree	3	Judicial Clerkship (3)
# unemployed and seeking employment	69	Military (1)
# not seeking employment	16	Private Practice (36)
% grads employed by school	1	Public Interest (3)
State for bar exam	IL	
Pass rate for first-time bar	83.3	

LEWIS & CLARK COLLEGE
LAW SCHOOL

INSTITUTIONAL
INFORMATION

Public/private	Private
Affiliation	No Affiliation
Student-faculty ratio	10:1
% faculty part-time	43
% faculty female	47
% faculty underrepresented minority	12
Total faculty	95

SURVEY SAYS...
Liberal students, Beautiful campus

STUDENTS

Enrollment of law school	752
% male/female	68/32
% from out-of-state	69
% part-time	36
% underrepresented minority	14
% international	1
# of countries represented	13
Average age of entering class	27

ACADEMICS

Academic Experience Rating	**75**
Profs interesting rating	77
Profs accessible rating	78
Hours of study per day	3.58

Academic Specialties
Commercial, Corporation Securities, Criminal, Environmental, International, Taxation, Intellectual Property, Animal, Public Interest

Advanced Degrees Offered
LLM Environmental & Natural Resources, 12-18 months; LLM Animal Law, 12-18 months M.S. Environmental Law Studies Program, 12-24 months

Combined Degrees Offered
JD/LLM in Environmental & Natural Resources Law, 3-1/2 years

Academics

Students who take the legal plunge at Lewis & Clark Law School in beautiful Portland, Oregon, enjoy professors who are "uniformly excellent and approachable for discussion about class topics and other issues striking your fancy." The small size of the law school allows for an extremely personalized educational experience, and students benefit from this cozy setup on multiple levels, "from an academic perspective as well as from a functional perspective." "I have been lucky enough to develop solid mentor relationships with specific professors that were particularly inspirational," says a second-year student. Practically everyone involved in running the school, from the dean to the cafeteria staff, "seem to truly like each other," and the well-regarded faculty is given an "unusual amount of influence in the way that the school is run, and [in the] the school's policies."

Lewis & Clark Law School has a relatively small course load of required classes and offers a night program, bringing a large contingent of older and more experienced students to the classrooms, which "adds a valuable, practical dimension to the learning experience." As one would expect from such an environmentally conscious institution, programs such as environmental and natural resources law and animal law are "unparalleled." No matter what their specialization, the faculty is considered to be "inspirational and knowledgeable enough to stimulate thinking beyond what's required by the curriculum," and the school's size "allows for an ideal student/teacher ratio that goes further to foster a highly effective teaching environment." Lewis & Clark's National Crime Victim Law Institute is another source of pride for the school, "leading the way in an emerging field of law."

Administrators are friendly, and accessible, "always willing to help out a student," and they keep the law school "running very smoothly." The research librarians are cited for being "very knowledgeable," and the Career and Professional Development Center also does its part to make sure students' needs are met, though some would like to see more non-metro area firms on campus. For students who are interested in staying in the area after graduation, there is "heavy support and involvement from the Portland legal community," and for others, "Alumni are distributed all around the world."

Since the school and its student body are known for being nature-friendly, it follows that the buildings on campus are all "green" and "tucked into a forested state park." This is nice, students say, because "when you are facing the gut-wrenching pain of law school, a 'walk in the park' goes a long way." Students are quite pleased with the library and the newer building, Wood Hall, but many are clamoring for an update of the other facilities. Portland is universally beloved as "a great place to live," though students say the parking situation could stand some improvements. A graduating student sums up life at the law school this way: "The professors are passionate about what they teach, and the students actually want to help each other get ahead in school. And where else do you get to study while in an overly large tree house?"

SHANNON DAVIS, ASSISTANT DEAN FOR ADMISSIONS
LEWIS & CLARK LAW SCHOOL, 10015 SW TERWILLIGER BOULEVARD, PORTLAND, OR 97219
TEL: 503-768-6613 FAX: 503-768-6793
E-MAIL: LAWADMSS@LCLARK.EDU • WEBSITE: WWW.LAW.CLARK.EDU

Life

No one would argue that "liberal" describes the majority of those enrolled at Lewis & Clark, and as one 3L warns, "If you are conservative, religious, or a meat-eating capitalist, be prepared." Fortunately, the laid-back nature of the majority of the student body means that there is "a complete void of competition"; absolutely "no one participates in the awful game of one-upmanship or cutthroat competition," and "The students are genuinely interested in helping and supporting each other." The day and night students don't often interact outside of class, but this doesn't seem to be a source of much tension. There are plenty of clubs in which they can relate if they so choose, and students here "are spoiled with the number of lunchtime events," including speakers and panels. "Everyone is accepted for who they are," coos a 2L. A second-year student puts it in another way: "Good people go here."

Getting In

The admission rate at Lewis & Clark is 55 percent—the majority of applicants are not admitted. The typical student has been in the work force for several years, which plays into the amount of weight placed on various admissions factors. GPA will factor in more heavily for recent grads, and applicants should make sure their letters of recommendation come from the appropriate sources (professors or employers). Recently admitted students at the 25th percentile had an LSAT score of 156 and an average GPA of 3.29, while admitted students at the 75th percentile had an LSAT score of 162 and a GPA of 3.65.

Clinical program required	No
Legal writing course requirement	Yes
Legal methods course requirement	Yes
Legal research course requirement	Yes
Moot court requirement	Yes
Public interest law requirement	No

ADMISSIONS

Selectivity Rating	79
# applications received	2,293
% applicants accepted	55
% acceptees attending	17
Median LSAT	160
LSAT Range (25th to 75th percentile)	156–162
Median undergrad GPA	3.47
Application fee	$50
Regular application deadline	3/15
Transfer students accepted	Yes
Evening division offered	Yes
Part-time accepted	Yes
CAS accepted	Yes

International Students

TOEFL required of international students	Yes

FINANCIAL FACTS

Annual tuition	$38,180
Books and supplies	$1,600
Fees	$50
Room & Board	$19,800
Financial aid application deadline	2/15
% first-year students receiving some sort of aid	92
% all students receiving some sort of aid	94
% of aid that is merit based	99
% receiving scholarships	61
Average grant	$12,584
Average loan	$48,068
Average total aid package	$59,580
Average debt	$109,419

EMPLOYMENT INFORMATION

Career Rating	88	
Total 2012 JD Grads	209	
% for whom you have useable information	99	
% grads employed nine months out	86	
Median starting salary	$58,500	
# employed full-time	155	
# employed part-time	24	
# employed bar required	135	
# employed JD preferred	26	
# employed professional/other	9	
# employed non-professional	9	
# pursuing advanced degree	5	
# unemployed and seeking employment	23	
# not seeking employment	0	
State for bar exam	OR	
Pass rate for first-time bar	90	

Prominent Alumni
Earl Blumenauer, US Representative; Phil Schirilo, Special Advisor to the President; Heidi Heitkamp, U.S. Senator, North Dakota.

Grads Employed by Field (%)
Business/Industry (18)
Government (12)
Judicial Clerkship (12)
Private Practice (49)
Public Interest (9)

LOUISIANA STATE UNIVERSITY
PAUL M. HEBERT LAW CENTER

Academics

The "very inexpensive" Louisiana State University Law Center boasts "the highest bar-passage rate in the state" pretty much every year and a unique program where graduates receive both a JD and Graduate Diploma in comparative law that provides "exposure to both common and civil law." You'll leave LSU Law with a Juris Doctor as well as a graduate diploma in comparative law, which is a mélange of European legal traditions. "The focus on the civil law at LSU is a definite plus because most of us remain in Louisiana to practice," explains a 2L. "It's a much different approach to problems than our common law colleagues use, and the training in the civil law happens early and often." The "first-year curriculum is rich and very demanding." Contracts, torts, civil procedure, constitutional law, and all your standard 1L courses are required. Students must also take course work in Louisiana's codes of torts, civilian property, and much else. After first year, "2Ls and 3Ls [are] more free to specialize and take advantage of the practical law courses available that would be applicable out of state." Some students complain that there aren't nearly enough electives, though. "LSU is small and so the range of courses available isn't very broad, and it's not always clear when a course will be taught." "Some courses offered in the school's course booklet haven't been offered in years," gripes a hardened 3L.

"The classrooms and facilities are phenomenal." Class attendance policies are "relatively stringent." It's a good thing, then, that the academic atmosphere is generally "excellent." "The great thing about LSU Law professors is that many of them have been incredibly influential in the development of Louisiana law," observes a 1L. "In preparing cases for classes, you can't help but notice how often the courts have relied on your professor's doctrinal works in formulating their decisions." "While some are intent on using the Socratic Method at all costs, most use it simply to ensure that you are paying attention and can answer their questions when called upon," relates a 3L. Not all faculty members are fabulous, though. "LSU has some of the best," advises a 2L, "but a couple have to be the worst." Outside of class, most faculty members are "more than willing to talk to students." "They are all accessible if you try a little bit." A few students tell us that the administration "emphasizes bureaucracy," but the overwhelming sentiment here is that top brass "truly works for the students" and is "remarkably responsive to the student body."

LSU Law offers "an abundance of opportunities to be involved" in journals and advocacy programs. There are clinical programs in immigration law, family law, mediation, and juvenile representation. "A well-connected externship program places second- and third-year students with justices and judges in the Louisiana Supreme Court and the U.S. Fifth Circuit Court of Appeals, among others," adds a 3L. A study abroad program in Lyon, France, is also popular. Over 150 employers recruit here each year, but opinion regarding LSU Law's ability to help students find jobs is split. Critics tell us that the Career Services office displays "callous indifference toward students who are not in the top five to ten percent of the class." Other students say that Career Services is "in touch with you from the beginning" and "goes the extra mile to help students and find opportunity for them." "This school does everything it possibly can to ensure that you pass the bar and get a job," beams a confident 1L.

MICHELE FORBES, DIRECTOR OF STUDENT AFFAIRS AND REGISTRAR
202 LAW CENTER, BATON ROUGE, LA 70803
TEL: 225-578-8646 FAX: 225-578-8647
E-MAIL: ADMISSIONS@LAW.LSU.EDU • WEBSITE: WWW.LAW.LSU.EDU

Life

"Students are generally serious and hardworking." "The student body and faculty lean conservative, but all walks of life are welcome" and it's a diverse group, "age-wise and experience-wise." LSU Law "has a collegial feel where there is a place for everyone." "The school is just the right size to allow getting to know everyone," explains a 2L. "No one is just a number. Everyone has the opportunity to be an individual." "We have gunners just like every law school," admits a 1L. For the most part, though, there is only "a mild dose" of competition. "There really isn't a lot of the cutthroat behavior." Students frequently "share outlines and help each other learn the law."

"Social life at LSU Law is great from the library to the tailgate." This school is "in the middle of Cajun country—great food, one of the best football teams in the nation, and good Southern people." "LSU is in the greatest location a student could ask for," gloats a 1L. "Baton Rouge is an amazing city, and the Law Center is located in the heart of one of the most vibrant undergraduate campuses in the nation." "There are many social programs running throughout the semester so that you get to know your classmates personally and you aren't just doing law school 24/7." "There are parties all the time." "There are free drinks nearly every weekend." "Intramural tournaments" are pretty popular, too. "Students strap on pads and play a charity football game once a year," just for instance, complete with tackling.

Getting In

Admitted students at the 25th percentile have LSAT scores around 155 and undergraduate grade point averages not much over 3.0. At the 75th percentile, LSAT scores are about 159 and GPAs are approximately 3.7.

Clinical program required	No
Legal writing course requirement	Yes
Legal methods course requirement	Yes
Legal research course requirement	Yes
Moot court requirement	No
Public interest law requirement	No

ADMISSIONS

Selectivity Rating	83
# applications received	1,374
% applicants accepted	45
% acceptees attending	32
Average LSAT	157
Median LSAT	157
LSAT Range (25th to 75th percentile)	153–160
Average undergrad GPA	3.34
Median undergrad GPA	3.38
Application fee	$50
Regular application deadline	3/1
Transfer students accepted	Yes
Evening division offered	No
Part-time accepted	No
CAS accepted	Yes

FINANCIAL FACTS

Annual tuition	$16,966
Books and supplies	$2,000
Fees (in-state out-of-state)	$1,652/$19,040
Room & Board (on/off campus)	$17,292/$19,788
% first-year students receiving some sort of aid	56
% all students receiving some sort of aid	68
% of aid that is merit based	57
% receiving scholarships	57
Average grant	$4,891
Average loan	$21,458
Average total aid package	$18,330
Average debt	$78,762

EMPLOYMENT INFORMATION

Career Rating	84	# unemployed and seeking employment	7
Total 2012 JD Grads	223	# not seeking employment	3
% for whom you have useable information	221	% grads employed by school	0
% grads employed nine months out	92	State for bar exam	LA
Median starting salary	$52,000	Pass rate for first-time bar	78
% job accepting grads providing useable salary information	89	**Grads Employed by Field (%)**	
		Academic (4)	
# employed full-time	200	Business/Industry (16)	
# employed part-time	3	Government (9)	
# employed bar required	171	Judicial Clerkship (11)	
# employed JD preferred	16	Private Practice (55)	
# employed professional/other	14	Public Interest (4)	
# employed non-professional	2		
# pursuing advanced degree	8		

LOYOLA MARYMOUNT UNIVERSITY
LOYOLA LAW SCHOOL

INSTITUTIONAL INFORMATION

Public/private	Private
Affiliation	Roman Catholic-Jesuit
Student-faculty ratio	15:1
% faculty part-time	43
% faculty female	32
% faculty underrepresented minority	14
Total faculty	145

SURVEY SAYS...

Diverse opinions accepted in class-rooms, Great research resources, Great library staff

STUDENTS

Enrollment of law school	1,238
% male/female	47/53
% from out-of-state	22
% part-time	18
% underrepresented minority	38
% international	2
# of countries represented	23
Average age of entering class	25

ACADEMICS

Academic Experience Rating	95
Profs interesting rating	96
Profs accessible rating	93
Hours of study per day	3.36

Academic Specialties

Civil, Criminal, Environmental, Civil Litigation, Corporate, Entertainment, Immigration, Public Interest, Trial Advocacy, Human Rights, International, Labor, Legal History, Taxation, Intellectual Property

Advanced Degrees Offered

LLM in Taxation, full-time, 1 year, part-time, 3 years; JD/LLM in Taxation, 3 years; LLM (for Foreign-Trained Attorneys), 1 year

Combined Degrees Offered

JD/MBA, 4 years; JD/LLM in Taxation, 3 years

Academics

Loyola Law School (affiliated with Loyola Marymount University, or the "mothership") is "an understated gem" in downtown Los Angeles that "seeks to create top lawyers who use the profession for the betterment of society and [to] give back to [the] legal community." It's a generally happy place that quite simply seeks to make good lawyers, send them out to the world, and repeat; all the people associated with the school, from students to staff, are accordingly pleasant and uncomplicated, if not a little resentful of the relative anonymity as compared to the other law schools in the area. As one 1L puts it, "Masochists would be disappointed at Loyola. For legal torture, look elsewhere in Los Angeles."

Professors are "smart [and] demanding yet understanding of the pressures of a first-year law student." They are of "the highest caliber" and "set the bar high, but [they] give you all of the tools to use at your discretion to meet that bar." Classes are "lively and enjoyable," and teachers keep their doors open for whatever's troubling the masses. "Every professor I have had seems to truly care about the success of their students, both inside and outside the classroom," says a student.

The curriculum itself offers "a strong foundation in legal theory but also the practical skills necessary to excel in the workplace," including a comprehensive legal research and writing program. There are a "broad range of specialists within a variety of fields" to help students narrow down their field of focus, and many "solid opportunities for public interest law," as well as "a tremendous trial advocacy program, moot court, and three law reviews." "A break in $40,000 tuition payments would be nice. For a school that boasts itself on public interest, taking out well over $100,000 in tuition loans doesn't exactly amend itself to accepting a $50,000 per year public interest job," says a 3L. Graduates of LLS mainly practice in California and L.A., so the school enjoys a much greater reputation within the state than it does nationally, and for those who do stay nearby (very much the majority), the alumni networking opportunities are strong.

As for the administrators, most here have little to no problems with the administration, which "not only talks the talk, but walks the walk." That is, aside from the Registrar's office, which "is like talking to a brick wall. They need to listen and think about what you are saying before they respond with the scripted answer." The law school has its own "cozy" and completely separate campus from Loyola Marymount, so there are "no undergrads taking up the library study rooms." The school operates a shuttle, which takes students to the financial district and the new L.A. Live entertainment complex every fifteen minutes, which means that "courts, law firms, and our city's phenomenal entertainment are basically our campus."

Life

As expected, happy students make for a happy campus. Competition is at a low here; notes and outlines "are regularly shared," and "There has not been one hint of dirty competition at all." "I can't imagine a better atmosphere considering the pressures of first year. The 2Ls and 3Ls have been amazingly supportive too," says one first-year. Even outside of the classroom, everyone is "peculiarly friendly"—one student was "caught off guard by how helpful everybody was." There is always something new and exciting going on, from "bowling to benefit the public interest law foundation, to lunches with European patent scholars, to social outings at hot bars and clubs around town." Panel lunches with industry leaders are well-attended at Loyola, and "You could probably go to a meeting and eat for free every day if you wanted."

One of the reasons the lunch hour is so heavily trafficked is the high number of commuters who go to school here, which limits after-class time as an option for socializing and means that "developing a large social network isn't as easy as it might be if everyone lived right next to campus" (where everyone also agrees that it would "be nice if we had a gym"). However, the SBA and student organizations "do a good job of scheduling social activities to bring students closer," and this social bunch obliges for the most part. Downtown L.A. has also undergone a massive revitalization effort, and everyone agrees that it is "incredibly convenient."

Getting In

To be considered for admission to Loyola Law School, students must submit undergraduate transcripts, LSAT scores, and a personal statement. Students also must submit at least one and up to three letters of recommendation, of which at least one should be from an academic source.

Clinical program required	No
Legal writing course requirement	Yes
Legal methods course requirement	Yes
Legal research course requirement	Yes
Moot court requirement	No
Public interest law requirement	Yes

ADMISSIONS

Selectivity Rating	86
# applications received	4,175
% applicants accepted	39
% acceptees attending	21
Average LSAT	160
Median LSAT	161
LSAT Range (25th to 75th percentile)	158–162
Average undergrad GPA	3.47
Median undergrad GPA	3.54
Application fee	$65
Regular application deadline	
Early application deadline	12/1
Early application notification	12/31
Transfer students accepted	Yes
Evening division offered	Yes
Part-time accepted	Yes
CAS accepted	Yes

FINANCIAL FACTS

Annual tuition	$43,660
Books and supplies	$1,370
Fees	$570
Room & Board	$16,038
Financial aid application deadline	3/15
% first-year students receiving some sort of aid	85
% all students receiving some sort of aid	85
% of aid that is merit based	16
% receiving scholarships	33
Average grant	$21,260
Average loan	$47,789
Average total aid package	$50,260
Average debt	$141,936

EMPLOYMENT INFORMATION

Career Rating	81
Total 2012 JD Grads	411
% for whom you have useable information	100
% grads employed nine months out	73
Median starting salary	$72,000
# employed full-time	247
# employed part-time	53
# employed bar required	236
# employed JD preferred	47
# employed professional/other	10
# employed non-professional	6
# pursuing advanced degree	4
# unemployed and seeking employment	82
# not seeking employment	11
% grads employed by school	8
State for bar exam	CA, IL, NV, WA
Pass rate for first-time bar	79.3

Prominent Alumni
Gloria Allred, Trial Attorney; Thomas (Tom) Girardi, Trial Attorney; Laura Wasser, Trial Attorney.

Grads Employed by Field (%)
Academic (1)
Business/Industry (14)
Government (3)
Judicial Clerkship (2)
Private Practice (41)
Public Interest (2)

LOYOLA UNIVERSITY—CHICAGO
SCHOOL OF LAW

INSTITUTIONAL INFORMATION

Public/private	Private
Affiliation	Roman Catholic
% faculty part-time	64
% faculty female	51
% faculty underrepresented minority	10
Total faculty	222

SURVEY SAYS...
Diverse opinions accepted in classrooms, Great library staff, Students love Chicago, IL

STUDENTS

Enrollment of law school	854
% male/female	49/51
% part-time	13
% underrepresented minority	27
# of countries represented	5
Average age of entering class	24

ACADEMICS

Academic Experience Rating	**85**
Profs interesting rating	77
Profs accessible rating	79
Hours of study per day	3.22

Academic Specialties
Corporation Securities, Criminal, International, Labor, Taxation, Intellectual Property

Advanced Degrees Offered
MJ Health Law-online, MJ in Children's Law and Policy-online; MJ in Business and Corporate Governance Law-online, 22 semester hours; LLM Health Law, LLM Child Law, LLM Tax Law, LLM Advocacy, LLM in Business Law, LLM in International Law, LLM in US Law for Foreign Lawyers (24–26 credit hours); LLM in Rule of Law for Development (27 credit hours, Rome Campus). Online LLM in Health Law. SJD Health Law, DLaw in Health Law, 2 years full-time.

Combined Degrees Offered
JD/MBA, JD/MSW, JD/MA Political Science, 4 years

Academics

Loyola University—Chicago's School of Law provides a "great well-rounded education" in a "very friendly and welcoming environment" from its location in "one of the most beautiful city blocks in Chicago." Founded in 1909 by the Society of Jesus, the school's "Jesuit values...permeate everything that goes on at the school." "The best thing about Loyola is that for a competitive law school that boasts many of Chicago's most well-known litigators, the personality of the institution is welcoming," a 2L says. This "extremely friendly" atmosphere receives endless praise from Loyola students. "I have heard horror stories of law schools that pit the students against each other," a 1L explains, "[but] it isn't like that at Loyola." "The Loyola name is highly respected in the Chicago area," and the "very good" and "very engaged" alumni "help Loyola Law students and will often hire them."

"Loyola's facilities are excellent," including the "beautiful," "large and spacious" classrooms that provide "great views of the city which make studying not seem as bad." The law school is located in a "new, state-of-the-art" building, but students point out that "the undergrads share the building with the law students." The "abysmal" law library is actually "out done by [the] undergraduate library" and "could stand to be re-done." However, the "library staff is excellent." Students also complain that "the cost of tuition is quite high." "I am very worried about getting a job after school that will allow me to pay off my debt," one student admits.

Students have praise for the school's "amazing" staff and faculty nearly across the board. "The staff is great!" says one student, while another declares "the administration is unlike any I've ever experienced." "I have been extremely impressed by the level of attention to detail the Loyola professors and non-academic staff place on managing the legal program," a happy 1L says. The "always available" professors will "talk and say hello in the hallways." While some say the professors have a "very broad range" of quality, most "really challenge you" and "are more like friends/mentors." Loyola "offers a wide variety of practical, hands on courses" as well as "great panels, symposiums, and networking events." The administration and faculty "really encourage getting outside experience while in school." Thus, "many students participate in externships" or find other opportunities in Chicago. "I have had a great experience at Loyola thus far and can't say enough good things about it," a 3L proudly says.

Life

The "excellent" student body is filled with "very nice people" that are "very cohesive and social." However, the student body is divided between "day and evening students," and there can be "limited interaction between" the two groups. This may be due to the "different situations...between the older evening students and the younger less experienced day students." Although another student says "day and evening students do interact quite often in social settings and after the first year, there is little distinction between them." In general, the culture at Loyola is "very nurturing" and many miles from "the stereotypical 'highly competitive' environment."

"The school is in the most perfect location one could hope for in an urban campus," giving students access to all of America's Second City. The "social scene" on campus "is very much catered to twenty-two-year-olds" due to the "very young student body." Since the law building is shared with the undergraduate school, "undergrad students and overall environment is a constant complaint." "There is plenty to do if you have extra time" on campus or off, and "there are ample opportunities for networking and for job searching while in school." "Loyola is real big on community service which you gotta love, there is always an opportunity to serve," one 3L says.

Getting In

Loyola University—Chicago's School of Law is very competitive. The median GPA and LSAT for the 2012 class were 3.35 and 160 respectively, so potential applicants will want to study, study, study. In addition to grades and scores, the Loyola looks closely at letters of recommendation and personal statement, and takes into account work experience as well as a perceived ability to overcome hardships.

Clinical program required	No
Legal writing course requirement	Yes
Legal methods course requirement	No
Legal research course requirement	Yes
Moot court requirement	No
Public interest law requirement	No

ADMISSIONS

Selectivity Rating	84
# applications received	4,225
% applicants accepted	41
% acceptees attending	17
Median LSAT	160
LSAT Range (25th to 75th percentile)	156–160
Median undergrad GPA	3.35
Application fee	$0
Regular application deadline	3/1
Regular notification	4/1
Early application deadline	1/15
Early application notification	2/15
Transfer students accepted	Yes
Evening division offered	Yes
Part-time accepted	Yes
CAS accepted	Yes

FINANCIAL FACTS

Annual tuition	$39,850
Books and supplies	$1,500
Fees	$732
Room & Board	$14,950
Financial aid application deadline	3/1
% first-year students receiving some sort of aid	93
% all students receiving some sort of aid	62
% of aid that is merit based	85
% receiving scholarships	63
Average grant	$12,000
Average loan	$47,000
Average total aid package	$59,364
Average debt	$117,699

EMPLOYMENT INFORMATION

Career Rating	88	
Total 2012 JD Grads	271	
% for whom you have useable information	100	
% grads employed nine months out	83	
Median starting salary	$60,000	
# employed full-time	203	
# employed part-time	23	
# employed bar required	172	
# employed JD preferred	31	
# employed professional/other	21	
# employed non-professional	2	
# pursuing advanced degree	13	
# unemployed and seeking employment	28	
# not seeking employment	4	
% grads employed by school	1	
State for bar exam	IL, CA, MI, TX, WI	
Pass rate for first-time bar	92	

Prominent Alumni
Lisa Madigan, Illinois Attorney General; Laurel Bellows, President American Bar Association (2012); John Cullerton, Illinois Senate President.

Grads Employed by Field (%)
Academic (4)
Business/Industry (24)
Government (8)
Judicial Clerkship (2)
Private Practice (56)
Public Interest (7)

LOYOLA UNIVERSITY—NEW ORLEANS
COLLEGE OF LAW

Academics

Loyola University—New Orleans College of Law is "hands down, the best place to study law," thanks to its "regional reputation, elite professors, great career resources, and guest speakers." Owing to "its location in one of the world's great cultural centers," students here aren't surprised with "the quality and accessibility of the professors," all within an "atmosphere that facilitates learning and making connections." The "top-notch" professors "bring a wealth of practical experience into the classroom" and are "willing to bend over backwards to help students in their career path." It helps that the professors "all have practical experience in their area of law" and "incorporate that [expertise] in the classroom." "It's great to have a professor who helped write the civil code and court opinions teach them to you," says a 3L. Administration can be "very good, very personal, and helpful," and the financial aid department recently acquired new staff, improving the department's efficiency. Those involved in the school's evening program would like to see the administration give them the same "availability of classes and special programs, such as internships or externships," as those in the regular program have. Others appreciate the lack of "long lines" and "red tape." "This law school is completely oriented around the students," says a 1L.

"There are continual opportunities to gain practical legal experience" at Loyola through "constant notices of internships, jobs, volunteer projects, and externships." "Professors share their advice for exam preparation and are very up front with expectations for exams," says a 2L. However, while nearly all students approve of the "moot court and trial advocacy programs," some would like to "have fewer required courses so that students can specialize in a particular area with more ease." Others think that "Loyola needs to do a much better job preparing students to actually practice law." "The odds are severely stacked against a recent graduate arguing anything to an appeals court, as most firms have attorneys with considerably more experience who handle all of the firm's appeals work," explains a 3L. "Therefore, the area in which Loyola could stand to improve the most is offering more trial court advocacy classes and giving those equal, if not greater, focus than moot court."

Opinions on Loyola's career services office range from "fantastic" to "a joke," though which side you'll fall on will likely depend on where you're from. "One area that I think the school could improve on is helping the common law students obtain jobs out of state," says a 3L. "Our career services is terrible if you're not from Louisiana," adds a 2L. That said, most students are happy to stay in New Orleans after graduating. "Loyola's great for people who want to practice in New Orleans," says a 2L. "It offers lots of connections and alumni in the area who like to give back to their own."

"Some of the classrooms, namely the newer ones, are top-notch," says a 1L. Others "are overcrowded and students are relegated to using stand-alone desks along the edges of the classrooms with inadequate surfaces for writing or computer usage." "The facilities could use a drastic update," says a 2L. While the library is "giant" with "many helpful resources," it's in "need of a twenty-first (or even twentieth) century makeover." Students also wouldn't mind having a place where they can "study late at night, segregated from the undergrads," along with "more food options for the law campus."

K. Michele Allison-Davis, Dean of Admissions
7214 Saint Charles Avenue, Box 904, New Orleans, LA 70118
Tel: 504-861-5575 Fax: 504-861-5772
E-Mail: ladmit@loyno.edu • Website: law.loyno.edu

Life

Students at Loyola "are generally helpful to each other" and "very friendly regardless of whether they are from the New Orleans area or not." "There is some competitiveness amongst the student body, but I would hesitate to say cutthroat," says a 2L. "Every student seems to view your own personal success as their own," adds a 1L. Though there's a lot of talk about "the rift between Civil and Common Law students," most agree, "It is best explained by the fact that students take largely different courses and study very different material over three years." That said, most admit that they "have never seen an argument or any social outcasting based on a student's choice of study." There's a fair amount of diversity in the student population. "I have never had a group of friends as diverse as what I have found here," says a 2L. "There is not another school that I am aware of that could foster such camaraderie among so diverse a population."

When it comes to social life at Loyola, all students have to do is step outside. Located in "Uptown New Orleans," students can readily hop a streetcar that "provides access to the French Quarter and Central Business District." "New Orleans has the best nightlife in the South," says a 3L. "The city environment is perfect for young professionals." "I would say that most students spend a majority of their social time in Uptown or in the Garden District rather than in the belligerent, tourist-packed French Quarter," says a 2L. "The nightlife in Uptown and the Garden District is much more tailored to the academic crowd." According to a 1L, "This year's 1L class hangs out together in a wide variety of ways, [whether it's] going to the Jay-Z concert as a big group or holding our own Mardi Gras party with the whole class invited to come, grab a drink, and watch the parades." Fundamentally, argues a 2L, "The music, food, and social justice opportunities should encourage anyone to come to law school at Loyola."

Getting In

Recently admitted students at Loyola Law have average undergraduate GPAs of 3.34 and LSAT scores of 154. The admissions office operates a unique Early Admit program that allows those who have completed three-fourths of their undergraduate degree requirements to be admitted. Those who take advantage of this option will be expected to have higher entering credentials than those who will be entering law school with an undergraduate degree.

Clinical program required		No
Legal writing course requirement		Yes
Legal methods course requirement		Yes
Legal research course requirement		Yes
Moot court requirement		Yes
Public interest law requirement		Yes

ADMISSIONS

Selectivity Rating	68
# applications received	1,617
% applicants accepted	67
% acceptees attending	22
Average LSAT	154
Median LSAT	152
LSAT Range (25th to 75th percentile)	150–155
Average undergrad GPA	3.20
Median undergrad GPA	3.21
Application fee	$45
Regular application deadline	
Transfer students accepted	Yes
Evening division offered	Yes
Part-time accepted	Yes
CAS accepted	Yes

FINANCIAL FACTS

Annual tuition	$40,362
Books and supplies	$1,500
Fees	$1,086
Room & Board	$20,700
% first-year students receiving some sort of aid	90
% all students receiving some sort of aid	87
% of aid that is merit based	51
% receiving scholarships	43
Average grant	$19,358
Average loan	$37,871
Average total aid package	$57,229
Average debt	$124,355

EMPLOYMENT INFORMATION

Career Rating	90	
Total 2012 JD Grads	231	
% grads employed nine months out	74	
# employed full-time	160	
# employed part-time	2	
# employed bar required	109	
# employed JD preferred	35	
# employed professional/other	21	
# employed non-professional	4	
# pursuing advanced degree	11	
# unemployed and seeking employment	42	
# not seeking employment	4	
State for bar exam	LA, TX, FL, GA, MS	
Pass rate for first-time bar	72	

Prominent Alumni
Pascal Calogero, Chief Justice, Louisiana Supreme Court; Moon Landrieu, Secretary of HUD, Mayor of New Orleans, etc.; Carl Stewart, U.S.Court of Appeals, 5th Circuit.

Grads Employed by Field (%)
Academic (2)
Business/Industry (11)
Government (9)
Judicial Clerkship (7)
Private Practice (41)
Public Interest (5)

MARQUETTE UNIVERSITY
LAW SCHOOL

INSTITUTIONAL INFORMATION

Public/private	Private
Affiliation	Roman Catholic
% faculty female	43
% faculty underrepresented minority	11
Total faculty	37

SURVEY SAYS...

Diverse opinions accepted in classrooms, Great library staff, Abundant externship/internship/clerkship opportunities

STUDENTS

Enrollment of law school	730
% male/female	57/43
% part-time	18
% underrepresented minority	20
# of countries represented	2
Average age of entering class	24

ACADEMICS

Academic Experience Rating	**73**
Profs interesting rating	79
Profs accessible rating	82
Hours of study per day	3.91

Academic Specialties

Civil Procedure, Commercial, Constitutional, Corporation Securities, Criminal, Environmental, International, Labor, Legal History, Property, Taxation, Intellectual Property

Advanced Degrees Offered

LLM in sports law for foreign attorneys, 1 year

Combined Degrees Offered

JD/MBA, JD/MBA Sports Business, JD/MA Political Science, JD/MA International Relations, JD/MA Philosophy, JD/MA in History of Philosophy, JD/MA Bioethics, all 4 year programs. Students may also earn the JD/Certificate in Dispute Resolution in 3 years.

Academics

The Law School at Wisconsin's Marquette University is a supportive environment where "students are interested in each other's success." The school encourages students to realize that their fellow students will be future colleagues and urges them to learn to respect each other with that fact in mind early on. This mindset is upheld by both students and faculty, making sure that the entire institution functions as "a cohesive unit." First year law students have no trouble scheduling their required courses because all 1Ls have their classes scheduled for them. Though this negates the stress of not getting a needed class, some students see it as "scheduling nightmare." After their first year though, students have an abundance of options within a vast variety of specializations in smaller classes. "Dean Kearney wants to make sure we learn the law, not the latest in pop sociology," says a student. Administration is known to be extraordinarily helpful. "Even if you're not talking to the right person, they'll get you there." With a new law building introduced in 2010, the school is constantly working to stay current, offering the most cutting-edge legal education. "The Administration goes above and beyond for their students! Any problem or need can be brought to them and with ease they solve the issue. No red tape, no jumping through hoops, they are simply the best!" says a 3L. The legal writing program is particularly popular on campus. "In clerkship after clerkship, the research and writing skills I gained in class have been complimented," says a student. Sports Law is another celebrated program at Marquette. Professors are lauded as "very knowledgeable, thought-provoking, and engaging," as well as "unforgettably intelligent and witty." The faculty is made up of individuals hailing from top universities and successful legal careers, yet still manage to "allow students room to debate legal issues in a cordial, professional manner." "It is amazing how a two-second question might turn into an hour discussion outside of class," says a 2L. "The professors have usually written many books on the subjects they're teaching" reveals a 2L. "Mostly the professors are caring and helpful. They are very open and one can learn a lot other than the subjects that they teach by spending time outside class talking to them," says a 3L. "I am continuously impressed with the knowledge, intelligence, and enthusiasm that the professors demonstrate in lecture as well as in individual student/professor relationships." Marquette prides itself on offering a "flexible evening program" and being "very accommodating to part-time students." Many classes are offered at night to accommodate "full-time work schedules and family lives." The school's Milwaukee location affords the school's career services center to provide "many opportunities to obtain practical experience through internships and clinic work in the legal community," making it possible for students to get hands-on training throughout their academic career. "The extensive clinical, internship, and externship program run by Professor Hammer offers a great opportunity to get practice in a wide variety of subject areas while building a network of attorneys. The faculty is also extremely accessible," says a 3L. "Especially the Academic Success Program, which provides 1Ls with access to 2Ls and 3Ls for study assistance," reflects a 1L. The school continues supporting its students past graduation with its state bar exam exemption program, which allows graduates to begin their career without having to take the nationwide exam. The program is one of two of its kind in the state of Wisconsin. "My school is in a community with lawyers who care about the law school. Students get numerous chances to interact with, work with, and learn from the lawyers in the city and around the state," says a 3L. "The new building is an amazing environment. It offers comfortable study space, a workout gym, and plenty of light," says a 3L. "The law school classrooms are like walking onto the bridge of a starship; projectors and screens hidden in the ceilings; automated lights, microphones, and blinds; touchscreens that control the entire room. It is the ultimate joining of cutting edge technology and media integration with the age-old study of law," a 2L chimes in. "There is a surplus of outlets, bathrooms, and study rooms. The library is an open, flowing concept,

SEAN REILLY, ASSISTANT DEAN FOR ADMISSIONS
ECKSTEIN HALL, ROOM 132, P.O. BOX 1881, MILWAUKEE, WI 53201-1881
TEL: 414-288-6767 FAX: 414-288-0676
E-MAIL: LAW.ADMISSION@MARQUETTE.EDU • WEBSITE: LAW.MARQUETTE.EDU

which means that there are stacks on each of the four floors. There is also a place to study for everybody—stereotypical silent library, forum and tables where groups of students can talk and study, and two floors where it is largely quiet and there are individual desks."

Life

Milwaukee itself is laid back and promotes the campus' communal spirit. There are an abundance of social activities on campus to make up for what the surrounding neighbor-hoods lack. Students enjoy student-faculty basketball games, intramural sports, or the "Malpractice Ball, Brewers games, Bucks games, and various NCAA Division I sports [games]." Thursday night is known as the Bar Review, "where most students go out to the same bar and blow off steam" and "relax and get ready to study for the weekend."

Because of the large part-time program there is a wide variety of ages within the student body. Older students that maintain full time jobs and families commute to and from cam-pus, causing a small divide between themselves and the younger students. Students say, though the overall feeling is inclusive, "students can be a little clique-y."

Marquette Law students are quick to let you know, however, that you won't find any cutthroat competitive streaks here. "I feel like I'm in the third round of 'American Idol.' Everyone is watching their own back, and everyone else's," says a student. "I broke my leg and had to miss two days. I had four sets of notes for each class in my e-mail inbox without soliciting them from anybody," says a 2L. Most students feel like the campus community here is small, which can sometimes give off "a high school-like feeling—everyone knows everyone else, who they are, and likely some detail of their life. Depending on what a person wants, that could be a good or bad thing."

Getting In

The law school employs a modified rolling admissions process, with the admissions committee typically beginning its evaluations in December. As is the case in all rolling admissions systems, there are more spaces available sooner rather than later—especially if you think you may be a borderline candidate quantitatively. An undergraduate GPA of B+ and an LSAT score in the high 150s would make you solidly competitive for admis-sion at Marquette.

Clinical program required	No
Legal writing course requirement	Yes
Legal methods course requirement	No
Legal research course requirement	Yes
Moot court requirement	No
Public interest law requirement	No

ADMISSIONS

Selectivity Rating	71
# applications received	1,549
% applicants accepted	66
% acceptees attending	20
Average LSAT	155
Median LSAT	155
LSAT Range (25th to 75th percentile)	153–158
Average undergrad GPA	3.33
Median undergrad GPA	3.4
Application fee	$50
Regular application deadline	4/1
Transfer students accepted	Yes
Evening division offered	Yes
Part-time accepted	Yes
CAS accepted	Yes

FINANCIAL FACTS

Annual tuition	$38,690
Books and supplies	$1,200
Fees	$0
Room & Board	$12,950
Financial aid application deadline	3/1
% first-year students receiving some sort of aid	94
% all students receiving some sort of aid	94
% of aid that is merit based	13
% receiving scholarships	48
Average grant	$12,695
Average loan	$46,015
Average total aid package	$49,104
Average debt	$120,904

EMPLOYMENT INFORMATION

Career Rating	87	
Total 2012 JD Grads	218	
% grads employed nine months out	86	
Median starting salary	$55,000	
# employed full-time	178	
# employed part-time	10	
# employed bar required	131	
# employed JD preferred	35	
# employed professional/other	20	
# employed non-professional	2	
# pursuing advanced degree	3	
# unemployed and seeking employment	19	
# not seeking employment	0	
% grads employed by school	0	
State for bar exam	TX, IL, MN, CA, WI	
Pass rate for first-time bar	93	

Prominent Alumni
Hon. Diane Sykes, U.S. Court of Appeals Judge; Hon. Janine Geske, Former WI Supreme Court Justice; Hon. James Wynn, U.S. Court of Appeals Judge.

Grads Employed by Field (%)
Academic (2)
Business/Industry (23)
Government (6)
Judicial Clerkship (5)
Military (1)
Private Practice (47)
Public Interest (3)

MERCER UNIVERSITY
WALTER F. GEORGE SCHOOL OF LAW

INSTITUTIONAL INFORMATION

Public/private	Private
Affiliation	Baptist
Student-faculty ratio	14:1
% faculty part-time	60
% faculty female	31
% faculty underrepresented minority	5
Total faculty	91

SURVEY SAYS...

Great research resources, Great library staff, Beautiful campus

STUDENTS

Enrollment of law school	438
% male/female	54/46
% from out-of-state	23
% underrepresented minority	22
% international	1
Average age of entering class	25

ACADEMICS

Academic Experience Rating	84
Profs interesting rating	91
Profs accessible rating	96
Hours of study per day	3.78

Academic Specialties
Criminal, International, Labor, Taxation, Intellectual Property

Advanced Degrees Offered
JD, 3 years; LLM, Federal Criminal Practice & Procedure, 1 year.

Combined Degrees Offered
JD/MBA, 3–4 years

Academics

Mercer University School of Law strikes the "perfect balance" between a "familial atmosphere" and one of "healthy competition" thanks to its "smaller size," which "allows for close relationships with other students and productive interaction with professors," and its "emphasis on practical training in the law." "I feel like I'm getting an Ivy League education, but without the higher price tag and without having to move to New England," explains a 1L. "The class sizes are very small compared to other law schools, which encourages thoughtful discussion in class, [and] the professors abide by an open-door policy and are always willing to provide extra help." Most students here agree that the "outstanding" faculty is "interesting," "engaging," and "very welcoming." "The professors that I have had thus far have all been brilliant academics, which can be intimidating at times—especially in the beginning—yet they have the ability to stimulate student thought through engaging discussion and have successfully trained me to 'think like a lawyer,'" says a 2L. The "helpful and friendly" administration gets similarly high marks for being "extremely accessible." "Many of the administrators are helpful, kind, and welcoming of suggestions and questions from the student body," says a 2L.

Students at Mercer Law consider the "outstanding" and "second-to-none" legal writing program—in particular, the Writing Certificate Program—to be one of the school's "greatest strengths." According to a 2L, "As I have seen from moot court competition, higher-ranked schools don't produce better writers than Mercer." A 3L adds, "The substantial emphasis that Mercer Law places on developing superior legal writing skills is an asset that will distinguish all graduates throughout their legal careers." However, students would like to see "more entertainment and [intellectual property] law classes" as well as a more relaxed curriculum. Mercer law addressed these issues through a curriculum redesign in 2011 designed to promote a greater flexibility for students in their choice of courses and create more opportunities for faculty advising in those choices.

When it comes to the Career Services Office, student opinion is divided between "terrible" and "wonderful." "Even in a recession, they have managed to produce a large number of opportunities for on-campus interviews, and for other job opportunities as well," says a 3L. However, another 3L would like to see Career Services "reach out to 3Ls who are struggling to find jobs in this terrible economy." The school's Career Services Office has met the challenges of the new economy and was ranked 25th in the ABA for full time placements requiring a bar certification for the class of 2012.

Though the "facilities probably won't win any beauty contests" due to "sterile" classrooms that could be "mistaken for conference rooms at a Holiday Inn," the "great" law school building itself draws plenty of praise for its "Southern charm." Students also appreciate the "well maintained" library and "renovations" that have provided a "comfortable work environment."

MARILYN E. SUTTON, ASST. DEAN OF ADMISSIONS AND FINANCIAL AID
1021 GEORGIA AVENUE, MACON, GA 31207
TEL: 478-301-2605 FAX: 478-301-2989
E-MAIL: ADMISSIONS@LAW.MERCER.EDU • WEBSITE: WWW.LAW.MERCER.EDU

Life

With a "class size of about 150 students," "everybody knows everybody" at Mercer Law. Despite "healthy competition," students are "very friendly and accepting," meaning that Mercer "does not suffer from the same cutthroat, book-stealing plague that runs rampant at the top-tier schools." "It is amazing how open and cooperative the student body here is," says a 1L. "I have yet to encounter any real drama or horror story concerning the cutthroat environment that I had heard about prior to entering law school." Due to Mercer's location in "the heart of the South," students note that "conservative students" will feel "right at home." "It's not unusual for a class discussion with a left-leaning political note to be interrupted by the harrumphs and disapproving commentary from much of the rest of the class," says a 2L.

Students insist that they're "very social outside of school," but as "it is law school," opportunities to kick back can be slim. Luckily, student clubs and associations "consistently host fun social events, such as charity auctions, dances, and other parties." When it comes to Mercer's location in Macon, students are a little less sunny. "The only problem with Mercer is that it is in Macon, and downtown Macon, though on the verge of improving, is pretty depressed," says a 1L. Macon's lack of excitement can be "a blessing" since it means there are "few, if any, distractions" from academics. However, many students admit that while Macon "isn't exactly the cultural capital of the world," it's "accessible" and "only an hour from Atlanta" if the need for more happening locales arises.

Getting In

Recently admitted students at Mercer Law at the 25th percentile have LSAT scores of 153 and GPAs in the 3.13 range. Admitted students at the 75th percentile have LSAT scores of 158 and GPAs of roughly 3.67.

Clinical program required	No
Legal writing course requirement	Yes
Legal methods course requirement	No
Legal research course requirement	Yes
Moot court requirement	No
Public interest law requirement	No

ADMISSIONS

Selectivity Rating	76
# applications received	1,290
% applicants accepted	53
% acceptees attending	19
Median LSAT	153
LSAT Range (25th to 75th percentile)	149–156
Median undergrad GPA	3.43
Application fee	$50
Regular application deadline	3/15
Transfer students accepted	Yes
Evening division offered	No
Part-time accepted	No
CAS accepted	Yes

FINANCIAL FACTS

Annual tuition	$36,960
Books and supplies	$1,482
Fees	$300
Room & Board	$16,532
Financial aid application deadline	4/1
% first-year students receiving some sort of aid	94
% all students receiving some sort of aid	87
% of aid that is merit based	18
% receiving scholarships	34
Average grant	$23,753
Average loan	$46,758
Average total aid package	$57,105
Average debt	$113,310

EMPLOYMENT INFORMATION

Career Rating	85	Prominent Alumni
Total 2012 JD Grads	142	Griffin Bell, Former Attorney General of the
% grads employed nine months out	82	United States; Honorable Hugh Thompson,
Median starting salary	$53,500	Justice, Georgia Supreme Court; Nathan
# employed full-time	113	Deal, Governor of Georgia.
# employed part-time	4	**Grads Employed by Field (%)**
# employed bar required	106	Academic (1)
# employed JD preferred	7	Business/Industry (7)
# employed professional/other	4	Government (5)
# employed non-professional	0	Judicial Clerkship (9)
# pursuing advanced degree	7	Private Practice (56)
# unemployed and seeking employment	11	Public Interest (6)
# not seeking employment	1	
% grads employed by school	1	
State for bar exam	GA,	
Pass rate for first-time bar	93.1	

MICHIGAN STATE UNIVERSITY
COLLEGE OF LAW

INSTITUTIONAL INFORMATION

Public/private	Private
Student-faculty ratio	14:1
% faculty part-time	58
% faculty female	52
% faculty underrepresented minority	16
Total faculty	100

SURVEY SAYS...

Diverse opinions accepted in classrooms, Great research resources, Great library staff

STUDENTS

Enrollment of law school	910
% male/female	54/46
% from out-of-state	49
% part-time	3
% underrepresented minority	18
% international	6
# of countries represented	12
Average age of entering class	24

ACADEMICS

Academic Experience Rating	90
Profs interesting rating	81
Profs accessible rating	88
Hours of study per day	4.92

Academic Specialties

Constitutional, Corporation Securities, Criminal, Environmental, Government Services, International, Taxation, Intellectual Property

Advanced Degrees Offered

LLM, 1 year; MJ, 1 year

Combined Degrees Offered

JD/MBA, JD/MS (Various Fields), JD/MA (Various Fields), 4 years

Academics

When students at Michigan State University say their school offers "the best of both worlds," they really mean it. As a private school affiliated with a large public institution, MSU Law offers "a small academic community where professors remember and really take an interest in their students," while simultaneously providing "access to all the benefits of a world-class Big Ten university." The school maintains an accomplished faculty, and "The professors have, for the most part, attended top schools and have great experience to share." "While all the professors have their own research and other legal work, the emphasis is on teaching" at MSU. Of course, "You'll have some professors that are better than others," but the majority are engaging and student-friendly. If you visit them during office hours or linger around after class, many professors will "talk about work experience, research they've done, [and] interesting cases they've worked on. Some of them will connect on a more personal level" and talk "about their families or cool places they have visited."

The JD curriculum is "quite rigorous," and "you have to be willing to put in the work to get the results"; however, MSU invests in its students' success. One student explains, "The law college is good at providing academic resources for students such as labs, advisement, and T.A.'s for 1Ls." In the library, "the research librarians are great at helping students find what they are looking for," as well as keeping the noise levels reasonable during exams. Highly student-friendly, the law school's administration is praised for their efficiency, friendliness, and contemporary approach to education, especially the school's "great Dean, who understands the current legal market and the changing legal education system." Throughout departments and processes, "The administration at MSU is actively involved in making sure you receive a high-quality legal education," and they "genuinely want to connect with students." For example, "The deans have a free lunch meeting once a month where they explain what is going on in the school and let students ask questions."

There are many ways to put your legal skills into practice at MSU, including the school's "excellent Moot Court and Law Review opportunities." Of particular note, "The emphasis on clinical experience and expansion of the clinical programs at MSU College of Law is second to none." Depending on your area of interest, "There are about seven or eight different clinics that 2Ls and 3Ls can enroll in, ranging from Tax and Housing to Chance at Childhood and Plea and Sentencing." Alternatively, MSU's "geographic location (adjacent to the state capitol, Lansing) enables students to pursue a variety of intern- and externships in lieu of the offered clinics." Those interested in government work can augment these experiences through the school's popular "semester in Washington, DC," which combines professional experience at a federal agency coupled with the ongoing coursework at MSU.

After graduation, students looking for work in Michigan appreciate the school's great local reputation. Propitiously located in the capital city of Lansing, "There are a lot of opportunities for work within a few miles of school," particularly for those interested in government-related positions. For those planning to practice outside of the Great Lakes state, note the words of one student in particular who affirms that "career services is an extremely useful department for in-state students. However, more could be done to improve the ability of out-of-state students to obtain internships and externships."

CHARLES ROBOSKI, ASSISTANT DEAN, ADMISSIONS AND FINANCIAL AID
230 LAW COLLEGE BUILDING, EAST LANSING, MI 48824-1300
TEL: (517) 432-0222 FAX: (517) 432-0098
E-MAIL: ADMISS@LAW.MSU.EDU • WEBSITE: WWW.LAW.MSU.EDU

Life

Those looking for a lively, well-rounded law school experience will be happy with the atmosphere at MSU. There is "great cooperative attitude among all students," and no lack of activities and events to fill up their free time. Between the law school and the larger university campus, there is "a wide range of extracurricular activities and organizations, from access to intramural sports through the university to law-student-specific groups that encompass just about every background, interest, and practice area." Students love attending college football games with their classmates, and they take advantage of the myriad fitness and recreational facilities on campus. Among other perks, "There are two golf courses on campus, and the driving range is heated so you can hit a bucket late into fall or early in spring."

The law school is located in an "excellent building," which is "newly renovated with wireless throughout." In addition to nice study spaces and common areas, "There are private study rooms for groups that can be reserved in advance." Plus, "Sparty's, the cafe in the law school, is a great spot to get caffeine before late nights or long classes." Located in a bustling "college town," law students benefit from an affordable and relaxed lifestyle in hometown Lansing. When they need a change of scenery, "E. Lansing and Lansing offer a wide range of cuisines and other activities that don't have to revolve around the school."

Getting In

Applications for the fall term are reviewed on a rolling basis starting in November. While the school will accept new applications through April 30, priority is given to students who apply before March 1. As with any rolling admissions program, changes of admission are better earlier in the application cycle. In recent years, the median LSAT score for incoming students was 157; with the upper quartile averaging a score of 160, their median undergraduate GPA was 3.54.

Clinical program required	No
Legal writing course requirement	Yes
Legal methods course requirement	No
Legal research course requirement	Yes
Moot court requirement	No
Public interest law requirement	No

ADMISSIONS

Selectivity Rating	87
# applications received	3,732
% applicants accepted	32
% acceptees attending	26
Median LSAT	157
LSAT Range (25th to 75th percentile)	152–160
Median undergrad GPA	3.54
Application fee	$60
Regular application deadline	4/30
Early application deadline	3/1
Transfer students accepted	Yes
Evening division offered	No
Part-time accepted	Yes
CAS accepted	Yes

FINANCIAL FACTS

Annual tuition	$34,452
Books and supplies	$1,368
Fees	$131
Room & Board	$10,886
Financial aid application deadline	4/1
% first-year students receiving some sort of aid	85
% all students receiving some sort of aid	85
% of aid that is merit based	80
% receiving scholarships	45
Average grant	$25,540
Average loan	$25,590
Average total aid package	$45,011
Average debt	$108,000

EMPLOYMENT INFORMATION

Career Rating	90	# not seeking employment	2
Total 2012 JD Grads	348	State for bar exam	MI, IL, OH, CA, NY
% for whom you have useable information	95	Pass rate for first-time bar	88
% grads employed nine months out	92	**Prominent Alumni**	
Median starting salary	$58,994	Dennis Archer, Leadership; Geoffrey Fieger, Trial Lawyer; Marrianne Battani, U.S. District.	
% job accepting grads providing useable salary information	26	**Grads Employed by Field (%)**	
# employed full-time	240	Academic (10)	
# employed part-time	60	Business/Industry (18)	
# employed bar required	151	Government (9)	
# employed JD preferred	111	Judicial Clerkship (7)	
# employed professional/other	23	Military (1)	
# employed non-professional	12	Private Practice (45)	
# pursuing advanced degree	16	Public Interest (5)	
# unemployed and seeking employment	9		

MISSISSIPPI COLLEGE
SCHOOL OF LAW

INSTITUTIONAL INFORMATION

Public/private	Private
Affiliation	Southern Baptist
% faculty part-time	77
% faculty female	41
% faculty underrepresented minority	8
Total faculty	110

SURVEY SAYS...
Abundant externship/internship/ clerkship opportunities

STUDENTS

Enrollment of law school	536
% male/female	59/41
% from out-of-state	55
% part-time	3
% underrepresented minority	12
% international	1
# of countries represented	6
Average age of entering class	25

ACADEMICS

Academic Experience Rating	**67**
Profs interesting rating	77
Profs accessible rating	80
Hours of study per day	3.16

Advanced Degrees Offered
JD, 3 years; LLM, 1 year (International Students—American Legal Studies)

Combined Degrees Offered
JD/MBA; JD (3 years), MBA (1 year)

Academics

At Mississippi College, a "positive learning environment" and friendly staff offset the inevitable challenges of a legal education. Rather than promoting cutthroat competition or scary Socratic questioning, "The faculty and staff at MC Law are a unique bunch filled with kindness and enthusiasm." Students praise their school's moderate size, saying it allows for a more rewarding academic experience. While one may have a few large lecture courses, many "smaller classrooms allow for more collaboration because students sit around round tables." Plus, the academic intimacy really pays off at MC, where students can find "M.S. state Supreme Court justices teaching seminars, Federal District Court judges leading lectures, and practicing attorneys from the city of Jackson and surrounding areas leading our legal writing program." Despite their all-star credentials, "The professors make a wonderful effort to ensure that you understand the concepts, whether you ask in class or out of class." That extra help can really pay off, as "the low GPA curve creates a more competitive environment than most people like to admit."

There is a "very strong emphasis on writing" throughout the MC curriculum, as well as an "exceptional legal research staff" in the library. For those with a specific legal interest, the school also offers several special centers, like the Bioethics and Health Law Center and the Public Service Law Center, which operate both academic and extracurricular programs, as well as the opportunity to earn special certificates at graduation. Nonetheless, a handful of students worry that "some of the professors are too theoretical" in their approach to the coursework, while others say, "The school should require more research classes." Fortunately, Mississippi College augments traditional classroom instruction with numerous hands-on learning tools, which "allow everyone an opportunity to see how law is practiced in a variety of fields while taking classroom courses." For example, "the training provided by the Moot Court program provides law students with the practical skills needed to make the transition into effective young attorneys." In addition to moot court, students are eager to point out that "there are other exceptional programs here such as the Adoption Clinic, the Externship Program, and the Pro Bono Certificate program that are rarely discussed." However, one area in which the school could improve its real-world credentials is the percentage of students who pass the bar the first time they take the test. Apparently, the "bar passage rate [is] below 80 percent for first time takers."

Yet, when it comes to the real world, "being in the state's capital is definitely a huge plus to attending school" at Mississippi College. "As the only law school in the capital city, MC Law students receive a unique opportunity to [receive] practical experience through many clerkships, externships, and internships." Through these practical programs, students make professional connections and have "contact with state and federal bench, bar, and state legislators on a regular basis." Back on campus, "The school strives to keep the classroom technologically updated and recently added a new mock courtroom and several classrooms." These amenities are certainly nice, but they also come at a price. As a private institution, "Tuition and books costs are very high" at Mississippi College. The good news is that students feel their investment is respected at MC, where everyone is "incredibly accommodating" and "willing to help you any way they possibly can." From financial aid to registrars, the "administration at MC is extremely friendly," including the school's "wonderful dean," who is "always around and very approachable." Believe it or not, one may even "see the dean weeding the landscaping or picking up trash in the parking lot."

ASSISTANT DEAN PATRICIA H. EVANS, DEAN OF ADMISSIONS
151 EAST GRIFFITH STREET, JACKSON, MS 39201
TEL: 601-925-7152 FAX: 601-925-7166
E-MAIL: HWEAVER@MC.EDU • WEBSITE: WWW.LAW.MC.EDU

Life

"MCSOL provides a comfortable environment conducive to learning," and most students say cooperation trumps competition in the classroom and in the courtroom. At Mississippi College, "Everyone is friendly and works together towards the one single goal of graduation and passing the bar…The school is small enough that you know most of the people in your classes, and can recognize everyone in the halls." A student shares, "I think that in any academic setting there will be factions and competition on some level. However, my experience was that most students were cordial, helpful, and conducted themselves as if they were part of one really big team moving toward one common goal—graduation."

Although some would love to see more "more campus activities" specifically planned for law students, they say there is a great social atmosphere at Mississippi College. There are parties and other activities organized by the Student Bar Association, as well as student-run clubs and associations. Overall, "The number of student run social events is pretty high, and it does allow for students to branch out and meet others." Nevertheless, one's level of involvement is individualized. "MC Law has a wonderful social base which is just right if you choose to be social, but is not overly pressured." Unfortunately, students note a "lack of quality social events" in surrounding Jackson, when they explain, "If one wants to experience great music and southern dining, then making the 2 and 1/2 hour drive north to Oxford is well worth it."

Getting In

Admission to Mississippi College School of Law is attainable, if you have the right Mississippi College seeks well-rounded applicants, evaluating students based on their academic record and LSAT scores, as well as their professional, military, and leadership experience. The median undergraduate GPA for incoming students is about 3.19. For top applicants, the school offers generous merit-based scholarships, which can help offset the cost of a private education. The admissions office accepts applications on a rolling basis from September 1 to June 1.

Clinical program required	No
Legal writing course requirement	Yes
Legal methods course requirement	No
Legal research course requirement	Yes
Moot court requirement	Yes
Public interest law requirement	No

ADMISSIONS

Selectivity Rating	68
# applications received	1,209
% applicants accepted	66
% acceptees attending	19
Average LSAT	149
Median LSAT	149
LSAT Range (25th to 75th percentile)	146–152
Average undergrad GPA	3.26
Median undergrad GPA	3.27
Application fee	$0
Regular application deadline	7/15
Transfer students accepted	Yes
Evening division offered	No
Part-time accepted	Yes
CAS accepted	Yes

FINANCIAL FACTS

Annual tuition	$28,950
Books and supplies	$1,200
Fees	$1,000
Room & Board	$12,375
Financial aid application deadline	7/1
% first-year students receiving some sort of aid	85
% all students receiving some sort of aid	83
% of aid that is merit based	100
% receiving scholarships	29
Average grant	$18,000
Average loan	$38,000
Average total aid package	$43,000
Average debt	$95,000

EMPLOYMENT INFORMATION

Career Rating	85	# not seeking employment	1
Total 2012 JD Grads	164	% grads employed by school	1
% for whom you have useable information	99	State for bar exam	MS, AL, TN, TX, GA
% grads employed nine months out	85	Pass rate for first-time bar	87
Median starting salary	$57,976	**Prominent Alumni**	
% job accepting grads providing useable salary information	34	Sharion Aycock, Federal District Judge; Mike Parker, Federal Magistrate Judge; Linda Anderson, Federal Magistrate Judge.	
# employed full-time	135	**Grads Employed by Field (%)**	
# employed part-time	4	Academic (3)	
# employed bar required	100	Business/Industry (8)	
# employed JD preferred	33	Government (13)	
# employed professional/other	3	Judicial Clerkship (8)	
# employed non-professional	3	Military (1)	
# pursuing advanced degree	4	Private Practice (49)	
# unemployed and seeking employment	19	Public Interest (3)	

NEW ENGLAND LAW | BOSTON

INSTITUTIONAL INFORMATION

Public/private	Private
Affiliation	No Affiliation
Student-faculty ratio	27:1
% faculty part-time	68
% faculty female	41
% faculty underrepresented minority	9
Total faculty	135

SURVEY SAYS...

Diverse opinions accepted in classrooms, Great library staff, Students love Boston, MA

STUDENTS

Enrollment of law school	1,137
% male/female	42/58
% from out-of-state	71
% part-time	28
% underrepresented minority	22
% international	2
# of countries represented	7
Average age of entering class	24

ACADEMICS

Academic Experience Rating	73
Profs interesting rating	84
Profs accessible rating	85
Hours of study per day	3.99

Academic Specialties

Criminal, Human Rights, International, Taxation, Intellectual Property

Advanced Degrees Offered

JD degree (3–4 years); LLM degree (1 year)

Academics

New England Law | Boston is "relatively small" (though classes can sometimes be large), and it's a "stand-alone school," unaffiliated with a larger university. "New England Law is not a flashy school by any means," explains a 2L, "but the education you receive will put you in a position to be successful." Schedules are "incredibly flexible, allowing evening students and part-time students to attend law school while working full-time and having families." "High-level theory" is certainly on offer here, but the approach tends to be more geared toward real life. "Opportunities for practical experience" are plentiful. A great assortment of practicum courses and seminars allows students "to apply their knowledge and really learn how to be a lawyer." A profusion of clinical options varies from pretty mundane to fascinating. An array of study abroad programs and externships involving various international criminal tribunals is another great perk.

Students have nothing but plaudits for New England Law's "passionate" and "extremely knowledgeable" professors. These "amazing human beings" are "absolutely brilliant, but scary as hell" in a good way. Most of them "have deep practical experience" "rather than being pure academics," and they combine "subject-matter mastery with an approach to teaching that is focused on both deep understanding and practical application." Outside the classroom, they're "extremely accessible and helpful." In a nutshell, the faculty is "the reason for going to this school." Like at most law schools, the staff receives more mixed reviews. According to some students, the administration is "very dedicated" and "approachable." "Communication within the school is seamless," one student tells us, and staffers "do a wonderful job." Other students assert that the different management fiefdoms are "unaware of what each is doing." Also, they say, "Registration is a mess."

New England Law's campus consists of four buildings. None of them is "much to write home about." In the main building, things are definitely "a little cramped." "Hundreds of students trying to move in opposite directions down a single hallway" poses annoying logistical difficulties on a daily basis. "The library isn't nearly big enough" either. "There are times when the library and student lounge are completely overcrowded." On the plus side, technology is "really quite good," and "The law librarians are absolute wizards at researching complicated areas of the law."

Nobody is particularly in love with Career Services. As a part of the program, there is a 1L career counseling requirement, a weekly career newsletter, and complementary membership to the Boston Bar Association for graduating students, yet some feel that New England Law "does not provide opportunities similar to other schools." "There is no grade inflation" either, and the tough grading creates problems because students face pretty tough local competition for law jobs. Nevertheless, students say that New England Law enjoys "an excellent reputation around Boston and Massachusetts." An "alumni network that is fiercely loyal" is an additional plus. Also, the location "in the middle of downtown Boston" provides easy access to "all of the downtown firms and government agencies," thus allowing numerous opportunities to gain real-world practice before graduation. "There are a lot of other, more prestigious, law schools in Boston," relates a 2L," but I am never embarrassed to say I am at New England. In fact, I'm always eager to tell people how great I think the school is."

MICHELLE L'ETOILE, DIRECTOR OF ADMISSIONS
154 STUART STREET, BOSTON, MA 02116
TEL: 617-422-7210 FAX: 617-422-7201
E-MAIL: ADMIT@NESL.EDU • WEBSITE: WWW.NESL.EDU

Life

Students here have a "scrappy, going-it-together attitude" and "a strong work ethic." "Frankly, I look forward to entering the legal community and knocking the socks off students from other Boston law schools," announces a 2L, "especially those from stuffy institutions across the river." New England locals comprise the largest segment of the student body, though the school draws students from across the country. Diversity in terms of ethnicity and age is respectable. Politic opinions run the gamut. "Massachusetts tends to be a liberal region, especially Boston," and New England Law reflects that reality. However, "There is a fairly large conservative base at school as well." The academic atmosphere is reportedly "very warm and welcoming." "While there is just enough competition to ensure you excel, there is enough friendly camaraderie to ensure you enjoy your time as well," says a 2L. "The students here support each other and care about the collective success of all classmates."

The social situation is fairly intimate. "After a little while, you recognize everyone in the building and it's a nice familial feeling," reflects a 3L. There's "a rumor about everything." Numerous student organizations "constantly hold fun and interesting events." "Law prom, softball tournaments," and assorted gatherings are commonplace. The food court across the street is loaded with students studying and socializing. The city of Boston also provides plenty of energy and excitement.

Getting In

Admission to New England Law is no great challenge. Entering students at the 25th percentile have LSAT scores of 151 or lower and undergraduate GPAs of 3.02 or lower. At the 75th percentile, LSAT scores are 154 or higher and GPAs are 3.49 or higher.

Clinical program required	No
Legal writing course requirement	Yes
Legal methods course requirement	Yes
Legal research course requirement	Yes
Moot court requirement	Yes
Public interest law requirement	No

ADMISSIONS

Selectivity Rating	66
# applications received	2,470
% applicants accepted	88
% acceptees attending	15
Median LSAT	149
LSAT Range (25th to 75th percentile)	145–153
Median undergrad GPA	3.06
Application fee	$65
Regular application deadline	3/15
Transfer students accepted	Yes
Evening division offered	Yes
Part-time accepted	Yes
CAS accepted	Yes

FINANCIAL FACTS

Annual tuition	$42,490
Books and supplies	$1,300
Fees	$80
Room & Board	$18,630
Financial aid application deadline	3/25
% first-year students receiving some sort of aid	93
% all students receiving some sort of aid	93
% of aid that is merit based	96
% receiving scholarships	49
Average grant	$17,940
Average loan	$45,422
Average total aid package	$49,507
Average debt	$132,634

EMPLOYMENT INFORMATION

Career Rating	78	**Prominent Alumni**
Total 2012 JD Grads	339	Leonard P. Zakim, NE Anti-Defamation
% grads employed nine months out	76	Leag., namesake, Boston bridge; The
Median starting salary	$53,138	Honorable Susan J. Crawford, Chief
# employed full-time	212	Justice, U.S. Ct of Appeals for Armed
# employed part-time	44	Forces; The Honorable John R. Simpson,
# employed bar required	145	Frmr Head of the U.S. Secret Service.
# employed JD preferred	65	**Grads Employed by Field (%)**
# employed professional/other	31	Academic (2)
# employed non-professional	15	Business/Industry (22)
# pursuing advanced degree	8	Government (9)
# unemployed and seeking employment	63	Judicial Clerkship (6)
# not seeking employment	1	Private Practice (34)
% grads employed by school	2	Public Interest (4)
State for bar exam	MA	
Pass rate for first-time bar	85	

New York Law School

INSTITUTIONAL INFORMATION

Public/private	Private
% faculty part-time	60
% faculty female	40
% faculty underrepresented minority	12
Total faculty	207

SURVEY SAYS...

Diverse opinions accepted in class-rooms, Liberal students, Students love New York, NY

STUDENTS

Enrollment of law school	1,503
% male/female	48/52
% from out-of-state	37
% part-time	27
% underrepresented minority	27
% international	1
# of countries represented	19
Average age of entering class	25

ACADEMICS

Academic Experience Rating	78
Profs interesting rating	83
Profs accessible rating	77
Hours of study per day	3.89

Academic Specialties
Civil Procedure, Commercial, Constitutional, Corporation Securities, Criminal, Government Services, Human Rights, International, Labor, Legal History, Property, Taxation, Intellectual Property

Advanced Degrees Offered
JD; LLM programs in Taxation, Real Estate, Financial Services Law and American Business Law; MA and cer-tificate program in Mental Disability Law (online); Certificate program in Financial Services and Real Estate

Combined Degrees Offered
JD/MBA with Baruch College; JD/MA in Forensic Psychology with John Jay College of Criminal Justice, CUNY; JD/LLM in Taxation and JD/LLM in Real Estate, JD/LLM in Financial Services Law.

Academics

New York Law School, a private institution in lower Manhattan, prides itself on pro-viding hands-on training to yield lawyers who pass the bar exam and who are "ready to make an impact on the legal profession." The program has a heavy focus on practical courses and offers "many opportunities to take part in real lawyering while you are still in law school" through coursework as well as externships. There are plenty of opportuni-ties to tailor your program to fit your professional needs with 250 elective courses offer-ing a host of specialized areas of law.

The NYLS campus employs "state-of-the-art facilities in a prime location of New York City. There are numerous courthouses within walking distance and students are encour-aged and sometimes required by professors to see the law in action first-hand," says a 1L.

The faculty at NYLS brings talent and expertise to each program making classes a pleasure. "Professors and deans make themselves accessible at all times, eager to help students in any way that he or she can, friendly in the hallways, want to get to know the student body," beams a 2L.

"The professors here actually care. They want their students to learn the law and join the legal field as competent and well trained lawyers. They focus less on theory and more on the challenges that we will face in practice. This is great, because most of us are here because we want to be practicing attorneys. For those who are interested in legal scholar-ship, the Law Review is a great way to get involved. Professors are generally more than happy to meet with students to give guidance on school, careers, and anything else," says one student.

"The assistant dean and registrar Oral Hope, is incredibly dedicated to his job and has more than once helped me organize a perfect class schedule. Professors are usually well qualified and like conveying their knowledge. They are also very accessible" says a 2L.

Some students are not as satisfied with the administration, charging that it can be "unavailable and hostile to criticism." Most students, however, view the management team as "present and very accessible to students," as well as "very responsive to stu-dents' needs." As of June 2012, NYLS welcomed a new Dean and President, a new Associate Dean for Academic Affairs, and a new Associate Dean for Career Planning.

The classes at NYLS may not be suited for students seeking small classes and indi-vidual attention. Many students cite classes as being "seriously overcrowded."

When it comes to career services offered by the program, reviews are mixed. Some prospective lawyers on campus say that "career opportunities for students outside the top tier seem to be few and far between." "Getting into prestigious law firms is extreme-ly difficult, and recruitment at NY Law is terrible." Of course students at the top of their class view things differently, reporting that "it's not difficult to get a big firm job here in NYC." Citing the "huge network of practicing alumni" who hold positions at big name organizations in government, public interest, and firms of all sizes as their defense.

"Like most things, law school is what you make it. NYLS has an enormous amount of resources available if one sought them out. If the school does not have something, they are willing to reach out to other institutions on your behalf. I have had the privilege of working with professors outside of the classroom, which has enabled me to further tap into the resources at NYLS," retorts a 2L.

Despite being a smaller campus, the facilities are impressive. Newer buildings are outfitted with state-of-the-art amenities, including "brand new classrooms, lounges," study rooms, and a new library. "The classrooms, library and building in general are state of the art. Wireless internet and wireless printing is accessible everywhere in the building. The classrooms are designed in such a way that you can always see and hear the professor," adds a 2L.

ADAM BARRETT, ASSOCIATE DEAN
NEW YORK LAW SCHOOL, 185 WEST BROADWAY, NEW YORK, NY 10013
TEL: 212-431-2888 FAX: 212-966-1522
E-MAIL: ADMISSIONS@NYLS.EDU • WEBSITE: WWW.NYLS.EDU

Life

Like the city in which the campus sits, NYLS is a melting pot where students of every age and part of the world converge to immerse themselves in their law education. Minorities make up a quarter of the student body but students say that there are only two types of students "those that are from the NYC area [and] those that are not."

NYLS maintains a competitive atmosphere but not overwhelmingly so. "People are more than willing to share notes, outlines, and briefs," they say. "I was very surprised at how cooperative students are with each other," relates a 1L.

There is plenty to do when students aren't studying. "Student groups are plentiful, and there are many leadership opportunities for students." As far as the social scene, reviews often vary. "Since New York Law School is not attached to a larger undergraduate institution, we are a more close-knit community," says a 1L, "like a large extended family." While other students feel a rift. "I would not say that there is a strong New York Law School social scene per se," reflects a 2L. "School spirit, community, and social life at the school should be improved."

All students agree, though, that there is no shortage of things to do when New York City is your campus. NYLS is located in the hip, trendy, and expensive neighborhood of Tribeca. Endless shopping and nightlife options are available in nearby Greenwich Village and Soho, with the rest of the city of Manhattan just a subway ride away.

Getting In

Admitted students at the 25th percentile have LSAT scores in the low 150s and GPAs around 3.0. Admitted students at the 75th percentile have LSAT scores of 157 or so and GPAs of around 3.3.

Clinical program required	No
Legal writing course requirement	Yes
Legal methods course requirement	Yes
Legal research course requirement	Yes
Moot court requirement	No
Public interest law requirement	No

ADMISSIONS

Selectivity Rating	**74**
# applications received	4,825
% applicants accepted	54
% acceptees attending	17
Median LSAT	152
LSAT Range (25th to 75th percentile)	149–154
Median undergrad GPA	3.13
Application fee	$0
Regular application deadline	6/1
Transfer students accepted	Yes
Evening division offered	Yes
Part-time accepted	Yes
CAS accepted	Yes

FINANCIAL FACTS

Annual tuition	$47,600
Books and supplies	$1,300
Fees	$1,625
Room & Board (on/off campus)	$22,800/$17,550
Financial aid application deadline	5/1
% first-year students receiving some sort of aid	92
% all students receiving some sort of aid	89
% of aid that is merit based	10
% receiving scholarships	35
Average grant	$12,729
Average loan	$54,314
Average total aid package	$54,082
Average debt	$153,836

EMPLOYMENT INFORMATION

Career Rating	**77**	
Total 2012 JD Grads	601	
% grads employed nine months out	80	
Median starting salary	$58,000	
# employed full-time	399	
# employed part-time	83	
# employed bar required	280	
# employed JD preferred	128	
# employed professional/other	36	
# employed non-professional	36	
# pursuing advanced degree	10	
# unemployed and seeking employment	82	
# not seeking employment	9	
% grads employed by school	3	
State for bar exam	NY, NJ, CA, PA, MD	
Pass rate for first-time bar	71	

Prominent Alumni
John Marshall Harlan, NYLS 1924, US Supreme Court Justice 1955-1971; Wallace Stevens, NYLS 1903, Pulitzer Prize-winning poet; David Kelley 1986, US Attorney for the Southern District of New York.

Grads Employed by Field (%)
Academic (2)
Business/Industry (25)
Government (7)
Judicial Clerkship (3)
Private Practice (38)
Public Interest (4)

NEW YORK UNIVERSITY
SCHOOL OF LAW

INSTITUTIONAL INFORMATION

Public/private	Private
Student-faculty ratio	9:1
% faculty part-time	30
% faculty female	35
% faculty underrepresented minority	10
Total faculty	240

SURVEY SAYS...

Great research resources, Students love New York, NY

STUDENTS

Enrollment of law school	1,471
% male/female	58/42
% part-time	0
% underrepresented minority	26
% international	4
Average age of entering class	24

ACADEMICS

Academic Experience Rating	98
Profs interesting rating	93
Profs accessible rating	83
Hours of study per day	3.58

Academic Specialties

Civil Procedure, Commercial, Constitutional, Corporation Securities, Criminal, Environmental, Government Services, Human Rights, International, Labor, Legal History, Legal Philosophy, Property, Taxation, Intellectual Property

Advanced Degrees Offered

LLM, JSD

Combined Degrees Offered

JD/LLM, JD/MBA, JD/MPA, JD/MPP, JD/MUP, JD/MSW, JD/MA, JD/Ph.D., JD/JD (Melbourne), JD/LLB (NUS)

Academics

New York University School of Law is a renowned, "rigorous," and "practically focused" legal powerhouse that offers a ridiculous array of courses and a stunning number of programs, colloquia, institutes, and centers. "The academic buildings are wonderful." Resources are world class and "fancy schmancy," including a "huge" library. Students have access to some thirty clinics and over a dozen full-time clinical faculty members. They also have unmatched resources for pursuing public interest opportunities. "The dedication to public interest is unrivaled in the area, and everyone knows it and talks about it," crows a 1L. Students collectively log thousands of volunteer hours, and thanks to "guaranteed" funding, roughly half of each first-year class secures public interest internships for the summer. There's plenty of international flavor here, as well. A few hundred foreign students study law at NYU each year, and there are study abroad opportunities at several of the most distinguished universities in the world.

Class sizes can be pretty large, particularly first year, but they're "not intimidating," and there are "interesting" discussions. Legal theory is part of the deal here, of course, but students also stress the fact that they're exposed to copious amounts of "real law." "The overall quality of the professors is mind-boggling." They're "top-notch academics from a very broad range of legal areas." The faculty is "constantly strengthened by new additions," as well. "NYU has worked tirelessly over the last two decades to amass a faculty that matches or surpasses any other in the country," brags a 1L, "and it has succeeded," largely by "poaching them from places like Harvard and Yale." "I guess money and the opportunity to live in the Village are too much to pass up," muses a 2L. While a few professors are "really inaccessible" "academic researchers" and "less well-regarded as teachers," most offer "real mentorship" and "want to get to know you." "The faculty is deeply committed to student engagement, and they seem to genuinely enjoy it," says a 1L. "The administration is extremely accommodating" as well.

Picky students complain that their degrees are "underappreciated outside of the Northeast," but the employment situation is nothing short of fabulous. There's arguably no law school on the planet that better prepares its graduates for a career in the public sector, and Career Services for those students is "actually as well-resourced as the private-sector employment track." "Anywhere you want to work in public interest law, there will be someone that the Public Interest Law Center can put you in touch with," guarantees a 1L. Students who want to work at big firms are also highly successful. The career and networking opportunities "are fantastic in the New York area." Many NYU Law graduates "with just average grades" have little trouble finding work at top-of-the-market compensation. "If you do well and want to work in a firm, you will," declares a 2L. Other students are a little less cocky, but they're still confident. "If you go to Career Services early enough in the game to fix what you're doing," relates a 2L, "you should be golden."

OFFICE OF ADMISSIONS
139 MacDougal Street, Suite C-201 New York, NY 10012
Tel: 212-998-6060 Fax: 212-995-4527
E-Mail: LAW.MOREINFO@NYU.EDU • Website: WWW.LAW.NYU.EDU

Life

"It is fantastically expensive to attend NYU, both because of tuition and living in Manhattan," but NYU students enjoy an "epic location" "in the middle of Greenwich Village." Simply put, it's "one of the most desirable locations in the world." Of course, if you're looking for a bucolic, cloistered academic experience, this isn't it. "It's New York City, so there are tons of things to do," explains a 2L. "Bars, movies, the theater—really whatever you want." "Students have a great time enjoying the city," "but it's hard to enjoy when you study so much."

Students at NYU Law describe themselves as "easygoing, yet hardworking." "The people here are accustomed to getting very good grades and have the discipline and focus necessary to achieve them." "There is definitely an air of superiority among some of the students." At the same time, the academic atmosphere is "incredibly cooperative and supportive." "The school has a real sense of community about it." "Classmates are excited to hear of the opportunities others have, and not jealous." "It's not competitive," says a 1L, "and it's the most interesting group of people I've been around." "They're musicians, athletes, playwrights, yoga aficionados, rabbis, musical theater talents, etc." In a nutshell, students at NYU Law are elated to be here. "The professors are great, the students are fantastic, and this is a great place to attend law school."

Getting In

Admission to NYU Law is tremendously competitive. Admitted students at the 25th percentile have LSAT scores approaching 170 and undergraduate GPAs around 3.6. At the 75th percentile, LSAT scores are a whopping 173, and GPAs are pretty close to perfect.

Clinical program required	No
Legal writing course requirement	Yes
Legal methods course requirement	Yes
Legal research course requirement	Yes
Moot court requirement	No
Public interest law requirement	No

ADMISSIONS

Selectivity Rating	95
# applications received	6,392
% applicants accepted	28
% acceptees attending	25
Median LSAT	171
LSAT Range (25th to 75th percentile)	169–173
Median undergrad GPA	3.69
Application fee	$85
Regular application deadline	2/15
Regular notification	4/30
Early application deadline	11/15
Early application notification	12/31
Transfer students accepted	Yes
Evening division offered	No
Part-time accepted	No
CAS accepted	Yes

FINANCIAL FACTS

Annual tuition	$51,150
Books and supplies	$1,500
Fees	$1,386
Room & Board	$21,720
Financial aid application deadline	4/15
Average grant	$23,056
Average debt	$149,336

EMPLOYMENT INFORMATION

Career Rating	99	Grads Employed by Field (%)
Total 2012 JD Grads	482	Academic (1)
% for whom you have useable information	100	Business/Industry (5)
% grads employed nine months out	97	Government (7)
Median starting salary	$160,000	Judicial Clerkship (8)
% grads employed by school	0	Private Practice (64)
State for bar exam	NY	Public Interest (15)
Pass rate for first-time bar	95.5	

NORTH CAROLINA CENTRAL UNIVERSITY
SCHOOL OF LAW

INSTITUTIONAL INFORMATION

Public/private	Public
Affiliation	No Affiliation
% faculty part-time	36
% faculty female	60
% faculty underrepresented minority	64
Total faculty	50

SURVEY SAYS...

Diverse opinions accepted in classrooms, Great research resources, Liberal students

STUDENTS

Enrollment of law school	582
% male/female	38/62
% from out-of-state	18
% part-time	18
% underrepresented minority	51
% international	1
# of countries represented	3
Average age of entering class	28

ACADEMICS

Academic Experience Rating	**71**
Profs interesting rating	82
Profs accessible rating	79

Academic Specialties

Constitutional, Taxation, Intellectual Property

Advanced Degrees Offered

JD Day Program, 6 semesters (3 years); JD Evening Program, 8 semester and 3 summer sessions (4 years)

Combined Degrees Offered

JD/MBA, 4 Years; JD/MLS, 4 Years

Academics

"I rave about my law school," gloats a 3L at the North Carolina Central University School of Law. By all accounts, NCCU is a "great value." It's unquestionably possible to graduate from here with little or no debt. The renovated law school building feels "very new" and it's "always well-kept." The facilities are state-of-the-art" and "extremely high-tech." "Practical training is strongly encouraged" and readily available. "NCCU has substantial opportunities for practical legal experience outside the classroom," explains a 1L. "Excellent" clinics, pro bono opportunities, externship programs, and hands-on skills courses provide real world experience galore. "The variety of clinics" (eighteen in all) includes criminal litigation, juvenile law, and a small business clinic—just to name a few. There's also a standard JD/MBA program, a JD/MLS program (for future law librarians), and a unique Biotechnology and Pharmaceutical Law Institute, where you can engross yourself in the labyrinth of prescription drug regulation. It's also worth noting that students here have easy access to the state and federal courts in the nearby state capital, Raleigh.

Inside the classroom, the "passionate, knowledgeable," and "very dedicated" faculty brings plenty of "real-world" know-how. For the most part, professors are also "very clear in explaining concepts." "The teachers are really encouraging, and they want to see each student succeed." "Motivation, guidance, and encouragement" are ample. "Faculty accessibility" is another huge plus. "They are tough but there for you in many ways." Faculty members are "very responsive" and "always available and willing to help" if you stay after class or stop by their offices.

Some students call NCCU "the total package" and wouldn't change a thing. Others, however, see areas that could be better. While some students tell us that management is "organized" and "always helpful," for example, others disagree. Also, despite the fact that a loyal alumni base works "to ensure that you have an opportunity to practice" and a recently reorganized Career Services Office has helped students with job placement, "other support services" could still use "an overhaul." A broader selection of electives would be another improvement. "We could offer a wider variety of classes in more concentrated areas," suggests a 3L.

Life

NCCU began in 1939 as North Carolina's only law school for African Americans. Today, it's quite a diverse bastion of legal education, ethnically and otherwise. "Students come from all over the country and all over the world." Ages run the gamut from students straight out of undergrad to those in their fifties who are training for a second (or third) career. "Different perspectives on life and law" are abundant. "Many schools claim to be diverse and accepting of diversity," observes one 3L. "Yet my school proves it every day. We are a family. It includes the good, the bad, and ugly."

STEPHANIE BARBEE WILLIAMS, ASSISTANT DEAN OF ADMISSION
640 NELSON STREET, DURHAM, NC 27707
TEL: 919-530-6517 FAX: 919-530-6030
E-MAIL: SBWILLIAMS@NCCU.EDU • WEBSITE: LAW.NCCU.EDU

NCCU's relatively small size lends an intimacy that you just won't find at larger schools. First-year sections are particularly cozy, and the atmosphere for all students is "very friendly." "We are a strong, supportive community," explains a 3L. "We help each other out and truly want each other to succeed." "Upperclassmen are mentors for new law students," and they offer advice "on a daily basis and on a variety of subjects and experiences." Nevertheless, and all of this social comfort notwithstanding, students are often competing for just a few precious A's. "The curve of our grading system can be devastating to a GPA," cautions a 2L," but it does force students to work their hardest to achieve good grades."

Students here are very satisfied with their lives outside of law school. "The campus has some problems with crime," but students stress that safety isn't much of an issue at all. Durham is a growing and revitalizing city that offers a low cost of living, some forty annual festivals, and unbeatable medical facilities. With about 15,000 students in town (at NCCU and at nearby Duke University), there are certainly plenty of lively social options. If you prefer laid-back ones, you can find those, too. An array of outdoorsy activities is available in every direction as well.

Gettin In

Though the acceptance rate at NCCU is low, you don't necessarily need outstanding grades and test scores to get admitted. Admitted students at the 25th percentile have LSAT scores of 145 or so and their undergraduate GPA is right around 3.0. Admitted students at the 75th percentile typically have LSAT scores around 151 and GPAs in B+ to A– territory.

Clinical program required	No
Legal writing course requirement	Yes
Legal methods course requirement	Yes
Legal research course requirement	Yes
Moot court requirement	No
Public interest law requirement	No

ADMISSIONS

Selectivity Rating	**86**
# applications received	1,400
% applicants accepted	34
% acceptees attending	45
Median LSAT	147
LSAT Range (25th to 75th percentile)	143–151
Median undergrad GPA	3.22
Application fee	$50
Regular application deadline	3/31
Transfer students accepted	Yes
Evening division offered	Yes
Part-time accepted	Yes
CAS accepted	Yes

FINANCIAL FACTS

Annual tuition (in-state out-of-state)	$8,050/$21,978
Books and supplies	$2,200
Fees	$3,325
Room & Board (on/off campus)	$10,712/$13,580
Financial aid application deadline	6/1
% first-year students receiving some sort of aid	98
% all students receiving some sort of aid	98
% of aid that is merit based	23
% receiving scholarships	41
Average grant	$4,500
Average loan	$28,500
Average total aid package	$32,000
Average debt	$72,000

EMPLOYMENT INFORMATION

Career Rating	70
Total 2012 JD Grads	165
% for whom you have useable information	55
% grads employed nine months out	43
Median starting salary	$50,000
# employed full-time	66
# employed part-time	5
# employed bar required	45
# employed JD preferred	18
# employed professional/other	17
# employed non-professional	0
# pursuing advanced degree	1
# unemployed and seeking employment	17
# not seeking employment	0
% grads employed by school	0
State for bar exam	NC
Pass rate for first-time bar	73.8

Prominent Alumni
Honorable Wanda Bryant, N.C. Court of Appeals; G. K. Butterfield, U.S. House of Rep.; Jason L. Groves, Executive VP/ General Counsel, Medifast.

Grads Employed by Field (%)
Academic (3)
Business/Industry (9)
Government (7)
Judicial Clerkship (1)
Private Practice (20)
Public Interest (3)

NORTHEASTERN UNIVERSITY
SCHOOL OF LAW

INSTITUTIONAL INFORMATION

Public/private	Private
Student-faculty ratio	15:1
% faculty part-time	47
% faculty female	48
% faculty underrepresented minority	19
Total faculty	86

SURVEY SAYS...

Abundant externship/internship/clerkship opportunities, Liberal students

STUDENTS

Enrollment of law school	604
% male/female	40/60
% from out-of-state	63
% part-time	0
% underrepresented minority	40
# of countries represented	2
Average age of entering class	24

ACADEMICS

Academic Experience Rating	80
Profs interesting rating	76
Profs accessible rating	79
Hours of study per day	4.10

Academic Specialties

Civil Procedure, Commercial, Constitutional, Corporation Securities, Criminal, Environmental, Human Rights, International, Labor, Property, Taxation, Intellectual Property

Advanced Degrees Offered

The Northeastern LLM program is designed to provide students with the opportunity to obtain the legal foundation and skills needed to succeed while affording students the freedom to tailor their coursework, legal placement and writing to meet their interests.

Combined Degrees Offered

Northeastern University School of Law's commitment to collaboration and cooperation extends far beyond our classrooms.

Academics

Northeastern University School of Law in Boston offers an absolute wealth of "practical hands-on learning," a "public interest focus," and "a very strong social-justice vibe." "Hands down," the best thing about this place is the cooperative legal education program. Students take traditional courses and have traditional semesters as 1Ls. Second- and third-year students are on a quarter system and "alternate classes with internships every three months." By the time they graduate, students at Northeastern have had "four full-time, law-related jobs." They are able to "test out different areas of the law" and gain "practical, real-world experience that most law students don't get." "Imagine leaving law school with forty-four weeks of legal experience on your resume," says a 1L. "There are numerous participating employers and students can get a chance to go across the country" and "all over the world." "I have had opportunities and experiences that I never would have had otherwise," gloats a 2L, "including clerking for a judge and working for an international investment bank in New York City." "Switching between co-op and classes every three months makes law school more bearable" as well. "You aren't stuck in school all year long," explains a 2L. "You go to school for eleven weeks, then you go do an awesome job."

Another unique feature at Northeastern is its evaluation system. There is no class rank here and there are no alphabet grades. Instead, students get narrative evaluations from both their professors and their co-op supervisors. Additionally, strong academic 2Ls and 3Ls receive honors and high honors designations. On one hand, "The grading system fosters a cooperative environment that really helps you learn from both the professors and the students you're with." On the other hand, "Excellent grades are indistinguishable from good grades." Regarding employment prospects after graduation, students say, "Northeastern has a great reputation in Boston." It's particularly awesome if you are looking to for a public interest career. If you want a job in the private sector, "The school prepares you well for that path," but you "must plan carefully" when selecting courses.

The faculty here is "overwhelmingly on the far left of the political spectrum." There are many "shining stars in their specialties" who "know the material like champs." Most professors are "extremely approachable" as well. There are also "a few egotistical nightmares," though, and "way too many adjuncts." Students happily attest that "administrators respond immediately to problems which are brought to their attention."

Facilities-wise, "The law campus is a little island in the undergrad campus, with two interconnected buildings of its very own and an underground labyrinth of offices, lockers, and study spaces." "The old building is drafty." The new building is "absolutely beautiful." The library is "sunny and pleasant," and "The library staff is phenomenal." There are "plenty of places to study." Classrooms are "bright and inviting," "with large windows and state-of-the-art equipment, including outlets for laptops at all seats."

Life

Students describe themselves as "welcoming, interesting, and smart." There are many students right out of college and a good percentage that are a little bit older. There's a big gay and lesbian population. Politically, "the student body at Northeastern is incredibly liberal and left-leaning." Some students tell us, "People are very receptive to differing views." Others disagree. A certain segment of the population is "offended by the most inane comments," they say. "If you are not super liberal," counsels a 3L, "do not bother applying." Politics notwithstanding, everyone seems to agree that the academic

CARRIE TAUBMAN, ASSISTANT DEAN AND DIRECTOR OF ADMISSIONS
400 HUNTINGTON AVENUE, BOSTON, MA 02115
TEL: 617-373-2395 FAX: 617-373-8865
E-MAIL: LAWADMISSIONS@NEU.EDU • WEBSITE: WWW.NORTHEASTERN.EDU/LAW

environment is "incredibly collegial." "Collaboration is encouraged." "Students study together, share notes, and help each other out when needed."

Northeastern is "located in an urban area of Boston," and there is plenty to do outside the confines of the law school. "There are great common areas for social gatherings and biweekly bar events around Boston." You definitely don't have to party to have a good time, though. Students here tend to be "less obnoxiously obsessed with drinking than seems to be the law school norm." Social life tends to be "clique-y," primarily because the co-op program is constantly shifting them back and forth from course work to internship work. People leave town for a few months on internships. "There are people who live two blocks away who are hardly ever on campus, and there are people who commute ninety minutes who are always around."

Getting In

Enrolled students at the 25th percentile have LSAT scores of about 155 and GPAs of roughly 3.3. Enrolled students at the 75th percentile have LSAT scores in the 164 range and GPAs a bit over 3.7. Early action applicants who are admitted are not required to attend, as the program is non-binding.

Clinical program required	No
Legal writing course requirement	Yes
Legal methods course requirement	Yes
Legal research course requirement	Yes
Moot court requirement	No
Public interest law requirement	Yes

ADMISSIONS

Selectivity Rating	85
# applications received	3,216
% applicants accepted	39
% acceptees attending	13
Median LSAT	161
LSAT Range (25th to 75th percentile)	154–163
Median undergrad GPA	3.52
Application fee	$75
Regular application deadline	3/1
Regular notification	4/15
Early application deadline	11/15
Early application notification	1/15
Transfer students accepted	Yes
Evening division offered	No
Part-time accepted	No
CAS accepted	Yes

FINANCIAL FACTS

Annual tuition	$42,940
Books and supplies	$5,548
Fees	$116
Room & Board	$17,100
Financial aid application deadline	2/15
% first-year students receiving some sort of aid	90
% all students receiving some sort of aid	96
% of aid that is merit based	80
% receiving scholarships	85
Average grant	$10,661
Average loan	$44,909
Average total aid package	$52,851
Average debt	$129,467

EMPLOYMENT INFORMATION

Career Rating	82
Total 2012 JD Grads	215
% for whom you have useable information	95
% grads employed nine months out	84
Median starting salary	$51,312
% job accepting grads providing useable salary information	48
# employed full-time	133
# employed part-time	39
# employed bar required	116
# employed JD preferred	41
# employed professional/other	10
# employed non-professional	5
# pursuing advanced degree	1
# unemployed and seeking employment	28
# not seeking employment	2
% grads employed by school	8
State for bar exam	MA
Pass rate for first-time bar	85.8

Prominent Alumni
Mary Bonauto, Civil Rights Project Director, Gay & Lesbian Advocates & Defenders; Scott Heekin-Canedy, President and General Manager, The New York Times; Joel Goldberg, General Counsel, Perkin Elmer.

Grads Employed by Field (%)
Academic (1)
Business/Industry (14)
Government (6)
Judicial Clerkship (7)
Military (1)
Private Practice (23)
Public Interest (21)

NORTHERN ILLINOIS UNIVERSITY
COLLEGE OF LAW

INSTITUTIONAL INFORMATION

Public/private	Public
Student-faculty ratio	15:1
% faculty part-time	24
% faculty female	41
% faculty underrepresented minority	29
Total faculty	34

SURVEY SAYS...

Diverse opinions accepted in classrooms, Great library staff, Students never sleep

STUDENTS

Enrollment of law school	103
% male/female	51/49
% from out-of-state	18
% part-time	1
% underrepresented minority	20
Average age of entering class	26

ACADEMICS

Academic Experience Rating	**66**
Profs interesting rating	70
Profs accessible rating	70

Combined Degrees Offered

JD/MPA. Other simultaneous enrollment options can be structured for students admitted to other graduate programs. Normally these programs are completed in 4–5 years.

Academics

As the only public school found within the environs of the greater Chicago area, NIUers are released into Illinois' sea of graduating law students equipped with a solid education at a fraction of the price. Known for its commitment to fostering a sense of community and responsibility and pointing its students in the direction of public service jobs, NIU places a high value on pro bono work and makes a number of "public interest stipends" available to its students each summer. The school "has placed a special emphasis on diversity, both amongst its faculty and its student body," and it shows in the number of "divergent viewpoints" that are represented both in and out of the classroom.

Professors are themselves one source of these divergent viewpoints, with many students claiming that "some of the professors are amazing while others clearly enjoy the benefits of tenure." While the vast majority of professors "are well above average" and "do a very good job," offering students a high level of approachability, many students claim to have had a few instructors who were below par. "Simply reciting material straight from the textbook is not teaching," observes a first-year student. For the most part, however, students are happy with the quality of teaching at NIU and say that the school is very good at balancing theory with practice. "A number of the professors go out of their way to expand on topics illustrated in the text and to relate their real-world experiences to the matters at hand. The professors as a group make themselves accessible to students who have issues that need to be discussed," affirms a student. "The faculty and administration practically begs students to come in and talk to them." Other students would like to see a broader spectrum of courses offered.

Although some students have grumbled about "1970s decor," the school recently repainted and refurnished several on-campus buildings, including the law library and the student lounge. One of the greatest resources offered to NIU students, many of whom are older, is the Career Opportunities Office, which "will definitively help you get started toward your career," especially if you're at the top of your class and looking to get into "big law." Though some students speak of the disadvantages facing NIU grads—particularly the distance of the school from Chicago proper—others are reassured by the Career Opportunities Office's strong networking prospects, which complement the school's well-established and reputable clinic and externship programs. "We have a lock on many state attorney and public defenders offices now, and an incredible number of alumni in the judiciary. If you want to be a government trial lawyer in Illinois, this is definitely the school to go to." As an exiting student avers, "The price was right, and if you are willing to do the work you can get a good education."

SARAH E. SCARPELLI, DIRECTOR OF ADMISSIONS & FINANCIAL AID
SWEN PARSON HALL-COLLEGE OF LAW-ROOM 151, DeKALB, IL 60115
TEL: 815-753-8595 FAX: 815-753-5680
E-MAIL: LAWADM@NIU.EDU • WEBSITE: NIU.EDU/LAW

Life

With a strong contingent of older, "second-career" individuals, "a high bar for maturity and professionalism within the student body" tends to be set on campus. Students are friendly enough, but hometown DeKalb can be a "pretty desolate place to kids accustomed to the party life of Champaign-Urbana, Bloomington-Normal, or other major college towns." DeKalb is "without much of the nightlife and amenities that students were accustomed to having from their undergrad experience." There are two fraternities on campus (one is "clearly the party frat, and the other is the academic frat"), and there are a number of student groups that students can join, though "a few struggle to survive" due to lack of participation. As for competition among students, a second-year student assures us, "The shark-eat-shark mentality of other law schools would not be tolerated here." "For one thing, the student body is too small, and we all know each other too well. For another, there's just more a sense of being practical and real-world here; we're 'type-A' people, surely, but we've also mellowed with more life experience than your average law student straight out of undergrad."

Getting In

Northern Illinois encourages students to submit their application early, though they do accept applications after the suggested priority deadline of April 1. Recently admitted students at the 25th percentile had an LSAT score of 150 and an average GPA of 3.20, while students at the 75th percentile had an LSAT score of 155 and a GPA of about 3.42.

Clinical program required	No
Legal writing course requirement	Yes
Legal methods course requirement	No
Legal research course requirement	Yes
Moot court requirement	Yes
Public interest law requirement	No

ADMISSIONS

Selectivity Rating	**80**
# applications received	1,058
% applicants accepted	45
% acceptees attending	22
Average LSAT	152
Median LSAT	152
LSAT Range (25th to 75th percentile)	150–155
Average undergrad GPA	3.20
Median undergrad GPA	3.2
Application fee	$50
Regular application deadline	
Early application deadline	4/1
Transfer students accepted	Yes
Evening division offered	No
Part-time accepted	Yes
CAS accepted	Yes

FINANCIAL FACTS

Annual tuition (in-state out-of-state)	$14,624/$29,246
Books and supplies	$1,600
Fees	$4,065
Room & Board	$13,982
Financial aid application deadline	3/1
% first-year students receiving some sort of aid	87
% all students receiving some sort of aid	95
% of aid that is merit based	23
% receiving scholarships	49
Average grant	$13,375
Average loan	$24,344
Average total aid package	$28,729
Average debt	$49,858

EMPLOYMENT INFORMATION

Career Rating	78	**Prominent Alumni**
Total 2012 JD Grads	97	Kathleen Zellner; Cheryl Niro; Dr. Kenneth
% grads employed nine months out	81	Chessick
Median starting salary	$47,584	**Grads Employed by Field (%)**
# employed full-time	66	Academic (4)
# employed part-time	12	Business/Industry (19)
# employed bar required	65	Government (13)
# employed JD preferred	7	Judicial Clerkship (4)
# employed professional/other	1	Military (3)
# employed non-professional	5	Private Practice (50)
# pursuing advanced degree	0	Public Interest (8)
# unemployed and seeking employment	15	
# not seeking employment	3	
% grads employed by school	0	
State for bar exam	IL, IN, WI	
Pass rate for first-time bar	82.2	

NORTHWESTERN UNIVERSITY
SCHOOL OF LAW

INSTITUTIONAL INFORMATION

Public/private	Private
Student-faculty ratio	8:1
% faculty part-time	33
% faculty female	27
% faculty underrepresented minority	5
Total faculty	174

SURVEY SAYS...
Students love Chicago, IL

STUDENTS

Enrollment of law school	259
% male/female	54/46
% from out-of-state	80
% part-time	0
% underrepresented minority	34
% international	5
Average age of entering class	26

ACADEMICS

Academic Experience Rating	**98**
Profs interesting rating	94
Profs accessible rating	92
Hours of study per day	3.98

Academic Specialties
Corporation Securities, Environmental, Human Rights, International, Taxation

Advanced Degrees Offered
JD, 3 years; LLM, 1 year; SJD, 5 years; LLM in taxation, 1 year; LLM in human rights, 1 year; JD for international lawyers, 2 years; Accelerated JD, 2 years

Combined Degrees Offered
JD/MBA, 3 years; JD/Ph.D., 6 years; JD/LLM International Human Rights, 4 years; JD/LLM Tax, 4 years; LLM/certificate in management (Kellogg), 1 year

Academics

Located "in the heart of Chicago," Northwestern University School of Law has a first-rate "national reputation" for "developing practical skills" and offering "world-class" clinics that give students "unbelievable" opportunities to work on "real cases." Many here agree, "It's hard to imagine getting a better mix of academic rigor and practical job training anywhere else." Other highlights at NU include study abroad programs all over the world, a highly touted JD/MBA program, and lots of "self-scheduled exams." One demerit is the "legal writing program" that students wish was "a pass/fail class" due to the "incredible amount of work" it requires.

Northwestern's "brilliant" and "very friendly" faculty is made up of "nationally and internationally renowned scholars" who have "a great sense of humor." Students have "an unparalleled opportunity to learn from the best, starting right at the beginning." "My classes and instruction have ranged from very good to simply outstanding," relates a 2L. "I'd go so far as to say that my Constitutional Law class was one of the most intellectually stimulating courses I've encountered." Professors are "accessible" and "seem to really enjoy talking to students outside of class." "It is not uncommon for them to stop me in the hallway and chat about a class topic, my journal comment, or even college football," explains a student. For the most part the administration is "receptive to student concerns" and "always approachable." "Everything goes pretty smoothly," and the atmosphere is "not very bureaucratic," though some note that "change is very slow to come" in regards to "accommodation for disabilities."

Students happily report, "If you do even moderately well in your 1L classes at Northwestern, you're going to have legal employers knocking down your door." "You'd be hard-pressed to find someone coming out of NU to a less-than-excellent job." "Most of us start out at big firms," adds a 1L. "The Chicago firms just love NU students." However, some students complain, "There should be a greater emphasis on public interest career choices," as "not everybody wants to go to a big law firm upon graduation."

The architecture here is "nice, consisting of both old, more traditional buildings, and a newer building." "A quiet atmosphere prevails" and the "gorgeous" library overlooks Lake Michigan. Also, trust us: Lincoln Hall is exactly what a law school classroom should look like. While "good," the classrooms could use some "updating," and "There aren't enough areas to study." Also, "lighting conditions" in the library are "bad," and though "wireless Internet continues to improve," it can still be "insufficient and annoying."

Life

"Northwestern places a huge emphasis on admitting students who have a couple years of work experience after undergrad, and it makes a huge difference," says one student. These future lawyers "come from a variety of backgrounds and offer amazing insights into a range of issues." They "are grounded and have balanced lives." "People have a better sense of the world around them and the realities of life beyond a classroom," observes a 2L. "This keeps the drama to a minimum and also assembles a group of people who've done some pretty interesting things—minor league ball, the military, symphonic bassoon, and so on." "There seems to be the misconception that the students at Northwestern are really old," clarifies another student. "For most students it is only about two years before we come to law school."

DON REBSTOCK, ASSOCIATE DEAN OF ENROLLMENT
375 EAST CHICAGO AVENUE, CHICAGO, IL 60611
TEL: 312-503-8465 FAX: 312-503-0178
E-MAIL: ADMISSIONS@LAW.NORTHWESTERN.EDU • WEBSITE: WWW.LAW.NORTHWESTERN.EDU

"Class sizes are small" and "The school goes to great lengths to create and foster a sense of community among the students." In this "collegial" atmosphere, students are "intelligent, friendly, [and] laid-back." "There are not too many gunners," reports one student. "We're smart, personable people who mix well socially while doing top-notch legal work," says a 2L. However, some students project an "'I-don't-study-at-all' attitude in the middle of the semester, trying to throw others off base. Then, suddenly, the same person who 'never studies' has a 150-page annotated outline with hyperlinks to all of its sections and subsections."

Outside of class, Northwestern is "a very fun place to attend school." "The school sponsors many events for students every week," and there are "free lunches almost every day," along with "random social events put on by the many, many student organizations." "Lunchtime speakers, panels, and club meetings provide great opportunities to explore different facets of the law school experience and the legal profession without taking up too much time." In addition, "Chicago is a great city" with "a great mix of...hustle and bustle and Midwestern friendliness"—all of which starts right "next door" to campus with "Michigan Avenue's Magnificent Mile."

Getting In

Northwestern claims to be the only law school in the country that strongly encourages all applicants to interview as a part of the admissions process. Knowing this, it behooves you to show up for an interview if you apply. With or without an interview, though, admission is unusually competitive. Admitted students at the 25th percentile have LSAT scores of 166 and GPAs of about 3.4. Admitted students at the 75th percentile have LSAT scores of 171 and GPAs of about 3.9.

Clinical program required	No
Legal writing course requirement	Yes
Legal methods course requirement	No
Legal research course requirement	Yes
Moot court requirement	Yes
Public interest law requirement	No

ADMISSIONS

Selectivity Rating	96
# applications received	4,390
% applicants accepted	24
% acceptees attending	25
Median LSAT	170
LSAT Range (25th to 75th percentile)	164–171
Median undergrad GPA	3.8
Application fee	$100
Regular application deadline	2/15
Early application deadline	12/1
Early application notification	1/31
Transfer students accepted	Yes
Evening division offered	No
Part-time accepted	No
CAS accepted	Yes

FINANCIAL FACTS

Annual tuition	$53,168
Books and supplies	$10,196
Fees	$300
Room & Board	$14,040
Financial aid application deadline	3/1
% first-year students receiving some sort of aid	85
% all students receiving some sort of aid	85
% of aid that is merit based	50
% receiving scholarships	32
Average grant	$28,623
Average debt	$156,791

EMPLOYMENT INFORMATION

Career Rating	98	**Prominent Alumni**
Total 2012 JD Grads	295	John Paul Stevens, Supreme Court
% grads employed nine months out	91	Justice; Ada Kepley, First American woman
Median starting salary	$160,000	to obtain a law degree; Jerry Reinsdorf,
% job accepting grads providing		Owner, Chicago Bulls and White Sox.
useable salary information	84	**Grads Employed by Field (%)**
# employed full-time	255	Academic (1)
# employed part-time	13	Business/Industry (13)
# employed bar required	236	Government (4)
# employed JD preferred	30	Judicial Clerkship (8)
# employed professional/other	2	Military (1)
# employed non-professional	9	Private Practice (60)
# pursuing advanced degree	12	Public Interest (4)
# not seeking employment	2	
% grads employed by school	4	
State for bar exam	IL	
Pass rate for first-time bar	96	

Nova Southeastern University
Shepard Broad Law Center

INSTITUTIONAL INFORMATION

Public/private	Private
Affiliation	No Affiliation
Student-faculty ratio	17:1
% faculty part-time	68
% faculty female	37
% faculty underrepresented minority	20
Total faculty	193

SURVEY SAYS...

Diverse opinions accepted in classrooms, Students love Fort Lauderdale, FL

STUDENTS

Enrollment of law school	1,029
% male/female	47/53
% from out-of-state	21
% part-time	19
% underrepresented minority	32
% international	2
# of countries represented	23
Average age of entering class	26

ACADEMICS

Academic Experience Rating	**73**
Profs interesting rating	77
Profs accessible rating	83
Hours of study per day	4.43

Academic Specialties
Civil Procedure, Commercial, Constitutional, Corporation Securities, Criminal, Environmental, Government Services, Human Rights, International, Labor, Legal History, Property, Taxation

Combined Degrees Offered
JD/MBA, JD/MS Conflict Resolution, JD/MS Computer Science, JD/Masters in Urban and Regional Planning. Each of these programs should take 3 years to complete if full-time and 4 years if part-time.

Academics

Nova Southeastern University's Law Center is a large law school not too far from Miami that offers "a strong emphasis on legal writing" and a "hands-on approach to legal education." Highfalutin theory definitely isn't the focus at NSU. Here, you "learn how to be a good legal practitioner." NSU's critical skills program coaches students on everything from the basics of briefing cases during first year to bar exam preparation during third year. An "invaluable" clinical program that includes options in seven different areas of law provides a tremendous number of students with "practical experience before becoming an attorney." There are certificate programs in health law and international law. NSU also offers a host of study abroad opportunities. Especially noteworthy are the dual-degree law programs in both Barcelona and Rome that allow students to study civil law systems in addition to American common law. Completion of either one results in two law degrees in two different countries, which is an undeniably impressive set of credentials.

A couple of students say that the administration is "prompt in addressing students' needs," but the overwhelming sentiment seems to be that "it takes forever to get anything done" and that the top brass is "out of touch." "However, the professors are in touch," promises a 1L. "The professors really do care about your success." Some faculty members "have inflated egos" or simply are "not that good." On the whole, though, the "intense, demanding, and entertaining faculty" is "worth every tuition dollar." "I am most pleased with the knowledge, practical experience, and teaching skills possessed by my professors," reflects a 3L. Outside of class, Nova Southeastern's faculty is "extremely approachable." "They are always willing to help outside of the classroom and are very encouraging," promises a 2L. "Almost everyone has an open-door policy." "Some of the professors will sit and talk with you at great length about topics relevant to class and irrelevant," adds a 1L.

The facilities here are mixed. "The campus is absolutely beautiful." "The buildings around the law school are beautiful," too. "The law school building itself is bland," though. It's "fairly industrial and has a built-on-a-budget feel." "The chairs are uncomfortable" in many classrooms. "The library is ugly" and "could definitely use more study rooms." Some students say that Internet connectivity is "great" while others call it "horrible." "The school is very advanced technologically," explains a 3L. "However, half the time the technology is not working."

Some students call the work of the Career Development Office "unparalleled." Others tell us that students are "on their own with regard to finding employment and getting internships." Sentiment regarding job prospects is similarly mixed. One faction of students says that Nova Southeastern is "very reputable locally" while another faction gripes that the school "lacks sufficient connections to major law firms."

WILLIAM PEREZ, ASSISTANT DEAN FOR ADMISSIONS
3305 COLLEGE AVENUE, FORT LAUDERDALE, FL 33314
TEL: 954-262-6117 FAX: 954-262-3844
E-MAIL: ADMISSION@NSU.LAW.NOVA.EDU • WEBSITE: WWW.NSULAW.NOVA.EDU

Life

Nova Southeastern is home to "a wide diversity of students" in terms of ethnicity, social class, age, background, and pretty much every other category. Students describe themselves as "bright and "motivated." They are "nice and considerate," too, except possibly when it comes to the delicate subject of class rank. Some students maintain that the academic atmosphere is "generally cooperative" even then. "Fellow students make sure that you know the information and help out as much as possible," promises a 2L. However, many others say that the struggle for precious A's is tense (especially among full-timers) because "overall grades are curved" pretty harshly. "This is a competitive classroom experience," flatly advises a 1L , though students only need to contend with the curve during their first year.

"Weekends are nonexistent" for a few die-hard studiers. However, those students who do choose to put away their books "generally get along" and manage to squeeze in a respectable amount of social activity. There are some commuter aspects here, but "it is easy to make friends" if you put forth the effort. "Students regularly hang out together when we aren't studying," reports a 1L. You can choose to become involved in "many organizations" on campus. "The school's location is definitely a big advantage" as well. It's warm and sunny most of the time, of course, and beautiful beaches aren't far away. Downtown Fort Lauderdale is nearby and Miami is not too far south.

Getting In

Nova Southeastern isn't impossible to get into for students with solid grades and test scores. Enrolled students at the 25th percentile have LSAT scores around 147 and GPAs in the 3.0 range. At the 75th percentile, LSAT scores are around 152 and GPAs are about 3.5. Also worth noting is a provisional admission program that allows some applicants who would otherwise be rejected to take two courses at Nova Southeastern in May and June. Those applicants need a cumulative GPA of 2.5 or better in those two courses to get admitted for 1L classes in the fall.

Clinical program required	No
Legal writing course requirement	Yes
Legal methods course requirement	No
Legal research course requirement	Yes
Moot court requirement	No
Public interest law requirement	No

ADMISSIONS

Selectivity Rating	75
# applications received	1,721
% applicants accepted	54
% acceptees attending	34
Average LSAT	150
Median LSAT	150
LSAT Range (25th to 75th percentile)	147–153
Average undergrad GPA	3.13
Median undergrad GPA	3.13
Application fee	$53
Regular application deadline	5/1
Transfer students accepted	Yes
Evening division offered	Yes
Part-time accepted	Yes
CAS accepted	Yes

FINANCIAL FACTS

Annual tuition	$33,730
Books and supplies	$2,356
Fees	$600
Room & Board (on/off campus)	$14,938/$17,028
Financial aid application deadline	4/15
% first-year students receiving some sort of aid	93
% all students receiving some sort of aid	89
% of aid that is merit based	40
% receiving scholarships	35
Average grant	$10,367
Average loan	$41,459
Average total aid package	$42,255
Average debt	$135,548

EMPLOYMENT INFORMATION

Career Rating	78	**Prominent Alumni**
Total 2012 JD Grads	354	Melanie G. May, Appeals Court Judge; Rob
% for whom you have useable information	100	Brzezinski, VP football operations, Minnesota Vikings; Ellyn Setnor
% grads employed nine months out	81	Bogdanoff, FLA House of Representatives.
Median starting salary	$50,000	**Grads Employed by Field (%)**
# employed full-time	257	Academic (1)
# employed part-time	28	Business/Industry (11)
# employed bar required	221	Government (8)
# employed JD preferred	38	Judicial Clerkship (0)
# employed professional/other	18	Private Practice (57)
# employed non-professional	8	Public Interest (3)
# pursuing advanced degree	12	
# unemployed and seeking employment	53	
# not seeking employment	4	
% grads employed by school	0	
State for bar exam	FL	
Pass rate for first-time bar	81	

THE OHIO STATE UNIVERSITY
MICHAEL E. MORITZ COLLEGE OF LAW

INSTITUTIONAL INFORMATION

Public/private	Public
Student-faculty ratio	15:1
% faculty part-time	28
% faculty female	31
% faculty underrepresented minority	19
Total faculty	83

SURVEY SAYS...

Great research resources, Abundant externship/internship/clerkship opportunities

STUDENTS

Enrollment of law school	700
% male/female	57/43
% from out-of-state	33
% part-time	0
% underrepresented minority	20
% international	2
# of countries represented	7
Average age of entering class	23

ACADEMICS

Academic Experience Rating	88
Profs interesting rating	84
Profs accessible rating	84
Hours of study per day	3.86

Academic Specialties

Civil Procedure, Commercial, Constitutional, Corporation Securities, Criminal, Government Services, International, Labor, Property, Taxation, Intellectual Property

Advanced Degrees Offered

Masters in the Study of Law, 1 Year; LLM International Students, 1 Year

Combined Degrees Offered

JD/MBA (4), JD/MHA (4), JD/MPA (4), JD/over 80 different individually designed (4–5)

Academics

The Ohio State University Moritz College of Law is a "kinder, gentler law school," which "supports creativity." "Through career workshops each week, setting students up with legal professionals as private mentors, and a wide breadth of clinics to satisfy each particular taste, OSU invests in its students. And their offerings keep expanding!" The new Entrepreneurial Business Clinic should ease any student fears arising from a perceived lack of focus on corporate law and "fill the one gap Moritz had." OSU advocates pro bono work, and plenty of clinics allow students to gain practical experience in the legal world. Students love this "hands-on" approach. Additionally, there is a strong criminal law program, and "The alternative dispute resolution program is one of the best in the nation." The legal writing program is also outstanding. Students praise the law school's "connection with the university as a whole." The school offers various joint-degree programs, including a master's of public policy that can be completed "for free and in no additional time." Students couldn't be happier with their classroom experience, and professors seem to love what they do. "Almost every professor I've had has been engaging, brilliant, and enthusiastic," says one student. Students agree there's an endless supply of "fantastic educators." Professors are "leaders in their research fields," and "great citizens," who give openly of their time and "have a real passion for instructing." "It's common to see faculty at student events and around the law school." They're "excellent facilitators of class conversation" and create a "friendly environment." "I had no idea how strong the faculty would be," one student proclaims. "I have yet to find a professor, who does not go above and beyond to meet with students and share insight."

The resources at OSU are "focused on student access." The administration doesn't "hesitate to interact with the students to give them advice or even just to have casual conversation." Also, "We are just a hop, skip, and a jump away from downtown Columbus, home of the Ohio Statehouse, Ohio Supreme Court, and many other courts, organizations, and firms." This is very helpful in acquiring externship opportunities and jobs within the community. Although there are "increasing career outreach opportunities through Career Services," some worry that outside the state of Ohio resources might be "limited." There's a strong "network of alumni," and even though some students did stress their concern over finding jobs out of state, one student offers, "Even if you don't plan to stay in Ohio, OSU has great regional ties throughout the Midwest and a strong national reputation." Another student says the alumni and the Columbus legal community believe in the school's mission and will continue to help out when they can. Still students emphasize concern over the lack of east coast firms coming to campus to recruit.

Students mention the "primarily left-leaning" nature of the faculty and student body. While some love this aspect, others disputed it as fact. Whichever way the pendulum might swing, at OSU "a strong current of tolerance pervades." In the classroom and outside it, all views are expressed and accepted. Facilities and technology are a worry at OSU. Both are described as "surprisingly lacking." However, they "just finished remodeling the student union and the main library," and one student admits, "The facilities have gotten much better this year."

JIMMI NICHOLSON, ASSISTANT DIRECTOR
104 DRINKO HALL, 55 WEST 12TH AVENUE, COLUMBUS, OH 43210
TEL: 614-292-8810 FAX: 614-292-1492
E-MAIL: LAWADMIT@OSU.EDU • WEBSITE: MORITZLAW.OSU.EDU

Life

OSU School of Law is referred to as both "supportive" and "surprisingly congenial," and a school in which "people will always share their notes." "While we acknowledge the curve as a fact of life, we have a strong sense of camaraderie." Some students believe competition exists, but that it "does not overshadow a great law school experience." Another student has "never really felt a competitive spirit among the students here." Age at the law school ranges from those just out of undergrad to older students, many of whom "are married and have children."

"The law school is literally right next to the center of campus social life." Most students agree its location is convenient. "Directly across the street is the brand new Ohio Union, twenty restaurants and bars, a concert venue, movie theaters, coffee shops, and more." There are a multitude of places for students to relax and gather before and after class. To further foster a sense of community, "Every weekday at noon, there are no classes and an impressive amount of group and club events, guest speaker presentations, debates, and other special events happen every day."

Getting In

The admissions committee considers LSAT scores, undergraduate GPAs, personal essays, and letters of recommendation all very important in the process of admission. Roughly one in three applicants is accepted. Admitted students in the 25th percentile have undergraduate GPAs around 3.4 and LSAT scores in the high 150s. Admitted students in the 75th percentile have GPAs around 3.8 and LSAT scores in the mid 160s.

Clinical program required	No
Legal writing course requirement	Yes
Legal methods course requirement	No
Legal research course requirement	No
Moot court requirement	Yes
Public interest law requirement	No

ADMISSIONS

Selectivity Rating	87
# applications received	2,300
% applicants accepted	39
% acceptees attending	23
Average LSAT	162
Median LSAT	163
LSAT Range (25th to 75th percentile)	159–165
Average undergrad GPA	3.61
Median undergrad GPA	3.63
Application fee	$60
Regular application deadline	3/15
Transfer students accepted	Yes
Evening division offered	No
Part-time accepted	No
CAS accepted	Yes

FINANCIAL FACTS

Annual tuition (in-state out-of-state)	$26,328/$41,278
Books and supplies	$3,980
Fees	$2,300
Room & Board	$15,876
Financial aid application deadline	2/15
% first-year students receiving some sort of aid	76
% all students receiving some sort of aid	81
% of aid that is merit based	77
% receiving scholarships	75
Average grant	$8,132
Average loan	$34,169
Average total aid package	$9,512
Average debt	$87,770

EMPLOYMENT INFORMATION

Career Rating	92
Total 2012 JD Grads	231
% grads employed nine months out	97
Median starting salary	$60,000
% job accepting grads providing useable salary information	53
# employed full-time	181
# employed part-time	32
# employed bar required	156
# employed JD preferred	45
# employed professional/other	10
# employed non-professional	2
# pursuing advanced degree	6
# unemployed and seeking employment	5
# not seeking employment	7
State for bar exam	OH, DC, NY, IL, CA
Pass rate for first-time bar	89

Prominent Alumni
Jack Creighton, Former CEO Weyerhauser Corp. and United Airlines; Brian Sandoval, Governor of Nevada; Erin Moriarity, 48 Hours/CBS News Journalist.

Grads Employed by Field (%)
Business/Industry (26)
Government (16)
Judicial Clerkship (6)
Military (1)
Private Practice (44)
Public Interest (5)

OKLAHOMA CITY UNIVERSITY
SCHOOL OF LAW

INSTITUTIONAL INFORMATION

Public/private	Private
Affiliation	Methodist
Student-faculty ratio	8:1
% faculty part-time	53
% faculty female	37
% faculty underrepresented minority	13
Total faculty	75

SURVEY SAYS...

Heavy use of Socratic method, Diverse opinions accepted in classrooms, Great library staff

STUDENTS

Enrollment of law school	539
% male/female	55/45
% from out-of-state	36
% part-time	12
% underrepresented minority	24
% international	1
# of countries represented	5
Average age of entering class	26

ACADEMICS

Academic Experience Rating	70
Profs interesting rating	82
Profs accessible rating	79
Hours of study per day	4.41

Academic Specialties
Commercial, Business Law, Indian Law, Energy and Natural Resources Law, Health Law

Advanced Degrees Offered
JD; 3 years

Combined Degrees Offered
JD/MBA; JD/Masters of Applied Sociology- Non-Profit Leadership

Academics

Students are held to high standards at Oklahoma City University School of Law. At this private college, professors "really make you work for your grade," and the school's tough curve inspires "students who have a strong work ethic to compete with each other" for the top spots. Despite the challenges, it is difficult to get lost in the lecture hall at OCU. "Professors and administrators alike know students' names outside of the classroom," and "smaller class sizes" ensure the opportunity "to get more individualized attention if need be from professors." A 1L enthuses, "I have a personal relationship with all my teachers, and they know me by name. That's an incredible feeling, especially when the material is hard." Outside the classroom, there are numerous ways for students to get extra help with the material, and "Oklahoma City University's staff is devoted to making the students that pass through the halls of this school successful." For example, the comprehensive Study for Success program offers a series of seminars and special workshops designed to help 1Ls adjust to law school. In this and other ways, students say they get a great return on investment. Yes, OCU is "expensive," but "the administration really goes out of the way to make sure you are getting what you pay for." A current student attests, "I cannot recall hearing 'there is no budget for that.' In fact I have watched complaints by a vocal minority answered with drastic action when the complaint was reasonable."

Students praise the academic experience at OCU, especially its "smart and talented" instructors. Bringing real-world knowledge to the classroom, "Professors are not only brilliant scholars but are also experienced attorneys in their respective fields." In addition to the broad core curriculum, "Oklahoma City University places special emphasis on legal research and writing skills." Students agree that the writing component is key to their education, but also "one of the most challenging aspects of the 1L year." Among other unique curricular and extracurricular offerings, the school's American Indian Wills Clinic, Immigration Law Clinic, and Innocence Clinic allow students to work directly with clients, under the supervision of a faculty member. In fact, OCU is "the top in the state, and one of the leading schools in the country for Native American law." OCU students can also gain course credit for externships at Oklahoma government agencies, state and federal courts, and in corporate counsel offices. Another feather in the school's cap includes the fact that OCU "has the highest bar pass rate in the state." Rather than expecting students to prepare on their own time, the school "takes bar prep very seriously, offering free bar prep classes weekly during the final year of school."

When it comes time to take their education out into the real world, OCU's "Alumni network is extensive and encouraging," with former students living across the United States, as well as internationally. OCU has a "solid employment record," but students say they would benefit from "more internship opportunities and more networking opportunities" during the program. While they tend to place well in Oklahoma City, students are eager to point out that, "a law degree from OCU could easily take you anywhere in the country or even internationally." For that reason, many say the school's most important goal is "getting its name out beyond just the local region."

LAURIE W. JONES, ASSOCIATE DEAN FOR ADMISSIONS
2501 N BLACKWELDER, OKLAHOMA CITY, OK 73106-1493
TEL: 405-208-5354 FAX: 405-208-5814
E-MAIL: LAWQUESTIONS@OKCU.EDU • WEBSITE: WWW.LAW.OKCU.EDU

Life

For penny-pinching students, Oklahoma City provides the attractive combination of "low cost of living and high quality of life." The school's main campus is "located close to downtown Oklahoma City, which is a growing and diverse community," now home to close to 1.2 million residents. Though it remains relatively affordable, Oklahoma City boasts an active nightlife, a growing arts district, and "a great NBA team, and many students share season tickets." The greater Oklahoma City University campus is home to over 4,000 students, adding a bustling backdrop to the law school. Law students tell us that the "campus is beautiful," though they also admit that "the classrooms are a little cramped sometimes." Fortunately, "the law school spent over $1 million renovating facilities—including the law library—this past year. Construction was a bit of an inconvenience but future students will be able to enjoy the benefits of the upgrades to the facilities."

Among law students, the school boasts a "close-knit environment," where a general sense of camaraderie prevails. While academics are tough, the "Student body isn't overly competitive." A student explains, "The difficulty of the experience binds us together." Students participate in events hosted by the Student Bar Association, or take part in one of the School of Law's numerous clubs and associations, from the Women Law Students' Association, to Military, International & National Security Law Association, to the Health Law Association.

Getting In

With its strong regional reputation and ties to the Oklahoma bar, OCU attracts many in-state students, while recruiting heavily from other western states. In addition to regular admission, the school offers the Alternate Summer Admission Program, or ASAP, through which students, whose basic LSAT scores or GPA do not meet requirements, are conditionally admitted. After completing a special, four-week summer program, these applicants may be admitted to the regular law school program. In 2011, the entering class had a median LSAT score and GPA or 151 and 3.13 respectively.

Clinical program required	No
Legal writing	
course requirement	Yes
Legal methods	
course requirement	Yes
Legal research	
course requirement	Yes
Moot court requirement	No
Public interest	
law requirement	No

ADMISSIONS

Selectivity Rating	70
# applications received	1,201
% applicants accepted	65
% acceptees attending	31
Average LSAT	149
LSAT Range	
(25th to 75th percentile)	147–153
Average undergrad GPA	3.19
Application fee	$50
Regular application deadline	8/1
Transfer students accepted	Yes
Evening division offered	Yes
Part-time accepted	Yes
CAS accepted	Yes

FINANCIAL FACTS

Annual tuition	$30,885
Books and supplies	$1,740
Fees	$3,405
Room & Board	$9,200
Financial aid application	
deadline	3/1
% first-year students receiving	
some sort of aid	93
% all students receiving	
some sort of aid	91
% of aid that is merit based	50
% receiving scholarships	56
Average grant	$16,000
Average loan	$38,349
Average total aid package	$39,404
Average debt	$93,475

EMPLOYMENT INFORMATION

Career Rating	79	Prominent Alumni
Total 2012 JD Grads	207	Reta Strubhar, First Woman on Oklahoma
% for whom you have useable		Court of Criminal Appeals; Andrew Benton,
information	93	President, Pepperdine University; Nona
% grads employed nine months out	85	Lee, VP and General Counsel, Arizona
Median starting salary	$55,014	Diamondbacks.
% job accepting grads providing		**Grads Employed by Field (%)**
useable salary information	50	Academic (3)
# employed full-time	83	Business/Industry (14)
# employed part-time	1	Government (13)
# employed bar required	60	Military (2)
State for bar exam OK, TX, IL, UT, MO		Private Practice (62)
Pass rate for first-time bar	87	Public Interest (5)

PACE UNIVERSITY
SCHOOL OF LAW

INSTITUTIONAL INFORMATION

Public/private	Private
Affiliation	No Affiliation
Student-faculty ratio	13:1
% faculty part-time	47
% faculty female	42
% faculty underrepresented minority	8
Total faculty	103

SURVEY SAYS...
Diverse opinions accepted in classrooms

STUDENTS

Enrollment of law school	702
% male/female	45/55
% from out of state	15
% part-time	22
% underrepresented minority	18
% international	1
Average age of entering class	25

ACADEMICS

Academic Experience Rating	**87**
Profs interesting rating	82
Profs accessible rating	80
Hours of study per day	4.32

Academic Specialties
Civil Procedure, Commercial, Constitutional, Corporation Securities, Criminal, Environmental, Government Services, Human Rights, International, Labor, Legal History, Property, Taxation, Intellectual Property

Advanced Degrees Offered
SJD in Environmental Law, 1 year; LLM in Environmental Law, 1–2 years; LLM in Comparative Legal Studies, 1 year

Combined Degrees Offered
JD/MBA with Pace University, 4–6 years; JD/MPA with Pace University, 4–6 years; JD/MEM with Yale University, 4–6 years; JD/MS with Bard College, 4–6 years; JD/MA with Sarah Lawrence College, 4–6 years

Academics

New York's Pace University School of Law has earned a regional reputation as a leader in its field because it has excelled in its specialty of environmental law. The "one-of-a-kind" environmental law curriculum wins praise for offering "a variety of courses" taught by faculty who are "highly respected and known in the environmental community." This "broad" program "offers a unique specialization within the legal profession" taught by "some of the greatest professors available," and one that has proven to be the best known aspect of Pace's law program. However, students point out that Pace is "not just an environmental law school...I think Pace has rested on this reputation for far too long."

Educators at Pace aim to ensure graduates are "readily prepared to enter the working field and perform at a high level." Internships abound, including study abroad opportunities that allow you to work at overseas law firms or intern with a war crime tribunal. The "amazing" professors here "are interested in their students' growth, understanding, and achievement and are for the most part available for help and talking outside of the classroom." Indeed, they will "frequently even give students their home phone numbers if they need to call for questions." Some suggest the quality of professors can be "hit or miss," with some going so far as to say that "the professors are either very good or very poor with very little in between." However, according to most these educators "are intelligent, love their jobs, and are always helpful." These teachers "work hard to help us and are excellent at the subjects they teach and conveying the subjects to us."

Student opinions on the administration are mixed, with some indicating that the administration's unwillingness to confront problems or ideas presented by students "detracts from all the great resources available to those who attend Pace." Other members of the faculty win praise. Many students note that "the librarians are fantastic at helping students and explaining research tools to students." Gripes with the administration aside, overall "the quality of the faculty coupled with the genuine care in preparation of students is unrivaled." The trick is letting people know—students would love to see Pace gain a wider reputation.

Life

With a campus in the Westchester County suburbs of New York City, life at Pace Law School can be as active as you want to make it. It is not cheap to live here—White Plains "is an expensive place to live"—but the school is proximate enough to the five boroughs of New York City, as well as the NYC suburbs, that commuting to school is common. The "extremely professional" and "extremely polite" people on campus, both staff and students alike, create an "intimate atmosphere" in which students feel "close to (their) peers." Student organizations are many, so "social life is there if you want it, but you're not an outcast if you don't."

LISA LANCIA, DIRECTOR OF ADMISSIONS
78 NORTH BROADWAY, WHITE PLAINS, NY 10603
TEL: 914-422-4210 FAX: 914-989-8714
E-MAIL: ADMISSIONS@LAW.PACE.EDU • WEBSITE: WWW.LAW.PACE.EDU

The situation with the campus itself is not as universally beloved. Despite its reputation as a cutting edge environmental law school, "there is nothing particularly cutting-edge about the technology on campus." Students complain that "the wireless is frequently down," and that the "windowless" auditorium-style classrooms lack natural lighting. Despite these complaints, one student summed up a common sentiment: "I consider myself to be very fortunate to be a Pace law student."

Getting In

LSAT scores of approximately 152 and GPAs a little less than 3.2 are typical for enrolled students at the 25th percentile. At the 75th percentile, those scores are close to 157 (LSAT) and about 3.6 (GPA). Pace has an accelerated program that allows students to start in January and graduate in two and a half years, if they are in a hurry to get their JD.

Clinical program required	No
Legal writing course requirement	Yes
Legal methods course requirement	Yes
Legal research course requirement	Yes
Moot court requirement	Yes
Public interest law requirement	No

ADMISSIONS

Selectivity Rating	**83**
# applications received	2,556
% applicants accepted	45
% acceptees attending	15
Median LSAT	154
LSAT Range (25th to 75th percentile)	152–156
Median undergrad GPA	3.4
Application fee	$65
Regular notification	rolling
Transfer students accepted	Yes
Evening division offered	No
Part-time accepted	Yes
CAS accepted	Yes

FINANCIAL FACTS

Annual tuition	$41,950
Books and supplies	$1,600
Fees	$248
Room & Board	$10,460

EMPLOYMENT INFORMATION

Career Rating	**75**	**Prominent Alumni**
Total 2012 JD Grads	230	John Cahill, Chief of Staff, Former NY
% for whom you have useable information	92	Governor George Pataki; Robert F. Kennedy Jr., Co-Director, Pace
% grads employed nine months out	86	Environmental Litigation Clinic; Gerry
Median starting salary	$57,500	Comizio, Partner, Paul, Hastings, Janofsky
# employed full-time	143	& Walker, LLP., Judith Lockhart, Carter
# employed part-time	11	Ledyard & Milburn
# employed bar required	139	**Grads Employed by Field (%)**
# employed JD preferred	25	Academic (2)
# employed professional/other	12	Business/Industry (23)
# employed non-professional	14	Government (11)
# pursuing advanced degree	2	Judicial Clerkship (8)
# unemployed and seeking employment	30	Private Practice (47)
% grads employed by school	7	Public Interest (9)
State for bar exam	NY	

PEPPERDINE UNIVERSITY
SCHOOL OF LAW

INSTITUTIONAL INFORMATION

Public/private	Private
Affiliation	Church of Christ
Student-faculty ratio	17:1
% faculty part-time	61
% faculty female	25
% faculty underrepresented minority	16
Total faculty	113

SURVEY SAYS...

Students love Malibu, CA

STUDENTS

Enrollment of law school	633
% male/female	50/50
% from out-of-state	45
% part-time	0
% underrepresented minority	17
% international	1
# of countries represented	2
Average age of entering class	24

ACADEMICS

Academic Experience Rating	94
Profs interesting rating	95
Profs accessible rating	99
Hours of study per day	3.76

Academic Specialties

Commercial, Corporation Securities, International, Taxation, Intellectual Property

Advanced Degrees Offered

LLM in Dispute Resolution

Combined Degrees Offered

JD/MBA, 4 years; JD/MDR, 3–4 years; JD/MPP, 4 years; JD/MDiv, 5 years

Academics

It's hard not to lead with the most obvious benefit of choosing Pepperdine for law school: "the panoramic view of the Pacific Ocean and Catalina Island as you enter just about make law school tolerable." Pepperdine's law campus is in fact located in stunning Malibu, CA, just outside Los Angeles, but to emphasize the beauty of its location would "wrongly connote a culture that may lack rigor or seriousness." Indeed, among Pepperdine's legal strengths are "top-notch dispute resolution curricula, wide variety of faculty from myriad professional and ideological backgrounds, and its top-tier student body." "The administration is currently in the process of evolving to update themselves with modern times and beliefs," and students see its recent changes as mostly positive ones that are "not yet complete" but "moving at a promising rate": "Our new dean is spectacular, and will continue to improve our law school in any way needed." "Dean Tacha could not be more optimistic, outgoing, or encouraging if she tried." Though Pepperdine is historically, and still, a Christian university, they recently instituted an LGBT student group, and students say Pepperdine's "is a growing community of diversity." Despite the fact that "technology has been updated recently," many students do echo the need for further updates: the "Wifi speed" is "miserable," there's a "lack of computers in classrooms, for professor/PowerPoint use," and "the interior of the Law Building looks as though it was plucked straight out of 1985." More importantly, a lot of students feel some lack in the school's career services, saying Pepperdine "could use heavy improvement in its career development office," but there's a "large alumni base in Los Angeles," where there's also an abundance of legal jobs.

Professors, for the most part, receive high marks from students: they're "absolutely excellent," "have a genuine open-door policy," and "have been nothing less than completely exceptional." "They truly invest in and care about the students and it makes law school much less stressful." A few voices dissent with this characterization, noting the prevalence of "very wealthy, conservative men, which makes expressing your (differing) opinions difficult." In spite of that, "I haven't met one professor who didn't seem completely passionate about both teaching law and encouraging every student to succeed." PBeyond Malibu, "the overseas study opportunities are numerous and very well run," and students praise Pepperdine's program in "dispute resolution," noting that "classes through the Straus Institute for Dispute Resolution...fill up quickly."

Life

It's hard not to love your time at Pepperdine when the "campus is set in an absolutely beautiful location," and students appreciate their "Wonderful peers as a result of such a warm environment." While "the competition is extremely high," "The student body is generally very warm." The staff also "Promotes both personal and intellectual growth": "The leadership and location are unmatched. Pepperdine's School of Law has been an extremely welcoming environment."

SHANNON PHILLIPS, EXECUTIVE DIRECTOR, ADMISSIONS
24255 PACIFIC COAST HIGHWAY, MALIBU, CA 90263
TEL: 310-506-4631 FAX: 310-506-7668
E-MAIL: SOLADMIS@PEPPERDINE.EDU • WEBSITE: LAW.PEPPERDINE.EDU

As a Christian university, Pepperdine leans right and could according to some be "More open to diversity in viewpoints," but "in my three years at Pepperdine I have never once felt out of place as a non-religious, liberal Democrat." Even if highers-up tend in conservative directions, "there are plenty of conservatives and liberals alike among the students," which creates a vibrant culture of discussion. "Because most students who choose Pepperdine share its religious values, it can create a dividing line among students. That being said, the faculty, staff, and students are all very welcoming and kind to every single student at Pepperdine regardless of their religious and political affiliations." Pepperdine is also "second to none among law schools in America today" in its commitment to making its law education available to veterans: "From being one of three top tier law schools in the country to offer full Yellow Ribbon support, housing allowance based on the Malibu Beach zip code, to dinner at the Dean's house on Veteran's Day, this law school truly strives to serve those who have served their country."

Getting In

Pepperdine's LSAT median is 162 (156–164, 25th–75th percentiles) and GPA median is 3.63 (3.35–3.75, 25th–75th percentiles). As noted above, aspiring lawyers who have served in the U.S. military are very welcome applicants.

Clinical program required	Yes
Legal writing course requirement	Yes
Legal methods course requirement	No
Legal research course requirement	Yes
Moot court requirement	Yes
Public interest law requirement	No

ADMISSIONS

Selectivity Rating	88
# applications received	2,655
% applicants accepted	32
% acceptees attending	26
Average LSAT	160
LSAT Range (25th to 75th percentile)	158–162
Average undergrad GPA	3.55
Application fee	$50
Regular application deadline	2/1
Transfer students accepted	Yes
Evening division offered	No
Part-time accepted	No
CAS accepted	Yes

FINANCIAL FACTS

Annual tuition	$35,460
Books and supplies	$800
Fees	$60
Room & Board	$15,110
% first-year students receiving some sort of aid	87
% all students receiving some sort of aid	87
% of aid that is merit based	30
% receiving scholarships	75
Average grant	$9,950
Average loan	$35,155
Average total aid package	$45,105
Average debt	$111,163

EMPLOYMENT INFORMATION

Career Rating	85	Grads Employed by Field (%)
% grads employed nine months out	97	Academic (3)
State for bar exam	CA	Business/Industry (20)
Pass rate for first-time bar	74	Government (13)
Prominent Alumni		Judicial Clerkship (1)
Pierre Prosper, Ambassador-at-Large for		Private Practice (44)
War Crime Issues; Rod Blagojevich,		Public Interest (3)
Govenor, Illinois; Todd Platts,		
Congressman, Pennsylvania.		

PHOENIX SCHOOL OF LAW

Academics

This brand-spanking new school received accreditation from the ABA in June 2010, making it the only private law school in Arizona with both full- and part-time programs. Though this lack of tradition means that many areas of the school can still be considered "reactive," students claim PhoenixLaw is "on the cusp," and its eventual reputation rests on its performance in the next few years. As of now, the rapidly growing (and somewhat expensive) school seems to be aiming to become a "unique, niche law school targeting nontraditional students with practice ready skills." Indeed, "practice readiness" is something the school not only proclaims it focuses on, but also "genuinely centers most of its activities toward."

"Phenomenal" professors are very devoted to their students and "will work with you on any issues and really encourage excellence." The mix of adjunct and full-time teachers "are very accessible, treat us as colleagues, and devote hours to practical, hands-on applications of the law." PhoenixLaw has "great teachers and very high expectations" (including a strict attendance policy and a C curve), making the achievement of the elusive A difficult, but there's ample help available from the "knowledgeable, intelligent" professors, and the school even offers intersession classes, which provides even more class availability. "There are many options for class times, if you are willing to take a night class." "The school's administration could not do more to try to help and encourage students to succeed. Every school activity and function is centered toward student success," says a student.

Though the name of the school could certainly use some rooftop screaming, its strong practical focus on experience is highly employable, which bolsters its reputation among those firms that are familiar with PhoenixLaw. The externship programs and Center for Professional Development are well-lauded, leading one student to claim that "more than any other school I researched, it really bridges the gap between law school and a law career." The school has also recently begun small-sized review classes, "which are very informative because they discuss how to approach bar questions."

Life

There's a lack of competition at PhoenixLaw, due to the friendly, Southwestern nature of the students. "When someone wants notes because they missed class, notes are provided. When someone needs help understanding something, there's always student help nearby. I think the cooperative nature of the student body is a huge asset of this school," says a 3L. Most students are from Phoenix and the sprawling suburbs, and many have come here to embrace a career change. The increased attempt by the administration to gain student opinions is reflected in their recent strides of reaching out to night students to help them to participate in school functions.

GLEN FOGERTY, ASSISTANT DEAN OF ADMISSIONS
ONE NORTH CENTRAL AVENUE, PHOENIX, AZ 85004
TEL: 602-682-6800 • FAX: 602-682-6999
E-MAIL: ADMISSIONS@PHOENIXLAW.EDU • WEBSITE: WWW.PHOENIXLAW.EDU

Though the school itself doesn't have much of a campus, "It feels like a law school" in its aesthetics. Classes are held in one building located in downtown Phoenix; outfitted with high tech classrooms and common areas designed to facilitate student collaboration. The library is "clean and organized, and the staff is incredibly helpful." Most students have some form of transportation at their disposal but "There is also a light rail and bus system with which people can get anywhere in the city." Social events do exist but typically occur in the city itself. The older average age of students means that many must attend to full-time jobs and families instead of socializing with their fellow classmates.

Getting In

Class sizes have only grown since the school's formation, as has the applicant pool. For the fall 2011, admitted students at the 25th percentile had LSAT scores around 145 and GPAs in the 2.7 range. Admitted students at the 75th percentile had LSAT scores in the low 150s and GPAs of approximately 3.38.

Clinical program required	No
Legal writing course requirement	Yes
Legal methods course requirement	No
Legal research course requirement	Yes
Moot court requirement	No
Public interest law requirement	Yes

ADMISSIONS

Selectivity Rating	67
# applications received	2,299
% applicants accepted	73
% acceptees attending	27
Average LSAT	148
Median LSAT	145
LSAT Range (25th to 75th percentile)	141–151
Average undergrad GPA	2.98
Median undergrad GPA	2.93
Application fee	$0
Regular application deadline	
Transfer students accepted	Yes
Evening division offered	Yes
Part-time accepted	Yes
CAS accepted	Yes

FINANCIAL FACTS

Annual tuition	$39,252
Books and supplies	$2,185
Fees	$1,860
Room & Board	$12,136
% first-year students receiving some sort of aid	84
% all students receiving some sort of aid	88
% of aid that is merit based	65
% receiving scholarships	46
Average loan	$54,415
Average total aid package	$54,035
Average debt	$135,655

EMPLOYMENT INFORMATION

Career Rating	87
Total 2012 JD Grads	181
% for whom you have useable information	99
% grads employed nine months out	90
Median starting salary	$55,000
% job accepting grads providing useable salary information	36
# employed full-time	129
# employed part-time	34
# employed bar required	98
# employed JD preferred	51
# employed professional/other	13
# employed non-professional	1
# pursuing advanced degree	7
# unemployed and seeking employment	9
# not seeking employment	1
% grads employed by school	9
State for bar exam	AZ, CA, NJ, NM, MI
Pass rate for first-time bar	76.6

Prominent Alumni
Julia Guinane, Kercsmar & Feltus, PLLC, Selected 2013 Southwest Rising Star Super Lawyer; Javier M. Leija, IP attorney with an expertise in copyright and trademark.

Grads Employed by Field (%)
Academic (3)
Business/Industry (15)
Government (12)
Judicial Clerkship (1)
Private Practice (48)
Public Interest (10)

QUINNIPIAC UNIVERSITY
SCHOOL OF LAW

INSTITUTIONAL INFORMATION

Public/private	Private
Affiliation	No Affiliation
Student-faculty ratio	13:1
% faculty part-time	47
% faculty female	32
% faculty underrepresented minority	6
Total faculty	72

SURVEY SAYS...
Great research resources, Beautiful campus

STUDENTS

Enrollment of law school	407
% male/female	58/42
% from out-of-state	48
% part-time	20
% underrepresented minority	11
% international	1
# of countries represented	10
Average age of entering class	25

ACADEMICS

Academic Experience Rating	**81**
Profs interesting rating	80
Profs accessible rating	88
Hours of study per day	4.38

Academic Specialties
Criminal, Taxation, Intellectual Property

Advanced Degrees Offered
JD, 3 years full-time, 4 years part-time; LLM in Health Law

Combined Degrees Offered
JD/MBA, 4 years; JD/MBA in Health Care Management, 4 years

Academics

Quinnipiac University School of Law is "a pretty, quaint, and intimate" "suburban" school with "nice and small" class sizes. At the same time, "The extracurricular opportunities are extraordinary" and students are afforded plenty of opportunities to gain "real-world experience." "It's possible to be a big fish in a small pond here and really amp up your resume," says a 2L. "Nearly every student participates in some sort of practical course, clinic, or externship," adds another 2L. "I've personally been able to do something practical every semester since my first year, and I know other students have had the same experience." There are six areas of concentration including health law, intellectual property, and tax law. "There are also numerous competition teams," and "Dispute resolution is a real strong point." Naturally, smaller schools tend to have fewer courses, and Quinnipiac is no exception. Beyond the concentrations, "There are relatively few courses that are helpful outside of a general practice."

Most students tell us that "the administration here is "receptive" and "visible." "You will never get lost in the mix or stuck on hold for thirty minutes waiting to talk to financial aid." The faculty is largely excellent except for a few "incredibly boring" "bad apples, like anywhere." "Most professors are entertaining," and they're "highly dedicated to helping students achieve success." Faculty members are also "approachable people, which can be hard to come by in law professor types." "They are readily available and willing to help," gushes a 1L. "The professors know you on a personal level and genuinely care about your success." "Many of them have taken a personal interest in my goals for the future," adds a 3L.

Quinnipiac has a steadily growing roster of helpful alums, and the school is nicely situated, close to New Haven and Hartford and not unreasonably far from both Boston and New York. Firms throughout Connecticut participate in on-campus interviews, and the headquarters of several gigantic conglomerates and financial institutions are located nearby, which leads to a lot of corporate positions. "Large firm jobs are hard to come by," however. "Unless you are in the top 5 percent of the class," advises a 2L, "don't expect to even be considered for a high-paying big firm job for the summer or straight out of school." Job prospects for students who want to work in Connecticut are solid, but the situation for students who want to work elsewhere is "insanely frustrating." "Any job you might be interested in outside of the state, you have to find yourself," though the Career Services office is trying to do more to help these students.

The campus of the larger university here is "beautiful." "Studying on the grass by the lake is the perfect environment in the spring." A state park across the street lends an additional visual appeal. The law school building is newer, and it "takes great advantage of natural lighting." The facilities are "set up very fluidly," and they range from "pretty good" to "state-of-the-art." Classrooms are "modern." The library is "extremely comfortable," and "It's a great place for research." Study carrels abound both in the library and around the building. "The building is breathtaking and a wonderful place to study," says a 2L. "It is extremely accommodating of commuters," at least once they overcome Quinnipiac's "impossible" parking "nightmare."

EDWIN WILKES, ASSOCIATE VICE PRESIDENT AND DEAN OF LAW SCHOOL ADMISSIONS
275 MOUNT CARMEL AVENUE, (LW-ADM), HAMDEN, CT 06518-1908
TEL: 203-582-3400 FAX: 203-582-3339
E-MAIL: LADM@QUINNIPIAC.EDU • WEBSITE: LAW.QUINNIPIAC.EDU

Life

A couple dozen states are represented among the law students at Quinnipiac but the majority of students hail from the Northeast. Students describe themselves as "intelligent," "decent, friendly human beings." There's a "rough" grading curve "that sometimes stinks," but students are mutually respectful and "supportive" in spite of it. "My classmates are extremely helpful and generous with notes and time," relates a 2L. "Our environment is comfortable and relaxed, which makes it easier to not only learn, but make friends."

"The student body is somewhat bifurcated between those who don't realize that they aren't living at a frat anymore and those who are actually serious about law school, though generally the serious students vastly outnumber the party students." If you do come to Quinnipiac seeking ribald fun, however, you're unlikely to find much locally. "Hamden is beautifully boring and therefore the perfect place to go to law school," but it doesn't offer much in the way of interesting activities. "City slickers that need constant action, clubs that stay open 'til 4:00 A.M., or any real nightclubs for that matter will not be satisfied," cautions a 2L. A solid contingent of students frequently heads to nearby New Haven, where fairly lively urban fare is "certainly available." When students need a taste of serious city life, they typically head to New York City or Boston.

Getting In

Admitted students at the 25th percentile have LSAT scores in the mid 150s and undergraduate GPAs around 3.0. At the 75th percentile, LSAT scores are close to 160, and GPAs are approximately 3.6.

Clinical program required	No
Legal writing course requirement	Yes
Legal methods course requirement	Yes
Legal research course requirement	No
Moot court requirement	Yes
Public interest law requirement	No

ADMISSIONS

Selectivity Rating	77
# applications received	1,355
% applicants accepted	52
% acceptees attending	15
Average LSAT	156
Median LSAT	156
LSAT Range (25th to 75th percentile)	153–159
Average undergrad GPA	3.40
Median undergrad GPA	3.42
Application fee	$65
Regular application deadline	
Transfer students accepted	Yes
Evening division offered	Yes
Part-time accepted	Yes
CAS accepted	Yes

FINANCIAL FACTS

Annual tuition	$46,260
Books and supplies	$1,200
Fees	$816
Room & Board (on/off campus)	$0/$15,454
Financial aid application deadline	4/15
% first-year students receiving some sort of aid	95
% all students receiving some sort of aid	92
% of aid that is merit based	56
% receiving scholarships	72
Average grant	$22,495
Average loan	$38,174
Average total aid package	$45,139
Average debt	$97,218

EMPLOYMENT INFORMATION

Career Rating	84	Grads Employed by Field (%)	
Total 2012 JD Grads	151	Academic	(1)
% for whom you have useable information	99	Business/Industry	(19)
% grads employed nine months out	84	Government	(16)
Median starting salary	$52,000	Judicial Clerkship	(7)
% job accepting grads providing useable salary information	54	Private Practice	(40)
		Public Interest	(1)
# employed full-time	119		
# employed part-time	8		
# employed bar required	64		
# employed JD preferred	49		
# employed professional/other	10		
# employed non-professional	4		
# pursuing advanced degree	1		
# unemployed and seeking employment	16		
# not seeking employment	6		
% grads employed by school	1		
State for bar exam	CT, NY, NJ, MA, RI		
Pass rate for first-time bar	90		

REGENT UNIVERSITY
SCHOOL OF LAW

INSTITUTIONAL INFORMATION

Public/private	Private
Affiliation	Nondenominational
% faculty part-time	0
% faculty female	34
% faculty underrepresented minority	17
Total faculty	29

SURVEY SAYS...

Conservative students, Beautiful campus

STUDENTS

Enrollment of law school	434
% male/female	56/44
% from out-of-state	60
% part-time	4
% underrepresented minority	4
Average age of entering class	25

ACADEMICS

Academic Experience Rating	**89**
Profs interesting rating	97
Profs accessible rating	93
Hours of study per day	5.01

Academic Specialties
Human Rights, International

Advanced Degrees Offered
LLM in American Legal Studies, 1 year

Combined Degrees Offered
JD/MBA, JD/MA in Management, JD/MA in Communication, JD/MA in Journalism, JD/MA in Counseling, JD/MA in Divinity, JD/MA in Government, 4 years; JD/M Div, 4–5 years

Academics

Tucked away in beautiful Virginia Beach, Regent University is molding the next generation of Christian lawyers and legal scholars. The program works diligently to maintain "a good sense of community" and the school as a whole feels "very cohesive." Academically, Regent places "a strong emphasis on legal research and writing." And while the course is "extremely rigorous and challenging," students admit they find it "incredibly useful" as they begin to tackle summer internships. Additionally, Regent boasts "first-class" moot court and ADR facilities. Even better; the "buildings and grounds are beautiful" to boot!

Moreover, Regent manages to attract some stellar professors. The vast majority are "very engaging in the classroom and are always available for one-on-one discussions." One third-year student agrees, remarking that "accessibility" is a common attribute of the faculty here. Indeed, "each professor, including the Dean, leaves their door open and students drop by all the time." Many professors also come to the classroom armed with "practical legal experience" which helps students thoroughly understand how to apply legal concepts within real-world settings. Students also greatly appreciate that professors use "multiple teaching techniques, methods and forms of evaluation."

Beyond the classroom, the "research librarians are always helpful with journal work and general library questions." As a pleased third-year shares, "They demonstrated a knowledge and skill in research I have never seen before." Another 3L expounds, "The law library staff is a tremendous help in guiding students to the right resources using Westlaw, Lexis, Bloomberg, and online resources like Google scholar. And the interlibrary loan program is extraordinarily helpful and fast when working on journal related items." However, some students do bemoan the fact that the law library is simply "the third floor of the general school library." This results in students frequently having to deal with loud, boisterous undergraduates.

By and large, students also speak highly of the "very nice" Career Services. The office "regularly hold events and [counselors] are always willing to meet with you regarding internships, resumes, cover letters, etc." They also "active[ly] provide students with opportunities to network." However, a first-year does caution that "they are extremely busy and you must book about two weeks in advance."

Finally, the "great" administration continually proves themselves to be "very responsive to students' needs." Generally, Regent's administrators are "well organized," "provide clear, succinct communication" and offer many "opportunities for student feedback." Overall, "the people who comprise the Regent School of Law make attending law school an absolute pleasure. The school embraces a motto "iron sharpening iron" as it seeks to fulfill a mission of service and leadership in the practice of law."

Bonnie Creef, Director of Admissions & Financial Aid
1000 Regent University Drive, Robertson Hall, Virginia Beach, VA 23464
Tel: 757-352-4584 Fax: 757-352-4139
E-Mail: lawschool@regent.edu • Website: www.regent.edu/Law

Life

An atmosphere of compassion and camaraderie certainly permeate Regent's campus. Indeed, it's truly evident that the "faculty and administration genuinely care about student success in the classroom as well as success in the future and in their personal lives." This definitely extends to the student body as well. As one third-year shares, "It's amazing how people pull together to help others whether it's related to school work or a personal issue." A pleased first-year pipes in, "Students are not at each other's throats[; instead] there is an atmosphere of teamwork and community for collective learning. Law school is stressful enough, but at Regent you have a village to support you." Additionally, the law school really "encourages personal development in scholarship, leadership, moral character formation, and skills practice." Therefore, not surprisingly, "opportunities for skills development, and exposure to guest speakers including state, federal, and community leadership" abound.

Getting In

Certainly, the admissions committee at Regent University's School of Law takes the typical factors into account. So, you can rest assured your undergraduate GPA and LSAT score will be closely considered. However, beyond the standard facets, Regent is also deeply interested in each candidate's relationship to his/her faith. Admissions officers favor applicants who are committed to incorporating Christian principles into their practice of law.

Clinical program required	No
Legal writing course requirement	Yes
Legal methods course requirement	Yes
Legal research course requirement	Yes
Moot court requirement	Yes
Public interest law requirement	No

ADMISSIONS

Selectivity Rating	85
# applications received	1,135
% applicants accepted	38
% acceptees attending	34
Average LSAT	154
Median LSAT	153
LSAT Range (25th to 75th percentile)	150–158
Average undergrad GPA	3.28
Median undergrad GPA	3.29
Application fee	$50
Regular application deadline	6/1
Early application deadline	2/1
Transfer students accepted	Yes
Evening division offered	No
Part-time accepted	Yes
CAS accepted	Yes

FINANCIAL FACTS

Annual tuition	$31,800
Books and supplies	$1,500
Fees	$740
Room & Board (on/off campus)	$10,890/$10,125
Financial aid application deadline	5/1
% first-year students receiving some sort of aid	93
% all students receiving some sort of aid	98
% of aid that is merit based	26
% receiving scholarships	81
Average grant	$8,757
Average loan	$39,051
Average total aid package	$53,461
Average debt	$108,068

EMPLOYMENT INFORMATION

Career Rating	75	
Total 2012 JD Grads	118	
% grads employed nine months out	77	
Median starting salary	$48,920	
# employed full-time	78	
# employed part-time	9	
# employed bar required	71	
# employed JD preferred	9	
# employed professional/other	2	
# employed non-professional	3	
# pursuing advanced degree	5	
# unemployed and seeking employment	19	
# not seeking employment	3	
% grads employed by school	2	
State for bar exam	VA, CA, TX, NY, NC	
Pass rate for first-time bar	82.3	

Prominent Alumni
Robert F. McDonnell, Governor of Virginia; Scott Dupont, North Carolina Circuit Court Judge; Ron Pahl, Oregon Circuit Court Judge.

Grads Employed by Field (%)
Academic (3)
Business/Industry (18)
Government (8)
Judicial Clerkship (3)
Private Practice (34)
Public Interest (5)

ROGER WILLIAMS UNIVERSITY
SCHOOL OF LAW

INSTITUTIONAL INFORMATION

Public/private	Private
Affiliation	No Affiliation
Student-faculty ratio	15:1
% faculty part-time	50
% faculty female	34
% faculty underrepresented minority	10
Total faculty	68

SURVEY SAYS...

Diverse opinions accepted in classrooms, Great research resources

STUDENTS

Enrollment of law school	506
% male/female	48/52
% from out-of-state	71
% part-time	0
% underrepresented minority	16
# of countries represented	6
Average age of entering class	25

ACADEMICS

Academic Experience Rating	**77**
Profs interesting rating	92
Profs accessible rating	88
Hours of study per day	4.96

Academic Specialties

Civil Procedure, Commercial, Constitutional, Corporation Securities, Criminal, Environmental, Human Rights, International, Labor, Property, Taxation, Intellectual Property

Advanced Degrees Offered

JD, 3 years full-time

Combined Degrees Offered

JD/MMA Masters Marine Affairs, 3.5 years; JD/MS Masters of Science in Labor Relations & Human Resources, 4 years; JD/MSCJ Masters of Criminal Justice, 3.5 years

Academics

Learning at Roger Williams University School of Law is not only academic, but also experiential. "Through initiatives like the Pro Bono Collaborative, which links law students with area practitioners to work on pro bono projects, the school is always working to integrate itself into the fabric of the RI legal community." The Office of Career Services sets up mock interviews with local attorneys to help students prepare for real interviews. They also regularly run "resume writing events, career fairs, and networking events." "The Feinstein Institute for Legal Service is an integral part of the school. Many students obtain excellent public interest internships and externships through this office." Students have "clerkships with judges," as well as "access to the federal system." The school makes certain that "we not only know the law, but we know how to apply it outside the academic realm." Roger Williams also offers an honors program, comprised of seminars, clinics, and international training for those who qualify. There are summer programs in London, England; Tianjin, China; and Buenos Aires, Argentina and "great human rights–based courses." Other strengths of RW are its public interest and pro bono programs, as well as a full maritime program. There are also criminal defense, immigration, and mediation clinics, which help students by providing "valuable, practical experience."

At RWU, most students agree there are "more than a few shining stars" within the faculty, offering "great insight and wisdom." One student says the professors "really have made a difference in my life." This probably arises from the fact that most professors have either practiced law seriously before holding their current positions or are simultaneously working within the Rhode Island legal system. "I have had the excellent opportunity to take classes with five judges in all different levels of the judiciary." Professors have "great practical stories to add to class" and feel they "are also here to mentor." Students who mentioned the dean spoke highly of him, one suggesting he "knows every student personally." Not only are the dean and professors accessible, but so is the entirety of the Rhode Island legal system. The school has "excellent connections with the local bar," and one student boasts, "I've already met both senators, the first circuit court of appeals judges, one congressman, and a RI Supreme Court judge in a semester and a half." Another rhetorically asks, "How many law schools have a U.S. Circuit Court of Appeals hear arguments in your mock court room." The connections between students, faculty, and the real-world of law are many and fortuitous. This may be because Roger Williams is the only law school in the small state of Rhode Island. Those students who wish to practice there after graduation are pleased with these connections, one claiming there's "a plethora of academic, clinical, and law firm opportunities." Some who wish to live and work elsewhere after their time at RW feel differently. Alternately, one student mentions that there's a "wide network of contacts and alumni working all across the nation."

As for the school itself, "Classrooms are always being updated," and "The school feels comfortable, but professional." There are some administrative "hiccups" and scheduling concerns, but overall, the students seem pleased. Students did express concern for the school's ranking; however, one suggested RWU was "quietly becoming a great institution."

MICHAEL DONNELLY-BOYLEN, ASSISTANT DEAN OF ADMISSIONS
10 METACOM AVENUE, BRISTOL, RI 02809-5171
TEL: 401-254-4555 FAX: 401-254-4516
E-MAIL: ADMISSIONS@LAW.RWU.EDU • WEBSITE: LAW.RWU.EDU

Life

"While there is a healthy competition among the students, there is also great encouragement and camaraderie." One student described life outside the classroom as "extremely social," while another suggests that same social world has a "huge range." A third says life at Roger Williams is "a perfect balance of work and social activities." "Our fifteen-plus clubs are extremely active and supported by funds and time from the Student Bar Association." Bristol is "serene and beautiful" but can at times feel "remote." "The location is lovely; however, winters can be pretty brisk." What do you expect when your campus sits "directly on the water," "literally ocean front property"? RWU is "a walk down the road from a historically zoned Main Street that has nice shops, excellent restaurants, and great views." One student describes Bristol as "gorgeous and wonderful, if not a little quaint and boring." Yet another says its "size is just right." One definite perk is free public transportation for students, and almost everyone can agree, "It's nice to be so close to Providence and Boston."

Getting In

The acceptance rate at Roger Williams is fairly high. The admissions committee considers LSAT scores, undergraduate GPAs, personal essays, and letters of recommendation all very important. Still valued, but not as much, are extracurricular activities and work experience. Admitted students in the 25th percentile have GPAs close to 3.0, and LSAT scores less than 150. Admitted students in the 75th percentile have GPAs of almost 3.5 and LSAT scores in the mid 150s.

Clinical program required	No
Legal writing course requirement	Yes
Legal methods course requirement	Yes
Legal research course requirement	Yes
Moot court requirement	Yes
Public interest law requirement	Yes

ADMISSIONS

Selectivity Rating	69
# applications received	1,253
% applicants accepted	79
% acceptees attending	15
Average LSAT	152
Median LSAT	151
LSAT Range (25th to 75th percentile)	147–156
Average undergrad GPA	3.22
Median undergrad GPA	3.3
Application fee	$60
Regular application deadline	4/1
Transfer students accepted	Yes
Evening division offered	No
Part-time accepted	No
CAS accepted	Yes

FINANCIAL FACTS

Annual tuition	$40,200
Books and supplies	$1,500
Room & Board (on/off campus)	$16,422/$15,885
Financial aid application deadline	2/15
% first-year students receiving some sort of aid	90
% all students receiving some sort of aid	95
% of aid that is merit based	22
% receiving scholarships	57
Average grant	$19,774
Average loan	$44,250
Average total aid package	$58,315
Average debt	$132,699

EMPLOYMENT INFORMATION

Career Rating	76	Prominent Alumni	
Total 2012 JD Grads	181	Eugene Bernardo, Partner, Partridge Snow	
% for whom you have useable information	95	Hahn LLP, Providence, RI; Peter Kilmartin, RI Attorney General, Providence, RI; Lucy	
% grads employed nine months out	72	Holmes Plovnick, Partner, Mitchell	
Median starting salary	$50,000	Silberberg & Knupp LLP, Washington DC.	
# employed full-time	115	**Grads Employed by Field (%)**	
# employed part-time	16	Academic (1)	
# employed bar required	100	Business/Industry (13)	
# employed JD preferred	11	Government (7)	
# employed professional/other	14	Judicial Clerkship (11)	
# employed non-professional	6	Military (1)	
# pursuing advanced degree	5	Private Practice (33)	
# unemployed and seeking employment	31	Public Interest (7)	
# not seeking employment	2		
% grads employed by school	1		
State for bar exam	MA, RI, NY, CT, NJ		
Pass rate for first-time bar	81		

RUTGERS, THE STATE UNIVERSITY OF NEW JERSEY—CAMDEN SCHOOL OF LAW

INSTITUTIONAL INFORMATION

Public/private	Public
Student-faculty ratio	12:1
% faculty part-time	37
% faculty female	44
% faculty underrepresented minority	9
Total faculty	101

SURVEY SAYS...

Diverse opinions accepted in classrooms, Great library staff

STUDENTS

Enrollment of law school	711
% male/female	65/35
% part-time	21
% underrepresented minority	22
# of countries represented	1
Average age of entering class	25

ACADEMICS

Academic Experience Rating	89
Profs interesting rating	89
Profs accessible rating	84
Hours of study per day	2.94

Academic Specialties

Health, Environmental, International, Commercial, Criminal, Labor, Child Advocacy and Women's Rights, Litigation and Advocacy

Advanced Degrees Offered

JD, 3 year full-time program or 4 year part-time program.

Combined Degrees Offered

JD/MBA, 4 years; JD/MPA Public Administration, 4 years; JD/MSW Social Work, 4 years; JD/MS Public Policy, 3.5 years; JD/MCRP City and Regional Planning, 4 years; JD/MD and JD/DO University of Medicine and Dentistry of New Jersey; JD/MPA Public Administration in Health Care Management and Policy, 4 years

Academics

If going to law school gives you the jitters, your fears will quickly be assuaged at Rutgers, The State University of New Jersey—Camden School of Law. Sure, just like other prestigious JD programs, Rutgers will treat you to a dose of the "Socratic thunderstorm approach," and there is the typical "never-ending workload" throughout the first year. However, Rutgers maintains a remarkably friendly and supportive academic environment. Students insist, "First-year classes don't intimidate you, as there's no fear of speaking your mind in class, and diversity in thinking is highly encouraged." Outside the classroom, Rutgers professors are personable, to say the least: "Every Wednesday afternoon, there's a veritable party in our torts professor's office during his office hours. So many students go to discuss both academic and non-textbook-related topics that there aren't enough chairs and people sit on the floor," recalls one 2L. In fact, "It's common for professors to take students out to lunch, to conferences, and even to show up at student-sponsored pub crawls." The administration draws similar praise from students, who believe it "tries to be very open-door and available for anything we could possibly need." A 1L jokes, "I came to Rutgers expecting to witness students getting 'burned' by professors every day in class. Instead the only burn I got was on the roof of my mouth while eating pizza with the dean."

Students are impressed with the caliber of the Rutgers faculty, describing them as "knowledgeable and passionate about their subjects" and able pedagogues to boot. In the lecture hall, "The faculty is as intelligent as they are witty. Anecdotes from [their] real-world experiences are common in the classroom and make some of the drudgery more interesting." Many also point out the strength of the adjunct staff, who "come from varied fields, providing a unique and practical perspective to current topics." Indeed, a practical approach is emphasized at Rutgers, and classes may even include "spontaneous fieldtrips to the federal courthouse across the street from the campus just so we can view real-world motions to dismiss, jury selection, and final arguments." The school's active alumni network is also called on to contribute to the JD experience, and students tell us that "in many courses, alumni return to give lectures on the practical aspects of the subject, and they have been willing to assist any student [who] has a question."

Among the greatest perks of Rutgers—Camden is its low tuition, offering a "fantastic and highly respected education at a very reasonable price." As a result, students do not experience the financial anxiety common to law students today. "Due to a scholarship and a summer internship at a Philadelphia law firm," reports one 2L, "I will graduate with a top-rate legal education and virtually no debt. That combination is hard to beat, and I expect it will free up my career options considerably."

The school takes advantage of the resources in the surrounding community to instruct students in the playing out of law in the real world. "The federal courthouse is literally around the corner, the county courthouse a couple of blocks [away]," and Rutgers students "have tremendous access to the judges in the area and several teach as adjuncts." Students also praise the fact that "the law school is very involved in the community through its pro bono clinics."

Rutgers is "located close to Philly, Trenton, and New York, so there are plenty of job opportunities." On that note, "Career Services are always on the job helping students get placed for both summer and permanent positions. They also expose students to the different options available to attorneys by having guests come to the law school to provide experiences in different areas." Rutgers is somewhat unique among law schools in that almost half of the graduating class takes judicial clerkship positions, more students than those who take positions in private practice.

Ass. Director Maureen O'Boyle, Assistant Director of Admissions
406 Penn Street, 3rd Floor, Camden, NJ 08102
Tel: 800-466-7561 Fax: 856-225-6537
E-Mail: admissions@camlaw.rutgers.edu • Website: www.camden.rutgers.edu

Life

Attracting students from all across the nation and the world, the Rutgers student body is "extremely diverse in all aspects, including gender, socioeconomics, age, and interests." On this multicultural campus "There is an organization for just about any interest a person may have, [and] the SBA and other clubs do a great job of providing numerous social functions nearly every week." A 2L explains, "The environment is positive and students are involved with the school. Whether it be moot court, law journals, or politics, students are engaged in society and provide for a very strong sense of community." Off campus, "People are always looking to get together to study or to just go out socially," though most prefer hanging out in Philly to hitting the bars in the surrounding town of Camden. While some describe Camden as "the pit of despair," others tell us that "the waterfront on both sides of the Delaware River is beautiful." In addition, many appreciate the fact that "Philadelphia is exactly a mile away and provides for plenty of social opportunities."

Students warn that there are "a handful of students who are hell-bent on getting a certain GPA." Most, however, value kindness and cooperation over competition. A 3L explains, "My school is both cooperative and competitive. Students here care deeply about being successful, but everyone is quick to lend a hand to bring someone else along for the ride." Indeed, many students praise the fact that "you can always find a good conversation outside after class."

Getting In

The Law school recognizes that the LSAT and UGPA may not be the best predictors of success in law school and the legal profession for all applicants. Therefore, approximately one-fourth of the class is admitted based on other factors, including educational and employment experience, leadership ability, maturity, a history of overcoming disadvantage, extraordinary accomplishment or success in a previous career. For other prospective students, the admissions process is standard fare: Rutgers admits student who have demonstrated a high level of academic achievement, as well as strong standardized test scored.

Clinical program required	No
Legal writing course requirement	Yes
Legal methods course requirement	Yes
Legal research course requirement	Yes
Moot court requirement	Yes
Public interest law requirement	No

ADMISSIONS

Selectivity Rating	86
# applications received	1,228
% applicants accepted	39
% acceptees attending	24
Average LSAT	157
Median LSAT	157
LSAT Range (25th to 75th percentile)	153–160
Average undergrad GPA	3.30
Median undergrad GPA	3.31
Application fee	$65
Regular application deadline	
Early application deadline	1/1
Early application notification	3/1
Transfer students accepted	Yes
Evening division offered	Yes
Part-time accepted	Yes
CAS accepted	Yes

FINANCIAL FACTS

Annual tuition (in-state out-of-state)	$22,746/$34,478
Books and supplies	$1,550
Fees	$2,733
Room & Board (on/off campus)	$12,208/$16,693
Financial aid application deadline	8/1
% all students receiving some sort of aid	89
% of aid that is merit based	28
% receiving scholarships	45
Average grant	$4,368
Average loan	$11,347
Average total aid package	$33,947
Average debt	$93,990

EMPLOYMENT INFORMATION

Career Rating	81
Total 2012 JD Grads	270
% grads employed nine months out	81
Median starting salary	$44,306
# employed full-time	206
# employed part-time	13
# employed bar required	177
# employed JD preferred	20
# employed professional/other	19
# employed non-professional	3
# pursuing advanced degree	3
# unemployed and seeking employment	42
# not seeking employment	3
% grads employed by school	0
State for bar exam	NJ, NY, PA
Pass rate for first-time bar	85.6

Prominent Alumni
Hon. James Florio, Former Governor/U.S. Congressman; Hon. Joseph Rodriguez and Robert Kugler, U.S. Federal District Judge; Brigadier General Flora D. Darpino, Commander of the U.S. Army Legal Services Agency and chief judge of the U.S. Army Court of Criminal.

Grads Employed by Field (%)
Business/Industry (13)
Government (6)
Judicial Clerkship (36)
Private Practice (25)
Public Interest (2)

RUTGERS, THE STATE UNIVERSITY OF NEW JERSEY—NEWARK
SCHOOL OF LAW

INSTITUTIONAL INFORMATION

Public/private	Public
Affiliation	No Affiliation
Student-faculty ratio	15:1
% faculty part-time	36
% faculty female	37
% faculty underrepresented minority	20
Total faculty	88

SURVEY SAYS...

Diverse opinions accepted in classrooms, Great library staff, Abundant externship/internship/clerkship opportunities

STUDENTS

Enrollment of law school	789
% male/female	55/45
% from out-of-state	33
% part-time	26
% underrepresented minority	39
% international	1
# of countries represented	26
Average age of entering class	25

ACADEMICS

Academic Experience Rating	84
Profs interesting rating	79
Profs accessible rating	75

Academic Specialties

Civil Procedure, Commercial, Constitutional, Corporation Securities, Criminal, Environmental, Government Services, Human Rights, International, Labor, Legal History, Legal Philosophy, Property, Taxation, Intellectual Property

Combined Degrees Offered

JD/MBA, 4 years; JD/MD, 6 years; JD/Ph.D. (Jurisprudence), 5 years; JD/MA (Criminal Justice), 4 years; JD/MCRP (City, Regional Planning), 4 years; JD/MSW, 4 years; JD/MA (Public Health), 4 years; JD/MA (Global Studies), 4 years

Academics

According to students, Rutgers School of Law—Newark is "truly a gem" "that deserves more respect than it sometimes gets." They also boast that their school offers "definitely the best bang for your buck" among the handful of law schools in or within commuting distance from Manhattan. The academic highlight here is the "very strong," very large, and generally "fantastic" clinical program. Opportunities to gain "incredibly valuable practical experience" while helping real clients with real legal problems are "probably some of the best of any law school in the country" and they are numerous. Nearly two-thirds of the students here participate in a clinic before graduation. Externships are also plentiful. Rutgers—Newark is "located in the same town as a federal court and a state court," and "Many state-sponsored fellowships and internships work specifically with the school." Many students also praise the legal research and writing program for providing "a strong foundation to use in all areas" of the law. Others, however, gripe that the program supplies "very little guidance and very little instruction." Also, "Popular courses are sometimes difficult to get into," and if you are an evening student, "The course selection leaves a lot to be desired."

"Class size is small," and the "diverse" and "really accomplished" faculty brings "a broad range of experiences and expertise to the classroom." As far as teaching, "It's a mixed bag." For the most part, though, professors here "do a great job of employing the Socratic Method, and, above all, have an uncanny ability to communicate and teach these dense and often boring subjects with ease." "They really go above and beyond anything that could be reasonably expected," gushes a 1L. They're also "truly interested in mentoring, teaching, and assisting students." The "very transparent" and "particularly accessible" administration is "on top of everything." Staff members are "the type of people who will stay late hours to help students resolve problems and get answers for their questions." "Every dean is pleasant, capable, and genuinely willing to help students in any way possible," swears a happy 2L.

Rutgers—Newark is located near a great legal market and it has "quite a good reputation among employers." The Office of Career Services is "in touch with students." Rutgers also has "a strong history of public interest" and is "constantly promoting the idea that lawyers have a special opportunity to improve the community." The "focus on public interest tends to alienate those looking for jobs in the private sector somewhat," though. Also, the Career Services staff sometimes works "against the students' interest by weighing them down with bureaucracy and encouraging them to settle on modest goals."

"The facilities are good but not great." "We have everything we need to do what we need to do," explains a 2L. It's a public school, though, and resources are perennially "limited." The big complaint concerns technology. Internet connectivity "leaves very much to be desired" and wireless issues "plague" the otherwise "amazing" library.

ANITA WALTON, ASSISTANT DEAN FOR ADMISSIONS
CENTER FOR LAW AND JUSTICE, 123 WASHINGTON STREET, NEWARK, NJ 07102
TEL: 973-353-5554 FAX: 973-353-3459
E-MAIL: LAWINFO@ANDROMEDA.RUTGERS.EDU • WEBSITE: LAW.NEWARK.RUTGERS.EDU

Life

Diversity of all kinds is "a great strength" here. Students come from "very varied backgrounds" "and are eager to learn." There are plenty of "professional, mid-career individuals"—especially in the evening program—and ethnic minorities make up over a third of the student population. "The administration's dedication to finding students that will not only become great lawyers but great people overall makes this school unique." "If you want to meet intelligent and successful people from an array of backgrounds," declares a 3L, "this is the school for you." Politically, it's "a very liberal school" and a "left-of-center atmosphere" is prevalent both inside and outside the classroom. Students describe the academic environment as generally "cooperative." The struggle for jobs with "with other New York/New Jersey–area schools makes the student body a little anxious" but "there is little to no mean-spirited competition."

A few students tell us there us "no sense of community" here. Many others say there is a "great quality of life." "It is a warm, accepting community and it is very easy to make friends," beams a 2L. "Because the school has students from such diverse backgrounds," submits a 1L, "it makes it easier for anyone to fit in and not feel like an outcast." "There are always lots of talks and events to attend" and "a lot of student organizations" "sponsor mixers and activities." Champions of Newark describe it as "a well-developed commercial city with many large law firms and tons of wonderful places to eat." "Newark simply is not as bad as people think," they insist. Other students call Newark a "dirty city that can be unsafe." "If you could build a wall around the school and never look beyond that wall," suggests a 3L, "the setting would be lovely." Luckily for Newark detractors, New York City is very nearby.

Getting In

Admitted students at the 25th percentile have LSAT in the mid 150s and undergraduate grade-point averages in the 3.1 range. At the 75th percentile, LSAT scores in the low 160s and GPAs are in the 3.6 range.

Clinical program required	No
Legal writing course requirement	Yes
Legal methods course requirement	Yes
Legal research course requirement	Yes
Moot court requirement	Yes
Public interest law requirement	No

ADMISSIONS

Selectivity Rating	84
# applications received	2,460
% applicants accepted	34
% acceptees attending	27
Average LSAT	158
Median LSAT	158
LSAT Range (25th to 75th percentile)	155–160
Average undergrad GPA	3.24
Median undergrad GPA	3.26
Application fee	$65
Regular application deadline	3/15
Transfer students accepted	Yes
Evening division offered	Yes
Part-time accepted	Yes
CAS accepted	Yes

FINANCIAL FACTS

Annual tuition (in-state out-of-state)	$23,428/$35,512
Books and supplies	$1,550
Fees	$2,661
Room & Board (on/off campus)	$13,771/$18,125
Financial aid application deadline	3/15
% all students receiving some sort of aid	95
% of aid that is merit based	15
% receiving scholarships	36
Average grant	$6,999
Average loan	$29,094
Average total aid package	$29,368
Average debt	$83,381

EMPLOYMENT INFORMATION

Career Rating	77
Total 2012 JD Grads	248
% for whom you have useable information	96
% grads employed nine months out	86
Median starting salary	$50,500
% job accepting grads providing useable salary information	73
# employed full-time	492
# employed part-time	10
# employed bar required	133
# employed JD preferred	33
# employed professional/other	32
# employed non-professional	4
# pursuing advanced degree	2
# unemployed and seeking employment	22

# not seeking employment	4
% grads employed by school	1
State for bar exam	NJ, NY, PA
Pass rate for first-time bar	81

Prominent Alumni

Robert Menendez, US Senator; Jaynee LaVecchia, NJ State Supreme Court Justice; Louis Freeh, Former FBI Director.

Grads Employed by Field (%)

Academic (4)
Business/Industry (17)
Government (5)
Judicial Clerkship (28)
Private Practice (23)
Public Interest (5)

SAMFORD UNIVERSITY
CUMBERLAND SCHOOL OF LAW

INSTITUTIONAL INFORMATION

Public/private	Private
Affiliation	Southern Baptist
Student-faculty ratio	18:1
% faculty part-time	57
% faculty female	25
% faculty underrepresented minority	9
Total faculty	53

SURVEY SAYS...

Great research resources, Great library staff, Students love Birmingham, AL

STUDENTS

Enrollment of law school	421
% male/female	57/43
% from out-of-state	42
% part-time	0
% underrepresented minority	14
Average age of entering class	24

ACADEMICS

Academic Experience Rating	91
Profs interesting rating	94
Profs accessible rating	95
Hours of study per day	3.99

Academic Specialties

Corporation Securities, Criminal, Environmental, Taxation, Intellectual Property

Advanced Degrees Offered

Master of Comparative Law

Combined Degrees Offered

JD/Master of Accountancy, JD/Master of Business Administration, JD/Master of Divinity, JD/Master of Public Administration, JD/Master of Public Health, JD/Master of Science in Environmental Management, JD/Master of Art in Theological Studies, and JD/Master of Science in Bioethics. All programs are 3.5–4 years, except the JD/Master of Divinity which is a 5 year program.

Academics

Students at Samford University's Cumberland School of Law say their school is "a little bit of a hidden gem" and "a great place to become a lawyer." The bar-passage rate is utterly fabulous. There are seven joint-degree programs and a "diverse array" of available courses. "Practical skills are the strength" here, though. The legal writing program is reportedly outstanding. Students have an "incredible amount of opportunity to get experience in trial competition." "As far as trial advocacy goes, you cannot find a better school in the country," vaunts a 3L. "Practicing litigation attorneys train students in specialized trial advocacy programs, and the trial teams consistently win major national tournaments." Externships and a wealth of community service programs also provide "unmatched" opportunities to gain practical experience.

Cumberland is a small school with small class sizes, and it is home to "a diverse faculty with impeccable credentials." The professors are "an amazing group." "There is always going to be that jerk who is a complete know-it-all and thinks he hung the moon in any law school," and Cumberland is no exception. As a rule, though, these professors are "extremely knowledgeable" and "hilarious yet simultaneously intimidating." They "have practice experience, which is helpful in class because it allows for personal experiences to be introduced," and they "emphasize what will actually be useful and necessary" when you are representing clients. "A wonderful open-door policy" is another plus. "Professors are willing to meet with students and discuss the subject matter at any point outside of class," and they "genuinely want to help students in whatever way they can." "I don't even know why they put 'office hours' in their syllabi," adds a happy 2L. Students also rave about their "hands-on," accessible, and "very personable" administration. "They actually know students' names and want to help." And if you want to "shoot the breeze" with the dean, you can.

Facilities-wise, "The campus is beautiful and is extremely convenient to all areas of Birmingham." The "comfortable" and "awesome" library is "a great place to study." "Also, the library resources are exceptional," and the librarians are "wonderful" if you are in a bind. The "outdated" classrooms aren't the greatest. They "can feel a little cramped," and they are "windowless." "In some ways, that is a good thing because it keeps you from getting distracted," explains a 1L. "The technology in the classrooms isn't the best," either.

Students are pretty satisfied with their career prospects, although the "extremely helpful" Career Services Office "could do a better job marketing the school's graduates outside of the Birmingham legal market," laments a 2L. "The alumni network of this school is incredible," beams a 2L. "Cumberland alums are always looking to hire the bright young Cumberland graduates. And if an alum can't help you out, they are always willing to refer you to someone who can."

JENNIFER Y. SIMS, ASSISTANT DEAN FOR ADMISSIONS
800 LAKESHORE DRIVE, BIRMINGHAM, AL 35229
TEL: 205-726-2702 FAX: 205-726-2057
E-MAIL: LAWADM@SAMFORD.EDU • WEBSITE: CUMBERLAND.SAMFORD.EDU

Life

Politically, liberals are seen occasionally, but the overall population leans "pretty far to the right." Academically, there may be "a behind-the-scenes competitiveness," but the atmosphere looks and feels "cooperative and collegial." "Most students are more than willing to help their classmates succeed."

Socially, Cumberland is a decidedly "Southern school." Hospitality is paramount, and "even the slightly awkward students are still warmly received." "There is a real community at Cumberland," relates a 2L. "We study together, hang out together, and have formed a tight bond with each other," adds another 2L. "There is a friendliness and warmth that you just won't find at other schools." "We interact with each other like friendly colleagues; we compete with each other like sibling rivals; and we support each other through the trials of life and death like family," reflects an already wistful 3L. "The school creates a 'work hard' culture but constantly has entertaining social events." Weekly bar reviews around the affordable, growing city of Birmingham are reportedly well attended. In the spring, Cumberland celebrates Rascal Day in honor of its long-deceased canine mascot. There's food and live music, and the dean and the school president lead a march through campus.

Getting In

Enrolled students at the 25th percentile at Cumberland have LSAT scores around 153 and GPAs at just about 3.30. At the 75th percentile, LSAT scores are approximately 157 and GPAs are a little over 3.5. If you want to get started on your law school career a few months early, Cumberland allows admitted students to take two law school electives during the summer before 1L courses begin.

Clinical program required	No
Legal writing course requirement	Yes
Legal methods course requirement	Yes
Legal research course requirement	No
Moot court requirement	Yes
Public interest law requirement	No

ADMISSIONS

Selectivity Rating	82
# applications received	1,361
% applicants accepted	41
% acceptees attending	22
Average LSAT	154
Median LSAT	153
LSAT Range (25th to 75th percentile)	151–158
Average undergrad GPA	3.30
Median undergrad GPA	3.35
Application fee	$50
Regular application deadline	7/1
Early application deadline	2/28
Transfer students accepted	Yes
Evening division offered	No
Part-time accepted	No
CAS accepted	Yes

FINANCIAL FACTS

Annual tuition	$35,876
Books and supplies	$2,000
Fees	$340
Room & Board (on/off campus)	$0/$13,500
Financial aid application deadline	3/1
% first-year students receiving some sort of aid	82
% all students receiving some sort of aid	85
% of aid that is merit based	94
% receiving scholarships	41
Average grant	$17,878
Average loan	$45,038
Average total aid package	$47,779
Average debt	$126,143

EMPLOYMENT INFORMATION

Career Rating	71	**Prominent Alumni**
Total 2012 JD Grads	166	Charles J. Crist, Jr., Former Governor of
% for whom you have useable information	100	Florida; Cordell Hull, Founder of United Nations; Howell E. Jackson, U.S. Supreme
% grads employed nine months out	81	Court.
Median starting salary	$59	**Grads Employed by Field (%)**
# employed full-time	124	Academic (0)
# employed part-time	10	Business/Industry (13)
# employed bar required	106	Government (34)
# employed JD preferred	19	Judicial Clerkship (6)
# employed professional/other	6	Military (2)
# employed non-professional	3	Private Practice (54)
# pursuing advanced degree	12	Public Interest (2)
# unemployed and seeking employment	15	
# not seeking employment	5	
% grads employed by school	0	
State for bar exam	AL	
Pass rate for first-time bar	92	

SANTA CLARA UNIVERSITY
SCHOOL OF LAW

INSTITUTIONAL INFORMATION

Public/private	Private
Affiliation	Roman Catholic-Jesuit
Student-faculty ratio	12:1
% faculty part-time	36
% faculty female	50
% faculty underrepresented minority	21
Total faculty	66

SURVEY SAYS...

Diverse opinions accepted in classrooms, Students love Santa Clara, CA

STUDENTS

Enrollment of law school	880
% male/female	53/47
% part-time	21
% underrepresented minority	41
% international	4
# of countries represented	10
Average age of entering class	25

ACADEMICS

Academic Experience Rating	78
Profs interesting rating	79
Profs accessible rating	77
Hours of study per day	4.07

Academic Specialties

Constitutional, Criminal, Environmental, Human Rights, International, Labor, Taxation, Intellectual Property

Advanced Degrees Offered

LLM in U.S. Law for Foreign Lawyers, 1 year; LLM in International and Comparative Law, 1 year; LLM in Intellectual Property Law, 1-3 years

Combined Degrees Offered

JD/MBA, 3.5–4 years; JD/MSIS, 3.5–4 years

Academics

Jesuit-affiliated Santa Clara University School of Law "in the heart of Silicon Valley" is a smaller school that manages to offer "a wide range" of courses across a host of legal areas. As you would expect given the location, Santa Clara Law boasts "one of the top-ranking high-tech programs in the nation." The course work in patent and intellectual property law is "tremendous," and students regularly intern with "the vast array" of existing mammoth corporations as well as the next generation of mammoth corporations here "in the venture-capital capital of the country." The international law program is also extensive and "incredible." Study abroad opportunities are mind-blowing. There are a dozen different programs in twenty cities around the globe including—just to cite a few—Istanbul, Budapest, and Shanghai. In addition, there are several unique international judicial externships and international internships available. Still another perk here is the prominent focus on public interest and social justice law. SCU is teeming with institutes, centers, and programs that allow students to do "great things for people."

"Real-world experience" is one of the hallmarks of the professors at Santa Clara Law. "Some are brilliant savants, but you just can't learn from them." On the whole, though, faculty members are "top-notch," "dedicated to teaching," and "obviously committed to their students." Professors are "approachable" as well. They "really engage students" outside of class" "about their past experiences and future hopes." Administratively, lower-level staff can be "somewhat surly," and sometimes the decisions of the top brass "leave much to be desired," but the general consensus is that management is "extremely accommodating" and "very concerned with student feedback." "It would be difficult to find another law school that cares so much about [its] students and actually does something about it," beams a 1L.

Santa Clara's lush, "peaceful" campus is "simply gorgeous and kept very nicely." It's also home to some "great facilities." The law school facilities are pretty mundane, though. "The classrooms are classrooms," says a 3L. The law library is "certainly adequate," but it's "fairly depressing." It's "dark, and the temperature controls suck." On the bright side, the undergrad library "right next door" is "incredibly awesome," and it's a regular haunt for law students.

Santa Clara has a stellar reputation in the Bay Area, and career prospects are solid. More than 80 percent of all newly minted graduates head off to the private sector, where median starting salaries are very impressive. Quite a few students take jobs in Silicon Valley. San Francisco is another common destination. Santa Clara Law's "very accessible, passionate, successful, and helpful alumni network" is a huge advantage when students are looking for work. They are "very willing to give back to the school and provide advice and opportunities to current students." "Sometimes it feels like the entire community of attorneys in the South Bay graduated from Santa Clara," explains a 3L, "especially when it comes to district attorneys, public defenders, and judges." The alumni base and the SCU brand name aren't as strong nationally, though. "Nobody knows about it outside of the San Francisco area," laments another 3L.

Jeanette J. Leach, Assistant Dean for Admissions & Financial Aid
500 El Camino Real, Santa Clara, CA 95053
Tel: 408-554-5048 Fax: 408-554-7897
E-Mail: lawadmissions@scu.edu • Website: law.scu.edu

Life

"The school's location allows it to attract a diverse group of highly educated students." In terms of ethnicity, Santa Clara Law is among the most diverse schools in the country. "Varying ages," radically different life experiences, and a solid geographic distribution also make for "a good mix." Academically, a few students "are jerks and should be quarantined," but "there usually is a positive vibe around the school." "It is a very welcoming environment that engenders very happy students." "We're a social tribe," explains a 1L. "We might be graded on a curve but you'd never know it from how everyone treats each other."

"Student life is collaborative." "There's a club or society for everything under the sun." "Stimulating" speakers including local corporate bigwigs are frequent, and "The school makes a real effort to engage its alumni and host events where students can meet them." "Social activities and opportunities for students to get together" are also commonplace. "We study hard, but we also go out a lot on the weekends and form some close-knit friendships," says a 3L. The cost of living in Silicon Valley is very high, and the city of Santa Clara is "decidedly not a college town." The locale is "green and sunny most of the year," though, and the Bay Area offers quite a bit to do. When students need a break from their casebooks or law school in general, heading up to San Francisco is pretty common.

Getting In

Enrolled full-time students at the 25th percentile have LSAT scores of 157 and grade point averages right around 3.02. At the 75th percentile, LSAT scores are 161 and GPAs are around 3.47. Stats for the part-time program are somewhat lower.

Clinical program required	No
Legal writing course requirement	Yes
Legal methods course requirement	Yes
Legal research course requirement	Yes
Moot court requirement	Yes
Public interest law requirement	No

ADMISSIONS

Selectivity Rating	78
# applications received	2,940
% applicants accepted	53
% acceptees attending	13
Average LSAT	158
Median LSAT	158
LSAT Range (25th to 75th percentile)	156–160
Average undergrad GPA	3.23
Median undergrad GPA	3.23
Application fee	$75
Regular application deadline	2/1
Early application deadline	11/1
Early application notification	12/20
Transfer students accepted	Yes
Evening division offered	Yes
Part-time accepted	Yes
CAS accepted	Yes

FINANCIAL FACTS

Annual tuition	$45,000
Books and supplies	$1,286
Fees	$0
Room & Board	$14,582
Financial aid application deadline	2/1
% first-year students receiving some sort of aid	92
% all students receiving some sort of aid	87
% of aid that is merit based	94
% receiving scholarships	51
Average grant	$13,753
Average loan	$47,565
Average total aid package	$46,263
Average debt	$129,621

EMPLOYMENT INFORMATION

Career Rating	86
Total 2012 JD Grads	298
% grads employed nine months out	76
Median starting salary	$90,000
# employed full-time	179
# employed part-time	46
# employed bar required	154
# employed JD preferred	60
# employed professional/other	4
# employed non-professional	7
# pursuing advanced degree	4
# unemployed and seeking employment	24
# not seeking employment	28
% grads employed by school	6
State for bar exam	CA, FL, OR, TX, NY
Pass rate for first-time bar	70

Prominent Alumni

Leon Panetta, Political Leader; Zoe Lofgren, Congresswoman, U.S. House of Representatives; Sam O'Rourke, Deputy General Counsel, Intellectual Property at Facebook.

Grads Employed by Field (%)

Academic (1)
Business/Industry (19)
Government (5)
Private Practice (42)
Public Interest (2)

SEATTLE UNIVERSITY
SCHOOL OF LAW

INSTITUTIONAL INFORMATION

Public/private	Private
% faculty part-time	41
% faculty female	40
% faculty underrepresented minority	21
Total faculty	117

SURVEY SAYS...
Great research resources

STUDENTS

Enrollment of law school	961
% male/female	49/51
% part-time	21
% underrepresented minority	28
# of countries represented	3
Average age of entering class	26

ACADEMICS

Academic Experience Rating	**80**
Profs interesting rating	77
Profs accessible rating	75
Hours of study per day	3.68

Academic Specialties
Commercial, Constitutional, Corporation Securities, Criminal, Environmental, Human Rights, International, Labor, Property, Taxation, Intellectual Property

Advanced Degrees Offered
Law School offers JD degrees.

Combined Degrees Offered
Along with the highly regarded Albers School of Business, we offer eight joint degree programs: Master of Business Administration (JD/MBA), Master of International Business (JD/MIB), a Master of Science in Finance (JD/MSF), or a Master of Professional Accounting (JD/MPAC). We also now offer a (JD/MPA) with the Institute for Public Service, a JD/Master of Sports Administration and Leadership (JD/MSAL) and a JD/Masters in Transformational Leadership (JD/MTL) with the School of Theology and Ministry.

Academics

Seattle University "[offers] a great academic experience" while fostering "a challenging but supportive environment." The "great faculty, tremendous core values, [and] excellent course selection," are influenced by the school's Jesuit tradition. This "mission of social justice" divides the opinions of students. Some praise it as "one of the greatest strengths of this school." The school's location in one of America's hippest cities "affords many opportunities for externships and doing pro bono work." Seattle offers many benefits, both socially and career-wise, to students. The school is very "connected to the local legal community."

"The facilities are outstanding" at Seattle University, with a "bright and open" building that is "really nice, modern, and inviting." The law school is "always a comfortable temperature," has "excellent wireless access," and features "plenty of places to study and plenty of plug ins for laptops." There are "tons of places to meet in groups or hide to study alone," especially in the library where you can even "eat and drink" while hitting the books. "The library staff [is] very accessible and helpful" and "even the custodial staff and the baristas are sweethearts."

Academically, the most constantly praised program is easily the "top notch" "number 1 ranked legal writing program." "The legal writing program really shines and local employers take that into account when making hiring decisions," a 1L explains. "It's the only reason anyone that has a job after graduation got that job," says a 3L. "One of the highlights really has to be the center for professional development," and students also praise the law clinics. The "very passionate" professors "literally beg students to come to office hours." Some do suggest professors can be "a mixed bag." "The professors and deans are very accessible and willing to talk to/work with students to solve any problems," and they work to ensure classes are "always a collaborative and encouraging but challenging environment." A 2L elaborates: "The teaching focus is traditional with modern twists: how would this rule of evidence apply to text messages? Is opening an email an unlawful search? What free sources of research are available on the internet?" However, one 2L fears that "the theme of 'social justice' has overrun the theme of creating employable lawyers." "I loved every class and for the first time in my educational career, I actually WANTED to do my homework!" one pleased student declares. The "very down to earth" administration also receives praise for being "more than capable of answering just about every question you could have." Some students do think the admiration should work to make "the night program more equal to the day program," and in general the administration should "focus more on preparing students for employment following graduation." A 2L sums up their experience thusly: "The entire focus of the program, from top to bottom, is: You CAN do this and you CAN be amazing at it."

CAROL COCHRAN, ASSISTANT DEAN FOR ADMISSION
901 12TH AVENUE, SULLIVAN HALL, P.O. BOX 222000, SEATTLE, WA 98122-1090
TEL: 206-398-4200 FAX: 206-398-4058
E-MAIL: LAWADMIS@SEATTLEU.EDU • WEBSITE: WWW.LAW.SEATTLEU.EDU

Life

Seattle University "hosts frequent events both social and otherwise," which fosters "comradery between students." The student body is somewhat divided "between the day and evening students," two groups that are "different and [do] not socialize with each other." This may be exacerbated by the fact that "most of the school events, activities, and classes are geared towards day-students." The school's location "the midst of a great Seattle neighborhood" provide plenty of nightlife and off-campus activities. "Seattle is definitely gray and rainy, but that is part of the package," and students enjoy "being located in such a progressive city."

Getting In

The 2012 class had a GPA range (25th to 75th percentile) of 3.07 to 3.54. The same LSAT range was 154 to 159. In addition to these scores, Seattle University says that personal accomplishments are heavily weighted in admission decisions. Applicants with a history of community service, individual talents, of other extracurricular activities should note this in their personal statements.

Clinical program required	No
Legal writing course requirement	Yes
Legal methods course requirement	No
Legal research course requirement	Yes
Moot court requirement	No
Public interest law requirement	No

ADMISSIONS

Selectivity Rating	81
# applications received	2,083
% applicants accepted	51
% acceptees attending	27
Average LSAT	156
Median LSAT	156
LSAT Range (25th to 75th percentile)	154–159
Median undergrad GPA	3.32
Application fee	$60
Regular application deadline	3/1
Transfer students accepted	Yes
Evening division offered	Yes
Part-time accepted	Yes
CAS accepted	Yes

FINANCIAL FACTS

Annual tuition	$39,810
Books and supplies	$1,172
Fees	$72
Room & Board	$11,565
Financial aid application deadline	2/15
% first-year students receiving some sort of aid	98
% all students receiving some sort of aid	95
% of aid that is merit based	53
% receiving scholarships	53
Average grant	$11,826
Average loan	$46,897
Average total aid package	$51,390
Average debt	$119,918

EMPLOYMENT INFORMATION

Career Rating	90
% grads employed nine months out	91
Median starting salary	$71,000
State for bar exam	WA, CA, OR, TX, IL
Pass rate for first-time bar	76.1

Prominent Alumni
Mark McLaughlin, President and CEO, Verisign, Inc.; Judge Charles Johnson, Washington State Supreme Court; Sean Parnell, Governor of Alaska.

Grads Employed by Field (%)
Academic (2)
Business/Industry (23)
Government (14)
Judicial Clerkship (5)
Private Practice (47)
Public Interest (8)

SETON HALL UNIVERSITY
SCHOOL OF LAW

INSTITUTIONAL INFORMATION

Public/private	Private
Affiliation	Roman Catholic
Student-faculty ratio	14:1
% faculty past-time	63
% faculty female	37
% faculty underrepresented minority	16
Total faculty	111

SURVEY SAYS...

Diverse opinions accepted in classrooms, Great research resources, Great library staff, Abundant externship/internship/clerkship opportunities

STUDENTS

Enrollment of law school	266
% male/female	53/47
% part-time	24
% underrepresented minority	14
Average age of entering class	24

ACADEMICS

Academic Experience Rating	**80**
Profs interesting rating	79
Profs accessible rating	80
Hours of study per day	3.68

Academic Specialties

Intellectual Property

Advanced Degrees Offered

JD, 3 years full-time, 4 years part-time; LLM, 1 year full-time, 2 years part-time MSJ, 1 year full-time, 2 years part-time

Combined Degrees Offered

JD/MD, 6 years; MD/MSJ, 5 years; JD/MBA, 4 years; JD/MADIR (Int'l Relations), 4 years; BS/JD, 3+3

Academics

Seton Hall University School of Law is a private, mid-size bastion of legal education, where you'll get an excellent foundation in both the theoretical and the practical aspects of law. Concentrations are available in health law and intellectual property. The Center for Social Justice is "a great resource" that provides "ample opportunities to get hands-on legal experience." It consists of five clinics, and it's among the most comprehensive clinical and pro bono programs in the region, which is quite impressive considering the competition. Opportunities to participate begin during first year. "Very cool study abroad trips" in places such as Cairo, Zanzibar, and Geneva are another nice perk.

The classroom environment at Seton Hall Law is "very conducive to discussion." "There aren't many horrible professors," and "Most rave about their professors." Students say the faculty is full of some of "the wittiest, most passionate, brilliant, best-looking legal minds in the country." "Each of the first-year professors I've had has been really impressive," reports a 1L. "Some of them are pretty idiosyncratic, which provides for some good entertainment outside the classroom, and behind their backs." The faculty is "very accessible," as well. Many students also find the administration "generally helpful." The support staff goes out of its way to accommodate and even anticipate student needs," says a 2L. "It is reliable and makes few mistakes." Other students charge, "The administration at this school is a tsunami of disorganization." We also hear a number of complaints about the legal writing program, which a 3L calls "abhorrent."

"There's very much an on-your-own-feel to finding a job," and some students with middling grades feel "left out in the cold." Nevertheless, most students are pretty satisfied with their job prospects. State and federal court houses "are very close," and "The school has a strong connection to the New Jersey judiciary, so a lot of students get judicial clerkships at graduation." The alumni network is notably loyal, and "Seton Hall Law has a good networking system set in place." "We have the run of New Jersey," boasts a 2L. However, students who want to work in Manhattan have only moderate success. "You can see the city from the library," observes a 1L, "but it seems more like a beautiful dream than a reality for most students." That's not necessarily a drawback, though. "There are plenty of pretty great law firms right here in Newark."

The facilities here are definitely above average. "There can be no debate about that." Not everyone loves "the modern-esque style of the interior," and "The classrooms are more functional than aesthetically pleasing," but upgrades are "constant," and students have few serious grievances. Technology is "particularly smooth." "The library is fantastic," declares a 3L. "It provides especially good electronic resources, even in obscure areas." "I love how everything is in one place," adds a 2L.

Life

The population of future attorneys at Seton Hall Law is reasonably diverse in pretty much every respect except geography. Students report that they have "serious drive, ambition, and talent." While the curve is "severe" and "things get a little competitive during finals time," the academic atmosphere is generally "friendly, fun, and helpful." "Student life at Seton Hall Law delicately balances that line between competition and team work," explains a 1L.

Ms. Gisele Joachim, Asst. Dean of Admissions and Financial Aid
One Newark Center, Newark, NJ 07102
Tel: 888-415-7271 Fax: 973-642-8876
E-Mail: admitme@shu.edu • Website: law.shu.edu

Outside of class, there are frequent seminars and tons of organizations and activities. Attitudes concerning the surrounding city of Newark are seriously mixed. Detractors call it "a notoriously terrible city" that's "lacking in sophistication and charm." "Newark may be the least desirable place to go to law school in the country," reckons a 2L. Other students insist that the Brick City's reputation is unwarranted. "Just because Newark looks crappy doesn't mean it's dangerous," they say. "I feel like a lot of the kids from New Jersey just hate Newark because they bring their prejudices with them," claims a 2L. "Downtown Newark is as safe—if not safer—than any block in NYC. It is a professionally developed area" full of courts and multiple government offices. Whatever the case, the school is "about two blocks from Penn Station, so it's easy enough to commute from a nice area." Despite the commuter ambience, students tell us that there's "a very vibrant social community" at Seton Hall Law. Events sponsored by the student bar association are "pretty awesome," and students "regularly" go out en masse in Hoboken or New York City.

Getting In

Overall, admitted students at the 25th percentile have LSAT scores around 155 and undergraduate GPAs of approximately 3.2. At the 75th percentile, LSAT scores are a little more than 160, and GPAs are around 3.6. Stats for the evening division are somewhat lower across the board.

Clinical program required	No
Legal writing course requirement	Yes
Legal methods course requirement	No
Legal research course requirement	Yes
Moot court requirement	Yes
Public interest law requirement	No

ADMISSIONS

Selectivity Rating	81
# applications received	2,779
% applicants accepted	54
% acceptees attending	14
Median LSAT	160
LSAT Range (25th to 75th percentile)	157–162
Median undergrad GPA	3.52
Application fee	$65
Regular application deadline	4/1
Transfer students accepted	Yes
Evening division offered	Yes
Part-time accepted	Yes
CAS accepted	Yes

FINANCIAL FACTS

Annual tuition (in-state out-of-state)	$47,330
Books and supplies	$1,500
Fees	$840
Room & Board	$13,860
Financial aid application deadline	4/1
% first-year students receiving some sort of aid	94
% all students receiving some sort of aid	91
% of aid that is merit based	25
% receiving scholarships	61
Average grant	$23,500
Average loan	$42,470
Average total aid package	$63,900
Average debt	$127,702

EMPLOYMENT INFORMATION

Career Rating	82
Total 2012 JD Grads	310
% grads employed nine months out	83
Median starting salary	$43,437
% job accepting grads providing useable salary information	44
# employed full-time	251
# employed part-time	7
# employed bar required	210
# employed JD preferred	34
# employed professional/other	11
# employed non-professional	1
# pursuing advanced degree	0
# unemployed and seeking employment	30
# not seeking employment	0
% grads employed by school	0
State for bar exam	NJ
Pass rate for first-time bar	83.27

Prominent Alumni
Michael Chagares, Judge on Third US Circuit Court of Appeals; Christopher Christie, Governor of the State of New Jersey; Loria B. Yeadon, CEO HIP, Inc., Honeywell International.

Grads Employed by Field (%)
Academic (3)
Business/Industry (14)
Government (5)
Judicial Clerkship (31)
Private Practice (31)
Public Interest (2)

SOUTH TEXAS COLLEGE OF LAW

Academics

South Texas College of Law "is a school for litigators." Arming students with the tools they need to succeed in the courtroom, "the school has great advocacy programs in several different fields of law," with a mock trial program that is considered "one of the best in the nation." The regular JD program incorporates intensive training in trial and appellate advocacy, and the school additionally operates a "Summer Trial Academy, as an additional option for practical preparation for those not able to compete or who don't have time in their schedule to do the regular advocacy courses." In addition, "there are a lot of clinics that will place you in a firm or court to gain experience" in the real world. The lively, litigious environment is a huge draw for many STCL students, who warn that quieter types "will be eaten alive" at this competitive school. But do not be startled, as one current student reassures, "Many come to the school for its mock and moot programs, but as a member of the law review's editorial board, I can assure you that opportunities exist in all areas of practice and academia."

As "a down and dirty trade school rather than a school for philosophers," South Texas' academic curriculum "provides a well-reasoned balance between theoretical and practical education," emphasizing critical thinking skills as well as hands-on applications. Through discussion, Socratic questioning, and assignments, "The professors truly try to get you to start thinking like a lawyer from day one. They ask you the right questions to lead you down the path to the answer on your own, without giving you the answer." Staffed by a cadre of accomplished attorneys, "The professors are all extremely qualified, and only a few are purely academic." They will also give you a broad understanding of the law, as "the school has strategically sought out professors from a wide range of backgrounds: some the typical academics (Harvard educated, brilliant resume of publications), some working for the government (such as the SEC or the EPA), and some as experts of their fields in private practice (such as the oil and gas fields, and the energy transactional fields)." Law school is a challenge anywhere, but South Texas students tell us that those that apply must be prepared to work especially hard at their school. A current student recounts, "You have God awful amounts of reading to do all day and all night, you learn more material in the first six months than entire undergrad experience." For anyone who is struggling to keep up, "The professors are, for the most part, extremely accessible and ready to help with clarifications or advice on how to study or understand the material."

When it comes to the nuts and bolts, the program runs smoothly, especially when you consider that it's split between the daytime and evening divisions. Evening students, who attend part-time, are pleased to report, "Almost every class is offered during the day and at night using the same professors." Attentive to students' needs, "the Dean and Associate Deans are accessible and work diligently to ensure we receive a first-rate legal education." Plus, "When some offices/groups within the administration do not uphold their responsibilities, the leadership has made great strides in correcting any problem areas swiftly." After graduation, South Texas students say it's best to look for a job locally. "South Texas is well respected in the Houston community," and "the networking availability is unparalleled" in the region. On the flip side, many students complain that the national rankings do not reflect the true quality of the law school, and that these rankings can have a negative influence on employment opportunities. When looking for a job outside Houston, students admit that, "In other cities, competition is harder." They further note, "The prestigious firms which recruit tier 1 students also recruit at STCL. The big firms may not take as many first year associates, but every firm still appears at on campus interviews."

ALICIA K. CRAMER, ASSISTANT DEAN OF ADMISSIONS
1303 SAN JACINTO STREET, HOUSTON, TX 77002
TEL: 713-646-1810 FAX: 713-646-2906
E-MAIL: ADMISSIONS@STCL.EDU • WEBSITE: WWW.STCL.EDU

Life

Despite the fact that South Texas has produced more championship advocacy teams than any other law school in the United States, students reported that they do not feel like minnows in a tank of trial sharks at South Texas College of Law. "Students at this college are extremely competitive," yet most agree that, "The student body is very friendly…the students help each other out and want to see each other succeed." With its dual daytime and evening programs, "One of the greatest strengths of this school is the diversity of experience in its student body, especially the part-time students. You have people from many different walks of life and careers. People with families. Single people. People in their 40s and 50s. People in their 20s."

Regular full-time students will get the full law school experience at South Texas College of Law. From Amnesty International to the Environmental Law Society, the student body maintains a range of "clubs and organizations that are either fun, competitive, or fun and competitive." Socially, students further benefit from an active community, where "there is always some group throwing a party during lunch or happy hour and plenty of students show up to enjoy good food, cheap drinks, and good company." On the flip side, evening students lament the fact that most "Socials and activities are scheduled during our class times or are scheduled so that we will get out 15 minutes before the social ends."

Getting In

Students are admitted to the full-time program during both the fall and spring semesters. Students entering the part-time program are admitted during the fall semester only. Both paper and online applications are accepted for either program. Students are accepted primarily on the basis of their LSAT and undergraduate GPA. However, a segment of each incoming class is selected on the basis of additional factors. Every attempt is made to evaluate each applicant as an individual, a prospective student, and a future professional.

Clinical program required	No
Legal writing course requirement	Yes
Legal methods course requirement	Yes
Legal research course requirement	Yes
Moot court requirement	No
Public interest law requirement	No

ADMISSIONS

Selectivity Rating	77
# applications received	2,062
% applicants accepted	53
% acceptees attending	37
Average LSAT	153
Median LSAT	153
LSAT Range (25th to 75th percentile)	151–156
Average undergrad GPA	3.15
Median undergrad GPA	3.14
Application fee	$55
Regular application deadline	2/15
Regular notification	5/25
Transfer students accepted	Yes
Evening division offered	Yes
Part-time accepted	Yes
CAS accepted	Yes

FINANCIAL FACTS

Annual tuition	$27,000
Books and supplies	$8,130
Fees	$600
Room & Board	$13,770
Financial aid application deadline	5/1

EMPLOYMENT INFORMATION

Career Rating	86	**Prominent Alumni**
Total 2012 JD Grads	377	Richard H. Anderson, CEO and Chairman,
% grads employed nine months out	86	Delta Airlines; Eva M. Guzman, Justice,
Median starting salary	$60,000	Texas Supreme Court; Janis Graham Jack,
# employed full-time	308	Judge, U.S. District Court, Southern
# employed part-time	3	District of Texas.
# employed bar required	274	**Grads Employed by Field (%)**
# employed JD preferred	17	Academic (1)
# employed professional/other	18	Business/Industry (24)
# employed non-professional	2	Government (10)
# pursuing advanced degree	6	Judicial Clerkship (1)
# unemployed and seeking employment	27	Private Practice (63)
# not seeking employment	17	Public Interest (2)
% grads employed by school	0	
State for bar exam	TX	
Pass rate for first-time bar	85.6	

SOUTHERN ILLINOIS UNIVERSITY
SCHOOL OF LAW

INSTITUTIONAL INFORMATION

Public/private	Public
Affiliation	No Affiliation
Student-faculty ratio	13:1
% faculty part-time	19
% faculty female	57
% faculty underrepresented minority	14
Total faculty	37

SURVEY SAYS...

Diverse opinions accepted in classrooms, Great research resources, Great library staff

STUDENTS

Enrollment of law school	348
% male/female	63/37
% part-time	1
% underrepresented minority	11
Average age of entering class	26

ACADEMICS

Academic Experience Rating	**79**
Profs interesting rating	79
Profs accessible rating	91
Hours of study per day	3.52

Academic Specialties

Health Law; Business & Transactional Law; International, Intellectual Property

Advanced Degrees Offered

JD, 3 years; MLS, 2 years; LLM, 2 years

Combined Degrees Offered

JD/MD, 6 years; JD/MBA, 4 years; JD/MPA, 4 years; JD/M.Acc, 4 years; JD/MSW, varies, JD/MSEd, varies; JD/MS ECE

Academics

Southern Illinois University is a "small school" where "the tuition is low" yet the "quality of education" is "high." From professors to staff, the school fosters a "friendly/familial feel" that includes "personal attention" to students' needs. "The atmosphere" at SIU "is friendly and respectful." "I'd say the best aspect is the rapport between the students, faculty and administration," a 1L says. "You can tell the day that you start, that everyone [wants] you to succeed." The school's small size appeals to many, but can also cause "a significant amount of 'little school syndrome.'" The "great facilities" provide plentiful resources for "legal research, IT help, and assistance from librarians." "From adequate parking space, to on-site tech support," "there are all of the resources" students at a law school need. "In the library there are computers and all of the rooms have outlets for our lap tops," and the school is open to students "24 hours a day."

The friendly atmosphere and "small" size means the "helpful, insightful and always accessible" administration "knows nearly all the students by name from day 1." "Students are very close with the administration" and the overall experience is "great and friendly." Although some students say the administration can be "quite disorganized and disorderly," most say that "when there is a problem, it is fixed before anyone notices." "[The administration is] willing to sit down and explain the law school process, as well as help in any way to balance law school, family, and social life," says one 2L. Students do wish that the school offered "more diverse classes." Academically, there is strong "emphasis on practical skills" and "emphasis on legal writing." "We gain practical skills that prepares us well for outside employment," one student reports. SIU makes sure to work with the local community, and "the volunteer hours the local attorneys give to talk with students, coach students, and mentor students is phenomenal." As for the faculty themselves, they "are amazingly approachable and supportive" professors that "care deeply about their students" and "always open to conversation, whether it was about law school or not." "The professors at SIU have an open door policy and encourage one-on-one encounters," leading students to be impressed by "how accessible they are to meeting with students outside of class." The professors here are "freely willing to give students their personal contact information." "It is very nice to have instructors that have not only written texts but also model rules and the current law in the state," a happy 1L says. In general, the faculty and staff work to foster a culture that "minimizes competition and promotes collaboration."

AKAMI MARIK, DIRECTOR OF ADMISSIONS & FINANCIAL AID
SIU SCHOOL OF LAW WELCOME CENTER, 1209 W. CHAUTAUQUA, MAILCODE 6811,
CARBONDALE, IL 62901
TEL: 618-453-8858 FAX: 618-453-8921
E-MAIL: LAWADMIT@SIU.EDU • WEBSITE: WWW.LAW.SIU.EDU

Life

Your experience at SIU is influenced greatly by whether you are "a city-slicker" or someone who will like "the great outdoors" and "the small town feel of Carbondale." Carbondale, with a population of around 25,000, has "some beautiful scenery" but otherwise is "blah." However, "there are some of the most beautiful state parks and federal lands in the mid-west within [a] 20 minute drive of the law school." Some students report "cabin-fever," but many come to SIU specifically for "the slower pace of the small town life." As one student says: "some come, love it, and never leave." The student body has a Midwest feel, being mostly composed of students "from across the region, with about 15% coming from outside the region." The student body is "not racially diverse," but everyone gets along. SIU is a place where "students can actually interact with each other instead of competing with each other." "We are a small community and we all care a lot for each other," a 1L explains. "Everyone is friendly and I truly think that relationships that I have formed are unique and special to our school."

Getting In

The 2012 class at SIU had an average GPA of 3.26 and an average LSAT score of 153.9. In addition to these scores, the administration says they look heavily at the letters of recommendation, personal statement, and work history shown on applicant resumes.

Clinical program required	No
Legal writing course requirement	Yes
Legal methods course requirement	Yes
Legal research course requirement	Yes
Moot court requirement	No
Public interest law requirement	No

ADMISSIONS

Selectivity Rating	74
# applications received	719
% applicants accepted	57
% acceptees attending	27
Average LSAT	154
Median LSAT	152
LSAT Range (25th to 75th percentile)	149–155
Average undergrad GPA	3.26
Median undergrad GPA	3.05
Application fee	$50
Regular application deadline	4/1
Transfer students accepted	Yes
Evening division offered	No
Part-time accepted	No
CAS accepted	Yes

FINANCIAL FACTS

Annual tuition (in-state out-of-state)	$13,642/$35,214
Books and supplies	$1,150
Fees	$3,353
Room & Board	$12,158
Financial aid application deadline	4/1
% first-year students receiving some sort of aid	92
% all students receiving some sort of aid	91
% of aid that is merit based	22
% receiving scholarships	50
Average grant	$26,089
Average loan	$37,324
Average total aid package	$43,807
Average debt	$67,885

EMPLOYMENT INFORMATION

Career Rating	74
Total 2012 JD Grads	128
% grads employed nine months out	72
Median starting salary	$45,000
# employed full-time	81
# employed part-time	11
# employed bar required	74
# employed JD preferred	6
# employed professional/other	6
# employed non-professional	6
# pursuing advanced degree	2
# unemployed and seeking employment	16
# not seeking employment	6
% grads employed by school	0
State for bar exam	IL, MO
Pass rate for first-time bar	88.3

Prominent Alumni
William Enyart, U.S. Congressman, 12th District of Illinois; Karen Kendall, Partner, Heyl, Royster, Voelker & Allen; Hon. William E. Holdridge, Illinois Appellate Court, 3rd District.

Grads Employed by Field (%)
Academic (3)
Business/Industry (7)
Government (8)
Judicial Clerkship (2)
Private Practice (48)
Public Interest (4)

Southern Methodist University
Dedman School of Law

INSTITUTIONAL INFORMATION

Public/private	Private
Affiliation	Methodist
Student-faculty ratio	15:1
% faculty part-time	39
% faculty female	36
% faculty underrepresented minority	13
Total faculty	133

SURVEY SAYS...

Beautiful campus, Students love Dallas, TX, Good social life

STUDENTS

% male/female	61/39
% part-time	29
% underrepresented minority	21
Average age of entering class	23

ACADEMICS

Academic Experience Rating	**92**
Profs interesting rating	82
Profs accessible rating	80
Hours of study per day	3.70

Advanced Degrees Offered
LLM (Taxation), 1 year; LLM (General), 1 year; LLM (for Foreign Law School Graduates), 1 year; SJD, varies.

Combined Degrees Offered
JD/MBA, 4 years; JD/MA (Economics), 4 years

Academics

Boasting "a great program...great size...in a city with great opportunity," the Dedman School of Law at Southern Methodist University has it all. "The local legal community draws heavily from the law school, and with a little initiative, a law student can easily network with numerous lawyers and judges in the area and beyond." "Diverse course offerings" in "everything from the philosophical to the tediously practical" define the curriculum here, and "The legal clinics are absolutely amazing." Externships and scholarly journals are abundant. Students say there are plenty of opportunities to get involved: "We have consistently won national moot court and mock trial competitions over the past two years, and the school has a great Trial Advocacy program co-taught by practitioners and judges." A unique JD/MA program allows students to study economics as well as law, and students have the opportunity to study abroad in Oxford each summer.

Academic complaints often revolve around the legal writing program, which "needs a massive overhaul" and, "while informational, [can] feel more like fifth grade English in the way [it is] approached." Fortunately, the "very distinguished" yet "easily approachable" professors "are very receptive to students and concerned with [their] learning" and "make an effort to be available." They are "demanding of their students," but "interesting and entertaining in the classroom."

Professors "make the classroom experience fun," gushes one student. "My civil procedure exam was one of the funniest things I have ever read, with witty undercurrents and subtle political satire." Opinions of the administration vary considerably. Some students say the deans seem "distant at times, but whenever you need them, they're available and helpful." Others tell us that the administration "does not care about the students" and gripe about "bureaucratic inefficiencies."

Job prospects are very promising for SMU grads. Career Services is "actually concerned with helping you find a job." "Dallas is a wonderful market that pays salaries on par with New York, but the quality of life is so much better," according to students. "If you want to stay and practice in Dallas, you could not go to a better school." SMU's "exceptionally strong relationship with the Dallas legal market" provides an "extensive network of attorneys" "in every field imaginable." "The alums are very supportive and willing to help out." "A lot of doors are opened by attending the SMU Dedman School of Law, regardless of your class rank." "I was able to secure a six-figure job without being on law review or moot court," says a 3L. "There is definitely a huge hurdle" for students to face who do not want to practice in Texas, though.

The "gorgeous" campus is full of "very pretty, collegiate-looking brick buildings" and "nestled in one of the nicest, most affluent neighborhoods in the Dallas area." "The law school itself is further cloistered away from the rest of the university and, once inside, it is easy to forget you are sitting in the middle of a bustling metropolis." "Large oak trees provide shady walkways, and outdoor study places are ample." "The majority of classrooms are "very comfortable and accommodating," and the "nearly flawless" wireless signal is "strong in every corner of the law school." The library is "amazing," "both with regard to holdings and ease of use."

JILL NIKIRK, ASSISTANT DEAN OF ADMISSIONS
P.O. BOX 750110, DALLAS, TX 75275-0110
TEL: 214-768-2550 FAX: 214-768-2549
E-MAIL: LAWADMIT@SMU.EDU • WEBSITE: WWW.LAW.SMU.EDU

Life

"Students in the full-time day program tend to be younger—either directly out of their undergraduate program or with only a year or two of work experience. Nevertheless, there are still many full-time students in their thirties or older." Most are "Texas natives," and all are "fun, attractive, and smart." Some students are "cooperative, collegial, and very supportive of one another." Others are "very competitive." "There are definitely a few trust fund kids, but a lot of us are living off student loans as well," says one student. "The parking garage does boast an unusual concentration of BMWs and Hummers," agrees a 2L. "But as a non-Texan who shares a beat-up Honda with my wife, I've never felt out of place." "Political views run the gamut, but the large majority of students are tolerant of opposing views." SMU is also "remarkably GLBT-friendly."

Regarding social events on campus, students say "There's a club for everyone, whether you're a gun-toting Second Amendment crusader or a die-hard liberal." "The students put together a lot of fun activities," ranging from happy hours to baseball games to tailgating events. "The highlight of everyone's week is Bar Review where the Student Bar Association gets drink specials at a different local bar every Friday." There's also "a picnic/sports spectacular every semester." SMU's ritzy location is "great" in terms of safety but "can make finding student housing right next to school virtually impossible." Beyond the neighborhood surrounding campus, "Big D" is one of the liveliest cities in the South and "a fun place to live." "You get a great all-around legal education and have the resources of the Dallas–Fort Worth Metroplex right at your doorstep."

Getting In

For the fall 2012 entering class the median LSAT score among applicants to the full-time program was 164 and the median GPA was 3.73. Applicants to the part-time evening program posted slightly lower numbers: the median GPA was 3.49 and the median LSAT score was 160.

Clinical program required	No
Legal writing course requirement	Yes
Legal methods course requirement	No
Legal research course requirement	Yes
Moot court requirement	Yes
Public interest law requirement	Yes

ADMISSIONS

Selectivity Rating	89
# applications received	2,370
% applicants accepted	34
% acceptees attending	31
Median LSAT	164
LSAT Range (25th to 75th percentile)	157–165
Median undergrad GPA	3.73
Application fee	$75
Regular application deadline	2/15
Regular notification	5/15
Early application deadline	11/1
Early application notification	1/31
Transfer students accepted	Yes
Evening division offered	Yes
Part-time accepted	Yes
CAS accepted	Yes

FINANCIAL FACTS

Annual tuition	$39,309
Books and supplies	$2,000
Fees	$4,709
Average loan	$26,770

EMPLOYMENT INFORMATION

Career Rating	**95**	**Prominent Alumni**
Total 2012 JD Grads	293	Michael Boone, Founding partner, Haynes
% for whom you have useable information	100	& Boone; Bill Hutchison, President, Hutchison Oil & Gas.
% grads employed nine months out	93	**Grads Employed by Field (%)**
Median starting salary	$80,000	Academic (1)
# employed full-time	260	Business/Industry (25)
# employed part-time	13	Government (7)
# employed bar required	230	Judicial Clerkship (4)
# employed JD preferred	21	Military (1)
# employed professional/other	21	Private Practice (60)
# employed non-professional	1	Public Interest (1)
# pursuing advanced degree	5	
# unemployed and seeking employment	6	
# not seeking employment	9	
State for bar exam	TX	
Pass rate for first-time bar	89	

SOUTHERN UNIVERSITY
LAW CENTER

INSTITUTIONAL INFORMATION

Public/private	Public
Student-faculty ratio	14:1
% faculty part-time	4
% faculty female	37
% faculty underrepresented minority	61
Total faculty	41

SURVEY SAYS...

Diverse opinions accepted in classrooms, Great research resources, Great library staff, Good social life

STUDENTS

Enrollment of law school	728
% male/female	47/53
% from out-of-state	15
% part-time	34
% underrepresented minority	66
# of countries represented	2
Average age of entering class	28

ACADEMICS

Academic Experience Rating	**70**
Profs interesting rating	75
Profs accessible rating	77
Hours of study per day	3.06

Academic Specialties

Civil Procedure, Commercial, Criminal, Environmental, Government Services, International, Taxation, Intellectual Property

Combined Degrees Offered

JD/MPA, 4Years

Academics

With roughly 600 full-time and part-time students, Southern University Law Center is "small and personable." "I don't feel like just another number at my school," says a 1L. "You feel that the people around you want you to be successful." SULC is also "ridiculously affordable." "While others will be coming out of law school hundred of thousands of dollars in debt, Southern grads will have debt that is approximately one fifth of the cost." Additional perks here include a decently broad selection of courses and six clinics that provide hands-on experience with the realities of practicing law for a very good percentage of students. If you want to pursue both a JD and MPA, the school offers a joint-degree program in cooperation with Southern's Nelson Mandela School of Public Policy and Urban Affairs. There's also a study abroad program in London, in which students take courses in international law.

Louisiana is a civil law jurisdiction (in the tradition of France and Continental Europe), while law in every other state is based on the common law tradition (of England). While SULC students learn both, the required curriculum focuses on civil law both substantively and procedurally. If you plan to practice in the Pelican State, Southern is a great choice. The "wealth of alums" doesn't hurt when it comes to finding a job, either. However, if you want to practice in another state, learning Louisiana's unique system of law and trying to apply it to another state's bar exam won't be the easiest thing in the world.

"Some profs can be very intimidating," but the full-time faculty is full of "sincere, challenging, intelligent people" who are "downright awesome." The faculty is notoriously approachable as well. Most professors are "always willing to help." "I have a great amount of respect for 90 percent of my professors," explains a 2L. "I feel that all of them have been knowledgeable in the subject matter." The "generally excellent" part-time program tends to have more adjunct professors. They're more of a mixed bag. "Some of the evening professors are practicing attorneys during the day and are not as accessible or as devoted as the full-time day professors." Students offer considerable praise for the "very professional" administration. Deans are "approachable and available," and they "work diligently in their efforts to help the students succeed" and to "know who their students are." Some students tell us that the financial aid process can be a "nightmare," though. The legal writing program is another complaint. Students say that it "could use a lot of improvement." SULC's "somewhat new facilities" are "very poorly maintained." Otherwise, they are "really good" and "very hospitable." Classrooms have wireless Internet and plenty of electrical outlets. The library is "stocked with great resource materials."

Life

"This school is probably the most diverse school in the country in terms of the student body," gushes a 2L. SULC is a historically black institution, and some 60 percent of the students are African American. Students come here "from all over the country," and they "have very interesting backgrounds." The range of ages is vast as well.

VELMA E. WILKERSON, COORDINATOR OF ADMISSION
A.A. LENOIR HALL, P.O. BOX 9294, 2 ROOSEVELT STEPTOE STREET, BATON ROUGE, LA 70813
TEL: 225-771-4976 FAX: 225-771-2121
E-MAIL: ADMISSION@SULC.EDU • WEBSITE: WWW.SULC.EDU

"Southern charm is alive and well at SULC." A "kind and friendly" "family atmo-sphere" reigns supreme, and "a strong sense of camaraderie and support is evident in every aspect." "Some people are competitive," says a 1L, "but I don't get that extremely competitive vibe from Southern." "It's a smaller law school," explains a 2L, "which allows students to work more cooperatively, instead of against each other as at most law schools." Most everyone "goes out of their way to help." The biggest social divide is probably between the day program, which is generally composed of younger students, and the evening program, which is "mostly older professionals."

During the school day, "the school regularly has speakers and attorneys come in dur-ing the noon hour to give practical advice on the practice of law." Students are split when it comes to life beyond the confines of campus. Some tell us that Baton Rouge—the state capital and the second largest city in Louisiana—is a student's Shangri-la, especially if you like music and food. Baton Rouge is home to unique art and culture, tons of festivals, and mouthwatering cuisine of every kind. When students take a break from hitting the books, a good number of bars and clubs and a raging live music scene keep life interesting. Other students aren't feeling the cultural love, though. "The main chances for socialization seem to be at a bar or a church," suggests a 2L. "What if you don't drink or believe?"

Getting In

Admitted students at the 25th percentile have LSAT scores around 142 and GPAs in the 2.6 range. Admitted students at the 75th percentile have LSAT scores of 149 or so and GPAs of around 3.2.

Clinical program required	No
Legal writing course requirement	Yes
Legal methods course requirement	No
Legal research course requirement	Yes
Moot court requirement	No
Public interest law requirement	No

ADMISSIONS

Selectivity Rating	84
# applications received	1,049
% applicants accepted	38
% acceptees attending	64
Average LSAT	147
Median LSAT	145
LSAT Range (25th to 75th percentile)	142–149
Average undergrad GPA	2.91
Median undergrad GPA	2.85
Application fee	$25
Regular application deadline	2/28
Transfer students accepted	Yes
Evening division offered	Yes
Part-time accepted	Yes
CAS accepted	Yes

FINANCIAL FACTS

Annual tuition (in-state out-of-state)	$21,980/$37,180
Books and supplies	$5,581
Room & Board	$8,727
Financial aid application deadline	4/15
% first-year students receiving some sort of aid	88
% all students receiving some sort of aid	90
% of aid that is merit based	20
% receiving scholarships	20
Average grant	$8,000
Average total aid package	$20,500
Average debt	$65,000

EMPLOYMENT INFORMATION

Career Rating	72
Total 2012 JD Grads	143
% for whom you have useable information	100
% grads employed nine months out	76
Median starting salary	$46,375
% job accepting grads providing useable salary information	56
# employed full-time	93
# employed part-time	16
# employed bar required	59
# employed JD preferred	24
# employed professional/other	18
# employed non-professional	8
# pursuing advanced degree	5
# unemployed and seeking employment	27
# not seeking employment	2
% grads employed by school	0
State for bar exam	LA, FL, GA, IL, TX
Pass rate for first-time bar	66

Prominent Alumni

Brian Jackson, Chief U.S. District Judge for the Middle District of LA; Stephanie Finley, U.S. Attorney, Western District of LA; Claire Babineaux-Fontenot, Sr. VP & Chief Tax Officer/Walmart.

Grads Employed by Field (%)

Academic (6)
Business/Industry (16)
Government (15)
Judicial Clerkship (8)
Private Practice (27)
Public Interest (4)

SOUTHWESTERN LAW SCHOOL

INSTITUTIONAL INFORMATION

Public/private	Private
% faculty part-time	32
% faculty female	45
% faculty underrepresented minority	23
Total faculty	100

SURVEY SAYS...

Diverse opinions accepted in classrooms, Great research resources

STUDENTS

Enrollment of law school	1,086
% male/female	46/54
% from out-of-state	15
% part-time	36
% underrepresented minority	37
% international	1
# of countries represented	15
Average age of entering class	26

ACADEMICS

Academic Experience Rating	**80**
Profs interesting rating	75
Profs accessible rating	73
Hours of study per day	3.82

Academic Specialties

Civil Procedure, Commercial, Constitutional, Corporation Securities, Criminal, Entertainment and Media Law, Environmental, Government Services, Human Rights, International, Labor, Legal History, Legal Philosophy, Property, Taxation, Intellectual Property

Advanced Degrees Offered

In addition to the JD degree, Southwestern offers the first LLM in Entertainment and Media Law, and an individualized LLM program.

Combined Degrees Offered

JD/MBA; offered in collaboration with The Drucker Graduate School of Management; JD/MA in Conflict Resolution, Negotiation and Peacebuilding in collaboration with California State University Dominguez Hills

Academics

Large, private, and independent Southwestern Law School boasts an "emphasis on practical skills" and an impressive array of bells and whistles. In addition to your standard full-time day and part-time evening programs, there's a very intensive two-year program that features small classes and integrates plenty of real-world training. There's also a part-time day program that helps nontraditional students juggle the demands of work, family, and school. A "broad" and "ever-increasing" range of courses includes summer law programs in Argentina, Canada, England, and Mexico. Clinics are available in immigration law, street law, and children's rights. "The externships are amazing and very available to all class ranks." There's a JD/MBA program allied with the Drucker Graduate School of Management. If you are interested in entertainment and media law, Southwestern is home to a huge contingent of professors who specialize in that area, and the school maintains impressive connections "within the entertainment industry." Another perk is Southwestern's unique "three-track approach" to legal writing. As a 1L, you can choose from specialized writing programs in trial practice, negotiation, or appellate advocacy. While Southwestern sort of exists in the shadow of other law schools in the local area with national reputations, students tell us that they are happy with their employment prospects. Career Services has "tons of resources," they say, and Southwestern has a "huge alumni network," "especially in the Los Angeles area."

The faculty is composed of "an array of ages, ethnicities, and eccentricities." There are "some really outstanding teachers" here "who could not be more dedicated to their craft," and the faculty as a whole is "helpful and accommodating." They "genuinely care about your success in law school." "They are engaging and really care about what each student takes away from their class," explains a 3L. "The school is attempting to teach us to be good lawyers," explains a 1L, "with less emphasis on maintaining the 'hide-the-ball' pedagogy of the Socratic Method." There's the stray "incompetent" prof here, though, and some of the older ones are "standard fare." "Most professors are available to students on a regular basis" once class ends. "I was surprised by the support from teachers and access to them outside of the classroom," reports a 1L. "This institution is committed to a student-first ideology." Some students say that the administration "treats everyone like an individual, not just another customer." Others say that there is "too much bureaucracy, in all aspects."

The facilities at Southwestern are within easy commuting distance to the downtown district of Los Angeles. Students say they are "world-class." The crown jewel is a legendary, enormous, and very distinctive Art Deco building. It used to be a fancy department store and now it is listed on the National Register of Historic Places. "The administration clearly takes pride in the campus upkeep." "Everything is new and high-tech." Classrooms are "really nice." "The library is beautiful and basically kicks the ass out of the other law school libraries in Los Angeles," pronounces a 1L. There are also ample study areas, terraces with sweeping city views, and a gigantic fitness center for student use. A new upscale on-campus student residential complex will open in Fall 2013.

LISA GEAR, ASSISTANT DEAN FOR ADMISSIONS
3050 WILSHIRE BOULEVARD, LOS ANGELES, CA 90010-1106
TEL: 213-738-6834 • FAX: 213-383-1688
E-MAIL: ADMISSIONS@SWLAW.EDU • WEBSITE: WWW.SWLAW.EDU

Life

By all accounts, diversity is "great" at Southwestern in every way. Students come here from pretty much every state and all walks of life. Ethnic minorities constitute about a third of the population. Roughly two-thirds of the students have either previous work experience or some kind of advanced degree already. The academic atmosphere is "very professional and collegiate." "It's very cooperatively competitive," explains a 3L. "Everyone wants to do better than the next person but is always willing to help the next person out." "There's a lot of mentoring that goes on at Southwestern" between 1Ls and upper-division students as well.

Southwestern's campus is "an oasis in seedy Koreatown." Some students contend that social life is pretty dismal. "There is a social disconnect at the school," laments a 1L. "Clubs are not really active and there is a commuter atmosphere." Other students strongly disagree. According to them, Southwestern is "very social." "Everyone is friendly with each other, which has made for a pleasant experience," declares a 3L. "I've created some bonds with certain students that I will cherish forever." Whatever the case, the inexhaustible sprawl of the metropolitan Los Angeles area offers something for every taste and predilection imaginable.

Getting In

Enrolled full-time students at the 25th percentile have LSAT scores in the low 150s and GPAs around 3.2. Enrolled students at the 75th percentile have LSAT scores around 156 and GPAs a little over 3.5. If you enroll in the two-year program, classes start in mid-summer.

Clinical program required	No
Legal writing course requirement	Yes
Legal methods course requirement	Yes
Legal research course requirement	Yes
Moot court requirement	Yes
Public interest law requirement	No

ADMISSIONS

Selectivity Rating	82
# applications received	2,307
% applicants accepted	44
% acceptees attending	25
Median LSAT	153
LSAT Range (25th to 75th percentile)	152–156
Median undergrad GPA	3.33
Application fee	$60
Regular application deadline	4/1
Transfer students accepted	Yes
Evening division offered	Yes
Part-time accepted	Yes
CAS accepted	Yes

FINANCIAL FACTS

Annual tuition	$43,650
Books and supplies	$1,250
Fees	$200
Room & Board	$19,620
Financial aid application deadline	6/1
% first-year students receiving some sort of aid	86
% all students receiving some sort of aid	90
% receiving scholarships	53
Average grant	$21,581
Average loan	$57,201
Average total aid package	$61,964
Average debt	$147,976

EMPLOYMENT INFORMATION

Career Rating	72	# not seeking employment	24
Total 2012 JD Grads	324	% grads employed by school	1
% for whom you have useable information	90	State for bar exam	CA, NY, UT, CO, AZ
% grads employed nine months out	71	Pass rate for first-time bar	62
Median starting salary	$65,000	**Prominent Alumni**	
% job accepting grads providing useable salary information	34	Tom Bradley, LA Mayor for 20 years; Stanley Mosk, Longest serving Cal. Sup. Ct. Justice; Hon. Vaino Spencer, 1st Afr-Amer woman Judge in Calif. & 3rd in the US.	
# employed full-time	208		
# employed part-time	17		
# employed bar required	152	**Grads Employed by Field (%)**	
# employed JD preferred	44	Academic (2)	
# employed professional/other	17	Business/Industry (20)	
# employed non-professional	10	Government (2)	
# pursuing advanced degree	4	Judicial Clerkship (1)	
# unemployed and seeking employment	34	Private Practice (42)	
		Public Interest (3)	

ST. JOHN'S UNIVERSITY
SCHOOL OF LAW

INSTITUTIONAL INFORMATION
Public/private   Private
Affiliation   Roman Catholic
Student-faculty ratio   15:1

SURVEY SAYS...
Diverse opinions accepted in classrooms, Great research resources, Great library staff, Abundant externship/internship/clerkship opportunities

STUDENTS
Enrollment of law school   930
% male/female   56/44
% part-time   16
% underrepresented minority   23
Average age of entering class   23

ACADEMICS
Academic Experience Rating   80
Profs interesting rating   77
Profs accessible rating   76
Hours of study per day   4.01

Advanced Degrees Offered
JD, 3 years (full-time day), 4 years (part-time evening); LLM in Bankruptcy, 1 year (full-time), 2–3 years (part-time); LLM in US Legal Studies for Foreign Lawyers 1 year (full-time), 2–4 years (part-time); LLM in Transnational Legal Practice; LLM in International and Comparative Sports Law

Combined Degrees Offered
JD/MBA; JD/MA(MS); BA (BS)/JD; JD/LLM

Academics

St. John's University School of Law "places an emphasis on how to actually become a lawyer, not an academic" and boasts a bar-passage rate that's consistently higher than the Empire State's overall percentage. St. John's also comes equipped with an impressive array of academic bells and whistles. "There are very strong programs in bankruptcy and labor and employment law." The host of clinics is "a big draw." Highlights include securities arbitration, and a couple interesting programs involving immigration rights. There's also "a wide range of courses," "numerous journals and organizations," and an "outstanding" speaker series.

"There are some really incredible professors and some really miserable professors" at St. John's Law. "There's no in-between." Students say that most fall in the incredible category, though. They "do an outstanding job of mixing the Socratic Method while making clear the purpose of each class." "Our professors make the law real," declares a 1L. "They make sure we know the legal theories, but they also make sure we know why the theories matter and how we'll use those theories in practice to advocate for our clients." Full-time professors are "always around and accessible." "They eat breakfast and lunch in the cafe and sit with students to chat with them." Adjuncts are often a very different story. "Meeting with adjunct professors without an office on campus can be so difficult to arrange, it's headache-inducing," grumbles a 2L. Some students say that the top brass takes "an active, positive role in students' lives." "The dean makes an effort to know the name of every student in the school," they say. Other students contend that bureaucracy is "nightmarish," particularly if you're unlucky enough to face anyone outside the law school. "I dread having to deal with the general university's administrators," notes a 2L.

Without question, St. John's has a "broad" and "engaged" alumni network, which is "invaluable, especially for students looking to practice in the New York area." "The alumni provide you with positions or connections in any way they can," beams a 1L. "Alumni give their time to a significant number of the school's activities, such as panels and mock interview programs." "Career Services could be better," though and students seeking to work in big firms face grimly stiff competition from the gaggle of big-name schools in the region. Networking with loyal alums is paramount because "few St. John's students" land plum jobs through traditional on-campus interviews.

The larger university is quiet by New York City standards. Although "the building is pretty run down," there's ample space and the facilities are "very modern." "The library is fantastic." "Classrooms are comfortable," but occasionally crowded. Climate control can be a problem. "The environmental control system cannot regulate the temperature properly," explains a 3L, "so you need to come dressed prepared for anything as each room has the potential to range from Arctic to Sahara."

ROBERT M. HARRISON, ASSISTANT DEAN FOR ADMISSIONS
8000 UTOPIA PARKWAY, QUEENS, NY 11439
TEL: 718-990-6474 FAX: 718-990-2526
E-MAIL: LAWINFO@STJOHNS.EDU • WEBSITE: WWW.LAW.STJOHNS.EDU

Life

Most students are from New York, or at least from the Northeast, and ethnic diversity is laudable. Students at St. John's Law describe themselves as "type-A personalities with something to prove." They have "a sense that they will only get ahead through hard work and actually learning how to practice the law." Nevertheless, they're "very pleasant to be around." "The student body is respectful of one another and welcoming to everyone," promises a 1L. "There are only a few people in every year who are competitive," adds a 2L, "and they are usually ridiculed." Note, however, that the grading curve here is on the unforgiving side, "so your average grades will be lower than that at other law schools."

The location "in the middle of nowhere Queens" hinders the social scene somewhat. The bright lights of Manhattan are a very reasonable train ride away, but "It can sometimes be inconvenient to get to the city from here." "The Queens campus is a crappy location if you don't have a car," flatly advises a 1L. Socially unhappy commuters say, "Most clubs are little more than resume boosters, and few of them hold more than one or two meetings per semester." "Sometimes the student body does not have the same sense of family that other law schools possess." However, a large number of students live on campus or in the "affordable surrounding neighborhoods," and they report a much higher level of "social life and school spirit." "There are some good restaurants within walking distance," and it's common for students to "meet at the bars for a drink after studying." "The school's community is what you make of it," reflects a 3L. "Opportunities abound, but you have to make an effort to find them."

Getting In

Admitted students at the 25th percentile have LSAT scores in the mid 150s and undergraduate GPAs close to 3.2. At the 75th percentile, LSAT scores are a little more than 160, and GPAs are around 3.7.

Clinical program required	No
Legal writing course requirement	Yes
Legal methods course requirement	Yes
Legal research course requirement	Yes
Moot court requirement	Yes
Public interest law requirement	No

ADMISSIONS

Selectivity Rating	**81**
# applications received	3,036
% applicants accepted	47
% acceptees attending	19
LSAT Range (25th to 75th percentile)	153–161
Application fee	$60
Regular application deadline	4/1
Transfer students accepted	Yes
Evening division offered	Yes
Part-time accepted	Yes
CAS accepted	Yes

FINANCIAL FACTS

Annual tuition	$48,070
Books and supplies	$5,784
Room & Board (on/off campus)	$18,320/$17,365
Financial aid application deadline	2/1
% first-year students receiving some sort of aid	93
% all students receiving some sort of aid	92
% of aid that is merit based	36
% receiving scholarships	55
Average grant	$30,475
Average loan	$49,051
Average total aid package	$61,108
Average debt	$95,182

EMPLOYMENT INFORMATION

		Grads Employed by Field (%)
Career Rating	**83**	
Total 2012 JD Grads	281	Academic (3)
% grads employed nine months out	78	Business/Industry (20)
Median starting salary	$64,350	Government (14)
# employed full-time	185	Judicial Clerkship (3)
# employed part-time	35	Private Practice (56)
# employed bar required	151	Public Interest (3)
# employed JD preferred	53	
# employed professional/other	6	
# employed non-professional	6	
# pursuing advanced degree	3	
# unemployed and seeking employment	45	
# not seeking employment	7	
% grads employed by school	4	
State for bar exam	NY	
Pass rate for first-time bar	83	

St. Thomas University

School of Law

Academics

St. Thomas University School of Law offers "a small, tight-knit community" that truly wants to see its students thrive and succeed. The school takes a practical approach to teaching law and students are quick to highlight the legal writing department, which they view as an "asset." Indeed, the in-depth curriculum requires "a closed memo, open memo, motion for summary judgment, client letter, affidavit, service lists, statement of the facts, complaint and answer to the complaint, interrogatories, request for admissions, request for documents, summons, and appeals brief (and argument in the presence of 3 judges)." As one second-year continues, "Legal writing [is] the cornerstone of [your] career. Therefore, the standards for memos, motions, etc. are high."

Moreover, law students here speak glowingly about their "tremendously helpful and supportive" professors. The vast majority seems to maintain "an open door policy," which really "allows students to visit professors freely to ask questions and review problems." Additionally many truly appreciate how STU professors "push their students to achieve legal and social excellence." Indeed, "they are always there to offer whatever they can to help students, which is always well researched or spoken from their extensive experience." This praise also extends to the administration, which tends to "greet the students with open arms and typically by first name." Impressively, they also operate under an open door policy, which "helps cater to the needs of students (ex: extending library hours during final exams)." As a second-year brags, "Anything the students want/need, the students feel free to bring up to the administration for their consideration. "

STU also provides "great" research facilities and on-campus resources. One second-year elaborates, "Not only do we have Westlaw and LexisNexis, we have access to other great databases such as JSTOR and HeinOnline. Campus offers unlimited, free printing which is helping when writing your law review comment and/or seminar paper." Even better, "The staff in the library is ALWAYS around to help. They will meet with you for however long you need; it is like having your own personal library assistant there for you along the way."

Students here are also extremely grateful for the professional opportunities a St. Thomas education affords them. As one second year elaborates, "The externship programs and on-campus interviews brought in from career services is phenomenal. The school places students in trial, appellate, and supreme courts for both state and federal systems." Another pleased student quickly follow up, "The reputation that our school has in South Miami has helped place these students in the judicial clerkships and various public offices (state attorney and public defenders)." Further, St. Thomas has "a unique relationship with the Pax Romana of the United Nations. Therefore, students can be selected to go to New York to the UN headquarters for a unique experience with ambassadors and diplomats."

Life

"This law school is very diverse." In fact, it's one of the most ethnically diverse bastions of legal education in the country. There is a very high Latino student enrollment. There is also "a substantial number of second-career types as well as attorneys from Latin American and other countries who are revalidating their degrees" in the United States. "About half of the student body came to St. Thomas via the 'traditional' student method," estimates a 1L, "and the other half is a little older and brings a wide range of practical understandings. This dichotomy leads to some truly enlightening classroom

305-623-2310, DIRECTOR OF ADMISSIONS
16401 NORTHWEST 37TH AVENUE, MIAMI GARDENS, FL 33054
TEL: 305-623-2310 FAX: 305-623-2357
E-MAIL: ADMITME@STU.EDU • WEBSITE: WWW.STU.EDU/LAWSCHOOL

discussions." Some students explain, "There is a good deal of competition" academically. Others say that students "join forces" and share notes regularly and copiously at exam time.

STU is situated on the main campus of the larger university in a suburb between Ft. Lauderdale and Miami. Some students tell us the location is "not so good." The cost of living in these parts isn't the cheapest, either. On the plus side, the weather in South Florida is "very relaxing" virtually year-round, and the Floridian campus boasts palm trees, ponds, and tennis courts. The area also offers tons of activities and nightlife. Bars, restaurants, shopping and cuisine are all world-class and, of course, "you always have the beaches." Perhaps more importantly, students at STU are privy to "rich experiences" and "fantastic events." A pleased third-year proudly shares, "Our Law Review just hosted a tremendous symposium on Media and the Law, in which Harvard Law Professor Charles Nesson was the keynote speaker." Additionally, "last semester, Justice Scalia came and talked to our school." Socially, there are "enough student organizations to find something you like." This law school is a pretty tight-knit place too. "Close relationships" are easily formed, and students know pretty much everyone in their class year. Also, "The school design invites socialization." "There is a breezeway always full of students talking and hanging out, sharing thoughts, and talking about the professors and classes."

Getting In

St. Thomas University School of Law nets a competitive applicant pool. Admitted students in the 25th percentile scored a 148 on the LSAT and achieved a GPA of 2.66. Admitted students in the 75th percentile scored a 153 on the LSAT and achieved a GPA of 3.32. The overall median LSAT score was 150 and the median GPA was 3.03.

Clinical program required	Yes
Legal writing course requirement	Yes
Legal methods course requirement	Yes
Legal research course requirement	Yes
Moot court requirement	Yes
Public interest law requirement	Yes

ADMISSIONS

Selectivity Rating	80
# applications received	2,628
% applicants accepted	40
% acceptees attending	22
Average LSAT	149
LSAT Range (25th to 75th percentile)	147–151
Average undergrad GPA	3.08
Application fee	$60
Regular application deadline	5/1
Transfer students accepted	Yes
Evening division offered	No
Part-time accepted	No
CAS accepted	Yes

FINANCIAL FACTS

Annual tuition	$25,340
Books and supplies	$1,000
Fees	$1,240
Room & Board (on/off campus)	$10,341/$10,575
Financial aid application deadline	4/1
% first-year students receiving some sort of aid	95
% all students receiving some sort of aid	98
% of aid that is merit based	30
% receiving scholarships	39
Average grant	$14,000
Average loan	$20,500
Average total aid package	$31,250
Average debt	$82,000

EMPLOYMENT INFORMATION

		Grads Employed by Field (%)
Career Rating	73	Academic (2)
% grads employed nine months out	71	Business/Industry (15)
Median starting salary	$54,292	Government (17)
State for bar exam	FL, NY, GA, CA	Judicial Clerkship (3)
Pass rate for first-time bar	73	Private Practice (53)
Prominent Alumni		Public Interest (10)

Prominent Alumni
Brett Barfield, Partner, Holland & Knight;
Mark Romance, Partner, Richman Greer;
Representative J.C. Planas, Florida House
of Representatives.

STANFORD UNIVERSITY
SCHOOL OF LAW

INSTITUTIONAL INFORMATION

Public/private	Private
Affiliation	No Affiliation
Student-faculty ratio	8:1
% faculty female	33
% faculty underrepresented minority	18
Total faculty	55

SURVEY SAYS...

Great research resources, Great library staff

STUDENTS

Enrollment of law school	575
% male/female	57/43
% underrepresented minority	38
Average age of entering class	24

ACADEMICS

Academic Experience Rating	99
Profs interesting rating	99
Profs accessible rating	92
Hours of study per day	3.69

Academic Specialties

Civil Procedure, Commercial, Constitutional, Corporation Securities, Criminal, Environmental, Government Services, Human Rights, International, Labor, Legal History, Legal Philosophy, Property, Taxation, Intellectual Property

Advanced Degrees Offered

MLS, 1 year; JSM, 1 year; LLM, 1 year; JSD, 4 years

Combined Degrees Offered

JD/MBA, 3 2/3–4 years; JD/MA, 3 years; JD/Ph.D., 6 years; JD/MA, 6 years

Academics

"People are happy" at Stanford Law School, and why wouldn't they be? There are "tons of programs," an array of specialized centers, and a couple dozen joint-degree options. The eleven clinics here include a Supreme Court litigation clinic and an IP Innovation clinic, just to list a couple. "The resources available to us at Stanford are fantastic, and sometimes unbelievable," gushes a 2L. The "amazingly brilliant" and "diverse" faculty is "a great mix of practically minded and experienced—professors and wild-minded theorists." Professors are "incredible lecturers and easy to approach outside of the classroom." "I have yet to meet a professor who is not only doing something amazing but is completely approachable and dying to help us get jobs and do research," gloats a 2L. Moreover, Stanford is "so small that everything is very easy to do." "All of my seminars have had fewer than ten people," gloats a 2L. "The university as a whole has a lot of red tape," but the law school's administration is "very receptive" and accessible at almost every level. "It's the opposite of the 'factory' feeling at large professional schools," explains a 3L. "If you want to do something new or nontraditional, just ask. Usually you can work something out."

The Stanford campus is "sprawling" and "beautiful," with "acres of rolling green hills for hiking, and palm trees everywhere." "The law school is hideous from the outside but, inside, it's quite nice." The library is a world-class research facility "and all law students have twenty-four-hour access to study there." "I can't study in any other university library," admits a comfortable 1L, "because I have become too accustomed to the law school's Aeron chairs."

A few students call Career Services "underwhelming," but "Pretty much everyone can get a firm job if they want one." They can get that job anywhere in the country, too. Less than 50 percent of all newly minted Stanford Law grads take jobs in California. Stanford is also "seriously committed to public interest law," and the "great loan repayment program" here is arguably the best in the country. Also worth noting is the impressive historical fact that more than 100 Stanford law graduates have clerked for one of the Supreme Court Justices.

Of course, nothing is perfect, even at Stanford. Some students love the pass/fail grading system while others say it provides little incentive to work hard. Despite these complaints, though, students call Stanford "the best law school west of the Appalachians," and they "have a hard time seeing why anyone would choose to go to law school anywhere else."

Life

"Small size makes for a more personal experience" at Stanford. Here, "You really get to know your classmates, and there is consequently no competitive behavior." The academic atmosphere is "very collaborative." There are "study groups galore." Students describe themselves as "ridiculously smart people" who are "highly ambitious" and "work extremely hard." "It easy to feel like you must have been admitted by mistake," confesses an awed 1L. There is "lots of diversity" in terms of age, background, ethnicity, and pretty much every attribute. Some students call the political environment "overwhelmingly liberal." Other students say "there's a critical mass of right-of-center students," and they point out that you definitely won't see too many protests among law students. "Perhaps that's because everyone harbors secret Supreme Court ambitions and wouldn't want to pigeonhole their position on an issue somewhere the Senate Confirmation Committee could find it," suggests a 1L.

Certainly, "you won't have to contend with snow or gloomy weather" at this school. "The weather is perfect 90 percent of the time." Some students call Palo Alto "a cultural wonderland" that has everything you need including "incredibly nice" graduate student housing located right next to the law school. Other students gripe, "Living in Palo Alto is like living in a suburb, which to anyone who is coming from an urban area will be a shock." "A big percentage of Stanford students are married, or commute from San Francisco, so they have their own lives away from the school." Extracurricular activity is constant for everyone, though. "Having the law school right in the middle of Silicon Valley allows for many practitioners, general counsels, venture capitalists," and the like to drop by. Student organizations are profuse. "Everyone at Stanford is president of a club, editor of a journal, director of a pro bono, and a board member of a society," claims a 2L. "Social events are plentiful," and they are "always a hoot." There is something of a fraternity-like culture if that's what you are looking for, but it's "not [an] overwhelming scene," and we aren't talking about people doing multiple keg stands. "You have to remember that everyone had to be pretty studious and dorky in order to get in here," says a 1L.

Getting In

Admission to Stanford Law is very competitive. Enrolled students at the 25th percentile have LSAT scores of about 167 and GPAs of roughly 3.74. Enrolled students at the 75th percentile have LSAT scores above 170 and GPAs pretty close to 4.0.

Clinical program required	No
Legal writing course requirement	Yes
Legal methods course requirement	No
Legal research course requirement	Yes
Moot court requirement	No
Public interest law requirement	No

ADMISSIONS

Selectivity Rating	99
# applications received	3,966
% applicants accepted	10
% acceptees attending	47
Average LSAT	171
LSAT Range (25th to 75th percentile)	168–173
Average undergrad GPA	3.83
Application fee	$100
Regular application deadline	2/1
Regular notification	4/30
Transfer students accepted	Yes
Evening division offered	No
Part-time accepted	No
CAS accepted	Yes

FINANCIAL FACTS

Annual tuition	$48,870
Books and supplies	$1,950
Fees	$1,395
Room & Board (on/off campus)	$19,005/$20,018
Financial aid application deadline	3/15
% first-year students receiving some sort of aid	82
% all students receiving some sort of aid	79
% of aid that is merit based	0
% receiving scholarships	56
Average grant	$24,212
Average loan	$39,901
Average total aid package	$55,261
Average debt	$108,683

EMPLOYMENT INFORMATION

Career Rating	96	Prominent Alumni
Total 2012 JD Grads	181	Sandra Day O'Connor, First female Supreme Court Justice (1981 to 2006); Warren Christopher, Former Secretary of State (1993 to 1997); Anthony Romero, Executive Director of ACLU (2001-Present).
% for whom you have useable information	100	
% grads employed nine months out	98	
# employed full-time	175	
# employed part-time	0	
# employed bar required	166	**Grads Employed by Field (%)**
# employed JD preferred	9	Academic (1)
# employed professional/other	0	Business/Industry (8)
# employed non-professional	0	Government (2)
# pursuing advanced degree	2	Judicial Clerkship (31)
# unemployed and seeking employment	3	Private Practice (50)
# not seeking employment	1	Public Interest (6)
% grads employed by school	1	
State for bar exam	CA, NY, MD, IL, WA	
Pass rate for first-time bar	93.9	

SUNY BUFFALO LAW SCHOOL—THE STATE UNIVERSITY OF NEW YORK

INSTITUTIONAL INFORMATION

Public/private	Public
Affiliation	No Affiliation
Student-faculty ratio	13:1
% faculty part-time	42
% faculty female	44
% faculty underrepresented minority	9
Total faculty	105

SURVEY SAYS...

Diverse opinions accepted in classrooms, Great research resources, Great library staff, Abundant externship/internship/clerkship opportunities

STUDENTS

Enrollment of law school	629
% male/female	55/45
% from out-of-state	6
% part-time	2
% underrepresented minority	14
% international	3
# of countries represented	8
Average age of entering class	24

ACADEMICS

Academic Experience Rating	72
Profs interesting rating	74
Profs accessible rating	69
Hours of study per day	3.75

Academic Specialties

Criminal, Environmental, International, Labor, Intellectual Property, Family Law

Advanced Degrees Offered

LLM in Criminal Law, 1 year ; LLM General, 1 year

Combined Degrees Offered

JD/MSW, 4 years; JD/MBA, 4 years; JD/MPH, 4 years; JD/MLS, 4 years; JD/MA Applied Economics, 3.5 years; JD/Ph.D., 6+ years; JD/MUP, 4 years; JD/Pharm.D., 6 years

Academics

SUNY Buffalo Law School is a practical and affordable option for future New York State lawyers. The school's three-year JD begins with a series of required classes in contracts, torts, and other basic areas. In the next two years, law students have the "ability to create a unique curriculum" through a "nice array of courses," including "timely classes that are relevant to the world and cover cutting edge legal issues (examples: class on international piracy, class on counterterrorism law, etc.)." The school offers curricular concentrations in nine fields, including civil litigation and intellectual property, and students note the array of "great human rights and international law classes." While they like the course diversity, many Buffalo students feel the school could dig even deeper into specialty topics and "incorporate more courses which teach practical lawyering skills in specific areas of the law." Fortunately, curricular improvements are being implemented with attention and efficiency. "The current administration is making a concerted effort to improve the look of the school and the opportunities available to students." In addition, many students praise the schools' supervisors and staff and attest, "School administrators seem to genuinely care about you from the moment you step in the door all the way up to graduation and beyond."

Buffalo offers "plenty of opportunity to get hands-on experience in legal jobs during law school." Traditional academics are augmented by "diverse opportunities for experiential learning," including "non-traditional course offerings like clinics and externships." Within the law school, "There are countless opportunities for moot court, trial team, and journal work," and "The law school's clinic program is excellent." Of particular note, "The school goes out of its way to help those interested in Public Interest work," with numerous clinics devoted to affordable housing, community economic advocacy, and social justice. Even so, some would also like to see the school build a "stronger presence in the greater Buffalo community," and point out the campus's isolated location in a northern suburb of the city. The events and culture generated from having over 24,000 undergraduate and graduate students on Buffalo's campus should not be discounted, though.

When it comes to the teaching staff, students praise Buffalo's "terrific adjunct professors," saying they love being taught by "faculty members who are still trying cases, rather than those who have been out of court for years." The school attracts a number of accomplished attorneys, and "some of the faculty [are] at the very pinnacle of their fields, with reputations that span the country." A current student enthuses, "On multiple occasions, my professors have actually worked on the cases we cover in class." Despite their many accolades, "faculty is hit or miss" in the classroom. Because SUNY is a "great research institution," it tends to attract "professors that are experts in their field with a significant amount of publishing in their background, but have no teaching skills and no ability to relate to the students." Outside of the classroom, teachers are diverse in the same manner. Some professors are friendly and student-oriented, while others "are not always accessible because they are busy."

Buffalo is a great choice for local lawyers, and the school maintains a great "reputation in New York, particularly in western New York." For many local students, cost was also a major factor in their decision to attend SUNY Buffalo. While "tuition increases and the new re-payment plans for government loans" have tempered the school's overall value, it still offers an "amazing education for the price." However, the value tuition is principally open to New York state residents, who, not surprisingly, comprise more than 90 percent of the school's population.

LILLIE V. WILEY-UPSHAW, VICE DEAN FOR ADMISSIONS AND FINANCIAL AID
309 O'BRIAN HALL, BUFFALO, NY 14260
TEL: 716-645-2907 FAX: 716-645-6676
E-MAIL: LAW-ADMISSIONS@BUFFALO.EDU • WEBSITE: WWW.LAW.BUFFALO.EDU

Life

Students seeking a "serious, but not overly competitive environment" will find a good match at SUNY Buffalo, where academic rigors are balanced by a "strong sense of community and camaraderie among the students." Most students are serious about their education, and "come ready to work every day." However, that sense of purpose never overrides the generally low-key and friendly atmosphere within the law school. A current student elaborates, "While we are all competitive, there is a "no 1L left behind," feeling to all of the classes. If you are having trouble with the material there are always countless students willing to sit down and thoroughly discuss the material until you grasp it." Both socially and professionally, the collegial atmosphere pays off. Here, "Networking is easy at UB because everyone is already your friend."

Within the law school, there are "myriad, valuable student organizations," and socially, one student proclaims, "There are always SO many events going on, it is literally impossible to keep up." In contrast, there isn't much happening in the surrounding area. The School of Law's campus is located in "suburban hell," north of Buffalo proper, and there is "nothing in walking distance. You have to drive everywhere to get or do anything." Not only is "there is no 'college town' feel," students remind us that, "The heart of Buffalo's legal community, including the state and federal courthouses and the major law firms, remains in downtown Buffalo."

Getting In

At the University at Buffalo, LSAT scores and GPA are the most important components of any law school application; however, the admissions officers will also consider other aspects of a prospective student's application, including the personal statement, recommendation, professional or volunteer experience. In the most recent incoming class, the median LSAT score was 156 and the median GPA was 3.51. About 37 percent of more than 1400 applicants were admitted, with around 175 enrolling.

EMPLOYMENT INFORMATION

Career Rating	82
Total 2012 JD Grads	209
% for whom you have useable information	97
% grads employed nine months out	86
Median starting salary	$50,144
# employed full-time	156
# employed part-time	17
# employed bar required	130
# employed JD preferred	27
# employed professional/other	10
# employed non-professional	4
# pursuing advanced degree	1
# unemployed and seeking employment	21
# not seeking employment	7
% grads employed by school	0
State for bar exam	NY, NJ, MA, CA, MN
Pass rate for first-time bar	83.4

Prominent Alumni
Hon. Julio Fuentes, US Court of Appeals for the 3rd Circuit; Mark Pearce, Chairman of the National Labor Relations Board; Hon. Paul Friedman, United States District Judge.

Grads Employed by Field (%)
Academic (3)
Business/Industry (17)
Government (5)
Judicial Clerkship (4)
Military (1)
Private Practice (49)
Public Interest (6)

Clinical program required	No
Legal writing course requirement	Yes
Legal methods course requirement	No
Legal research course requirement	Yes
Moot court requirement	No
Public interest law requirement	No

ADMISSIONS

Selectivity Rating	84
# applications received	1,436
% applicants accepted	44
% acceptees attending	32
Average LSAT	156
Median LSAT	156
LSAT Range (25th to 75th percentile)	152–158
Average undergrad GPA	3.42
Median undergrad GPA	3.51
Application fee	$75
Regular application deadline	3/1
Early application deadline	11/15
Early application notification	12/15
Transfer students accepted	Yes
Evening division offered	No
Part-time accepted	No
CAS accepted	Yes

FINANCIAL FACTS

Annual tuition (in-state out-of-state)	$20,730/$35,220
Books and supplies	$1,194
Fees	$1,894
Room & Board (on/off campus)	$10,919/$14,345
Financial aid application deadline	3/1
% first-year students receiving some sort of aid	88
% all students receiving some sort of aid	89
% of aid that is merit based	10
% receiving scholarships	50
Average grant	$5,554
Average loan	$27,327
Average total aid package	$27,862
Average debt	$72,681

STETSON UNIVERSITY
COLLEGE OF LAW

INSTITUTIONAL INFORMATION

Public/private	Private
Student-faculty ratio	16:1
% faculty part-time	56
% faculty female	36
% faculty underrepresented minority	8
Total faculty	124

SURVEY SAYS...

Diverse opinions accepted in classrooms, Great research resources

STUDENTS

Enrollment of law school	1,004
% male/female	52/48
% from out-of-state	24
% part-time	23
% underrepresented minority	25
# of countries represented	20
Average age of entering class	24

ACADEMICS

Academic Experience Rating	84
Profs interesting rating	78
Profs accessible rating	83
Hours of study per day	3.74

Academic Specialties

Environmental, International, Advocacy, Elder Law, Social Justice

Advanced Degrees Offered

JD, 3 years full-time, 4 years part-time; LLM: Advocacy, Elder Law and International Law, typically 1–2 years

Combined Degrees Offered

JD/MBA, 3 years full-time (longer for part-time); JD/MPH with University of South Florida (approximately 4–5 years); JD/Grado with University of Granada, Spain, 4 years; JD/MICL (French Graduate Degree through Universtiy of Toulouse), minimum 4 years

Academics

Stetson University College of Law in Florida offers "a good mix of practicality and theory." Points of pride here include a serious first-year emphasis on research and writing. "The pace and the intensity of it are not matched by other schools," declares a 1L. There's a "wide variety of" "excellent" internships and clinics as well, and pro bono opportunities abound." While four certificate programs are available (in advocacy, elder law, international law, and environmental law), advocacy is far and away the principal focus here. Students gloat that Stetson is home to "the best trial advocacy school in the country." "Every week, a different trial team is out competing and winning something." "For a litigator who wants to practice in Florida, or an appellate practitioner who wants access to judicial internships in the area," counsels a 2L, "Stetson is ideal." "You will know your way around a courtroom long before graduating." However, some students say that this school overemphasizes litigation. However, some students say that this school overemphasizes litigation, despite a variety electives, including state-specific topics such as Florida Criminal Procedure and Florida Civil Procedure. Students also note that Stetson isn't cheap. "I had considered transferring just to save money," admits a 3L, "but I had such a great environment at Stetson. I couldn't leave."

There are quite a few adjunct professors, who teach one or two classes per year while maintaining their practice as attorneys or judges. Some full-time professors "can make a semester seem unbearable," but by and large, the faculty at Stetson Law is "caring," "very dedicated," "and eager to make your learning experience successful." Professors are "knowledgeable in both their areas of expertise and general law and life." They're also "available and approachable." Students brag that Stetson has "one the most accessible faculties imaginable." "Despite their busy schedules, they always make time for students and are happy to do so," relates a 3L. Some members of the administration "go to great lengths to get to know students on a personal basis." Others are "arrogant [and] incompetent" and "seem to manage to screw over their students on biweekly basis."

On the employment front, "One of the biggest assets is that Stetson is the only law school in the Tampa Bay Area." Students tell us that Stetson has an excellent reputation locally. "Judges rave about Stetson's professionalism," asserts a 3L. The name carries some weight throughout the Sunshine State as well, though "There just are not too many firms that are recruiting" on campus. Views concerning Career Development are conflicting. Some students call the staff "outstanding." Others gripe that Career Services "has little connection with practicing alumni in the area and is not very organized overall."

The facilities here are generally impressive. "The campus is exclusively a law school," and the hacienda-style architecture creates a kind of "old resort" vibe, which "takes away some of the sting of having to go to class." "The school has plenty of room, with large classrooms that are modern and comfortable and several gorgeous, usable courtrooms on campus." Library resources are "very impressive," and "the librarians are the best around." A 2L likens them to "fairy godmothers of legal research." Technology is a bit of sore spot, though. The server "seems to be down once a week," and "There are constant problems" with various gadgetry. Also, bring a sweater because "the air-conditioning is freezing cold."

LAURA ZUPPO, EXECUTIVE DIRECTOR OF ADMISSIONS & STUDENT FINANCIAL PLANNING
1401 61ST STREET SOUTH, GULFPORT, FL 33707
TEL: 727-562-7802 FAX: 727-343-0136
E-MAIL: LAWADMIT@LAW.STETSON.EDU • WEBSITE: WWW.LAW.STETSON.EDU

Life

Students tell us that there's "a family-like atmosphere" here. "Stetson is very open," relates a 1L. "There is a great sense of community between the students, faculty, and staff." The academic atmosphere is amicable. "Students are generally very helpful to each other, and the environment is friendly and noncompetitive for the most part. Competition is healthy rather than cutthroat or underhanded."

When students aren't hitting the books, it's easy "to get involved in organizations," and everyone here is pretty social. Students also say that they're situated in an ideal place to learn the law. "You cannot beat the location," wagers a 1L. Obviously, this is a "year-round warm place," which has numerous advantages. Stetson's "affordable, tranquil" suburban environs make for an ideal atmosphere to work, study, and play. World class beaches are a short drive away. The reasonably lively city of St. Petersburg is also close, and the broader Tampa Bay Area is a growing, bustling region of close to three million people.

Getting In

Admitted students at the 25th percentile have LSAT scores in the mid 150s and under-graduate GPAs close to 3.2. At the 75th percentile, LSAT scores approach 160, and GPAs are close to 3.7.

Clinical program required	No
Legal writing course requirement	Yes
Legal methods course requirement	Yes
Legal research course requirement	Yes
Moot court requirement	Yes
Public interest law requirement	Yes

ADMISSIONS

Selectivity Rating	83
# applications received	2,157
% applicants accepted	44
% acceptees attending	25
Median LSAT	155
LSAT Range (25th to 75th percentile)	152–158
Median undergrad GPA	3.3
Application fee	$55
Regular application deadline	5/15
Transfer students accepted	Yes
Evening division offered	Yes
Part-time accepted	Yes
CAS accepted	Yes

FINANCIAL FACTS

Annual tuition	$35,848
Books and supplies	$1,730
Fees	$320
Room & Board	$15,922
% first-year students receiving some sort of aid	87
% all students receiving some sort of aid	97
% receiving scholarships	32
Average grant	$20,347
Average loan	$47,495
Average total aid package	$50,483
Average debt	$131,178

EMPLOYMENT INFORMATION

Career Rating	80	**Prominent Alumni**
Total 2012 JD Grads	341	Chief Justice Carol Hunstein, Supreme
% grads employed nine months out	84	Court of Georgia; Hon. Elizabeth
Median starting salary	$43,403	Kovachevich, USDC Middle District Florida;
# employed full-time	272	Rich McKay, President & CEO, Atlanta
# employed part-time	15	Falcons.
# employed bar required	216	**Grads Employed by Field (%)**
# employed JD preferred	34	Academic (1)
# employed professional/other	30	Business/Industry (15)
# employed non-professional	7	Government (16)
# pursuing advanced degree	14	Judicial Clerkship (4)
# unemployed and seeking employment	21	Military (2)
# not seeking employment	17	Private Practice (40)
% grads employed by school	0	Public Interest (7)
State for bar exam	FL	
Pass rate for first-time bar	88.9	

SUFFOLK UNIVERSITY
LAW SCHOOL

INSTITUTIONAL INFORMATION

Public/private	Private
Student-faculty ratio	18:1
% faculty part-time	51
% faculty female	36
% faculty underrepresented minority	11
Total faculty	140

SURVEY SAYS...

Great research resources, Beautiful campus, Students love Boston, MA

STUDENTS

Enrollment of law school	1,632
% male/female	49/51
% from out-of-state	43
% part-time	34
% underrepresented minority	22
% international	2
# of countries represented	43
Average age of entering class	26

ACADEMICS

Academic Experience Rating	71
Profs interesting rating	79
Profs accessible rating	76
Hours of study per day	3.04

Academic Specialties

International, Intellectual Property, Health/Biomedical

Advanced Degrees Offered

JD, 3 years full-time, 4 years part-time. LLM in Global Law and Technology, LLM in General Law, one year, full-time, 3 years, part-time. SJD, 1 to 3 years

Combined Degrees Offered

JD/MBA, JD/MPA, JD/MS in International Economics, JD/MS in Finance, JD/MS in Criminal Justice. Each program can be completed in 4 years of full-time study or 5 years of part-time study. There is a 3 year JD/MBA program as well.

Academics

A very strong evening program, "high level of pro bono participation," and a fantastic bar passage rate are just a few of the many attributes that make Suffolk Law students love their school. Students say the peer-mentoring program, Academic Support Services, and specialized tutoring, as well as the school's top clinic programs, many journals, and student organizations "make for a rich law school experience." "I participated in the Juvenile Defenders Clinic, and…have been able to appear in court nearly a dozen times on behalf of my clients," says a 3L. "The practical experience you can acquire, should you desire such experience, is unparalleled." Because of the school's connection with the legal community of greater Boston, Suffolk "has a large number of current and former judges on its faculty, which provides for an excellent learning experience."

The school offers a "vast array" of different courses in all specialty areas of the law (as well as a thorough legal writing program), and the "tough but understanding" professors are "consummate professionals and experts in their field." "I have found that respectful dissenting opinions, even radical ones, are met with enthusiasm and serious consideration," says a student. These teachers are the "best part" of Suffolk, "come from all walks of life," and "are not using their positions to launch their career somewhere else." "I even had a tax law professor (a subject I dreaded) who made tax interesting and, dare I say, exciting," says a 3L.

The administration here receives similar kudos for its "fair" treatment of student concerns, particularly the Registrar's Office. "Everyone is willing to work with you [administration, registrar, faculty], but no one is going to work for you," sums up a student. Academic support and bar prep are both "excellent," though Career Services "needs to do better about reaching out to students and professionals in the field to actually place students while in law school," by "building alumni connections within private employers in the city."

Another perk of Suffolk Law is the strong alumni network, which, "in a city with so many law schools…is very important." "Anywhere you go, anywhere you work, there will be a Suffolk grad," says a 1L. A 2L puts it a little less delicately: "I think we're all aware that we're probably not getting by on the name of the school like other Boston schools, so everybody is really focus[ed] on building their networks and learning the skills they need."

The facilities here are brand-new and "outstanding." "I feel like I am part of a grand tradition of lawyers, yet have access to state-of-the-art classrooms," says a 3L. Still, many students wish the school's reputation had more of a "national presence," as the name "doesn't immediately curry the same sort of respect as a more highly ranked school." "Something is holding the school back from being respected as a top law school. It is not the faculty and it is not the students," says one of many puzzled students.

Life

The "fairly large student body" is divided into 1L sections upon entrance to the school, which does a lot "to create close friendships and collaborative relationships between new students." The school is pretty much composed of "nice, young people, mostly from the Boston area," which makes for "a cohesive bunch—none of that *Paper Chase* nonsense." "I am so happy to be at a school where I feel challenged by my classmates, but not threatened," says a student. A surprising number of students refer to the "professionalism" of their classmates, possibly due to the frequent intermingling of day and evening students

JENNIFER Y. SIMS, ASSISTANT DEAN OF ADMISSIONS AND FINANCIAL AID
120 TREMONT STREET, BOSTON, MA 02108-4977
TEL: 617-573-8144 FAX: 617-523-1367
E-MAIL: LAWADM@SUFFOLK.EDU • WEBSITE: WWW.LAW.SUFFOLK.EDU

in evening classes, which "is of benefit to both, with the evening students bringing a lot of real-world experience to class discussions." On the flip side, "It's hard to get involved in the social side of life at Suffolk when you're in the evening program."

The central Boston location "couldn't be better," and lends to the school the quality of a "social paradise, with frequent events at school and local bars." "You're [a] ten-minute walk from the Prudential Center, a five-minute walk from Faneuil Hall, a two-minute walk from Pemberton Square, ten minutes from the BMC, and thirty seconds from the Boston Common or the State House." Most first-year students "gather at the local water-ing hole on Friday afternoon to let off steam and talk trash about the other sections" in a good-natured way. There are also "consistent events throughout the academic year" involving clubs, job opportunities, networking seminars, political groups, and more.

Getting In

Suffolk's Admissions Committee seeks candidates who are poised to contribute to the life of the campus community as well as to the future of the legal profession. Prospective students can demonstrate their potential in these areas by getting involved in community service, extracurricular undergraduate organizations, and pre-professional societies and are also evaluated on the growth and maturity exhibited by work experience since graduation. The 2011 incoming class scored a mean score of 155 on the LSAT and boasted a 3.3 median undergraduate GPA.

Clinical program required	No
Legal writing course requirement	Yes
Legal methods course requirement	Yes
Legal research course requirement	Yes
Moot court requirement	Yes
Public interest law requirement	No

ADMISSIONS

Selectivity Rating	68
# applications received	2,999
% applicants accepted	73
% acceptees attending	17
Average LSAT	151
Median LSAT	152
LSAT Range (25th to 75th percentile)	147–155
Average undergrad GPA	3.22
Median undergrad GPA	3.24
Application fee	$60
Regular application deadline	3/1
Early application deadline	3/1
Transfer students accepted	Yes
Evening division offered	Yes
Part-time accepted	Yes
CAS accepted	Yes

FINANCIAL FACTS

Annual tuition	$44,934
Books and supplies	$1,000
Fees	$120
Room & Board	$18,486
Financial aid application deadline	3/1
% first-year students receiving some sort of aid	86
% all students receiving some sort of aid	85
% of aid that is merit based	49
% receiving scholarships	40
Average grant	$15,054
Average loan	$42,405
Average total aid package	$50,845
Average debt	$119,096

EMPLOYMENT INFORMATION

Career Rating	75	
Total 2012 JD Grads	517	
% for whom you have useable information	95	
% grads employed nine months out	74	
Median starting salary	$58,000	
% job accepting grads providing useable salary information	58	
# employed full-time	333	
# employed part-time	47	
# employed bar required	236	
# employed JD preferred	88	
# employed professional/other	38	
# employed non-professional	18	
# pursuing advanced degree	13	
# unemployed and seeking employment	80	
# not seeking employment	10	
% grads employed by school	0.5	
State for bar exam	MA, NY, RI	
Pass rate for first-time bar	82	

Prominent Alumni
John Joseph Moakley, U.S. Congressman; James Bamford, Author; Kristen Kuliga, Principal, K Sports and Entertainment.

Grads Employed by Field (%)
Academic (2)
Business/Industry (29)
Government (13)
Judicial Clerkship (5)
Military (1)
Private Practice (45)
Public Interest (5)

SYRACUSE UNIVERSITY
COLLEGE OF LAW

INSTITUTIONAL INFORMATION

Public/private	Private
Student-faculty ratio	11:1
% faculty female	42
% faculty underrepresented minority	17
Total faculty	65

SURVEY SAYS...

Diverse opinions accepted in classrooms, Great library staff, Abundant externship/internship/clerkship opportunities, Good social life

STUDENTS

Enrollment of law school	663
% part-time	0
Average age of entering class	24

ACADEMICS

Academic Experience Rating	72
Profs interesting rating	75
Profs accessible rating	79
Hours of study per day	4.84

Academic Specialties

Corporation Securities, Criminal, Human Rights, International, Property, Taxation, Intellectual Property

Advanced Degrees Offered

LLM for non-U.S. lawyers. 12 months.

Combined Degrees Offered

JD/MPA (Pub. Adm.); JD/MS (Acc't., Lib. Sci., Comm., News/ Mag., Media); JD/MBA (Bus. Adm.); JD/MA (Econ., Hist., Int'l Rel); JD/ MS in Educ. (Disability Studies); JD/ MS (Forensic Science); JD/MSW (Soc. Work); JD/MS or JD/Ph.D. in Envir. Stud.; JD/MS Engin. & Comp Sci.; JD/MA (Poli. Sci.; Eng.; Phil.) Most can be completed in 3–3.5 years; JD/MBA, 4 years

Academics

Syracuse University College of Law is an institution that "offers many resources [to ensure] that...students fulfill their potential." The school emphasizes "the importance of acquiring research skills" and many stress the uniqueness of the legal writing and research program. "The LCR staff come from different professional backgrounds making our legal communication and research skills adaptable." Students also value the school's connection to the "fast-rising business school (Whitman School of Management), the Maxwell School of Citizenship and Public Affairs, [along with] other departments as part of [the larger university system.]" They can also take advantage of joint-degree programs with the State University of New York- College of Environmental Science and Forestry, earning a Masters in environmental sciences or natural resources management. Additionally, the "international program is fantastic." A handful of respondents also highlight "the National Security and Counterterrorism Program [along with the myriad of] opportunities for clinics/externships."

By and large, students declare that "the faculty is incredible" and represents some of the "preeminent scholars in their respective fields"; however, what they value most is just how "accessible and completely dedicated to their students success" professors have demonstrated themselves to be. As one second year explains, "They go to extreme lengths to ensure that their students understand the material. Further they are available all the time to help students." A pleased classmate adds, "They are really here to make sure students learn, not just to do research." The administration is also "extremely helpful and supportive." They take "student concerns serious[ly] and provide a lot of programming to keep us all balanced." Though a few do caution that there is "a lot of bureaucracy, which can be quite annoying to deal with if you are not a traditional law student (I am a JD/MBA). I often feel like I have to jump through hoops and fill out form after useless form just to do what is required by my program."

Though Syracuse is "building a brand new law school building for the start of the 2014-2015 academic year," students state that the current facilities are "manageable and serviceable." While many concede that the library is "small," they also assure us that "it packs a punch" and offers students "access to dozens of databases." Many also appreciate how "there are places to study if you are feeling social and places for when you need to study alone." Perhaps more importantly, the "library staff is incredible. They are knowledgeable, accessible and helpful."

Students here are also incredibly grateful for their alumni network, which is a "fabulous resource." As one pleasantly surprised second-year elaborates, "I have found that many alumni genuinely care and are willing to go above and beyond what they are asked to help ensure that my goals are given their best chance to succeed." Many also applaud the efforts of the Office of Professional and Career Development. "They connect you with alumni, provide fast but thorough critiques of resumes and cover letters, and do a whole host of trainings to help you prepare for internship and job searches." However, others complain that "the resources available to the students seem to be limited." A 1L suggests, "Improving programming, on-campus networking events, and developing a larger database for off-campus job opportunities would strengthen this department."

Life

Many students at Syracuse proclaim that the school manages to foster "a fun environment." Indeed, the "law school holds ample events, and the university is a Division I athletics school and competitive in the Big East in most sports." There are also organized weekly social nights as well as a seasonal flag football league. A handful of people also socialize through the student-run Syracuse Law Review. Moreover, there are a multitude of law journals for them to join as well as moot court competitions. The surrounding area also offers "great bars [and] great restaurants." As one knowledgeable third-year expounds, "Syracuse is affordable. There is enough to do on the one night a weekend you venture out as a law student, including some really great local restaurants. [Additionally, it's only a] short drive to larger cities like Rochester and New York. Summers [in] Syracuse are the best: sunshine, moderate temperatures, and tons of festivals!" Though one pragmatic student does counter that Syracuse can be "trying in the winter."

When it comes to their peers, law students at Syracuse are decidedly mixed. Some steadfastly assert that their fellow students are "competitive." However, others assure us that they "[are] not cutthroat" and blame the competitive nature on a curve "which can be unforgiving." And plenty more outright disagree, confidently stating that their peers are "generous and helpful to others." One happy student goes as far as saying that "It feels like a family." Further, for older students who might have children or separate lives, the school attempts to foster "a sense of community" by "organizing monthly get-togethers." Whether you attend is up to you, and essentially, "The experience is what you make of it."

Getting In

Accepted students in the 25th percentile earned an LSAT score of around 153 and had an undergraduate GPA around 3.10. Accepted students in the 75th percentile earned an LSAT score of around 157 and had an undergraduate GPA of 3.56. The median LSAT score is 155 and the median GPA is 3.36.

Clinical program required	No
Legal writing course requirement	Yes
Legal methods course requirement	Yes
Legal research course requirement	Yes
Moot court requirement	No
Public interest law requirement	No

ADMISSIONS

Selectivity Rating	80
# applications received	2,905
% applicants accepted	47
% acceptees attending	18
Average LSAT	153
Median LSAT	153
LSAT Range (25th to 75th percentile)	152–156
Median undergrad GPA	3.28
Application fee	$75
Regular application deadline	4/1
Transfer students accepted	Yes
Evening division offered	No
Part-time accepted	No
CAS accepted	Yes

FINANCIAL FACTS

Annual tuition	$44,000
Books and supplies	$1,570
Fees	$1,690
Room & Board	$11,190
Financial aid application deadline	2/15
% first-year students receiving some sort of aid	94
% all students receiving some sort of aid	92
% of aid that is merit based	69
% receiving scholarships	83
Average grant	$14,842
Average loan	$42,608
Average total aid package	$52,333
Average debt	$138,073

EMPLOYMENT INFORMATION

Career Rating	81	% grads employed by school	1
Total 2012 JD Grads	185	State for bar exam	NY, NJ, CA, PA, MA
% for whom you have useable information	94	Pass rate for first-time bar	76.2
% grads employed nine months out	83	**Prominent Alumni**	
Median starting salary	$58,000	Joseph R. Biden, Jr., Vice President of the United States; Theodore A. McKee, Federal Appeals Court Judge; David Gordon, Managing Partner, Latham & Watkins.	
% job accepting grads providing useable salary information	60		
# employed full-time	117	**Grads Employed by Field (%)**	
# employed part-time	27	Academic (1)	
# employed bar required	99	Business/Industry (27)	
# employed JD preferred	27	Government (14)	
# employed professional/other	7	Judicial Clerkship (7)	
# employed non-professional	11	Military (2)	
# pursuing advanced degree	6	Private Practice (42)	
# unemployed and seeking employment	19	Public Interest (7)	
# not seeking employment	4		

TEMPLE UNIVERSITY
JAMES E. BEASLEY SCHOOL OF LAW

INSTITUTIONAL
INFORMATION

Public/private	Public
% faculty female	43
% faculty underrepresented minority	18
Total faculty	67

SURVEY SAYS...

Diverse opinions accepted in classrooms, Great research resources, Liberal students

STUDENTS

Enrollment of law school	861
% male/female	57/43
% from out-of-state	67
% part-time	20
% underrepresented minority	27
% international	1
# of countries represented	7
Average age of entering class	24

ACADEMICS

Academic Experience Rating	85
Profs interesting rating	85
Profs accessible rating	82
Hours of study per day	3.86

Academic Specialties

Commercial, Constitutional, Corporation Securities, Criminal, Environmental, Government Services, Human Rights, International, Taxation, Intellectual Property

Advanced Degrees Offered

JD, 3 years full-time/4 years part-time; LLM in Trial Advocacy, 1 year; LLM in Taxation, 1 semester to 1 year; LLM in Transnational Law, 1 semester–1 year; Graduate Teaching Fellowships, 2 years; LLM for Graduates of Foreign law schools, 1 year; SJD

Combined Degrees Offered

JD/MBA (3–4 years), JD/MPH (3–4 years), JD/LLM degree programs in Taxation and Transnational Law (3.5 years), JD, individually designed joint degrees.

Academics

Founded in the late 19th century, Temple University's James E. Beasley School of Law is known for its a commitment to practical learning, skills classes, and clinicals, a goal which is achieved through hands-on courses and makes for "an enjoyable place to study law." Lots of "capable, intelligent people walking through these halls" pay a "very afford-able in-state tuition" to get "the biggest bang for your buck in Pennsylvania/New Jersey." "Given its low cost and its plentiful regional connections, if you intend to practice in the Philadelphia area it's probably the most sensible school to attend," says a student.

The school understands that law school must go beyond the theoretical, and to that end "helps students find internships for the summers or for the academic year, even giving students a chance to earn academic credit for unpaid internships." The heavy emphasis on practical experience means that by the time a student is out of law school, they have likely had "two summer internships, a part-time legal job or internship during the school year, and have been exposed to many areas of law in school." The trial advocacy department is "pretty amazing" and "gives students an opportunity to gain extremely important skills in both civil and criminal litigation that makes us stand out to employers." The school also has a Federal Judicial Clinical program that places 3L students in a Federal Judge's chambers and allows them to do substantive legal work on real cases.

The professors "are exceptional, both personally and professionally" and "are always willing to accommodate a student's schedule," which is especially important to students in the evening division. The Career Planning Office "is not the most helpful place, and "most students feel that they get more out of going to certain professors for career advice than they do to career planning." Luckily, this system works out well. "Numerous professors of mine have offered to help my friends and I find summer jobs and have provided excellent guidance," says a 2L. Fear not, though: even though students have to compete with other area law schools for summer positions, "the Temple Law alumni network is quite extensive throughout the city." "Temple has a strong presence in Philadelphia, so if you do well your first year, you should be able to find a great summer job."

JOHANNE L. JOHNSTON, ASSISTANT DEAN FOR ADMISSIONS & FINANCIAL AID
1719 NORTH BROAD STREET, PHILADELPHIA, PA 19122
TEL: 800-560-1428 FAX: 215-204-9319
E-MAIL: LAWADMIS@TEMPLE.EDU • WEBSITE: WWW.LAW.TEMPLE.EDU

Life

The atmosphere at Temple is "extremely congenial," and the" faculty, administration, the students, and even the security guard at the front door are all immensely friendly, supportive, and community-minded." Unfortunately, the physical building is "outdated" and "not as comfortable as it could be," but the library and research facilities are "ample and available" and "the library staff are amazingly knowledgeable." "What Temple lacks in flash it makes up in grit and determination!"

While most law students do not live on campus, there are specific neighborhoods in which students concentrate. Day students (which make up the vast majority of each class) are "typically in their 20s or 30s," and there is "definitely a sense of community in the evening students" as well. "Temple Law has a family feel, which helps during the dark days of finals," says a 3L. "Section bonding" is quite common, and the school has weekly to bi-weekly social events with a few more popular annual events (such as Barristers Ball and Lunar Banquet). There are "tons of social opportunities at Temple because of the myriad clubs," and these "offer both social bonding and networking, as many attorneys attend these, as well."

Getting In

At Temple, enrolled students at the 25th percentile have LSAT scores of 158 and GPAs in the 3.17 range. At the 75th percentile, the LSAT score is 163 and GPAs are about 3.64. Be warned, however: Temple's highly competitive admission process is designed to look at the whole person. Your personal statement and recommendation letters will be carefully considered by the admissions committee.

Clinical program required	No
Legal writing course requirement	Yes
Legal methods course requirement	No
Legal research course requirement	Yes
Moot court requirement	No
Public interest law requirement	No

ADMISSIONS

Selectivity Rating	84
# applications received	3,254
% applicants accepted	41
% acceptees attending	19
Average LSAT	160
Median LSAT	161
LSAT Range (25th to 75th percentile)	158–163
Average undergrad GPA	3.39
Median undergrad GPA	3.42
Application fee	$60
Regular application deadline	3/1
Transfer students accepted	Yes
Evening division offered	Yes
Part-time accepted	Yes
CAS accepted	Yes

FINANCIAL FACTS

Annual tuition (in-state out-of-state)	$19,148/$32,078
Books and supplies	$1,500
Fees	$640
Room & Board	$11,865
Financial aid application deadline	3/1
% all students receiving some sort of aid	85
% of aid that is merit based	96
% receiving scholarships	44
Average grant	$8,825
Average loan	$30,689
Average total aid package	$22,185
Average debt	$87,794

EMPLOYMENT INFORMATION

Career Rating	91	# not seeking employment	4
Total 2012 JD Grads	319	% grads employed by school	9
% for whom you have useable information	99	State for bar exam	PA
		Pass rate for first-time bar	92
% grads employed nine months out	92	**Grads Employed by Field (%)**	
Median starting salary	$60,000	Academic (3)	
% job accepting grads providing useable salary information	51	Business/Industry (14)	
		Government (8)	
# employed full-time	262	Judicial Clerkship (11)	
# employed part-time	30	Military (1)	
# employed bar required	227	Private Practice (37)	
# employed JD preferred	41	Public Interest (6)	
# employed professional/other	15		
# employed non-professional	9		
# pursuing advanced degree	3		
# unemployed and seeking employment	18		

TEXAS TECH UNIVERSITY
SCHOOL OF LAW

INSTITUTIONAL INFORMATION

Public/private	Public
% faculty part-time	13
% faculty female	41
% faculty underrepresented minority	21
Total faculty	56

SURVEY SAYS...

Diverse opinons accepted in classrooms, Great research resources, Great library staff

STUDENTS

Enrollment of law school	688
% male/female	54/46
% from out-of-state	10
% part-time	0
% underrepresented minority	28
% international	1
# of countries represented	5
Average age of entering class	24

ACADEMICS

Academic Experience Rating	89
Profs interesting rating	91
Profs accessible rating	99
Hours of study per day	4.38

Academic Specialties

Commercial, Constitutional, Corporation Securities, Criminal, Environmental, International, Property, Taxation, Intellectual Property

Advanced Degrees Offered

LLM, 1 year

Combined Degrees Offered

JD/MBA, 3 or 4 years, JD/MPA, 3 years, JD/MS Agricultural and Applied Economics, 3 or 4 years, JD/MS Accounting (Taxation), 3 or 4 years, JD/MS/Environmental Toxicology, 3 or 4 years; JD/PFP Personal Financial Planning, 3 or 4 years; JD/MS Biotechnology, 3 or 4 years; JD/M.Engr, 3 or 4 years; JD/MD Doctor of Medicine, 6 years

Academics

Students dole out praises for Texas Tech's rigorous and practical JD program, which really "teaches you what you need to know to be a good lawyer." From day one, real-world principles are incorporated into the learning experience, and throughout the program "the instruction [features] a good balance of the Socratic Method with practical advice." During the 1L curriculum, "emphasis is put on legal writing and research so that we are able to go straight into practice during the summer of our first year." 1Ls have a "year-long legal practice requirement," which "gives you a fantastic foundation before you step your foot in the real world." In addition to curricular offerings, the school offers an incredible breadth of "opportunities to gain practical experience through procedure classes, barrister competitions, clinics, and national competitions."

While the JD curriculum is "rigorous and demanding," it would be very difficult to slip through the cracks at Texas Tech. When they start the program, students are grouped into sections that serve as a support network during 1L, and "all of the first-year classes have upper-level students as tutors to supplement your classroom hours." The teaching staff is also committed to student success, and maintains consistent office hours so that students "can stop by and talk to professors at any time." A totally user-friendly experience, "the resources provided by the school are top-notch and they've designed everything to revolve around the student and their schedule." To top it all off, the school has completed the construction of the Lanier Professional Development Center building, which added 34,000 square feet to the law school building. The school is already equipped with a first-rate library, and "the library staff is amazing and always available."

When it's time to start looking for a job or clerkship, Texas Tech maintains "a great reputation in the Texas legal markets as producing hard-working, effective lawyers." Students choose Tech precisely for this reputation and are proud of the results. A third-year student asserts, "I've been told on several occasions that a firm would rather pick up a Tech Law graduate who knows what to do when he steps foot in the office than some Ivy League grad who knows more about theory and less about how to get the job done." While career placement is highly successful in Texas, many students feel that the school could improve its national reputation and help "out-of-state students find jobs in their home states." In general, students would like their top school to take a more leading role in the national legal community, urging the administration to "spend more money to attract more nationally known, rather than regionally known, guest speakers and employers."

Life

The surprisingly friendly and open atmosphere at Texas Tech is all due to students who aren't afraid to "help one another, encourage one another, and be kind to one another." No need for first-year jitters. You'll quickly feel at home at Texas Tech, thanks to a "tremendous student-run mentoring program for incoming students." Within the law school, there are a number of students clubs and organizations—plus many more in the larger university—and if you're married, there are "resources and social networking opportunities for students with spouses and their families." Conservative politics predominate, but students reassure us that "you can survive as a liberal." In fact, "the Tech democrats are more active than the republicans," and everyone listens to and respects different opinions.

STEPHEN M. PEREZ, ASSISTANT DEAN FOR ADMISSIONS & RECRUITMENT
TEXAS TECH UNIVERSITY SCHOOL OF LAW 1802 HARTFORD AVENUE, LUBBOCK, TX 79409
TEL: 806-742-3990 FAX: 806-742-4617
E-MAIL: ADMISSIONS.LAW@TTU.EDU • WEBSITE: WWW.LAW.TTU.EDU

If you've never been to West Texas, a student dryly describes it for us as "a vast, treeless, invariably flat expanse of dirt…They even have tumbleweeds here—like out of a John Wayne movie or *Looney Tunes*." Although it sounds a bit inhospitable, students say the advantage to Lubbock's small city environment and arid landscape is that there are fewer distractions, which makes it easier to focus on your homework. More importantly, "Lubbock is a great environment for law students to partner with local lawyers and learn the ropes." "The Lubbock legal community is extremely strong and polite, and the relationship is emphasized over the case," one student says.

If you are looking for nightlife and social outlets, "Lubbock is not the most exciting town on the universe." However, students guarantee us that the lively campus community can make life surprisingly entertaining. For sports fans, "There is a very good football team on the field," and the basketball team isn't too shabby either. On top of that, the law school's friendly students "have managed to carve out a pretty decent social life. The bars here are okay, but the law students will sponsor various events and they are typically very fun."

Getting In

Texas Tech evaluates students based on their previous academic performance, LSAT scores, letters of recommendation, and personal statements. While no specific pre-law curriculum is required, the admissions committee favors students who have reading and writing skills, an understanding of public institutions and government, and the ability to think both creatively and critically.

Clinical program required	No
Legal writing	
course requirement	Yes
Legal methods	
course requirement	Yes
Legal research	
course requirement	Yes
Moot court requirement	No
Public interest	
law requirement	No

ADMISSIONS

Selectivity Rating	81
# applications received	1,688
% applicants accepted	48
% acceptees attending	28
Average LSAT	155
Median LSAT	156
LSAT Range	
(25th to 75th percentile)	152–158
Average undergrad GPA	3.44
Median undergrad GPA	3.48
Application fee	$50
Regular application deadline	2/15
Early application deadline	11/1
Early application notification	1/15
Transfer students accepted	Yes
Evening division offered	No
Part-time accepted	No
CAS accepted	Yes

FINANCIAL FACTS

Annual tuition (in-state	
out-of-state)	$17,927/$27,557
Books and supplies	$1,200
Fees	$4,440
Room & Board	$8,802
Financial aid application	
deadline	3/1
% all students receiving	
some sort of aid	85
% of aid that is merit based	100
% receiving scholarships	72
Average grant	$4,921
Average loan	$26,373
Average total aid package	$32,305
Average debt	$69,596

EMPLOYMENT INFORMATION

Career Rating	90
Total 2012 JD Grads	216
% grads employed nine months out	85
Median starting salary	$65,688
# employed full-time	171
# employed part-time	11
# employed bar required	144
# employed JD preferred	26
# employed professional/other	9
# employed non-professional	3
# pursuing advanced degree	2
# unemployed and seeking employment	25
# not seeking employment	2
% grads employed by school	3
State for bar exam	TX, NM, UT
Pass rate for first-time bar	90.7

Prominent Alumni
Mary Alice McLarty, Litigator in Dallas, Texas; Pres. Amer. Assn. for Justice; Philip Johnson, Texas Supreme Court Justice.

Grads Employed by Field (%)
Academic (3)
Business/Industry (15)
Government (14)
Judicial Clerkship (1)
Military (1)
Private Practice (51)
Public Interest (0)

Thomas M. Cooley Law School

INSTITUTIONAL INFORMATION

Public/private	Private
Affiliation	No Affiliation
% faculty part-time	60
% faculty female	38
% faculty underrepresented minority	11
Total faculty	327

SURVEY SAYS...

Diverse opinions accepted in classrooms, Great research resources, Great library

STUDENTS

Enrollment of law school	3,095
% male/female	50/50
% part-time	81
% underrepresented minority	30
% international	6
Average age of entering class	27

ACADEMICS

Academic Experience Rating	77
Profs interesting rating	82
Profs accessible rating	79
Hours of study per day	4.57

Academic Specialties

Commercial, Constitutional, Corporation Securities, Environmental, Government Services, Human Rights, International, Taxation, Intellectual Property, Canadian Law, Homeland and National Security

Advanced Degrees Offered

JD, 2–5 years; LLM Taxation, 1 year full-time, part-time variable; LLM Intellectual Property, 1 year full-time, part-time variable; LLM Corporate Law & Finance, 1 year full-time, part-time variable; LLM Insurance Law, 1 year full-time, part-time variable; LLM Self-Directed, 1 year full-time, part-time variable; LLM U.S. Legal Studies for Foreign Lawyers, 3 consecutive semesters; LLM Homeland and National Security

Academics

The Thomas M. Cooley Law School in Michigan is the "the largest law school" in the United States in terms of enrollment. There are four Michigan campuses—one in the state capital of Lansing, one in the northern suburbs of Detroit, one in Grand Rapids and and one in Ann Arbor. Cooley's newest campus in Tampa Bay, Florida opened in May 2013. Cooley prides itself on "flexible" and "accommodating" scheduling. There are "daytime, nighttime, and weekend" classes. There are "three terms year-round" as well, and you can start in January, May, or September. Students tell us the price tag is "very affordable." Either way, Cooley offers "a lot of financial aid and scholarship opportunities." Technology is also "cutting-edge," and the law library is one of the most extensive in the country.

Students here describe Cooley as an "underrated" "lawyer-making machine." It's not the place for you if you want to imbibe legal theory, though. "The school promotes practical application so you are ready to jump into your career" immediately upon graduation. Real legal experience "is required." Every student must complete a clinic, internship, externship, or otherwise demonstrate the equivalent in work experience. "Lectures are practical and grounded instead of theoretical." Course selection is broad and specializations are available but the number of mandatory courses is "a little ridiculous," and it "may prevent you from taking many electives and delving deeply into a particular area of interest." Basically, "Cooley's thinking is that if it is tested on the bar, it should be a required class." "This law school prepares you for the bar exam." Period.

Some students love the "hard-working" administration. Others say that the top brass is "frigid." Far and away, the biggest administrative complaint is that Cooley takes its sweet time posting grades. Like, "forever." The faculty is "interesting, entertaining, and knowledgeable," and it's full of professors who have "actually practiced law." There are also "many adjunct professors." They're typically judges, partners at big law firms, or general counsel for major corporations. Outside of class, faculty members are very approachable. "The accessibility of the professors is second to none," beams a 3L.

The "rigorous" academic atmosphere here is "not for the faint hearted." "Class sizes tend to be quite large." Professors generally "employ the Socratic Method and are always seeking to test your knowledge of the material." "The majority of students get C's." "Exams are tough, and an A is well earned." "Cooley lowers the bar for admissions, but after that you are on your own to sink or swim," warns a 1L. "Cooley is very hard to stay in." Although the school has a fully staffed academic support resouce center, students uniformly promise that "you will struggle to survive through all three of your years here." "You better know the law," they say. "If you slack off, you'll fail out."

Life

Cooley "accepts just about anyone and everyone." The student population is "a mixture of students who didn't get in any place else and students who are on full scholarships because their LSAT and GPA were so high." An overwhelming majority of students are enrolled part time. Diversity of all kinds is a fabulous strength. Well more than half the future attorneys here come from some state other than Michigan. About one third represent an ethnic minority. There are "nontraditional students from many different professions." "Age, background, and socioeconomic status" really run the gamut. "Cooley is so diverse that one could not even attempt to discriminate without confusing himself," declares a 3L. On the one hand, the vast assortment of students "makes for excellent class discussions." On the other hand, "people divide into cliques easily" outside the classroom.

The five campuses each have their own identity. In Lansing, students have a "beautiful" building downtown "by the capitol." However, the surrounding area is largely "bleak" and "depressing." The Grand Rapids campus is similarly located in "a refurbished old building in the heart of downtown," and it's not in the greatest neighborhood, either. The decidedly suburban Auburn Hills campus is a nice and new facility "tucked away in a wooded compound" that feels like "a generic corporate headquarters." Ann Arbor's building was designed by renowned architect and Frank Lloyd Wright apprentice, Alden B. Dow. The stunning new Tampa Bay campus is situated on 8.8 acres in suburban Riverview.

Social life can be hit or miss. Cooley is home to a tremendous number of student organizations," and "most students are nice people." However, there isn't much of a community. "A lot of people come to class and then leave immediately after," explains a 1L. "Building a social life takes effort." The fact that "grades are impossible during the first few terms" certainly doesn't help. "Those who are social butterflies mostly ended up failing out after one or two semesters," cautions a 2L. "People get along, but it's best to focus on studying."

Getting In

Cooley is one of the easiest law schools to get admitted to in the country. The acceptance rate hovers at about 70 percent annually. Admitted students at the 25th percentile have LSAT scores around 142 and GPAs of roughly 2.6. Admitted students at the 75th percentile have LSAT scores of 151 or so and their undergraduate GPA is about 3.3.

Combined Degrees Offered

JD/MPA, 3-6 years with Western Michigan University; JD/MBA, 3-6 years with Western Michigan University; JD/MSW, 3-6 years with Western Michigan University; JD/MBA, 3-6 years with Oakland University; JD/MPA, 3-6 years with Oakland University; JD/LLM 3-6 years; JD/MBA, 3-6 years with Davenport University; LLM/MBA in Insurance Law, 1-3 years with Olivet College

Clinical program required	Yes
Legal writing course requirement	Yes
Legal methods course requirement	Yes
Legal research course requirement	Yes
Moot court requirement	No
Public interest law requirement	No

ADMISSIONS

Selectivity Rating	66
# applications received	3,688
% applicants accepted	73.6
% acceptees attending	28.8
Median LSAT	145
LSAT Range (25th to 75th percentile)	142–151
Median undergrad GPA	3.02
Application fee	$0
Transfer students accepted	Yes
Evening division offered	Yes
Part-time accepted	Yes
CAS accepted	Yes

FINANCIAL FACTS

Annual tuition	$37,140
Books and supplies	$1,400
Fees	$40
Room & Board	$7,800
Financial aid application deadline	9/1
% all students receiving some sort of aid	94
% of aid that is merit based	15
% receiving scholarships	55
Average debt	$122,398

EMPLOYMENT INFORMATION

Career Rating	74	
Total 2012 JD Grads	1,079	
% grads employed nine months out	69.67	
Median starting salary	$50,000	
% job accepting grads providing useable salary information	42.61	
# employed full-time	575	
# employed part-time	105	
# employed bar required	352	
# employed JD preferred	160	
# employed professional/other	124	
# employed non-professional	44	
# pursuing advanced degree	29	
# unemployed and seeking employment	215	
# not seeking employment	49	
% grads employed by school	0.4	
State for bar exam	MI, NY, IL, PA, CA, TX, MD, NJ, OH	
Pass rate for first-time bar	72.14	

Prominent Alumni
John Engler, Former Governor of Michigan; Bart R. Stupak, U. S.; Representative; Jane Markey, Judge, Michigan Court of Appeals

Grads Employed by Field (%)
Academic (2.65)
Business/Industry (26.11)
Government (12.68)
Judicial Clerkship (6.34)
Private Practice (49.12)
Public Interest (3.10)

TOURO COLLEGE
JACOB D. FUCHSBERG LAW CENTER

INSTITUTIONAL INFORMATION

Public/private	Private
Affiliation	Jewish
Student-faculty ratio	17:1
% faculty part-time	42
% faculty female	42
% faculty underrepresented minority	11
Total faculty	84

SURVEY SAYS...

Diverse opinions accepted in classrooms, Great research resources, Beautiful campus

STUDENTS

Enrollment of law school	805
% male/female	54/46
% part-time	28
% underrepresented minority	25
Average age of entering class	26

ACADEMICS

Academic Experience Rating	79
Profs interesting rating	81
Profs accessible rating	80
Hours of study per day	3.71

Academic Specialties
Commercial, Criminal, Human Rights, International, Intellectual Property

Advanced Degrees Offered
JD, 2.5–3 years full-time; 3.5–5 years part-time; LLM for Foreign law graduates, 1 year full-time; 3 semesters part-time; LLM General Studies, 1 year full-time; 3 semesters part-time.

Combined Degrees Offered
Dual Degree Programs: JD/MBA; JD/MPA; JD/MSW

Academics

Long Island's Touro may not receive national accolades, but "the quality of the education at Touro is exceptionally better than the school's reputation." Students say there is "no difference" between professors here and those at more prestigious schools; they are "of the same caliber as professors of top tier law schools." "Brilliant and caring," these "passionate" professors "convey not only legal theory, but the practical points which are necessary to know in the new legal economy." Even outside the classroom, they make the time necessary to guide you through the curriculum. "I have never had a problem with scheduling a meeting with a professor," one student notes. Though TLC is "not too large," it boasts "excellent library resources" and a staff who "are always there to help." Overall, at Touro, students feel the "helpful, kind and compassionate" administration "is committed to the success of each and every student."

Touro's Long Island location may not seem like a prime destination for law students, but in fact, the school's location is one of its great strengths. Having a "close proximity to the state and federal court houses" means that students here enjoy "opportunities that are unavailable to most other law schools." That access to real law being practiced in real courts, as well as its "great relationship with the judges and attorneys," means "it feels like the courts are part of our educational experience on a daily basis because we frequently visit them to watch trials, and we also have some of the judges teaching in our school."

That access is important to the primary goal here: providing you with the framework necessary to have a thriving career. Faculty members "want to ensure that every student has an opportunity to achieve a solid job opportunity after graduation." The "challenging but fruitful" education students enjoy at Touro "fosters academic and professional development" that, when coupled with the access students have to lawyers and judges— "we can get clerkships much easier than many other schools," one student notes—allows graduates to quickly be on course for their career pursuits. As one student boasts, "lawyers who graduate from our school are more competent and better equipped to practice law than most other third and fourth tier schools."

Life

When making "awesome new friends" is set alongside meeting "some excellent attorneys, district attorneys, assistant US attorneys and judges," it's easy to see why students appreciate life at Touro, even if opportunities for good times on the weekend are relatively limited in the quiet community of Central Islip. (New York City is an hour away, and is a prime destination for those looking for excitement.) Though everyone here is working hard, don't expect a cutthroat atmosphere. Those at Touro "share a spirit more of camaraderie than competition." Your fellow students will not be homogenous, either. "TLC encompasses a diverse student body—not just in terms of race and gender, but also diversity of backgrounds, walks of life, and stages of life."

SUSAN THOMPSON, DIRECTOR OF ENROLLMENT
225 EASTVIEW DRIVE, CENTRAL ISLIP, NY 11722
TEL: 631-761-7010 FAX: 631-761-7019
E-MAIL: ADMISSIONS@TOUROLAW.EDU • WEBSITE: WWW.TOUROLAW.EDU

The people and atmosphere may be inviting, but there are complaints about the facilities. The elevators are "a nightmare," and "horrible acoustics" and "obstructed view seats" make lectures halls less than pleasant places to be. Even the layout wins some scorn for being unnecessarily complex; "going from the third floor in the library to third floor in the school, ten feet away, you must travel six flights of stairs." In addition, be prepared to work around a schedule influenced by the college's Jewish affiliation. Though the school promotes non-secular activities, "the school and library are closed at 2:30 P.M. on Friday afternoons" and most Saturdays, which for some "makes it extremely hard to put in 100 percent." That said, the building is "relatively new," with wireless available "everywhere."

Getting In

Students recently admitted to Touro Law Center at the 25th percentile have LSAT scores of approximately 150 and GPAs of approximately 2.8. Meanwhile, admitted students at the 75th percentile have LSAT scores of 153 and GPAs of roughly 3.4.

Clinical program required	No
Legal writing course requirement	Yes
Legal methods course requirement	Yes
Legal research course requirement	Yes
Moot court requirement	No
Public interest law requirement	Yes

ADMISSIONS

Selectivity Rating	78
# applications received	1,652
% applicants accepted	52
% acceptees attending	31
LSAT Range (25th to 75th percentile)	148–153
Application fee	$60
Regular application deadline	
Early application deadline	5/1
Transfer students accepted	Yes
Evening division offered	Yes
Part-time accepted	Yes
CAS accepted	Yes

FINANCIAL FACTS

Annual tuition	$41,770
Books and supplies	$
Fees	$120
Room & Board	$20,084
Financial aid application deadline	5/1
% first-year students receiving some sort of aid	74
% all students receiving some sort of aid	51
% of aid that is merit based	95
% receiving scholarships	60
Average grant	$7,650
Average loan	$37,000
Average total aid package	$40,500
Average debt	$132,302

EMPLOYMENT INFORMATION

Career Rating	73	**Prominent Alumni**
Total 2012 JD Grads	221	Lewis Lubell, Justice, NYS Supreme Court;
% for whom you have useable information	97	Kathleen Rice, Nassau County District Attorney; Seymour Liebman, Corporate
Median starting salary	$66,742	Counsel, Canon USA.
# employed full-time	153	**Grads Employed by Field (%)**
# employed part-time	17	Academic (1)
# employed bar required	144	Business/Industry (14)
# employed JD preferred	15	Government (19)
# employed professional/other	10	Judicial Clerkship (5)
# employed non-professional	1	Private Practice (58)
# pursuing advanced degree	1	Public Interest (3)
# unemployed and seeking employment	41	
# not seeking employment	3	
State for bar exam	NY, NJ, CT	
Pass rate for first-time bar	77.4	

TULANE UNIVERSITY
LAW SCHOOL

INSTITUTIONAL INFORMATION

Public/private	Private
Affiliation	No Affiliation
Student-faculty ratio	14:1
% faculty part-time	40
% faculty female	31
% faculty underrepresented minority	6
Total faculty	84

SURVEY SAYS...

Students love New Orleans, LA, Good social life

STUDENTS

Enrollment of law school	743
% male/female	50/50
% from out-of-state	62
% underrepresented minority	18
% international	3
# of countries represented	20
Average age of entering class	24

ACADEMICS

Academic Experience Rating	**86**
Profs interesting rating	86
Profs accessible rating	83
Hours of study per day	3.52

Academic Specialties
Environmental, International, Intellectual Property

Advanced Degrees Offered
SJD, 2–3 years depending on length of time to complete dissertation; Master of Laws, 1 year full-time, 2 years part-time; Master of Laws in Admiralty, 1 year full-time, 2 years part-time; Master of Laws in Energy and Environment, 1 year full-time, 2 years part-time; Master of Laws in International and Comparative Law, 1 year full-time, 2 years part-time; Master of Laws in American Law, 1 year full-time.

Combined Degrees Offered
JD/MBA, JD/MHA, JD/MPH, JD/MSW, JD/MACCT, JD/MS International Development, all 4 years.

Academics

Tulane University Law School is "extremely enjoyable because it provides you with the same resources as all the top law schools, with a more laid-back atmosphere." "The quality of teaching is superb." The "world-renowned faculty" here is full of "experts and kick-ass attorneys" who are "funny, extremely smart, and extremely approachable." "They are highly qualified and accomplished but remain accessible and down-to-earth." Some students call the administration "ridiculously awesome," too. The deans are "nice and helpful," they say, "and most of them teach a 1L or 2L class, which gives you the opportunity to be exposed to them early on in your career." More critical students call the management merely "vaguely competent."

Tulane is home to "quite a few unique programs and strengths." In addition to "exceptional clinical opportunities" and a host of dual-degree programs, students edit no fewer than eight journals. Tulane also offers certificates in international and comparative law, admiralty law, environmental law, sports law, and civil law. Also, Louisiana is a civil law state (whereas every other state is a common law state), so students are exposed to two very different legal systems. "The ability to follow a common law or civil law track not only opens up opportunities in Louisiana, but it also makes an international law career more feasible." The big academic complaint here is the research and writing program. "I am not sure whoever designed it has ever heard the term 'best practices,'" speculates a 1L. "If you came as a strong technical writer, you will leave with no new skills. If you did not, you are on your own."

Students note that the academic program is competitive and challenging, and it is important to maintain strong performance if you want to gain the interest of local employers. Tulane is "extremely active in helping everyone secure summer employment and beyond." Students also note that their school's brand name is often a real advantage on a resume. "We're the best law school in Louisiana, and the firms know it," brags a 2L. "We are not all competing for the same thirty spots at the top law firm in our city because our goals are incredibly diverse," adds a 2L.

Facilities wise, Tulane has "a wonderful library." Some students say that "classrooms are nice." Others disagree. "The actual building and classrooms are forgettable," they tell us. "The horrid ergonomics of it all!" bemoans a 2L. "To plug in your laptop can take two minutes and can set the stage for an awkward encounter with the person sitting next to you while you fumble around under the table like a teenager on a first date."

Life

New Orleans is definitely located in "the American South, and many students come from the South." Geographic diversity is pretty abundant, though. Some 85 percent of the students come from a state other than Louisiana. About 20 percent of the students represent an ethnic minority. There's a "wide range of International Students" and plenty of "diversity of opinion and background." Some students insist that "there's no cutthroat competition here." They say that the typical student is as "friendly, cooperative, and as laid-back as a stressed law student could possibly be." Others tell us that competition exists "but it's not as prevalent until exam time."

Outside of class, Tulane students are an "extremely social," "fun-loving bunch." There are "plenty of cliques, largely organized according to special interests areas of law, ethnicity, and age." At the same time, the environment is "very collegial." "The community atmosphere is a definite plus." Quite a few students "enjoy a good party." There are "a lot

ADAM KANCHER, ASSISTANT DIRECTOR
WEINMANN HALL, 6329 FRERET STREET, NEW ORLEANS, LA 70118
TEL: 504-865-5930 FAX: 504-865-6710
E-MAIL: ADMISSIONS@LAW.TULANE.EDU • WEBSITE: WWW.LAW.TULANE.EDU

of the smart kids who had fun in undergrad" here, and their good times continue unabated in law school. "Socializing is in overdrive at TLS," cautions a 2L, "which can be a distraction from your studies if you let it." "Most people go out at least once or twice a week." "Whether it's a run-of-the-mill bar review or renting out a restaurant on the Mardi Gras parade route, there's always a social event on the horizon."

Off campus, the Big Easy is reportedly "the most relaxed city in the USA" and "a perfect place to unwind on weekends or after finals." Students love the food, the nightlife, and the "warm winter weather." There's the debauchery of Bourbon Street, of course, but there's also an array of "incredible" streets and neighborhoods. "The sidewalk bistros and beautiful, lush scenery add significant character to your day-to-day experience as a law student." Beyond the city of New Orleans, "there are lots of good places for weekend trips in the area" as well.

Getting In

Tulane has a fabulous regional reputation and a very good national reputation. Admitted students at the 25th percentile have LSAT scores around 158 and GPAs not much less than 3.4. Admitted students at the 75th percentile have LSAT scores of 163 or so and GPAs around 3.7.

Clinical program required	No
Legal writing course requirement	Yes
Legal methods course requirement	No
Legal research course requirement	Yes
Moot court requirement	Yes
Public interest law requirement	Yes

ADMISSIONS

Selectivity Rating	82
# applications received	2,271
% applicants accepted	48
% acceptees attending	23
Average LSAT	160
Median LSAT	161
LSAT Range (25th to 75th percentile)	156–163
Average undergrad GPA	3.44
Median undergrad GPA	3.46
Application fee	$60
Regular application deadline	
Transfer students accepted	Yes
Evening division offered	No
Part-time accepted	No
CAS accepted	Yes

FINANCIAL FACTS

Annual tuition	$41,500
Books and supplies	$7,550
Fees	$3,780
Room & Board	$13,440
% first-year students receiving some sort of aid	88
% all students receiving some sort of aid	88
% receiving scholarships	59
Average grant	$19,452
Average loan	$47,399
Average total aid package	$58,005
Average debt	$115,029

EMPLOYMENT INFORMATION

Career Rating	60*	Prominent Alumni
Total 2012 JD Grads	269	Edith Clement, US Court of Appeals judge;
% grads employed nine months out	87	Jacques Wiener, US Court of Appeals
# employed full-time	215	judge; John Minor Wisdom, judiciary.
# employed part-time	19	**Grads Employed by Field (%)**
# employed bar required	185	Academic (2)
# employed JD preferred	31	Business/Industry (20)
# employed professional/other	11	Government (8)
# employed non-professional	7	Judicial Clerkship (11)
# pursuing advanced degree	12	Military (1)
# unemployed and seeking employment	15	Private Practice (42)
# not seeking employment	2	Public Interest (4)
% grads employed by school	0	
State for bar exam	NY, LA, TX, FL, CA	

THE UNIVERSITY OF AKRON
SCHOOL OF LAW

INSTITUTIONAL INFORMATION

Public/private	Public
Affiliation	No Affiliation
Student-faculty ratio	13:1
% faculty female	37
% faculty underrepresented minority	9
Total faculty	35

SURVEY SAYS...

Diverse opinions accepted in classrooms, Great research resources, Great library staff

STUDENTS

Enrollment of law school	563
% male/female	63/37
% from out-of-state	28
% part-time	41
% underrepresented minority	14
# of countries represented	2
Average age of entering class	26

ACADEMICS

Academic Experience Rating	**74**
Profs interesting rating	79
Profs accessible rating	78
Hours of study per day	3.61

Academic Specialties

Corporation Securities, Criminal, International, Labor, Taxation, Intellectual Property

Advanced Degrees Offered

LLM in Intellectual Property: 1 year full-time or 2–3 years part-time

Combined Degrees Offered

JD/Master in Business Administration; JD/Master in Taxation; JD/Master in Public Administration; JD/Master in Applied Politics—these progs. usually take 1 additional semester to finish, may be completed with summer hours. JD/LLM in Intellectual Property Law, 100 hours total, can be completed in 3 years (full-time) or 4 years (part-time).

Academics

The University of Akron School of Law is an "undervalued," "regional law school" that offers a lot of perks. "The tuition is very reasonable," especially if you can claim residency in Ohio. The bar-passage rate is solid. Course load options are "extremely flexible." It's very easy to switch between the full-time and part-time programs. The four specialized centers here "are very well-known." The "high-powered" certificate program in intellectual property is particularly notable. There's also a certificate in litigation and areas of concentration galore. Akron Law also boasts five joint-degree programs, a couple of "pretty freaking amazing" journals, and the chance to study abroad in Geneva, Switzerland. The curriculum here focuses primarily on the hard-boiled application of law. "If you want a legal education that emphasizes practical skills needed in the real-world," declares a 1L, "Akron Law is for you." The trial advocacy program is "outstanding" and the trial team is "one of the best" in the nation, routinely bagging trophies at national tournaments. Clinics are "very strong" and reportedly a cinch to get into. One of the clinics is the Clemency Project, which aids low-income people who have been convicted of crimes in securing pardons from the state governor. Another is the new business legal clinic, which helps people start businesses in the Akron area. As far as academic complaints, some students call the legal writing program "poor." Also, "Internships and externships placements are not readily available," and grading can be "pretty harsh."

Students heap praise on both the faculty and the administration. "The professors at Akron are the crown jewel of the school," beams a 1L. "They make even esoteric, archaic concepts like the rule against perpetuities interesting and understandable." "It is evident that they are passionate about teaching." "Many could probably make double or triple their salary by working in a big-city law firm." Faculty accessibility outside of class is "great," too. Professors here are "really interested in helping you find your way as a lawyer." They are "constantly walking the halls and willing to chit-chat." "Every professor I have had in class knows my name," reflects a 3L. The "ultra-helpful" and "very flexible" administration is "also very accessible and interested in the students" and "willing to work with" them.

While you can find Akron Law graduates all over the country, the great mass of alumni ends up practicing in northeast Ohio. While critics charge that the Office of Career Planning "does not do a great job at placing students," most students seem pretty happy with their post-law school employment prospects. The school has a "good reputation in the region." "The local bar association has a very close relationship with Akron Law," and "The school provides countless opportunities for" mentoring and networking.

Students tell us, "Akron is in the process of building a brand-new law school." In the meantime, the current facility "isn't grotesque-looking" but it's "less than stellar" and it just "doesn't feel like a law school." "The physical plant is a mess," explains a 3L. "The law school is actually two buildings that were combined in the cheapest way possible." "Areas of the building can seem cramped." "The heating and cooling system is consistently broken." On the plus side, classrooms are adequate. "They are all equipped for wireless Internet access and have plug-ins for every student laptop." Also, the location is excellent. City, county, state, and federal courts "are all steps from the door of the school."

Lauri S. Thorpe, Asst. Dean of Admission, Fin. Aid, Student Svcs.
The University of Akron School of Law, 302 Buchtel Common, Akron, OH 44325-2901
Tel: 800-425-7668 Fax: 330-258-2343
E-Mail: lawadmissions@uakron.edu • Website: www.uakron.edu/law

Life

The vast majority of students at Akron Law are residents of Ohio. They describe themselves as "pretty outgoing and friendly." "The biggest surprise about law school is the fact that the other students are normal," relates a 1L. "I was expecting snobs and nerds but I have found people that I look forward to seeing every day." Student opinion concerning the academic atmosphere is decidedly split. Some students perceive "healthy amounts of competition." Others don't. "You see your fellow classmates as colleagues," says a 1L. "Students here aren't that competitive," adds a 3L. "I have helped several students and others have helped me study for exams."

Beyond the confines of the classroom, a respectable number of speakers come to campus and the student bar association is "very active." Socially, "There is quite a divide between day and evening students" and "there are a lot of cliques." The city of Akron is "a small, insular community." It's not the worst place in the world, but it's certainly not a world-class city, either. "Downtown Akron is not, shall we say, appealing in many ways," explains a 2L. "Some areas are nice, but some areas abutting campus are sketchy."

Getting In

Admitted full-time students at the 25th percentile have LSAT scores in the low 150s and undergraduate grade point averages a little under 3.2. At the 75th percentile, LSAT scores are close to 160 and GPAs are in the 3.7 range. Stats for admitted part-time students are somewhat lower.

Clinical program required	No
Legal writing course requirement	Yes
Legal methods course requirement	Yes
Legal research course requirement	Yes
Moot court requirement	No
Public interest law requirement	Yes

ADMISSIONS

Selectivity Rating	76
# applications received	1,647
% applicants accepted	54
% acceptees attending	20
Average LSAT	153
Median LSAT	153
LSAT Range (25th to 75th percentile)	151–156
Average undergrad GPA	3.33
Median undergrad GPA	3.35
Application fee	$0
Regular application deadline	
Transfer students accepted	Yes
Evening division offered	Yes
Part-time accepted	Yes
CAS accepted	Yes

FINANCIAL FACTS

Annual tuition (in-state out-of-state)	$18,977/$31,532
Books and supplies	$900
Fees	$2,897
Room & Board	$11,134
Financial aid application deadline	3/1
% first-year students receiving some sort of aid	90
% all students receiving some sort of aid	92
% of aid that is merit based	97
% receiving scholarships	47
Average grant	$11,931
Average loan	$23,744
Average total aid package	$27,808
Average debt	$67,948

EMPLOYMENT INFORMATION

Career Rating	89	**Prominent Alumni**
Total 2012 JD Grads	116	Deborah Cook, Judge, U.S. Court of
% for whom you have useable information	100	Appeals-Sixth Circuit; Rochelle Seide, Partner, Schwegman Lundberg Woessner;
% grads employed nine months out	91	John Vasuta, VP, Gen. Counsel & Sec.,
Median starting salary	$54,000	Bridgestone Firestone.
# employed full-time	100	**Grads Employed by Field (%)**
# employed part-time	5	Academic (3)
# employed bar required	68	Business/Industry (32)
# employed JD preferred	17	Government (19)
# employed professional/other	9	Judicial Clerkship (7)
# employed non-professional	11	Private Practice (37)
# pursuing advanced degree	0	Public Interest (2)
# unemployed and seeking employment	6	
# not seeking employment	5	
% grads employed by school	0	
State for bar exam	OH, NY, VA, CA	
Pass rate for first-time bar	90	

THE UNIVERSITY OF ALABAMA—TUSCALOOSA
SCHOOL OF LAW

INSTITUTIONAL INFORMATION
Public/private	Public
Student-faculty ratio	10:1
Total faculty	75

SURVEY SAYS...
Great research resources, Great library staff, Abundant externship/internship/clerkship opportunities

ACADEMICS
Academic Experience Rating	**82**
Profs interesting rating	88
Profs accessible rating	98
Hours of study per day	3.21

Advanced Degrees Offered
LLM Concentrations in Taxation and Business Transactions, 2 years part-time; International LLM Program, 1 year, full-time

Combined Degrees Offered
JD/MBA, 3 or 4 years several dual enrollments with various University graduate programs

Academics

Alabama prides itself on offering a tremendous legal education at an affordable price. Though the school definitely places an "emphasis...on corporate law," students are grateful that there are also "amazing faculty members with interests in academia, public interest and environmental law." And according to one-second year, these professors are "huge assets to students with no desire to go to a big firm or to vote Republican." Overall, many find their academic experience to be "exceptional." As another second year notes, "The quality of classes I've taken has been amazing, especially compared to classes I sat in on at other (higher ranked) law schools prior to enrolling. There are incredible academics willing to oversee guided research topics and help you get published." Students also highlight Alabama's international programs, which offer "even more opportunities to work with professors in different areas of law in different countries." Moreover, they note that "the school's administrators and professors have an open door policy and are always amenable to speaking with students. The administrators and professor genuinely care about the students and their success in the classroom and beyond."

One gripe students at UA do have is with the perceived "bias against students with low GPAs." As a frustrated second-year notes, "While I had hoped that a lower GPA might merit extra attention, especially since I am paying full-price to attend the Law School, I have found that students with high GPAs by far receive the most praise and attention from administrators." Another student concurs adding, "Furthermore, like many law schools, my school's administration and faculty tends to place favor and preference upon those with higher GPAs, a practice that outcasts those of us with a strong work ethic who fell victim to the mandatory curve." Fortunately, the low student to teacher ratio means struggling students can meet individually with their professors if they need extra help. In addition, the school hosts several skills workshops open to the entire law school.

Students feel that there remains room for improvement when it comes to career services. However, they appreciate the strides the office has made. "Our career services are still adjusting to our improving national reputation. They are making increased efforts at providing useful business contacts outside of Alabama, but could still improve." A frustrated second year adds, "We do not attract a lot of attention from prestigious firms because they assume we are all uninformed rednecks—an assumption that is both unfortunate and inaccurate." However, another more content second-year counters, "As a native Alabamian, I am interested in finding long-term employment either in my home state or in Washington, DC. The school has been very helpful in creating connections for me, both through UA Law alumni and through the DC externship program."

Life

UA manages to foster a warm and welcoming environment and this collegial atmosphere certainly extends to the law students. Indeed, "Alabama has heart, ambition, and an attitude that really encourages teamwork. Outlines and notes circulate through so many students—there is no required 'quid pro quo' in that regard. We just believe in each other." A second year student concurs stating, "Everyone operates with a sense of respect and professionalism toward one another...with a little 'Southern Hospitality,' everyone always lends a helping hand, so the competition is outweighed by our southern charm."

Ms. Claude Reeves Arrington, Associate Dean
Box 870382, Tuscaloosa, AL 35487
Tel: 205-348-5440 Fax: 205-348-5439
E-Mail: ADMISSIONS@LAW.UA.EDU • Website: WWW.LAW.UA.EDU

"The average student is young and direct from college," and "usually" comes directly from Alabama "or from a neighboring state." Students describe themselves as "very smart" and "down-to-earth." Politically, it is a pretty conservative atmosphere, though you will find students with a range of interests and viewpoints nonetheless. While the UA law population is "not very diverse," "in recent years, racial and geographic diversity has been a priority of the law school. The average age of law students has increased as well." One ecstatic third year buoys this sentiment sharing, "I'm a Yankee, but the people down here are second to none. I wouldn't trade any of them for anything."

While most students here are diligent workers, one-second year also assures us that they "know how to have a little fun" as well. A fellow student agrees adding, "It has been very easy for me to make several good friends among very diverse individuals with differing interests. While we study a great deal we also find time to hit up the bars in large groups." Additionally, "The Student Bar Association throws parties every other week, and the students all socialize together." Tuscaloosa offers "great weather" and "it's a great college town." Be forewarned though, for those not "super interested" in football "[it is considered] sacrilegious down here." Indeed, Alabama's social scene generally "revolves around sports," and "football is a near-religious experience." Devotion to the Crimson Tide certainly extends to the law school. In fact, students have their own cheering section, "right there with the fraternities." As a first year student admits, "We schedule our work so we can attend Crimson Tide ball games." If you "don't like football you'll probably have a harder time finding your niche." However, others assure us that "it is possible to escape and do your own thing." "Birmingham is an awesome city a mere forty-five minutes away from Tuscaloosa and it offers everything an urbanite could need," including "fantastic shopping, excellent restaurants, lots of young singles, a sense of community, and even a little bit of the hipster scene (somewhat of a rarity in Alabama)."

Getting In

Admitted applicants in the 25th percentile earned an LSAT score around 158 and a GPA around 3.31. Admitted applicants in the 75th percentile earned an LSAT score around 167 and a GPA around 3.94. The median LSAT score is 165 and the median GPA 3.83.

Clinical program required	No
Legal writing course requirement	Yes
Legal methods course requirement	No
Legal research course requirement	Yes
Moot court requirement	Yes
Public interest law requirement	No

ADMISSIONS

Selectivity Rating	95
# applications received	1,679
% applicants accepted	25
% acceptees attending	35
Median LSAT	165
LSAT Range (25th to 75th percentile)	158–167
Median undergrad GPA	3.83
Application fee	$40
Transfer students accepted	Yes
Evening division offered	No
Part-time accepted	No
CAS accepted	Yes

FINANCIAL FACTS

Annual tuition (in-state out-of-state)	$19,660/$32,920
Books and supplies	$1,400
Room & Board	$11,850

EMPLOYMENT INFORMATION

Career Rating	85	# not seeking employment	2
Total 2012 JD Grads	172	State for bar exam	AL, GA, FL, TX, VA
% grads employed nine months out	94	Pass rate for first-time bar	95
# employed full-time	155	**Grads Employed by Field (%)**	
# employed part-time	3	Academic (4)	
# employed bar required	136	Business/Industry (8)	
# employed JD preferred	15	Government (14)	
# employed professional/other	3	Judicial Clerkship (14)	
# employed non-professional	4	Military (1)	
# pursuing advanced degree	7	Private Practice (52)	
# unemployed and seeking employment	1	Public Interest (7)	

UNIVERSITY OF ARIZONA
JAMES E. ROGERS COLLEGE OF LAW

INSTITUTIONAL INFORMATION

Public/private	Public
Affiliation	No Affiliation
Student-faculty ratio	12:1
% faculty part-time	42
% faculty female	40
% faculty underrepresented minority	20
Total faculty	83

SURVEY SAYS...

Great research resources, Beautiful campus, Students love Tucson, AZ

STUDENTS

Enrollment of law school	460
% male/female	50/50
% from out-of-state	30
% part-time	0
% underrepresented minority	28
% international	1
# of countries represented	3
Average age of entering class	26

ACADEMICS

Academic Experience Rating	85
Profs interesting rating	76
Profs accessible rating	90
Hours of study per day	3.86

Academic Specialties

Commercial, Constitutional, Corporation Securities, Criminal, Environmental, Human Rights, International, Legal History, Legal Philosophy, Property, Taxation, Intellectual Property

Advanced Degrees Offered

JD, 85 units; LLM in International Trade Law; LLM in Indigenous Peoples Law and Policy; SJD

Combined Degrees Offered

JD/Ph.D. in Phil., Psyc. or Econ. (6 years); JD/MBA (4 years); JD/MPA (4 years); JD/MA in American Indian Studies (4 years); JD/MA in Econ. (4 years); JD/MA in Women's Studies (4 years); JD/MA in Latin American Studies (4 years); JD/MMF Management Finance

Academics

The University of Arizona James E. Rogers College of Law offers "small class sizes"; "a very friendly, welcoming environment"; and "a price tag that lets students pursue careers in public service and nonprofit organizations" without racking up a gargantuan debt. Opportunities to gain practical experience are plentiful. The "strong" judicial externship program "can accommodate students interested in everything from bankruptcy court to superior court to district court." Clinics offer "hands-on experience" in eight areas including immigration, child advocacy, and indigenous peoples' law.

"This school is the most student-focused academic institution I have ever attended," says a happy 3L. Faculty members "truly care about their students" and "are available constantly." In the classroom, professors "make every effort to make the classes interesting and enjoyable," and "The small-section format during first year allows students to build a relationship with at least one professor." "They encourage discussion before and after class and are more than willing to provide letters of recommendation and reference." "They are approachable, friendly, and most even greet you by name as they pass you in the lobby or going to and from class." "Most are around campus all day and not just available during their office hours." "I e-mailed my property professor on a Sunday at roughly 10:30 P.M., with a pretty lengthy question," describes a 2L. "The question was answered at length by 10:45 P.M." "The administration is great too," enthuses a 1L. "Everyone is very helpful and interested in you getting a good education." "The quality of instruction is outstanding, and the responsiveness of the faculty and staff are remarkable. I am so very happy that I ended up at the U of A," sums up one pleased student.

Some students tell us that the "very helpful" Career and Professional Development Office at the U of A is "active in helping students connect with amazing internship and job opportunities in both the public sector and in law firms" in Arizona, California, and other Western states. If a student "is clear about where she wants to live or what she wants to do, the Career Office will give that student personal attention to strategize a plan to get there," although some complain that "they don't care what job you get, as long as you get one somewhere."

Facilities on campus are impressive. "The new building is gorgeous, especially the library. Tons of technology and connectivity. Little things like plugs at every desk and the latest projectors for classrooms make a big difference." Another student concurs, "The classrooms are brand-new and state-of-the-art—in my Family Law Class last semester we were able to video conference with a teacher in Canada to talk about divorce law without any extraneous equipment. Everything we needed to videochat was in the classroom!"

Life

There is a "relaxed Arizonan attitude" among the "amazingly friendly, smart" students at the U of A. "There is definitely competition here, as is unavoidable, but the school has a very laid-back atmosphere that allows you to keep things in perspective." "The second- and third-year students are very active in assisting the first-years adapt to law school through tutorials for all first-year classes," and teaching assistants "help with briefing and outlining." "Despite the curve, grades are not a big issue among students, and we tend to be excited for others' successes," declares a 1L. "This place is the opposite of cutthroat. Small sections for first-year students "are really conducive to forming lasting friendships." "I became very close with the other twenty-six students in my small section and continue to be good friends with several of them," says a 2L. "There is an overriding sense that everyone, from faculty to administration to students, really wants to be at the school and wants to see the school succeed."

The social atmosphere is "very vibrant." "There are thirty-plus student organizations that cover different religious, political, social and ethnic categories." That translates into lots of events. " "I have had so much fun in law school," gushes a 1L. "Almost every day, there are informative and thought-provoking guest speakers, panel discussions, or film screenings, especially during the lunch hour." Intramural sports are also popular. Social life tends to be "polarized between younger people coming straight out of college and older students with families." "The crowd divides into three groups," elaborates a 3L, "the married/serious relationship/older crowd, the nerds who rarely go out, and those who are trying to extend their undergraduate experience by going to law school." Without question, if you are "interested in partying, you cannot beat the University of Arizona bar scene."

The U of A campus itself is "beautiful, complete with palm trees and a gigantic, ideal student union." "The weather is ideal." The low cost of living is "fabulous, especially from a student's perspective." If you like outdoor activity, there are "myriad" activities within minutes of campus, including hiking, biking, swimming, and rock climbing.

Getting In

Admitted students at the 25th percentile have LSAT scores in the range of about 158 and GPAs in the range of 3.3 or so. Admitted students at the 75th percentile have LSAT scores of about 164 and GPAs approaching 3.8.

Clinical program required	No
Legal writing course requirement	Yes
Legal methods course requirement	No
Legal research course requirement	Yes
Moot court requirement	No
Public interest law requirement	No

ADMISSIONS

Selectivity Rating	88
# applications received	2,284
% applicants accepted	31
% acceptees attending	22
Average LSAT	161
LSAT Range (25th to 75th percentile)	157–164
Average undergrad GPA	3.50
Application fee	$50
Regular application deadline	2/15
Early application deadline	11/15
Early application notification	12/23
Transfer students accepted	Yes
Evening division offered	No
Part-time accepted	No
CAS accepted	Yes

FINANCIAL FACTS

Annual tuition (in-state out-of-state)	$17,768/$28,574
Books and supplies	$1,000
Fees	$0
Room & Board (on/off campus)	$8,864/$12,688
Financial aid application deadline	3/1
% first-year students receiving some sort of aid	80
% all students receiving some sort of aid	82
% of aid that is merit based	50
% receiving scholarships	75
Average grant	$5,000
Average loan	$13,500
Average total aid package	$18,000
Average debt	$50,000

EMPLOYMENT INFORMATION

		Grads Employed by Field (%)
Career Rating	96	Academic (8)
% grads employed nine months out	95	Business/Industry (7)
Median starting salary	$70,000	Government (15)
State for bar exam	AZ, CA, WA, NV, DC	Judicial Clerkship (22)
Pass rate for first-time bar	94	Military (3)
Prominent Alumni		Private Practice (42)
Morris K. Udall, Former Congressman;		Public Interest (3)
Stewart Udall, Former Congressman &		
Sec'y of Interior; Dennis DeConcini,		
Former Senator.		

UNIVERSITY OF ARKANSAS—FAYETTEVILLE

SCHOOL OF LAW

INSTITUTIONAL INFORMATION

Public/private	Public
Affiliation	No Affiliation
Student-faculty ratio	14:1
% faculty part-time	51
% faculty female	48
% faculty underrepresented minority	10
Total faculty	46

SURVEY SAYS...

Diverse opinions accepted in classrooms, Great research resources, Students love Fayetteville, AR

STUDENTS

Enrollment of law school	392
% male/female	61/39
% from out-of-state	31
% part-time	0
% underrepresented minority	17
Average age of entering class	24

ACADEMICS

Academic Experience Rating	**88**
Profs interesting rating	84
Profs accessible rating	86
Hours of study per day	3.49

Advanced Degrees Offered

LLM in Agricultural & Food Law, 1 academic year

Combined Degrees Offered

JD/MBA 3/1.5 years; JD/MPA 3/1 years; JD/MA 3/1.5 years

Academics

The University of Arkansas School of Law in Fayetteville is "a smaller school" that offers a "five-star, New York restaurant quality education for a McDonald's price." "In choosing a school that has very low in-state tuition, I gained an extremely valuable education at a fraction of the cost I would have paid at other institutions," brags a miserly 3L. "It's a pretty unbelievable education for the cost." "Various trial and counseling competitions are a few of the greatest strengths" here. Clinical courses and certified skills courses offer "excellent opportunities to get hands-on experience with the actual practice of law." In addition to traditional judicial externships, there are legislative externships and corporate counsel externships. A "strong legal writing program" is another plus. "You'll hear the students whining about it around the time appellate briefs are due," promises a 3L, "but we finish the program with excellent practical writing skills."

"The faculty is comprised of both older professors using more traditional teaching styles such as the Socratic Method, and younger professors that bring helpful insight[s] into today's practice of law into the classroom," explains a 2L. While a few professors here "would be better suited to write articles all day long and not get anywhere near the classroom," the quality of the instruction is fantastic" overall. "Most of the professors are really energetic and relevant," says a 1L, "and they encourage lively discussion." This faculty is also "devoted" and "almost always accessible" outside of class. The "very accessible and accommodating" administration is "always putting the students first" and "committed to raising the school's profile." "I have never had a problem too big or too small for them to address," reminisces a 3L. "It has been great." Upper-level students can choose from a range of elective courses in fields like health law, refugee and asylum law, entertainment law, and immigration policy, though some students would like the school to "add more electives" to the program.

Career Services isn't perfect but the staff is generally "wonderful" and employment prospects are reportedly excellent. Starting salaries are lower than what you'll find in more populous places. Arkansas is very inexpensive, though, and it's one of those states where everybody seems to know everybody else. Consequently, "the networking abilities within the city and state" are definitely a strength. Also, with Wal-Mart and gargantuan food conglomerate Tyson "just down the road," Northwest Arkansas is a relatively booming area of the country that "provides many unique opportunities for employment with both law firms and major corporations." "We have some students who go 'big law' in the major cities; we have some students who set up shop in rural Arkansas; we have some who go in-house; and we have a lot of government employees, too," says a 3L.

"The facilities are old in some areas but brand-new in others," and there are "lots of small nooks to study in." The old classrooms that are still used for nearly all of the first-year classes are "okay" at best. "The wood paneling is dark and depressing and reminiscent of an old station wagon," describes a 2L. A newer wing has "ergonomic and aesthetically pleasing" classrooms that are "technology-friendly." "The research facilities are great" in the "comprehensive" library. There's an onsite coffee shop, too, "which is great for study breaks when you need to recaffeinate."

JAMES K. MILLER, ASSOCIATE DEAN FOR STUDENTS
UNIVERSITY OF ARKANSAS SCHOOL OF LAW, FAYETTEVILLE, AR 72701
TEL: 479-575-3102 FAX: 479-575-3937
E-MAIL: JKMILLER@UARK.EDU • WEBSITE: LAW.UARK.EDU

Life

Some students describe the academic atmosphere as "very competitive." It's "cut-throat" during the first year, they allege. Other students dispute that characterization. "Students here are pretty laid-back," rejoins a 1L. "We work hard but it's not a cutthroat environment where people are trying to claw their way to the top of the class no matter what."

According to one view, social life can be hard for transplants because a lot of students come preequipped with their own cliques. "People who went to undergraduate school here seem to hang out with each other," says a 3L. "Many of the groups do not appear to be very inclusive of other students not in their normal social circle." Other students describe the environment as "very communal." "You get to know your fellow students and professors very well," says a 2L. Socially satisfied students also point to the "wide availability" of clubs and organizations and the fact that the student bar association is "active in providing events outside of the law school to…[help] get your mind off of classes." Campus sporting events are another big draw—especially football—and the surrounding Ozarks provide plenty of options for adventure activity. Fayetteville is very much a college town with "a unique feel that allows for people of many different cultures and backgrounds to feel at home." Dickson Street, the hub of Fayetteville nightlife, adjoins the campus, so you can revel with party-hardy undergrads any time you want to blow off your cases.

Getting In

Admitted students at the 25th percentile have LSAT scores around 153 and undergraduate grade point averages of about 3.19. At the 75th percentile, LSAT scores approach 160 and GPAs are 3.7 or so.

Clinical program required	No
Legal writing course requirement	Yes
Legal methods course requirement	No
Legal research course requirement	No
Moot court requirement	No
Public interest law requirement	No

ADMISSIONS

Selectivity Rating	86
# applications received	1,083
% applicants accepted	37
% acceptees attending	34
Median LSAT	156
LSAT Range (25th to 75th percentile)	153–158
Median undergrad GPA	3.52
Application fee	$0
Regular application deadline	4/1
Transfer students accepted	Yes
Evening division offered	No
Part-time accepted	No
CAS accepted	Yes

FINANCIAL FACTS

Annual tuition (in-state out-of-state)	$11,019/$24,156
Books and supplies	$1,278
Fees	$1,496
Financial aid application deadline	4/1
% first-year students receiving some sort of aid	86
% all students receiving some sort of aid	87
% of aid that is merit based	65
% receiving scholarships	40
Average grant	$6,289
Average loan	$20,672
Average total aid package	$21,439
Average debt	$57,873

EMPLOYMENT INFORMATION

Career Rating	90	# not seeking employment	1
Total 2012 JD Grads	132	State for bar exam	AR, GA, MO, OK, TX
% for whom you have useable information	99	Pass rate for first-time bar	85
% grads employed nine months out	90	**Prominent Alumni**	
Median starting salary	$60,000	Mark Pryor, U.S. Senator from Arkansas; George Haley, Former Ambassador to Gambia; Mike Beebe, Governor of Arkansas.	
% job accepting grads providing useable salary information	30		
# employed full-time	119	**Grads Employed by Field (%)**	
# employed part-time	0	Academic (1)	
# employed bar required	93	Business/Industry (21)	
# employed JD preferred	20	Government (7)	
# employed professional/other	3	Judicial Clerkship (5)	
# employed non-professional	3	Private Practice (51)	
# pursuing advanced degree	6	Public Interest (5)	
# unemployed and seeking employment	5		

University of Arkansas—Little Rock
William H. Bowen School of Law

INSTITUTIONAL INFORMATION

Public/private	Public
Affiliation	No Affiliation
Student-faculty ratio	13:1
% faculty part-time	65
% faculty female	33
% faculty underrepresented minority	15
Total faculty	124

SURVEY SAYS...

Heavy use of Socratic method, Diverse opinions accepted in classrooms, Great research resources, Great library staff

STUDENTS

Enrollment of law school	490
% male/female	54/46
% from out-of-state	38
% part-time	31
% underrepresented minority	20
% international	1
# of countries represented	2
Average age of entering class	27

ACADEMICS

Academic Experience Rating	83
Profs interesting rating	75
Profs accessible rating	79
Hours of study per day	3.23

Academic Specialties

Civil Procedure, Commercial, Constitutional, Corporation Securities, Criminal, Environmental, Government Services, International, Labor, Legal History, Property, Taxation

Combined Degrees Offered

JD/MBA, JD/MPA, JD/MPH (Master of Public Health), JD/MPS (Master of Public Service), JD/MST (Master of Science in Taxation), JD/PharmD (Doctor of Pharmacy) (3.5–4 years); JD/MD (7 years)

Academics

The "perfectly sized" University of Arkansas—Little Rock William H. Bowen School of Law is located "right in the heart of downtown Little Rock"—"the economic and government center of the state"—and it is thoroughly "tied into the local community through its connections with legislators, judges, government agencies, and private firms." Clerkships and externships are "bountiful." Access to part-time jobs at law firms is "second to none." Other perks at UALR include three clinical programs, five dual-degree programs, and "a bargain-basement price." There are around twenty different areas of concentration here and some students tell us that "the overall breadth of course choices makes it possible to study almost any topic you find particularly interesting." Others grumble that course selection is actually pretty limited. "Students here get a strong, basic legal education," says a 2L. "However, if you want more variety in more subject-specific courses, you won't really find them at this school."

Professors "expect you to come to class prepared." The faculty is "highly qualified, and there is a great mix of" adjuncts who teach specialized courses. Not every professor is great but most are "dedicated" teachers "who really want to see their students learn." "They make sure we understand," says a 1L, "and if we don't, they go back over it." Students also laud the legal writing program and say that the "writing instructors epitomize true excellence in their fields." Outside of class, faculty members are reportedly "very approachable." "The student body is small enough that you can have ample one-on-one time with the profs after hours," reports a 3L, "if you're brave enough." Student opinion concerning the administration is drastically split. Some students call management "incompetent." "The school is run like a low-budget movie set," charges a 2L. Other students contend that UALR is "very well-run." "The administration is very helpful and accessible," they contend, and the deans make "an effort to hear student comments and feedback, and implement changes accordingly."

The law school itself is "ugly-looking from the outside" and it's "in a rough section of town." The facility is "very pretty" on the inside, though, "with great marble stairs" and "nice views" from the upper levels. Incidentally, we think the "haunted floors" are just a legend. "Classrooms are top-notch" "with plenty of outlets" for laptops. "This law school is one of the only schools in the nation with state-of-the-art video lecture capture in nearly every room," beams a 3L. "Missed something in class? Watch it again, including any slides or videos that were shown." The building is also "fully equipped for Wi-Fi access and remote printing." There's a fabulous student lounge, too. Even "parking is awesome," which is something law students at many schools complain about to high heaven. "Overall, our school works to provide us with a comfortable environment," says a 2L. The spacious library is "the law library for the state of Arkansas, so it is excellent," too. The staff is "phenomenal." It's a public library, though, and "There are definitely some pro se misfits who can be distracting."

Life

Some students call UALR "a diverse school." Others argue, "There is not much diversity," beyond a solid contingent of nontraditional, older students. Views of the academic atmosphere also vary. "There are some students who are very competitive," relates a 3L, "and there are others like me who do the best that I can regardless of what others do." Other students say, "There is no rivalry" when it come to grades. "There is a definite sense that we are all in this together," says a 1L, "and most everyone is willing to help out a fellow student if that students asks."

VALERIE N. JAMES, ASSISTANT DEAN FOR ADMISSIONS
1201 MCMATH AVENUE, LITTLE ROCK, AR 72202-5142
TEL: 501-324-9903 FAX: 501-324-9433
E-MAIL: LAWADMISSIONS@VALR.EDU • WEBSITE: UALR.EDU / LAW

Socially, it's "a very congenial atmosphere." "There are plenty of student organizations." In addition, there are "wonderful lunch meetings and seminars, as well as dinner programs on a regular basis that accommodate both part-time and full-time students." "The school is intimate and definitely allows for getting acquainted with people," reports a 2L, though "if you're not from Arkansas it is a lot harder to find a social niche." Also, "there does seem to be a line" between the students who find it "hard turning down the temptation of going out" and those who would rather crack the books all day, every day. Beyond the confines of the law school, Little Rock is "the largest city in Arkansas," but it's "still a small town" that approximates "a suburb" when compared to a lot of bigger cities. "There is not a whole lot to do in Little Rock outside of school," explains a 2L. "There is a downtown area with bars and shops, but nothing huge."

Getting In

For admitted students at the 25th percentile, LSAT scores hover a little over 150 and undergraduate grade point averages are in the 3.0 range. At the 75th percentile, LSAT scores are around 157 and GPAs are a little under 3.6.

Clinical program required	No
Legal writing course requirement	Yes
Legal methods course requirement	Yes
Legal research course requirement	Yes
Moot court requirement	No
Public interest law requirement	No

ADMISSIONS

Selectivity Rating	90
# applications received	1,514
% applicants accepted	27
% acceptees attending	38
Median LSAT	154
LSAT Range (25th to 75th percentile)	151–157
Median undergrad GPA	3.27
Application fee	$0
Regular application deadline	4/15
Early application deadline	1/1
Transfer students accepted	Yes
Evening division offered	Yes
Part-time accepted	Yes
CAS accepted	Yes

FINANCIAL FACTS

Annual tuition (in-state out-of-state)	$10,062/$22,058
Books and supplies	$1,250
Fees	$1,395
Room & Board	$8,000
Financial aid application deadline	7/1
% receiving scholarships	36
Average grant	$5,090
Average loan	$19,500
Average total aid package	$19,500
Average debt	$26,000

EMPLOYMENT INFORMATION

Career Rating	81	**Grads Employed by Field (%)**
% grads employed nine months out	82	Academic (2)
Median starting salary	$50,000	Business/Industry (23)
State for bar exam	AR, TN, TX, GA, FL	Government (18)
Pass rate for first-time bar	86	Judicial Clerkship (5)
Prominent Alumni		Private Practice (49)
Vic Snyder, Member,U.S. Congress;		Public Interest (3)
Annabelle Imber Tuck, State Supreme		
Court; Colette Honorable, State Public		
Service Commission.		

UNIVERSITY OF CALIFORNIA
HASTINGS COLLEGE OF THE LAW

INSTITUTIONAL INFORMATION

Public/private	Public
Affiliation	No Affiliation
% faculty part-time	44
% faculty female	38
% faculty underrepresented minority	18
Total faculty	128

SURVEY SAYS...

Diverse opinions accepted in class-rooms, Great research resources, Great library staff, Abundant externship/internship/clerkship opportunities, Liberal students

STUDENTS

Enrollment of law school	1,100
% male/female	47/53
% from out-of-state	8
% part-time	0
% underrepresented minority	42
% international	1
# of countries represented	8
Average age of entering class	24

ACADEMICS

Academic Experience Rating	**86**
Profs interesting rating	79
Profs accessible rating	74
Hours of study per day	3.69

Academic Specialties

Criminal, International, Taxation, Intellectual Property

Advanced Degrees Offered

JD, 3 years; LLM, 1 year; MSL, 1 year

Combined Degrees Offered

JD and LLM degrees offered at Hastings; may combine JD with other institutions' masters' degrees, with some cross-crediting (e.g. JD/MBA can be completed together in 4 rather than 5 years separately)

Academics

UC Hastings is at the forefront of the legal education reformation. Indeed, the program staunchly places an emphasis on "practice [over] theory." This evolution is evident in Hastings' curriculum which only mandates a relatively small number of required courses. In turn, this allows students "to easily specialize and spend their time interning or externing." Additionally, the school provides what is arguably one of the "nation's best" moot courts and offers a "number of clinics" of which students can take advantage.

For the most part, students are impressed with their classroom experience. Although the average class size is fairly large, Hastings manages to accomplish the seemingly impossible and create an "intimate" feel. A first-year explains, "Despite the fact that there are 80 students in my section, I have made personal connections with each of my professors and feel as comfortable with them as I would expect if my section had ten students."

Speaking of professors, Hastings has managed to attract "a number of leaders in their respective fields." One fortunate first-year quickly chimes in, "The professors are not only highly regarded scholars, that many times have written the text for the course, but have also been great teachers with ample time for students." Overall, the faculty offers a "great mix of personalities, interests, backgrounds, credentials, etc." This might offer some insight into why they fervently "encourage and acknowledge different opinions." Finally, just as essential, professors are "always…approachable and willing to engage with students."

Perhaps one of Hastings greatest strengths is its Career Center. Counselors are "always available and work with every student association, and the administration to make getting a job easy and to ensure that students feel prepared for the future." An incredulous first-year quickly adds, "They even have a program to help you determine what kind of LIFE you want to have, and whether it even includes typical lawyering." Beyond the Career Center, students can also tap into a "huge alumni base, particularly in the Bay area" when seeking employment.

Students also happily report that Hastings administrators are a "supportive" bunch. Generally, they "are responsive to any issues and remedy problems as quickly as possible." One particularly pleased third-year student expresses gratitude to them for swiftly "eliminating bad professors upon negative feedback from students." However, there are a handful of students who feel that the administration could "communicate better with students and keep them more informed."

GREG CANADA, ASSISTANT DEAN OF ADMISSIONS
200 MCALLISTER STREET, SAN FRANCISCO, CA 94102
TEL: 415-565-4623 FAX: 415-581-8946
E-MAIL: ADMISS@UCHASTINGS.EDU • WEBSITE: WWW.UCHASTINGS.EDU

Life

There's a lot of which to take advantage outside the classroom at Hastings. To begin with, "The alumni and career centers put on interesting and informational lawyer and alumni panels on a weekly basis." Additionally, there are also "excellent health and counseling resources" and there "are always lots of social events to attend." A content third-year offers some more insight, "I saw three Supreme Court Justices speak, attended panels and symposiums with top lawyers, even work[ed] with several super lawyers."

Further, Hastings prime location in San Francisco's Tenderloin neighborhood also means that students have a myriad of professional opportunities at their fingertips. As a third-year brags, "we are so close to so many law firms and attorneys- the networking opportunities and proximity to firms/externships is unparalleled." A second-year adds, "UC Hastings is walking distance from both state and federal trial and appellate courts, in addition to numerous government agencies. I can take a class that begins ten minutes after my externship ends at the US.. Attorney's Office (and not be late)." Finally, yet another classmate confirms declaring, "there is no better legal mecca than our area. It is also centrally located in the city and on main public transportation, making it easy for commuters."

Getting In

Hastings maintains a competitive application process. The median undergraduate GPA for accepted candidates is 3.59 and the median LSAT score is 162. Applicants who think Hastings might be their first choice are encouraged to apply via the program's early commitment option.

Clinical program required	No
Legal writing course requirement	Yes
Legal methods course requirement	No
Legal research course requirement	Yes
Moot court requirement	Yes
Public interest law requirement	No

ADMISSIONS

Selectivity Rating	89
# applications received	4,811
% applicants accepted	30
% acceptees attending	22
Median LSAT	162
LSAT Range (25th to 75th percentile)	157–165
Median undergrad GPA	3.58
Application fee	$75
Regular application deadline	3/1
Regular notification	4/30
Transfer students accepted	Yes
Evening division offered	No
Part-time accepted	No
CAS accepted	Yes

FINANCIAL FACTS

Annual tuition (in-state out-of-state)	$43,486/$49,486
Books and supplies	$1,150
Fees	$3,089
Room & Board	$14,040
Financial aid application deadline	3/1
% first-year students receiving some sort of aid	92
% all students receiving some sort of aid	92
% of aid that is merit based	1
% receiving scholarships	83
Average grant	$16,281
Average loan	$44,050
Average total aid package	$57,870
Average debt	$114,736

EMPLOYMENT INFORMATION

Career Rating	83
Total 2012 JD Grads	443
% for whom you have useable information	98
% grads employed nine months out	74
Median starting salary	$74,500
% job accepting grads providing useable salary information	64
# employed full-time	256
# employed part-time	73
# employed bar required	283
# employed JD preferred	35
# employed professional/other	7
# employed non-professional	4
# pursuing advanced degree	3
# unemployed and seeking employment	94
# not seeking employment	3
% grads employed by school	7
State for bar exam	CA, NY, AZ, FL, NV
Pass rate for first-time bar	78.1

Prominent Alumni
Marvin Baxter, Associate Justice, CA Supreme Court; Willie Brown, Former Mayor, San Francisco; Carol Corrigan, Associate Justice, CA Supreme Court.

Grads Employed by Field (%)
Academic (2)
Business/Industry (9)
Government (12)
Judicial Clerkship (2)
Private Practice (42)
Public Interest (7)

UNIVERSITY OF CALIFORNIA—BERKELEY
BERKELEY LAW

INSTITUTIONAL INFORMATION

Public/private	Public
% faculty female	36
% faculty underrepresented minority	20
Total faculty	144

SURVEY SAYS...
Great library staff, Liberal students, Students love Berkeley, CA

STUDENTS

Enrollment of law school	916
% male/female	47/53
% from out-of-state	44
% part-time	0
% underrepresented minority	47
Average age of entering class	24

ACADEMICS

Academic Experience Rating	**97**
Profs interesting rating	85
Profs accessible rating	86
Hours of study per day	3.47

Academic Specialties
Corporation Securities, Environmental, International, Intellectual Property

Advanced Degrees Offered
LLM; JSD; Ph.D. in Jurisprudence and Social Policy.

Combined Degrees Offered
JD/MA; JD/MBA School of Business; JD/MA Asian Studies; JD/MA International Area Studies; JD/MCP Department of City and Regional Planning; JD/MJ Graduate School of Journalism; JD/MPP School of Public Policy; JD/MSW School of Social Welfare; JD/MA. Information Management Systems; JD/MS Energy and Resources Group. JD/Masters combined degrees average 4 years to completion.

Academics

UC Berkeley School of Law is indisputably one the nation's most celebrated citadels of legal education. The curriculum includes a great mix of legal theory and practical courses, and the breadth of specialized courses is dazzling. "Students have the opportunity to pursue virtually any sub-genre of the law and receive credit for it," says a satisfied 3L. "There are extensive externship opportunities at nonprofit organizations and governmental agencies." There are nearly a dozen journals. Unlike at most law schools, all of them (except for the Law Review) are open membership, and students are allowed to participate immediately. Students tell us that the immense clinical opportunities "are the absolute highlight of Boalt," though. "We get to start clinical opportunities, just like journals, from day one," gloats a 1L. "There are a number of 1L clinics in employment, education, immigration and asylum, tenant rights, homeless aid—you name it."

The "illustrious" faculty at Berkeley Law is crammed with "almost frighteningly brilliant" professors who are "some of the most well-known and well-respected scholars in the field." The "quality of instruction can vary widely" "from the poor to the most excellent," but it's always worth showing up to lectures for the dynamic classroom interaction. "Boalt's intellectual rigor is most evident in class discussions," reports a 2L, "where students' learnedness, insightfulness, and curiosity come shining through." Outside of class, professors are "incredibly devoted," "always approachable," and "want to develop relationships." Sipping coffee with faculty members is practically customary, and it's not uncommon to go to a professor's house "for sushi and great wine, while discussing the Uniform Commercial Code." Some students are "disgruntled" with the top brass, especially in light of ever-increasing tuition. However, even the harshest critics admit that management "runs things fairly smoothly." "The administration is always ready to help," declares a 1L, "whether it's dealing with the crashing of a laptop during a final or hearing and considering an idea for school improvement."

Like every other law school, Berkeley Law is engaged in "a constant arms race to be better positioned for firm hiring." The difference is that Berkeley usually wins. The "name has street cred," and the Career Development Office "can and will help you find a job." Job opportunities are beyond plum, and the school's prestigious reputation helps students land summer associate jobs and extravagantly salaried full-time positions at prestigious firms around the country. Also, the loan repayment assistance program for students who choose to go work in the public interest is one of the best in the nation.

"No one picks Boalt for its facilities," and "Boalt's exterior will never be much to write home about." However, the interior of the school is "generally quite up-to-date," if not "freaking gorgeous." "Classrooms are pretty standard, not really good or bad," but they're "modern and laptop friendly." The newly renovated library boasts a pretty striking reading room and, as you would expect, world-class resources.

Life

Students at Berkeley Law are "weird" and "wildly intelligent, but not wildly egotistical." "Diversity is wonderful." "Every student at Berkeley is passionate about something, and it is just incredible to hear their experiences," gushes a 2L. Views of the political landscape are conflicting. Some students find it "overly politically correct." "The liberal Bezerkeley mania occasionally—not as often as you'd expect—takes over the student body and affects the tenor of class discussions," says a 1L. However, liberalism isn't unconditionally pervasive. "I am very conservative and haven't even noticed which side of the political scale most people fall on," relates a 1L, "because no one really shoves

EDWARD TOM, ASSISTANT DEAN OF ADMISSIONS
2850 TELEGRAPH AVENUE, SUITE 500, BERKELEY, CA 94705-7220
TEL: 510-642-2274 FAX: 510-643-6222
E-MAIL: ADMISSIONS@LAW.BERKELEY.EDU • WEBSITE: WWW.LAW.BERKELEY.EDU

it in your face, especially the professors." "There are weirdos from the right and the left here," adds a wizened 3L, "who all come together to learn and grow."

Academically, "The culture is fantastic." It's "an atmosphere that's as noncompetitive as you can hope for with a building full of law students." "Even the gunners are relaxed." The relatively tolerant grading scale (which is sort of an all-or-nothing curve) relieves a lot of pressure. Still, "No matter how smart you are, you have to try hard." Beyond the confines of the classroom, a multitude of clubs and organizations forms the backbone of student life. "Boalt is a collegial place," reports a 2L. "Students have fun studying together, partying together, and just hanging out." "Berkeley quirkiness," "great weather" at all times of the year, and the fact that "you get to live and work in the Bay Area" are also fabulous perks. "If you have to spend three years studying law," counsels a happy 2L, "there's no better place than Berkeley to do it."

Getting In

It's extremely difficult to get admitted to Berkeley Law. Admitted students at the 25th percentile have LSAT scores around 162 and undergraduate GPAs just higher than 3.6. At the 75th percentile, LSAT scores are approximately 170, and GPAs are pretty close to 3.9.

Clinical program required	No
Legal writing course requirement	Yes
Legal methods course requirement	Yes
Legal research course requirement	Yes
Moot court requirement	Yes
Public interest law requirement	No

ADMISSIONS

Selectivity Rating	99
# applications received	7,024
% applicants accepted	12
% acceptees attending	32
Median LSAT	161
LSAT Range (25th to 75th percentile)	164–170
Median undergrad GPA	3.81
Application fee	$75
Regular application deadline	2/1
Regular notification	4/1
Transfer students accepted	Yes
Evening division offered	No
Part-time accepted	No
CAS accepted	Yes

FINANCIAL FACTS

Annual tuition (in-state/out-of-state)	$46,348/$50,335
Books and supplies	$1,446
Fees	$3,990
Room & Board	$1,602
Financial aid application deadline	3/2
% first-year students receiving some sort of aid	78
% all students receiving some sort of aid	78
% of aid that is merit based	3
% receiving scholarships	44
Average grant	$1,448
Average loan	$51,770
Average total aid package	$59,692
Average debt	$141,053

EMPLOYMENT INFORMATION

Career Rating	98	Grads Employed by Field (%)
% grads employed nine months out	96	Academic (1)
Median starting salary	$160,000	Business/Industry (1)
State for bar exam	CA	Government (7)
Pass rate for first-time bar	91.6	Judicial Clerkship (11)
		Private Practice (69)
		Public Interest (111)

UNIVERSITY OF CALIFORNIA—DAVIS
SCHOOL OF LAW

INSTITUTIONAL INFORMATION

Public/private	Public
Affiliation	No Affiliation
% faculty part-time	24
% faculty female	41
% faculty underrepresented minority	31
Total faculty	74

SURVEY SAYS...

Diverse opinions accepted in class-rooms, Great library staff, Liberal students

STUDENTS

Enrollment of law school	569
% male/female	53/47
% from out-of-state	17
% part-time	0
% underrepresented minority	39
% international	3
Average age of entering class	24

ACADEMICS

Academic Experience Rating	**92**
Profs interesting rating	93
Profs accessible rating	93
Hours of study per day	3.42

Academic Specialties

Criminal, Environmental, Human Rights, International, Taxation, Intellectual Property

Advanced Degrees Offered

JD, 3 years; LLM, 1 year

Combined Degrees Offered

JD/MBA, 4 years; JD/MA or JD/MS, 4 years

Academics

The "cozy" University of California—Davis, School of Law is "one of the smallest law schools in California." The "dynamic" professors here "know what they're talking about" and are "passionate about teaching." Sure, some teachers are less student-oriented but overall, "The faculty is the best part of King Hall." "Most use some form or other of the Socratic Method." "My professors have at least added humor to my life, ranging from role play (like arresting people in class) and poking fun at our being stumped over relatively simple questions just because it's sometimes terrifying to be called on," relates a 2L. These "incredibly approachable" professors are also "willing to help in anyway they can to enhance your education or career goals." Tutors in the highly praised teaching assistant program "hold office hours and review sessions to solidify big-picture concepts" for 1Ls. The UCD administration is good at "seeking student involvement in decision-making."

The whopping twelve clinics at UCD "are a great way to really understand how to practice law." The prison law clinic in particular "has enjoyed a great deal of success and acclaim." There are certificate programs in public service law and environmental law, and students say they are "truly are committed to public interest work." "We take the fact that we are named after Martin Luther King Jr. very seriously," asserts a 2L. "It's great to be in an environment where people truly care about cause lawyering." However, many students pine for more of a course selection. "About one-fourth of a class has the opportunity to take Pre-Trial Skills, but there are so many classes like Latinos and the Law and Disability Rights with classrooms that sit half empty."

As for employment, alumni are "supportive," and with San Francisco and Sacramento nearby, "Davis is conveniently connected to two powerful cities that are full of federal, state, and local agencies as well as important judicial offices." The school has responded to students' complaints that Career Services "needs to get its act together" by hiring new staff, including a new Assistant Dean. "'Big-law' possibilities are fairly good," and "approximately 25 percent of the student body will work in a large law firm after graduation." There is "an awesome loan forgiveness program" for graduates who pursue public interest careers.

The King Law building recently underwent a massive expansion and renovation, which included the construction of new classrooms and offices, as well as a new appellate courtroom. The library is an "exceptional" research facility, but it's "grungy," "with a little bit of a 1960s industrial feel." "Fortunately the school is about to undergo a dramatic facelift." "Future classes should have newer and more spacious facilities." The library rennovations are scheduled for completion at the end of 2012.

Life

Student diversity is comparatively strong on campus, with a visible "Asian and Pacific Islander" presence and a "decent" Hispanic student population. "There are active Jewish, Muslim, and Catholic student groups in the law school, as well as a feminist forum, a pro-choice group, a GLBT group, and a Federalist society." Politically, "Students are often very liberal or very conservative," and "Moderates aren't very vocal."

SHARON L. PINKNEY, DIRECTOR OF ADMISSION
SCHOOL OF LAW-KING HALL, 400 MRAK HALL DRIVE, DAVIS, CA 95616-5201
TEL: 530-752-6477
E-MAIL: ADMISSIONS@LAW.UCDAVIS.EDU • WEBSITE: WWW.LAW.UCDAVIS.EDU

"There is certainly competition" among students, but "the King Hall Spirit" "keeps it from getting dirty or uncomfortable." "A laid-back atmosphere" permeates. "People loan notes and books without a qualm." "Not that we all hold hands in the hallway and sing Kumbaya," elaborates a 3L, "but everybody is very respectful and has a good time together." Socially, "Most people find a niche," and events and parties occur "pretty much every weekend." "There are a large number of traditions at King Hall that students really get into" as well, including "softball and bowling leagues, the law school talent show, and a law school prom." "While these may seem lame and tacky, they are actually really fun, and the large majority of students get involved," explains a 3L. There's also "a co-op nursery, so students with children can drop their kids off while in class."

"The city of Davis is a delightful college town." "You don't have to fight traffic, and people are just downright friendly." "Armies of students ride bicycles to classes, and the fun downtown area is a short walk from campus." There is a "dearth of interesting restaurants," but "The weather is nice." "You can focus," notes a 3L, because "It's quiet." "Davis is a fantastic place to spend three years of graduate school," adds another 3L.

"Sacramento is fifteen minutes away and the Bay Area is only an hour [away]." "Great skiing" and "wine country" are not far. Davis is also "a town where hippies settle down after...making high salaries." As a result, apartments aren't cheap. "The housing crunch cannot be overstated enough," warns a 2L. "Students considering Davis should immediately check Craigslist and do everything in their power to get housing secured as soon as they accept."

Getting In

Admitted students at the 25th percentile have LSAT scores of 161 and GPAs of nearly 3.5. Admitted students at the 75th percentile have LSAT scores of 165 and GPAs of 3.8. UC Davis will consider all LSAT scores and asks that applicants add an addendum explaining increases of 5 points or more for multiple LSAT scores.

Clinical program required	No
Legal writing course requirement	Yes
Legal methods course requirement	Yes
Legal research course requirement	Yes
Moot court requirement	No
Public interest law requirement	No

ADMISSIONS

Selectivity Rating	87
# applications received	3,499
% applicants accepted	36
% acceptees attending	15
Average LSAT	163
Median LSAT	164
LSAT Range (25th to 75th percentile)	161–165
Average undergrad GPA	3.60
Median undergrad GPA	3.63
Application fee	$75
Regular application deadline	2/1
Early application deadline	2/1
Transfer students accepted	Yes
Evening division offered	No
Part-time accepted	No
CAS accepted	Yes

FINANCIAL FACTS

Annual tuition (in-state out-of-state)	$0/$12,245
Books and supplies	$1,014
Fees	$46,570
Room & Board (on/off campus)	$0/$12,113
Financial aid application deadline	3/2
% first-year students receiving some sort of aid	85
% all students receiving some sort of aid	85
% of aid that is merit based	26
% receiving scholarships	75
Average grant	$23,000
Average loan	$37,920
Average total aid package	$60,920
Average debt	$96,664

EMPLOYMENT INFORMATION

Career Rating	89	% grads employed by school	13
Total 2012 JD Grads	202	State for bar exam	CA, NY, MA, NV, OR
% for whom you have useable information	98	Pass rate for first-time bar	80
% grads employed nine months out	88	**Prominent Alumni**	
Median starting salary	$69,000	Tani Cantil-Sakauye, Chief Justice, California Supreme Court; Darrell Steinberg, President Pro Tem, California State Senate; George Miller, Member, US House of Representatives, CA 7th district.	
% job accepting grads providing useable salary information	72		
# employed full-time	144		
# employed part-time	33	**Grads Employed by Field (%)**	
# employed bar required	135	Academic (15)	
# employed JD preferred	29	Business/Industry (10)	
# employed professional/other	3	Government (10)	
# employed non-professional	0	Judicial Clerkship (2)	
# pursuing advanced degree	5	Military (1)	
# unemployed and seeking employment	12	Private Practice (43)	
# not seeking employment	3	Public Interest (6)	

UNIVERSITY OF CALIFORNIA—LOS ANGELES
SCHOOL OF LAW

INSTITUTIONAL INFORMATION

Public/private	Public
% faculty part-time	37
% faculty female	33
% faculty underrepresented minority	13
Total faculty	181

SURVEY SAYS...

Great research resources, Great library staff, Students love Los Angeles, CA

STUDENTS

Enrollment of law school	994
% male/female	55/45
% from out-of-state	33
% part-time	0
% underrepresented minority	17
% international	1
# of countries represented	11
Average age of entering class	25

ACADEMICS

Academic Experience Rating	**96**
Profs interesting rating	87
Profs accessible rating	85
Hours of study per day	3.41

Academic Specialties

Constitutional, Corporation Securities, Criminal, Environmental, Human Rights, International, Labor, Legal Philosophy, Property, Taxation, Intellectual Property

Combined Degrees Offered

JD/MA (African American Studies), JD/MA (American Indian Studies), JD/MBA, JD/Ph.D. (Philosophy), JD/MPH, JD/MA (Public Policy), JD/MSW (Social Welfare), and JD/MURP (Urban and Regional Planning). Students may also create a tailored program by undertaking work from multiple disciplines within UCLA an apply to the JD program; or students may design a joint program with another school with administrative approval.

Academics

At UCLA's law school, "The professors are all studs in their field, and most teach 1L courses. It's pretty cool to have a famous professor as a teacher in your first year." Students feel like a priority to their professors and administrators despite the size of the student population, saying "Considering UCLA is a large university, the law school feels small and friendly." They laud their professors, especially, for being "some of the most incredible, engaging and intelligent people I have ever met" and appreciate that they've been invited "to meals with or been at the homes of most of my professors." UCLA's "brilliant, renowned, accessible, kind" professors do a great job balancing professional and pedagogical responsibilities: "the number of professors who are considered authorities within their realm of expertise is unreal, and to know that these highly-reputed figures are willing to open their office for you because they truly care about your learning is incredible." Indeed, students perceive their professors to be "completely committed to forming talented attorneys who will contribute to society."

UCLA law is "very progressive" and forward-looking in the legal field, resulting in an "incredibly impressive" "diversity of classes, opinions, [and] extracurricular programs." "The David J. Epstein Program in Public Interest Law and Policy and the Critical Race Studies Program are two very unique and well-run specializations", and many "in-depth classes in particular areas" engage students. "The quality of discussion in the classroom is superb" across the board, and students credit this partially to the program's "ample diversity." When it comes to grading, the curve is kind: "The curve once you're in upper division classes is at a B+, so that's quite nice."

In their interactions with the administration, students often report that they've "greatly benefited from the services and support" of particular programs like "the Public Interest Law Program and the Critical Race Studies Program. I have a post-graduation job already thanks to the advice and support I received from the Public Interest Law Program's office." For budding attorneys looking to practice in California (who may be the best served by a UCLA degree, as some students complain that the school has "no network on the east coast"), UCLA offers "access to more people and resources in the entertainment industry than any school in the country," as well as "great connections to the legal community and access to jobs and internships." In general, students find that "The administration is unbelievably supportive and communicative", while also encountering that, not unusually for a large, public university, "There is a lot of red tape when trying to do anything out of the ordinary." "In terms of facilities", they critique, "The law school building itself is a bit of a mixed bag. I think they're in the process of renovating rooms continuously, so every semester a new room gets redone, but the two really big lecture halls are pretty outdated."

ROBERT SCHWARTZ, DEAN OF ADMISSIONS AND FINANCIAL AID
71 DODD HALL, BOX 951445, LOS ANGELES, CA 90095-1445
TEL: 310-825-2080 FAX: 310-206-7227
E-MAIL: ADMISSIONS@LAW.UCLA.EDU • WEBSITE: WWW.LAW.UCLA.EDU

Life

Socially, "The culture is competitive (it's law school, after all) while still being friendly and collegial." "Overall, students here are very cooperative and helpful", and value the "community atmosphere" that the program cultivates. They're incredibly proud of the school's "Diversity": "The school is full of people who come from different backgrounds and ethnicity, and there is absolutely no barrier between them." Conservative-leaning students sometimes feel the university could do better at "Offering a more politically balanced and neutral environment."

Unsurprisingly, the perks of UCLA's geographic location are popular: "Though you have no life as a 1L here, there is something amazing about being able to study on the beach in 70 degree whether in the middle of December." "In between classes and at lunch, everyone hangs out in the central courtyard and soaks in the LA sunshine." This contributes, undoubtedly, to the "congenial student body" and an greater environment that students extol as "challenging, diverse, and rewarding."

Getting In

For the class of 2015, the median LSAT spread was 164-169, and the median GPA spread was 3.58 to 3.89. Students say UCLA does an unusually good job integrating JD and LLM candidates.

Clinical program required	No
Legal writing course requirement	Yes
Legal methods course requirement	Yes
Legal research course requirement	Yes
Moot court requirement	No
Public interest law requirement	No

ADMISSIONS

Selectivity Rating	94
# applications received	6,117
% applicants accepted	24
% acceptees attending	21
Median LSAT	168
LSAT Range (25th to 75th percentile)	164–169
Median undergrad GPA	3.78
Application fee	$75
Regular application deadline	2/1
Early application deadline	11/15
Early application notification	12/31
Transfer students accepted	Yes
Evening division offered	No
Part-time accepted	No
CAS accepted	Yes

FINANCIAL FACTS

Annual tuition (in-state out-of-state)	$47,464/$53,959
Books and supplies	$1,812
Room & Board	$14,172
Financial aid application deadline	3/2
% first-year students receiving some sort of aid	87
% all students receiving some sort of aid	89
% receiving scholarships	77
Average grant	$17,954
Average loan	$45,776
Average total aid package	$52,049
Average debt	$109,539

EMPLOYMENT INFORMATION

Career Rating	97
Total 2012 JD Grads	333
% grads employed nine months out	91
Median starting salary	$135,000
# employed full-time	266
# employed part-time	36
# employed bar required	280
# employed JD preferred	20
# employed professional/other	2
# employed non-professional	0
# pursuing advanced degree	4
# unemployed and seeking employment	19
# not seeking employment	5
% grads employed by school	12
State for bar exam	CA
Pass rate for first-time bar	89

Prominent Alumni

Senator Kirsten Gillibrand '91, United States Senator, New York; David Steiner '86, Chief Executive Officer, Waste Management, Inc.; The Honorable Alex Kozinski '75, Chief Judge of the United States Court of Appeals for the Ninth Circuit.

Grads Employed by Field (%)

Academic (1)
Business/Industry (8)
Government (8)
Judicial Clerkship (7)
Military (1)
Private Practice (55)
Public Interest (11)

THE UNIVERSITY OF CHICAGO
LAW SCHOOL

INSTITUTIONAL INFORMATION

Public/private	Private
% faculty part-time	20
% faculty female	30
% faculty underrepresented minority	14
Total faculty	138

SURVEY SAYS...
Heavy use of Socratic method, Diverse opinions accepted in classrooms, Great research resources, Great library staff, Abundant externship/internship/clerkship opportunities

STUDENTS

Enrollment of law school	610
% male/female	57/43
% from out-of-state	86
% part-time	0
% underrepresented minority	27
% international	3
Average age of entering class	24

ACADEMICS

Academic Experience Rating	99
Profs interesting rating	99
Profs accessible rating	98
Hours of study per day	3.47

Academic Specialties
Civil Procedure, Commercial, Constitutional, Corporation Securities, Criminal, Environmental, Government Services, Human Rights, International, Labor, Legal History, Legal Philosophy, Property, Taxation, Intellectual Property

Advanced Degrees Offered
JD, 3 years; LLM, 1 year; JSD (depends on Dissertation) (up to 5 years)

Combined Degrees Offered
JD/MBA, 4 years; JD/Ph.D. in conjunction with Graduate School of Business (depends on dissertation); JD/MA Public Policy, 4 years; JD/MA International Relations, 4 years

Academics

The rigorous and ultra-prestigious Law School at The University of Chicago offers "an incredibly dynamic educational environment full of quirky but brilliant professors and an eclectic mix of students." "Expectations are high" and a unique trimester system means "There is little rest for the weary." Even so, students report, "There is no other place like The University of Chicago when it comes to intellectual curiosity." Course work is cerebral and highly analytical. Classes "have a strong theoretical bent" and are "geared to those who like thinking about the law." Chicago is virtually synonymous with the interdisciplinary combination of law and economics. The humanities, the social sciences, and the natural sciences are all integrated into the curriculum as well.

Students swear that their school has, "without a doubt, the best faculty in the country." The professors are "unquestionably the greatest part of this school." Somehow "they manage to produce brilliant work" while maintaining "a real emphasis on teaching" and making students "feel like top priority." "It's incredible to take classes from...Richard Epstein, and numerous others as a 1L, and to find out how accessible they are," beams one satisfied student. These "rock stars of legal academia" "treat students with respect," "are often in the common areas, and readily have lunch with students." "I have been amazed by the accessibility of my professors, particularly considering who they are," says a 3L. "They are always available for office hours." "The professors can help you get amazing jobs, can impart unparalleled wisdom, and are the people who write the books you use," explains another student. "I don't know where they find the time."

The administration "makes the experience seamless" and is quite popular with most students. "I would call the administration extremely overqualified if it weren't for the negative implications of that label," says a 1L. "I can't imagine a more enthusiastic and at-your-service administration." "The law school tries harder than any other school I've heard of to make its students happy," declares another student. Career Services does a good job too. There are "no worries about jobs." "Over 400 employers compete for only 190 students in each class," so "everyone will get a great job (public or private) making top dollar." There are some complaints, though. "The grading system is a little bizarre. It's tough on the ego because nearly everyone gets the same grade." Students must "lottery" into many seminars and clinical programs. Once in, however, students say the law school's fifteen clinics are "great" for real-world experience. Though the recent introduction of a summer public interest program has guaranteed funding for public interest jobs, the majority of students become corporate lawyers.

"The facilities are state of the art" at the U of C, though the "boringly modern" architecture won't exactly elevate your soul—unless, of course, a floating-cube-of-glass design is your idea of beautiful. Inside the law school, "The 1L classrooms are gorgeous but cramped." The library has undergone extensive renovation recently and boasts "a great number of resources and a willing and helpful staff."

Life

Chicago is "small" and home to "an intense intellectual environment." "It's quite an experience to know that some of my friends will clerk for the Supreme Court and work at the highest level in the field," relates one student. Debates are "constant and vibrant." "Our faculty and student body has many liberals, libertarians, moderates, and conservatives," explains a 2L. "The political views...range from ultra-liberal to ultra-conservative, but all

ANN PERRY, ASSOCIATE DEAN FOR ADMISSIONS
1111 EAST 60TH STREET, CHICAGO, IL 60637
TEL: 773-702-9484 FAX: 773-834-0942
E-MAIL: ADMISSIONS@LAW.UCHICAGO.EDU • WEBSITE: WWW.LAW.UCHICAGO.EDU

viewpoints are respected. Great weight is placed on academic inquiry and discussion, as opposed to vacuous politicking." "People are very interested in learning and maturing as legal thinkers."

Many students tell us that the academic environment is "easygoing" and "mostly non-competitive." "It is an extremely friendly school with a low degree of competition," they say, where "2L and 3L students frequently offer their assistance to the 1L class." However, other students tell us "The competition is tough." "Students are definitely not laid-back about getting jobs," observes a 3L. "Even though everyone ends up with plenty of great job offers, students are intense and cutthroat."

Socially, there is "community atmosphere" and "a great attitude on campus." People are "interesting and cool" and "genuinely excited to be a part of the law school." "Lots of people…participate in social events." Because many people hail from outside the Midwest, everyone arrives looking for friends. "The 1L class bonds quickly." "The small class size is a phenomenal advantage because I feel as if I get to know everyone," comments a 1L. Also, "weekly events such as Wine Mess and Coffee Mess" are perennial social institutions where students mingle with classmates and professors. "Nearly every day there is free food for some political or legal guest speaker," which is great if you like "sandwiches, pizza, or Thai food." The biggest complaint about life here appears to be the law school's affordable but "inconvenient" Hyde Park location. When students need to get away for work or any other reason though, downtown Chicago is "easy enough to live in and get to school" by car, bike, or public transportation.

Getting In

If you can get admitted here, you can get admitted to virtually any law school in the country. Admitted students at 25th percentile have LSAT scores of about 169 and GPAs of about 3.6. Admitted students at 75th percentile have LSAT scores of 173 and GPAs over 3.8. If you take the LSAT a second time, Chicago will consider your higher score.

Clinical program required	No
Legal writing course requirement	Yes
Legal methods course requirement	Yes
Legal research course requirement	Yes
Moot court requirement	Yes
Public interest law requirement	No

ADMISSIONS

Selectivity Rating	98
# applications received	4,458
% applicants accepted	20
% acceptees attending	21
Median LSAT	171
LSAT Range (25th to 75th percentile)	167–173
Median undergrad GPA	3.9
Application fee	$75
Regular application deadline	2/1
Early application deadline	12/1
Early application notification	12/31
Transfer students accepted	Yes
Evening division offered	No
Part-time accepted	No
CAS accepted	Yes

FINANCIAL FACTS

Annual tuition	$49,875
Books and supplies	$1,755
Fees	$930
Room & Board	$13,590
Financial aid application deadline	2/1
% first-year students receiving some sort of aid	90
% all students receiving some sort of aid	84
% of aid that is merit based	75
% receiving scholarships	47
Average grant	$18,702
Average loan	$55,000
Average debt	$135,307

EMPLOYMENT INFORMATION

		Grads Employed by Field (%)
Career Rating	99	Business/Industry (4)
Total 2012 JD Grads	215	Government (3)
% for whom you have useable information	100	Judicial Clerkship (17)
% grads employed nine months out	99	Private Practice (67)
Median starting salary	$160,000	Public Interest (8)
# employed full-time	210	
# employed part-time	3	
# employed bar required	207	
# employed JD preferred	5	
# employed professional/other	1	
# employed non-professional	0	
# pursuing advanced degree	1	
# unemployed and seeking employment	1	
# not seeking employment	0	
% grads employed by school	0	
State for bar exam	IL, NY	
Pass rate for first-time bar	95.3	

UNIVERSITY OF CINCINNATI
COLLEGE OF LAW

INSTITUTIONAL INFORMATION

Public/private	Public
Student-faculty ratio	11:1
% faculty part-time	51
% faculty female	40
% faculty underrepresented minority	14
Total faculty	65

SURVEY SAYS...

Diverse opinions accepted in classrooms, Great library staff, Abundant externship/internship/clerkship opportunities, Good social life

STUDENTS

Enrollment of law school	386
% male/female	60/40
% part-time	0
% underrepresented minority	14
% international	1
Average age of entering class	24

ACADEMICS

Academic Experience Rating	74
Profs interesting rating	77
Profs accessible rating	85
Hours of study per day	3.79

Academic Specialties

Commercial, Corporation Securities, Criminal, Environmental, Human Rights, International, Labor, Taxation, Intellectual Property

Advanced Degrees Offered

JD, 3 years; LLM, 1 year

Combined Degrees Offered

JD/MBA, 4 years; JD/MCP, 4.5 years; JD/MA in Women's, Gender, and Sexuality Studies, 4 years; JD/MA in Political Science, 4 years

Academics

Students at the University of Cincinnati get the "small class sizes" and "intimate environment" typical of a private college while paying the comfortable, low tuition you would expect from a public institution. With roughly 125 students in each entering class, the school strikes an "excellent" balance with "its affordability, reputation, small class size, and excellent faculty. Students agree that UC professors are an "amazing and diverse group of people who care just as much for teaching and students as they do about publishing their own work." UC is particularly noted for its focus on "public interest" and "international" law; however, "There is no shortage of brilliant legal minds in a broad range of subjects—that goes for students as well as the professors." In addition to the accomplished tenured faculty, students rave about the school's recent acquisition of "exceptional young faculty members that have great teaching skills to match their great scholarship." A 2L sums it up, "As one of the smallest public law schools in the country, I feel my educational experience has been fantastic, and yet, at very little cost. Because our class consists of only 128 people, all of my professors know my name."

University of Cincinnati runs several "amazing" legal institutes and research centers focused on unique topics such as domestic violence, law and psychiatry, and corporate law. Through these centers, students can earn credit hours while doing fulfilling and useful work in the community. Many students make particular note of the Ohio Innocence Project, an institute at the University of Cincinnati through which students conduct substantive work to impact legislative reform, and work on real criminal cases. The institute also brings notable speakers to campus. Students also have the opportunity to research and write for the school's renowned publications, including the Human Rights Quarterly, Law Review, and Freedom Center Journal. While students at other schools might scramble for spots on the school's law review or clinic programs, "Since the school is small, each student can participate in and get involved in a number of organizations."

Thanks to an "ambitious but not overly competitive student body," the learning environment is charged, but not cutthroat, at University of Cincinnati. A 3L attests, "While academic achievement is always a numbers game in law school, the atmosphere at UC is nonpretentious and noncontentious." When it comes to the job and internship placements, University of Cincinnati maintains a "deep and well-regarded history as a legal educational institution" both locally and nationally. As a result, most students say the school "is a great place for students with all different kinds of career aspirations, and especially has a public interest/human rights orientation that I think is unparalleled in the Midwest." In fact, "Public interest students can actually obtain funding for their summer jobs through the school's Summer Public Interest Fellowship Program." Most UC grads stay in the Cincinnati area and meet with good results while those looking outside the region must do a little extra legwork to find a good placement. "While plenty of our grads go on to excellent careers in major firms, federal clerkships, and other government positions, I don't feel like our school does enough PR work to get out-of-town employers interested in our students," says one student.

Life

For starving students/aspiring lawyers, Cincinnati is an excellent home base offering the unbeatable combination of "small town prices (housing, dining, entertainment) with big city amenities." For both professional and recreational pursuits, the UC campus is pleasantly located "close to downtown so it's easy to get to work, ballgames, and entertainment." While Cincinnati has its charms, students complain that the law school could use "more outlets and better lighting." "Windows would be nice," adds another. However, students are optimistic that the school will consider remodeling the law school along with other campus projects. The good news is that "the new parking garage has been built, and there are brand-new (and attractive) living units pretty much right across the street." Not to mention that a few "ice cream shops have opened within a short walk from school."

Despite the rigors of the academic curriculum, "The students that are here create a suitable balance between academic and social life. There are plenty of opportunities to go out and have fun and not be completely overwhelmed with school." On and off campus, "There are frequently SBA social events for students, such as happy hours at local bars." In fact, the SBA is very active and "most of the students are friends and spend time together outside of the law school." On the other hand, students remind us that Cincinnati also attracts "a large contingent of commuter students who spend little if no time involved in the school outside of actual class."

Getting In

To apply to the University of Cincinnati College of Law, students must submit LSAT scores and register with the Law School Credential Assembly Service Report. If the LSAT was taken more than once, the highest score will be considered by the Admissions Committee. More than 1,300 hopefuls applied for 125 spots in the JD program. Students in the 25th percentile had LSAT scores of 156 and GPAs of 3.2, while those in the 75th percentile had LSAT scores of 161 and GPAs of 3.73.

Clinical program required	No
Legal writing course requirement	Yes
Legal methods course requirement	No
Legal research course requirement	Yes
Moot court requirement	No
Public interest law requirement	No

ADMISSIONS

Selectivity Rating	75
# applications received	1,356
% applicants accepted	59
% acceptees attending	13
Median LSAT	158
LSAT Range (25th to 75th percentile)	156–161
Median undergrad GPA	3.5
Application fee	$35
Regular application deadline	3/1
Early application deadline	12/1
Early application notification	1/15
Transfer students accepted	Yes
Evening division offered	No
Part-time accepted	No
CAS accepted	Yes

FINANCIAL FACTS

Annual tuition (in-state out-of-state)	$21,876/$39,384
Books and supplies	$1,539
Fees	$1,660
Room & Board	$16,797
Financial aid application deadline	3/1
% receiving scholarships	69
Average grant	$8,159
Average debt	$84,140

EMPLOYMENT INFORMATION

Career Rating	75
Total 2012 JD Grads	140
% for whom you have useable information	71
% grads employed nine months out	86
Median starting salary	$55,000
% job accepting grads providing useable salary information	44
# employed full-time	99
# employed part-time	21
# employed bar required	89
# employed JD preferred	19
# employed professional/other	6
# employed non-professional	6
# pursuing advanced degree	2
# unemployed and seeking employment	14
# not seeking employment	2
% grads employed by school	4
State for bar exam	OH, KY, NY, IN, IL

Prominent Alumni
Major General John D. Altenberg, Military; Cris Collinsworth, Journalist; Billy Martin, Wash, DC based high profile case attorney

Grads Employed by Field (%)
Academic (6)
Business/Industry (19)
Government (9)
Judicial Clerkship (2)
Military (4)
Private Practice (40)
Public Interest (6)

UNIVERSITY OF COLORADO
LAW SCHOOL

Academics

Colorado provides aspiring lawyers with an "intellectually challenging" environment and a myriad of opportunities in which "to begin honing [their] experiential skills." Indeed, the "emphasis on clinical programs and practical experience is second to none." When it comes to environmental law, Colorado is a powerhouse. As one second-year brags, "Our environmental law program is either one of the best or the best in the country depending on who you ask."

Students at Colorado are also privy to "topnotch" facilities and "excellent computer and library resources." A thrilled third-year adds, "The physical building that houses Colorado Law is stunning. It's hard to complain about spending a Saturday studying when you can see the mountains from the library windows." Additionally, the fantastic library staff is always "eager to help with research." They continually "partner with legal writing professors to introduce students to resources early on in the year." The Career Development Office also receives high marks. The office is "comprised of outstanding individuals who always make time to work with students, inform them of opportunities that interest them, and advise whenever required."

However, what "really makes Colorado Law stand out is the accessibility—and quality—of its faculty." For starters, the professors here continually show "genuine... interests in students." Another second-year boasts that, "every professor I have had at CU has known not only who I am, but my academic interests and how they correspond to their own." A deeply satisfied third-year interjects, "Most of the professors here are brilliant intellectuals and wonderful people. I will have lasting relationships with many of them long after I am graduated."

Echoing the care and openness displayed by the faculty, administrators are also heralded as "highly responsive" to the students' needs. A veteran third-year explains, "CU is such a small law school that I see everyone from the Deans to the Registrar, to the office assistants regularly, and I feel comfortable going to any of them with questions or problems that I need help resolving." Moreover, "they also go out of their ways to get to know students, share relevant information, and make it a positive academic experience."

Life

Though one might not associate legal education with the notion of good vibes, the sentiment does ring true for Colorado. Indeed, "The students who comprise CU Law are reflective of the friendly, caring administration and faculty. It's hard to stay cross at CU Law for more than an hour, because the positive atmosphere engulfing you makes you appreciate how good you have it." Truly, "this school's trump card is its quality of life." The "students, faculty, and staff here are all exceptionally friendly, and almost all seem to recognize that being a person should come before being an attorney."

KRISTINE JACKSON, ASSISTANT DEAN FOR ADMISSIONS & FINANCIAL AID
403 UCB, BOULDER, CO 80309-0403
TEL: 303-492-7203 FAX: 303-492-2542
E-MAIL: LAWADMIN@COLORADO.EDU • WEBSITE: WWW.COLORADO.EDU / LAW

Additionally, Colorado offers many educational opportunities beyond the classroom. As a second-year shares, "The school has gotten great guests during my two years (two Supreme Court justices, the Colorado Supreme Court, the 10th Circuit, the Federal Circuit, the Colorado Court of Appeals, and countless stars from the public and private sectors)." Of course, there are plenty of opportunities to kick back as well. In fact, "many students arrange their schedules so as not to have class on Friday so they can go skiing all weekend, and I have personally had an adjunct prof cancel a Thursday night class so he could go to Steamboat Springs with his family." Further, "there are loads of people who go out on weekends, whether it be partying, camping, exercising, or travelling. If you want to become a lawyer AND have a good time doing it, this is the place for you."

Getting In

The Colorado admissions office maintains some impressive stats. Amongst accepted applicants, the median undergraduate GPA is 3.65 and the median LSAT score is 164. While the school does not require any specific pre-law curriculum, classes that place an emphasis on analytical and writing skills are highly recommended. Finally, the program operates on a rolling admissions basis. Therefore, the earlier you apply the stronger your chances.

Clinical program required	No
Legal writing course requirement	Yes
Legal methods course requirement	Yes
Legal research course requirement	Yes
Moot court requirement	No
Public interest law requirement	No

ADMISSIONS

Selectivity Rating	87
# applications received	2,802
% applicants accepted	34
% acceptees attending	16
Average LSAT	162
Median LSAT	164
LSAT Range (25th to 75th percentile)	159–166
Average undergrad GPA	3.56
Median undergrad GPA	3.65
Application fee	$65
Regular application deadline	3/15
Regular notification	4/30
Transfer students accepted	Yes
Evening division offered	No
Part-time accepted	No
CAS accepted	Yes

FINANCIAL FACTS

Annual tuition (in-state out-of-state)	$29,718/$36,504
Books and supplies	$1,800
Fees	$1,777
Room & Board	$18,692
Financial aid application deadline	4/1
% first-year students receiving some sort of aid	82
% all students receiving some sort of aid	85
% of aid that is merit based	18
% receiving scholarships	61
Average grant	$12,546
Average loan	$38,930
Average total aid package	$39,758
Average debt	$100,813

EMPLOYMENT INFORMATION

Career Rating	86	**Prominent Alumni**
Total 2012 JD Grads	175	Wiley B. Rutledge, Former Associate
% for whom you have useable information	99	Justice, US Supreme Court; Bill Ritter, Jr., former Governor of Colorado; Roy Romer,
% grads employed nine months out	90	former Governor of Colorado.
Median starting salary	$50,100	**Grads Employed by Field (%)**
% job accepting grads providing useable salary information	79	Academic (1)
		Business/Industry (7)
# employed full-time	134	Government (13)
# employed part-time	24	Judicial Clerkship (15)
# employed bar required	116	Military (1)
# employed JD preferred	30	Private Practice (32)
# employed professional/other	9	Public Interest (11)
# employed non-professional	0	
# pursuing advanced degree	0	
# unemployed and seeking employment	10	
# not seeking employment	5	
% grads employed by school	9	
State for bar exam	CO, MN, IL, CA, TX	
Pass rate for first-time bar	89.3	

UNIVERSITY OF CONNECTICUT
SCHOOL OF LAW

INSTITUTIONAL INFORMATION

Public/private	Public
Affiliation	No Affiliation
Student-faculty ratio	11:1
% faculty part-time	63
% faculty female	31
% faculty underrepresented minority	10
Total faculty	119

SURVEY SAYS...

Great research resources, Great library staff, Beautiful campus

STUDENTS

Enrollment of law school	697
% male/female	55/45
% from out-of-state	30
% part-time	30
% underrepresented minority	21
% international	2
# of countries represented	10
Average age of entering class	25

ACADEMICS

Academic Experience Rating	**86**
Profs interesting rating	77
Profs accessible rating	75
Hours of study per day	3.65

Academic Specialties
Civil Procedure, Commercial, Constitutional, Corporation Securities, Criminal, Environmental, Government Services, Human Rights, International, Labor, Legal History, Legal Philosophy, Property, Taxation, Intellectual Property

Advanced Degrees Offered
JD, 3–4 years; LLM, U.S. Legal Studies, 1 year; LLM, Insurance, 1 year; SJD, 1 year.

Combined Degrees Offered
JD/MBA, JD/MLS, JD/MPA, JD/MSW, JD/MPH, JD/LLM Insurance Law. Each dual degree program is 4 years full-time.

Academics

The University of Connecticut School of Law is located in Hartford, the state's capital. The institution boasts all of "the resources of a large, public institution with the feel of a small, private school." The low in-state tuition is great for Connecticut residents looking for a deal.

The program has cultivated a "strong relationship with pretty much every firm/agency/government office in the state," though most students warn other law school applicants who are looking to practice outside of the state upon graduation to do their research. Career Services at UConn Law has a reputation of being "Connecticut-oriented" and "most of the recruitment is self-selecting/self-motivating," says a 3L.

The administration here is "excellent, very accessible, and very responsive to student needs and concerns." With the exception of the required curriculum, most students find professors to be "approachable" as well, says a 1L.

Once students reach the higher-level courses and specialties, they engage with teachers who possess valuable field experience and provide more practice-oriented instruction to prepare students for their career ahead. "I really get the sense that no one wants me to fail," says a 1L. "Many of the professors have been in the state for a number of years, and many of the lawyers and judges in Hartford, and Connecticut more generally, are alumni, which make opportunities for internships/clerkships very accessible," says a 2L. Overall, many students feel that they have the faculty's full support.

"The University of Connecticut offers a unique program, which allows students to spend a semester working at a federal agency in Washington, D.C. While participating in the program, my fellow classmates and I had exclusive access to the White House, Pentagon, and other various high profile Washingtonian landmarks," says a 3L.

Some students yearn for more evening classes while others just wish for "more classes" overall. In contrast students see the program's opportunities for specialization as its "greatest strength." One student sees this manifested in "the ability to conduct your own research project, as well as [to] compete in trial and appellate competitions across the country and conferences around the world."

However, one aspect of the school that students can agree upon is their love of the clinics offered on campus. "With a little work on your part it is relatively easy to get an externship experience that looks fantastic on a resume. Attorneys that I talk to look to see experiential learning and UCONN gives you that opportunity," says a 3L.

The recent renovation of the school's library has done much to enhance the productivity and esthetic of the UConn Law campus. "The library is absolutely beautiful and we have access to every resource imaginable. The library staff is very friendly and knowledgeable. The classrooms were recently updated and the courtrooms are impressive," informs a 3L.

Students gush about the school's "historic look, with a modern interior." Buildings have "state-of-the-art research capabilities and plenty of private study areas with full Internet access at every desk." "In my last seminar class, the flat screen television started ringing and we began a satellite conference call with someone in England," says a student.

Life

Students at UConn Law value the school's small size despite the fact that it's a public institution. The campus "really fosters a sense of community among students." "The community of students at UConn Law are some of the most diverse and friendly people I have met," says one 3L. "Every student is incredibly bright, but except for a couple students, each student supports his/her classmates. That is, the environment highly fosters friend-

KAREN DeMEOLA, ASSISTANT DEAN FOR ADMISSIONS AND STUDENT FINANCE
45 ELIZABETH STREET, HARTFORD, CT 06105
TEL: 860-570-5100 FAX: 860-570-5153
E-MAIL: ADMISSIONS@LAW.UCONN.EDU • WEBSITE: WWW.LAW.UCONN.EDU

ship and support for one another's achievements. It also enhances the learning environment." The "student body [is] deeply involved in student organization [and is] deeply involved in the greater Hartford area," says a 1L.

The city of Hartford is academically rich and is home to both UConn and Trinity College. The school has worked to improve the safety of its students on and around the school area.

On campus there is plenty to do in one's spare time despite the large number of commuter and part-time students. "Many activities [are] both structured and informal, in which the younger, full-time students make time to participate."

UConn Law also makes a concerted effort to be "very welcoming to LGBT students," displaying diversity in its student body as well as in its faculty. This, students say, enhances classes and "makes for very lively and interesting discussions."

Getting In

Students are admitted to UConn School of Law once annually, for entry in the fall semester. No numeric index is used to rank applicants to UConn School of Law (though the LSAT is required) and each applicant is considered individually; the school is also veteran-friendly. Connecticut residents receive special consideration in an admissions decision, though no absolute preference is given. Of the 182 1Ls accepted for the entering class of 2010, the undergraduate GPA was median 3.42 and the LSAT score was median 159.

Clinical program required	No
Legal writing course requirement	Yes
Legal methods course requirement	Yes
Legal research course requirement	Yes
Moot court requirement	Yes
Public interest law requirement	No

ADMISSIONS
Selectivity Rating	88
# applications received	1,897
% applicants accepted	31
% acceptees attending	23
Average LSAT	159
Median LSAT	159
LSAT Range (25th to 75th percentile)	157–163
Average undergrad GPA	3.42
Median undergrad GPA	3.45
Application fee	$60
Regular application deadline	3/15
Transfer students accepted	Yes
Evening division offered	Yes
Part-time accepted	Yes
CAS accepted	Yes

FINANCIAL FACTS
Annual tuition (in-state out-of-state)	$22,416/$43,632
Books and supplies	$1,390
Fees	$876
Room & Board	$12,160
Financial aid application deadline	3/15
% first-year students receiving some sort of aid	87
% all students receiving some sort of aid	80
% of aid that is merit based	7
% receiving scholarships	76
Average grant	$12,645
Average loan	$23,354
Average total aid package	$36,024
Average debt	$65,639

EMPLOYMENT INFORMATION

		Grads Employed by Field (%)
Career Rating	89	Academic (4)
Total 2012 JD Grads	179	Business/Industry (18)
% for whom you have useable information	93	Government (9)
% grads employed nine months out	83	Judicial Clerkship (12)
Median starting salary	$65,000	Military (2)
% job accepting grads providing useable salary information	66	Private Practice (50)
# not seeking employment	6	Public Interest (4)
% grads employed by school	0	
State for bar exam	CT, NY, MA	
Pass rate for first-time bar	90	

UNIVERSITY OF DAYTON
SCHOOL OF LAW

INSTITUTIONAL INFORMATION

Public/private	Private
Affiliation	Marianist
% faculty part-time	33
% faculty female	51
% faculty underrepresented minority	13
Total faculty	53

SURVEY SAYS...

Diverse opinions accepted in classrooms, Great research resources, Great library staff, Beautiful campus

STUDENTS

% part-time	0
Average age of entering class	26

ACADEMICS

Academic Experience Rating	65
Profs interesting rating	76
Profs accessible rating	81
Hours of study per day	3.82

Academic Specialties
Civil Procedure, Criminal, Property, Intellectual Property

Advanced Degrees Offered
JD, 3 years or 2.5 years (5 semester option)

Combined Degrees Offered
JD/MBA, 2–4 years

Academics

A small, Catholic-affiliated private school with a strong reputation in Ohio, the University of Dayton School of Law offers two JD options: a traditional three-year program and an accelerated two-year degree. No matter which course of study one chooses, the curriculum begins with ten core courses, followed by elective classes and upper-level seminars. When evaluating their academic experience, students dole out praises for the "incredible writing program," often citing the writing coursework as the school's greatest strength. They also love the fact that "classes are small," so students feel like "more than just a number to your professors"; although, they would love to see a "wider range of courses" offered to upper-level students.

Those who choose this "serious" school should come prepared to work hard. At this fast-paced program, students insist, "We study just as hard as any first year law student possibly could—the bar is set high, and those who do not meet it after their first semester are asked not to return." The good news is that "professors are extremely accessible" and "genuinely concerned with the success of their students," often "more than willing to meet with students outside of office hours and [to] make previous exams available." A 1L shares this rather reassuring advice, "If you do not study (the workload is considerable) you will fail, but if a person wants to be here, they just need to put in the work and they will be fine."

While UDSL recruits accomplished faculty, "The professors vary as far as quality" in the classroom. The majority of students maintain that "the professors are, for the most part, wonderful. They are all very knowledgeable and are willing to provide as much outside assistance as necessary." Many will even "incorporate trending interests such as pop, music, movies into their teaching materials." Unfortunately, a few UDSL professors love the sound of their own voice, making it "very difficult to learn and share opinions in class." Still, a few bad classes amount to "a small and limited experience" when measured up against the program as a whole. Students dispute the administration's effectiveness in managing the program, though they agree that the school's deans and officers are "quick to respond to student concerns and are very personable." Here, "both the Dean of Students and the Dean of the law school know most of the students by name"; however, frequent administrative glitches can be highly upsetting for students. For example, "grades are routinely incorrectly recorded," which can lead to problems when calculating a student's class rank.

Throughout the program, there is a "strong emphasis on real world preparation and bar passage." Traditional academics are complemented by courses in writing and research, clinical experience, and a capstone course, in which students must apply their skills to a real-world situation. Through the school's clinical programs, students also get experience "preparing all aspects of a case, from the initial client interview to preparing for trial and possibly even participating in a trial"; plus, "every student is required to take an externship somewhere in a legal office so that we get hands-on legal training." When it comes to hiring, students say the school has a "mostly regional appeal," with most students seeking employment in surrounding Dayton. A big benefit in the job market is that "the alumni are very involved," and the "school's alumni base stretches past the Midwest," reaching as far as western New York and other states.

JANET L. HEIN, ASST. DEAN, DIR. OF ADMISSIONS AND FINANCIAL AID
UNIVERSITY OF DAYTON SCHOOL OF LAW, 300 COLLEGE PARK, 112 KELLER HALL,
DAYTON, OH 45469-2760 • TEL: 937-229-3555 FAX: 937-229-4194
E-MAIL: LAWINFO@NOTES.UDAYTON.EDU • WEBSITE: WWW.UDAYTON.EDU/LAW

Life

In contrast to the rigors of the academic program, one student asserts, "There is a pervasive, pleasant, [and] professional atmosphere at this small school, and my fellow students tend to help one another out rather than compete with each other." Unlike some law programs, "people support one another here—those Midwestern values of honesty, decency, forthrightness, and fairness one hears about in the abstract have an actual, everyday existence here in Dayton." Beyond academics, "students are involved in student organizations," and "there are always school and non-school gatherings to attend" when you want to blow off steam. A 3L remembers, "Most (and I mean most) students went out numerous nights a week, partying and drinking at bars close to the law school." Though some choose the school for its Catholic affiliation, the school's Marianist ties are "downplayed" in most cases. For those who would like to incorporate Catholic ethics into their educational experience, "rich opportunities are present to get involved with the Catholic mission of the university."

Throughout the law school, students love the University of Dayton's atmosphere. "The building at UDSL is spectacular in terms of the library, classrooms, and the ease at using computers." Around them, "the undergraduate school is expanding; new buildings are sprouting all around campus." Sadly, "Dayton is a dying city," which offers fewer social and recreational activities than some students would like; however, "the surrounding area, such as Kettering or Oak Wood, are very safe and classy."

Getting In

Every year, University of Dayton strives to admit a diverse incoming class, comprised of students from a range of professional and personal backgrounds. While LSAT scores and undergraduate GPA are important factors, the school also looks at an applicant's professional experience, interests and extracurricular activities, graduate work, volunteer history, and background. The school operates a rolling admissions program from November 1 to April 1, and most applicants will receive a response in two to six weeks of submitting a completed application. For the most recent incoming class, the median undergraduate GPA was 3.1, with a 25th-75th percentile range of 2.78-3.37.

Clinical program required	Yes
Legal writing course requirement	Yes
Legal methods course requirement	Yes
Legal research course requirement	Yes
Moot court requirement	No
Public interest law requirement	No

ADMISSIONS

Selectivity Rating	67
# applications received	1,402
% applicants accepted	69
% acceptees attending	14
Median LSAT	149
LSAT Range (25th to 75th percentile)	146–152
Median undergrad GPA	3.11
Application fee	$0
Regular application deadline	5/1
Transfer students accepted	Yes
Evening division offered	No
Part-time accepted	No
CAS accepted	Yes

FINANCIAL FACTS

Annual tuition	$32,160
Books and supplies	$1,500
Fees	$398
Room & Board	$17,500
Financial aid application deadline	5/1
% first-year students receiving some sort of aid	72
% all students receiving some sort of aid	82
% of aid that is merit based	79
% receiving scholarships	82
Average grant	$10,857
Average loan	$36,862
Average total aid package	$39,997
Average debt	$118,333

EMPLOYMENT INFORMATION

Career Rating	79	State for bar exam	OH, NY, IL, PA, IN
Total 2012 JD Grads	174	Pass rate for first-time bar	73.1
% for whom you have useable information	93	**Prominent Alumni**	
% grads employed nine months out	82	Barbara Gorman, Judge, Common Pleas Court; Hinton Lucas, VP of Dupont; Honorable Mary Donovan, Justice of 2nd District Court of Appeals, Michael Coleman, Mayor, Columbus, Ohio.	
Median starting salary	$49,500		
# employed full-time	122		
# employed part-time	10		
# employed bar required	98	**Grads Employed by Field (%)**	
# employed JD preferred	15	Academic (3)	
# employed professional/other	12	Business/Industry (22)	
# employed non-professional	7	Government (14)	
# pursuing advanced degree	2	Judicial Clerkship (3)	
# unemployed and seeking employment	22	Military (3)	
# not seeking employment	3	Private Practice (50)	
% grads employed by school	0	Public Interest (5)	

UNIVERSITY OF DENVER
STURM COLLEGE OF LAW

Academics

The University of Denver's Sturm College of Law is "an outstanding school" in "a beautiful building in a beautiful city." The city of Denver provides a great boon to students, as there are "great networking events and close ties with the greater Denver law community." "Our greatest strength is that we feed into the city of Denver with our only other real competition being a smaller class from CU [University of Colorado] every year," a 1L brags. The "gorgeous" and "modern" law building has up-to-date technology "including wireless throughout, power and cable Ethernet hookups at each desk." Most classrooms have "lots of light" although "those with no windows feel like caverns." "The library is pretty well equipped" and there are "lots of places to study alone, converse with others, work on projects—whatever you need." Did we mention the "awesome views of the Rockies from third and fourth floors"?

The Sturm College of Law "places a large emphasis on experiential learning" although "there are many opportunities to explore the theoretical as well." This "focus on practical skill and real life application" means students are ready to work as soon as they graduate. While "the available courses are fairly diverse," one student says there is "too much focus on firms/corporate rather than government work, public interest, non-traditional, or novel/up-and-coming areas of law." The "focus on experiential learning...sets [Denver] students ahead of others in terms of being able to practice law" upon graduation. The "friendly, accessible, and helpful" professors "love working with students," even going so far as to "share their personal cell phone numbers for last minute questions before finals." Several students did feel that many of the first year professors "need to be re-evaluated" but empathized that the "upper level writing profs are great!" These professors are "not only knowledgeable about the theory of law, they are passionate and require students to apply the law in practical ways" with a focus on "hands on learning" such as the "mock trial program. Denver has a "really good faculty/student ratio and the classes are usually no more than 20 once you get past your first year." "The Academic Achievement Program and accessibility of faculty really bolster the academic success of the students at DU Law," a 1L notes.

"Everything runs smoothly with the administration," and the dean "is particularly accessible." The administration "is very concerned with employability of the students and it shows through the many program offerings available throughout the week." However, the downside to the administration is the "incredibly rude" registrar's office that is not "willing to accommodate student needs." The career services office gets mixed reviews, some saying they are "extremely helpful and accessible" and others saying point blank: "The career services DO NOT HELP in finding a job." Overall, students deem the Denver law experience "excellent. Period." "The bar preparation/success program has helped raise DU's bar passage rates well into 90 percent!" a 3L boasts.

YVONNE CHERENA-PACHEO, ASSOCIATE DIRECTOR OF ADMISSIONS
2255 E. EVANS AVENUE, DENVER, CO 80208
TEL: 303-871-6135 FAX: 303-871-6992
E-MAIL: ADMISSIONS@LAW.DU.EDU • WEBSITE: WWW.LAW.DU.EDU

Life

The academic atmosphere "is really friendly and not ultra-competitive" while the "social atmosphere at DU is great." Students work hard, but there are still "many many opportunities to socialize and drink together." Denver fosters a "tight knit community" where "students compete with themselves but not with each other," although "most law students are type-A, stressed out, and cliquey." The party atmosphere with "a lot of drinking (happy hours are a common club social)" appeals to younger students, while some "older students who may have families/spouses" might find less to do. Students love Denver, noting that many opportunities off campus and calling it "a wonderful place to live."

Getting In

Competition is fierce at Denver, with the law school getting almost 2,500 applicants in 2012. This means students will want to study, study, and study more to achieve the right GPA and LSAT scores. The school weighs those two scores more heavily than any other part of the application. The 2012 class had an average GPA and LSAT of 3.39 and 158 respectively.

Clinical program required	No
Legal writing course requirement	Yes
Legal methods course requirement	Yes
Legal research course requirement	Yes
Moot court requirement	· No
Public interest law requirement	Yes

ADMISSIONS

Selectivity Rating	83
# applications received	2,382
% applicants accepted	47
% acceptees attending	26
Average LSAT	158
Median LSAT	159
LSAT Range (25th to 75th percentile)	155–161
Average undergrad GPA	3.4
Median undergrad GPA	3.46
Application fee	$65
Regular application deadline	
Transfer students accepted	Yes
Evening division offered	Yes
Part-time accepted	Yes
CAS accepted	Yes

FINANCIAL FACTS

Annual tuition	$40,710
Books and supplies	$1,800
Fees	$708
Room & Board	$10,746
Financial aid application deadline	2/15
% first-year students receiving some sort of aid	87
% all students receiving some sort of aid	88
% of aid that is merit based	55
% receiving scholarships	44
Average grant	$20,544
Average loan	$39,641
Average total aid package	$45,161
Average debt	$127,420

EMPLOYMENT INFORMATION

Career Rating	87
Total 2012 JD Grads	317
% grads employed nine months out	89
Median starting salary	$56,000
# employed full-time	227
# employed part-time	54
# employed bar required	194
# employed JD preferred	53
# employed professional/other	28
# employed non-professional	6
# pursuing advanced degree	3
# unemployed and seeking employment	23
# not seeking employment	6
% grads employed by school	10
State for bar exam	CO, TX, NY, CA, AZ
Pass rate for first-time bar	88

Prominent Alumni
Don Sturm, LLB '58, Banking; Doug Scrivner, JD '77, Former General Counsel of Accenture; Secretary Jim Nicholson, JD '72, Secretary of Veterans Affairs.

Grads Employed by Field (%)
Academic (7)
Business/Industry (14)
Government (17)
Judicial Clerkship (8)
Military (2)
Private Practice (34)
Public Interest (7)

UNIVERSITY OF THE DISTRICT OF COLUMBIA
DAVID A. CLARKE SCHOOL OF LAW

INSTITUTIONAL INFORMATION

Public/private	Public
Affiliation	No Affiliation
% faculty part-time	53
% faculty female	44
% faculty underrepresented minority	51
Total faculty	45

SURVEY SAYS...
Liberal students, Students love Washington, D.C.

STUDENTS

Enrollment of law school	366
% male/female	44/56
% part-time	41
% underrepresented minority	48
% international	2
# of countries represented	4
Average age of entering class	28

ACADEMICS

Academic Experience Rating	**69**
Profs interesting rating	74
Profs accessible rating	73
Hours of study per day	4.06

Advanced Degrees Offered
JD, 3 years for full-time students, 4 years for part-time students; LLM, 2 years

Academics

The David A. Clarke School of Law at the University of the District of Columbia is founded on an "enthusiasm for equality and justice." It's a small school, one of only six ABA-accredited law schools at Historically Black Colleges and Universities. The school offers training to those underrepresented at the bar. Its mission is "to serve the public and equip lawyers who will promote social justice." Students don't just study law, but "Learn how to make the legal system work for the most vulnerable populations in our society." UDC is "on the cutting-edge of clinical practice." There's a required 700 hours of clinical experience, within which are a "great variety" of fields to choose from. In clinic, students are responsible for their own cases and clients and "have a chance to hone their research and writing skills." Unique to UDC School of Law is a "complete public interest focus and a commitment to serving the impoverished." The school operates by the credo, "Tolerance, service, and commitment to ensuring equal access to justice." After graduation, students say they feel confident taking on their own cases due to the heavy clinical requirement.

"Our professors are committed to educating the next generation of public interest lawyers." "They are by far the best thing going for the institution. Their experience and expertise is priceless." Professors choose to teach at UDC School of Law because they believe in its mission. They're "truly passionate" and try to prepare students for the "issues most of us will face as public interest attorneys." "I had the opportunity to learn from a D.C. Superior Court Judge, a nationally renowned civil rights attorney whose record and experience comprise nearly fifty years of service to the profession and to society, and an Ivy League–educated criminal defense superstar from D.C.'s Public Defender Service." These professors represent the "spirit of tolerance, dedication, and advocacy." The curriculum is "designed to equip each graduate with not merely an intellectual grasp of the law, but also the skills required to make practice of the law a reality." Students feel prepared for the real world of law outside the doors of UDC and also praise the professors' "compassion for humanity."

Students are divided on the usefulness of the administration. One says they're both "helpful" and "attentive," and another claims they do a good job "making the school feel like a community." However, others feel quite the opposite. "The school's administration often leaves students very frustrated," and "UDC Law is sometimes crippled by bureaucracy." Most of the complaints come from part-time students who wish the administration kept better hours. They would also like more opportunities to fulfill the clinical requirement and participate in student organizations. Yet another claims, "The administration here knows individuals by name, and it is not uncommon for an administrator to e-mail an important deadline reminder to a forgetful student."

Students agree, "It would be nice if the law school had a bit more room." The law school is growing, and in August 2011, the law school moved to a new, more spacious building, alleviating student complaints of about classrooms and equipment. One student says, "I've never had an instance where I was unable to find a research tool I needed." Another student claims the library as a "second home."

VIVIAN CANTY, ASSISTANT DEAN OF ADMISSION
4200 CONNECTICUT AVENUE, NW, BUILDING 38, WASHINGTON, D.C. 20008
TEL: 202-274-7336 FAX: 202-274-5583
E-MAIL: VCANTY@UDC.EDU • WEBSITE: WWW.LAW.UDC.EDU

Life

Students "come in all shades, ages, income levels, and backgrounds." UDC law is left-leaning, and no matter what your ethnicity or sexual orientation may be, you'll fit in well, as diversity is the school's "greatest strength." The atmosphere is "noncompetitive" and, "UDC-DCSL doesn't keep class ranks, because, well, everyone is encouraged to succeed." Students say it's an "extremely positive environment." Fellow classmates "help each other succeed" and, even more, are "invested" in that success. "I never feel isolated," another student adds.

The majority of students are recent graduates of their undergraduate institutions. Students love D.C. for the location! The school is "minutes from the historic streets and monuments of downtown D.C. The location is great for available transportation, travel to the many other D.C. law schools and colleges, and all types of recreation and entertainment for singles, couples, families, and the young at heart."

Getting In

The admissions committee focuses on work experience, extracurricular activities, letters of recommendation, and the personal essay. Roughly one in four candidates is accepted. Admitted students in the 25th percentile had GPAs around 2.8 and LSAT scores just about 150. Admitted students in the 75th percentile had GPAs just beneath 3.4 and LSAT scores at 155.

Clinical program required	Yes
Legal writing course requirement	Yes
Legal methods course requirement	No
Legal research course requirement	Yes
Moot court requirement	Yes
Public interest law requirement	Yes

ADMISSIONS

Selectivity Rating	85
# applications received	1,548
% applicants accepted	27
% acceptees attending	30
Average LSAT	151
Median LSAT	151
LSAT Range (25th to 75th percentile)	148–153
Average undergrad GPA	2.97
Median undergrad GPA	2.95
Application fee	$35
Regular application deadline	3/15
Transfer students accepted	Yes
Evening division offered	Yes
Part-time accepted	Yes
CAS accepted	Yes

FINANCIAL FACTS

Annual tuition (in-state out-of-state)	$10,620/$21,240
Books and supplies	$2,000
Fees	$630
Room & Board	$20,200
Financial aid application deadline	3/30
% first-year students receiving some sort of aid	93
% all students receiving some sort of aid	90
% of aid that is merit based	75
% receiving scholarships	57
Average grant	$4,806
Average loan	$35,838
Average total aid package	$40,644
Average debt	$119,004

EMPLOYMENT INFORMATION

Career Rating	70
Total 2012 JD Grads	93
% for whom you have useable information	92
% grads employed nine months out	57
Median starting salary	$40,000
% job accepting grads providing useable salary information	43
# employed full-time	46
# employed part-time	7
# employed bar required	30
# employed JD preferred	13
# employed professional/other	8
# employed non-professional	2
# pursuing advanced degree	6
# unemployed and seeking employment	20
# not seeking employment	7
% grads employed by school	0
State for bar exam	MD, DC, VA, CA, NY
Pass rate for first-time bar	66

Prominent Alumni

Thomas Kilbride, Illinois Supreme Court Justice; Kim Jones, Founder and Director, Advocates for Justice in Education; Tom Devine, Legal Whistleblower Attorney and Director, Government Accountability Project.

Grads Employed by Field (%)

Academic (4)
Business/Industry (30)
Government (15)
Judicial Clerkship (9)
Private Practice (26)
Public Interest (15)

UNIVERSITY OF FLORIDA
LEVIN COLLEGE OF LAW

INSTITUTIONAL INFORMATION
Public/private   Public
% faculty part-time   0
% faculty female   37
% faculty underrepresented
minority   22
Total faculty   51

SURVEY SAYS...
Diverse opinions accepted in class-rooms, Great research resources, Good social life

STUDENTS
Enrollment of law school   960
% male/female   59/41
% from out-of-state   10
% part-time   0
% underrepresented minority   30
% international   3
Average age of entering class   23

ACADEMICS
Academic Experience Rating   88
Profs interesting rating   82
Profs accessible rating   80
Hours of study per day   3.45

Academic Specialties
Criminal, Environmental, International, Taxation, Intellectual Property

Advanced Degrees Offered
LLM in Taxation, 1 year; LLM in International Taxation, 1 year; LLM in Comparative Law, 1 year; LLM in Environmental and Land Use Law, 1 year; SJD in Taxation, multi-year.

Combined Degrees Offered
More than 30 joint degree programs (JD/Masters & Ph.D.); length of program varies.

Academics

Holding students to "high academic standards," the University of Florida's Levin College of Law offers students an excellent "balance between legal theory and practical courses." Certainly a "well respected institution," many students are quick to assert that the school's "value is very good for [the] price." As a pleased 3L boasts, "The greatest strength is how cheap it is, at least relative to other law schools, for the top law school in Florida." Students also enjoy that "there are several certificate programs" available including environmental and land law use, family law, intellectual property and international and comparative law. Though some wish there were "more practical skills courses," others tell us that "clinics and trial practice classes are very hands-on." Further, students here love the extensive opportunities to study abroad in exotic locales such as Costa Rica and South Africa.

Importantly the "professors are a great mix of race, background, experience, and knowledge. They are very approachable and in their offices any time to answer a question." Indeed, "most have an open door policy and welcome student questions." Fortunately, "many professors seek research assistants, which is a very valuable experience." However, some students do caution that first-year classes are "too large for good interaction and discussion." Therefore, it's sometimes possible to feel "totally lost in the shuffle."

While some students have experienced "the significant red tape" that is often part and parcel with a massive state university, many proclaim the administration here is "very responsive to student requests." As a grateful 3L explains, "The school administration here is very helpful and listens to student concerns and does its best to redress any issues raised. The dean [even] meets regularly over coffee with students." A content 2L echoes these sentiments sharing, "Everyone at the Levin College of Law is extremely helpful. I have gone to various offices on campus for help and have not been let down."

Students are quite happy with the "fantastic facilities," which they find "very well kept and modern." Classrooms "all have great seating, lighting, visual, and audio." What's more, the "new advocacy center is a state-of-the-art new building to practice and learn advocacy skills in a realistic full courtroom." In addition, the library is "first-rate" and definitely conducive to long study sessions; although, some students do gripe that it's starting to become overrun with undergraduates.

Finally, students highlight the alumni network which is "vast and plays a major role in obtaining positions." As a pleased 3L recounts, "The greatest strength is the distinguished alumni pool around the state, region, and country who always come back, give back, and are open to help out students in the employment search. The resources and connections of the school are great as well and completely prepare all students who take advantage of them to build great attorneys and connect them with hiring employers." However, a disgruntled 2L counters, "The school is stuck in a cycle of creating a job placement system that benefits only the top 10 percent of the students and handcuffing the bottom 75 percent. Essentially the bottom 75 percent of the students gets no benefit from the career services department and thus must scramble to find their own jobs."

Life

The overwhelming majority of students here are Florida residents. Otherwise, "UF Law is unique in its ability to achieve diverse incoming class." Ethnic minorities make up a pretty considerable contingent, and all kinds of students enroll here. "The best part of law school is conversing with people of different backgrounds and history," says a thrilled 2L. "It's fascinating." Some students "can be cutthroat," but for the most part, the law student population is "intelligent and harmonious." Indeed, "there is a nice sense of community." "You will be able to find a friend or two to study with regularly and many friends to interact with socially," promises a 1L. Students do tend to stick to their sections first year, but "there's a lot of cross-section interaction starting second year."

Despite a "problematic" parking situation, "Gainesville is nice." With big-time college sports, the University of Florida is certainly hard to beat. As one proud 3L notes, "[Even] our faculty members appreciate the prominence and breadth of Gator Nation, even though our football team didn't live up to the Gator standard last year." The "sunny weather" is spectacular, provided one enjoys heat and a constant dose of humidity. Hometown Gainesville is a quintessential college town and students can take advantage of numerous restaurants, performing arts venues, cultural events and, of course, bars. Unfortunately though, the law school is located in a rather remote part of the campus, and some students complain that it is "not within walking distance of any dining options and the on-campus options are paltry." On the positive side, should students ever tire of the scene in Gainesville, within driving distance lie Jacksonville, Orlando and Tampa – all fairly large cities.

Getting In

Gaining that coveted acceptance letter is no simple feat at the University of Florida. Accepted students in the 25th percentile earned around a 160 on the LSAT and an undergraduate GPA of 3.43. Accepted students in the 75th percentile earned around a 164 on the LSAT and an undergraduate GPA of 3.82. The median LSAT score is 162 and the median GPA is 3.64.

Clinical program required	No
Legal writing course requirement	Yes
Legal methods course requirement	No
Legal research course requirement	Yes
Moot court requirement	No
Public interest law requirement	No

ADMISSIONS

Selectivity Rating	89
# applications received	2,686
% applicants accepted	33
% acceptees attending	32
Average LSAT	161
Median LSAT	161
LSAT Range (25th to 75th percentile)	160–164
Average undergrad GPA	3.53
Median undergrad GPA	3.59
Application fee	$30
Regular application deadline	3/15
Regular notification	4/30
Transfer students accepted	Yes
Evening division offered	No
Part-time accepted	No
CAS accepted	Yes

FINANCIAL FACTS

Annual tuition	$18,912
Books and supplies	$2,460
Fees	$21,874
Room & Board (on/off campus)	$10,000/$10,550
Financial aid application deadline	4/15
% first-year students receiving some sort of aid	92
% all students receiving some sort of aid	86
% of aid that is merit based	6
% receiving scholarships	32
Average grant	$7,916
Average loan	$28,750
Average total aid package	$29,114
Average debt	$72,974

EMPLOYMENT INFORMATION

Career Rating	86
Total 2012 JD Grads	333
% grads employed nine months out	79
Median starting salary	$57,000
# employed full-time	228
# employed part-time	36
# employed bar required	196
# employed JD preferred	49
# employed professional/other	12
# employed non-professional	7
# pursuing advanced degree	19
# unemployed and seeking employment	29
# not seeking employment	12
% grads employed by school	4
State for bar exam	FL, GA, NY, MA, NC
Pass rate for first-time bar	98.4

Prominent Alumni
Martha Barnett, Holland & Knight LLP; ABA President 2000; W. Reece Smith Jr., Carlton, Fields; ABA President 1980; Stephen Zack, Boies, Schiller & Flexner; ABA President, 2010.

Grads Employed by Field (%)
Academic (2)
Business/Industry (10)
Government (13)
Judicial Clerkship (4)
Military (1)
Private Practice (39)
Public Interest (7)

UNIVERSITY OF GEORGIA
SCHOOL OF LAW

INSTITUTIONAL INFORMATION

Public/private	Public
Student-faculty ratio	12:1
% faculty part-time	22
% faculty female	37
% faculty underrepresented minority	15
Total faculty	60

SURVEY SAYS...

Diverse opinions accepted in classrooms, Great research resources, Great library staff, Good social life

STUDENTS

Enrollment of law school	669
% male/female	57/43
% from out-of-state	33
% underrepresented minority	19
% international	3
# of countries represented	3
Average age of entering class	23

ACADEMICS

Academic Experience Rating	97
Profs interesting rating	96
Profs accessible rating	89
Hours of study per day	4.56

Academic Specialties

Civil Procedure, Commercial, Constitutional, Corporation Securities, Criminal, Environmental, Government Services, Human Rights, International, Labor, Legal History, Legal Philosophy, Property, Taxation, Intellectual Property

Advanced Degrees Offered

LLM, 1 year

Combined Degrees Offered

JD/Master of Business Administration (4 years); JD/Master of Historic Preservation (4 years); JD/Master of Public Administration (4 years); JD/Master of Social Work (4 years); JD/Master of Education in Sports Studies (4 years); JD/MA, various fields (varies); JD/Ph.D., various fields (varies).

Academics

At the University of Georgia Law, students rave about the education they receive for a "bargain price." Non-resident students may apply for in-state rates after the first year, and many out-of-state residents receive scholarships for their first year, which waive the tuition difference. That's not to mention the school's "great academic reputation" and position as a "feeder to the most prominent city in the South." "It is really nice to be able to afford a JD from a reputable school and not be faced with the 'golden handcuffs,'" says a student not looking to work at a firm. All in all, "The professors, the people, the curriculum, and the facilities contribute to an overall competitive and comprehensive program that still embodies southern hospitality."

The "stellar" teachers at Georgia Law are "compassionate, while still demanding excellence," and it's "very easy to meet with professors and discuss things unrelated to class," as well as many student groups that allow for diverse ideas and discussions among students. "They genuinely care about us as individuals and have never been too busy to assist," says a student. Though students "are definitely left to figure things out on our own in many respects" ("Communication about how to get grades, etc., are somewhat lacking."), the school "provides a wide range of clinical opportunities for its students," as well as its nationally recognized moot court and mock trial programs and three major journals. It also offers study and work abroad programs to help reinforce its focus on global issues, and concurrent enrollment with the university's other programs is an option.

There's a wide variety of courses from which students can choose their electives, and the school has a unique approach to grading in the "intense" first year. Students don't receive grades for the first semester (with the exception of criminal law and civil procedure), and at the end of 1L, fall semester performance counts toward the final grade, but it's weighted significantly less than spring exam scores. The school wants students to focus on their studies and discourages 1Ls from taking jobs during the first year of law school.

Georgia Law has one of the largest law libraries in the nation—students love its "huge, picturesque windows and accommodating seating and tables"—and it's embarking on a renovation and expansion that will only improve the quality of life. Classroom facilities are "also great," and the school produces an enthusiastic alumni base that helps during interview season. Still, many students do wish that more job opportunities outside of Georgia found their way to the UGA Law campus.

Life

Students say that the "small Southern town" of Athens, with its coffee shops and music scene, is the "quintessential college town," but one that can be "somewhat limiting for older students." Though the school is just a couple of blocks from downtown, "Housing options are pretty limited around the law school and most students live two to three miles away," and often must drive to school as "the Athens bus service is not great." Atlanta is about an hour-and-a-half away, so students who must frequently travel for their internships have a bit of a hike, but it's still close enough that its myriad entertainment options can be enjoyed without much trouble. "The camaraderie of the students, an awesome social scene, and proximity to Atlanta make a good educational experience that much better," says a student.

PAUL ROLLINS, ASSOCIATE DEAN FOR ADMINISTRATION
225 HERTY DRIVE, ATHENS, GA 30602-6012
TEL: 706-542-7060 FAX: 706-542-5556
E-MAIL: UGAJD@UGA.EDU • WEBSITE: WWW.LAW.UGA.EDU

UGA Law offers a "great balance between traditional legal education and strong social environment." Small class sizes mean, "Everyone is very independently driven," providing at most a "friendly competition," instead of a cutthroat one, but "Grabbing a beer with friends after a long Friday full of classes makes law school really bearable." "No one is hiding books; no one is refusing to help. We are all in this together and at the end of the day, the person next to you is a future referral and professional colleague," says a 2L. "One thing that Dean White reminds all incoming 1Ls at orientation is that our classmates are our colleagues, not our competition, and students really take this to heart," says another student.

Getting In

Admission to the University of Georgia is selective, and the school prides itself on the diverse backgrounds that its students bring. Members of the class of 2013 include a professional baseball player in Israel, the lead singer of a band, a published author, an intern for the SEC, and a former Miss Georgia. The school has received record numbers of applications in recent years. There was a 39 percent increase for the class of 2012 from the previous year. The class of 2013 had a median LSAT of 164 and a median undergraduate GPA of 3.7.

Clinical program required	No
Legal writing course requirement	Yes
Legal methods course requirement	No
Legal research course requirement	Yes
Moot court requirement	No
Public interest law requirement	No

ADMISSIONS

Selectivity Rating	90
# applications received	2,461
% applicants accepted	32
% acceptees attending	24
Average LSAT	164
LSAT Range (25th to 75th percentile)	158–165
Average undergrad GPA	3.67
Application fee	$50
Regular application deadline	4/1
Early application deadline	11/1
Early application notification	12/15
Transfer students accepted	Yes
Evening division offered	No
Part-time accepted	No
CAS accepted	Yes

FINANCIAL FACTS

Annual tuition (in-state out-of-state)	$16,506/$34,176
Books and supplies	$1,768
Fees	$2,234
Room & Board (on/off campus)	$15,266/$12,266
Financial aid application deadline	7/1
% first-year students receiving some sort of aid	90
% all students receiving some sort of aid	90
% of aid that is merit based	25
% receiving scholarships	69
Average grant	$11,468
Average loan	$26,735
Average total aid package	$28,930
Average debt	$59,473

EMPLOYMENT INFORMATION

Career Rating	**89**	**Grads Employed by Field (%)**
Total 2012 JD Grads	227	Academic (2)
% for whom you have useable information	100	Business/Industry (12)
% grads employed nine months out	87	Government (10)
Median starting salary	$55,000	Judicial Clerkship (15)
# employed full-time	175	Military (1)
# employed part-time	15	Private Practice (53)
# employed bar required	159	Public Interest (8)
# employed JD preferred	17	
# employed professional/other	12	
# employed non-professional	2	
# pursuing advanced degree	9	
# unemployed and seeking employment	23	
# not seeking employment	0	
% grads employed by school	3	
State for bar exam	GA	
Pass rate for first-time bar	93	

UNIVERSITY OF HAWAII—MANOA
WILLIAM S. RICHARDSON SCHOOL OF LAW

INSTITUTIONAL INFORMATION

Public/private	Public
Affiliation	No Affiliation
% faculty part-time	50
% faculty female	44
% faculty underrepresented minority	44
Total faculty	62

SURVEY SAYS...

Diverse opinions accepted in classrooms, Students love Honolulu, HI

STUDENTS

Enrollment of law school	370
% male/female	41/59
% from out-of-state	10
% part-time	26
% underrepresented minority	71
% international	3
# of countries represented	3
Average age of entering class	27

ACADEMICS

Academic Experience Rating	93
Profs interesting rating	85
Profs accessible rating	83
Hours of study per day	3.97

Academic Specialties
Environmental, International

Advanced Degrees Offered
Full-Time JD, 3 years evening, part-time JD, 4 years or more.

Combined Degrees Offered
JD/MA (varies), JD/MBA (varies), JD/MS (varies), JD/MSW (varies), JD/Ph.D. (varies)

Academics

Life at the University of Hawaii – Manoa's William S. Richardson School of Law is not as carefree and relaxing as its gorgeous island setting might make you imagine. The course load is "demanding," but since there is a "tremendous feeling of support from both peers and administration" the school has managed to develop "a proud and loyal student body." The "amazingly accessible" staff at Manoa are "here to make sure that we succeed and that we enjoy this process." Richardson may be small, but "the faculty is a distinguished group with diverse backgrounds and experience." A few students do feel that "more intense attention should be given to developing legal writing/research skills," but not for lack of resources. Research tools available to students are "more than adequate," the "amount of books available in the library is quite good," and librarians and researchers "teach strategies and practical skills."

Some have had a "mixed" experience, with some courses offering "a lot about topics relevant to my career interests" and other courses taught by replacement teachers who "had no experience in teaching the topic." Overall, however, students feel they have "received a great legal education" by being "challenged academically" at Richardson. Key is the idea that professors "encourage discussion and questions," with a hands-on process that "allows students to play with the hypotheticals" rather than simply absorb lectures.

Students here do not feel cut off from the administration of the school, either. Faculty are supportive of all, even "talented students who may not aspire to law review but will still serve as assets to the profession. " "When we feel that any part of the school's facilities is lacking, there are avenues we can take to express our concerns, and there is often action taken to address our problems." The administration is even "willing to work with students in order to adjust finals and class schedules." While some complain "there is a lot of red tape to go through if you want to accomplish anything," results are the bottom line, and most students agree that the administration is "eager to help students" and "take the time to get to know us." Students have even "had discussions with the various deans passing in the courtyard."

"Antiquated" facilities vex some students, however, with "unreliable" Internet access and classrooms "not all equipped for the mandatory use of laptops." The IT staff at Richardson completed a wireless expansion in April 2013. This is balanced by "some of the most competent and experienced professors ever," an "amazing" group of educators who display "passion for teaching" and a "willingness to personally engage with their students." As one student notes, these traits "add value to my education and growth."

Life

Expect a more welcoming environment than Richardson's reputation may lead one to believe. In the past people have talked about "haole bias," or bias against mainlanders, but these days many feel "there is way too much emphasis on any strife between islanders and mainlanders." The degree to which this division exists is not just "overstated," it's a situation that "has changed a lot over the past few years. " As one student notes, "in my experience, there has been no conflict among the groups on campus. I would certainly not consider it merely civil." Whether from the mainland or the island, students in recent classes "quickly gelled" and "respect each other." Indeed, the small student population means you do get "better responses when students are in crisis" from the "friendly, supportive environment."

ELISABETH STEELE HUTCHISON, DIRECTOR OF ADMISSIONS
2515 DOLE STREET, HONOLULU, HI 96822
TEL: 808-956-3000 FAX: 808-956-3813
E-MAIL: ESTEELE@HAWAII.EDU • WEBSITE: HTTPS://WWW.LAW.HAWAII.EDU

While Richardson does boast more diversity than many other law schools—"women and minorities are well represented"—that diversity can be a little misleading because "they largely come from privileged backgrounds." Without great access to scholarship money for the financially disadvantaged, the school may "increasingly be reserved for rich kids." The fact that "we do not have large endowments or a wealthy alumni base" does not help in this regard. But for those who can attend, opportunities outside the classroom are unlike those anywhere else in the nation thanks to the stunning tropical setting.

Getting In

The University of Hawaii—Manoa Richardson School of Law is the only ABA-accredited law school in the Pacific Asia region, therefore it can afford to be selective. Anyone looking to practice law in the area, whether local talent or from the mainland, can expect to compete for a limited number of seats. Richardson is strict about deadlines; all applications must be received by February 1. Each year, the Admissions Committee selects ten to twelve applicants to join the first year class as part of the Ulu Lehua Scholars Program. Criteria include a record of overcoming social, educational, economic, or other sources of adversity; and activities and/or employment manifesting a strong commitment to social justice, the public interest, and service to legally, socially, and economically disadvantaged communities.

Clinical program required	Yes
Legal writing course requirement	Yes
Legal methods course requirement	Yes
Legal research course requirement	Yes
Moot court requirement	No
Public interest law requirement	Yes

ADMISSIONS

Selectivity Rating	95
# applications received	697
% applicants accepted	29
% acceptees attending	43
Average LSAT	158
Median LSAT	158
LSAT Range (25th to 75th percentile)	155–161
Average undergrad GPA	3.32
Median undergrad GPA	3.38
Application fee	$75
Regular application deadline	2/1
Regular notification	3/15
Transfer students accepted	Yes
Evening division offered	Yes
Part-time accepted	Yes
CAS accepted	Yes

FINANCIAL FACTS

Annual tuition (in-state out-of-state)	$17,424/$33,816
Books and supplies	$3,094
Fees	$670
Room & Board (on/off campus)	$10,029/$12,831
Financial aid application deadline	3/1
% first-year students receiving some sort of aid	76
% all students receiving some sort of aid	83
% of aid that is merit based	3
% receiving scholarships	54
Average grant	$7,144
Average loan	$24,507
Average total aid package	$34,575
Average debt	$64,000

EMPLOYMENT INFORMATION

Career Rating	80
Total 2012 JD Grads	106
% grads employed nine months out	88
Median starting salary	$53,000
% job accepting grads providing useable salary information	48
# employed full-time	76
# employed part-time	6
# employed bar required	62
# employed JD preferred	16
# employed professional/other	2
# employed non-professional	2
# pursuing advanced degree	2
# unemployed and seeking employment	10
# not seeking employment	2
% grads employed by school	2
State for bar exam	HI
Pass rate for first-time bar	75

Prominent Alumni
John Waihee, former Governor of Hawaii; Sabrina McKenna, Hawaii Supreme Court; Alexa Fujise, Associate Judge, Hawai`i Intermediate Court of Appeals.

Grads Employed by Field (%)
Academic (5)
Business/Industry (6)
Government (17)
Judicial Clerkship (30)
Military (2)
Private Practice (30)
Public Interest (8)

UNIVERSITY OF HOUSTON
LAW CENTER

Academics

As large and lively as the state of Texas, the University of Houston Law Center enrolls fewer than 900 students in its diverse and challenging JD, LLM, and joint-degree programs. Drawing top names from the Houston legal community, professors are "either extremely accomplished attorneys or nationally renowned experts in a particular field of law." Though they represent the top of their field, "There are no 'bigger than Texas' egos with any of the faculty." In fact, "The entire faculty is very accessible and willing to help students learn in any way they can." Students agree that their professors are "not only available during office hours, many professors host lunches or parties in their homes to learn more about their students."

In the classroom, the professors are "very much focused on teaching us to think creatively" and throughout the JD program the "Practical aspects of lawyering are stressed." Things here begin with a bang as "All first-year students are required to take part in a moot court competition, and it's a great experience for everyone." In addition, "There are six different law journals in which a student may participate, including the Houston Law Review, which consistently ranks in the top fifty of all Law Reviews in the country." What's more, the school operates a number of clinics and research institutes that augment classroom experiences with hands-on experience. "I have spent three semesters working at the Immigration [Clinic] and Civil [Practice] Clinic and will always remember this time as the most exciting and rewarding aspect of my law school experience," explains one clinic participant. "We are given enormous responsibility for our clients and the experience has given me an invaluable opportunity to learn actual lawyering skills."

Those looking for great value relative to cost in their education will be extremely satisfied with U of H. Students love that they get a "high-value education for a low cost in a great legal market." If you can manage a "scholarship" or are "a Texas resident" it only sweetens the proverbial deal. Even so, students admit there are some sacrifices associated with a U of H education, particularly with regard to the school's facilities which most agree "need improvement." There are no ivy-lined walls at U of H; instead, think "East German bunker school of architecture." However, most students take the environs in stride. "Students who enter with high expectations of facilities will be disappointed," says one student. "But you learn at this school in an environment conducive to learning." On that note, U of H "fosters a community and not a rivalry among students. Fellow students are always willing to answer a question, share notes, and form study groups."

Outside the classroom, "There are lots of opportunities to work with major law firms and other community organizations during the summer and during the school year," and the Career Development Office "is particularly helpful for summer job opportunities." After graduation, Houston is a well-suited environment for future attorneys, boasting its reputation as one of the "largest legal markets in the country." A current student insists, "If you want to succeed, you can, and you can get a great job when you graduate too—with all the top firms in Texas including all the elite New York satellite offices."

Life

Students say the school is a great place to work on your powers of persuasion as there's lots of debate on the U of H campus. A student explains, "Because the student body is fairly conservative, but, at the same time, lawyers generally exhibit liberal thinking (at least in the social realm), you get a nice balance of liberal and conservative, often

JAMIE WEST DILLON, ASSISTANT DEAN FOR ADMISSIONS
100 LAW CENTER, HOUSTON, TX 77204-6060
TEL: 713-743-2280 FAX: 713-743-2194
E-MAIL: LAWADMISSIONS@UH.EDU • WEBSITE: WWW.LAW.UH.EDU

leading to lively debate absent from more liberal institutions." Even so, don't expect "any cutthroat type of competitive environment" here since students agree that "even if they have polar opposite views in the classroom, afterwards they hang out."

On campus, the prevailing atmosphere is "friendly" with "an awesome SBA that is very active in helping make UHLC a better place." Students tend to form strong friendships in their first-year sections, and when the weekend arrives "Plenty of people…go out on a regular basis." Night students are generally less involved in the campus community, admitting that there is something of a "social divide between part-time and full-time students"; many complain that events and activities take place during the day (while they are working) and that "most of the social events are geared toward single people or those without children."

Unfortunately, the campus isn't much of a social hub because "It is in a part of Houston that nobody really cares to live in, so most people come in for class and then head home." However, the cosmopolitan city of Houston is a great place to live, offering "a standing symphony, opera, and ballet, NFL, NBA, MLB, and MLS sports teams (and minor league ice hockey) a great zoo and museums, and a multitude of golfing opportunities."

Getting In

There is no set minimum LSAT score or undergraduate GPA required for acceptance to the University of Houston Law Center; all applicants are reviewed individually. In 2012, the lowest LSAT score accepted was in the lower 140s, while the median score for accepted applicants was 163. The median GPA was 3.54. Non-Texans comprise approximately 7 percent of the student population and the acceptance rate is equally competitive for out-of-state and in-state residents.

Clinical program required	No
Legal writing course requirement	Yes
Legal methods course requirement	Yes
Legal research course requirement	Yes
Moot court requirement	Yes
Public interest law requirement	No

ADMISSIONS

Selectivity Rating	91
# applications received	3,059
% applicants accepted	30
% acceptees attending	23
Average LSAT	161
Median LSAT	161
LSAT Range (25th to 75th percentile)	159–163
Average undergrad GPA	3.44
Median undergrad GPA	3.47
Application fee	$70
Regular application deadline	2/15
Regular notification	5/15
Early application deadline	11/15
Early application notification	2/15
Transfer students accepted	Yes
Evening division offered	Yes
Part-time accepted	Yes
CAS accepted	Yes

FINANCIAL FACTS

Annual tuition (in-state out-of-state)	$24,467/$34,418
Books and supplies	$2,900
Fees	$5,281
Room & Board (on/off campus)	$8,600/$10,600
Financial aid application deadline	4/1
% first-year students receiving some sort of aid	52
% all students receiving some sort of aid	80
% of aid that is merit based	58
% receiving scholarships	58
Average grant	$2,000
Average loan	$30,598
Average debt	$81,721

EMPLOYMENT INFORMATION

Career Rating	**97**	**Prominent Alumni**
Total 2012 JD Grads	262	Hon. Vanessa Gilmore, United States
% for whom you have useable information	100	District Court Judge, Southern District of Texas; Hon. Gray H. Miller, United States
% grads employed nine months out	86	District Court Judge, Southern District of
Median starting salary	$120,000	Texas; Hon. Ruby Kless Sondock, First
% job accepting grads providing		female Texas Supreme Court justice, cur-
useable salary information	40	rently a mediator; Hon. Michael H.
# employed full-time	214	Schneider, Sr., United States District Court
# employed part-time	11	Judge, Eastern District of Texas.
# employed bar required	175	**Grads Employed by Field (%)**
# employed JD preferred	32	Academic (<1)
# employed professional/other	16	Business/Industry (26)
# employed non-professional	1	Government (8)
State for bar exam	TX	Judicial Clerkship (2)
Pass rate for first-time bar	88.72	Private Practice (61)
		Public Interest (2)

UNIVERSITY OF IDAHO
COLLEGE OF LAW

INSTITUTIONAL INFORMATION

Public/private	Public
Affiliation	No Affiliation
Student-faculty ratio	15:1
% faculty part-time	7
% faculty female	56
% faculty underrepresented minority	15
Total faculty	27

SURVEY SAYS...

Diverse opinions accepted in classrooms, Great library staff, Students never sleep, Conservative students

STUDENTS

Enrollment of law school	102
% male/female	63/37
% from out-of-state	41
% part-time	0
% underrepresented minority	13
% international	1
# of countries represented	1
Average age of entering class	26

ACADEMICS

Academic Experience Rating	**65**
Profs interesting rating	75
Profs accessible rating	80
Hours of study per day	4.47

Academic Specialties

Commercial, Corporation Securities, Environmental, Intellectual Property, Native American Law, Litigation and Alternative Dispute Resolution

Combined Degrees Offered

Dual JD/MS/Ph.D. in Water Resources (Law, Management, and Policy): JD/MS 8 semesters, Ph.D. varies; Dual JD/MS Environmental Science: 8 semesters; Dual JD/Professional Masters of Science: 8 semesters; Dual JD/MS Accountancy: 8 semesters; Dual JD/MS Accountancy, Taxation Emphasis (offered in conjunction with Boise State University): 8 semesters. JD/MS Bioregional Planning and Community Design: 8 semesters

Academics

A "great value," University of Idaho College of Law is a small yet affordable place to get a JD Citing the school's strong regional ties and low in-state tuition, students declare, "If one wants to practice law in Idaho especially, going to UofI makes sense from an educational and financial standpoint." With a total enrollment of about 350, students benefit from a surprisingly small and intimate campus environment. A 2L explains, "Even though this is a public institution, I feel like I get as much attention as if I paid more and went to a private law school. My professors' doors are always open." A first-year student adds, "All five of my professors knew my name by the end of my first week. Most of them sincerely care about our success and are happy to answer questions about life after law school." When it comes to their pedagogical skills, "There are some very good professors and some very poor professors" at UI. However, faculty members are generally accomplished in their fields and "bring a lot of experience" to the classroom. In fact, "For being in a relatively small town, we have faculty from very diverse backgrounds who could definitely teach at more prestigious universities." In that regard, the University of Idaho experience is deeply influenced by its location in the small town of Moscow. Far from the capital in Boise, "The campus and community are very isolated," and some students feel that "the school could improve in diversity and the welcoming of diverse people and diverse viewpoints," both within the student body and within the faculty. It is important to note that qualified students may take classes at the satellite campus in Boise in their third year if they so choose. Fortunately, with the concerted effort of the administration, "There are still some very good speakers and events that come through here."

Academically, the school specializes in environmental law, Native American law, business and entrepreneurship, and litigation and alternative dispute resolution. Students would like to see a greater emphasis on real-world skills, complaining that a number of professors "work too much with theory and not enough with practical application" in the classroom. Fortunately, the school offers "a plethora of opportunities to gain practical legal skills" through clinics, and "the administration also does an excellent job in getting internship opportunities for the students." When it comes to the job hunt, "career services is understaffed" (the size of the staff has tripled for 2013) and the largest in-state job market in Boise is far away, but, despite these obstacles, graduates have a lot going for them. A boon to anyone hoping to practice in the region, UI is "the only law school in the state (accredited). That means all the law firms and courts are packed with our graduates and they protect the opportunities for our students." For those who'd like to practice further afield, "the administration is good at recognizing that there are a lot of students that want to practice out of state, so they cater to that diversity in instruction and events we host."

Life

Students differ personally, professionally, and philosophically at UI. There is a "substantial Mormon population" within the law school, which tends to be more politically and socially conservative, offset by a "sizable body of politically moderate students." Clashing political views is a source of tension on campus. According to some students, "If you consider yourself conservative or libertarian in any fashion, you will quickly find yourself outnumbered, politically isolated, and regarded as offensive and problematic to the staff and faculty." Others claim, "There's a large and outspoken religious majority at the school that tends to jump at any comment they feel is disparaging while loudly asserting their own freedom of speech." Idaho residents make up about 60 percent of the

CAROLE WELLS, JD, DIRECTOR OF ADMISSIONS
6TH & RAYBURN, MOSCOW, ID 83844-2321
TEL: 208-885-2300 FAX: 208-885-5709
E-MAIL: LAWADMIT@UIDAHO.EDU • WEBSITE: WWW.LAW.UIDAHO.EDU

student body, with the remaining 40 percent hailing from across the country. Though most students are just a few years out of college, University of Idaho is "accessible to nontraditional students."

There are around 11,700 undergraduates and 1,700 graduate students on the University of Idaho campus in Moscow, lending a fun, vibrant, student-friendly backdrop to the law school environment. Within the law school itself, "everything is in one building. It gives the students and the faculty easy access to each other." "About half of the students socialize on a regular basis," and there are a range of student groups and recreational activities hosted on the larger campus, as well as through the law school. Home to about 24,000 residents, "Moscow is truly a charming college town that provides decent access to a range of outdoor pursuits." In complement to the school's low tuition, "the cost of living is affordable" in Moscow, and students enjoy the "large food co-op," "impressive farmer's market," and many "great parks" in town. It is "easy to walk anywhere." Students can also cross the state line into Pullman, Washington, another college town that is home to Washington State University, only eight miles away.

Getting In

To be eligible for admission to the University of Idaho, students must have an undergraduate degree from an accredited college, recent LSAT scores, and a Credential Assembly Service account. Dedicated to accepting a diverse entering class, the University of Idaho evaluates each applicant's academic preparedness, test scores, personal statement, and other life experiences when making an admissions decision. The application deadline for the fall semester is March 1; applications are accepted after that date, though chances of admission are smaller.

Clinical program required	No
Legal writing course requirement	Yes
Legal methods course requirement	No
Legal research course requirement	Yes
Moot court requirement	Yes
Public interest law requirement	Yes

ADMISSIONS

Selectivity Rating	72
# applications received	588
% applicants accepted	65
% acceptees attending	27
Median LSAT	153
LSAT Range (25th to 75th percentile)	149–156
Median undergrad GPA	3.21
Application fee	$50
Regular application deadline	3/1
Regular notification	3/15
Early application deadline	12/1
Early application notification	12/15
Transfer students accepted	Yes
Evening division offered	No
Part-time accepted	Yes
CAS accepted	Yes

FINANCIAL FACTS

Annual tuition (in-state out-of-state)	$15,036/$27,824
Books and supplies	$1,474
Room & Board	$9,278
Financial aid application deadline	6/1
% first-year students receiving some sort of aid	100
% all students receiving some sort of aid	100
% of aid that is merit based	100
% receiving scholarships	41
Average grant	$7,683
Average debt	$96,406

EMPLOYMENT INFORMATION

Career Rating	83
Total 2012 JD Grads	104
% for whom you have useable information	100
% grads employed nine months out	92
Median starting salary	$50,000
# employed full-time	75
# employed part-time	21
# employed bar required	68
# employed JD preferred	12
# employed professional/other	9
# employed non-professional	7
# pursuing advanced degree	3
# unemployed and seeking employment	4
# not seeking employment	1
% grads employed by school	0
State for bar exam	ID, WA, UT, OR, CA
Pass rate for first-time bar	78.6

Prominent Alumni
Linda Copple Trout, Past Chief Justice, Idaho Supreme Court; Georgia Yuan, Deputy Under Secretary of Education; Frank Shrontz, Former CEO and Chairman of the Boeing Co.

Grads Employed by Field (%)
Academic (2)
Business/Industry (15)
Government (13)
Judicial Clerkship (15)
Private Practice (43)
Public Interest (4)

UNIVERSITY OF ILLINOIS
COLLEGE OF LAW

INSTITUTIONAL INFORMATION

Public/private	Public
Student-faculty ratio	12:1
% faculty part-time	51
% faculty female	38
% faculty underrepresented minority	16
Total faculty	103

SURVEY SAYS...

Diverse opinions accepted in classrooms, Great research resources, Great library staff

STUDENTS

Enrollment of law school	627
% male/female	57/43
% part-time	0
% underrepresented minority	31

ACADEMICS

Academic Experience Rating	88
Profs interesting rating	84
Profs accessible rating	88

Advanced Degrees Offered

LLM, 1 year; JSD, minimum 3 years

Combined Degrees Offered

JD/ Masters in: business administration, chemistry, computer science, human resources and industrial relations, journalism, medicine, natural resources and environmental sciences, philosophy, political science, urban planning; JD/Ph. D.: philosophy, political science , veterinary medicine.

Academics

"You'll definitely get the bang for your buck" at the University of Illinois College of Law, "a jewel amid the cornfields [that boasts] the best mix of academic excellence, social interaction, and human decency for the best price available." Tuition is especially affordable for in-state students. The "tireless [administration] is also very accessible" and extraordinarily popular among students. "The new dean is extremely supportive of the students and does a wonderful job of building community."

Students at the U of I tell us emphatically that "the faculty is the school's greatest strength." The "tough but not unreasonable" professors are "prolific writers [who are] clearly brilliant and accomplished." Students say the professors "are, for the most part fantastic, both in and out of the classroom [and] always able to clarify concepts that are confusing. More significant, they are completely available [and] genuinely interested in teaching and working with students." The professors make an effort to be reached in that they "have open-door policies and are available for discussions with students about class, a job, or just life in general." Students also note that the school "employs a nice mix of tenured and adjunct faculty, which makes for a perfect balance of legal theory and real-world experience. The primary complaint that students have with regard to the faculty is "keeping the good professors around. "One student explains, "There's not much reason for them to stay in central Illinois. The school really needs to make an effort to not let the good ones get away."

Graduates enjoy "a great employment rate" thanks to an aggressive Office of Career Planning and Professional Development. As one transfer student attests, "I'm in a unique position in that I've seen how two different law schools operate. I was blown away by the quality of the Career Services Department at the University of Illinois. The administration goes to great lengths to make sure that not only do all University of Illinois College of Law graduates get jobs, but that they get the jobs they want." "If you do well here, nothing in Chicago will be off limits." However, students complain that the college "needs to broaden its resources [and] expand beyond the Midwestern market." Until that happens, "It is difficult to get much traction" on either coast "when searching for jobs in Champaign."

The facilities at the U of I "are good" in that large chunks "are wired," and the research resources of the library are as abundant as you'll find anywhere. Overall, though, the "rather Spartan [College of Law] could use some serious help." Suffice it to say, the "incredibly ugly and cheap-looking [building] does not give anyone goose bumps for the grand study of the law." One student writes, "There are no windows in any of the rooms." It's like going to school in a casino." Students note, "Sometimes seats are scarce [in the] crowded" classrooms, as well as in the "cramped" library, though now that the school has reduced the size of the incoming class, this should help to alleviate the problem. Also, wear layers because "There also seems to be a bit of a temperature control problem" no matter what the season.

Life

If they do say so themselves, the students at the U of I are "very amiable, noncompetitive, [and] very intellectually minded, yet not stuck on themselves." These are the "brightest [and] most fun" people—"all the cool, smart kids." Students at the U of I are also "a bit neurotic [and] love to hear their own voices." The student population "has a wonderful mix of student ethnicities, religions, sexual orientation, and gender." There is

REBECCA RAY, ASSISTANT DEAN FOR ADMISSIONS AND FINANCIAL AID
504 EAST PENNSYLVANIA AVENUE, ROOM 201, MC-594, CHAMPAIGN, IL 61820
TEL: 217-244-6415 FAX: 217-244-1478
E-MAIL: LAW-ADMISSIONS@ILLINOIS.EDU • WEBSITE: WWW.LAW.ILLINOIS.EDU

also a laid-back atmosphere on campus. "Everybody really cares about you. They want you to succeed, and it's almost difficult not to."

"The school truly is a community because of its manageable size. Lunches with the dean" are common, and there are "endless other ways to connect with the other students and, more important, the faculty." One content student writes, "The cafeteria has good food and, best of all, they carry Starbucks coffee." Students also say, "Although U of I is located in the corn fields of Illinois, it is impossible to feel isolated" because the administration "is constantly bringing in lecturers, symposiums, and guest speakers." In addition, the College of Law sponsors "a weekly happy hour, [at which] professors and administrators act as the celebrity bartenders."

Life outside the classroom has many positive aspects. Students are very "sports-oriented" and say "It is great to be on a Big Ten campus and be able to devote yourself to the study of law full-time," and surprising though it seems, "There is actually a lot to do in Urbana-Champaign." There are "great bars, coffee houses, [and] centers for the arts." There is also "a progressive music scene." Some students gripe that "social life can seem dominated by a frat/sorority type atmosphere," even at the law school level. "The town is basically designed for college students, so it gets a little dullsville at times." Many students would "prefer to be in a larger city," with Chicago being the example of choice. "Socially, we do the best we can with the town we're in," asserts one student. "That means we drink a lot [and] go en masse to football and basketball games."

Getting In

The average LSAT score for admitted students is 166. The median GPA is 3.5. Those numbers are serious but not forbidding. Note also that, while it's substantially cheaper for Illinois residents to attend the college, residency in the Land of Lincoln will not get you one iota of special treatment from the admissions office.

Clinical program required	No
Legal writing course requirement	Yes
Legal methods course requirement	No
Legal research course requirement	Yes
Moot court requirement	No
Public interest law requirement	No

ADMISSIONS

Selectivity Rating	90
# applications received	2,699
% applicants accepted	42
% acceptees attending	17
Median LSAT	163
LSAT Range (25th to 75th percentile)	158–165
Median undergrad GPA	3.55
Application fee	$0
Regular application deadline	3/15
Regular application notification	rolling
Transfer students accepted	Yes
Evening division offered	No
Part-time accepted	No
CAS accepted	Yes

FINANCIAL FACTS

Annual tuition (in-state out-of-state)	$38,497/$45,917
Books and supplies	$1,800
Financial aid application deadline	3/15
% of aid that is merit based	100
% receiving scholarships	96
Average debt	$95,803

EMPLOYMENT INFORMATION

Career Rating	60*	Grads Employed by Field (%)	
Total 2012 JD Grads	213	Academic	(5)
% for whom you have useable information	98	Business/Industry	(12)
% grads employed nine months out	81	Government	(8)
# employed full-time	168	Judicial Clerkship	(5)
# employed part-time	5	Private Practice	(61)
# employed bar required	146	Public Interest	(9)
# employed JD preferred	21		
# employed professional/other	5		
# employed non-professional	1		
# pursuing advanced degree	5		
# unemployed and seeking employment	22		
# not seeking employment	7		
% grads employed by school	10		
State for bar exam	IL		
Pass rate for first-time bar	93		

THE UNIVERSITY OF IOWA
COLLEGE OF LAW

INSTITUTIONAL INFORMATION
Public/private   Public
Student-faculty ratio   11:1
% faculty part-time   23
% faculty female   38
% faculty underrepresented
     minority   14
Total faculty   56

SURVEY SAYS...
Diverse opinions accepted in class-rooms, Great research resources, Great library staff

STUDENTS
Enrollment of law school   527
% male/female   57/43
% from out-of-state   52
% part-time   0
% underrepresented minority   18
% international   3
# of countries represented   8
Average age of entering class   25

ACADEMICS
Academic Experience Rating   84
Profs interesting rating   84
Profs accessible rating   78
Hours of study per day   3.43

Academic Specialties
International

Advanced Degrees Offered
LLM, 24 hours of academic credit and a thesis, 1 year

Combined Degrees Offered
JD/MBA, 4 years; JD/MA, 4 years; JD/MHA, 4 years; JD/MSW, 4 years; JD/MPH, 3.5 years; JD/MS, 4 years; JD/MD, 6 years

Academics

Students at the affordable University of Iowa College of Law are unanimous on one point: Iowa is "the most underrated school in the country." "If you want to learn from the best without giving an arm and a leg for tuition," they say, "come to this school." The "sympathetic" faculty at Iowa is "very concerned with providing the best academic experience." "Professors are demanding in a way that I know will make me a better lawyer," relates 2L. "They are brilliant yet not egomaniacs." "Some scare the crap out of you, and some create a warm classroom environment." Outside of class, "The professors are, for the most part, interesting and cool people," and interaction between students and professors is exceedingly common. Sure, they are "awkward socially," but "Even the most distinguished professors welcome you into their offices, and it's not uncommon to go out to dinner with your professor and a few classmates."

Classes here "tend toward the theoretical." "Iowa presents kind of a contradiction," proffers a 2L. "It is a theory-driven program that produces mostly practicing attorneys." Iowa's ten practice clinics are "very strong," "and there are plenty of slots available" (though you do have to lottery into them). "The Iowa City / Cedar Rapids area has opportunities to practice while in law school, but those opportunities are somewhat limited." The legal writing program garners mixed reviews. "We are learning to write legal briefs and memos from the best," contends a satisfied 1L. Others feel "cheated." "We could use a lot more hands-on training with writing and research," says one student. Pretty much everyone who mentions the moot court program is unhappy with it. "The faculty can't be bothered to provide meaningful coaching or instruction," laments one student.

The Career Services staff here "is a group of all-stars" that provides "all of the assistance you need." "The top 25 to 30 percent of students don't seem to have any trouble finding work in cities across the country, including New York, San Francisco, Los Angeles, and Boston." By and large, though, students end up practicing in one of "several large markets" throughout the Midwest. Some students complain that "Iowa could do better in attracting and encouraging employers outside of the Midwest." "If you want to work in the Midwest, this school is considered good, and employers are eager to interview you," advises a 2L. "If you want to work anywhere else, go to law school in that region."

The "really space-constrained" law school building is "functional, though it looks pretty awful." "It was built in the early '80s, and I think at that time people thought it was cool and futuristic," adds a 2L, "but now it just looks like something out of *Star Trek IV*." "Classrooms are pretty typical," though students "appreciate the plentiful outlets and wireless Internet." "There is no shortage of PCs available in the computer labs," and "The school also has very friendly tech gurus." The "extensive" law library is "a little bubble of greatness." It's "open late" and "always staffed by friendly librarians who know more about the law than anyone ever should."

Life

Students are "mostly white and from Iowa or Illinois," but there is also "a surprisingly large number of kids from the coasts." "I was actually surprised by how many non-Midwestern students are currently at the school," admits a 1L. Overall, it's "a good mix

JAN BARNES, ADMISSIONS COORDINATOR
320 MELROSE, IOWA CITY, IA 52242
TEL: 319-335-9095 FAX: 319-335-9646
E-MAIL: LAW-ADMISSIONS@UIOWA.EDU • WEBSITE: WWW.LAW.UIOWA.EDU

of people from all walks of life." There are "some very conservative points of view" but "young crazy liberals" predominate. There are "a lot of do-gooders who are very socially conscious and commit a tremendous amount of time to community and national issues." "U of I law students and most of the professors have a definite liberal slant," says a 2L. "If you're conservative and not articulate and able to defend your opinions, you'll never survive classroom discussion."

"Students at Iowa are competitive, certainly." "I was surprised by how many gunners there actually are," relates a 3L. It's "friendly" gunning, though. Iowa students are "a group of people who have their priorities in order, who are willing to lend a hand, and who are remarkably grounded in reality." "There's an earnestness and commitment to integrity and excellence that Iowa students, faculty, and staff all share," enthuses a 3L. "It makes Iowa a unique place, and it makes me hopeful for the legal profession as a whole. As a jaded California native and East Coast private college graduate, I never cease to be surprised by the quality and professionalism I've found here in the heartland."

Socially, though "People tend to buckle down when it is demanded," "You can be sure to find friends out at a bar" on virtually any given weekend night. "Everyone is very good friends with each other," and Iowa City is "a fun town." Coffee shops, libraries, bookstores, and great restaurants abound. There are "weekly Law Nights held at a local drinking establishment." "There's no such thing as a grad student bar in Iowa City," and there is "a pretty big divide between people who took time off and people who came straight from undergrad."

Getting In

Admitted students at the 25th percentile have LSAT scores of 158 and GPAs in the range of 3.5. Admitted students at the 75th percentile have LSAT scores of 164 and GPAs of around 3.8.

Clinical program required	No
Legal writing course requirement	Yes
Legal methods course requirement	Yes
Legal research course requirement	Yes
Moot court requirement	Yes
Public interest law requirement	No

ADMISSIONS

Selectivity Rating	83
# applications received	1,463
% applicants accepted	49
% acceptees attending	22
Average LSAT	161
Median LSAT	162
LSAT Range (25th to 75th percentile)	158–164
Average undergrad GPA	3.61
Median undergrad GPA	3.64
Application fee	$60
Regular application deadline	3/1
Transfer students accepted	Yes
Evening division offered	No
Part-time accepted	No
CAS accepted	Yes

FINANCIAL FACTS

Annual tuition (in-state out-of-state)	$25,608/$46,056
Books and supplies	$2,300
Fees	$1,736
Room & Board	$10,350
% first-year students receiving some sort of aid	89
% all students receiving some sort of aid	91
% of aid that is merit based	21
% receiving scholarships	67
Average grant	$21,864
Average loan	$33,848
Average total aid package	$47,995
Average debt	$95,574

EMPLOYMENT INFORMATION

Career Rating	89	
Total 2012 JD Grads	185	
% for whom you have useable information	100	
% grads employed nine months out	94	
Median starting salary	$57,408	
# employed full-time	158	
# employed part-time	16	
# employed bar required	141	
# employed JD preferred	19	
# employed professional/other	5	
# employed non-professional	9	
# pursuing advanced degree	2	
# unemployed and seeking employment	10	
# not seeking employment	7	
% grads employed by school	1	
State for bar exam	IA, IL, MN, NY, CA	
Pass rate for first-time bar	91	

Prominent Alumni
Kimberly Teehee, Senior Policy Advisor for Native American Affairs, Washington, DC; The Honorable Michael J. Melloy, Senior Judge, US Court of Appeals for the Eighth Circuit, Cedar Rapids; Mary K.W. Jones, Senior Vice President and General Counsel, Deere & Company, Moline.

Grads Employed by Field (%)
Academic (3)
Business/Industry (21)
Government (14)
Judicial Clerkship (12)
Military (2)
Private Practice (43)
Public Interest (5)

UNIVERSITY OF KANSAS
SCHOOL OF LAW

INSTITUTIONAL INFORMATION
Public/private   Public
Affiliation   No Affiliation
% faculty part-time   33
% faculty female   38
% faculty underrepresented
minority   10
Total faculty   58

SURVEY SAYS...
Great research resources

STUDENTS
Enrollment of law school   441
% male/female   61/39
% underrepresented minority   16
% international   2
# of countries represented   6
Average age of entering class   24

ACADEMICS
Academic Experience Rating   81
Profs interesting rating   81
Profs accessible rating   85
Hours of study per day   3.57

Academic Specialties
Commercial, Constitutional,
Corporation Securities, Criminal,
Environmental, International, Tribal,
Media, Taxation, Intellectual
Property

Advanced Degrees Offered
LLM in American Legal Studies,
LLM Program in Elder Law; Doctor
of Juridical Science (SJD) Degree

Combined Degrees Offered
JD/Master of Business
Administration; JD/ Master in East
Asian Languages and Cultures; JD/
MA in Economics; JD/MA in Global
Indigenous Studies; JD/Master of
Health Services Administration; JD/
MS in Journalism; JD/MA in
Philosophy; JD/Master of Public
Administration; JD/MA in Political
Science; JD/MA in Russian, East
European and Eurasian Studies; JD/
Master of Social Work; JD/Master of
Urban Planning.

Academics

Kansas Law is certainly considered a legal powerhouse in the Midwest. The university "offers a wide variety of classes that suit all types of students interested in an array of legal areas." As one third-year shares, "I've never found it challenging to find classes I'm interested in taking. [In fact,] there are usually too many classes and I have to narrow it down to what fits into my schedule the best." Moreover, students benefit from a curriculum that manages to deftly balance a "mix of traditional legal theory with practical skills." Another satisfied third-year adds, "The clinical programs are numerous and diverse. A student could have practical experience in every semester as an upperclassman, just through the clinics and externships provided by the school." However, some students do grumble that "the mandatory grade curve puts KU students at a disadvantage compared to other law schools within the region."

Students at KU seem to fully enjoy their time in the classroom. This can certainly be attributed to "absolutely fantastic professors" who are "brilliant, approachable, and want to be there." It's readily apparent that they "genuinely love their job and love the university." As one knowing third-year succinctly states, "They are very knowledgeable in their subject areas, friendly, accessible, and willing to help each student succeed."

One area that could use a little improvement is the actual law school building. Many say that it feels "dated" and a first-year colorfully suggests that it resembles an "old airport." Further, a disgruntled second-year laments that it's "crowded with print resources no one uses, lacking moot court space, lacking group study space [and] lacking effective air conditioning." Fortunately, though the law building might leave some wanting, the university's "research resources are also quite simply - wonderful." A first-year explains, "Our library is well stocked, and our librarians are very helpful, as well as available to us at all times. KU Law also provides us with Westlaw, LexisNexis, and Bloomberg research trainings, and representatives from those companies are available 24/7."

Finally, students also greatly appreciate the fact the administration is "very hands on." In fact, even the "Dean teaches classes and takes the time to mingle with the students constantly." As one excited first-year pleasantly sums up, "KU Law is still the most welcoming, diverse, inclusive, and supportive group of individuals I've yet to meet, and I would recommend it to anybody looking to law as a profession."

Life

Students at Kansas speak highly of their peers, finding them (among other choice adjectives) friendly, caring and helpful. As a second-year emphatically states, "The greatest strength of KU Law is that it is very congenial among the students. You hear these horror stories when you apply to law school of students stealing notes or destroying each other's outlines for a competitive edge, but the experience here at KU is much different. While people are still competing for rank, they are still willing to help each other out and compete in an honest and fair way. This, I believe, leads to a much more conducive environment for learning and excelling." A first-year concurs adding that "all of the 2Ls and 3Ls are very kind and supportive to new 1Ls and everyone looks out for one another."

STEVEN FREEDMAN, ASSISTANT DEAN OF ADMISSIONS
1535 W. 15TH STREET, LAWRENCE, KS 66045-7577
TEL: 785-864-4378 FAX: 785-864-5054
E-MAIL: ADMITLAW@KU.EDU • WEBSITE: WWW.LAW.KU.EDU

Beyond a warm and welcoming vibe, KU Law also provides students with a myriad of professional opportunities. As one proactive third-year delights in sharing, "I have had the opportunity to participate in an externship/clinic, serve on a legal publication, and work as a research assistant for a professor." Moreover, due to "KUs geographical location, it is midway between Kansas City and Topeka, there is an extensive range of externship options, either in a big city or in a state capital." Of course, fear not; these future JDs are also able to indulge in a little R & R every now and again. Indeed, we've been assured that KU offers a "great balance of school and fun" and students find plenty of time to "go out and socialize with [their] law school friends." Not surprisingly, everyone loves supporting the Jayhawks!

Getting In

KU's admissions process is fairly by the book. First and foremost, the committee considers each applicant's undergraduate GPA and LSAT score. Following these quantitative assessments, admissions officers carefully analyze personal statements, recommendations and employment history. The only admissions requirements are an undergraduate degree from an accredited university, sitting for the LSAT and registering with the Law School Admissions Council Credential Assembly Service.

Clinical program required	No
Legal writing course requirement	Yes
Legal methods course requirement	Yes
Legal research course requirement	Yes
Moot court requirement	No
Public interest law requirement	No

ADMISSIONS

Selectivity Rating	80
# applications received	962
% applicants accepted	54
% acceptees attending	27
Average LSAT	157
Median LSAT	157
LSAT Range (25th to 75th percentile)	154–159
Average undergrad GPA	3.45
Median undergrad GPA	3.51
Application fee	$55
Regular application deadline	5/1
Transfer students accepted	Yes
Evening division offered	No
Part-time accepted	No
CAS accepted	Yes

FINANCIAL FACTS

Annual tuition (in-state out-of-state)	$18,664/$31,474
Books and supplies	$1,000
Fees	$888
Room & Board	$10,474
Financial aid application deadline	4/1
Average debt	$74,454

EMPLOYMENT INFORMATION

Career Rating	85	
Total 2012 JD Grads	154	
% grads employed nine months out	86	
# employed full-time	123	
# employed part-time	8	
# employed bar required	104	
# employed JD preferred	23	
# employed professional/other	3	
# employed non-professional	1	
# pursuing advanced degree	2	
# unemployed and seeking employment	20	
# not seeking employment	1	
% grads employed by school	2	
State for bar exam	KS, MO, CA, CO, TX	
Pass rate for first-time bar	93	

Prominent Alumni
Hon. Mary H. Murgia, 9th Circuit Judge; Gov. Sam Brownback, State of Kansas Governor; Mary Beck Briscoe, 10th Circuit Judge.

Grads Employed by Field (%)
Academic (3)
Business/Industry (21)
Government (15)
Judicial Clerkship (7)
Military (2)
Private Practice (47)
Public Interest (5)

UNIVERSITY OF KENTUCKY
COLLEGE OF LAW

INSTITUTIONAL INFORMATION

Public/private	Public
Affiliation	No Affiliation
Student-faculty ratio	12:1
% faculty part-time	0
% faculty female	41
% faculty underrepresented minority	15
Total faculty	34

SURVEY SAYS...

Heavy use of Socratic method, Diverse opinions accepted in classrooms, Students love Lexington, KY

STUDENTS

Enrollment of law school	402
% male/female	57/43
% part-time	0
% underrepresented minority	15
% international	12
# of countries represented	1
Average age of entering class	23

ACADEMICS

Academic Experience Rating	81
Profs interesting rating	80
Profs accessible rating	82
Hours of study per day	3.41

Combined Degrees Offered

JD/MPA, JD/MBA, JD/Masters in Diplomacy and International Commerce, 4 years

Academics

The University of Kentucky's College of Law is a relatively small flagship state law school that attracts just as many out-of-state students as in-state, due to its solid academics and the accessibility of deans and professors. Small classes, combined with the commitment of this "dedicated" faculty indicate that "there are plenty of opportunities for interaction with professors." "The quality of instruction and the reputation of the school within the state of Kentucky are excellent," says a student.

Though many agree "the building itself is not much to look at" since it is "poorly laid out [and] falling apart," the professors inside its walls "are absolutely superb" and "open to discussion and opinions in class." "UK Law is the epitome of the Rule Against Judging a Book by Its Cover. While our building is outdated, the professors that teach in them are first class." What the facilities lack is "made up for in the general quality of professors and the approachability of the entire law school staff." Their doors are often open, "whether you want to discuss an issue from class or seek career advice," says a student. One professor even hugs her students as they leave the final, and "gets her feelings hurt if they don't stay in touch." In addition to flexible office hours, the professors and deans have had students "to their homes for dinner, participated in school intramural events and other outside activities such as tailgates that the law school hosts."

The "very communicative" administration is similarly caring and "seems to want to improve the school"; they try to provide as many resources as possible, but "because funding is low, we just don't have a lot of resources to work with." That being said, "you quickly learn which administrators to seek out when there are problems," as most agree "the school administration could do a better job communicating long term vision to students"; although "they do host feedback sessions /Town Hall meetings." Technology assistants are also "well-trained and will help with even non-school related computer issues."

The "excellent" first year legal writing and research program at UK places students in classes of 12, which leads to "extensive one-on-one time" to help hone in on these important, crucial skills. The program provides "detailed, practical experience." However, students say that beyond this program, "the school doesn't offer enough skills-based classes," and there aren't many areas in which to specialize. Yet, "you will find a well-rounded legal education," and UK does "a great job in setting up on campus interviews and providing externship opportunities." "If I had to choose a school again, I would no doubt choose UK," says one satisfied student.

Life

Lexington is "an excellent place to live," and everyone in this "involved student body" becomes "friends and helps each other out." The school naturally focuses "much more on individual progress," and "the competitiveness is at a minimum," providing "a community feel rather than a cutthroat atmosphere." This aura of laid-back professionalism "is conducive to collaboration among students." Since many UK students are from out-of-state, friends are easy to come by, and Student Bar Association events, speakers, and local flair offer plenty of places to interact.

DRUSILLA V. BAKERT, ASSOCIATE DEAN
209 LAW BUILDING, LEXINGTON, KY 40506-0048
TEL: 859-257-6770 FAX: 859-323-1061
E-MAIL: DBAKERT@EMAIL.UKY.EDU • WEBSITE: WWW.UKY.EDU/LAW

Clinical program required	No
Legal writing course requirement	Yes
Legal methods course requirement	No
Legal research course requirement	Yes
Moot court requirement	Yes
Public interest law requirement	No

UK is a town within itself, and "$5 student UK basketball tickets" help to provide a downtime respite. "The best part about UK Law School is the basketball team (Go Big Blue)." As with the classrooms, students say that "better facilities to accommodate the rigors of law school would make the place much nicer," including a lunch area, more bathrooms, and a parking lot closer to the school. Though school seems to keep everyone busy enough, the general collegiality of the student body means that social involvement is easy to find. "I have had the pleasure of interacting with outstandingly talented professors AND student colleagues," says one student.

Getting In

The University of Kentucky starts with a prospective student's LSAT scores and GPA when making an admissions decision. However, all applications are reviewed in full and other academic factors (such as writing ability, grade trends, and letters of recommendation) are also considered. Last year, the school extended just 456 offers of admission to more than 1,100 candidates, the majority of which were not residents of Kentucky. The median LSAT score for the entering class was 159 and their median GPA was 3.57.

ADMISSIONS

Selectivity Rating	**86**
# applications received	1,168
% applicants accepted	51
% acceptees attending	23
Median LSAT	158
LSAT Range (25th to 75th percentile)	155–161
Median undergrad GPA	3.51
Application fee	$50
Regular application deadline	3/1
Transfer students accepted	Yes
Evening division offered	No
Part-time accepted	No
CAS accepted	Yes

FINANCIAL FACTS

Annual tuition (in-state out-of-state)	$19,404/$33,618
Books and supplies	$900
Room & Board	$11,680
Financial aid application deadline	3/15
% first-year students receiving some sort of aid	90
% all students receiving some sort of aid	83
% of aid that is merit based	0
% receiving scholarships	68
Average grant	$7,500
Average loan	$26,400
Average total aid package	$30,000

EMPLOYMENT INFORMATION

Career Rating	**91**	
Total 2012 JD Grads	135	
% for whom you have useable information	100	
% grads employed nine months out	96	
Median starting salary	$47,500	
% job accepting grads providing useable salary information	57	
# employed full-time	119	
# employed part-time	10	
# employed bar required	104	
# employed JD preferred	14	
# employed professional/other	4	
# employed non-professional	7	
# pursuing advanced degree	1	
# unemployed and seeking employment	4	
# not seeking employment	1	
% grads employed by school	0	
State for bar exam	KY	
Pass rate for first-time bar	96	

Prominent Alumni
Mitch McConnell, U.S. Senator; Ben Chandler, U.S. Representative; Steve Reed, Former U.S. Attorney.

Grads Employed by Field (%)
Academic (2)
Business/Industry (19)
Government (7)
Judicial Clerkship (18)
Military (1)
Private Practice (49)
Public Interest (4)

UNIVERSITY OF MAINE
SCHOOL OF LAW

INSTITUTIONAL INFORMATION
Public/private	Public
Affiliation	No Affiliation
Student-faculty ratio	14:1
% faculty part-time	43
% faculty female	42
% faculty underrepresented minority	0
Total faculty	42

SURVEY SAYS...
Diverse opinions accepted in classrooms, Great library staff, Students love Portland, ME

STUDENTS
Enrollment of law school	286
% male/female	54/46
% from out-of-state	31
% part-time	4
% underrepresented minority	7
% international	2
# of countries represented	3
Average age of entering class	28

ACADEMICS
Academic Experience Rating	**75**
Profs interesting rating	88
Profs accessible rating	86
Hours of study per day	4

Advanced Degrees Offered
The law school recently began offering an LLM primarily intended for foreign students and practitioners who have earned a law degree outside the United States. The LLM program normally is completed in 1 academic year, which begins for all new students in late August. The program requires completion of 24 semester hours of credit.

Combined Degrees Offered
JD/MA Public Policy & Mgt, 4 years; JD/MCP Community Planning & Mgt, 4 years; JD/MS Health Policy and Mgt, 4 years; JD/MBA Business Administration, 4 years

Academics

The University of Maine School of Law is "a small school with many opportunities to develop personal, professional relationships." Students tell us there's a nice balance of academic legal subjects and practical lawyering skills. In addition to the standard tenets of legal theory, there's a pretty good selection of clinics. Internships and externships are ample, as well. There's also a patent law program and a notable marine law institute. While "the cost of tuition is not low for out-of-state students," it's worth noting that Maine Law accepts a limited number of students from New Hampshire, Rhode Island, and Vermont at a reduced tuition rate.

Students tell us, "The very small class size—as compared to other law schools—is a great advantage." Small class sizes let students "become familiar with the entire student body and the faculty" and "encourage class participation, which in turn encourages thoughtful interaction with the subject matter of the class." By virtually all reports, the faculty is "absolutely amazing." Professors are "very interactive and caring." "The professors are as talented as they are accessible and make students feel like they are names instead of numbers," says a 1L. Outside of class, faculty members are "easily accessible." The "lovely" administration "likewise is very approachable." There's some red tape, though. Sometimes, students have "no idea what is going on, which is not a good thing for such a small school." Registration can be problematic, as well. "There are way too many lottery classes," vents a 2L. "Students are sometimes stuck with taking classes they are not truly interested in taking."

Maine Law is "the only law school in Maine," and if you're looking to hang out your shingle or otherwise find legal work in the Pine Tree State, there's really no question that this school is the place for you. Students enjoy "unparalleled access to externships and jobs in public interest law, private practice, the judiciary, and governmental agencies." "You will make connections and network with your Maine peers in a way that just wouldn't be possible at an out-of-state school," promises a 2L. Career Services is reportedly "very kind, warm, and helpful," as well. You can "ask a question without needing an appointment or waiting in a line."

Despite "significant improvements," the overall state of the accommodations here remains "pretty terrible." "Don't come to Maine expecting top-notch facilities," warns a 2L. "The school itself is a physically strange building." We have to agree with the 3L, who calls it a "concrete toilet-paper roll." Technology is merely adequate, and there's a "lack of community space to chat with students and professors between classes or hold study groups." On the plus side, "Library resources are as good as you'll find anywhere."

Life

The student population isn't very ethnically diverse, but "There are individuals from all walks of life and many differing ages and opinions" at Maine Law. Nontraditional students "with families and children and prior careers" are fairly common. "Weirdoes abound." The political spectrum runs the gamut. "There is a nice mix at the school," relates a 1L, "conservatives and liberals, environmentalists and capitalists." "Most anybody would feel welcome to engage in a friendly debate here, regardless of their leanings."

The "low-competition" academic atmosphere is "warm and inviting." All first-year students "take almost all of their classes together and get to know each other." "There is a real sense of community," and "Nothing about the school is cutthroat." "Maine Law is

ALISON BEYEA, DIRECTOR OF ADMISSIONS
246 DEERING AVE, PORTLAND, ME 04102
TEL: 207-780-4341 FAX: 207-780-4239
E-MAIL: LAWADMISSIONS@MAINE.EDU • WEBSITE: MAINELAW.MAINE.EDU

as small as it gets, so it naturally engenders a close-knit community," explains a 1L. "How people present themselves during their three years at Maine Law will very likely carry forward into their future legal careers. There's a good chance that most Maine Law students will practice law in Maine, and the legal community in Maine is small, too. Our classmates of today will be our professional peers of the future."

The social scene at Maine Law is generally solid. Student events are widely attended and opportunities to gather at various bars are common. Portland is the largest city in Maine, but that's not saying much. Portland does have great oceanfront scenery and kind of an old New England feel, and it's a fantastic little city for living and working. The bright lights of Boston are within reasonable driving distance. A handful of ski resorts and a multitude of outdoor activities are also nearby.

Getting In

The admissions profile at Maine Law is slightly more competitive than your average public law school in a sparsely populated state. Admitted students at the 25th percentile have LSAT scores about 153, and undergraduate GPAs average just less than 3.2. At the 75th percentile, LSAT scores approach 160, and GPAs are about 3.6.

Clinical program required	No
Legal writing course requirement	Yes
Legal methods course requirement	No
Legal research course requirement	Yes
Moot court requirement	No
Public interest law requirement	No

ADMISSIONS

Selectivity Rating	**74**
# applications received	929
% applicants accepted	56
% acceptees attending	17
Average LSAT	155
Median LSAT	155
LSAT Range (25th to 75th percentile)	152–157
Average undergrad GPA	3.28
Median undergrad GPA	3.31
Application fee	$50
Regular application deadline	4/15
Early application deadline	11/15
Early application notification	12/30
Transfer students accepted	Yes
Evening division offered	No
Part-time accepted	Yes
CAS accepted	Yes

FINANCIAL FACTS

Annual tuition (in-state out-of-state)	$23,610/$34,680
Books and supplies	$1,500
Fees	$1,270
Room & Board	$14,200
Financial aid application deadline	2/15
% of aid that is merit based	100
% receiving scholarships	33
Average grant	$7,442
Average total aid package	$34,995
Average debt	$91,060

EMPLOYMENT INFORMATION

Career Rating	**72**	**Prominent Alumni**
Total 2012 JD Grads	87	Hon. John A. Woodcock, Chief District
% for whom you have useable information	100	Judge, United States District Court of Maine; Hon. Leigh I. Saufley, Chief Justice
% grads employed nine months out	72	of the Maine Supreme Judicial Court;
Median starting salary	$44,500	Janet T. Mills, Attorney General of Maine.
% job accepting grads providing useable salary information	51	**Grads Employed by Field (%)**
# employed full-time	52	Business/Industry (18)
# employed part-time	11	Government (10)
# employed bar required	40	Judicial Clerkship (13)
# employed JD preferred	11	Private Practice (28)
# employed professional/other	6	Public Interest (2)
# employed non-professional	6	
# pursuing advanced degree	4	
# unemployed and seeking employment	17	
# not seeking employment	1	
% grads employed by school	0	
State for bar exam	ME	
Pass rate for first-time bar	74.6	

University of Maryland
Francis King Carey School of Law

INSTITUTIONAL INFORMATION

Public/private	Public
Affiliation	No Affiliation
% faculty part-time	46
% faculty female	43
% faculty underrepresented minority	15
Total faculty	127

SURVEY SAYS...

Diverse opinions accepted in classrooms, Great research resources, Beautiful campus

STUDENTS

Enrollment of law school	906
% male/female	49/51
% from out-of-state	40
% part-time	22
% underrepresented minority	36
% international	5
# of countries represented	17
Average age of entering class	25

ACADEMICS

Academic Experience Rating	84
Profs interesting rating	77
Profs accessible rating	75
Hours of study per day	3.80

Academic Specialties

Commercial, Constitutional, Corporation Securities, Criminal, Environmental, Human Rights, International, Labor, Taxation, Intellectual Property

Advanced Degrees Offered

JD, 3 years full-time day; 4 years evening; LLM 1 year full-time

Combined Degrees Offered

JD/Ph.D. Public Policy, 7 years; JD/MA Public Policy, 4 years; JD/MBA, 4 years; JD/MA Public Management, 4 years; JD/MA Criminal Justice, 3.5–4 years; JD/MSW, 3.5–4 years; JD/MA Liberal Arts, 4 years; JD/MA Community Planning, 4 years; JD/Pharm.D. Pharmacy 7 years; JD/MPH, 4 years

Academics

With "great opportunities for hands-on lawyering," and low in-state tuition for residents, the University of Maryland School of Law is "very well-connected to the Baltimore/Maryland legal community," with a "strong commitment to public service and social justice," and recognized legal specialties in health, environmental law, clinical law, and trial advocacy. The school "has tremendous relationships with organizations in Washington, D.C., the Maryland legislature, and many congressional offices," which makes it "extremely easy" to gain the kind of practical experience legal employers will be looking for come hiring season. The clinical offerings here are both required and "hard to beat": "Not only was I able to argue before a state appellate court during my second year, but I have also received credit for doing to externships during my third year," says a 3L.

Seven professional schools all share the same campus in Baltimore, which can overburden some of the administrative offices; students cite the financial aid office's lag time, and a career development office that "generally lacks important contacts in the work field." Still, the school boasts an active recruiting program and a high job placement rate, while the main head honchos at the school are very accessible, and "many of the deans also teach classes and are available to all students, even if you don't have them as a professor." The school's great strength is "teaching you how to be a smart and effective lawyer," through a few students say there is relatively little class time devoted to "cutting-edge legal scholarship and critical theory," and complain that "the popular courses are filled so quickly."

Maryland professors are "top-notch," being both "incredibly smart legal thinkers and, more importantly, fantastic teachers in the classroom." Nearly all of the professors "have practiced law for a decade or more before coming to the law school," which not only contributes to their legal experience, but to their sympathy for the demands of the profession. Professors and staff are all "very accommodating" to students trying to get through law school while working—night classes are made available to students in their second and third years—and faculty are "very helpful in advising students on how to mitigate stress and handle the competing interests of law school." "I have had a number of brilliant and committed adjunct professors who understand the burdens associated with working and going to school full-time," says a student. "Even if you are not in their class, they help you with course-related questions, study skills, and exam strategies," says another.

Life

As a whole, there is a presiding "positive attitude" among the "friendly" student body, which is "smart and capable." Cliques do tend to form within sections (as with many law schools), and "day students are way more social than the evening students," but there is definitely a sense of "we're all in it together." The student body is also quite diverse, and people "don't have the sense that cultural groups self-segregate here."

While the law school itself is "beautiful," and "new and gorgeous with all the technical bells and whistles," the location of the law school is "truly the worst...although that is not really the school's fault." "Baltimore is an impressive city in many respects, but the campus is not located in one of the city's many pleasant neighborhoods," says a student of the surrounding area, where "things around school shut down as soon as it is dark." There is

CONNIE BEALS, ASSISTANT DEAN OF ADMISSIONS & STUDENT RECRUITING
500 WEST BALTIMORE STREET, BALTIMORE, MD 21201
TEL: 410-706-3492 FAX: 410-706-1793
E-MAIL: ADMISSIONS@LAW.UMARYLAND.EDU • WEBSITE: WWW.LAW.UMARYLAND.EDU

"no need to go out and buy a Kevlar vest or anything," but "just be sure to do your research, and if you have a chance to, come look around before signing a lease—I would advise that." Students who live on campus are often disappointed with restaurant and nightlife options, and some students feel that finding entertainment "is difficult if you don't own a car," as the social life at the school struggles "because many students commute...and this damages the sense of community." On-campus activities tend to be based on legal issues and career-building, rather than pure socialization, though law students can take advantage of the gym, pool, and student lounge at the brand new campus center.

The law school curve does incite a bit of competition among students, which is more "collaborative" than cutthroat, but it still creates an atmosphere "with enough competition to encourage a race to the top." "Although we all compete against each other, I do not think that anyone at this law school would sabotage another student in anyway," says one, and everyone seems to agree.

Getting In

The school prides itself on a "holistic review" of each applicant's file, which takes into account the background and experiences that students might bring to help diversify classroom discussions. Students may also transfer to the school after completing a year of law school elsewhere. Admitted students for the entering class of 2011 at the 25th percentile have LSAT scores of approximately 156 and GPAs around 3.3. Admitted students at the 75th percentile have LSAT scores of 163 and GPAs in the 3.75 range.

Clinical program required	Yes
Legal writing course requirement	Yes
Legal methods course requirement	Yes
Legal research course requirement	Yes
Moot court requirement	Yes
Public interest law requirement	Yes

ADMISSIONS

Selectivity Rating	90
# applications received	3,068
% applicants accepted	27
% acceptees attending	26
Average LSAT	158
Median LSAT	162
LSAT Range (25th to 75th percentile)	151–164
Average undergrad GPA	3.50
Median undergrad GPA	3.65
Application fee	$70
Regular application deadline	4/15
Transfer students accepted	Yes
Evening division offered	Yes
Part-time accepted	Yes
CAS accepted	Yes

FINANCIAL FACTS

Annual tuition (in-state out-of-state)	$24,426/$36,042
Books and supplies	$1,725
Fees	$1,667
Room & Board (on/off campus)	$22,469/$28,139
Financial aid application deadline	3/1
% first-year students receiving some sort of aid	86
% all students receiving some sort of aid	82
% of aid that is merit based	63
% receiving scholarships	36
Average grant	$5,795
Average loan	$32,381
Average total aid package	$57,133
Average debt	$122,349

EMPLOYMENT INFORMATION

Career Rating	88	**Prominent Alumni**
Total 2012 JD Grads	319	Christine A. Edwards, Partner, Winston &
% grads employed nine months out	91	Strawn; Benjamin R. Civiletti, former US
Median starting salary	$60,000	Attorney General; Senior Partner, Venable;
% job accepting grads providing		The Honorable Andre M. Davis, U.S. Court
useable salary information	80	of Appeals for the Fourth Circuit.
# employed full-time	261	**Grads Employed by Field (%)**
# employed part-time	30	Academic (6)
# employed bar required	201	Business/Industry (16)
# employed JD preferred	62	Government (14)
# employed professional/other	28	Judicial Clerkship (19)
# employed non-professional	0	Military (1)
# pursuing advanced degree	4	Private Practice (27)
# unemployed and seeking employment	19	Public Interest (9)
# not seeking employment	4	
% grads employed by school	8	
State for bar exam	MD	
Pass rate for first-time bar	81	

UNIVERSITY OF MEMPHIS
CECIL C. HUMPHREYS SCHOOL OF LAW

Academics

While it may not have Ivy League name recognition, the University of Mephis Cecil C. Humphreys School of Law's "reputation far exceeds [its] rank." As "the only law school in Memphis", the University of Mephis' students over and over again call it "a gem" and "a diamond in the rough." "I came to this school despite options to go to tier 1 schools in the US News and World Report Rankings. The academic life is as rigorous as any intellectual could want, and the social atmosphere of the school as is team-oriented as it gets." The U of M's professors, who are "down to earth, speak for their chosen fields eloquently, and very respectful", "combine Ivy League educations with real-world experience to create classroom experiences that are both challenging and relevant." "I was surprised at how approachable and genuinely interested the administration and professors were in students' opinions and their overall well-being." While approachable, the faculty is "entrenched in the Socratic method" and rigorous. One student notes a noticeable reduction in the size of his class "mostly because of those old-school "I will haze you by employing the Socratic Method" type profs." Some students say they wish the law program was "more practical", or had more "curriculum diversity": the "abundance of opportunities to work in criminal law, family law, elder, and housing in Memphis" may make it harder to practice an "area of the law that is not so much in need here (business, intellectual property)."

Also among the U of M's prime features are shining facilities: the school recently "opened in a new, restored historic courthouse and customs building, and all of the facilities, library, and classrooms were (and still are) top notch." Classrooms boast "great wireless internet, acoustics, and seating arrangement", and students take pride in their "beautiful" surroundings, asserting that "since the move into the renovated building downtown, there's no way we can't compete with any school in the country on facilities."

What students arguably love the most, though, is how the University of Memphis competes in "bang for your buck." "The price...is very low compared to the national average, and in my book that meant getting a huge value for my legal education." This value doesn't sacrifice job readiness: students report that the university is "dedicated to ensuring our graduates hit the ground running." Extracurricular and internship opportunities include the "Law Review, Mock Trial (both inter and intra school competitions), clinics, and the school's dynamic Memphis Association of Law and Business", as well as "opportunities to volunteer for first year students, such as the Saturday Legal Clinic and the weekday divorce clinic", and "networking opportunities with local professionals and the Memphis Bar Association."

Dr. Sue Ann McClellan, Assistant Dean for Law Admissions
1 N. Front Street, Memphis, TN 38103-2189
Tel: 901-678-5403 Fax: 901-678-0741
E-Mail: lawadmissions@memphis.edu • Website: www.memphis.edu/law

Life

"The school's location in the heart of downtown" Memphis strikes students as "perfect": "The proximity of the campus to downtown restaurants, national and college sports arenas, and other venues really make the school appealing." There's "a great connection between the school and the city" both socially and professionally; U of M students enjoy a campus situated "within blocks of all the courts and numerous attorney offices which makes for easy field trips or internships." Apart from the job-seeking grind, popular activities and destinations include local "Grizzlies games", and "Beale Street", where it's easy to run into "my boss and other lawyers" and "build relationships." Plenty of amenities are available on campus, as well: "The law building sits right on the Mississippi river and has a great book/food store and also some recreational equipment in the lounge." "Our small class sizes create a friendly atmosphere both inside and outside the classroom", and students "cannot stress enough how awesome it is to live, go to school, gain outside experience, and have a fun social life all within half a mile."

Getting In

For the entering class of 2012, the median LSAT was 154 and the median GPA 3.25.

Clinical program required	No
Legal writing course requirement	No
Legal methods course requirement	Yes
Legal research course requirement	Yes
Moot court requirement	No
Public interest law requirement	Yes

ADMISSIONS

Selectivity Rating	86
# applications received	817
% applicants accepted	34
% acceptees attending	39
Average LSAT	154
Median LSAT	154
LSAT Range (25th to 75th percentile)	152–157
Average undergrad GPA	3.25
Median undergrad GPA	3.25
Application fee	$25
Regular application deadline	3/1
Regular notification	4/1
Transfer students accepted	Yes
Evening division offered	No
Part-time accepted	Yes
CAS accepted	Yes

International Students

TOEFL required of international students	Yes

FINANCIAL FACTS

Annual tuition (in-state out-of-state)	$15,086/$36,958
Books and supplies	$1,912
Fees	$1,748
Room & Board	$9,265
Financial aid application deadline	5/1
% first-year students receiving some sort of aid	86
% all students receiving some sort of aid	88
% of aid that is merit based	9
% receiving scholarships	37
Average grant	$8,887
Average loan	$24,665
Average total aid package	$25,269
Average debt	$72,993

EMPLOYMENT INFORMATION

Career Rating	84
Total 2012 JD Grads	134
% grads employed nine months out	85
Median starting salary	$52,000
% job accepting grads providing useable salary information	70
# employed full-time	101
# employed part-time	9
# employed bar required	86
# employed JD preferred	16
# employed professional/other	7
# employed non-professional	1
# pursuing advanced degree	2
# unemployed and seeking employment	14
# not seeking employment	4
% grads employed by school	0
State for bar exam	TN, CA, GA, CO, MS
Pass rate for first-time bar	88.6

Prominent Alumni
Honorable Bernice Donald, Judge, U.S. 6th Circuit Court of Appeals; Steve Cohen, US Congressman, TN 9th District; Caroline Hunter, Commissioner, Federal Election Commission.

Grads Employed by Field (%)
Academic (1)
Business/Industry (15)
Government (9)
Judicial Clerkship (5)
Military (2)
Private Practice (63)
Public Interest (5)

UNIVERSITY OF MIAMI
SCHOOL OF LAW

INSTITUTIONAL INFORMATION

Public/private	Private
% faculty part-time	57
% faculty female	43
% faculty underrepresented minority	20
Total faculty	190

SURVEY SAYS...

Great library staff, Students love Coral Gables, FL, Good social life

STUDENTS

Enrollment of law school	447
% male/female	58/42
% from out-of-state	42
% underrepresented minority	36
% international	3
# of countries represented	10
Average age of entering class	23

ACADEMICS

Academic Experience Rating	**82**
Profs interesting rating	78
Profs accessible rating	75
Hours of study per day	3.74

Academic Specialties

Civil Procedure, Commercial, Constitutional, Corporation Securities, Criminal, Environmental, Government Services, Human Rights, International, Labor, Property, Taxation, Intellectual Property

Advanced Degrees Offered

International Law; Estate Planning; Ocean and Coastal Law; Real Property Development and Taxation.

Academics

Set in one of the "most unique cities in the U.S.," students flock to the University of Miami School of Law for its "incredibly diverse" student body, "accomplished, approachable" professors and the incredible "weather." UM Law provides all of the advantages of being on the doorstep of a vibrant legal and business community while also offering a location on the university's beautiful main campus in Coral Gables. Corporate, international, and intellectual property law are among the school's strengths. In addition to pursuing a typical JD degree, UM Law offers five LLM programs including International Law, Ocean and Coastal Law, Real Estate Law, Estate Planning, and Tax Law. Students also have the opportunity to pursue joint degree programs, combining their JD/LLM degrees and JD/master's degrees in Business Administration, Music Business and Entertainment Industries, Marine Affairs, Communications, and Public Health.

The student body at UM is "incredibly diverse in terms of work and life experience." Some say, "The student body is too large for comfort," but at least the crowd is impressive. Students say their peers are "highly intelligent, driven people."

Students say they are "quite impressed with professors and their accomplishments." "Beyond office hours, they are available to their students." Given the large class sizes, "Professors expect students to be prepared for class and to work hard." In return, "They take an active interest in the students' learning, and generally treat students as younger colleagues." When it comes to professorial accolades, students say that, for the most part, there are plenty of opportunities to learn from the best: "Miami is a flashy city with lots to do, and the accolades of the faculty speak to that big-city, flashy, sleek, Miami feel especially well."

The administration is "very diverse, intelligent, and engaging." "We gain access to a variety of famous speakers and experts in the legal community." Due to Miami's reputation of being an international hub, "particularly with South America we receive great visiting professors from that area in the fields of international transactions and arbitration/mediation." Despite the beauty of the law school's campus, the facilities themselves "are aging," and the classrooms are "too small," and are "not up-to-date in terms of technology." Fortunately, "New facilities are in the works" and a project to upgrade the technology standards both within the classroom and school facilities was completed in 2013. As it stands, "The law library and undergrad library are outstanding. Although it lacks computers, everyone has laptops complete with wireless network accessibility." The librarians "continually provide training in both Lexis and Westlaw which [is] quite helpful." Others note, "The new administration has started to overhaul how the school is run." "I am very optimistic about the direction the law school is taking under Dean Patricia White. She has already done wonderful things in [a] short time at the law school. Her accomplishments range from grand (a new building scheduled to be completed in two years in addition to a complete overhaul of our writing program) to subtle (more clinical space, no increase in tuition, and greater accessibility to the students than the prior administration)." In recent years, "UM [has] made significant increases in clinical opportunities. There are so many clinical opportunities now that picking between them is a tough choice."

Beyond the occasional griping about the facilities, students' only major complaint is the limited resources for students planning on practicing outside the Florida area. However, for those looking to put down their legal roots in Florida, "as the only premier

THERESE LAMBERT, DIRECTOR OF STUDENT RECRUITMENT
1311 MILLER DR, ROOM F203, CORAL GABLES, FL 33124-8087
TEL: 305-284-6746 FAX: 305-284-4400
E-MAIL: ADMISSIONS@LAW.MIAMI.EDU • WEBSITE: WWW.LAW.MIAMI.EDU

law school in the South Florida–area...students [here] have a tremendous advantage in the local (Miami, Fort Lauderdale, etc.) job markets. Local employers love Miami Law students, and it makes networking very easy." The school also recently created the Legal Corp program, a postgraduate fellowship that places recent law graduates in public sector organizations nationwide.

Life

The University of Miami campus, as a whole, "is a beautiful tropical oasis, with a large lake, fountains, and tropical landscaping everywhere." "The campus is beautiful; it looks like a country club," which provides "a very peaceful and pleasant environment." However, students note, the law school facilities "are getting a little rundown, but rumor has it that a new facility is in the works for sometime in the next year or two."

The student body at UM "is relatively easygoing and likes to work hard and play hard." Those drawn to study here are a mirror of the city itself, "elite in intelligence and social skills compared to most law schools." Others add, "It's Miami, enough said. Beautiful campus, beautiful people, perfect weather. We wear shorts to class almost every day." When it comes to socializing, nightlife in the city is spectacular. On campus, "There are many ways to get involved in students org[anization]s and meet people." "Football games are a blast, the student bar association provides a tailgate for law students where games are played and food and beer are provided."

Getting In

UM reigns supreme in the legal community of South Florida. If you want to practice in this region, you can't do much better than this school. The average undergraduate GPA for the fall 2012 entering class was 3.36 with an average LSAT of 157.

Combined Degrees Offered

JD/LLM/MBA; JD/MBA; JD/MPH Public Health; JD/MPS Marine Affairs; JD/MM Music Business & Entertainment Industries; JD/MA Arts Presenting and Live Entertainment Management; JD/MA Communications; JD/MSEd Community & Social Change; JD/LLM International Law; JD/LLM Ocean and Coastal Law; JD/LLM Real Property Development; JD/LLM Taxation; JD/ PhD Environmental Science & Policy

Legal writing course requirement	Yes
Legal methods course requirement	Yes
Legal research course requirement	Yes
Moot court requirement	No
Public interest law requirement	No

ADMISSIONS

Selectivity Rating	82
# applications received	4,729
% applicants accepted	46
% acceptees attending	20
Average LSAT	157
LSAT Range (25th to 75th percentile)	156–160
Average undergrad GPA	3.36
Application fee	$60
Regular application deadline	7/31
Early application deadline	2/3
Transfer students accepted	Yes
Evening division offered	No
CAS accepted	Yes

FINANCIAL FACTS

Annual tuition	$42,000
Books and supplies	$1,200
Fees	$938
Room & Board	$21,216
Financial aid application deadline	3/1
% first-year students receiving some sort of aid	79
% all students receiving some sort of aid	86
% of aid that is merit based	14
% receiving scholarships	33
Average grant	$11,414
Average loan	$33,042
Average total aid package	$38,401
Average debt	$1140,032

EMPLOYMENT INFORMATION

Career Rating	87	**Prominent Alumni**
Total 2012 JD Grads	461	The Honorable Fred Lewis, Chief Justice,
% grads employed nine months out	86.1	Florida Supreme Court; Carolyn B. Lamm,
Median starting salary	$60,000	Partner, White & Case (DC); Former ABA
% job accepting grads providing		President; Roy Black, Prominent Criminal
useable salary information	47.5	Defense Attorney, Legal Expert.
# employed full-time	385	**Grads Employed by Field (%)**
# employed part-time	12	Academic (2)
# employed bar required	327	Business/Industry (15)
# employed JD preferred	54	Government (10)
# employed professional/other	14	Judicial Clerkship (4)
# employed non-professional	2	Military (1)
# pursuing advanced degree	17	Private Practice (46)
# unemployed and seeking employment	8	Public Interest (8)
# not seeking employment	26	
% grads employed by school	9.1	
State for bar exam	FL, NY, NJ, CA, MA	
Pass rate for first-time bar	81.6	

UNIVERSITY OF MICHIGAN
LAW SCHOOL

INSTITUTIONAL INFORMATION

Public/private	Public
% faculty part-time	30
% faculty female	33
% faculty underrepresented minority	11
Total faculty	129

SURVEY SAYS...

Great research resources, Beautiful campus

STUDENTS

Enrollment of law school	1,124
% male/female	55/46
% from out-of-state	78
% part-time	0
% underrepresented minority	10
% international	3
# of countries represented	42
Average age of entering class	25

ACADEMICS

Academic Experience Rating	98
Profs interesting rating	94
Profs accessible rating	86
Hours of study per day	3.99

Academic Specialties

Civil Procedure, Commercial, Constitutional, Corporation Securities, Criminal, Environmental, Government Services, Human Rights, International, Labor, Legal History, Legal Philosophy, Property, Taxation, Intellectual Property

Advanced Degrees Offered

LLM Master of Laws; International Tax LLM; MCL Master of Comparative Law; and SJD Doctor of the Science of Law

Academics

As a consistently top ten law school, the University of Michigan has a lot to brag about in terms of "name recognition, academic reputation, [and] alumni network". That said, even though "everyone at Michigan is really proud to be here", they're not really bragging types: the "Michigan Difference" provides "a superior legal education while avoiding the snottiness that ordinary accompanies it—and employers recognize it." U of M professors "are brilliant, accessible, and committed to the classroom", and "frequently attend happy hours or invite us into their homes. They are seriously wonderful, friendly people." Indeed, many students underscore the fact that professors represent "a fantastic array of ...theoretical and political perspectives" and are "more friendly or open with students at other top law schools." Some students express a desire for "more diversity in course offerings", and their comments frequently reflect the opinion that the "Transnational Law course requirement is a waste", but they generally agree that the "academic experience at Michigan has been out of this world."

Though "the alumni network is massive", job placement is "top notch", and "if you throw a rock in a big law firm, you're likely to hit a Michigan Law grad excited to dish about the school", some students argue that the "school needs a better career services office that is better adapted to the post-recession legal market." Equally do they report, though, that the "Administration is phenomenal," "friendly, accessible, and responsive," and "responds to emails with amazing promptness and a willingness to help." Students looking to cast a wide net in job placement benefit from Michigan's Midwestern location: "I love how well Michigan places nationally—it is very nice to not be married to one market."

U of M's students adore the law school facilities, which "are not only functionally amazing but spectacular to look at as well. Easily the most aesthetically pleasing law school in the country, and new renovations to the Lawyer's Club should make it better than ever." "Classrooms are well-equipped, with the newer facilities providing 9 whiteboards, hydraulic podiums, and individual microphones for every student", and "the buildings are architectural gems, especially the Reading Room." This, of course, comes at a cost: Michigan doesn't give as significant an in-state tuition break as many other state universities (though they do give a competitive amount of financial aid), and "Like any law school, debt is a huge problem." Broadly speaking, students express a high degree of satisfaction with the education they're paying for: "Michigan students rarely want for anything in terms of opportunities, experiences, or facilities."

SARAH C. ZEARFOSS, ASSISTANT DEAN AND DIRECTOR OF ADMISSIONS
625 SOUTH STATE STREET, ANN ARBOR, MI 48109-1215
TEL: 734-764-0537 FAX: 734-647-3218
E-MAIL: LAW.JD.ADMISSIONS@UMICH.EDU • WEBSITE: WWW.LAW.UMICH.EDU

Life

Michigan students, "genuine and decent people who are simply fun", take pride in their humility: "Everyone here is smart, but nobody is a jerk about it. Employers know that, too." "The friendly, relatively noncompetitive atmosphere is why I chose Michigan Law, and I am so grateful for it every single day." Many of them picked Michigan over other choices because "the cut-throat, unhappy reputation of other schools is the exact opposite of what you find at Michigan" and "the collegiality of the students and professors here is so refreshing." The university encourages this dynamic: "the school seems to make life, especially during finals period, as easy as possible, going the length of increasing/making free printing, keeping facilities open longer, etc."

They're also delighted by their surroundings, joking that the "law quad" is so "gorgeous" it's like "we basically go to school at Hogwarts." The excellent facilities augment quality of life on campus, offering "ample room to study, relax, socialize, and bask in the awe of one of the most beautiful academic buildings on the planet."

Getting In

Though Michigan follows ABA requirements to consider the highest score of any applicant who has taken the LSAT more than once, they do consider the average score as well. Its median LSAT range is 166-170 and median GPA range is 3.58-3.83. It's possible to start in the summer if you apply accordingly, and as a Teach for America partner school, TFA corps members or alumni can have their application fees waived by contacting the school.

Combined Degrees Offered

JD/MBA; JD/Ph.D. Economics; JD/MA Modern Middle Eastern & North African Studies; JD/Master Public Policy; JD/MS Natural Resources; JD/Master Health Services Administration; JD/MA Russian & East European Studies; JD/MA World Politics; JD/MSW; JD/Master Science Information; JD/Master Public Health; JD/MA Japanese Studies; JD/Master Urban Planning; JD/MA Chinese Studies

Clinical program required	No
Legal writing course requirement	Yes
Legal methods course requirement	Yes
Legal research course requirement	Yes
Moot court requirement	No
Public interest law requirement	No

ADMISSIONS

Selectivity Rating	96
# applications received	5,062
% applicants accepted	24
% acceptees attending	28
Median LSAT	169
LSAT Range (25th to 75th percentile)	166–170
Median undergrad GPA	3.73
Application fee	$75
Regular application deadline	2/15
Early application deadline	11/15
Early application notification	12/15
Transfer students accepted	Yes
Evening division offered	No
Part-time accepted	No
CAS accepted	Yes

FINANCIAL FACTS

Annual tuition (in-state out-of-state)	$48,012/$51,010
Books and supplies	$6,700
Fees	$244
Room & Board	$12,000
% first-year students receiving some sort of aid	94
% all students receiving some sort of aid	94
% receiving scholarships	69
Average grant	$15,414
Average loan	$50,663
Average total aid package	$52,993
Average debt	$120,136

EMPLOYMENT INFORMATION

Career Rating	97	
Total 2012 JD Grads	388	
% for whom you have useable information	99	
% grads employed nine months out	93	
Median starting salary	$130,000	
% job accepting grads providing useable salary information	80	
# employed full-time	348	
# employed part-time	7	
# employed bar required	335	
# employed JD preferred	18	
# employed professional/other	1	
# employed non-professional	1	
# pursuing advanced degree	6	
# unemployed and seeking employment	16	
# not seeking employment	7	
% grads employed by school	3	
State for bar exam	NY, IL, CA, MI, MD	
Pass rate for first-time bar	92.7	

Grads Employed by Field (%)
Academic (1)
Business/Industry (6)
Government (6)
Judicial Clerkship (12)
Military (1)
Private Practice (53)
Public Interest (12)

UNIVERSITY OF MINNESOTA
LAW SCHOOL

INSTITUTIONAL INFORMATION

Public/private	Public
Student-faculty ratio	11:1
% faculty female	42
% faculty underrepresented minority	13
Total faculty	69

SURVEY SAYS...
Great research resources, Liberal students, Students love Minneapolis, MN

STUDENTS

Enrollment of law school	759
% male/female	57/43
% from out-of-state	62
% part-time	0
% underrepresented minority	22
% international	6
# of countries represented	13
Average age of entering class	25

ACADEMICS

Academic Experience Rating	90
Profs interesting rating	82
Profs accessible rating	74
Hours of study per day	3.82

Academic Specialties
Corporation Securities, Criminal, Environmental, Human Rights, International, Labor

Advanced Degrees Offered
JD, LLM for foreign lawyers, 1 year

Combined Degrees Offered
JD/MBA, 4 years; JD/MPA, 4 years; JD/MA; JD/MD; JD/MPP, 4 years; JD/MURP, 4 years; JD/MS, 4 years; JD/Ph.D; JD/MBT; JD/MBS; JD/MPH

Academics

The "world class" faculty of the University of Minnesota Law School are "dedicated to the students" and tend to be "very helpful, especially the professors' assistants." Styles vary. "Some professors prefer a more Socratic style, some a more discussion based approach," but regardless of whether they prefer lectures, discussion, or a mixture of both, "all are available to talk to students whenever." One 1L noted that they have "always felt completely welcome to talk to all my professors, and that has continued on as a 2L."

Due in part because "the professors are experts and heavily published in their fields, the program here is "very research driven." However, the professors having successful outside-of-school pursuits causes some students to complain that "professors care more about their research than their teaching." By and large, however, they are "well-respected in their fields and usually great teachers to boot." Their real-world experience means for many, "they've been very helpful in learning the nuts and bolts of the profession." Regardless of what other distractions they have, professors are "universally welcoming and eager to work with students."

That said, the "dated" facilities can be "gloomy and depressing." Being educated in the basement "feels oppressive in the dead of winter," but it's not all bad when it comes to the facilities. "U of M takes pride in the size of the law library," one student notes, "and I think that pride is well-earned." The school also makes it a point to give students a sense for how their studies will apply to the real world. A mock trial competition team, for example, "is an example of how the school makes sure to promote the practical aspects of the law and integrate the scholastic elements of the education."

Opportunities in the Twin Cities abound. From a wide range of classes to the "large number of journals" to mock courts, an "active student organization community," and a legal community that embraces those in the U of M program, "there are more opportunities than I have time in which to partake." Because this is a top 20 school, "there is a strong drive among students for big firm jobs." At one time that was reflected in the curriculum, too, but these days the school "has made significant progress in recognizing and meeting the needs of students interested in public interest, government, and policy or research oriented positions."

Life

The city of Minneapolis is "amazing," with a bustling nightlife–the music scene is legendary, arts and culture abound, and it's a growing Mecca for craft beer–and "many opportunities to get out there" when it comes to networking with those in the profession. "The legal community is very approachable and welcomes 1Ls (and 2L/3Ls) to many of their events," offering "numerous opportunities to network." If the people and city win accolades, the facilities, which are "unfortunately located in a basement," do not. They "are clean and well-kept, but not attractive." Still, while the "lack of natural light in most classrooms" has resulted in the facilities being nicknamed "the dungeon," they are still "modern" and "tech-equipped," with "comfortable seats, and plugs for everybody's laptops."

NICK WALLACE, DIRECTOR OF ADMISSIONS
290 MONDALE HALL, 229 19TH AVENUE SOUTH, MINNEAPOLIS, MN 55455
TEL: 612-625-3487 FAX: 612-626-1874
E-MAIL: JDADMISSIONS@UNM.EDU • WEBSITE: WWW.LAW.UMN.EDU

But it is the people who win out in the end. "People are happy to be here" for a reason. The faculty and student body alike "works hard to promote an environment of collegiality, where the students work hard with each other as colleagues instead of against each other as competitors." In fact, "given our career choice … students are not as outwardly assertive as you'd think they'd be." Even though everyone is working hard to succeed, "nobody will flaunt their grades or job prospects." In addition, "diversity is truly valued," especially when it comes to student achievement. Students here "support each other as long as the effort is honest, because it all comes out in finals."

Getting In

Expect competition when trying to gain admission to the University of Minnesota Law School. Interested candidates will need a strong undergraduate record along with excellent LSAT scores, as well as the ability to demonstrate that they can handle rigorous course work and that they've acquired solid communication skills. In addition, the admissions committee will consider factors such as previous work experience, public service, other graduate work and ethnic background. Because admission is granted on a rolling basis, the earlier an applicant applies the better.

Clinical program required	No
Legal writing course requirement	Yes
Legal methods course requirement	No
Legal research course requirement	Yes
Moot court requirement	No
Public interest law requirement	No

ADMISSIONS

Selectivity Rating	93
# applications received	3,225
% applicants accepted	23
% acceptees attending	27
Average LSAT	163
Median LSAT	167
LSAT Range (25th to 75th percentile)	158–168
Average undergrad GPA	3.60
Median undergrad GPA	3.8
Application fee	$75
Regular application deadline	4/1
Regular notification	4/1
Early application deadline	11/15
Early application notification	12/31
Transfer students accepted	Yes
Evening division offered	No
Part-time accepted	No
CAS accepted	Yes

FINANCIAL FACTS

Annual tuition (in-state out-of-state)	$34,896/$43,560
Books and supplies	$1,666
Fees	$1,924
Room & Board	$10,188
Financial aid application deadline	5/1
% all students receiving some sort of aid	85
% receiving scholarships	64
Average grant	$17,911
Average loan	$36,025
Average total aid package	$44,428
Average debt	$100,166

EMPLOYMENT INFORMATION

Career Rating	**80**	
Total 2012 JD Grads	230	**Prominent Alumni**
% for whom you have useable information	100	Walter F. Mondale, Former Vice President of The United States; Keith Ellison, U.S. Representative; Jean E. Hanson, Partner Fried, Frank, Harris, Shriver, & Jacobson.
Median starting salary	$67,000	
# employed full-time	205	**Grads Employed by Field (%)**
# employed part-time	10	Academic (4)
# employed bar required	186	Business/Industry (18)
# employed JD preferred	19	Government (5)
# employed professional/other	4	Judicial Clerkship (18)
# employed non-professional	2	Private Practice (39)
# pursuing advanced degree	5	Public Interest (9)
# unemployed and seeking employment	5	
# not seeking employment	5	
% grads employed by school	7	
State for bar exam	MN	
Pass rate for first-time bar	97.2	

University of Mississippi
School of Law

INSTITUTIONAL INFORMATION

Public/private	Public
% faculty part-time	30
% faculty female	31
% faculty underrepresented minority	13
Total faculty	52

SURVEY SAYS...

Diverse opinions accepted in classrooms, Great library staff, Students love University, MS

STUDENTS

Enrollment of law school	531
% male/female	54/46
% from out-of-state	16
% part-time	0
% underrepresented minority	17
# of countries represented	1
Average age of entering class	24

ACADEMICS

Academic Experience Rating	87
Profs interesting rating	84
Profs accessible rating	83
Hours of study per day	2.55

Academic Specialties

Commercial, Corporation Securities, Criminal, Environmental, International, Taxation

Advanced Degrees Offered

None

Combined Degrees Offered

JD/MBA, 4 years; JD/MA, Tax, 4 years; JD/MA, Accounting, 4 years

Academics

Students at Ole Miss love the combination of "a down-home, small-town atmosphere where everyone knows your name" and a law degree that is "given much credit within the state." Though "academically strenuous," the school's "laid-back atmosphere" prevails, and students praise the "easily accessible" staff, the "large student mall with plenty of couches and chairs for discussions between classes," and the "professors with awesome senses of humor." By all accounts, Ole Miss is not a school that "makes you feel like they are trying to weed you out." As one student explains, "I love the dynamics of the classes and the size of the student body. It is nice to be friends with 2Ls and 3Ls and not feel like a freshman again." "Everyone in the administration is incredibly friendly and helpful," a classmate adds. "If you have any question, even if it has nothing to do with their particular job, they will do everything they can to get you the right answer." Professors here hail from "a broad diversity of backgrounds" and "are all extremely knowledgeable and very experienced." Not only do they "present the material in an entertaining way," they "take a special interest" in students, "which can help build up [students'] confidence and help them to excel."

The professors at Ole Miss are a major reason why its students say the school is a "great value." "It is not nearly as expensive to go to school here as the other schools to which I applied or was accepted," says one student. "I can still get pretty much any job I want coming out of Ole Miss, yet I have zero debt." Other students, however, temper such expectations, noting that while Ole Miss' "Career Services Office is always there to help with a resume or to provide Tylenol during exams," securing a job outside of Mississippi can be an uphill battle. That said, this situation seems to be on the upswing thanks to the school's "great relationship with alumni" and also in that "Ole Miss changed their grading curve [a few years ago] and that has significantly helped those who are looking to get a job out of state."

Students consistently report that the faculty is one of the school's "greatest strengths." "They take away the mundane, stereotypical experience of law school and present the material in an entertaining way without compromising the integrity of the institution," says one student. Many feel that "there is a lot of potential in the legal writing and research classes"; however, they are damaged by "the lack of communication between...departments." Others would like "more classes to choose from," particularly in the area of entertainment law. Students are divided on the school's aesthetics, finding that the "great library" is "extremely up to date with the latest technology" while the building itself is "not very pretty" and "somewhat outdated." A 1L provides some perspective, explaining that "the law school building would be aesthetically pleasing at most major schools, but when compared to the columned architecture and tree-lined walkways of the rest of the campus, you can immediately tell it is a relic of the early 1970s...Instead of being 'post-modern,' it simply looks out of place." However, "a new state-of-the-art building" "will soon be under construction."

Life

Ole Miss students emphasize that theirs is a "relaxed learning environment," one that "promotes collaboration between students instead of the cutthroat competition that you hear about at other law schools." The school divides 1Ls into sections of "about sixty

BARBARA VINSON, DIRECTOR OF ADMISSIONS
OFFICE OF ADMISSIONS, P.O. BOX 1848, LAMAR LAW CENTER, UNIVERSITY, MS 38677
TEL: 662-915-6910 FAX: 662-915-1289
E-MAIL: LAWMISS@OLEMISS.EDU • WEBSITE: WWW.LAW.OLEMISS.EDU

students." While this can be "good for making friends" and forming "study groups and TV nights," it can at times seem "like high school all over again with the distinct social circles." "In true Southern form," law students at Ole Miss "like to work hard and play hard," and "There is a huge effort to make sure that students do more than study." "There is a great Law School Social Board that throws parties, organizes intra-mural teams, and puts together community-service projects so that students have a way to get to know each other and put the books down for a few hours," a 1L reports. When they do take a break, Ole Miss students find themselves in a pleasant location. The university's campus is "beautiful," and hometown Oxford is "a unique place" with "a healthy social scene." Though most will tell you that "drinking is a big part of social life" here, popular opinion states that "you can absolutely have a good time without drinking." "There are two great new movie theaters, and there are plans to open a 'New Square,'" says one student. "Oxford is constantly growing, and hopefully there will be a lot more for students to do soon." One thing that students agree could be improved a more "diverse student body."

Getting In

The early bird gets the worm at Ole Miss since admitted first-year students can begin their studies during the summer. Certain factors, such as "residency, undergraduate institution, difficulty of major, job experience, social, personal or economic circumstances, non-academic achievement, letters of recommendation and grade patterns and progression," can impact your application favorably, according to the school. Admitted students at the 25th percentile have an LSAT score of 151 and a GPA of 3.25. Admitted students at the 75th percentile have an LSAT score of 157 and a GPA of 3.76.

Clinical program required	No
Legal writing course requirement	Yes
Legal methods course requirement	Yes
Legal research course requirement	Yes
Moot court requirement	No
Public interest law requirement	No

ADMISSIONS

Selectivity Rating	87
# applications received	1,656
% applicants accepted	32
% acceptees attending	33
Median LSAT	155
LSAT Range (25th to 75th percentile)	151–157
Average undergrad GPA	3.49
Median undergrad GPA	3.49
Application fee	$40
Regular application deadline	3/1
Regular notification	4/30
Transfer students accepted	Yes
Evening division offered	No
Part-time accepted	No
CAS accepted	Yes

FINANCIAL FACTS

Annual tuition (in-state out-of-state)	$9,350/$19,620
Books and supplies	$1,300
Room & Board	$18,832
% of aid that is merit based	90
Average grant	$5,788
Average loan	$15,334
Average debt	$41,632

EMPLOYMENT INFORMATION

Career Rating	93	**Grads Employed by Field (%)**
% grads employed nine months out	96	Academic (3)
Median starting salary	$64,025	Business/Industry (11)
State for bar exam	MS, TN, GA, FL, TX	Government (14)
Pass rate for first-time bar	90	Judicial Clerkship (17)
Prominent Alumni		Private Practice (50)
C. Trent Lott, Former U.S. Senator; Thad		Public Interest (5)
Cochran, U.S. Senator; John Grisham, Author.		

UNIVERSITY OF MISSOURI
SCHOOL OF LAW

INSTITUTIONAL INFORMATION

Public/private	Public
Affiliation	No Affiliation
Total faculty	67

SURVEY SAYS...
Diverse opinions accepted in class-rooms, Great research resources, Great library staff

STUDENTS

Enrollment of law school	412
% male/female	63/37
% part-time	2
% underrepresented minority	18
# of countries represented	2
Average age of entering class	25

ACADEMICS

Academic Experience Rating	76
Profs interesting rating	74
Profs accessible rating	70

Academic Specialties
Commercial, Criminal, Environmental, Government Services, International, Labor, Property, Taxation, Intellectual Property

Advanced Degrees Offered
LLM in Dispute Resolution, which is typically a 1 year program.

Combined Degrees Offered
JD/MBA, 4 years; JD/MPA (Public Administration), 4 years; JD/MHA (Health Administration), 4 years; JD/MA (Economics) 4 years; JD/MA/MS (Human Development and Family Studies), 4 years; JD/MA (Educational Leadership & Policy Analysis), 4 years; JD/MA (Journalism), 4 years; JD/Ph.D. (Journalism), 6 years; JD/MLS (Library and Information Science), 4 years; JD/MS (Personal Financial Planning), 4 years

Academics

The University of Missouri School of Law, "provides a high-quality legal education at an affordable price." Its small size, collegial atmosphere and "absolutely outstanding" faculty make Mizzou a "place where you can find all the challenge you want in a law school, without unnecessary stress on top of it." In the words of one student, "If you want to practice in the state of Missouri, there's no better place. Our law school consistently produces the future leaders of Missouri."

Students offer nothing but the utmost praise for their faculty. "The professors are intelligent yet not intimidating; they really care about the students." They "are leading scholars in their field yet available outside the classroom." "Although the Socratic Method is used throughout the first year, and often in other classes, it is used effectively, to help teach students to think like lawyers, but not to embarrass them." Of particular note, one student expresses pleasure in discovering that "classes integrate well with each other, in that professors seem aware of the other classes students are taking, and they draw connections between various fields of the law, thus helping students see how the law comes together." In the words of one particularly enthusiastic student, "The university is the reason I chose MU School of Law, but the faculty is why I would recommend it to any future students. Go Tigers!"

Similar feelings resonate over the administration. One student shares, "The dean of the law school teaches one of my classes. That's probably one of the coolest things about the law school—everyone is so attainable. The administration knows me, and probably every other student in the school, and they genuinely do have our best interests in sight." An older student returning to school after having a family, remarks, "The administration and professors are willing to work with students when those pesky issues of life come along and interfere with the school schedule." Another fan declares, "Law school is hard, MU made it easier."

Academically, students are challenged "within the comfort of a community." Students appreciate "the rigor and intensity of the curriculum" and especially call attention to Mizzou's noteworthy program in alternative dispute resolution. However, of greatest frustration to students are course offerings that conflict with scheduling. One student explains, "Although the course catalog offers a nice variety, students sometimes will have only one opportunity to take a particular class during their student careers, since some 2L/3L classes are offered only every other year." Unfortunately, the wait for in-demand classes can range from a semester to a year, depending on availability.

Career services receive mixed reviews. One student feels that "Career Services does an excellent job with the top 25 percent of the class, but the other three-fourths could use more attention, in my opinion." Another agrees, remarking that "the career development services are probably the most deserving of attention." Specifically, some feel that "the Career Office could do a better job attracting employers from more geographical areas." Fortunately, it appears that Career Services is addressing some of these issues; as one student reports, due to recent changes, "Career Services has done a much better job at providing job and internship opportunities for the students."

MICHELLE KECK, ASSISTANT DEAN
103 HULSTON HALL, COLUMBIA, MO 65211
TEL: 573-882-6042 FAX: 573-882-9625
EMAIL: MULAWADMISSIONS@MISSOURI.EDU • WEBSITE: WWW.LAW.MISSOURI.EDU

While instructional technology is current, the facilities have some shortcomings. "The classrooms do not have electrical outlets, which makes it difficult to take notes on a computer when you have class for four hours straight." As a result, "Students are commonly seen lugging around extension cords" with them on campus. Additionally, students feel that "physical facilities are starting to show their age and need to be remodeled."

Life

"Mizzou is a great place for law school, the vast majority of people get along well with everyone else, and we all socialize together as well." "As [for] social life—you can get exactly what you want out of it. If you want to be involved, you got it. If you want to be a hermit and just come in for class," go ahead. "It is an environment that allows people to be flexible with their time, but it is also demanding in a sense that it has the proper time constraints to get people motivated." "Furthermore, Columbia is a great city, and the law school is right in the heart of campus with easy access to the recreation center as well as all of the amenities of downtown."

The degree of competition varies depending on who you ask. One student notes, "The thing I like best about this school is that very few individuals are worried about hiding books from each other in the library in order to get that cutthroat best grade." Another explains, "Students are friendly, but not shy about competition. We are here to learn how to be good lawyers, not to tear each other up." "MU is not a love fest though; people are here because they want to succeed."

Getting In

While application decisions are made on a rolling basis as long as the entering class has openings (class size is 135), the school recommends early application, preferably in the fall of the year prior to enrollment. Admitted students at the 25th percentile have an LSAT score of 156 and a GPA of 3.2. Admitted students at the 75th percentile have an LSAT score of 160 and a GPA of 3.7.

Clinical program required	No
Legal writing course requirement	Yes
Legal methods course requirement	Yes
Legal research course requirement	Yes
Moot court requirement	Yes
Public interest law requirement	No

ADMISSIONS

Selectivity Rating	80
# applications received	707
% applicants accepted	56
% acceptees attending	34
Median LSAT	157
LSAT Range (25th to 75th percentile)	152–159
Median undergrad GPA	3.5
Application fee	$60
Regular application deadline	3/1
Early application deadline	11/15
Early application notification	12/31
Transfer students accepted	Yes
Evening division offered	No
Part-time accepted	Yes
CAS accepted	Yes

FINANCIAL FACTS

Annual tuition (in-state out-of-state)	$17,475/$34,503
Books and supplies	$1,624
Fees	$1,144
Room & Board	$10,612
Financial aid application deadline	3/1
% first-year students receiving some sort of aid	93
% all students receiving some sort of aid	93
% of aid that is merit based	13
Average grant	$6,562
Average loan	$26,690

EMPLOYMENT INFORMATION

Career Rating	60*	Prominent Alumni
Total 2012 JD Grads	147	Claire McCaskill, US Senator; Jay Nixon,
% grads employed nine months out	92	Governor of Missouri; John R. Gibson, US
# employed full-time	124	Ct of Appeals-8th Cir.
# employed part-time	9	**Grads Employed by Field (%)**
# employed bar required	106	Academic (2)
# employed JD preferred	23	Business/Industry (14)
# employed professional/other	0	Government (16)
# employed non-professional	5	Judicial Clerkship (5)
# pursuing advanced degree	1	Military (1)
# unemployed and seeking employment	6	Private Practice (46)
# not seeking employment	1	Public Interest (7)
% grads employed by school	0	
State for bar exam	MO, IL, CA, GA, TN	

UNIVERSITY OF MISSOURI—KANSAS CITY
SCHOOL OF LAW

INSTITUTIONAL INFORMATION

Public/private	Public
Student-faculty ratio	14:1
% faculty part-time	27
% faculty female	42
% faculty underrepresented minority	7.5
Total faculty	66

SURVEY SAYS...

Diverse opinions accepted in classrooms, Students love Kansas City, MO

STUDENTS

Enrollment of law school	463
% male/female	62/38
% from out-of-state	21
% part-time	6
% underrepresented minority	12
% international	1
# of countries represented	7
Average age of entering class	26

ACADEMICS

Academic Experience Rating	85
Profs interesting rating	83
Profs accessible rating	87
Hours of study per day	3.56

Academic Specialties
International, Taxation, Intellectual Property, Family Law, Advocacy

Advanced Degrees Offered
LLM, 1-3 years

Combined Degrees Offered
JD/MBA, 3–4 years, JD/MPA 3–4 years, JD/LLM, 3.5–4 years

Academics

The University of Missouri-Kansas City School of Law offers "relatively low" tuition and "really focuses on" "nuts-and-bolts legal skills." Six emphasis areas include litigation, business and entrepreneurial law, child and family law, international, comparative and foreign law; urban land use and environmental law; and intellectual property law. There are also three dual-degree options. The clinical programs here include a tax clinic and the Midwestern Innocence Project, which provides pro bono legal and investigative services to wrongfully convicted prisoners. Also, opportunities to spend the summer abroad are spectacular. They include a program that takes students on a whirlwind tour of Ireland (with a stop in Wales) and an "outstanding" Beijing program "at China's premier university," which offers lectures in the mornings and cultural field trips in the afternoons. The legal writing program at UMKC is "very intensive," but "needs a little work."

"The professors here genuinely care about the well-being and success of their students," and they make "even the most mundane topics intriguing." "Some teachers use humor to get points across and to enhance memorization, while others will use scare tactics and examples of bar complaints or malpractice suits to teach a lesson," relates a 3L. "Overall, when the semester has ended, one way or another, the knowledge is retained." Faculty members are also "very accessible and willing to help students." "The open-door policy of every professor is incredibly beneficial," observes a 2L. Depending on the students you talk to, the administration is "always on the ball" and "never seems too far away" or "seems to be a bit flustered at times."

Students who are fond of Career Services say that the staff places "a very big emphasis on helping its students obtain internships, externships, and jobs during school" and "has a lot of information and connections to attorneys in the area." Students who don't like Career Services charge that the staff is "notably absent" and "wonder what they are doing sometimes." Most students agree that the career outlook is largely positive, though. To improve that experience, the career services center hired a new director and assistant director in 2012. "UMKC alums dominate" the legal scene throughout Kansas City, and "Connections to the local market" are a big draw. "The school is geographically located very close to the action in downtown Kansas City," adds a 1L. "Many UMKC Law grads are very active and do a lot to support students." Also, the school's unique mentorship program, which is called the Inns Program, provides students with valuable opportunities to build relationships with the local practitioners.

The biggest source of dissatisfaction among students concerns the "admittedly dated" and "borderline embarrassing" law school building at UMKC. "It needs a face-lift without question," laments a 1L. "The furniture looks and feels like it was donated in the 1970s," gripes a 3L. Parking is another perennial source of frustration. "Unless you arrive early in the morning, you probably get to enjoy a nice walk." Generally, though, "The problems are largely cosmetic," and this place is "not a dump by any stretch of the imagination." Many classrooms are "modern and comfortable." "The library is accommodating, and the research resources are pretty comprehensive." Technology is "up-to-date." "Another huge asset is the computer technician dedicated to fixing law students' computers free of charge," says a 1L. "My computer has crashed twice since school began, and each time, the computer technician has rebuilt the device and had it back in my possession within a week's time."

Life

The UMKC School of Law is home to an impressive variety of people. "The diversity of age, work experience, and background of the students is very interesting and enriches the learning environment," declares a 1L. While many students come to UMKC right out of college, there's also a large number of students "commuting in each day" who have been out of school for many years. Opinions concerning the academic atmosphere are mixed. According to some students, the vibe is "generally friendly and helpful with little trace of competition." Other students tell us that tough grading policies produce "quite a competitive atmosphere."

Students report that there are plenty of ways to fill up your free time here. "Awesome" clubs and organizations "are always putting on events for law school students to lessen the turbulence and stress." Also, UMKC is not far from "all the coolest hangouts in Kansas City." Some of the greatest barbecue in the world is also available if you're into that sort of thing. "The social life here is very, very active," promises a 1L. "UMKC students love to" have a good time.

Getting In

Admitted students at the 25th percentile have LSAT scores in the low 150s, and undergraduate GPAs of about 3.0. At the 75th percentile, LSAT scores are around 157 and GPAs are very close to 3.6. Part-time stats are typically a little lower.

EMPLOYMENT INFORMATION

Career Rating	88	**Prominent Alumni**
Total 2012 JD Grads	153	Harry S. Truman, President of the United
% for whom you have useable		States; Charles E. Whittaker, U.S. Supreme
information	100	Court Justice; Clarence Kelley, FBI Director.
% grads employed nine months out	90	**Grads Employed by Field (%)**
Median starting salary	$49,250	Academic (3)
% job accepting grads providing		Business/Industry (21)
useable salary information	68	Government (10)
# employed full-time	132	Judicial Clerkship (9)
# employed part-time	6	Military (1)
# employed bar required	105	Private Practice (52)
# employed JD preferred	25	Public Interest (4)
# employed professional/other	7	
# employed non-professional	1	
# pursuing advanced degree	3	
# unemployed and seeking employment	7	
# not seeking employment	4	
% grads employed by school	1	
State for bar exam	MO, KS, CO	
Pass rate for first-time bar	94	

Clinical program required	No
Legal writing course requirement	Yes
Legal methods course requirement	No
Legal research course requirement	Yes
Moot court requirement	Yes
Public interest law requirement	No

ADMISSIONS

Selectivity Rating	85
# applications received	731
% applicants accepted	58
% acceptees attending	36
Average LSAT	153
Median LSAT	152
LSAT Range (25th to 75th percentile)	149–156
Average undergrad GPA	3.23
Median undergrad GPA	3.22
Application fee	$60
Regular application deadline	
Transfer students accepted	Yes
Evening division offered	No
Part-time accepted	Yes
CAS accepted	Yes

FINANCIAL FACTS

Annual tuition (in-state out-of-state)	$17,058/$32,853
Books and supplies	$1,650
Fees	$827
Room & Board (on/off campus)	$11,552/$8,372
Financial aid application deadline	3/1
% first-year students receiving some sort of aid	91
% all students receiving some sort of aid	87
% of aid that is merit based	17
% receiving scholarships	42
Average grant	$7,815
Average loan	$10,693
Average total aid package	$31,535
Average debt	$87,102

UNIVERSITY OF NEBRASKA—LINCOLN
COLLEGE OF LAW

INSTITUTIONAL INFORMATION

Public/private	Public
% faculty part-time	51
% faculty female	36
% faculty underrepresented minority	1
Total faculty	55

SURVEY SAYS...
Great research resources, Great library staff, Beautiful campus

STUDENTS

Enrollment of law school	392
% male/female	61/39
% from out-of-state	25
% part-time	1
% underrepresented minority	6
% international	1
# of countries represented	3
Average age of entering class	24

ACADEMICS

Academic Experience Rating	82
Profs interesting rating	78
Profs accessible rating	90
Hours of study per day	3.43

Academic Specialties
Commercial, Corporation Securities, Environmental, International, Labor, Taxation, Intellectual Property

Advanced Degrees Offered
JD, 3 years; MLS, 1 year; LLM in Space, Cyber & Telecommunications, 1 year

Combined Degrees Offered
Law & Masters of Business Administration (JD/MBA, 4 years); Law & Masters of Professional Accountancy (JD/MPA, 4 years); Law & Psychology (JD/MA, 4 years; or JD/Ph.D., 6 years); Law & Community & Regional Planning (JD/MRCP, 4 years); Law & Journalism (JD/MA, 4 years); Law & Political Science (JD/MA, 4 years); Law and Gerontoloty (JD/MA, 4 years); Law & Public Health (JD/MPH, 4 years)

Academics

The University of Nebraska College of Law offers a high-quality education at an unbeatable price. With costs and tuition totaling far less than comparable schools, one student incredulously declares, "Where else can you get a top-rate legal education for that cheap?" Students say that Nebraska offers a first-rate education with a "brilliant and very approachable" faculty and staff. "Not only are the professors walking through the library, talking to the students and answering questions, but the staff throughout the college is amazing."

The administration, faculty, and research staff undoubtedly serve as the law school's greatest assets. One student remarks, "Honestly, I don't think that one could find a better school administration or research librarians. They always meet you with a helpful smile," and are willing to do all that they can to assist students. Another notes, "The faculty and staff at Nebraska Law care about the success of each student," and help "student[s] find their place within the law." According to many, professors are "extremely engaging" and "are able to connect the subject matter to practical experience and real-life cases, which makes class more interesting."

Students warn, "The first year is extremely demanding, especially spring semester [since most of] our classes are a year long and most of the tests in the spring are cumulative," though two semester long courses will replace yearlong courses beginning in the 2012-2013 academic year. While April and May in the first year might be "almost unbearable," one seasoned 3L reassures us, "During my three years at UNL, most of my classes have been very interesting. Some of them have changed my life and outlook on the world." Students rave about Nebraska's prosecutorial clinic, as it is one of the few of its kind amongst an array of defense clinics. One student emphatically declares it "the best class that I took at UNL. Another student is of the opinion that though "there are a lot of classes in varying subjects, [the law school] is lacking in public interest/pro bono–type classes or topics for students wanting a different type of experience," though the school's Pro Bono Initiative has helped ameliorate matters, including an Immigration Clinic where students would with low-income clients.

Students are divided when it comes to the subject of employment after graduation. One student expresses an appreciation for "how UNL is trying to branch out and help students land jobs outside of Nebraska." Another argues that while "The school is great for finding jobs for students with higher grades that want to stay in Nebraska," "There is not enough emphasis on employment after law school if a student wants to work in public interest." One 3L would like "employers more involved in recruiting for clerkships," but in the same breath concedes that "most [students] were able to get clerkships if they wanted them as a 2L."

"It's great having brand new classrooms and facilities, as well as complete access to technology anywhere in the building." The almost fully renovated classrooms are "extremely comfortable" and "all have wireless access and plugs for laptops." Overall, students seem content with the refurbished facilities and as one satisfied 1L affirms, "After six years on the East Coast, the beautiful library and outstanding professors made returning to the Midwest an easy decision."

TRACY WARREN, ASSISTANT DEAN FOR ADMISSIONS
P.O. BOX 830902, LINCOLN, NE 68583-0902
TEL: 402-472-2161 FAX: 402-472-5185
E-MAIL: LAWADM@UNL.EDU • WEBSITE: LAW.UNL.EDU

Life

"UNL recruits some very intelligent and exceptionally talented students," and students agree, "The law school does a really good job of creating community among the students." Specifically, the small class size creates a "close-knit group mentality" and particularly helpful is the practice of scheduling first years "so they have at least one class with most of the students" in their cohort. One reassured student remarks from experience, "I know that if I need any help, albeit from a librarian, administrator, faculty member, or fellow law student, that I will receive it."

There is no shortage of social opportunities at Nebraska. "People take the initiative to organize mixers and activities to help people get to know one another and to keep law school stress at bay as much as possible." The SBA, Women's Law Caucus and American Constitution Society and the law fraternities routinely host speakers, discussion panels and philanthropic events. Academic groups like Moot Court and Client Counseling also bring students together in social-academic environments that don't revolve around the bar scene. The bottom line remains clear as expressed in one student's words, "students aren't just classmates—we're friends."

Getting In

LSAT scores and undergraduate GPA are the main factors that the Admissions Committee considers when evaluating applications. Admitted students at the 25th percentile have an LSAT score of 153 and a GPA of 3.3. Admitted students at the 75th percentile have an LSAT score of 159 and a GPA of 3.79. The law school tries hard to create a class that is diverse.

Clinical program required	No
Legal writing course requirement	Yes
Legal methods course requirement	No
Legal research course requirement	Yes
Moot court requirement	No
Public interest law requirement	No

ADMISSIONS

Selectivity Rating	82
# applications received	825
% applicants accepted	48
% acceptees attending	32
Median LSAT	157
LSAT Range (25th to 75th percentile)	153–159
Median undergrad GPA	3.51
Application fee	$50
Regular application deadline	3/1
Transfer students accepted	Yes
Evening division offered	No
Part-time accepted	No
CAS accepted	Yes

FINANCIAL FACTS

Annual tuition (in-state out-of-state)	$10,783/$26,862
Books and supplies	$1,378
Fees	$3,104
Room & Board (on/off campus)	$14,310/$13,858
Financial aid application deadline	5/1
% of aid that is merit based	93
% receiving scholarships	51
Average loan	$8,200
Average debt	$22,196

EMPLOYMENT INFORMATION

Career Rating	85	**Prominent Alumni**
Total 2012 JD Grads	130	Ted Sorensen, Special Counsel to
% for whom you have useable information	97	President John F. Kennedy; Harvey Perlman, Chancellor, University of
% grads employed nine months out	88	Nebraska-Lincoln; Ben Nelson, U.S.
Median starting salary	$50,000	Senator and former Governor of Nebraska.
% job accepting grads providing useable salary information	63	**Grads Employed by Field (%)**
# employed full-time	106	Academic (2)
# employed part-time	8	Business/Industry (25)
# employed bar required	82	Government (13)
# employed JD preferred	16	Judicial Clerkship (3)
# employed professional/other	8	Military (1)
# employed non-professional	8	Private Practice (49)
# pursuing advanced degree	2	Public Interest (6)
# unemployed and seeking employment	9	
# not seeking employment	1	
State for bar exam	NE, IA, MO, SD, CO	
Pass rate for first-time bar	91	

UNIVERSITY OF NEVADA—LAS VEGAS
WILLIAM S. BOYD SCHOOL OF LAW

INSTITUTIONAL INFORMATION

Public/private	Public
% faculty part-time	5
% faculty female	41
% faculty underrepresented minority	19
Total faculty	58

SURVEY SAYS...
Diverse opinions accepted in classrooms, Great research resources

STUDENTS

Enrollment of law school	157
% male/female	56/44
% from out-of-state	29
% part-time	30
% underrepresented minority	35
Average age of entering class	25

ACADEMICS

Academic Experience Rating	**80**
Profs interesting rating	74
Profs accessible rating	86

Combined Degrees Offered
JD/MBA, 4 years; JD/MSW, 4 years; JD/Ph.D. in Education, 4 years

Academics

ABA-accredited in 2003, many students feel, "The greatest strength of Boyd is its newness," which lends a sense of optimism, excitement, and challenge to the campus. Because it's not "steeped in tradition, there's an entrepreneurial spirit here. Everyone senses we're building something special." With a quality teaching staff, top-notch facilities, a talented student body, and reasonable tuition costs, students are confident that their school will continue to climb in the ranks. In fact, this sense of excitement extends throughout the city and state. Boyd is the only law school in Nevada; students report, "The legal community and the community in general are excited to have us here and the whole city [and state] is invested in all of us succeeding."

Professors boast impressive educational and professional backgrounds and are known to be both "intelligent and well-respected in their fields." More important, they are "stimulating individuals who are skilled teachers." Students are "consistently amazed by the ease with which the faculty so effectively employs the Socratic Method, such that the student body...is able to break down even the most complex legal scenarios and digest them as fully understandable rules and concepts." Outside the classroom, "Professors are extremely approachable, even for a shy student."

The administration is generally regarded as "accessible and very pro-student." A 2L affirms, "The administrators I deal with on any sort of regular basis are fantastic. Not only do they know their stuff; they are anxious to help and are just all-around fabulous people." Students particularly applaud the efforts the administration has made to help new students make the transition into law school, citing the "optional thirty-minute classes once a week where we are taught exam skills, note-taking, and outlining tips."

Classrooms at Boyd are "new and clean" and very high-tech. The "top quality facilities" include "wireless Internet and cable Internet hook-ups throughout the building," as well as "a state-of-the-art library." Off campus, students say, "Being the only law school in Nevada, in the middle of one of the fastest-growing economies in the United States, opportunities abound." For example, UNLV students "have opportunities for something close to eighty-five judicial externships each year (out of a class of 150)" and additionally "have extraordinary access to the local, regional, and state governments." When it comes to landing a job after graduation, UNLV is extremely well located. In the city of Las Vegas, "The local law firms are eager to hire graduates, and the private sector opportunities in gaming, hospitality, real estate, corporate, entertainment, and litigation are abundant and highly lucrative."

ELIZABETH KARL, ADMISSIONS & RECORDS ASSISTANT
4505 MARYLAND PARKWAY, BOX 451003, LAS VEGAS, NV 89154-1003
TEL: (702) 895-2440 FAX: (702) 895-2414
E-MAIL: REQUEST@LAW.UNLV.EDU • WEBSITE: WWW.LAW.UNLV.EDU

Life

While located in the heart of Las Vegas, "Most of the students commute into campus… and that can put a strain on the nearby social scene." In lieu of a hopping campus life, "Student organizations are great and have become central to social events at the school." Students have no trouble making friends among their interesting and talented classmates since "The people make the school." One student writes, "I love coming to school because I've made really great friends and don't mind seeing them everyday."

Commuter student or not, "Being in the center of Las Vegas, there is always something to do and somewhere new to go." You may be surprised to learn, however, that law school in Sin City is actually quite serious. Some students feel the competitiveness is a product of the high caliber of the student body. A 1L explains particularly in the school's early years many "of the students in the entering class are in their forties, and several of them are doctors and dentists, so the bar is set quite high." Though the level of commitment remains the same, the profile of the average entrant may have changed over time as the school's applicant pool has widened in terms of age and experience. In addition to their diligence, UNLV students are a fairly homogenous and quite conservative group. One student points out that some of "the faculty is comprised of very liberal individuals from a diverse background, whereas a majority of the students are very conservative and tend to have similar life experiences."

Getting In

When selecting applicants, the Admissions Committee looks for students with demonstrated academic capability, including depth and breadth of undergraduate course work, grades, concurrent work experience, and extracurricular activities. The school also considers non-academic factors, such as community service and work experience. Older students should feel particularly welcomed at Boyd.

Clinical program required	No
Legal writing course requirement	Yes
Legal methods course requirement	Yes
Legal research course requirement	Yes
Moot court requirement	No
Public interest law requirement	Yes

ADMISSIONS

Selectivity Rating	92
# applications received	1,755
% applicants accepted	23
% acceptees attending	39
Average LSAT	158
LSAT Range (25th to 75th percentile)	155–160
Average undergrad GPA	3.44
Application fee	$50
Regular application deadline	3/15
Regular notification	4/30
Transfer students accepted	Yes
Evening division offered	Yes
Part-time accepted	Yes
CAS accepted	Yes

FINANCIAL FACTS

Annual tuition (in-state out-of-state)	$18,000/$30,000
Books and supplies	$1,080
Fees	$500
Room & Board	$8,370
Financial aid application deadline	2/1
% first-year students receiving some sort of aid	88
% all students receiving some sort of aid	86
% of aid that is merit based	90
% receiving scholarships	33
Average grant	$7,400
Average loan	$26,200
Average total aid package	$28,000
Average debt	$55,700

EMPLOYMENT INFORMATION

Career Rating	92	
% grads employed nine months out	94	
Median starting salary	$75,532	
State for bar exam	NV, AZ, UT, CA	
Pass rate for first-time bar	75	

Grads Employed by Field (%)
Academic (2)
Business/Industry (12)
Government (10)
Judicial Clerkship (16)
Private Practice (55)
Public Interest (4)

UNIVERSITY OF NEW HAMPSHIRE
SCHOOL OF LAW

INSTITUTIONAL INFORMATION

Public/private	Private
Student-faculty ratio	16:1
% faculty part-time	63
% faculty female	50
% faculty underrepresented minority	8
Total faculty	87

SURVEY SAYS...

Diverse opinions accepted in classrooms

STUDENTS

Enrollment of law school	304
% male/female	59/41
% from out-of-state	74
% part-time	<1
% underrepresented minority	13
% international	3
# of countries represented	11
Average age of entering class	27

ACADEMICS

Academic Experience Rating	**81**
Profs interesting rating	80
Profs accessible rating	87
Hours of study per day	5.05

Academic Specialties

Commercial, Criminal, Human Rights, International, Intellectual Property, Social Justice

Advanced Degrees Offered

MIP (Master of IP)(1 year); MCT (Master of Commerce & Technology Law)(1 year); MICL&J (Master of Int'l Criminal Law & Justice)(1 year); LLM-IP (Master of Laws in IP)(1 year); LLM-CT (Master of Laws in Commerce & Technology Law) (1 year); LLM-ICL&J (Master of Laws in Int'l Criminal Law & Justice)(1 year); DIP (Diploma in IP)(6 months))

Academics

Formerly Franklin Pierce Law Center, the University of New Hampshire is the only law school in the state, yet it attracts a high class of students from all over the country, primarily due to its focus on creating "practice-ready" lawyers and because of its Intellectual Property Program, which "is by far the greatest strength of this school." There are many resources available to students when it comes to IP: the library is the biggest IP library in US, "many graduates are willing to speak to us about their experience," and the program in Commerce and Technology includes a razor edge focus on e-Law.

The school has an "excellent focus on practice," which is buoyed by its externship programs and allows students to work in their fields of interest for up to a full semester while receiving credit. The Daniel Webster Scholar Honors Program "offers every real world experience a future attorney could ask for " and is the only practice-based bar exam alternative in the nation. The emphasis on practical, skills-based lawyering "is not just an advertisement - it really happens in the classroom." There are "endless" internship, externship, and clinical opportunities, as well as a number of classes that focus on what you will do in practice, rather than just theory. "If a student evades a tough question, the professor will often ask 'What would you tell your client?'" "I really enjoy learning how we'll be able to apply what we learn in the real world," says a student.

Small class size means the "dynamic, high energy" faculty "really gets to know the students." Everybody at UNH Law is very accessible. "I even see the Dean walking around in the hallways," says a 1L. "Many professors have an open door policy," and "there are teaching assistants who can help you in the rare times when you can't find the professor." "There was never a time when I needed to locate someone and I just couldn't," says a student. Some professors even give out their phone numbers "just in case," and students "don't have to fight through 23 TAs before actually getting in touch with them." One contracts professor even stays until 11 pm at times when students need help preparing for finals. Several students take note and appreciate this apparent dedication. Almost all of the professors still practice or have practiced before they begin teaching, which allows them "actual practice-based knowledge to share with the students, [which is] a huge asset to the student body." Similarly, "the administration and overall management of our school is great." "Because it's such a small school, you know all of the administrative staff, and they are very responsive to your needs," says a 2L.

As the main legal game in the state, the school attracts "a wide variety of speakers from judges, governors, senators, to well known commentators in the legal field on a weekly basis," which makes for "endless opportunities for networking as a result." Some externs are sent to the New Hampshire Supreme Court, and students "also have the ability to extern at the first circuit and other federal courts"; however, some feel like other concentrations of law besides IP "could use a little boost." "If one was to practice something else and travel out of state they might not have much luck," says a student.

Life

The school has "a strong sense of community," and although it "has limited facilities" due to its size ("the building is very nice; not too big and not too small"), the facilities the school does have "are pristine, and run very smoothly," including a "beautiful" courtroom that is available for students to use whenever a class is not in session. The "close-knit" Concord coterie means that plenty of campus life takes place off-campus. "I

ROBIN INGLI, ASSISTANT DEAN FOR ADMISSIONS
TWO WHITE STREET, , CONCORD, NH 03301
TEL: 603-228-9217 • FAX: 603-229-0425
E-MAIL: ADMISSIONS@LAW.UNH.EDU • WEBSITE: WWW.LAW.UNH.EDU

frequently see professors and fellow students working out at the local YMCA," says a student. Concord "doesn't have a great night life, but there are plenty of things to do here." The bars that are here "are enough to keep you satisfied," and "there are also a lot of great things to do around the city that don't involve drinking." Parking can sometimes be problematic, but "most students walk to school."

The "intimate environment" fostered on campus is apparent everywhere. "Professors interact with the students outside of class on a daily basis and seem to generally care about how each student is doing." The student body itself is composed of "diverse groups of students of all ages and from all backgrounds." Although the students are competitive, they "all get along well and work together, creating a strong network in the long term." Most of the students here are right out of undergrad or have spent 1-2 years outside of school before applying to law school.

Getting In

The school's Intellectual Property program is a huge draw to students from all over the country, so residence is irrelevant and acceptance is fairly easy; around one out of every two students gets in. A B-average and a decent LSAT score should do the trick numerically, but beyond that, UNH Law has a very small admissions department that carefully reviews applications to make sure that the student will bring a fresh perspective and added ambition to the mix. Note: there is no part-time program or spring entry.

Combined Degrees Offered

Dual JD/MBA (3 years)	
Clinical program required	No
Legal writing course requirement	Yes
Legal methods course requirement	Yes
Legal research course requirement	Yes
Moot court requirement	Yes
Public interest law requirement	No

ADMISSIONS

Selectivity Rating	77
# applications received	800
% applicants accepted	59
% acceptees attending	16
Average LSAT	156
Median LSAT	156
LSAT Range (25th to 75th percentile)	151–159
Average undergrad GPA	3.28
Median undergrad GPA	3.28
Application fee	$55
Regular application deadline	4/1
Transfer students accepted	Yes
Evening division offered	No
Part-time accepted	No
CAS accepted	Yes

FINANCIAL FACTS

Annual tuition (in-state out-of-state)	$36,100/$41,100
Books and supplies	$1,448
Fees	$90
Room & Board	$10,998
Financial aid application deadline	3/15
% first-year students receiving some sort of aid	96
% all students receiving some sort of aid	93
% of aid that is merit based	86
% receiving scholarships	83
Average grant	$8,272
Average loan	$43,245
Average total aid package	$60,184
Average debt	$116,234

EMPLOYMENT INFORMATION

Career Rating	77	State for bar exam	NH
Total 2012 JD Grads	138	Pass rate for first-time bar	90
% for whom you have useable information	100	**Prominent Alumni**	
% grads employed nine months out	88	Dawn Buonocore-Atlas, VP-Enforcement and Assistant General Counsel, Calvin	
Median starting salary	$58,000	Klein; Donna Edwards, US Representative-	
% job accepting grads providing useable salary information	30	Maryland; David Koris, General Counsel, Shell International; Tim Ryan, US	
# employed full-time	117	Representative-Ohio; Douglas Wood,	
# employed part-time	4	Partner, Reed Smith	
# employed bar required	100	**Grads Employed by Field (%)**	
# employed JD preferred	13	Academic (3)	
# employed professional/other	5	Business/Industry (24)	
# employed non-professional	3	Government (11)	
# pursuing advanced degree	2	Judicial Clerkship (1)	
# unemployed and seeking employment	7	Military (2)	
# not seeking employment	8	Private Practice (49)	
% grads employed by school	11	Public Interest (10)	

UNIVERSITY OF NEW MEXICO
SCHOOL OF LAW

INSTITUTIONAL INFORMATION

Public/private	Public
% faculty female	52
% faculty underrepresented minority	42
Total faculty	33

SURVEY SAYS...

Great library staff, Abundant extern-ship/internship/clerksip opportuni-ties, Students love Albuquerque, NM

STUDENTS

Enrollment of law school	346
% male/female	53/47
% from out-of-state	11
% part-time	1
% underrepresented minority	42
# of countries represented	2
Average age of entering class	26

ACADEMICS

Academic Experience Rating	87
Profs interesting rating	80
Profs accessible rating	90
Hours of study per day	3.15

Academic Specialties

Environmental

Advanced Degrees Offered

JD, 3 years (full-time program). A limited number of students may elect to participate in the Flexible Time Legal Education Program and take 10 credit hours per semester during the first year of law school and as few as 8 credit hours per semester in the second and later years of law school. Students taking part in the Flexible Time program must complete the JD degree in no more than 5 years, including sum-mers.

Combined Degrees Offered

JD/MBA, JD/MA in Latin American Studies, JD/MA in Public Administration, 4 years

Academics

"The essence of the University of New Mexico School of Law is community," sums up one student. Community "demonstrated through our professors' and administrators' ease in accessibility to students, alumni involvement, and peer[s'] competitive yet supportive spirit." In addition, students are drawn here for "the required clinic program, the small class sizes, the diversity of faculty, staff, and students, and the laid-back atmosphere." The Family Law and Criminal Law curricula are popular, and certificates are available in Natural Resources Law and in the legendary Native American Law pro-gram. Dual-degree programs include a JD/MA in Latin American Studies, a JD/MPA in Public Administration, and a JD/MBA. The school also boasts study abroad programs in Mexico, Tasmania, and Canada.

Due to the small class sizes, UNMSOL "creates a unique opportunity to connect with your professors, administrators, and classmates providing for further personal and professional development." This tight-knit atmosphere also "fosters a less competitive learning environment unlike other law schools." When it comes to instructors, by and large the professors here "are an extremely diverse and prestigious group." "It's incred-ible to learn about Con Law from someone who has argued in front of the Supreme Court and written countless appellate briefs for them." Others warn it can be a bit of a mixed bag, "I have had some excellent professors and some [that are just] okay."

The highlight of the program here is the mandatory clinic experience, which is univer-sally lauded as an "outlet where students learn how their legal classes apply to actual practice." In addition, "UNMSOL collaborates with the New Mexico Court of Appeals so that students can take classes with the judges, have them for moot court coaches, and participate in summer externships." One student elaborates, "One of the highlights of my law school experience at UNMSOL was arguing before three of our state's Supreme Court justices and two of our state's appellate court judges in preparation for a moot court competition. Our state's legal community, at every level, is exceptionally generous with its budding lawyers. The strength and depth of this partnership between the legal community and the law school is one of the unique advantages of a law school experi-ence at UNMSOL." In addition to the exceptional clinical opportunities, there is also "ample opportunity to compete for a position on one of the school's three academic journals: the Natural Resources Journal, the New Mexico Law Review, and the Tribal Law Journal."

When it comes to gastronomical concerns, students are left to grovel among "poor food offerings in the building." They also offer a word to the wise about post-law school place-ment; "This can be a boon if you plan to practice here, or in the Southwest. However, [career opportunities] are lacking in a more broad, federal sense."

SUSAN MITCHELL, ASSISTANT DEAN FOR ADMISSIONS & FINANCIAL AID
MSC 11-6070, 1 UNIVERSITY OF NEW MEXICO, ALBUQUERQUE, NM 87131-0001
TEL: 505-277-0958 FAX: 505-277-9958
E-MAIL: ADMISSIONS@LAW.UNM.EDU • WEBSITE: LAWSCHOOL.UNM.EDU

Life

Relations among students at UNMSOL "are great." It is "a very cooperative learning environment." "Everyone is treated the same by both their peers and the professors with no regard for ethnicity, sex, or any other personal background." In addition to "a large percentage of minority and female students," "there is a substantial diversity in age background at UNM." This leads to a "feisty group." "We all have strong opinions, but still help each other out." On the whole, students here tend to be "extremely liberal"; however, "The school is very supportive of diversity, allowing for a broad range of ethnic and political backgrounds." In fact, students say, "The greatest strength in the law school is the community atmosphere." UNM has "a strong collaborative environment where all are intent on making sure that everyone comes through together." The "cutthroat competition that one hears so much about at many law schools is nonexistent here" which "makes for a much better learning environment." The "only issue as far as community goes" is the lack of graduate campus housing. While some rent condos, apartments, or townhouses near the school, you will find law students "living all over the city."

The surrounding city of Albuquerque is an "extremely affordable place to live." The warm, temperate climate makes New Mexico a haven for outdoorsy types. Summers are relatively hot during the day with cool dry evenings. During the winter, there is skiing in the nearby mountains.

Getting In

The admissions committee at University of New Mexico School of Law "gives a decided preference to New Mexico residents." In addition, "the committee recognizes that special prelaw programs for underrepresented and disadvantaged applicants provide valuable information about an applicant's ability to succeed in law school, and participation in such programs is taken into account." The average undergraduate GPA for the fall 2010 entering class was 3.32. The average LSAT scores for the fall 2010 entering class was 156.

Clinical program required	Yes
Legal writing course requirement	Yes
Legal methods course requirement	No
Legal research course requirement	Yes
Moot court requirement	No
Public interest law requirement	No

ADMISSIONS

Selectivity Rating	89
# applications received	749
% applicants accepted	31
% acceptees attending	49
Average LSAT	155
Median LSAT	156
LSAT Range (25th to 75th percentile)	152–158
Average undergrad GPA	3.37
Median undergrad GPA	3.39
Application fee	$50
Regular application deadline	2/15
Transfer students accepted	Yes
Evening division offered	No
Part-time accepted	No
CAS accepted	Yes

FINANCIAL FACTS

Annual tuition (in-state out-of-state)	$15,098/$33,908
Books and supplies	$1,701
Room & Board (on/off campus)	$8,312/$8,774
Financial aid application deadline	3/1

EMPLOYMENT INFORMATION

Career Rating	87	State for bar exam	NM, CO, CA, TX, MD
Total 2012 JD Grads	119	Pass rate for first-time bar	85.5
% for whom you have useable information	100	**Prominent Alumni**	
% grads employed nine months out	95	The Honorable Edward L. Chavez, Justice, New Mexico Supreme Court; Tom Udall, US Senator, United States Senate; Gary King, New Mexico Attorney General.	
Median starting salary	$50,000		
% job accepting grads providing useable salary information	80	**Grads Employed by Field (%)**	
# employed full-time	87	Business/Industry (6)	
# employed part-time	14	Government (18)	
# employed bar required	85	Judicial Clerkship (8)	
# employed JD preferred	8	Private Practice (40)	
# employed professional/other	5	Public Interest (12)	
# employed non-professional	2		
# pursuing advanced degree	7		
# unemployed and seeking employment	8		
# not seeking employment	2		
% grads employed by school	0		

THE UNIVERSITY OF NORTH CAROLINA AT CHAPEL HILL
SCHOOL OF LAW

INSTITUTIONAL INFORMATION

Public/private	Public
% faculty part-time	0
% faculty female	41
% faculty underrepresented minority	14
Total faculty	59

SURVEY SAYS...

Diverse opinions accepted in classrooms, Great research resources, Great library staff, Students love Chapel Hill, NC

STUDENTS

Enrollment of law school	737
% male/female	49/51
% from out-of-state	27
% part-time	0
% underrepresented minority	28
% international	1
# of countries represented	11
Average age of entering class	23

ACADEMICS

Academic Experience Rating	97
Profs interesting rating	89
Profs accessible rating	87
Hours of study per day	3.04

Academic Specialties

Civil Procedure, Commercial, Constitutional, Corporation Securities, Criminal, Environmental, Government Services, Human Rights, International, Labor, Legal History, Legal Philosophy, Property, Taxation, Intellectual Property

Advanced Degrees Offered

JD, 3 years

Combined Degrees Offered

JD/MBA, 4 years; JD/MPA, 4 years; JD/MPPS, 4 years; JD/MPH, 4 years; JD/MRP, 4 years; JD/MSW, 4 years; JD/MASA, 4 years; JD/MALS or MSIS, 4 years; JD/MAMC, 4 years

Academics

The School of Law at The University of North Carolina at Chapel Hill is, according to students, "one of the best public law schools in the country." Many claim that "the faculty here couldn't be more down to earth and accessible." They have "a literal 'my-door-is-open-all-the-time policy' and never hesitate to "[take] the time to talk to every single student before class." Still, some students feel that "there is a strong liberal bias at the school" and that professors sometimes "bring their political views with them into the classroom." To correct this, they are calling for the law school to "improve on fostering a more diverse political atmosphere." UNC Law's "excellent" and "accessible" administration is "unparalleled" in its efforts to promote a "positive and supportive environment for the study of law." Everyone here seems to practice "the 'We're all family at UNC' motto to a fault."

Most UNC survey respondents are pleased about their employment prospects. One student credits the Career Services Office as being "the greatest strength of UNC. Even when they are too busy for a brief meeting about resumes or cover letters, you can just leave your stuff under the door, and someone will get it back to you by the next day with recommendations about what you should fix." However, some feel that it could "stand to improve, particularly with communicating jobs to 1Ls." However, jobs in North Carolina and neighboring states are fairly abundant, though, in large part because the law school maintains "strong connections" with in-state employers.

Student organizations and learning opportunities are aplenty. According to one student, "There are lots of organizations to get involved in, and the pro bono program is one of the best." About 60 percent of all students do some kind of pro bono work—many during the summer or during winter or spring breaks. Students who have performed more than seventy-five hours of pro bono service receive certificates of acknowledgment from the state bar association, and those who perform more than 100 hours of pro bono service get special shout-outs at graduation. Other notables include UNC's clinical programs, in which students handle more than 350 civil and criminal cases every year and "really get a lot of hands-on experience" along with "solid academic[s]" in the process. Joint-degree programs include the standard JD/MBA as well as master's of public policy science and a handful of others. UNC also offers a summer program down under in Sydney, Australia, that concentrates on Pacific Rim issues and semester-long programs in Europe and Mexico.

The general consensus is that facilities at UNC are middling, but in terms of the availability of information, "The resources are outstanding." Also, "The school is improving the technology of each classroom every year." In the meantime, a cry of "more parking!" can be heard throughout campus.

MICHAEL J. STATES, JD, ASSISTANT DEAN FOR ADMISSIONS
CB# 3380, VAN HECKE-WETTACH HALL, UNC SCHOOL OF LAW—ADMISSIONS,
CHAPEL HILL, NC 27599-3380
TEL: 919-962-5109 FAX: 919-843-7939
E-MAIL: LAW_ADMISSIONS@UNC.EDU • WEBSITE: WWW.LAW.UNC.EDU

Life

"Carolina offers a healthy balance between academic and student life." UNC is home to "diverse, interesting, charming, and intelligent people." One student exclaims, "I am constantly amazed by how interesting my classmates are." Most agree that "everyone gets along" in this "very friendly" and "very cooperative" academic atmosphere. "It is competitive but not necessarily with each other. It seems we all want to see everyone do well," explains one student.

Students insist that "there is no better college town in the United States than Chapel Hill," a Southern hamlet of about 54,000 souls that offers a good supply of part-time jobs, affordable housing, and a mild climate. These fine qualities have not gone unnoticed: *Money* magazine has before named the Raleigh-Durham-Chapel Hill area the "Best Place to Live in the South," in 2000, and *Sports Illustrated* named Chapel Hill "the Best College Town in America" a few years earlier. "It's a great place to live," says one student. "The people are amazing" and the "campus and city are breathtaking." As one student puts it, "While you don't go to law school for the social life, it makes a big difference to have something to do when you actually do find free time."

"Social life is good" at Chapel Hill because "on the whole, students are very social outside of class." There are always a multitude of "school-sponsored social events in town" and "parties being thrown by law students to celebrate a wide array of milestones" (for instance, there is a "we just took our second practice exam" party). However, some students lament that there is little to do "for someone who does not drink."

Getting In

While perhaps easier than you might think, admissions here is no cakewalk. Admitted students at the 25th percentile have an LSAT score of 161 and a GPA of 3.4. Admitted students at the 75th percentile have an LSAT score of 165 and a GPA of 3.8. If applying as a non-resident, keep in mind that you'll want to be ready to dazzle with your academic prowess as around 70 percent of each admitted year at Chapel Hill are residents of North Carolina, and competition for the remaining slots in the class is stiff.

Clinical program required	No
Legal writing course requirement	Yes
Legal methods course requirement	No
Legal research course requirement	Yes
Moot court requirement	Yes
Public interest law requirement	No

ADMISSIONS

Selectivity Rating	98
# applications received	2,576
% applicants accepted	18
% acceptees attending	54
Median LSAT	163
LSAT Range (25th to 75th percentile)	161–165
Median undergrad GPA	3.51
Application fee	$75
Regular application deadline	3/1
Transfer students accepted	Yes
Evening division offered	No
Part-time accepted	No
CAS accepted	Yes

FINANCIAL FACTS

Annual tuition (in-state out-of-state)	$19,012/$34,120
Books and supplies	$1,150
Room & Board	$14,990
Financial aid application deadline	3/1
% first-year students receiving some sort of aid	100
% all students receiving some sort of aid	92
% of aid that is merit based	11
% receiving scholarships	88
Average grant	$4,636
Average loan	$26,299
Average total aid package	$29,676
Average debt	$76,642

EMPLOYMENT INFORMATION

Career Rating	95	State for bar exam	NC, NY, FL, GA, VA
Total 2012 JD Grads	247	Pass rate for first-time bar	93
% for whom you have useable information	97	**Prominent Alumni**	
% grads employed nine months out	91	Jim Delany, Big 10 Conference Commissioner; Julius Chambers, Civil Rights Attorney.	
# employed full-time	206		
# employed part-time	8	**Grads Employed by Field (%)**	
# employed bar required	178	Academic (1)	
# employed JD preferred	23	Business/Industry (18)	
# employed professional/other	2	Government (8)	
# employed non-professional	11	Judicial Clerkship (10)	
# pursuing advanced degree	6	Military (1)	
# unemployed and seeking employment	14	Private Practice (48)	
# not seeking employment	5	Public Interest (11)	
% grads employed by school	0		

University of North Dakota
School of Law

INSTITUTIONAL INFORMATION

Public/private	Public
% faculty part-time	44
% faculty female	36
% faculty underrepresented minority	8
Total faculty	25

SURVEY SAYS...

Diverse opinions accepted in classrooms, Great research resources, Great library staff, Abundant externship/internship/clerkship opportunities

STUDENTS

Enrollment of law school	241
% male/female	53/47
% from out-of-state	46
% part-time	0
% underrepresented minority	12
% international	7
# of countries represented	6
Average age of entering class	27

ACADEMICS

Academic Experience Rating	78
Profs interesting rating	78
Profs accessible rating	89
Hours of study per day	2.81

Advanced Degrees Offered

JD, 3 years

Combined Degrees Offered

JD/MPA, 4 years; JD/MBA, 4 years

Academics

Located in Grand Forks, the "underrated" University of North Dakota School of Law is home to one of the smallest law student populations. The resulting small class sizes make for "a better learning experience" than some larger schools, as "you get to hear opinions from all of the students" rather than just a few. Those who attend UND relish the intimacy this affords. "The first year class starts at eighty-five students, and that is as high as it will go," says a student. "Anything beyond that would be too big." UND School of Law "will prepare you to be a real legal practitioner." "You will be confident in your ability to handle your clients when you graduate," says a 1L.

The professors here "are the school's greatest resource." These "wonderful" and "accessible" teachers "are very willing to just meet with students to chat," and the faculty offices are in a location that is "very inviting" to students. "They all know my name and are eager to meet whenever possible. This proved very helpful as a nervous 1L," says a student. Most have plenty of legal experience and are able to bring those experiences into the classroom in order to "help contextualize the complicated content in a way that allows the students to make sense of it." The deans are "very nice and personable," and the Dean has a "commanding presence"; she "is cleaning house of mediocre professor[s]," meaning that "newly hired professors are proving to be definitely outstanding and fresh. "The administration is similarly receptive, and "students are very involved in the process" of running the law school. Students are kept well-informed about administration through "Dean's forums, email and word-of-mouth."

One of the greatest strengths of UND is "how well connected it is in the state of North Dakota." The federal externship program offers UND students opportunities that can be scarce at other law schools, and though students admit that the school's reputation has not exactly spread nationwide among employers, "North Dakotans take care of their own." The legal job market in the state is strong and "embraces us exclusively": "UND grads hire UND grads." The state legislature is also very supportive, especially through its legislative internship semester program; however, as strong as in-state job prospects are, the Career Services Office has quite a few naysayers when it comes to those seeking to go further. "Individual work needs to be done by students who are looking to be employed outside of the state," says a student. "Most of the help this office provides is generic information regarding resumes, cover letters, etc."

The size allows for courses to be "conducted with the students needs as the focus," but it also implies that "specializ[ing] is very hard to do at this particular school." There are two certificate options through the school (in Native American law and another in Aviation law), but outside of those two areas, a student is hard pressed to focus on the curriculum unless he or she forms a project with a professor, "which does not happen often. "In order to branch out, UND Law students do have the option to participate in the school's summer Norway Exchange Program.

The building classrooms are definitely "outdated." There are only two classrooms that can fit the full class of eighty-five students, but "the school is making improvements." During the 2013 legislative session, the state legislature appropriated $11.4 million for an addition and renovation project for the School of Law. The library is an excellent resource—"far better than using the online tools. The library staff goes above and beyond to help the students find what they need."

BEN HOFFMAN, DIRECTOR OF ADMISSIONS & RECORDS
CENTENNIAL DRIVE, P.O. BOX 9003, GRAND FORKS, ND 58202
TEL: 701-777-2260 FAX: 701-777-2217
E-MAIL: HOFFMAN@LAW.UND.EDU • WEBSITE: WWW.LAW.UND.EDU

Life

The combination of "low tuition for residents, low cost of living in North Dakota, [and a] booming economy in North Dakota" make UND Law a wise decision for in-state students and allow for a comfortable three years. The student body may "lack diversity" culturally, but there is "quite an age range," and though "everyone gets along great… there is a slight social divide." The younger students "have more time and freedom from familial obligations to go downtown on the weekends," but fun events also exist, which include: "the malpractice bowl, annual golf scramble, Halloween party, law school prom, and numerous other student organization led gatherings that most, if not all, students attend." There is also an annual Art Auction in which the graduating class raises money for their graduation party and class gift to school. At this auction, students bid "on such things as gourmet dinner parties prepared by professors and held at their homes, ice climbing with a professor, bowling with a professor, or the dean's parking spot for a week."

Grand Forks itself "is a small town with few activities to speak of." The weather can really be "a downer," though students claim it helps motivate them to study. The overall small law school size "allows the student[s] to get to know everyone quite well if they choose to," which can create excellent friendships among "future colleagues," not to mention "a friendly, understanding, and cooperative atmosphere." "Personally, these relationships have been vitally important for my overall well-being and experience," says a first year student.

Getting In

The admissions committee considers the following when considering candidates for admission: LSAT scores, undergraduate GPAs, personal essays, and letters of recommendation. It also considers oral and written communication skills. For the Class of 2013, the average undergraduate grade point average was 3.32 and the median LSAT score was 151.

Clinical program required	No
Legal writing	
course requirement	Yes
Legal methods	
course requirement	Yes
Legal research	
course requirement	Yes
Moot court requirement	No
Public interest	
law requirement	No

ADMISSIONS

Selectivity Rating	**82**
# applications received	422
% applicants accepted	44
% acceptees attending	44
Average LSAT	150
Median LSAT	150
LSAT Range	
(25th to 75th percentile)	145–153
Average undergrad GPA	3.27
Median undergrad GPA	3.26
Application fee	$35
Regular application deadline	4/1
Transfer students accepted	Yes
Evening division offered	No
Part-time accepted	No
CAS accepted	Yes

FINANCIAL FACTS

Annual tuition (in-state	
out-of-state)	$7,172/$19,478
Books and supplies	$1,533
Fees	$2,916
Room & Board	$8,520
% first-year students receiving	
some sort of aid	77
% all students receiving	
some sort of aid	84
% of aid that is merit based	16
% receiving scholarships	39
Average grant	$6,339
Average loan	$22,589
Average total aid package	$23,340
Average debt	$64,100

EMPLOYMENT INFORMATION

Career Rating	**85**	**Prominent Alumni**
Total 2012 JD Grads	90	Earl Pomeroy, Congressman, ND; H.F.
% for whom you have useable		Gierke, Chief Justice, US Armed Forces
information	98	Court of Appeals; Kermit Bye, Judge, 8th
% grads employed nine months out	88	Circuit Court of Appeals.
# employed full-time	73	**Grads Employed by Field (%)**
# employed part-time	4	Business/Industry (10)
# employed bar required	62	Government (14)
# employed JD preferred	9	Judicial Clerkship (12)
# employed professional/other	2	Military (2)
# employed non-professional	4	Private Practice (47)
# pursuing advanced degree	1	Public Interest (3)
# unemployed and seeking employment	6	
# not seeking employment	4	
% grads employed by school	0	
State for bar exam	ND, MN, CA, SD, MT	
Pass rate for first-time bar	80.5	

UNIVERSITY OF NOTRE DAME
LAW SCHOOL

INSTITUTIONAL INFORMATION
Public/private	Private
Affiliation	Roman Catholic
Student-faculty ratio	9:1
% faculty part-time	40
% faculty female	37
% faculty underrepresented minority	9
Total faculty	115

SURVEY SAYS...
Diverse opinions accepted in classrooms, Great library staff, Beautiful campus

STUDENTS
Enrollment of law school	545
% male/female	56/44
% from out-of-state	92
% underrepresented minority	28
% international	2
# of countries represented	6
Average age of entering class	23

ACADEMICS
Academic Experience Rating	95
Profs interesting rating	97
Profs accessible rating	89
Hours of study per day	4.16

Academic Specialties
Criminal, Human Rights, International

Advanced Degrees Offered
LLM in International Human Rights (1 year); JSD in International Human Rights (3–5 years, including 2 years of residency); LLM in International and Comparative Law (London campus only) (1 academic year)

Combined Degrees Offered
JD/MBA, 4 years; JD/ME, 3 years; JD/MA in English, 3–4 years; JD/MS, 3–4 years; JD/Ph.D., length dependent upon program selection. Where appropriate and with the approval of the departments involved, other dual degree programs may be fashioned to suit individual interests or needs.

Academics

Notre Dame, named for the Virgin Mary of the school's Catholic faith, provides a "great education," a "strong" brand, and "academic freedom" all tinged with a "Catholic character." The Catholic roots provide a "strong moral compass" and helps Notre Dame have "an intangible that you just can't put your finger on. It feels special." Notre Dame's great brand name comes complete with a "close-knit" and "nationwide" alumni base. This is "tremendously useful to young lawyers due to its active and engaged membership base" and "leads to stronger networking/ job opportunities." "The experience here has been second to none," a happy 1L says. Notre Dame "respects and encourages public service." One 3L says that "of all the law schools I contemplated attending, none respected and encouraged public service like Notre Dame."

Students rave about the school's facilities, dubbing them "state of the art," "top notch," "outstanding," and "of the highest caliber." "I don't think there is a better place to study law," one student says of the building. "The law school is still brand new" and the "beautiful" library is "conveniently located on campus." "The technology is top of the line" in this "spacious" "new" building, including "strong wifi throughout and monitors/ projectors to assist in classroom presentation." "It's modern and yet has the rich feel of an old and prestigious school. It's like Hogwarts, especially during the winter," a 3L says while invoking Harry Potter.

The academic environment is one "where the faculty and administration truly care about the success and growth of their students." "While many law schools may be very cut-throat and competitive," a 3L explains, "Notre Dame emphasizes a more collaborative, cohesive atmosphere." Career services "is diligent and genuinely cares," while the administration is labeled by many as "superb." However, several students note that the "inaccessible" dean "has a very poor reputation amongst the students." The "outstanding faculty" gets high marks, "particularly the younger faculty." These "fantastic" professors are each "a distinguished scholar in the subject that they teach." The faculty garners "a great deal of respect" from the students, especially for how they are "willing to speak to students and help the students out in any way they can." "Sure, their resumes are astounding, but they also are dedicated to teaching," a 3L explains. If there is a downside, it is that the faculty have "a strong conservative and/or religious presence" and some students wish they would have a more balanced faculty and bring in "more professors with liberal perspectives." Most students label "the overall academic experience" as "very rewarding." As a 1L puts it: "Notre Dame Law has been around a long time—they know what they're doing."

MELISSA FRUSCIONE, DIRECTOR OF ADMISSIONS AND FINANCIAL AID
NOTRE DAME LAW SCHOOL, P.O. BOX 780, NOTRE DAME, IN 46556
TEL: 574-631-6626 FAX: 574-631-5474
E-MAIL: LAWADMIT@ND.EDU • WEBSITE: LAW.ND.EDU

Life

"The best part" of life at Notre Dame "is the community, which includes the students, faculty, and alumni. Everyone takes pride in being part of Notre Dame." "The student body is fairly relaxed" although the law school "needs to improve [its student body] diversity." "Everyone in the school seems to have the same socioeconomic background," a 3L says. In addition, students think it is time that the program stopped discriminating. "It is 2013. It is unacceptable that this place will not allow an LGBT group," a 3L says. Students love "the atmosphere" at Notre Dame. "Unlike other programs that are cut throat and uber-competitive, the class at Notre Dame bonds together in a very unique way" and consequentially "there is a high level of trust, honesty, and appreciation for one another" that is not present at all law schools. You cannot think about Notre Dame without thinking football, and students here love to go to games and shout "Go Irish."

Getting In

Notre Dame's strong brand is built on accepting only the strongest applicants. For the 2012 class, the range (25th to 75th percentile) in GPA and LSAT were 3.43 to 3.8 and 161 to 167 respectively. The school takes great pride in its mission as a Catholic Law School, and looks for students that will respect the traditions and goals that entails.

Clinical program required	No
Legal writing course requirement	Yes
Legal methods course requirement	No
Legal research course requirement	Yes
Moot court requirement	Yes
Public interest law requirement	No

ADMISSIONS

Selectivity Rating	94
# applications received	2,852
% applicants accepted	24
% acceptees attending	26
Median LSAT	166
LSAT Range (25th to 75th percentile)	161 –167
Median undergrad GPA	3.66
Application fee	$75
Regular application deadline	3/15
Transfer students accepted	Yes
Evening division offered	No
Part-time accepted	No
CAS accepted	Yes

FINANCIAL FACTS

Annual tuition	$45,500
Books and supplies	$9,050
Fees	$480
Room & Board	$9,050
Financial aid application deadline	2/28
% of aid that is merit based	95
Average debt	$101,512

EMPLOYMENT INFORMATION

Career Rating	94	**Grads Employed by Field (%)**
Total 2012 JD Grads	196	Academic (3)
% for whom you have useable information	100	Business/Industry (12)
% grads employed nine months out	83	Government (9)
Median starting salary	$80,000	Judicial Clerkship (11)
# employed full-time	158	Military (3)
# employed part-time	5	Private Practice (43)
# employed bar required	134	Public Interest (2)
# employed JD preferred	24	
# employed professional/other	2	
# employed non-professional	3	
# pursuing advanced degree	0	
# unemployed and seeking employment	28	
# not seeking employment	2	
% grads employed by school	2	
State for bar exam	NY, IL, CA, IN, OH	
Pass rate for first-time bar	91.6	

UNIVERSITY OF OKLAHOMA
COLLEGE OF LAW

INSTITUTIONAL INFORMATION

Public/private	Public
Affiliation	No Affiliation
Student-faculty ratio	13:1
% faculty part-time	25
% faculty female	33
% faculty underrepresented minority	11
Total faculty	57

SURVEY SAYS...

Great research resources, Great library staff, Beautiful campus

STUDENTS

Enrollment of law school	505
% male/female	55/45
% from out-of-state	36
% part-time	0
% underrepresented minority	20
# of countries represented	1
Average age of entering class	25

ACADEMICS

Academic Experience Rating	90
Profs interesting rating	88
Profs accessible rating	83
Hours of study per day	2.94

Academic Specialties
Civil Procedure, Commercial, Constitutional, Corporation Securities, Criminal, Environmental, Human Rights, International, Labor, Legal History, Property, Taxation, Intellectual Property

Advanced Degrees Offered
None

Combined Degrees Offered
JD/MBA, 4 years; JD/MPH, 4 years; JD/Generic Dual Degree, 4 years

Academics

It is a "pleasure to attend" the University of Oklahoma College of Law, an affordable, forward-thinking, and thoroughly student-friendly institution, located on a "gorgeous" campus in Norman. While the school has established a strong reputation locally, "OU Law is constantly improving," overseen by an administration that is "extremely committed to raising the profile of OU Law through fundraising, community outreach, and increased academic opportunity." Of particular note, the program dean and the dean of students "have brought fresh, new ideas and programs to the student body, faculty, and staff," which have created "a buzz about what is to come for the law school." As the program evolves, students feel their voices are heard. "The administration at OU Law is keyed into the students' perspective in a unique way. The dean often mingles with students in the common areas and it is easy to get a meeting with any administration official."

The University of Oklahoma JD begins with a core curriculum in legal fundamentals, including a strong "focus in [the] 1L year on research and writing." Thereafter, students can tailor their legal education through elective courses. In addition to the school's excellence in Native American law, "Our world leadership in the area of oil and gas law makes OU stand out among so many law schools." A current students adds, "As energy becomes more and more important to this state and this nation, OU will continue to be more important in training future professionals in the energy industry." For those who don't want to practice in the oil and gas industry, the school also has "a genuine and earnest commitment to public service, and the cost of attendance allows students to pursue that kind of work after graduating without having to harvest organs on the side." On that note, it's worth looking into the school's strengths and weaknesses before enrolling. "Certain academic areas are well developed (e.g. torts and litigation skills) while others are fairly marginal (e.g. environmental law)." In addition to coursework, students can take advantage of "multiple international summer programs, legal clinics, as well as research positions with professors." It is also worth noting that the school's "externship programs in the area of American Indian Law and International Human Rights law are among the best in the country."

Combining an intimate academic environment with an attractive in-state price tag, "University of Oklahoma is a great place to go if you're looking for affordable legal education with all of the upside of a top-tier institution." Experts in their fields, OU's "professors come from a variety of different backgrounds and many are very animated, making classes more interesting." Thanks to the school's low enrollment, "the quality of professors, coupled with the small class sizes, facilitates unmatched educational opportunities." While academics are "rigorous," OU understands that law school doesn't have to be unpleasant. Unique for a public school, "OU places a great deal of emphasis on serving student needs," and throughout the program, "faculty and staff and students work together to help everyone succeed and have a positive experience." Students are treated as adults, and academic policies are reasonable, rather than punitive. For example, one OU "professor teaches three sections of the same class because he enjoys it so much and allows students to sit in on other sections in case they can't make it to their own class. This gives us the opportunity to handle life as it comes, and doesn't punish us for missing class due to uncontrollable circumstances." Adding to the overall good vibes, the law school building is "state-of-the-art, with technology in almost every classroom,

VICKI FERGUSON, ADMISSIONS COORDINATOR
ANDREW M. COATS HALL, 300 TIMBERDELL ROAD, NORMAN, OK 73019
TEL: 405-325-4728 FAX: 405-325-0502
E-MAIL: VFERGUSON@OU.EDU • WEBSITE: WWW.LAW.OU.EDU

making learning more interactive." Without batting an eyelash, OU students explain the "facilities are some of the best in the nation," which include "breathtaking" courtrooms for trial practice and a library boasting "a vast array of resources and very knowledgeable staff."

Life

University of Oklahoma Law School is a "very cooperative and fun environment," where it's easy to make friends and get involved in campus life. There are about 150 students in each 1L class, and this is further divided into sections of "around 45 people, which allows for great interaction with teachers and also fosters a lot of friendships." Through curricular and extracurricular activities, students forge the personal and professional connections they will rely on throughout their career. "The legal community in Oklahoma is small, and we all know these are people we will be working with the rest of our lives." Some OU students would like to see the school make an effort to "recruit a more diverse student body," though they also feel that "opinions in class on politics and society are surprisingly varied." In terms of politics, one student declares, "The student body, while more conservative than other places in the country, is MUCH more liberal than Oklahoma overall."

Overall, the student body is "cohesive and social," and the staff does "a great job of planning and executing several social events for students." From law journals to social clubs, "student organization participation is excellent and very accessible for incoming 1L students." For a bit of diversion, "OU football is amazing," and in the surrounding town of Norman, there are "oodles of churches, volunteering opportunities, organizations, and hot spots where a student looking to branch out from the law school can network."

Getting In

For prospective students, University of Oklahoma offers local recruitment events, including the opportunity to meet OU's popular dean. Admission to the program is fairly selective. The average LSAT score for incoming students is 158, and the average undergraduate GPA is 3.48. The admissions committee only considers one's highest LSAT score. Students are admitted once a year for a fall start-date.

Clinical program required	No
Legal writing course requirement	Yes
Legal methods course requirement	No
Legal research course requirement	Yes
Moot court requirement	Yes
Public interest law requirement	No

ADMISSIONS

Selectivity Rating	87
# applications received	982
% applicants accepted	38
% acceptees attending	41
Median LSAT	158
LSAT Range (25th to 75th percentile)	155–161
Median undergrad GPA	3.48
Application fee	$50
Regular application deadline	3/15
Early application deadline	3/15
Transfer students accepted	Yes
Evening division offered	No
Part-time accepted	No
CAS accepted	Yes

FINANCIAL FACTS

Annual tuition (in-state out-of-state)	$14,190/$24,615
Books and supplies	$1,500
Fees	$5,573
Room & Board	$18,208
Financial aid application deadline	3/1
% first-year students receiving some sort of aid	94
% all students receiving some sort of aid	91
% of aid that is merit based	63
% receiving scholarships	85
Average grant	$4,000
Average loan	$27,419
Average total aid package	$20,500
Average debt	$77,146

EMPLOYMENT INFORMATION

Career Rating	85	% grads employed by school	0
Total 2012 JD Grads	188	State for bar exam	OK, TX, CO, MO, KS
% for whom you have useable information	100	Pass rate for first-time bar	88.7
% grads employed nine months out	89	**Prominent Alumni**	
Median starting salary	$50,000	Frank Keating, Former Gov. of Oklahoma; David L. Boren, Pres. of OU (Former U. S. Senator); Jerry Stritzke, COO & President of Coach.	
% job accepting grads providing useable salary information	88		
# employed full-time	151	**Grads Employed by Field (%)**	
# employed part-time	10	Academic (2)	
# employed bar required	133	Business/Industry (22)	
# employed JD preferred	24	Government (13)	
# employed professional/other	9	Judicial Clerkship (3)	
# employed non-professional	1	Military (1)	
# pursuing advanced degree	4	Private Practice (54)	
# unemployed and seeking employment	12	Public Interest (5)	
# not seeking employment	5		

UNIVERSITY OF OREGON
SCHOOL OF LAW

INSTITUTIONAL INFORMATION

Public/private	Public
Student-faculty ratio	15:1
% faculty part-time	40
% faculty female	48
% faculty underrepresented minority	12
Total faculty	58

SURVEY SAYS...

Liberal students, Beautiful campus

STUDENTS

Enrollment of law school	480
% male/female	58/42
% part-time	0
% underrepresented minority	17
% international	1
# of countries represented	4
Average age of entering class	25

ACADEMICS

Academic Experience Rating	76
Profs interesting rating	77
Profs accessible rating	77
Hours of study per day	4.47

Academic Specialties

Civil Procedure, Commercial, Constitutional, Corporation Securities, Criminal, Environmental, Government Services, Human Rights, International, Property, Taxation, Intellectual Property

Advanced Degrees Offered

2 year master's degree program in Conflict and Dispute Resolution; LLM degree in Environmental and Natural Resources Law.

Combined Degrees Offered

JD/MBA Business & Law; JD/MA or JD/MS Environmental Studies; JD/MA International Studies; JD/MA or JD/MS Conflict & Dispute Resolution; JD/MA or JD/MS & Journalism; JD/MA or JD/MS in Community and Regional Planning; JD/MA or JD/MS in Public Administration; and a JD/MS in Water Sciences with Oregon State University.

Academics

As the state's only public law, the University of Oregon's School of Law provides numerous opportunities for interdisciplinary learning that go beyond the traditional curriculum (such as intersections with journalism, conflict resolution, and environmental studies), and a robust commitment to public service and public interest law. The school's clinics and externship opportunities and "amazing" legal writing and research program round out the affordable and respected degree on offer here.

Every faculty and staff member at Oregon is "extremely focused on the student experience." "You can always get ahold of your professor, and the Dean even holds office hours, allowing you to go and discuss whatever you'd like with him," says a student. For common occurrences like clinics, externships and registration, the "amazingly helpful" administration "has made everything flow very easily." Conversely, if you have a special situation, "administrators are always available to meet and discuss solutions with you." "The school is small enough that you really get to know the faculty and administration, and they will help you in any way they can to network and get jobs," says a 2L (though some admit that the school "could use more career services related to jobs out of state"). The school's major focus is on public interest law, but it has "a high number of specialized programs and great faculty that allow for students to get a great education in their area of interest," and "is very supportive of students who want to pursue non-Big Law careers."

The classroom experience is "very collaborative," and members of the "empowered student body" are supportive of one another all hours of the day. Students do worry that the University of Oregon (and law schools in general) are "not concerned enough about practical lawyering skills," and wish that the administration could hurry along the process for creating even more clinics. "In order for the legal job market to weather this ongoing crisis, law schools must take swift measures to make law schools more affordable, practical, and efficient," says one. Top programs and centers such as the Appropriate Dispute Resolution Center, the Wayne Morse Center for Law and Politics, and the Center for Law and Entrepreneurship's Small Business Clinic (which assists small and microbusinesses) help to offset this need and add to the school's reputation.

The law school has addressed these issues through offering 9 different clinical opportunities each year wither between 110 and 180 seats. There is also a robust externship program. Top programs and centers such as the Appropriate Dispute Resolution Center, the Wayne Morse Center for Law and Politics, and the Center for Law and Entrepreneurship's Small Business Clinic (which assists small and microbusinesses) help to offset most other experiential complaints and add to the school's reputation.

Life

Oregon is "a pretty white state," so "while the administration does a lot of outreach to attract minority students, the overall population is really white." The school and students may tend towards younger and liberal, but "there is a healthy dose of differing opinions and political backgrounds." The "tech-savvy" school "makes most students feel welcome in what is a very stressful environment": "Everyone is very friendly," the law school "has a great vibe," the building is "amazing," and the library is "great." The city of Eugene itself is "generally a pretty great place to live," and students also get "free tickets to Ducks football," which helps relax the soul and bolster school spirit.

"Student groups are very active on campus," and this social bunch take advantage whenever they can find the time. The "geographically breathtaking location" provides "biking trails, hills to climb, [and]outdoor activities galore," which is par for the course of any Oregonian (less than half of the student body is an Oregon resident when they enroll).

Getting In

When applying to a strong law program located in a gorgeous setting, expect some competition. Oregon's admitted students at the 25th percentile have LSAT scores of 155 and GPAs of 3.09. Admitted students at the 75th percentile have LSAT scores of 160 and GPAs of 3.63.

Clinical program required	No
Legal writing course requirement	Yes
Legal methods course requirement	No
Legal research course requirement	Yes
Moot court requirement	No
Public interest law requirement	No

ADMISSIONS

Selectivity Rating	79
# applications received	1,545
% applicants accepted	53
% acceptees attending	18
Median LSAT	158
LSAT Range (25th to 75th percentile)	155–160
Median undergrad GPA	3.33
Application fee	$50
Regular application deadline	3/1
Transfer students accepted	Yes
Evening division offered	No
Part-time accepted	No
CAS accepted	Yes

FINANCIAL FACTS

Annual tuition (in-state out-of-state)	$27,054/$34,074
Books and supplies	$1,600
Fees	$1,300
Room & Board	$10,854
Financial aid application deadline	3/1
% first-year students receiving some sort of aid	90
% all students receiving some sort of aid	93
% of aid that is merit based	15
% receiving scholarships	69
Average grant	$7,177
Average loan	$36,883
Average total aid package	$38,733
Average debt	$100,169

EMPLOYMENT INFORMATION

Career Rating	71	**Prominent Alumni**
Total 2012 JD Grads	161	Ron Wyden, U.S. Senator; Alfred T.
% grads employed nine months out	70	Goodwin, Former Chief Judge, US Ct. of
Median starting salary	$44,152	Appeals, Ninth Cir.; Jim Carter, VP &
# employed full-time	90	General Counsel, Nike.
# employed part-time	23	**Grads Employed by Field (%)**
# employed bar required	82	Academic (1)
# employed JD preferred	25	Business/Industry (9)
# employed professional/other	4	Government (15)
# employed non-professional	1	Judicial Clerkship (14)
# pursuing advanced degree	6	Private Practice (21)
# unemployed and seeking employment	35	Public Interest (10)
# not seeking employment	2	
% grads employed by school	8	
State for bar exam	OR, CA, WA, NY, AZ	
Pass rate for first-time bar	74	

University of the Pacific
McGeorge School of Law

INSTITUTIONAL INFORMATION

Public/private	Private
Affiliation	No Affiliation
Student-faculty ratio	15:1
% faculty part-time	57
% faculty female	40
% faculty underrepresented minority	12
Total faculty	105

SURVEY SAYS...

Diverse opinions accepted in classrooms, Beautiful campus

STUDENTS

Enrollment of law school	916
% male/female	53/47
% from out-of-state	23
% part-time	28
% underrepresented minority	28
% international	1
# of countries represented	20
Average age of entering class	23

ACADEMICS

Academic Experience Rating	85
Profs interesting rating	84
Profs accessible rating	87
Hours of study per day	3.92

Academic Specialties

Criminal, Environmental, Government Services, International, Property, Taxation, Intellectual Property

Advanced Degrees Offered

JD, 3 years; JD, 4 years; JSD International Water Law, LLM Transnational Business Practice, 1 year. LLM International Law, 1 year; LLM Public Law & Policy, 1 year; LLM Experiential Law Teaching, 1 year

Combined Degrees Offered

JD/MBA, JD/MPPA, JD/MA or MS upon approval (all concurrent degrees are planned for 4 years)

Academics

Located in the state capital of Sacramento, McGeorge School of Law's proximity to the courts understandably leads to an emphasis on lawyering skills and the reality of legal practice. The unique locale also offers "amazing access to California state government opportunities," and its status as the "largest law school campus in the world" (resting on 13 acres) is made even more resounding by the fact that the campus is entirely devoted to the law school. "No MBA students, undergrad, or the like—everyone here is either going through what you are or can help in some way," says a 1L.

Most here say that McGeorge's great strength is its "awesome professors." "Very few of them are the dry, stuffy professors you expect to have in law school"; instead, they're "witty, friendly, very accessible, and sociable." "It's refreshing to see that they don't take themselves too seriously. Law school is just that much more fun when a professor is willing to show up to class wearing a twisted-balloon bow tie," says a student. They "are always willing to meet and talk with a student" and also "great about not only attending school sponsored events but also show up to unofficial events." For the most part, the "strong trial advocacy programs" and comprehensive curriculum "is well tailored to the student body," and professors "want more than anything for us students to become that knowledgeable and quick."

Another strength is the faculty scholarship. "I am constantly recommending to friends at other law schools supplements that were authored by Pacific McGeorge faculty simply because they are the best supplements," says a second year. Administration is as accessible as the faculty, and "the Dean herself is holding a resume review session to give individuals advice on their resumes." The writing program could use some work to become more flexible, according to some, because "although the program sounds good on paper, it fails to achieve its goals because of the way it is implemented." The global lawyering skills (GLS) program "emphasizes legal writing and oral argument, which is essential for becoming a skilled lawyer"; while it is not without its merits, many agree that it "takes up too many credit hours," and "the idea that it is known in the region is not, in all likelihood, a function of its success."

Classrooms are "nice and clean," and a renovation of the library has been completed: it is "large, aesthetic," and "gorgeous," making it "a good place to study." The library staff goes "above and beyond the call of duty in locating difficult-to-find sources." Job placements "could be much better," however, and students agree that a better reputation would help out greatly. "Your degree is only worth what job it gets you," says one. Luckily, for those remaining in the area, "the school faces little competition from other schools," and alumni "are always anxious to help out students." Some wish the bar passage rates would go up, and agree that "it would be helpful if we were specifically told which electives we should take that would increase our chances of passing the bar."

ELLA MAE S. ESTRADA, DIRECTOR OF ADMISSIONS
3200 FIFTH AVENUE, SACRAMENTO, CA 95817
TEL: 916-739-7105 FAX: 916-739-7301
E-MAIL: ADMISSIONSMCGEORGE@PACIFIC.EDU • WEBSITE: WWW.MCGEORGE.EDU

Life

The students in the "very welcoming community" of McGeorge are "great," and "experiences here are memorable," according to one. Students are "much less competitive than at the majority of other law schools"; since there is no mandatory grading curve, there is "a much stronger sense of community, unlike the cutthroat atmosphere" at some other law schools. "I came to McGeorge for the atmosphere, and it hasn't disappointed. My 1L section was like family," says a second year student.

While the neighborhood around the school is "less than ideal," the campus "is constantly working to ensure the students feel safe," and public safety is "always available and easily accessible." There is a "lack of on-campus housing," so most students commute to school every day. The campus itself is lovely, with brick buildings, "massive trees," and a gorgeous quad with a gazebo. "The campus is extremely beautiful and it has all the resources one could wish for a law school to have," says a student. McGeorge also cares about the environment: there's an on-campus community garden and a student-run sustainability committee which works with the administration to make the school more sustainable.

Getting In

The most important factors in admissions' decisions are a student's previous academic record, LSAT scores, graduate school or post-college career experience, and community service or extracurricular activities. For last year's entering day class, LSAT scores at the 25th percentile were 155, and GPAs were 3.09; for the 75th percentile, LSATs were 160, and GPAs were 3.57. Although the admissions office has access to all LSAT scores (for applicants who take the test multiple times), the highest score is used for purposes of admission.

Clinical program required	No
Legal writing course requirement	Yes
Legal methods course requirement	No
Legal research course requirement	Yes
Moot court requirement	Yes
Public interest law requirement	No

ADMISSIONS

Selectivity Rating	84
# applications received	3,555
% applicants accepted	39
% acceptees attending	16
Average LSAT	158
LSAT Range (25th to 75th percentile)	155–160
Average undergrad GPA	3.40
Median undergrad GPA	3.32
Application fee	$50
Regular application deadline	5/1
Early application deadline	3/15
Early application notification	5/1
Transfer students accepted	Yes
Evening division offered	Yes
Part-time accepted	Yes
CAS accepted	Yes

FINANCIAL FACTS

Annual tuition	$41,320
Books and supplies	$2,250
Fees	$73
Room & Board	$9,738
% first-year students receiving some sort of aid	94
% all students receiving some sort of aid	90
% of aid that is merit based	49
Average grant	$11,320
Average loan	$44,444
Average total aid package	$48,938
Average debt	$138,267

EMPLOYMENT INFORMATION

Career Rating	85	**Prominent Alumni**
Total 2012 JD Grads	303	Scott Boras, Sports Agent/Baseball; Bill
% grads employed nine months out	83	Lockyer, Attorney General/CA Gvt; Steve
Median starting salary	$65,000	Martini, Novelist.
# employed full-time	178	**Grads Employed by Field (%)**
# employed part-time	61	Academic (3)
# employed bar required	199	Business/Industry (13)
# employed JD preferred	17	Government (23)
# employed professional/other	20	Judicial Clerkship (4)
# employed non-professional	3	Military (1)
# pursuing advanced degree	3	Private Practice (45)
# unemployed and seeking employment	56	Public Interest (11)
# not seeking employment	0	
% grads employed by school	11	
State for bar exam	CA, NV, HI, OR, DC	
Pass rate for first-time bar	81	

UNIVERSITY OF PENNSYLVANIA
LAW SCHOOL

INSTITUTIONAL INFORMATION

Public/private	Private
% faculty part-time	45
% faculty female	39
% faculty underrepresented minority	15
Total faculty	118

SURVEY SAYS...
Great research resources, Great library staff

STUDENTS

Enrollment of law school	776
% male/female	50/50
% part-time	0
% underrepresented minority	30
% international	3
# of countries represented	20
Average age of entering class	24

ACADEMICS

Academic Experience Rating	98
Profs interesting rating	89
Profs accessible rating	80
Hours of study per day	3.65

Academic Specialties
Civil Procedure, Commercial, Constitutional, Corporation Securities, Criminal, Environmental, Government Services, Human Rights, International, Labor, Legal History, Legal Philosophy, Property, Taxation, Intellectual Property

Advanced Degrees Offered
JD; LLM; SJD; LLCM

Combined Degrees Offered
3 Years: JD/MBA; JD/MA or MS (Criminology); JD/MSEd (Ed. Policy); JD/MSEd (Higher Ed.); JD/MES (Environ. Studies); JD/MPA (Government); JD/MA (Int. Studies); JD/MBE (Bioethics); JD/MSSP (Social Policy); JD/MA (Global Business Law); JD/MSW (with a BSW), JD/LLM (Hong Kong). 4 years: JD/MCP (City & Regional Planning); JD/MPH (Public Health); JD/AM (Islamic Studies); JD/MSW;

Academics

Founded in 1850, Penn Law is one of the country's most outstanding law schools, boasting a "stellar" academic reputation and a cross-disciplinary program nearly unrivalled by other schools. The school "has a lot of resources and ensures that it remains a place of cutting edge legal thinking and teaching," and the environment is one that fosters "academic success and personal friendships at the same time." Overall, the school is "the perfect mix of academic rigor, opportunity, and collegial environment," according to a 2L.

The professors are "incredible," comprising a faculty of "nothing but pure geniuses." They "genuinely care about the students and take the time to mentor them," and many seem "to genuinely enjoy working through legal issues or discussing legal scholarship with their students." Faculty members are "interesting people who've had extraordinary careers," and most feel that "it's an honor to learn from them." Students are also able to take classes outside of the law school in their second and third years in order to broaden their horizons. Currently, the Legal Writing program is getting "a much-needed makeover," and the appellate advocacy courses and moot court opportunities "are strong and can accommodate most if not all students who wish to participate." Clinics are "great... if you can get into one," as they tend to be small, meaning many students ultimately may not be able to capitalize on the school's strong clinical programming.

The "extremely visible" administration garners similar enthusiasm, delivering "excellence with a smile." They "consistently put in extra effort to improve your learning experience, to bring a speaker to the law school, or to implement a concern or suggestion you have to improve the law school." As examples, a student cites the staff member in the registrar's office who "emailed me a syllabus for a course I hoped to register for, so I could be current on the readings," and the times that "the library researchers will hold an impromptu meeting to help find a tricky resource." "It would be easy for Student Affairs to hear out student complaints or suggestions and never act on them. Our administrators, however, really seem invested in making this a positive experience for the students and respond with action a majority of the time."

There are "lots of pro bono opportunities" that provide practical experience, but a few students do wish that more practical opportunities were available, "particularly ones geared toward transactional, legal practice." Fortunately, professors are "very willing to help with clerkships, externships, and outside research." The lack of practical opportunities is the only resource complaint that Penn students have, yet many agree that the professors "make sure we have what we need and that we know how to use this stuff." Registering for classes can be "a hassle" though, and students gripe about the "archaic process" of having to go to the office and write your name on a waitlist, which is a slightly tedious process.

Penn alumni are very involved, returning to Penn Law to teach elective courses and to offer their support in the recruiting process; it is because of the alumni's solid reputation that "employers look at a resume that has 'Penn Law' on it."

RENEE POST, ASSOCIATE DEAN, ADMISSIONS AND FINANCIAL AID
3501 SANSOM STREET, PHILADELPHIA, PA 19104-6204
TEL: 215-898-7400 FAX: 215-898-9606
E-MAIL: CONTACTADMISSIONS@LAW.UPENN.EDU • WEBSITE: WWW.LAW.UPENN.EDU

Life

"I love being at Penn," says a happy student. "The size of the student body is large enough that I am still meeting people, but small enough that it feels like a real community." Penn is composed of "superbly accomplished individuals who are relatively humble about their achievements," which makes for a "superior learning environment, where everyone works to their highest capacity, but everyone is still kind and generous to others." This general feeling of being the best of the best takes a load off of the tension that can be found in many graduate programs: "Everyone is very confident that they will get a great job when they graduate, so there is no sense of competition that I hear about from my friends at comparable schools." Students "share notes and outlines at the drop of a hat, and there's a genuine feeling that we're all in it together." The school is also very LGBTQ friendly and supportive.

The facilities at Penn are "visually pleasing and practical," and classroom facilities are "mostly very high-tech and new, especially with the addition of our new building." There are always "good places to study, socialize, eat, hold events, and whatever else you want to do." The school is small, and the way it is laid out "really makes it feel friendly and like a community. You run into everyone all the time, professors and students." "Penn is as good as everyone says, and better," says a pleased student. "Law school's a tough three years. Given a choice to do it all over again, I can't imagine wanting to go anywhere else."

Getting In

Last year, the University of Pennsylvania received close to 5,000 applications for an entering class of around 266 students. The entering class had an LSAT score of 171 in the 75th percentile (and a GPA of 3.93), and a 166 in the 25th percentile (GPA of 3.58). Penn evaluates an applicant's entire academic history, including grade trends and rigor of undergraduate course work. The admissions committee also evaluates a candidate's writing ability, as well as leadership experience, personal background, and achievements.

JD/MBA; JD/DMD (Dental Medicine); JD/MS (Historic Preservation). PhD programs (6 years): JD/PhD (American Legal History); JD/PhD (Philosophy), JD/PhD (Psych.); JD/PhD (Communications). JD/EdD (Ed.) and JD/MD in Medicine. a within Penn.

Clinical program required	No
Legal writing course requirement	Yes
Legal methods course requirement	Yes
Legal research course requirement	Yes
Moot court requirement	No
Public interest law requirement	Yes

ADMISSIONS

Selectivity Rating	98
# applications received	5,848
% applicants accepted	16
% acceptees attending	27
Median LSAT	170
LSAT Range (25th to 75th percentile)	164–171
Median undergrad GPA	3.87
Application fee	$80
Regular application deadline	3/1
Early application deadline	11/15
Early application notification	12/31
Transfer students accepted	Yes
Evening division offered	No
Part-time accepted	No
CAS accepted	Yes

FINANCIAL FACTS

Annual tuition	$49,900
Books and supplies	$7,720
Fees	$3,238
Room & Board	$13,672
Financial aid application deadline	3/1
% first-year students receiving some sort of aid	86
% all students receiving some sort of aid	77
% of aid that is merit based	13
% receiving scholarships	47
Average grant	$17,377
Average loan	$44,517
Average total aid package	$61,893
Average debt	$116,689

EMPLOYMENT INFORMATION

Career Rating	99	
Total 2012 JD Grads	270	
% for whom you have useable information	100	
% grads employed nine months out	98	
Median starting salary	$160,000	
# employed full-time	263	
# employed part-time	2	
# employed bar required	258	
# employed JD preferred	7	
# employed professional/other	0	
# employed non-professional	0	
# pursuing advanced degree	0	
# unemployed and seeking employment	5	
# not seeking employment	0	
State for bar exam	NY, PA	
Pass rate for first-time bar	95	

Prominent Alumni
Michael Richter, Chief Privacy Officer, Facebook; Libby Liu, President, Radio Free Europe; Leo E. Strine, Jr., Chancellor, Delaware Court of Chancery.

Grads Employed by Field (%)
Business/Industry (4)
Government (2)
Judicial Clerkship (15)
Private Practice (73)
Public Interest (4)

UNIVERSITY OF PITTSBURGH
SCHOOL OF LAW

INSTITUTIONAL INFORMATION

Public/private	Public
% faculty part-time	73
% faculty female	34
% faculty underrepresented minority	9
Total faculty	160

SURVEY SAYS...

Great research resources, Students love Pittsburgh, PA

STUDENTS

Enrollment of law school	709
% male/female	56/44
% from out-of-state	41
% part-time	1
% underrepresented minority	16
% international	2
# of countries represented	5
Average age of entering class	24

ACADEMICS

Academic Experience Rating	81
Profs interesting rating	80
Profs accessible rating	83
Hours of study per day	3.45

Academic Specialties

Civil Procedure, Environmental, International, Taxation, Intellectual Property

Advanced Degrees Offered

Master of Laws LLM for foreign-trained attorneys

Combined Degrees Offered

JD/MPA, Law and Urban and Public Administration, 4 years; JD/MPIA, Law and International Affairs, 4 years; JD/MBA, Law and Business Administration, 3.5 years; JD/MPH, Law and Public Health, 3.5 years; JD/MA, Law and Medical Ethics, 3.5 years; JD/MS, Law and Public Management, 4 years (in conjunction with Carnegie Mellon University); JD/MBA (in conjunction with Tepper School Carnegie Mellon University; JD/MSW with the School of Social Work, 4 years

Academics

The University of Pittsburgh School of Law's long history of turning out educated, practical attorneys dates back more than 110 years, and the school (located in the lively Oakland neighborhood of Pittsburgh) continues to uphold the standards of excellence set into place way back when. Those who want to focus or broaden their expertise can enroll in one of seven joint degree programs (including two partnerships with Carnegie Mellon University) or five certificate programs, which come with possibilities for international externships, skills instruction by teams of practicing litigators, or membership on an intellectual property moot court team.

Pitt Law often flies under the radar, but boasts "a surprisingly impressive faculty and staff" and an "incredible and very accessible" Dean. "I often joke that I accidentally went to the best school I applied to without knowing it," says a 1L. The "extremely high quality" professors are "fantastic," "universally reasonable, engaged and knowledgeable," and are "accessible without any reservation." Some "will even give personal phone numbers to contact in case of emergency or to arrange a meeting outside the law school." "I've been impressed at how passionate a lot of the professors are about their subjects. If you go talk to them, you may pick up a bit of that passion, too," says another.

The "breadth of available academic concentrations and hands-on skills courses" afforded to students are what really drive home the value of a Pitt Law degree; the health law and international law programs are "of a very high caliber" and offer "diverse opportunities and successful job placement," and Pitt Law students can also serve as editors at JURIST, the world's only web-based, student-powered legal news source, which is based at the law school. Students can also take advantage of "the help and resources of Pitt Law's internal organizations" such as the Center for International Legal Education, which helps to organize international internships and other opportunities, and the Innovation Practice Institute, which connects law students with local start-ups.

The financial aid and admissions offices "are run more smoothly than any other school of which I know," according to a student. Career services "has often seemed meandering in focus," but "the new head of the career services office is more aggressive in pursuing opportunities for students." She is "incredibly well networked and goes above and beyond to assist students in finding and landing internships and jobs." The alumni network is also quite expansive, and most former students "seem to hold a special place in their hearts for their alma mater and a strong willingness to help current students achieve their goals."

CHARMAINE C. MCCALL, ASSISTANT DEAN FOR ADMISSIONS AND FINANCIAL AID
3900 FORBES AVENUE, PITTSBURGH, PA 15260
TEL: 412-648-1413 FAX: 412-648-1318
E-MAIL: ADMITLAW@PITT.EDU • WEBSITE: WWW.LAW.PITT.EDU

Life

Pittsburgh "is pretty much the perfect city for law school" ("the city as a whole is united around the sports teams"), and the school's location is in a neighborhood known for being the city's bustling academic and cultural center. Regrettably, the law school building is "a 1970s concrete monstrosity" ("The architecture of this place kills me every time," says a student); the facilities inside are "well-equipped [and] sufficient for learning," but" you will never have a classroom lit with natural light." Pitt Law is in the middle of a remodeling project to address these aesthetic issues. The library is "outstanding," though. The school goes out of its way to "ensure that we have access to a wide breath of electronic resources." Also, "professional research librarians are always on duty to help whenever the library is open."

One of the greatest boons to Pitt Law life is the "strength of the community," in which one's peers "can routinely be described as collaborative." "The goal is to learn the material, not to beat each other," says a 2L. This "hard-working yet friendly student body" creates "a community atmosphere where classmates drive each other to succeed." Everyone "cheers each other on and shares in motivating each student to achieve everything they wish to pursue."

Getting In

Admitted students at the 25th percentile have LSAT scores of roughly 155 and GPAs of 3.09. Admitted students at the 75th percentile have LSAT scores of about 160 and GPAs of just over 3.6. Pitt's administration says that it will consider your highest score if you take the LSAT multiple times. Decisions are based on many factors (it is strongly recommended that you submit a resume), and the admissions committee requires online applications through LSAC starting September 1 through March 1. Applications are considered for only the current year for the full semester.

Clinical program required	No
Legal writing course requirement	Yes
Legal methods course requirement	No
Legal research course requirement	Yes
Moot court requirement	No
Public interest law requirement	No

ADMISSIONS

Selectivity Rating	80
# applications received	1,973
% applicants accepted	50
% acceptees attending	21
Average LSAT	157
Median LSAT	158
LSAT Range (25th to 75th percentile)	155–160
Average undergrad GPA	3.31
Median undergrad GPA	3.34
Application fee	$65
Regular application deadline	3/1
Early application deadline	12/1
Early application notification	12/31
Transfer students accepted	Yes
Evening division offered	No
Part-time accepted	No
CAS accepted	Yes

FINANCIAL FACTS

Annual tuition (in-state out-of-state)	$28,728/$35,704
Books and supplies	$1,560
Fees	$842
Room & Board	$16,052
Financial aid application deadline	3/1
% first-year students receiving some sort of aid	93
% all students receiving some sort of aid	89
% of aid that is merit based	60
% receiving scholarships	53
Average grant	$14,543
Average loan	$35,905
Average total aid package	$39,110
Average debt	$94,879

EMPLOYMENT INFORMATION

Career Rating	81
Total 2012 JD Grads	222
% grads employed nine months out	76
Median starting salary	$60,000
# employed full-time	116
# employed part-time	10
# employed bar required	126
# employed JD preferred	35
# employed professional/other	6
# employed non-professional	2
# pursuing advanced degree	1
# unemployed and seeking employment	37
# not seeking employment	1
% grads employed by school	0
State for bar exam	PA, VA, MD, NY, CA
Pass rate for first-time bar	84

Prominent Alumni
Richard Thornburg, Former U.S. Attorney General; Orrin Hatch, Senator,Utah; Joseph Weis, Senior Judge for the Third Circuit.

Grads Employed by Field (%)
Business/Industry (19)
Government (7)
Judicial Clerkship (6)
Military (2)
Private Practice (41)
Public Interest (2)

UNIVERSITY OF RICHMOND
SCHOOL OF LAW

INSTITUTIONAL INFORMATION

Public/private	Private
Affiliation	No Affiliation
Student-faculty ratio	11:1
% faculty female	42
% faculty underrepresented minority	14
Total faculty	36

SURVEY SAYS...

Diverse opinions accepted in classrooms, Great research resources, Great library staff, Beautiful campus, Students love Richmond, VA

STUDENTS

Enrollment of law school	460
% male/female	56/44
% from out-of-state	47
% part-time	0
% underrepresented minority	16
% international	2
# of countries represented	4
Average age of entering class	24

ACADEMICS

Academic Experience Rating	97
Profs interesting rating	89
Profs accessible rating	97
Hours of study per day	3.85

Academic Specialties

Civil Procedure, Commercial, Constitutional, Corporation Securities, Criminal, Environmental, International, Labor, Legal History, Property, Taxation, Intellectual Property

Advanced Degrees Offered

JD, 3 years

Combined Degrees Offered

JD/MBA (Masters in Business Administration); JD/MURP (Masters in Urban and Regional Planning); JD/MHA (Masters in Health Administration); JD/MSW (Masters in Social Work); JD/ MPA (Masters in Public Administration); each 4 years

Academics

Those looking to receive a first-rate law education while enjoying "Southern hospitality at its finest" would be wise to look into University of Richmond School of Law, where students say "The open dialogue among students and between students and professors is truly special." By all accounts, a "very friendly," "almost family-like" atmosphere prevails at this small school. "It amazes me that I'm able to walk down the hallway and have even professors whose classes I have not taken greet me by name," a satisfied 3L writes. The "well-educated, well-published" faculty members here are "dedicated to bettering their students and compassionate to their needs as individuals." The majority of professors "offer their home numbers and cell phone numbers so that we can call whenever we need help, or even just a little advice."

Professorial love is of the tough variety in the classroom, where students say "the use of the Socratic Method" "can be a bit intimidating," particularly for first-year students, though "It makes class entertaining and ensures that you are prepared," a 1L offers. All students here go through "an outstanding lawyering skills program. During these courses, our legal writing and actual courtroom skills are emphasized in very precise, methodical ways," a 2L writes. If students run into academic difficulties, they can take advantage of Richmond's Academic Success Program, which provides a full-time faculty member to assist students with their course work. The downside to the school's small size is "limited course selection," and "only one section" of most upper-level classes each semester. To expand its offerings, the School of Law partners with other schools within the University of Richmond—for example, the Robins School of Business and the Jepson School of Leadership Studies—to offer students a "diversity of dual degrees" which allows students "to really focus on particular fields of interest."

Richmond enjoys "a tremendous reputation in the Commonwealth of Virginia" and students believe that "the fact that there are so many opportunities for legal experience in Richmond," the state capital, "is a great strength" of the school. "We have access to county, state, and district courts and often have lectures and course[s] taught by Virginia Supreme Court Justices," a sanguine student writes. Many clerkships and externships are made possible through a "highly involved alumni community" in the area and help students to figure out what type of practice they would like to enter when they graduate. Because many students "fall in love with the city," the school's Career Development Office (CDO) has historically taken a somewhat regional approach. However, it "recently hired a new dean and two new staff members," and students are beginning to feel that the CDO "has the resources to help any student find a job anywhere in the world." The law school also provides guaranteed summer stipends to first- and second-year law students who obtain unpaid government or public-interest internships.

Administrators are described as "doting," and all maintain an "open-door policy." While there are a few reports of disorganization, the vast majority here believe the "personal approach" and lack of red tape transcend the minor difficulties. The "entire campus has wireless Internet access," which allows students to "study anywhere." In addition, "You are provided your own personal study carrel in the library, which functions as a locker and, most importantly, a nice quiet place to study." If students require more incentive to head to the library, "ample" staffing ensures that all customers "find what they are looking for." The student body's biggest complaint is that Richmond is "very underappreciated." "I have friends at Georgetown, UNC, Wake Forest, Duke, NYU, and UVA law schools, and none of them are as happy as I am at Richmond," a 2L boasts.

MICHELLE RAHMAN, ASSOCIATE DEAN FOR ADMISSIONS
LAW SCHOOL ADMISSIONS OFFICE, 28 WESTHAMPTON WAY, UNIVERSITY OF RICHMOND, VA 23173
TEL: 804-289-8189 FAX: 804-287-6516
E-MAIL: LAWADMISSIONS@RICHMOND.EDU • WEBSITE: LAW.RICHMOND.EDU

Life

Not only is the University of Richmond campus "one of the most beautiful in the country," it is "surrounded by a safe and pristine neighborhood that is also easily affordable." Adding to the pleasant environment, "Competition among students is healthy and not overwhelming." "I almost enjoy the daily grind of law school when I can so easily relate to my fellow students," a 2L reports. "Little things, like taking lunch breaks at the dining hall or going through flashcards together during exams, [have] helped me find a comfortable niche here." Richmond is "a very social school," and "numerous events and groups meetings" are held "every week." In addition, "The school sponsors monthly happy hours in order to encourage students and faculty/staff to interact," and "There is always the opportunity for free food." The student body can be cliquey, however, "especially if you don't fit in with the pretty and party-oriented mid-twenties crowd." Fortunately, "There's plenty to do in Richmond. I went to the opera with one of my friends and his wife," a 2L writes. Bars in the Fan district, "in the heart of Richmond," are very popular with students of all ages.

In recent years, "the school has significantly improved its minority enrollment," and "they are well integrated (I am one of them) and treated exactly as any individual regardless of race or gender by students, faculty and staff alike." A former bastion of conservatism, Richmond is "middle of the road these days, and there is a definite liberal presence on campus."

Getting In

Students frequently mention "the Admissions Office ladies" as a major resource of Richmond. "Literally, if you need a hug, they are there," a 2L reports. Their "personal acceptance phone call" initiates students to an environment in which "Every student is given plenty of attention." The advice the associate dean provides on the law school's website is another way in which the staff here goes above and beyond the call of duty.

Clinical program required	No
Legal writing course requirement	Yes
Legal methods course requirement	Yes
Legal research course requirement	Yes
Moot court requirement	No
Public interest law requirement	No

ADMISSIONS

Selectivity Rating	92
# applications received	2,823
% applicants accepted	21
% acceptees attending	25
Median LSAT	162
LSAT Range (25th to 75th percentile)	158–163
Median undergrad GPA	3.5
Application fee	$50
Regular application deadline	4/15
Regular notification	3/31
Early application deadline	12/15
Early application notification	12/24
Transfer students accepted	Yes
Evening division offered	No
Part-time accepted	No
CAS accepted	Yes

FINANCIAL FACTS

Annual tuition	$36,850
Books and supplies	$1,400
Fees	$0
Room & Board (on/off campus)	$10,330/$11,070
Financial aid application deadline	2/25
% first-year students receiving some sort of aid	75
% all students receiving some sort of aid	91
% of aid that is merit based	88
% receiving scholarships	60
Average grant	$16,050
Average loan	$38,375
Average total aid package	$43,490
Average debt	$107,960

EMPLOYMENT INFORMATION

Career Rating	75
Total 2012 JD Grads	148
% for whom you have useable information	97
% grads employed nine months out	84
Median starting salary	$60,000
% job accepting grads providing useable salary information	55
# employed full-time	119
# employed part-time	6
# employed bar required	86
# employed JD preferred	33
# employed professional/other	1
# employed non-professional	4
# pursuing advanced degree	0
# unemployed and seeking employment	10
# not seeking employment	8
% grads employed by school	0
State for bar exam	NC, NY, FL, VA, DC

Prominent Alumni
Lawrence L. Koontz, Justice, VA Supreme Court; Harvey E. Schlesinger, U.S. District Court Judge, Middle Dist. of FL; Frederick P. Stamp, Jr., U.S. District Court Judge, Northern District of WV.

Grads Employed by Field (%)
Business/Industry (24)
Government (10)
Judicial Clerkship (16)
Private Practice (33)
Public Interest (1)

UNIVERSITY OF SAN DIEGO
SCHOOL OF LAW

Academics

The University of San Diego School of Law boasts a lengthy 50-year history, an ideal location, and an alumni roster of 60 judges and two members of Congress, including the Chairman of the House Ways and Means Committee. The well-reputed national mock trial team and appellate moot court program all make for a "wonderful experience" and a "grand" academic life. At USD, "the opportunities are endless, it doesn't matter what field you want to enter."

The "great" faculty members here "genuinely like teaching" and "make an effort beyond the classroom to reach out to students." There is "supportive academic advising in every aspect of learning," and "professors are very interested in helping their students excel." Research opportunities are also readily available. Many of the first year professors use the Socratic method, but this becomes less and less frequent as a student advances, and the legal writing course was recently changed to being graded instead of pass/fail, which means that "if you let it, it will consume much more of your time." Some of the more popular classes "are really hard to get into, especially if a particular professor is good." Several professors are practitioners in the San Diego legal community, and offer "current, pertinent information necessary to 'survive' in the legal world today." The Lawyering Skills Department is a standout here among students, as it "teaches us legal research and writing during our 1L year, and is a great program." Students also appreciate the legal clinics on campus that service low-income families in a variety of legal areas. A few students do wish that there was a "bar course integrated into the education," as the post-graduate bar prep courses can be pricey.

The administration is "flexible and willing to change with the times and adapt to unsuccessful programming, classes, or past precedent." A staff that "knows you by name" proves to be "highly desirable as a law student," as many here are paying a great deal of money and "don't want to just be another number."

The "service oriented" administration at USD may be "great," but the office of career services is a mixed bag. Some say it is "very helpful" and "run very well," while others wish it could do more. "I go there every few weeks but never really get much out of them," says one student. It definitely helps that the "small market of San Diego yields constant opportunity to network and build your personal brand." "My school is well-ranked within the city, which allowed me to work at the ACLU and the IRS. If I went to a school of a similar ranking in LA, I doubt I would have had the same opportunities. Or if I went to Iowa, neither of those organizations have offices there," says a student.

CARL EGING, ASSISTANT DEAN OF ADMISSIONS AND FINANCIAL AID
OFFICE OF ADMISSIONS AND FINANCIAL AID, 5998 ALCALA PARK, SAN DIEGO, CA 92110
TEL: 619-260-4528 FAX: 619-260-2218
E-MAIL: JDINFO@SANDIEGO.EDU • WEBSITE: WWW.LAW.SANDIEGO.EDU

Life

As one student puts it, "Law school is challenging enough, you do not need your school making it harder than it needs to be. USD makes the transition into law school life so smooth and effortless." This "quaint" school truly has a "student body that is willing to help each other succeed." It "feels small and it feels like you know everyone." The pleasant mood of students here flows easily, since the school is located five minutes from the beach "in a beautiful setting" and is laid out "very conveniently in regards to the classrooms and research center." "The San Diego area is wonderful, but also the campus culture is laid back and cooperative rather than combative," says one student.

The school also has a good understanding of the need for creature comforts and stress-relieving practices: it "provides coffee and snacks during finals," "there is candy in every office, [and] the dean's mixers are well attended and delicious."

Getting In

While there are no pre-legal courses required for entry to the USD law program, all applicants must have a bachelor's degree from an accredited college. LSAT scores and GPA are important to an admissions decision, as are the personal qualities and skills demonstrated by your personal statement and letters of recommendation. The 2011–2012 entering class had a median LSAT score of 160 and a median GPA of 3.43.

Clinical program required	No
Legal writing course requirement	Yes
Legal methods course requirement	Yes
Legal research course requirement	Yes
Moot court requirement	Yes
Public interest law requirement	No

ADMISSIONS

Selectivity Rating	**85**
# applications received	4,314
% applicants accepted	38
% acceptees attending	18
Average LSAT	160
Median LSAT	160
LSAT Range (25th to 75th percentile)	158–162
Average undergrad GPA	3.41
Median undergrad GPA	3.43
Application fee	$50
Regular application deadline	
Early application deadline	2/1
Transfer students accepted	Yes
Evening division offered	Yes
Part-time accepted	Yes
CAS accepted	Yes

FINANCIAL FACTS

Annual tuition (in-state out-of-state)	$42,540
Books and supplies	$1,403
Fees	$214
Room & Board	$21,048
Financial aid application deadline	3/1
% first-year students receiving some sort of aid	93
% all students receiving some sort of aid	92
% of aid that is merit based	46
% receiving scholarships	46
Average grant	$21,581
Average loan	$41,347
Average total aid package	$49,901
Average debt	$110,625

EMPLOYMENT INFORMATION

Career Rating	**80**
Total 2012 JD Grads	318
% for whom you have useable information	99
% grads employed nine months out	86
Median starting salary	$67,600
# employed full-time	203
# employed part-time	68
# employed bar required	210
# employed JD preferred	36
# employed professional/other	13
# employed non-professional	12
# pursuing advanced degree	3
# unemployed and seeking employment	34
# not seeking employment	3
% grads employed by school	4
State for bar exam	CA, NV, AZ

Prominent Alumni
Shelley Berkeley, Congresswoman from Nevada; Theodore Epstein, President of Baseball Operations, Chicago Cubs; Hon. Thomas Whelan, U.S. District Court, So. California.

Grads Employed by Field (%)
Academic (3)
Business/Industry (23)
Government (6)
Judicial Clerkship (3)
Private Practice (47)
Public Interest (4)

UNIVERSITY OF SAN FRANCISCO
SCHOOL OF LAW

Academics

Jesuit-affiliated University of San Francisco School of Law puts a "sincere focus on public interest work" proclaims a 2L. USF's Public Interest Law Foundation demonstrates its support by "offering grants to students working in the public interest over the summer, and there is a loan forgiveness program for graduates pursuing public interest careers."

USF also works towards goals of producing graduates who are ready to practice and make an impact on the legal community. "USF is very good at developing lawyers who can actually practice when they graduate," says a 3L. There are eight clinical programs offered, which cover a plethora of legal areas of interest. "I worked in the predatory lending clinic, which was life-changing for me," reflects a 3L. "It helped me get perspective on the practice of law and what it means to work with low-income clients."

Students are encouraged to explore international affairs through summers abroad in Ireland and the Czech Republic. There are additional summer internships in developing nations including Cambodia, India, and Argentina.

Though academic complaints are limited, many students note "the class selection is interesting, but not very broad." "They want to teach you as much as you are willing to learn," said a part-time student. The legal research and writing program garners mixed reviews. Some students say it is "not up to par at all" while others maintain that it is "extremely thorough and practical." The high cost of tuition is also somewhat of an issue.

The school's Bay Area campus helps "USF attract and retain many truly excellent professors," and most students indicate that "professors for the most part really want to be there and are incredibly supportive and smart." They are known to "make ample time to meet with students" and "take a personal stake" in their students' success.

The administration is equally well liked, with a reputation of being "transparent" and "approachable." One student mentions a memorable moment he experienced. "Dean Brand passed by as I was working in the hall and asked me what I was doing. When he learned what I was taking on, he gave me a few words of encouragement. Even the most socratic, toughest professors have been supportive and available—they want everyone to succeed." The alumni network is strong at USF. "Alumni of the school are loyal to helping current students and are prevalent in the Bay area." A particular emphasis is placed on "alumni connections at public-interest law firms, governmental agencies, and nonprofits" where USF students are "very well-positioned to get summer jobs with the district attorney, public defender, or other criminal law employers" following their first year.

Despite these resources, the legal market that surrounds USF is extremely competitive. This, coupled with the opinion among students that the Office of Career Planning "is not very aggressive about actual job placement," can make things difficult after graduation if one does not plan properly. Students say they combat this by finding support in each other. "[There is a] spirit of community among my fellow classmates. There is never any doubt we are all in competition with each other but it never FEELS that way," says a 1L. USF made major changes to the Office of Career Planning in the summer of 2012, bringing in a new leader who has focused on aggressively expanding career opportunities for USF students and preparing students to take an entrepreneurial approach to their job searches.

The campus of the University of San Francisco receives high marks among students who say the law school facilities are "wonderful, clean, and modern." "The rooms are all

ALAN GUERRERO, DIRECTOR OF ADMISSIONS
2130 FULTON STREET, SAN FRANCISCO, CA 94117
TEL: 415-422-6586 FAX: 415-422-5442
E-MAIL: LAWADMISSIONS@USFCA.EDU • WEBSITE: WWW.LAW.USFCA.EDU/LAW

up-to-date with the highest tech equipment." "The library is awesome and the librarians are amazingly helpful and useful." "The law school is beautiful and small enough that you get an individualized experience."

Life

Law candidates at USF relish in the vast amount of diversity their campus has to offer. "More than 40 percent of our 1L class was non-white, in my section of ninety there are at least ten people who are 29+, and there are students from all over the US. I love the diversity of this school; it really makes the classes more interesting. People bring in their experiences and help the professors make what we're learning more applicable to real life, reflects one student." "The diverse student body at USF Law is a true reflection of American society and contributes to both the academic strength and rich culture of the law school."

When students decide to take a break from the books they are met with many options. The school provides programs including "many reputable speakers," and "there are lots of free lunches and events that make school less stressful." "Weekly Thursday night bar nights" are also well attended.

The City of San Francisco is beautiful, affording students endless opportunities for work and play. "You've got everything that San Francisco and the Bay Area have to offer" to help you relax. "Public transportation is really accessible," and the culture, restaurants, and nightlife are plenty. For the student on a budget, though, the "cost of living in San Francisco can be pretty steep."

Getting In

Admitted students at the 25th percentile have LSAT scores of approximately 155, and undergraduate GPAs just higher than 3.0. At the 75th percentile, LSAT scores are a little higher than 160, and GPAs are about 3.6.

Clinical program required	No
Legal writing course requirement	Yes
Legal methods course requirement	No
Legal research course requirement	Yes
Moot court requirement	Yes
Public interest law requirement	No

ADMISSIONS

Selectivity Rating	81
# applications received	3,454
% applicants accepted	44
% acceptees attending	14
Median LSAT	156
LSAT Range (25th to 75th percentile)	153–159
Median undergrad GPA	3.26
Application fee	$60
Regular application deadline	2/1
Transfer students accepted	Yes
Evening division offered	Yes
Part-time accepted	Yes
CAS accepted	Yes

FINANCIAL FACTS

Annual tuition	$42,284
Books and supplies	$8,360
Fees	$80
Room & Board (on/off campus)	$15,000/$14,400
Financial aid application deadline	2/15
% first-year students receiving some sort of aid	91
% all students receiving some sort of aid	90
% of aid that is merit based	14
% receiving scholarships	34
Average grant	$15,320
Average loan	$43,904
Average total aid package	$48,476
Average debt	$145,524

EMPLOYMENT INFORMATION

Career Rating	80	**Prominent Alumni**
Total 2012 JD Grads	222	Justice Ming Chin, CA Supreme Court;
% for whom you have useable		Judge Martin Jenkins, California Court of
information	94	Appeal for the First District; Judge
% grads employed nine months out	78	Saundra B. Armstrong, U.S. District Court
Median starting salary	$70,000	Northern California.
% job accepting grads providing		**Grads Employed by Field (%)**
useable salary information	46	Academic (5)
# employed full-time	122	Business/Industry (20)
# employed part-time	51	Government (5)
# employed bar required	111	Judicial Clerkship (1)
# employed JD preferred	39	Private Practice (38)
# employed professional/other	20	Public Interest (9)
# employed non-professional	3	
# pursuing advanced degree	2	
# unemployed and seeking employment	26	
# not seeking employment	8	
% grads employed by school	10	
State for bar exam	CA, WA, NY, VA, PA	
Pass rate for first-time bar	70	

UNIVERSITY OF SOUTH CAROLINA
SCHOOL OF LAW

INSTITUTIONAL INFORMATION

Public/private	Public
Affiliation	No Affiliation
Student-faculty ratio	15:1
% faculty part-time	34
% faculty female	34
% faculty underrepresented minority	10
Total faculty	53

SURVEY SAYS...

Diverse opinions accepted in classrooms, Great library staff

STUDENTS

Enrollment of law school	630
% male/female	59/41
% part-time	0
% underrepresented minority	15
% international	1
Average age of entering class	24

ACADEMICS

Academic Experience Rating	**77**
Profs interesting rating	79
Profs accessible rating	82
Hours of study per day	3.75

Advanced Degrees Offered

JD, 3 years

Combined Degrees Offered

4 year programs: Master of Accountancy (MACC), Master of Criminology and Criminal Justice (MCJ), Master of Earth and Environmental Resource Management (MEERM), Master of Economics, Master of Studies in Environmental Law and Policy (with Vermont Law School) (MELP), Master of Health Services Policy & Management (MHA), Master of Human Resources (MHR), International Master of Business Administration (IMBA), Master of Mass Communication (MMC), Master of Public Administration (MPA), Master of Social Work (MSW).

Academics

Conveniently located on the campus of the state's flagship university, the University of South Carolina School of Law is in the state capital, which also doubles as the state's largest city. With many of the state's courts in such close proximity of school grounds, opportunities for finding internships and making pertinent connections are right outside students' doors.

On the internal side, law students at the University of South Carolina have the option of participating in a variety of extracurricular activities and joint-degree programs to help them succeed. The Pro Bono program is celebrated as well as the five clinics covering nonprofit organizations, criminal practice, consumer bankruptcy, child protection advocacy, and federal litigation. "This university places a special emphasis on developing students into professionals that will promote society and the common good, regardless of the chosen field. Pro Bono efforts are praised and encouraged," says a 1L.

Law students that have an interest in working in the realm of family court, juvenile cases, or child welfare have an opportunity to gain experience by representing litigants in family court with the school's Children's law externships. Partnerships with schools and firms in London make it possible for students interested in foreign practice to work or study abroad for three weeks.

However, the most popular amenity at USC is the school's faculty, according to gushing students. "The school's administration is top notch, and ready to serve the student body. They are accessible, informed, and frank with their advice. The faculty treats you like the adult that you are and expect a lot out of you in return." The students aren't the only ones that think so either, "The school administration and professors are well respected in the legal community," one reveals.

"The school administration is on the up-and-up. The new Dean is doing an excellent job fixing any problems that may have existed with the school in the past. There is a real new energy in the building. This is reflected in a new curriculum and the addition of new externships and clinical courses, and the continued expansion of offerings for upper-level courses that cover both substantive law, theory of laws, and practical skills," says an excited 3L.

The support, coupled with the top-notch resources, makes USC a fertile ground for producing lawyers ready to become contenders in the law arena upon graduation. The law library is among the largest in the southeast. "The librarians are super helpful and great resources." "The University of South Carolina School of Law gives students challenging and rigorous curriculum lead by phenomenal faculty for a reasonable price," says a 3L.

Alumni ties to USC are strong in South Carolina so if you plan to practice at any firm, large or small, in this state, this is the school for you. That being said, it's important to note that the curriculum and programs are geared toward working locally. If your goal is to practice out of state you may be at a disadvantage. "Someone once told me that if you want to practice law in South Carolina, you better have a darn good excuse if you didn't go to USC. That is really the truth," counsels a 3L. Jobs in the private sector make up two-thirds of the positions taken upon graduation, including a significant amount of students opting for the judicial clerkship route.

LEWIS L. HUTCHISON, JR., ASSISTANT DEAN FOR ADMISSIONS
701 SOUTH MAIN STREET, COLUMBIA, SC 29208
TEL: 803-777-6605 FAX: 803-777-7751
E-MAIL: USCLAW@LAW.SC.EDU • WEBSITE: WWW.LAW.SC.EDU

Clinical program required	No
Legal writing course requirement	Yes
Legal methods course requirement	No
Legal research course requirement	Yes
Moot court requirement	No
Public interest law requirement	No

ADMISSIONS

Selectivity Rating	81
# applications received	1,771
% applicants accepted	50
% acceptees attending	24
Median LSAT	157
LSAT Range (25th to 75th percentile)	154–159
Median undergrad GPA	3.32
Application fee	$60
Regular application deadline	3/1
Transfer students accepted	Yes
Evening division offered	No
Part-time accepted	No
CAS accepted	Yes

FINANCIAL FACTS

Annual tuition (in-state out-of-state)	$21,668/$43,398
Books and supplies	$1,000
Fees	$400
Room & Board	$12,376
Financial aid application deadline	4/1
% receiving scholarships	64
Average grant	$12,198
Average debt	$75,718

Life

The majority of the students at USC come from South Carolina or the surrounding states; however, those who choose to study here have many things in common. They: "work hard, play harder, make connections, root for each other, [and] build each other." While you'll find that the majority of the student body is rather conservative, there is enough diversity of political beliefs and backgrounds for almost anyone to find their niche," promises a 1L. "There are lots of liberals in the student body" and Columbia is, "almost without question, the most liberal place in South Carolina (for whatever that's worth)." Ethnic minorities make up about 12 percent of the population.

On campus students find it easy to get along and to fit in. "The students treat each other with kindness and respect no matter where they stand on the law school hierarchy." "We all help each other out and share notes," adds a 1L. "The professors and fellow law students have a strong interest in maintaining balance between school and personal life." When time is not spent studying, students often find plenty to do around the city of Columbia. "We go out on the weekends, go to sporting events, [and] study together." The cost of living and playing here is very affordable in this college town. The "big university feel" is unmistakable, providing a wealth of entertainment, including "a number of bars."

Getting In

Getting into USC Law isn't easy. Admitted students at the 25th percentile have LSAT scores around 155 and undergraduate grade point averages a little over 3.0. At the 75th percentile, LSAT scores are right at 160 and GPAs are approximately 3.6.

EMPLOYMENT INFORMATION

Career Rating	73	**Prominent Alumni**
Total 2012 JD Grads	226	Richard W. Riley, Former U.S. Secretary of
% for whom you have useable information	92	Education; Lindsey Graham, US Senate; Karen J. Williams, 4th Circuit Court of
Median starting salary	$55,774	Appeals.
% job accepting grads providing useable salary information	17	**Grads Employed by Field (%)** Academic (2)
# employed bar required	150	Business/Industry (25)
# employed JD preferred	14	Government (4)
# employed professional/other	12	Judicial Clerkship (22)
# employed non-professional	5	Military (2)
# pursuing advanced degree	8	Private Practice (39)
# unemployed and seeking employment	14	Public Interest (6)
# not seeking employment	5	
State for bar exam	SC, NC, GA, FL	
Pass rate for first-time bar	86.6	

THE UNIVERSITY OF SOUTH DAKOTA
SCHOOL OF LAW

INSTITUTIONAL INFORMATION

Public/private	Public
% faculty part-time	8
% faculty female	34
Total faculty	15

SURVEY SAYS...
Diverse opinions accepted in classrooms, Great library staff

STUDENTS

Enrollment of law school	217
% male/female	60/40
% from out-of-state	41
% part-time	0
% underrepresented minority	8
Average age of entering class	27

ACADEMICS

Academic Experience Rating	**64**
Profs interesting rating	78
Profs accessible rating	83
Hours of study per day	4.09

Advanced Degrees Offered
None

Combined Degrees Offered
JD/MBA, JD/MPA (Professional Accountancy, JD/M Education Administration, JD/M English, JD/M History, JD/M Political Science, JD/M Public Administration), JD/M Psychology, JD/M Administrative Studies

Academics

Despite being the only law school in the entire state, the School of Law and The University of South Dakota attract students from across the region, with nearly half of all those enrolled coming from out of state. Many students find their education "perfect for practice in rural America," and others go on to larger urban practices, yet the cost of tuition is "fairly inexpensive." "Having gone to a NY private school for undergrad and paying the private NY school price, when I got my first bill from USD I thought maybe they had left something major off," says one student.

The "mostly excellent" professors provide students with practical applications for the workplace and "focus on the real world more than just understanding case law and the bar exam materials." There are very few professors who "don't care about actually teaching you in class, they just get through the material," but for the most part, "all of the professors really care about your education at USD and are willing to meet outside of class to discuss exams or just to chat." This "diverse, non-judgmental, reputable, and highly knowledgeable" faculty aptly maintains "a youthful and inexperienced cognizant approach when proffering to that particular audience," and "more than make up for any of the limitations with resources."

There are no formal law specialization options at USD; students say that "specialization" here means taking a few "mostly overview courses" in Native American or environmental law, for which "there is no indication on your degree that you specialized in a particular field." The administration helps by "supplanting our academic needs with a broad range of extern and internships, and facilitate our transition from layman to lawyer."

However, this same administration can often be unresponsive and "disorganized," but hopefully the arrival of a new dean will help set it right. As a smaller school, "it's hard NOT to get to know your professors." The professor that teaches criminal procedure and evidence trains police officers and "is one of the best teachers I have ever had," according to one student. The civil procedure and insurance law professor is "nationally renowned in the area of ERISA," and the Native American Law professor is on the Rosebud Supreme Court. "Not only that, but you can watch him read poetry on YouTube."

Understandably, the school has an excellent relationship with the state bar association, the Circuit Court, and the State Supreme Court, which convenes here every year. Unfortunately, Career Services and on-campus recruitment does not fare as well in the students' opinions. There is "a constant anxiety over getting jobs because according to one student. Luckily, "there is a strong alumni" group that is willing to help students out when and where they can. "I think the school does the best with what it has," says a 2L transfer student.

Life

Vermillion, though small, has "a lot of cultural and entertainment opportunities—you just have to look." The law school itself has plenty of opportunities to socialize, students "just have to be open to them." Having Sioux Falls and Sioux City so close "makes it an ideal environment for law school," as "there are few distractions within the city but plenty of distractions within 45 minutes when you need one."

JEAN HENRIQUES, ADMISSION OFFICER/REGISTRAR
414 EAST CLARK STREET, VERMILLION, SD 57069-2390
TEL: 605-677-5444 FAX: 605-677-5417
E-MAIL: LAW.@USD.EDU • WEBSITE: WWW.USD.EDU/LAW

With such a small student body, everyone does know everyone, which "can be annoying during stressful times of the year, but by graduation time, I have a feeling we will all love each other like a family." "During my first semester there was a death in my family and the whole law-school staff, professors, and students were very supportive. Accommodations and help was readily available from everyone," says one student. There is still competition among the students, but "it is a fair competition that is to be expected in coming to law school—not cutthroat and downright mean."

Facilities are universally disliked. They are "outdated but functional" because of certain particular drawbacks in some of the buildings. There "are no windows in two of the four classrooms," and the walls are "gray cinderblock, [so] when you sit in class, it feels like you're sitting in a prison." The library is transitioning towards "offering more services and relying more on electronic research for non-South Dakota State codes," but the computer lab is "small and ancient." Students do like that they each have their own carrel in which they can study in between classes. One student explains that "[you're] able to trust leaving your stuff there when [you're] not studying."

Getting In

Admission to USD is moderately competitive, with more than half of all applicants getting in. The grades of incoming students are evaluated more closely than their LSAT scores. Admitted students at the 25th percentile have LSAT scores around 150 and undergraduate GPAs close to 3.05. At the 75th percentile, LSAT scores are about 156, and GPAs are just higher than 3.59. The Law Screening Program offers applicants who are not regularly admitted to the School of Law an opportunity to prove themselves.

Clinical program required	No
Legal writing course requirement	Yes
Legal methods course requirement	Yes
Legal research course requirement	Yes
Moot court requirement	No
Public interest law requirement	No

ADMISSIONS

Selectivity Rating	69
# applications received	326
% applicants accepted	66
% acceptees attending	29
Average LSAT	150
Median LSAT	149
LSAT Range (25th to 75th percentile)	146–153
Average undergrad GPA	3.29
Median undergrad GPA	3.28
Application fee	$35
Regular application deadline	
Transfer students accepted	Yes
Evening division offered	No
Part-time accepted	Yes
CAS accepted	Yes

FINANCIAL FACTS

Annual tuition (in-state out-of-state)	$7,162/$20,754
Books and supplies	$1,400
Fees	$6,000
Room & Board (on/off campus)	$6,264/$7,569
% first-year students receiving some sort of aid	85
% all students receiving some sort of aid	88
% of aid that is merit based	90
% receiving scholarships	27
Average grant	$2,976
Average loan	$26,358
Average total aid package	$26,312
Average debt	$77,925

EMPLOYMENT INFORMATION

Career Rating	82	
Total 2012 JD Grads	76	
% for whom you have useable information	100	
% grads employed nine months out	89	
Median starting salary	$46,000	
% job accepting grads providing useable salary information	42	
# employed full-time	63	
# employed part-time	4	
# employed bar required	51	
# employed JD preferred	13	
# employed professional/other	4	
# pursuing advanced degree	3	
# unemployed and seeking employment	5	
State for bar exam	SD, IA, MN, CO	
Pass rate for first-time bar	84	

Prominent Alumni
Tim Johnson, U.S. Senator; David Gilbertson, chief justice, SD Supreme Ct.; CAPT Carol Ricciardello, JAGC, USN (ret), admin. Judge and former (2001-04) chief trial judge, Navy-Marine Corps Trial Judiciary; Harvey C. Jewett IV, attorney, educator, and business executive, including SD Board of Regents, Education Assistance Corp., and The Rivett Group, LLC.

Grads Employed by Field (%)
Business/Industry (16)
Government (18)
Judicial Clerkship (18)
Private Practice (28)
Public Interest (10)

UNIVERSITY OF SOUTHERN CALIFORNIA
GOULD SCHOOL OF LAW

INSTITUTIONAL INFORMATION

Public/private	Private
Student-faculty ratio	13:1
% faculty part-time	15
% faculty female	34
% faculty underrepresented minority	17
Total faculty	134

SURVEY SAYS...

Diverse opinions accepted in classrooms, Great research resources, Great library staff, Good social life

STUDENTS

Enrollment of law school	637
% male/female	55/45
% from out-of-state	32
% underrepresented minority	39
% international	2
Average age of entering class	23

ACADEMICS

Academic Experience Rating	88
Profs interesting rating	79
Profs accessible rating	83
Hours of study per day	3.21

Academic Specialties

Civil Procedure, Commercial, Constitutional, Corporation Securities, Criminal, Government Services, Human Rights, International, Labor, Legal Philosophy, Property, Taxation, Intellectual Property

Advanced Degrees Offered

JD; LLM; MCL

Combined Degrees Offered

JD/MBA; JD/MPA; JD/Ph.D. in Economics; JD/MA in Economics; JD/MA in International Relations; JD/MA in Communications Management; JD/MA in Philosophy; JD/MSW; JD/Master of Real Estate Development; JD/Masters of Business Taxation; JD/MS in Gerontology; JD/MPP; JD/PH.D. in Social Science with California Institute of Technology; JD/MA in Political Science; JD/Ph.D. in Political Science

Academics

Many students come to USC's Gould School of Law for "the weather," but all end up "staying for the professors" and "friendly student body." The faculty here is highly praised as being "very approachable" as well as "brilliant and engaging." "[They're] some of the brightest professors I've ever had," says a 2L. "They strike the right balance between learning the material and making sure we stay interested and involved throughout the course." This enthusiasm extends even to those unhappy with their studies. "I hate law school, but I adore USC," says a 3L. "USC has made what could have been an absolutely nightmarish three years into a tolerable and occasionally even fun experience. Our students are brilliant, funny, and strange. Our professors are either unapologetically academic or real, live working attorneys with loads of hilarious horror stories and practical advice...When you join USC, you join it forever. That's a good thing. Everyone is miserable in law school, but at least here, you can be miserable together." Students admit that while "there may be the typical 'red tape'" when dealing with the administration, the school "wants everyone to succeed" and offers "many resources to help students along." "The administration is very impressive and accessible," says a 1L. "They are supportive of students making the transition to law school." Some find that while being "very organized," the administration can "often treat students like they're children," but overall, if students are willing to "ask for help," the "school administration takes [their] concerns very seriously."

Most professors are "very influenced by the Law and Economics movement," meaning that "there aren't many alternative theoretical perspectives presented convincingly, but they are very good at what they do." Some students would like to see "more emphasis on teaching practical skills in the practical skills courses," as well as "higher-quality professors for some of the big, basic bar classes." Others wouldn't mind more "criminal law" courses. "Also, there is too much focus on firm practice, with much less attention given to students who aren't interested in working for a large firm." The issue of Big Firm versus Public Interest careers is a contentious one at USC Law—many feel that the school "puts too much of a focus on entering the big firm marketplace," while another majority feels that the school "encourages students to go into public interest." "I know more people who are going into public interest and governmental positions than working in big law firms," says a 3L.

It's no secret that jobs can be scarce in the current economic climate; however, students find that "the location and reputation of the school are an invaluable asset" when job hunting. That said, many students aren't so impressed with the Career Services department. As one 2L explains, "I'm not 100 percent sold on the effectiveness of the Career Center—it feels like our awesome alumni connections makes them complacent." On the upside, the office "keeps a constant supply of coffee and hot chocolate," and at least one student says the "career service people played an essential role in my employment."

Despite being located on a "beautiful campus," the law building is "outdated" and "unimpressive." "Most of the classrooms are less than aesthetically inspiring, and are, at times, technologically awkward (as in, plugging in your laptop into the sockets under the tops of desks can bring you dangerously close to violating your neighbor's very personal space)," explains a 1L. Fortunately, students can find a more pleasant atmosphere and some nice places to eat at the brand new Tutor Campus Center, located just a stone's throw from the law school. Plus, students are hopeful that a new building is on the way. "Meetings have already been held with students regarding elements they want to see,

CHLOE REID, ASSOCIATE DEAN
USC LAW SCHOOL, LOS ANGELES, CA 90089-0074
TEL: 213-740-2523 FAX: 213-740-4570
E-MAIL: ADMISSIONS@LAW.USC.EDU • WEBSITE: WWW.LAW.USC.EDU

and plenty of windows and a 'less sucky' wireless Internet have been promised," says a 2L. There's more good news: USC now has a metro stop, so students can ride the light rail to campus.

Life

USC Law doesn't just boast a "competitive, yet modest and cooperative student body," but a "community" otherwise known as "the Trojan Family." "A lot of emphasis is placed on a sense of camaraderie and that we are all in this together," says a 2L. "My experience at USC could not be further from those law school horror stories regarding competition…Students routinely share each others' notes and outlines without a second thought." The "great" student population is "on the younger side," but "an amazing social life" is the result. Students are also "very diverse," and "every student has an interesting background and a different view because of it."

Thanks to its "tight-knit, family-like atmosphere," social opportunities "abound for more outgoing students," but "less socially active students still have a place as well." By all accounts, the bar reviews, often held at "top Hollywood hotspots," are "extremely well-attended," which, according to some, can lead to "lots of intermingling among the law students." However, it's estimated that "outside of the weekly bar reviews," a "good 80 percent of the people at the law school never really see Los Angeles." "It's like pulling teeth trying to get people at the law school to do anything that doesn't involve the chance for alcohol or food (preferably both), which is actually pretty sad, considering the amazing things that Los Angeles has to offer," says a 2L. Though being in Los Angeles is "great," the "area around USC is a bit sketch." But, "once you get over the traffic" and seek out the "diverse, large, and exciting city" of Los Angeles, "You'll never find yourself with a lack of things to do."

Getting In

Recently admitted students at USC Law at the 25th percentile have LSAT scores of 166 and GPAs in the 3.47 range. Admitted students at the 75th percentile have LSAT scores of 169 and GPAs of roughly 3.73.

Clinical program required	No
Legal writing course requirement	Yes
Legal methods course requirement	No
Legal research course requirement	Yes
Moot court requirement	Yes
Public interest law requirement	No

ADMISSIONS

Selectivity Rating	91
# applications received	5,012
% applicants accepted	29
% acceptees attending	13
Median LSAT	167
LSAT Range (25th to 75th percentile)	165–168
Median undergrad GPA	3.73
Application fee	$75
Regular application deadline	2/1
Transfer students accepted	Yes
Evening division offered	No
Part-time accepted	No
CAS accepted	Yes

FINANCIAL FACTS

Annual tuition	$52,814
Books and supplies	$1,990
Fees	$1,960
Room & Board	$16,000
Financial aid application deadline	3/1
% first-year students receiving some sort of aid	81
% all students receiving some sort of aid	85
Average grant	$20,000
Average loan	$43,874
Average total aid package	$55,551
Average debt	$136,241

EMPLOYMENT INFORMATION

Career Rating	97	% grads employed by school	5
Total 2012 JD Grads	221	State for bar exam	CA, NY, DC, WA, TX
% for whom you have useable information	98	Pass rate for first-time bar	88
% grads employed nine months out	86	**Prominent Alumni**	
Median starting salary	$145,000	Justice Joyce Kennard, California Supreme Court; Larry Flax, Co-founder California Pizza Kitchen; Judge Dorothy Nelson, US Ninth Circuit Court of Appeals.	
# employed full-time	181		
# employed part-time	8		
# employed bar required	169	**Grads Employed by Field (%)**	
# employed JD preferred	20	Academic (3)	
# employed professional/other	0	Business/Industry (16)	
# employed non-professional	0	Government (3)	
# pursuing advanced degree	2	Judicial Clerkship (8)	
# unemployed and seeking employment	19	Private Practice (66)	
# not seeking employment	6	Public Interest (4)	

UNIVERSITY OF ST. THOMAS
SCHOOL OF LAW

INSTITUTIONAL INFORMATION

Public/private	Private
Affiliation	Roman Catholic
% faculty part-time	64
% faculty female	38
% faculty underrepresented minority	11
Total faculty	110

SURVEY SAYS...

Beautiful campus, Students love Minneapolis, MN

STUDENTS

Enrollment of law school	448
% male/female	57/43
% from out-of-state	44
% part-time	1
% underrepresented minority	14
% international	1
# of countries represented	4
Average age of entering class	25

ACADEMICS

Academic Experience Rating	82
Profs interesting rating	95
Profs accessible rating	97
Hours of study per day	3.99

Combined Degrees Offered

Four joint-degree programs with College of Business (JD/MBA), Catholic Studies (JD/MA); Public Policy (JD/MA); Social Work (JD/MSW)—all about 4 years

Academics

The University of St. Thomas School of Law is a "small," and steadfastly Catholic bastion of legal education in downtown Minneapolis with an "intense" legal writing program and a "strong focus on doing the right thing over the profitable thing." A Catholic mass is held every weekday in UST Law's chapel, and the trappings of faith are very visible. At the same time, students are quick to call attention to the fact that "the curriculum is not permeated with dogma." "You can't go to St. Thomas and completely miss the fact that it's a Catholic law school," relates a 1L, "but, after the first week, it's fairly easy not to notice it anymore." You probably will notice the "commitment to public interest law" and the "emphasis on public service," though, because students here are required to perform at least fifty hours of community service work before graduation. Although St. Thomas has a relatively small student body, the school has made an effort to offer a diverse range of courses, adding multiple sections of key courses to meet demand and increasing the number of clinics in over the past few years. The school does participate in a consortium with three other nearby law schools, which allows for students to cross-register for classes not offered at their own school.

In addition to the required service hours, there's a "unique," innovative, and mandatory mentor externship program that "allows for networking from the outset." Students pair up an attorney or judge in the area "to shadow intermittently throughout the year." Employment prospects are solid. Students say that "the school has developed a great reputation in the Minneapolis–St. Paul area in a short amount of time." The budding alumni community is "extremely supportive." However, "There is not a strong alumni network" because the school hasn't been around that long. "It still needs to build its reputation for job placement." "I feel like right now we are a well-kept secret," laments a 2L, "a great, new law school that no one knows about." Most students seem more optimistic, though. "I think our credibility in the community is growing," says a 3L. "More and more of our graduates are landing top clerkships and jobs."

The administration here is full of "exceptionally responsive" and "effective managers and organizers." The "eccentric and eclectic" faculty is full of "engaging," "kind," and "extremely personable" professors who "come from diverse geographic and legal backgrounds, yet share a common passion for teaching." "They are remarkable educators and interesting and down-to-earth people." Professors are "visible, available, and approachable" outside of class as well. "Their office doors line the hallways," and e-mails are answered promptly.

The "bright and welcoming" facilities at St. Thomas are "impressive architecturally and comfortable for late night studying." "There's natural light through the whole building, which is therapeutic during long Minnesota winters." "The technology in the classroom is top-of-the-line." The library is also excellent. "It's big enough never to be overcrowded, but yet small enough to not get lost in." The school is also "blocks away" from a bevy of Minneapolis firms, and it "provides skyway access most everywhere," "which is especially great to avoid the cold weather." "Taking study breaks and getting to the coffee shop is a breeze."

CARI HAALAND, ASSISTANT DEAN FOR ADMISSIONS
1000 LaSalle Av, MSL 124, Minneapolis, MN 55403
Tel: (651) 962-4895 Fax: (651) 962-4876
E-Mail: LAWSCHOOL@STTHOMAS.EDU • Website: WWW.STTHOMAS.EDU/LAW

Life

UST Law could "be a lot more diverse" ethnically and otherwise. Nevertheless, "There is an incredible sense of community" among the students here as well as a "sense of building something great." The academic atmosphere includes "a healthy level of competition." "There are a few gunners who'd probably throw you under the bus," admits a 2L, "but they are outnumbered by the nice, fun, and not-super-high-strung students." Mostly, "People are extremely cooperative in class, often sharing notes and ideas with people who need them before they are requested." "The culture is so inclusive and congenial that I wouldn't want to be anywhere else," gushes a 1L. "You always have someone to go to," adds a 3L, "whether it is a fellow student, professor, or administrative personnel."

"Discussions about morality, particularly morality in the law, happen in and out of classrooms," and there's a reasonably thriving social scene. "A weekend does not go by where I am not made aware of three or four separate events that the students have organized to hang out with each other," observes a 1L. Students also tell us, "It is tough to beat the location in the heart of downtown Minneapolis," "within walking distance of" virtually anything you need. "A downtown atmosphere without the big-city feel is the perfect atmosphere for a law school," enthuses a 3L.

Getting In

Admitted students at the 25th percentile have LSAT scores in the mid 150s and undergraduate GPAs close to 3.0. At the 75th percentile, LSAT scores are just higher than 160, and GPAs are about 3.5.

Clinical program required	No
Legal writing course requirement	Yes
Legal methods course requirement	No
Legal research course requirement	Yes
Moot court requirement	No
Public interest law requirement	Yes

ADMISSIONS

Selectivity Rating	71
# applications received	999
% applicants accepted	67
% acceptees attending	21
Average LSAT	156
Median LSAT	155
LSAT Range (25th to 75th percentile)	152–160
Average undergrad GPA	3.34
Median undergrad GPA	3.39
Application fee	$0
Regular application deadline	7/1
Transfer students accepted	Yes
Evening division offered	No
Part-time accepted	No
CAS accepted	Yes

FINANCIAL FACTS

Annual tuition	$35,796
Books and supplies	$1,600
Fees	$308
Room & Board	$18,145
Financial aid application deadline	7/1
% first-year students receiving some sort of aid	98
% all students receiving some sort of aid	97
% of aid that is merit based	100
% receiving scholarships	82
Average grant	$20,666
Average loan	$36,675
Average total aid package	$47,558
Average debt	$96,659

EMPLOYMENT INFORMATION

Career Rating	85	
Total 2012 JD Grads	161	
% for whom you have useable information	100	
% grads employed nine months out	88	
Median starting salary	$50,000	
% job accepting grads providing useable salary information	51	
# employed full-time	121	
# employed part-time	21	
# employed bar required	88	
# employed JD preferred	36	
# employed professional/other	6	
# employed non-professional	12	
# pursuing advanced degree	3	
# unemployed and seeking employment	14	
# not seeking employment	2	
% grads employed by school	1	
State for bar exam	MN, WI, IL	
Pass rate for first-time bar	89	

Prominent Alumni
Jake Schunk, Trial Attorney, United States Department of Justice; Matt Dushek, Associate, Baker & McKenzie; Laura Hammargren, Associate, Mayer Brown LLP.

Grads Employed by Field (%)
Academic (2)
Business/Industry (29)
Government (7)
Judicial Clerkship (11)
Military (2)
Private Practice (34)
Public Interest (3)

THE UNIVERSITY OF TENNESSEE
COLLEGE OF LAW

INSTITUTIONAL INFORMATION

Public/private	Public
Affiliation	No Affiliation
% faculty part-time	41
% faculty female	43
% faculty underrepresented minority	10
Total faculty	87

SURVEY SAYS...
Great research resources, Beautiful campus

STUDENTS

Enrollment of law school	443
% male/female	60/40
% from out-of-state	11
% part-time	0
% underrepresented minority	24
% international	1
# of countries represented	2
Average age of entering class	24

ACADEMICS

Academic Experience Rating	**88**
Profs interesting rating	84
Profs accessible rating	88
Hours of study per day	4.29

Advanced Degrees Offered
JD, 3 years (6 semesters)

Combined Degrees Offered
JD/MBA, 4 years; JD/MPA, 4 years

Academics

Affordable, practical, and blessed with a touch of Southern charm, the University of Tennessee is a friendly place to study the law and to learn to be a lawyer. Across the board, UT students praise their school's unequivocal "emphasis on practical and 'real' lawyering instead of just philosophical theory." The school's fleet of faculty is equipped with impressive real-world credentials, and "Several classrooms are laid out exactly like courtrooms" to help students hone their litigation skills. In addition to the tenured staff, the "Adjunct professors for skills-based classes are a wonderful resource." UT students can further augment course work through the school's ample and long-standing clinical programs, which teach lawyering skills through real-world experience, including a pro bono clinic for indigent clients. They can also pursue a specialization in advocacy through the Center for Advocacy and Dispute Resolution. While the practical offerings are outstanding, many students mention that they would like to see more diverse academic specializations. A student clarifies, "Classes in a wide number of specialties are available, but it wouldn't hurt to hire a few more professors to have more options available in a given semester. It would seem the school has taken a "quality-over-quantity" approach in this regard."

Although University of Tennessee is a stalwart Southern institution, "There are numerous professors that cater to a wide range of philosophical beliefs and legal theories ...from the far-left stereotypical 'academics' all the way to the right side with Instapundit.com creator Glenn Reynolds." A stimulating academic atmosphere, "The class discussions that ensue between such a faculty and the geographically and academically diverse student body are most rewarding." The notorious Socratic method remains a classroom favorite; however, it's never used to torture or embarrass. Rather, it "is a tool to encourage learning, and professors and students are seen as partners in that endeavor, as opposed to adversaries." Outside the classroom, "Teachers are willing to meet you after class and help you in anyway possible," and students reassure us, "There isn't a faculty member I would feel intimidated approaching." A satisfied student sums it up: "The laid-back attitude juxtaposed with expert instruction and the feeling that the UT College of Law, while already well-ranked, is one of the most underrated schools and is by all means a rising star among law schools nationwide."

When transitioning to the real world, UT grads are prepared to hit the ground running. A 3L shares: "I worked at a big New York firm last summer with several Ivy Leaguers. Everyone was very smart, but many of them were just as lost when it came to advocacy skills (namely trial practice and negotiation). What I learned at Tennessee gave me an opportunity to shine in these areas." Another 3L chimes in, "I have a great job in Atlanta after graduation. When I was clerking down there this summer, I really enjoyed surprising people with how well-prepared I am to practice." On that note, career placement is no problem for UT grads—especially those looking to work in the South; however, generally speaking, "The Career Services Center is geared toward students who want to practice in Tennessee or in big law firms elsewhere. Other career options are usually up to the students to pursue."

Life

The UT campus is a pleasant place for work and play, and students admit, "The beautiful classrooms and library make coming to school a lot easier." In and out of the classroom, "The majority of students are very friendly and cooperative," and most strike a good balance between recreation and study. To burn some calories and blow off steam,

Dr. Karen R. Britton, Director of Admissions and Financial Aid
Director, The Betty B.Lewis Career Center
1505 West Cumberland Avenue, Suite 161, Knoxville, TN 37996-1810
Tel: 865-974-4131 Fax: 865-974-1572
E-Mail: lawadmit@utk.edu • Website: www.law.utk.edu

there are "law school teams in several of the intramural sports leagues on campus." When its time for a study break, there is a social event for almost every night of the week in Knoxville, a first-rate college town, boasting "a good music scene, an independent film theater, and lots of local festivals." Law students get together for "mixers every Thursday, bowling every Monday in the spring semester, and tailgates every Saturday in the fall." In addition to the weekly gatherings at local watering holes, the school sponsors many special events including "the yearly Halloween party called Chilla" and the enticing (or so students assure us) Learned Hand Bowling League. Within this tight-knit community, "Even if you don't go out every night you still develop good friendships with your peers."

Despite the social vibe, a student admits, "We have had some racial tension. We are trying to work on it and have less social segregation." Another student adds this perspective: "There are different social circles, but it is natural that people with common interests will be drawn to one another. On the whole, I feel that we have active and amiable community here."

Getting In

UT received more than 1,400 applications for an entering class of about 150 students. Undergraduate GPA and LSAT scores are important to an admissions decision; however, the school also considers qualitative factors including strength of undergraduate institution, extracurricular activities, and professional experience. The school has no minimum LSAT requirement; however, 75 percent of the entering class had an LSAT score 161 or lower, and 25 percent had an LSAT score of 157 or lower. Tennessee residents made up more than 70 percent of entering students.

Clinical program required	No
Legal writing course requirement	Yes
Legal methods course requirement	Yes
Legal research course requirement	Yes
Moot court requirement	No
Public interest law requirement	No

ADMISSIONS

Selectivity Rating	87
# applications received	1,055
% applicants accepted	37
% acceptees attending	31
Average LSAT	158
Median LSAT	160
LSAT Range (25th to 75th percentile)	156–161
Average undergrad GPA	3.52
Median undergrad GPA	3.6
Application fee	$15
Regular application deadline	2/1
Transfer students accepted	Yes
Evening division offered	No
Part-time accepted	No
CAS accepted	Yes

FINANCIAL FACTS

Annual tuition (in-state out-of-state)	$15,168/$31,596
Books and supplies	$1,902
Fees	$2,810
Room & Board	$11,522
Financial aid application deadline	3/1
Average grant	$6,716
Average loan	$25,317
Average total aid package	$25,317
Average debt	$76,381

EMPLOYMENT INFORMATION

Career Rating	**84**	**Prominent Alumni**
Total 2012 JD Grads	155	Howard H. Baker, Jr., Govenment/Public
% for whom you have useable		Service; Joel A. Katz, Entertainment
information	98	Lawyer; Dan Adomitis, President, Firestone
% grads employed nine months out	82	Natural Rubber Company.
Median starting salary	$60,000	**Grads Employed by Field (%)**
% job accepting grads providing		Academic (3)
useable salary information	60	Business/Industry (10)
# employed full-time	119	Government (8)
# employed part-time	6	Judicial Clerkship (11)
# employed bar required	104	Military (3)
# employed JD preferred	19	Private Practice (62)
# employed professional/other	2	Public Interest (3)
# employed non-professional	0	
# pursuing advanced degree	2	
# unemployed and seeking employment	18	
# not seeking employment	7	
% grads employed by school	1	
State for bar exam	TN	
Pass rate for first-time bar	85	

THE UNIVERSITY OF TEXAS AT AUSTIN
SCHOOL OF LAW

Academics

At the University of Texas, bigger is better. "The large size of the school provides opportunities to specialize in or explore almost any area of law" through diverse coursework, clinics, student organizations, journals, and other top-notch programs for future lawyers. The three-year JD program kicks off with a series of core courses in civil procedure, property, and other fundamental areas. These courses are often "fantastic," as "the school is very good about getting its top faculty members to teach 1L classes, exposing us to the best professors early rather than making us wait three years," says one student. Another student comments on the strength of the JD and states, "The legal writing program has recently been overhauled and is now a huge point of emphasis for first year students—which is a big strength, I think, given that every practicing attorney I've ever talked to has stressed the importance of effective legal writing." A team of attorneys with "stellar credentials,"…"the faculty at Texas has the right balance of prestige and accessibility." As at most schools, "Some are better teachers than others," and not all of them are focused on students. "Some professors go out of there way to keep up with student progress," while others prefer to concentrate on their own careers or research. Fortunately, "Most legitimately care about educating and some will go out of their way to make students understand and feel capable." In fact, "several professors even throw parties for students, raffle off brunch to the class and offer a variety of other ways to get to know them better in a far less formal setting."

UT's size does come with some downfalls. Specifically, students battle with the reams of red tape typical to large public institutions. "Since the law school is only one small part of the huge bureaucratic entity that is the University of Texas, things can sometimes get confusing—paying tuition, for instance, is done through one entity (not the law school), obtaining a student ID is done through another, financial aid through another, residency through another, etc." Students also note that there have been recent upheavals in the administration, and "a lot of faculty drama that happens behind the scenes." At the same time, the school works to mitigate the class size by dividing students into smaller study groups through a program known as the society system, to good effect: "The society system, which makes the large class size manageable and gives each student a smaller social group to interact with on a regular basis, helps greatly in personalizing the school and allaying feelings of being overwhelmed and alone in the school environment." Overall, students at UT Austin agree that, "the experience is comparable to an elite private school," but without the hefty price tag. With its low in-state tuition costs, "UT is probably the best value law school in the country for in-state students," while qualified "out-of-staters can either acquire residency (and get in state tuition) after a year at UT, or else can negotiate an in-state rate as a kind of scholarship offer."

Real-world preparation is taken seriously at UT Law. In addition to substantive courses in the curriculum, "students can and should participate in novice mock trial and moot court if they want more "hands on" courtroom experience, even as 1Ls." "Being located in the state capital provides many government-related opportunities not available elsewhere," and the school offers "a lot of clinics and internship programs that allow students to get tons of real-world practice in law." Widely considered the "best in Texas," UT's "greatest strength is its regional ties. It is well-placed among two very large legal markets (Dallas and Houston), which boast salaries on par with New York, DC, and LA along with a much lower cost of living." For better or for worse, one would be hard pressed to find a particular angle in recruiting either. "The school seems to place well enough in firms, nonprofits, and government, but does not excel in any one of those."

MONICA INGRAM, ASSISTANT DEAN FOR ADMISSIONS AND FINANCIAL AID
727 EAST DEAN KEETON STREET, AUSTIN, TX 78705-3299
TEL: 512-232-1200 FAX: 512-471-2765
E-MAIL: ADMISSIONS@LAW.UTEXAS.EDU • WEBSITE: WWW.UTEXAS.EDU/LAW

Life

The law school campus at UT may not win awards for beauty, but it is not a bad place to spend three years. Within the law school, "most of the classrooms don't have windows, which can get very depressing at times," and "the facilities are mediocre" at best. While not entirely ideal, students reason that "this is to be expected with the insanely low cost of attendance." On the upside, "the library is huge, and there is not the problem of undergrad kids trying to use our facilities like at other law schools."

On the whole, the law school maintains a very "laid-back environment," populated by students who are "accomplished, mature, and professional." When it comes to making friends and networking, UT's size is again a benefit. "The school is big enough that you can find any crowd you want to hang out with, and study anything you want with an expert in the field." Competitiveness is generally kept under wraps, and most people "seem to have a good sense of humor about our experience which does wonders for our morale." Off campus, opportunities for nightlife and recreation abound. A nationally famous, fun, and funky metropolis, "Austin is a terrific city and everyone wants to stay once they come to school here."

Getting In

Admission to UT Law is competitive, especially for out-of-state students. By state law, only 35 percent of the student body can come from outside Texas, so these spots are highly coveted. To be considered for admission, students must have a minimum undergraduate GPA of 2.2. Other than that, UT has no set standards for successful applicants; each prospective student is evaluated individually. For recent entering classes, the LSAT range for the middle 50 percent was 165-170.

Clinical program required	No
Legal writing course requirement	Yes
Legal methods course requirement	No
Legal research course requirement	Yes
Moot court requirement	Yes
Public interest law requirement	No

ADMISSIONS

Selectivity Rating	93
# applications received	4,316
% applicants accepted	27
% acceptees attending	26
Average LSAT	167
LSAT Range (25th to 75th percentile)	163–169
Average undergrad GPA	3.67
Application fee	$70
Regular application deadline	3/1
Regular notification	4/1
Early application deadline	11/1
Early application notification	1/31
Transfer students accepted	Yes
Evening division offered	No
Part-time accepted	No
CAS accepted	Yes

FINANCIAL FACTS

Annual tuition (in-state out-of-state)	$33,162/$49,244
Books and supplies	$5,466
Fees	$0
Room & Board	$10,946
Financial aid application deadline	3/15
% first-year students receiving some sort of aid	74
% all students receiving some sort of aid	72
% of aid that is merit based	43
% receiving scholarships	58
Average grant	$13,700
Average loan	$35,874
Average total aid package	$49,574
Average debt	$86,312

EMPLOYMENT INFORMATION

Career Rating	96	**Prominent Alumni**
Total 2012 JD Grads	373	Joseph D. Jamail, Jr., Jamail & Kolius Law
% for whom you have useable information	99	Firm; Kay Bailey Hutchison, United States Senator; Frederico Pena, Former Secretary
% grads employed nine months out	92	of Transportation.
Median starting salary	$91,750	**Grads Employed by Field (%)**
% job accepting grads providing useable salary information	71	Business/Industry (11)
# employed full-time	333	Government (11)
# employed part-time	9	Judicial Clerkship (11)
# employed bar required	313	Private Practice (50)
# employed JD preferred	27	Public Interest (8)
# employed professional/other	0	
# employed non-professional	2	
# pursuing advanced degree	7	
# unemployed and seeking employment	13	
# not seeking employment	7	
State for bar exam	TX, NY, CA	
Pass rate for first-time bar	96	

UNIVERSITY OF TOLEDO
COLLEGE OF LAW

INSTITUTIONAL INFORMATION

Public/private	Public
Affiliation	No Affiliation
Student-faculty ratio	12:1
% faculty part-time	34
% faculty female	39
% faculty underrepresented minority	8
Total faculty	46

SURVEY SAYS...

Diverse opinions accepted in class-rooms, Great research resources, Abundant externship/internship/clerkship opportunities

STUDENTS

Enrollment of law school	387
% male/female	62/38
% from out-of-state	37
% part-time	21
% underrepresented minority	15
% international	1
# of countries represented	5
Average age of entering class	25

ACADEMICS

Academic Experience Rating	**79**
Profs interesting rating	80
Profs accessible rating	87
Hours of study per day	3.62

Academic Specialties

Criminal, Environmental, International, Labor, Intellectual Property

Combined Degrees Offered

JD/MBA, 3.5–4 years; JD/MSE, 3.5–4; JD/Masters in Public Administration-3.5–4; JD/Masters in Criminal Justice, 3.5–4; JD/MD–6 years

Academics

The University of Toledo College of Law offers an affordable and welcoming, yet structured atmosphere designed to "accommodate, relax, and train students." The school has climbed in stature last year, yet retains its rather "humble, calm nature," partially due to its "intelligent, caring, involved, and self-regulating" students and decidedly non-arrogant professors who "are truly incredible individuals." "Every aspect of the school strikes the perfect balance between professionalism and personal attention," says a 2L. Students speak overwhelmingly of the school's obvious care and concern for their future, and the faculty's "willingness to sit and chat with students about class at any time, while connecting what we learn to real-life use." Thanks to the smaller number of students, "Everyone is able to develop personal relationships with faculty and staff." In an effort to keep anxiety levels down, a lot of the professors stay away from the old version of the Socratic Method, which too often "puts you on edge." If you do want to discuss flagging grades or class issues, all professors "go out of their way to make themselves available to students." "It is not uncommon for professors to 'hang out' in the forum chatting with students," says one. "I feel I can approach them with everything: my fears, thoughts, and course questions," says another. The "relatively new" administration "takes a personal and vested interest in seeing us succeed," and "Everything and everyone is very easily and readily accessible." Students do wish for a "more formalized joint degree program" and a "broader variety of courses," as well as a less rigid attendance policy.

The research and writing program is "very thorough and puts an emphasis on real-world concerns," and the school furthers each student's practical background through almost-weekly opportunities to attend speeches or lectures, like one given by U.S. Supreme Court Justice Antonin Scalia. Law Career Services "has put a great deal of effort" into the school's Public Service Externship programs to ensure that students have the opportunity to network while still in school. There's a "very big involvement of [the] Toledo Bar Association and Federal Bar Association in the school's life." The office "[does] it's best to help us in this tough economy," although the employment rate after graduation leaves something to be desired. However, students complain that much of this is due to the "oversaturated" Toledo and Midwest market, and the school's lack of national name recognition means that more help is needed in other regions.

Aside from the somewhat archaic building and library, which are "more appropriate to an era of bellbottoms and platform shoes," the law school's facilities are up-to-date (though definitely "not glamorous"), with wireless Internet access available in "every corner of the building" and Smart Boards in every classroom.

Life

Racial diversity isn't exactly at United Colors of Benetton levels here, but it "is quite good for this area of the country," and the faculty is very sensitive to both racial and gender issues. The political views also "follow a Midwestern range," ranging from liberal to conservative. The student body remains uncompetitive and "gets along great," even though many students (especially 1Ls) have GPA-based scholarships, and there's a great camaraderie among classes. The student mentor program receives raves, and to further this sense of interconnectedness, intramural sports are big. "There are many organizations to get involved with," and the Student Bar Association does "a very good job at bringing students together through social events (including weekly bar reviews) and volunteer opportunities."

JESSICA MEHL, ASSISTANT DEAN FOR ADMISSIONS
2801 WEST BANCROFT, TOLEDO, OH 43606
TEL: 419-530-4131 FAX: 419-530-4345
E-MAIL: LAW.ADMISSIONS@UTOLEDO.EDU • WEBSITE: LAW.UTOLEDO.EDU

"Toledo isn't exactly a party town," and it's "not the most enjoyable place to be," so there aren't too many distractions from school, but for those looking to blow off steam, "There are amazing metro parks, art, music, a zoo, and baseball and hockey games to attend." As one might expect of a small school in a small city, "The sense of community that Toledo strives for is amazing and then stems into the larger Toledo legal community." UT Law is also located within an hour of Detroit and Sandusky, within two hours of Dayton and Cleveland, and within four hours of Chicago, Indianapolis, Columbus, and Cincinnati. Still, when students are on campus, "It's difficult to get any kind of food after 11:00 P.M.," and the law school doesn't have any food options that can accommodate for the late hours students normally spend here.

Getting In

The college enrolls about 110 full-time students in each entering class, for which the college receives approximately 1,000 applications (including two required letters of recommendation) annually. The part-time program has slightly less competitive admissions requirements. Currently, the top quartile of the 1L class has an LSAT of 156 with a GPA of 3.5, while the median has an LSAT of 153 and a GPA of 3.22.

Clinical program required	No
Legal writing course requirement	Yes
Legal methods course requirement	No
Legal research course requirement	Yes
Moot court requirement	No
Public interest law requirement	No

ADMISSIONS

Selectivity Rating	76
# applications received	1,032
% applicants accepted	50
% acceptees attending	20
Average LSAT	152
Median LSAT	152
LSAT Range (25th to 75th percentile)	149–154
Average undergrad GPA	3.23
Median undergrad GPA	3.26
Application fee	$0
Regular application deadline	
Transfer students accepted	Yes
Evening division offered	Yes
Part-time accepted	Yes
CAS accepted	Yes

FINANCIAL FACTS

Annual tuition (in-state out-of-state)	$19,883/$31,431
Books and supplies	$4,660
Fees	$1,190
Room & Board (on/off campus)	$9,758/$12,468
Financial aid application deadline	8/1
% first-year students receiving some sort of aid	95
% all students receiving some sort of aid	94
% of aid that is merit based	21
% receiving scholarships	58
Average grant	$10,607
Average loan	$30,269
Average total aid package	$38,073
Average debt	$93,628

EMPLOYMENT INFORMATION

Career Rating	83	**Prominent Alumni**
Total 2012 JD Grads	147	Honorable Judith Lanzinger, Justice, Ohio
% grads employed nine months out	83	Supreme Court; Robert E. Latta, Ohio Fifth
Median starting salary	$53,000	Congressional District; Chief Justice C.
# employed full-time	97	Ray Mullins, U.S. Bankruptcy Ct, Northern
# employed part-time	25	District of Georgia.
# employed bar required	90	**Grads Employed by Field (%)**
# employed JD preferred	22	Academic (3)
# employed professional/other	4	Business/Industry (22)
# employed non-professional	5	Government (9)
# pursuing advanced degree	0	Judicial Clerkship (3)
# unemployed and seeking employment	14	Military (1)
# not seeking employment	6	Private Practice (43)
% grads employed by school	0	Public Interest (3)
State for bar exam	OH, MI	
Pass rate for first-time bar	88	

THE UNIVERSITY OF TULSA
COLLEGE OF LAW

INSTITUTIONAL INFORMATION

Public/private	Private
Affiliation	Presbyterian
% faculty part-time	39
% faculty female	41
% faculty underrepresented minority	11
Total faculty	44

SURVEY SAYS...

Diverse opinions accepted in classrooms, Great research resources, Great library staff

STUDENTS

Enrollment of law school	110
% male/female	58/42
% from out-of-state	52
% part-time	4
% underrepresented minority	20
% international	2
# of countries represented	4
Average age of entering class	25

ACADEMICS

Academic Experience Rating	90
Profs interesting rating	87
Profs accessible rating	87
Hours of study per day	3.18

Academic Specialties
Environmental, International

Advanced Degrees Offered
LLM in American Indian and Indigenous Law; LLM in American Law for Foreign Graduates, includes a concentration in energy law

Combined Degrees Offered
JD/MA degrees in Anthropology, Clinical Psychology, Computer Science, English, History, and Industrial Organization Psychology; JD/MS in Biological Sciences, Finance and Geosciences; JD/MBA. Each joint degree program takes approximately 4 years to complete.

Academics

Students at the University of Tulsa College of Law call their law school "amazing." "If you want a practical legal education in a happy environment," advises a 2L, "TU is certainly your best option." "Some essential courses are not offered every semester, but you'll find "a broad range of opportunities to engage in practical, professional development activities" here. There are quite a few joint-degree programs available. "Both journals are excellent." Areas of concentration include a "highly regarded energy law program" and a "strong," in-depth certificate program in Native American law. Also, the "top-notch" immigration rights clinic, which provides representation to non-citizens in immigration matters, "does great things and gives students practical experience."

Tulsa Law is on the smaller side, and "small class sizes" are the norm. "Lousy professors" do exist, but "Most of the professors are really good at conveying the black-letter law, policy considerations, as well as practical info." "Professors are willing to engage personally with students" as well. The faculty is "firm but fair," "dedicated to student success and achievement," and "willing to help you at the drop of the hat." "They are easy to talk with, accessible, friendly, and genuinely concerned with students' academic and professional success," declares a 2L. Reviews of management are more mixed. "The administration is dedicated first and foremost to serving the students," decrees a 3L. Some students find staffers "difficult to talk to," though. "The administration tends to spring mandatory meetings on us as well," adds a 2L.

The consensus here seems to be that "the school needs to do a better job placing students outside of Oklahoma." Students with professional destinations, "such as Dallas, Kansas City, and Denver," must be prepared to sell themselves. Otherwise, though, employment prospects are respectable, and most students are satisfied. Tulsa Law has a "reputation within and throughout the state of Oklahoma" and "strong ties" locally. "The integration of the Tulsa legal community with the law school is incredible," boasts a 2L. "On a daily basis, you will see attorneys, judges, scholars, and other alumni walking around." "The Professional Development Office is also very helpful in offering mock interviews, assisting with resumes and cover letters, offering workshops in guiding students to meet their full potential, and offering a multitude of networking opportunities."

The campus at the University of Tulsa is beautiful, and the law school building, John Rogers Hall, was completely renovated in the summer of 2011, with updated classrooms and administrative facilities. "The Internet is temperamental at times," but technology is generally "state-of-the-art," and the research facilities are "wonderful." The "huge" and "exceptionally clean" library is "pretty fantastic," which "makes for a positive studying experience." The librarians are "invaluable," and "There are plenty of study areas and meeting rooms."

Life

Tulsa Law "attracts students from many states," and more than half the students hail from outside of Oklahoma. This school is highly regional, though. "Most of the students who aren't from Oklahoma are from one of the surrounding states." The academic atmosphere generally ranges from "close-knit" to "cooperative to a fault." "With the exception of a few bad apples, the students are extremely supportive of one another," says a 2L. "Competition seems to be something reserved for the mock trial teams." "There seems to be a collective understanding that the student body will cooperate and help one other, and we'll just leave the academic curve up to the professors," relates a 1L.

Tulsa Law's ideal size enhances life outside the classroom. "Gossip is rampant," but students tell us, "The social life at the school is fantastic." "At TU, you really get a chance to meet and grow closer to a small group of students," reflects a 3L. The Student Bar Association is very active, and "Student organizations put on many different events," such as talent shows, pub crawls, and various auctions. The law school is located on the campus of the larger university "in a mixed residential and business neighborhood" about "a five-minute drive from downtown." The surrounding city of Tulsa has devotees as well as detractors. Aficionados point out that it's a fairly large metropolis that's home to a decent number of large corporations. "Getting around Tulsa is usually easy and stress free." It's the perfect size for anyone who doesn't want to live in crowded cities, but who also doesn't want to be stuck in the middle of nowhere. Critics disagree. They say Tulsa itself is "very boring"

Getting In

Reasonable grades and test scores will do the trick in most cases here. Admitted students at the 25th percentile have LSAT scores in the lower 150s and undergraduate GPAs right about 3.0. At the 75th percentile, LSAT scores are a little lower than 160, and GPAs are a little higher than 3.6.

Clinical program required	No
Legal writing course requirement	Yes
Legal methods course requirement	Yes
Legal research course requirement	Yes
Moot court requirement	No
Public interest law requirement	No

ADMISSIONS

Selectivity Rating	85
# applications received	1,442
% applicants accepted	36
% acceptees attending	21
Average LSAT	156
Median LSAT	156
LSAT Range (25th to 75th percentile)	153–158
Average undergrad GPA	3.39
Median undergrad GPA	3.38
Application fee	$30
Regular application deadline	
Early application deadline	2/1
Transfer students accepted	Yes
Evening division offered	No
Part-time accepted	Yes
CAS accepted	Yes

FINANCIAL FACTS

Annual tuition	$31,836
Books and supplies	$1,500
Fees	$334
Room & Board (on/off campus)	$16,536/$20,110
% first-year students receiving some sort of aid	100
% all students receiving some sort of aid	77
% of aid that is merit based	20
% receiving scholarships	58
Average grant	$16,000
Average loan	$35,890
Average total aid package	$49,015
Average debt	$104,785

EMPLOYMENT INFORMATION

Career Rating	89
Total 2012 JD Grads	134
% grads employed nine months out	92
Median starting salary	$55,000
% job accepting grads providing useable salary information	22
# employed full-time	115
# employed part-time	8
# employed bar required	95
# employed JD preferred	18
# employed professional/other	8
# employed non-professional	2
# pursuing advanced degree	2
# unemployed and seeking employment	2
# not seeking employment	6
% grads employed by school	2
State for bar exam	OK, TX, CO, MO, MD
Pass rate for first-time bar	89

Prominent Alumni
Layn R. Phillips, Member, Irell & Manella; former U.S. District Judge, Western District of OK; Hon. Elizabeth Crewson Paris, U.S. Tax Court Judge; Curtis Frasier, Shell Oil Co. (Americas), EVP & GC.

Grads Employed by Field (%)
Academic (6)
Business/Industry (18)
Government (12)
Judicial Clerkship (0)
Private Practice (61)
Public Interest (3)

UNIVERSITY OF UTAH
S. J. QUINNEY COLLEGE OF LAW

INSTITUTIONAL INFORMATION

Public/private	Public
% faculty part-time	59
% faculty female	11
% faculty underrepresented minority	7
Total faculty	37

SURVEY SAYS...

Diverse opinions accepted in classrooms, Great research resources, Students love Salt Lake City, UT

STUDENTS

Enrollment of law school	382
% male/female	59/41
% from out-of-state	26
% part-time	0
% underrepresented minority	10
# of countries represented	1
Average age of entering class	27

ACADEMICS

Academic Experience Rating	**87**
Profs interesting rating	82
Profs accessible rating	84
Hours of study per day	3.60

Academic Specialties
Constitutional, Corporation Securities, Criminal, Environmental, International, Intellectual Property

Advanced Degrees Offered
LLM, Environmental and Resources Law, 1 year

Combined Degrees Offered
JD/MPA, 4 years; JD/MBA, 4 years; JD/MSW, 4 years; JD/MPP, 4 years

Academics

At S. J. Quinney College Of Law, expect an "excellent selection of classes" and "diverse professors" that give students an opportunity to pursue a broad array of law specializations. Though there are "many more resources devoted to environmental issues than anything else," students can pursue specializations such as "global justice/international law, and the center for law and biomedical sciences, which ranges from health policy and care systems to patent law issues." In addition to the in-classroom experience, "the school offers multiple clinical experiences to put into practice the theory that has been taught in the classroom."

This is spearheaded by a staff of educators that win major praise from students. Professors' strong credentials as published experts are important, but "the school values teaching ability just as much as academic publishing." "Marvelous, very kind and accessible," these educators "teach a wide variety of classes" that rival even some "very high-priced, private undergraduate institutions." They make themselves readily available to students, too. Indeed, this "great group of professors" are "always willing to help students understand the material or plan a career path." Basically, "if you don't develop a good relationship with them, it's because you are trying to avoid them." In fact, "some professors will even give out their personal cell phone numbers and actually expect you to call them if you have a question."

Praise for the administration, on the other hand, is mixed. Administrators make you "feel like you've inconvenienced them by being present," according to some students. But that view is far from universal, with other students saying that members of the administration are "in general more than willing to help." That same administration has constantly sought to evolve, a trait some dub "reactionary" but which others say displays a desire to improve "student experience, academic quality, and transition to real-world practice." The result is an administration that is "helpful in preparing students to succeed in law school and plan for graduation."

When it comes to the days after graduation, location plays a major role in a U of U student's success. "Practical business teaching is in short supply," and while the PDO office is good at placing people with smaller firms, they are "not very good at placement with larger firms, even when the students are fully qualified for those positions." The location, however, goes a long way towards making up for any such shortcomings. The downtown Salt Lake City campus is "minutes away from the federal and state courthouses," meaning that "getting a judicial externship is very easy." Though the current building is "older and inadequate," the class of 2014/2015 should have the privilege of being the first to graduate from a brand new facility.

Life

Though "bright and engaging," U of U students are "not the typical Type A law students" because the "top notch" students here are "willing to help each other out." Indeed, they will go the extra mile for one another. "Fellow students freely give outlines, class notes and exam advice to each other. You can walk in the day of the final exam with a question and your fellow classmates will answer your question." While there is some competition among students, it generally does not show itself "until you are actually taking your exams." Overall, "it's a small school with a small student body, an environment in which you'll know practically everyone by your second year."

SUSAN BACA, OPERATIONS MANAGER FOR ADMISSIONS & FINANCIAL AID
ADMISSIONS, 332 SOUTH 1400 EAST, ROOM 101, SALT LAKE CITY, UT 84112-0730
TEL: 801-581-7479 FAX: 801-581-6897
E-MAIL: ADMISSIONS@LAW.UTAH.EDU • WEBSITE: WWW.LAW.UTAH.EDU

Salt Lake City is a beautiful town, but it's not a particularly exciting town. The city is a conservative one, and public school or not, the Mormon influence is clear. Expect few raging parties and wild weekends. On the other hand, do expect a clean, safe environment in a part of the country filled with natural wonders. What it lacks in urban excitement, however, it makes up for in opportunities. Being near downtown Salt Lake City putting students "close to the U.S. Attorney's office, the District Attorney, the Securities and Exchange Commission, every law firm," and other opportunities.

Getting In

Students admitted recently at the 25th percentile have LSAT scores of 157 and GPAs of nearly 3.4. At the 75th percentile, recently admitted students have LSAT scores of 163 and GPAs of about 3.8. Utah will use the highest score if you take the LSAT more than once.

Clinical program required	No
Legal writing course requirement	Yes
Legal methods course requirement	Yes
Legal research course requirement	Yes
Moot court requirement	No
Public interest law requirement	No

ADMISSIONS

Selectivity Rating	88
# applications received	878
% applicants accepted	35
% acceptees attending	31
Median LSAT	160
LSAT Range (25th to 75th percentile)	156–162
Median undergrad GPA	3.61
Application fee	$60
Regular application deadline	2/15
Transfer students accepted	Yes
Evening division offered	No
Part-time accepted	No
CAS accepted	Yes

FINANCIAL FACTS

Annual tuition (in-state out-of-state)	$21,464/$41,603
Books and supplies	$1,916
Fees	$943
Room & Board	$9,072
Financial aid application deadline	4/1
% first-year students receiving some sort of aid	0
% all students receiving some sort of aid	90
% receiving scholarships	52
Average grant	$6,854
Average loan	$29,536
Average total aid package	$36,390
Average debt	$80,608

EMPLOYMENT INFORMATION

Career Rating	77
Total 2012 JD Grads	134
% grads employed nine months out	88
Median starting salary	$56,000
# employed full-time	106
# employed part-time	12
# employed bar required	98
# employed JD preferred	15
# employed professional/other	4
# employed non-professional	1
# pursuing advanced degree	2
# unemployed and seeking employment	8
# not seeking employment	3
% grads employed by school	1
State for bar exam	UT, NV, CA, OR, ID

Prominent Alumni
Kelli L. Sager, Chair, Media Practice, Davis, Wright, Tremaine; Hon. Stephen Anderson, 10th Circuit Court of Appeals; Gary Kennedy, General Counsel & V.P. for American Airlines.

Grads Employed by Field (%)
Academic (3)
Business/Industry (15)
Government (14)
Judicial Clerkship (9)
Military (1)
Private Practice (56)
Public Interest (2)

UNIVERSITY OF VIRGINIA
SCHOOL OF LAW

INSTITUTIONAL INFORMATION

Public/private	Public
Student-faculty ratio	11:1
% faculty part-time	50
% faculty female	24
% faculty underrepresented minority	5
Total faculty	177

SURVEY SAYS...
Great research resources, Great library staff, Good social life

STUDENTS

Enrollment of law school	1,078
% male/female	55/45
% from out-of-state	68
% part-time	0
% underrepresented minority	24
% international	1
Average age of entering class	24

ACADEMICS

Academic Experience Rating	**99**
Profs interesting rating	98
Profs accessible rating	95
Hours of study per day	3.58

Academic Specialties
Civil Procedure, Commercial, Constitutional, Corporation Securities, Criminal, Environmental, Government Services, Human Rights, International, Labor, Legal History, Legal Philosophy, Taxation, Intellectual Property

Advanced Degrees Offered
LLM (1 year); SJD (2–5 years)

Combined Degrees Offered
JD/MA in English, Government or Foreign Affairs, History, Philosophy (3–4 years); JD/MS in Accounting (3.5 years); JD/MPH (4 years); JD/MBA (4 years); JD/Masters in Urban and Environmental Planning (4 years); JD/MPP (4 years); JD/MPA (4 years); JD/MA in Law and Diplomacy (4 years); JD/MA in International Relations (4 years)

Academics

Founded by Thomas Jefferson himself, the University of Virginia School of Law is one of the oldest law schools in the country, and has educated generations of lawyers and turned out hundreds of law firm heads, law clerks, and judges. This "unique and great place" is one of the country's most selective law schools, and currently offers six dual degrees, twenty clinics, six international exchange programs, and ten student-run academic journals, including the prestigious Virginia Law Review. UVA is on "a very positive trajectory" at the moment, with student quality on the rise, improved fundraising, ongoing facilities improvements, and good job placement rates.

One of the first things students are made aware of is how "pulled together" UVA feels. "Everyone I spoke with in administration, as well as the faculty, was focused on making the law school an excellent place to learn and grow as a future lawyer," says a 2L of his first visit. There is a wide variety of classes to choose from (including a selection of short courses in January), and there are "plenty of opportunities to get practical experience through a well-developed pro bono program" and the clinics. "For example, right now I'm taking an estate planning class where I actually get to draft wills and trusts under the guidance of two leading practitioners," says a 2L.

The focus on the student experience is "apparent throughout the entire law school," and the faculty is "incredibly accessible," which gives students the "unparalleled" opportunity to rub elbows with "some of the best legal scholars in the nation." Many members of the faculty have previously served in high level government positions, or are former federal prosecutors, to name a few. The school's reputation among lawyers is "phenomenal," and the Career Services department "gives fantastic advice, works hard to help students make connections to markets all across the US, and are incredibly friendly and accessible." The staff "walk us through every step of finding and getting jobs that we are excited about." There is a ton of engagement with the institution at UVA, "precisely because students don't vanish into the ether once class ends for the day." Students also have many opportunities to have "a significant influence" on the law school's governance and policies through the Student Bar Association. The school is generally receptive of student influence in the improvement and alteration of academic policies, "which is quite empowering for students."

Life

Everyone is" friendly and helpful, from the Dean to the librarians to the people who work in the coffee shop." The UVA peer advisory system, in which each 1L section is assigned six upper-class mentors to welcome them to school, helps ease new students into life at this "friendly, welcoming, and well-organized environment," and provides guidance on "everything from learning how to brief cases to applying for jobs to navigating the social scene." This type of mentorship "is invaluable" and "fosters UVA's famous sense of collegiality from year to year."

ANNE RICHARD, SENIOR ASSISTANT DEAN
580 MASSIE ROAD, CHARLOTTESVILLE, VA 22903-1738
TEL: 434-924-7351 FAX: 434-982-2128
E-MAIL: LAWADMIT@VIRGINIA.EDU • WEBSITE: WWW.LAW.VIRGINIA.EDU

Classrooms are well-equipped with the latest technology, and there are "plenty of comfortable and well-lit places to study throughout the law school." The student services wing of the law school building was "beautifully renovated" over the summer to expand the admissions, career services, and clinic offices, and the city of Charlottesville is "amazing." There's "a lot to do around here for such a relatively small place," including "great food, great music, UVA sports ....[and] good hiking nearby," and DC is jut a couple of hours away. "I think that it is telling that 3Ls dislike talking about having to leave the law school at the end of the year, wishing that their law school careers could last longer," says a happy student.

Getting In

Admitted students at the 25th percentile have LSAT scores of roughly 164 and GPAs of about 3.5. Admitted students at the 75th percentile have LSAT scores of about 171 and GPAs of just over 3.9. In the case of multiple LSAT scores, UVA gives the most weight to the highest submitted LSAT score; however, the school evaluates all information submitted as part of the application for admission, and encourages applicants with a significant difference in LSAT scores to include with their application any information that may be relevant to the interpretation of test results, such as illness or testing conditions. Keep in mind that this is a holistic approach, and at no point in admissions deliberations are numbers employed in a way that would trigger an automatic decision to offer or deny admission.

Clinical program required	No
Legal writing course requirement	Yes
Legal methods course requirement	Yes
Legal research course requirement	Yes
Moot court requirement	No
Public interest law requirement	No

ADMISSIONS

Selectivity Rating	98
# applications received	6,063
% applicants accepted	15
% acceptees attending	39
Median LSAT	170
LSAT Range (25th to 75th percentile)	164–171
Median undergrad GPA	3.87
Application fee	$80
Regular application deadline	3/1
Regular notification	4/15
Transfer students accepted	Yes
Evening division offered	No
Part-time accepted	No
CAS accepted	Yes

FINANCIAL FACTS

Annual tuition (in-state out-of-state)	$43,976/$48,294
Books and supplies	$4,400
Fees	$3,106
Room & Board	$16,000
Financial aid application deadline	2/17
% first-year students receiving some sort of aid	80
% all students receiving some sort of aid	81
% receiving scholarships	39
Average grant	$27,134
Average loan	$51,041
Average total aid package	$56,052
Average debt	$104,264

EMPLOYMENT INFORMATION

Career Rating	96	
Total 2012 JD Grads	364	
% for whom you have useable information	99	
% grads employed nine months out	98	
# employed full-time	357	
# employed part-time	0	
# employed bar required	344	
# employed JD preferred	11	
# employed professional/other	2	
# employed non-professional	0	
# pursuing advanced degree	2	
# unemployed and seeking employment	1	
# not seeking employment	2	
% grads employed by school	0	
State for bar exam	VA, NY, CA, TX, MD	
Pass rate for first-time bar	95	

Grads Employed by Field (%)
Academic (1)
Business/Industry (4)
Government (9)
Judicial Clerkship (18)
Military (1)
Private Practice (56)
Public Interest (10)

UNIVERSITY OF WASHINGTON
SCHOOL OF LAW

INSTITUTIONAL INFORMATION

Public/private	Public
Student-faculty ratio	10:1
% faculty part-time	29
% faculty female	43
% faculty underrepresented minority	17
Total faculty	77

SURVEY SAYS...

Great research resources, Great library staff, Beautiful campus, Students love Seattle, WA

STUDENTS

Enrollment of law school	528
% male/female	41/59
% from out-of-state	40
% part-time	0
% underrepresented minority	21
% international	2
# of countries represented	8
Average age of entering class	25

ACADEMICS

Academic Experience Rating	85
Profs interesting rating	70
Profs accessible rating	70

Academic Specialties

Civil Procedure, Commercial, Constitutional, Corporation Securities, Criminal, Environmental, Government Services, Human Rights, International, Labor, Legal History, Legal Philosophy, Property, Taxation, Intellectual Property

Advanced Degrees Offered

LLM Asian Law, Law of Sustainable International Development, Taxation, Intellectual Property. 1 year full-time programs. Taxation/IP are evening degree programs and may be full- or part-time.

Combined Degrees Offered

Can set up with 90 graduate programs at UW

Academics

The University of Washington School of Law, one of three law schools in the country on the quarter system, offers great opportunities to control your own legal education and lots of opportunities for learning and experience outside class. The school is well known for its numerous student organizations, many of which have a big public interest/community volunteering aspect; there's also a public service requirement that has "spawned many interesting externship and clinic opportunities for students." Still, students say that despite the touting of public service law, most of the events and funding are driven almost solely by these groups, and the school "doesn't offer much formal curriculum in that area." The Contorts program here is especially "spectacular," as it "allows students to look at a legal problem from a variety of perspectives which you don't get by looking at torts and contracts individually." Small section sizes help make UW seem cozier, and while the forced curve and the newly introduced class rankings system does mean that it can be a competitive place, this competition is "mostly because people want to do well, not because they want others not to do well."

The collaborative atmosphere between the students and faculty is a great boon to the school and makes for a great working environment and a very collegiate atmosphere, so "gunners and ultra-competitive attitudes are frowned on here." Many of the professors are brilliant in their field, and they "bring their own expertise and practical real world experience in the field in ways that really animate and extend the subject matter." Their willingness to discuss almost anything outside of class is deeply appreciated by students, even if there are "a few professors that should never be allowed anywhere near 1Ls." The law building is new and built with a grant from Bill Gates, so classrooms and study areas are "clean and up-to-date," and the building itself is "light and spacious" and has incredible views out over the sound and downtown Seattle. Classes are recorded and podcast for those with parental responsibilities (an accommodation "especially invaluable to student-parents") and the law library is amazing and gorgeous, with librarians that "are among the best anywhere."

The administration is genuine in their care for students, and one of the deans even hired an on-call psychologist for students to use for free in the interest of helping them to maintain their mental health, but the two hands-down weakest areas are found in Financial Aid and Career Services. The single administrator who runs all of the Financial Aid accounts for the law school is "unable to answer routine questions" and "can tell you the ins and outs of computer solitaire, but wouldn't know where to find a grant or extra loan if it bit him on the butt," and the Career Services office is "great if you want to work in a private law firm" or stay in Washington to practice, but "if you want to work in international human rights/ humanitarian law or domestic nonprofit law" the institutional resources aren't really there, and "job postings themselves are mostly centered in the Pacific Northwest." "They are more talk than action and somewhat out of touch with what employers are really looking for," says a student.

KATHY SWINEHART, ADMISSIONS SUPERVISOR
WILLIAM H. GATES HALL, BOX 353020, SEATTLE, WA 98195-3020
TEL: 206-543-4078 FAX: 206-543-5671
E-MAIL: LAWADM@U.WASHINGTON.EDU • WEBSITE: WWW.LAW.WASHINGTON.EDU

Life

Like any other law-school, UW has their share of type-A's, but the personality clashes are minimal. It's a small and tight-knit community, so naturally gossip can travel at the speed of light, but "it's all good natured and there is rarely, if ever, any rancor or backbiting." Competitiveness is kept to a minimum, and one student says that if he were to miss class, "several people would e-mail and offer to review the material with me." UW's rather long orientation really bonds folks, and many people report having made some of the best friends of their lives in their classes. Located in a neighborhood of Seattle that "is reasonably funky and fun, and not too far from the center of town," there are also a lot of student groups at the law school that are active, as well as intramural sports and school-organized weekly meet-ups at bars, so students can easily find something to match their interests. "There are not parties every weekend, but there are plenty of social events if you make the effort to find out about them and get involved," says a student. The left-leaning school is really committed to diversity and as a result, there's a wide range of age, experience, class, nationality, ethnicity, and disability; the sizeable older crowd "is great in the school environment, but socially nonexistent outside the school."

Getting In

It's tough getting admitted to the University of Washington, but the school follows your basic law school admissions policy: It puts heavy weight on applicants' undergraduate records and LSAT scores, also considering letters of recommendation, work and volunteer experience, and personal statements. The vast majority of enrollees (about 70 percent) are residents of Washington State; however, residency is not a major factor in an admissions decision.

Clinical program required	No
Legal writing course requirement	Yes
Legal methods course requirement	Yes
Legal research course requirement	Yes
Moot court requirement	No
Public interest law requirement	Yes

ADMISSIONS

Selectivity Rating	94
# applications received	2,585
% applicants accepted	23
% acceptees attending	31
Average LSAT	162
LSAT Range (25th to 75th percentile)	159–165
Average undergrad GPA	3.65
Application fee	$50
Regular application deadline	1/15
Regular notification	4/1
Transfer students accepted	Yes
Evening division offered	No
Part-time accepted	No
CAS accepted	Yes

FINANCIAL FACTS

Annual tuition (in-state out-of-state)	$17,846/$26,231
Books and supplies	$1,500
Room & Board	$16,626
Financial aid application deadline	2/28
% first-year students receiving some sort of aid	85
% all students receiving some sort of aid	85
% of aid that is merit based	10
% receiving scholarships	43
Average grant	$7,500
Average loan	$22,500
Average total aid package	$30,000
Average debt	$65,507

EMPLOYMENT INFORMATION

Career Rating	96	**Grads Employed by Field (%)**
% grads employed nine months out	97	Academic (2)
Median starting salary	$90,000	Business/Industry (7)
State for bar exam	WA	Government (14)
Pass rate for first-time bar	90	Judicial Clerkship (16)
Prominent Alumni		Private Practice (54)
Tom Foley, Former Speaker, U.S. House of		Public Interest (6)
Representatives; Gerry Alexander, Chief		
Justice, Washington Supreme Court; Betty		
Fletcher, Judge, U.S. Court of Appeals (9th		
Circuit).		

UNIVERSITY OF WISCONSIN—MADISON
LAW SCHOOL

INSTITUTIONAL INFORMATION

Public/private	Public
Affiliation	No Affiliation
Student-faculty ratio	11:1
% faculty part-time	45
% faculty female	46
% faculty underrepresented minority	13
Total faculty	125

SURVEY SAYS...
Students love Madison, WI

STUDENTS

Enrollment of law school	215
% male/female	61/39
% from out-of-state	45
% part-time	1
% underrepresented minority	24
% international	4
# of countries represented	5
Average age of entering class	24

ACADEMICS

Academic Experience Rating	**86**
Profs interesting rating	81
Profs accessible rating	76
Hours of study per day	3.64

Academic Specialties
Criminal, Environmental, International, Labor, Property, Intellectual Property

Advanced Degrees Offered
JD, 3 years; LLM, 1–2 years; SJD, 4–5 years

Combined Degrees Offered
Dual degree master's programs generally take four years to complete. Programs include but are not limited to: business, environmental studies, Latin American studies, library and information studies, public affairs, public health, philosophy, political science and sociology. Several dual Ph.D. programs are also available.

Academics

University of Wisconsin Law School is considered to be "the flagship law school in the state [of Wisconsin]," offering "a great legal education" and hosting some of "the best and brightest legal minds" on its illustrious faculty. Though students admit that professors can "vary in teaching styles" and "in their teaching abilities," nearly all agree that "it's clear that our professors are respected in Wisconsin and the nation." "It's exciting taking criminal law courses with professors who wrote the criminal code in Wisconsin and have an ongoing impact on criminal law in the state," says a 2L. "There are professors that are former Wisconsin Supreme Court Justices, former 'big law' partners, current appointees on national and international committees, and other well-respected scholars in their field." Professors teach "subjects that they enjoy and can shed real-life experience on, which really helps you to imagine using that law in practice." At the same time, "Many of the professors are old," and, as they retire, students would like the school to "bring in younger, top-notch professors." Along those lines, UW recently hired new faculty in tax, constitutional law, civil procedure, and other key areas. The administration can be "very accessible and accommodating of students," though some feel that it is "too disconnected" and a "little slow in getting out the class schedules."

Classes become "relatively small" after 1L (where "eighty [students in class] is the norm"), giving "everyone [the] opportunity to speak and learn in a smaller setting." But that's not to say there aren't small classes for 1Ls. "Keeping the 1L legal writing courses at only twelve students always increases interaction between each student and professor," says a 1L. Despite its intimacy, some students felt the "the legal writing program could be improved [as the school] does not put enough emphasis on writing or provide courses that teach students how to write the documents they are most likely to write as lawyers." In response, the UW hired a new Legal Writing Director, who has redesigned the program. On the upside, there are "significant opportunities" for "practical experience" through legal clinics and electives, but taking part in these relies on students being motivated to seek them out. "[UW Law] doesn't work to make sure that students are getting the practical 'Law in Action' experience they need in the classroom," says a 2L. "It's left to the students to get involved in a clinical. Yet, due to the realities of law school and the economy, this is not always a feasible option."

On the job front, the common consensus among students is that "Career Services needs to be revamped." UW Law answered these concerns by hiring an experienced Assistant Dean and new Director. A 2L adds, "I think that Career Services could be a little more creative, knowledgeable, and proactive." Luckily, the school's "proximity" to Chicago means that students have a large job market nearby in which they can "visit law firms" and "interview for jobs."

The law building is "located on Bascom Hill," considered to be "the focal point of the campus," however students aren't positive it deserves such a prominent view. "The older parts of the building are beyond outdated," says a 1L. A 2L concurs: "Although the building is in good condition and well-maintained, the furniture in the classrooms and library could be nicer." Classrooms have "wireless Internet, electric outlets, and projection screens," and while the building itself doesn't have the "elegant wood floors and paneling of some places," it's "more modern and functional than [other schools]." "Some of the technology in the classrooms is not as 'spiffy' as private schools, but the wonderful professors and overall supportive academic environment more than make up for these shortcomings," says a 1L.

REBECCA L. SCHELLER, ASSISTANT DEAN FOR ADMISSIONS AND FINANCIAL AID
975 BASCOM MALL, MADISON, WI 53706
TEL: 608-262-5914 FAX: 608-263-3190
E-MAIL: ADMISSIONS@LAW.WISC.EDU • WEBSITE: LAW.WISC.EDU

Life

Students at UW Law note the "strong sense of community" and "cooperation" that "permeates the student body" and allows them "to work at a higher level than if there was a more cutthroat environment." Though it can get "competitive during finals and tryouts for prestigious organizations," students "all help each other" and "no one is ripping pages out of books in the library." Diversity is "promoted heavily" and students "interact [both] within and outside of their ethnic/sexual orientation/political groups." "The school is accessible for all kinds of students [whether they're] right out of college or in their thirties married with kids," says a 1L. "Every group of students has their own active organization, putting [on] events and volunteering. Everyone can find someone to get along with here."

When students need a break from their studies, "Madison's nightlife being geared toward undergrads," students here "make do with what they have." Madison is a "great college town" and an "amazing place to go to law school." It "has all the resources of a city but feels like a town." With the law school "situated right on the Hill in the heart of campus" students are "close to everything," such as "restaurants, bars, and [other] things to do." And what might those other things be? According to these "word hard, play hard" types, "It's not uncommon to study until 9:00 P.M. and then go out to the bars."

Getting In

Recently admitted students at UW Law at the 25th percentile have LSAT scores of 158 and GPAs in the 3.39 range. Admitted students at the 75th percentile have LSAT scores of 164 and GPAs of roughly 3.78.

Clinical program required	No
Legal writing course requirement	Yes
Legal methods course requirement	Yes
Legal research course requirement	Yes
Moot court requirement	No
Public interest law requirement	No

ADMISSIONS

Selectivity Rating	87
# applications received	2,153
% applicants accepted	37
% acceptees attending	27
Average LSAT	161
Median LSAT	162
LSAT Range (25th to 75th percentile)	157–164
Average undergrad GPA	3.56
Median undergrad GPA	3.61
Application fee	$56
Regular application deadline	4/1
Early application deadline	11/15
Early application notification	12/15
Transfer students accepted	Yes
Evening division offered	No
Part-time accepted	Yes
CAS accepted	Yes

FINANCIAL FACTS

Annual tuition (in-state out-of-state)	$21,350/$40,040
Books and supplies	$2,390
Room & Board	$9,790
Financial aid application deadline	4/1
% first-year students receiving some sort of aid	90
% all students receiving some sort of aid	90
% receiving scholarships	49
Average grant	$12,905
Average debt	$77,077

EMPLOYMENT INFORMATION

Career Rating	93
Total 2012 JD Grads	234
% for whom you have useable information	99
% grads employed nine months out	90
Median starting salary	$59,987
% job accepting grads providing useable salary information	43
# employed full-time	235
# employed part-time	21
# employed bar required	186
# employed JD preferred	36
# employed professional/other	27
# employed non-professional	7
# pursuing advanced degree	6
# unemployed and seeking employment	17
# not seeking employment	2
State for bar exam	WI, IL, NY, MN, CA
Pass rate for first-time bar	100

Prominent Alumni
Tommy Thompson '66, Former U.S Secretary of Health and Human Services, Former Governor of Wisconsin; Tammy Baldwin '89, U.S. Senator, Former U.S. Congresswoman; David Ruder '57, Former Chairman of the SEC; Emeritus Professor and Former Dean of Northwestern Law.

Grads Employed by Field (%)
Academic (5)
Business/Industry (20)
Government (12)
Judicial Clerkship (6)
Military (1)
Private Practice (46)
Public Interest (10)

UNIVERSITY OF WYOMING
COLLEGE OF LAW

INSTITUTIONAL INFORMATION

Public/private	Public
Student-faculty ratio	11:1
% faculty part-time	31
% faculty female	44
% faculty underrepresented minority	14
Total faculty	36

SURVEY SAYS...

Diverse opinions accepted in class-rooms, Great research resources, Great library staff

STUDENTS

Enrollment of law school	229
% male/female	56/44
% from out-of-state	117
% part-time	0
% underrepresented minority	11
% international	4
# of countries represented	9
Average age of entering class	26

ACADEMICS

Academic Experience Rating	71
Profs interesting rating	75
Profs accessible rating	85
Hours of study per day	3.80

Advanced Degrees Offered
JD, 3 years

Combined Degrees Offered
JD/MPA, 3 years–4 years; JD/MBA, 3.5–4 years; JD/MA Environment & Natural Resources, 3 years–4 years

Academics

"Small but mighty," University of Wyoming's College of Law is the state's premiere law school. Its intimate size guarantees that "you are a name and a face not a number," and its students are privy to "individualized attention and amazing opportunities." The school offers some phenomenal programs including "excellent environmental and natural resources law" and many "practical experiences...through the legal clinics...and the summer trial institute." The "legal clinics [allow] students [to] get actual lawyering experience help[ing] low-income individuals in many different areas of law, and several students have even had the opportunity to argue in front of the state supreme court." Even more impressive, "the WY Supreme Court and the 10th Circuit Court of Appeals come here and hear oral arguments at least once a year in our state of the art moot court room." The school is also "very affordable, even for out of state students." It is also "one of the few to still give merit-based scholarships 2L and 3L year for substantial amounts." And many laud the fact that the university "is not a school that tries to be a lawyer factory. They focus on quality, not quantity."

Students at Wyoming also speak glowingly of their professors. To begin with, the faculty "is more than happy to address specific legal questions, issues about students' future practice of law, or to just chat." They've even been to known "to share a beer on [a] Friday." And a 1L shares, "the professors are not guarded in ivory towers but [are] always available (they usually supply their cell numbers) for supplemental questions as well as mentoring relationships." This openness also extends to the administration which most find to be "very accessible and strongly committed to ensuring a successful education for the students enrolled here." They "do a great job of advocating on our behalf and are wonderful overall advocates of the school and University in general."

Importantly, students find career services to be "a great resource." They help to "facilitate job opportunities...by hosting weekly panels from regional professionals/alumni, workshops on interviewing and resume writing, as well as developing externship programs throughout the region for Wyoming students." One pleasantly surprised 2L interjects, "The director will look over your resume at a moment's notice...The faculty here [has] an open door policy so you don't need to make appointments—you can stop by their offices at any time and they will take the time to meet with you." Certainly, attending law school "in a state with only one law school provides students the best opportunity for judicial clerkships, clinic placements, and internships." Also of note, "For students that wish to stay in the Rocky Mountain inter-west region, the job opportunities are plentiful—especially for energy related legal careers."

Life

Though most students are recent graduates and in their mid-twenties, the school nets a number of older students as well. And while Wyoming encourages its students to invite their "spouses, kids, dogs and friends to school functions," many feel these efforts often fall short. As an insightful 1L shares, "I would agree that the administration could do more to embrace the needs of individual students sometimes. There are a lot of married/parent students and sometimes the schedule of events is hard for those students." One 3L feels "successful completion of competitions is highly regarded, yet competitions are held at times when one is required to hire a baby sitter." Fortunately, the small classes really help to foster relationships and many students find "lifelong friends." Furthermore, many find their peers "very friendly" and insist "the competition is not cutthroat," and that there is "a great sense of community pride" and "more of a coopera-tive environment." "We cheer for high achievers and encourage those who aren't." Indeed, this student body "takes care of one another and [is] quick to help each other in tough times."

Hometown Laramie is a "quaint community" and while "winters may be harsh, the summers are beautiful and the people are friendly." In addition, "There is most always a sports event or cultural event to attend and hiking, skiing, and snowshoeing are close, as is Cheyenne to get in some bigger shopping or attend an oral argument." The university is a "very short drive to big cities like Denver, CO."; however, "if you are a fan of the outdoors...this is a perfect place for you." And the best part is that "because it's a small town, it is easy to find classmates and law students out in the community almost all the time."

Getting In

Admission requirements at University of Wyoming College of Law are pretty stan-dard. Accepted students in the 25th percentile earned around a 150 on the LSAT and an undergraduate GPA of 3.13. Accepted students in the 75th percentile earned around a 157 on the LSAT and an undergraduate GPA of 3.60.

Clinical program required	No
Legal writing course requirement	Yes
Legal methods course requirement	Yes
Legal research course requirement	Yes
Moot court requirement	Yes
Public interest law requirement	No

ADMISSIONS

Selectivity Rating	**82**
# applications received	574
% applicants accepted	46
% acceptees attending	29
Average LSAT	153
Median LSAT	153
LSAT Range (25th to 75th percentile)	149–156
Average undergrad GPA	3.43
Median undergrad GPA	3.43
Application fee	$50
Regular application deadline	3/1
Regular notification	4/1
Early application deadline	12/31
Early application notification	1/15
Transfer students accepted	Yes
Evening division offered	No
Part-time accepted	No
CAS accepted	Yes

FINANCIAL FACTS

Annual tuition (in-state out-of-state)	$13,428/$26,628
Books and supplies	$1,200
Fees	$1,005
Room & Board	$10,835
Financial aid application deadline	3/1
% of aid that is merit based	75
Average grant	$5,342
Average loan	$24,791
Average total aid package	$30,133
Average debt	$61,831

EMPLOYMENT INFORMATION

Career Rating	**73**	**Prominent Alumni**
Total 2012 JD Grads	75	Mike Sullivan, Former Ambassador to
% for whom you have useable information	96	Ireland & Governor, Wyoming; Gerry Spence, Trial Lawyer, Author, TV personali-
% grads employed nine months out	79	ty; Alan K. Simpson, Former U.S. Senator-
Median starting salary	$50,000	Wyoming, Political Commentator.
% job accepting grads providing useable salary information	56	**Grads Employed by Field (%)** Academic (4)
# employed full-time	51	Business/Industry (7)
# employed part-time	8	Government (8)
# employed bar required	43	Judicial Clerkship (12)
# employed JD preferred	11	Military (1)
# employed professional/other	1	Private Practice (44)
# employed non-professional	4	Public Interest (3)
# pursuing advanced degree	3	
# unemployed and seeking employment	10	
# not seeking employment	0	
% grads employed by school	0	
State for bar exam	WY, CO, TX, UT, SD	
Pass rate for first-time bar	68	

VANDERBILT UNIVERSITY
LAW SCHOOL

INSTITUTIONAL INFORMATION

Public/private	Private
Affiliation	No Affiliation
Student-faculty ratio	13:1
% faculty part-time	75
% faculty female	41
% faculty underrepresented minority	13
Total faculty	122

SURVEY SAYS...

Diverse opinions accepted in classrooms, Beautiful campus, Students love Nashville, TN, Good social life

STUDENTS

Enrollment of law school	580
% male/female	56/44
% from out-of-state	85
% part-time	0
% underrepresented minority	24
% international	3
# of countries represented	9
Average age of entering class	23

ACADEMICS

Academic Experience Rating	**96**
Profs interesting rating	98
Profs accessible rating	87
Hours of study per day	3.22

Academic Specialties

Civil Procedure, Commercial, Constitutional, Corporation Securities, Criminal, Environmental, Government Services, Human Rights, International, Labor, Legal History, Legal Philosophy, Property, Taxation, Intellectual Property

Advanced Degrees Offered

LLM Program, 1 year; JD/Ph.D. in Law and Economics, 6 years

Combined Degrees Offered

JD/MBA, JD/MA, 4 years; JD/Ph.D., 7 years, JD/MDiv, JD/MTS, 4 years; JD/MD, 6 years; JD/MPP, 4 years; LLM/MA of Latin American Studies, 2 years; Ph.D. in Law and Economics, 5–6 years

Academics

Motivated legal eagles tend to fall in love with Vanderbilt University Law School's "collegial, relaxed environment." This "collegiality sets it apart from most other law schools of similar academic reputation." "The people are incredible, the classes are interesting and challenging, the building is beautiful, and [hometown] Nashville is the best city in the world." Others add, "You get all the benefits of a top-five law school, both faculty-wise and job-wise, but in a comfortable and low-key environment."

Academically speaking, Vanderbilt offers an array of joint-degree, specialized, interdisciplinary and clinical offerings. Education here begins with "an orientation week 'boot-camp' course called Life of the Law," during which "all 1L's are brought up to speed. [The course] gives everyone a sense of what law school [will] be like." Though many tout the overall academic experience at Vanderbilt as "fantastic," with "great faculty" and "bright, sociable students," some students desire "more practical experiences. The only classes that really focus on skills are limited enrollment and/or clinical courses (our clinic is *awesome* by the way)."

The top brass has taken steps to implement classes that remain on "the cutting edge of legal education." Students who have felt the effect of these changes say, "There are numerous specialization programs you can choose from. The most well-known and demanding is probably the law and business program." Students in this specialization benefit from "the ability to...gain practical experience from actual practitioners." The legal writing program, however, continues to be "less than inspiring" and "somewhat weak, as compared to the rest of the curriculum."

Professors at Vanderbilt "are outstanding; they challenge you to find good arguments and are very fair with students. You can tell they want to teach, not just do research." In addition, there are "outstanding opportunities for practical experience (externships, clinics)." When it comes to outside help, "Professors are beyond accessible." They "invite us to their houses for dinner and go out of their way to find us jobs." Overall students say the administration "is super involved in student life." "You can easily find a Dean with whom you feel comfortable." "The administration goes above and beyond to look out for the well-being of the students, especially during the first year when students are adjusting to law school." Others have a more mixed view, pointing out that though the administration tries to be "helpful and responsive to student needs," "they don't listen to what we actually need versus what they think we need."

In the wake of recent renovations, classrooms at Vanderbilt are "comfortable and up-to-date on technology with remote-control everything. Many of the smaller classrooms are beautiful conference rooms with high-tech amenities. Even the hallways are littered with lounge furniture." When it comes to students' list of gripes, very few rumblings are heard save for a few complaints about the "tough job market." Some feel that Career Services "does not do enough to give us access to alumni or search out alternative career paths." Others cite a "strong alumni network" and applaud "a strong Career Services staff" that has "eased the stress of the floundering economy." As one student aptly appends, "law school opens doors, but the extent to which certain doors will always [be open] depends on the student."

G. TODD MORTON, ASSISTANT DEAN FOR ADMISSIONS
131 21ST AVENUE SOUTH, NASHVILLE, TN 37203
TEL: 615.322.6452 FAX: 615.322.1531
E-MAIL: ADMISSIONS@LAW.VANDERBILT.EDU • WEBSITE: WWW.LAW.VANDERBILT.EDU

Life

Students here "are without a doubt the most social group of law students in the top twenty and Vandy facilitates this." A mixture of book smart and social butterfly, students say the typical Vanderbilt law student tends to be "a little bit younger on average than some other law schools." The law school here "is extremely collegial" and there is never a lack of social activities; "Mondays are trivia night at the local bars. We all get together for bar review on Thursdays. Fridays are free dinner and drinks at the law school...People gather around the free drink station across from our mailboxes in the mornings, and there are talks by industry giants (with free lunch) nearly every day." These institutional opportunities for connecting with colleagues "serves [you] well when you need class notes, a study group, or just some stress relief." Overall, quality of life "is exceptional."

Hometown Nashville is "a fine city with a vibrant nightlife and excellent restaurants." Others add, it's "a fantastic town to go to law school in because it's chill, young, and fun." One lighthearted law student here jokes, "It is February 19th and it's sixty-one degrees, eat your heart out, Harvard." Known to foster a "balance of work and play," Vanderbilt "is big enough to be nationally competitive and to offer a huge variety of courses and activities, and small enough that you will know most of the people at the weekly Friday kegger. And yes, we really do have (free) weekly Friday keggers. It's awesome."

Getting In

A plethora of qualified candidates apply to Vanderbilt each year, and the school's rolling admission policy allows it to take the time it needs to consider each application carefully. The median undergraduate GPA for the fall 2012 entering class was 3.71 with a median LSAT of 169.

Clinical program required	No
Legal writing course requirement	Yes
Legal methods course requirement	No
Legal research course requirement	Yes
Moot court requirement	No
Public interest law requirement	No

ADMISSIONS

Selectivity Rating	91
# applications received	3,757
% applicants accepted	30
% acceptees attending	15
Median LSAT	169
LSAT Range (25th to 75th percentile)	163–170
Median undergrad GPA	3.71
Application fee	$50
Regular application deadline	4/1
Regular notification	5/1
Transfer students accepted	Yes
Evening division offered	No
Part-time accepted	No
CAS accepted	Yes

FINANCIAL FACTS

Annual tuition	$46,400
Books and supplies	$1,788
Fees	$404
Room & Board	$13,340
Financial aid application deadline	2/15
% first-year students receiving some sort of aid	96
% all students receiving some sort of aid	82
% of aid that is merit based	75
% receiving scholarships	75
Average grant	$20,000
Average loan	$42,790
Average total aid package	$70,146
Average debt	$124,493

EMPLOYMENT INFORMATION

Career Rating	97
Total 2012 JD Grads	196
% for whom you have useable information	99
% grads employed nine months out	92
Median starting salary	$105,000
# employed full-time	149
# employed part-time	32
# employed bar required	168
# employed JD preferred	6
# employed professional/other	4
# employed non-professional	1
# pursuing advanced degree	4
# unemployed and seeking employment	5
# not seeking employment	1
% grads employed by school	0
State for bar exam	TN, NY, GA, CA, TX
Pass rate for first-time bar	93

Prominent Alumni
Greg Abbott, Texas Attorney General; Fred Thompson, Senator; Counsel Watergate Committee, Actor; Martha Daughtrey, US Circuit Court Judge.

Grads Employed by Field (%)
Business/Industry (7)
Government (12)
Judicial Clerkship (16)
Military (1)
Private Practice (49)
Public Interest (7)

VERMONT LAW SCHOOL

INSTITUTIONAL INFORMATION

Public/private	Private
% faculty part-time	0
% faculty female	58
% faculty underrepresented minority	9
Total faculty	70

SURVEY SAYS...

Liberal students, Beautiful campus

STUDENTS

Enrollment of law school	512
% male/female	50/50
% from out-of-state	90
% part-time	0
% underrepresented minority	12
% international	2
# of countries represented	9
Average age of entering class	25

ACADEMICS

Academic Experience Rating	71
Profs interesting rating	82
Profs accessible rating	91
Hours of study per day	4.60

Academic Specialties

Criminal, Environmental, Government Services, Human Rights, International

Advanced Degrees Offered

JD, 2–4 years; MELP (Master of Environmental Law and policy), 1 year; MERL (Master of Energy Regulation and Law), 1 year; LLM (in Environmental Law or American Legal Studies), 1 year; LLM in Energy Law, 1 year

Combined Degrees Offered

JD/Master of Environmental Law and Policy (MELP), 3 years total (6 regular semesters and 2 summer semesters); JD/Master of Energy Regulation and Law (MERL), 3 years total (6 regular semesters and 2 summer semesters)

Academics

At Vermont Law School, the students, faculty and staff "are anything but 'typical.'" Students are drawn here for the school's "environmental focus, non-competitive atmosphere, great professors with a variety of legal experience, and the willingness of professors/students to help you." As one student notes, "The high moral and ethical fiber of the school's community cannot be overstated." Vermont Law provides an "educational environment [which] emphasizes community above competition and everyone is encouraged to use their legal degree to give back." In essence, "Vermont Law is the place to go if you want to feel like you're part of a community."

Many choose VLS for its "stellar reputation in environmental law"; however, others say they are "equally impressed by their international law program and their unbelievable foreign exchange and dual-degree opportunities." "At the end of my law school career, I hope to be eligible to take the bar in both France and the U.S., and to practice environmental law on an international scale," says one student. Administration and professors here "are all highly regarded in their respective fields and are completely available and willing to help students with intern/externships and employment opportunities." On the whole, instructors "are intelligent, kind, and accessible people." "It is easy to find a mentor you connect with because our faculty possess[es] a broad range of experience and specialties." Perhaps unsurprisingly, others note, "Much of the faculty is overly liberal. However, they are also extremely approachable and always willing to assist outside of class. If you are looking to study environmental law, there's no place on Earth like VLS. The number and depth of environmental classes is unbeatable." In addition, "The Academic Success Program is an excellent resource and utilizes student mentors to make asking for help a lot less frightening."

Classroom and research facilities on campus "are brand-new, state-of-the-art, and are comfortable." True to the school's sustainable roots, "Even the desks and podiums in the classrooms are made by local Vermont woodworkers with local materials." In addition, "The majority of the buildings that VLS students frequent (i.e., those that house all the classrooms, the cafeteria, the student center, the library, student mailboxes, the Environmental Law Center, and IT) are all interconnected—which is ideal during cold and snowy Vermont winters!" The library "is beautiful" with "a lot of sunlight on the top floor." Whatever it may be "lacking in books in-house," it is "helpful in acquiring through interlibrary loan." The IT department, however, "is a nightmare. E-mail tends to be slow, the Internet connection on campus is often slower than at home, and the servers use unsecured certificates."

When it comes to post-law school placement, some students feel "career development and alumni relations are very, very weak and need a huge revamping." However, "The administration is awesome. They always have their doors open to all students no matter what our issues may be. Especially Dean J, she's an amazing woman that inspires me to be a better person and motivates me to change the world around me."

Life

Attending Vermont Law School "is a lot like summer camp." "The location is unlike any other." Located in the Green Mountains with the White River running through campus "(complete with a nearby rope swing and kayak/tubing drop-in point)," the school's

KATHY HARTMAN, ASSOCIATE DEAN FOR ENROLLMENT MANAGEMENT
CHELSEA STREET, SOUTH ROYALTON, VT 05068-0096
TEL: 888-277-5985 FAX: 802-831-1174
E-MAIL: ADMISS@VERMONTLAW.EDU • WEBSITE: WWW.VERMONTLAW.EDU

facilities "even offer composting toilets, which give it an outhouse sort of feeling (don't worry, we have real toilets, too.)" Some say hometown South Royalton "is a perfect example of a small, New England village." "You're about thirty minutes from the nearest 'city.'" Others say, the "town is quaint but in the middle of nowhere and has no facilities. I mean none. One bar, [one] small grocery, one restaurant. [You] have to drive over twenty minutes for anything more." Basically," If you love doing outdoor activities every day, this place is for you. If you have any ambivalence about your feelings toward outdoor sports, seriously evaluate how happy you would be here."

Students are quick to add, "What we lack in access to shopping or amenities, we make up for in community." "Most of the events on campus (I'd estimate 90 percent or more) are student-organized and student-run. This includes educational dinners, speaking events, talent shows, costume contests, movie nights, outdoor adventures, competitions, festivals, and blood drives." The "summer camp feel" also translates "into a high level of camaraderie." "Everybody is always willing to lend a hand, a book, a ride, or a shovel." And shovel they do! "We are in the middle of nowhere and it is very cold and snowy during the winter. However, I like that everyone socializes together on the weekends. We go to parties hosted by our friends or the one pub in town. We are inspired to create our own social events."

The campus itself "is beautiful; it's in rural Vermont which affords wonderful opportunities to do activities outdoors: skiing, hiking, floating down the river, etc." Amenities-wise, students complain that the current gym is "embarrassingly unattractive and budget-looking."

Getting In

Undergraduate GPA for the fall 2010 entering class ranged from 3.13 (25th percentile) to 3.55 (75th percentile). LSAT scores in the same range were 153 (25th percentile) to 159 (75th percentile).

Clinical program required	No
Legal writing course requirement	Yes
Legal methods course requirement	Yes
Legal research course requirement	Yes
Moot court requirement	Yes
Public interest law requirement	No

ADMISSIONS

Selectivity Rating	66
# applications received	916
% applicants accepted	83
% acceptees attending	23
Median LSAT	152
LSAT Range (25th to 75th percentile)	149–158
Median undergrad GPA	3.21
Application fee	$60
Regular application deadline	3/1
Regular notification	4/1
Early application deadline	3/1
Early application notification	12/15
Transfer students accepted	Yes
Evening division offered	No
Part-time accepted	No
CAS accepted	Yes

FINANCIAL FACTS

Annual tuition	$45,207
Books and supplies	$1,500
Fees	$675
Room & Board	$18,100
Financial aid application deadline	3/15
% first-year students receiving some sort of aid	93
% all students receiving some sort of aid	98
% of aid that is merit based	76
% receiving scholarships	73
Average grant	$13,436
Average loan	$43,400
Average total aid package	$59,840
Average debt	$132,000

EMPLOYMENT INFORMATION

Career Rating	73	
Total 2012 JD Grads	206	
% grads employed nine months out	78	
Median starting salary	$47,250	
# employed full-time	143	
# employed part-time	15	
# employed bar required	108	
# employed JD preferred	38	
# employed professional/other	8	
# employed non-professional	4	
# pursuing advanced degree	9	
# unemployed and seeking employment	25	
# not seeking employment	11	
% grads employed by school	1	
State for bar exam	VT, NY, NH, MA, AK	
Pass rate for first-time bar	73.9	

Prominent Alumni
Glenn Berger, Partner, Skadden Arps; Charles Di Leva, Lead Environmental Counsel, World Bank; Linda Smiddy, Professor of Law, Vermont Law School.

Grads Employed by Field (%)
Academic (3)
Business/Industry (18)
Government (15)
Judicial Clerkship (11)
Military (1)
Private Practice (34)
Public Interest (17)

VILLANOVA UNIVERSITY
SCHOOL OF LAW

INSTITUTIONAL INFORMATION

Public/private	Private
Affiliation	Roman Catholic
Student-faculty ratio	18:1
% faculty part-time	53
% faculty female	39
% faculty underrepresented minority	17
Total faculty	119

SURVEY SAYS...
Great research resources, Great library staff, Beautiful campus

STUDENTS

Enrollment of law school	765
% male/female	57/43
% from out-of-state	49
% part-time	0
% underrepresented minority	19
% international	1
# of countries represented	5
Average age of entering class	23

ACADEMICS

Academic Experience Rating	82
Profs interesting rating	77
Profs accessible rating	82
Hours of study per day	3.99

Advanced Degrees Offered
JD, 3 years; LLM Taxation, 24 credits

Combined Degrees Offered
JD/MBA, 3–4 years; JD/LLM Taxation, 3.5 years; JD/LLM in International Studies (third year abroad), 3 years

Academics

At Villanova University School of Law, students find "a good balance in an interactive and educational atmosphere" through a blend of lecture, discussion, and serious hands-on experience. Students say the "absolutely wonderful" professors are the heart and soul of the program. "Instructors are all extremely intelligent and have a wealth of real-world experience, yet remain in touch with students," says a 1L. In fact, he tells us, "My law school professors are much more helpful and approachable than my undergrad professors were." Another student agrees that the "professors' knowledge and experience is fundamental to the Villanova experience." Many here happily report a lack of the "heavy competitive atmosphere that you hear about at other schools," noting, "We all encourage each other to do well."

Villanova takes a fairly traditional approach to introductory course work, and students say, "There is still a heavy reliance on the Socratic Method and many classes use a lecture format (especially in the first year)." In the next two years, students continue studying the basic principals of law, while adding elective courses to their schedule. Experiential learning is emphasized throughout the curriculum, and students dole out praise for the school's strong legal writing and research courses, simulation programs, clinics, and externships. The school has a "clear emphasis" on "solidifying students' legal writing skills." In addition, students take on real legal work thanks to the school's "strong commitment to community service and pro bono work."

For a Catholic institution, it should come as no surprise that a "Catholic identity" reigns supreme. However, some students wish opportunities for service were not restricted by the administration's commitment to Catholic values. ("No 'regular hours' in the forty-hour work week can be spent helping efforts to litigate for women's reproductive freedom, and the participating organization must be aware of the policy.") Ultimately, many wonder "how the administration will balance the school's Catholic mission with its mission as a legal institution."

Villanova's eagerly anticipated, state-of-the-art law school facility opened in August 2009 on a site adjacent to the university's suburban Philadelphia campus. Law students no longer have cause to bemoan the "severe lack of classrooms, computers, parking spots, hallways, lockers, and space in general" that they complained about in years prior as the new facility offers twice as much space as the old building and a new 500-car parking garage, to boot. While they may complain that the campus has a "high school atmosphere," students also say they leave Villanova well-prepared for their professional career in the adult world. Students insist that "opportunities for practical experience are abundant," and the "Career Services Department works really hard to help students find jobs in the private and public sectors." They note that the school has "strong professional contacts in Pennsylvania, New Jersey, and Delaware" and that "major firms routinely interview on campus and hire many Villanova graduates."

NOE BERNAL, ASSISTANT DEAN FOR ADMISSIONS
299 NORTH SPRING MILL ROAD, VILLANOVA, PA 19085
TEL: 610-519-7010 FAX: 610-519-6291
E-MAIL: ADMISSIONS@LAW.VILLANOVA.EDU • WEBSITE: WWW.LAW.VILLANOVA.EDU

Life

When they are not hitting the books, Villanova students live the high life at the many bars, clubs, and restaurants in Philadelphia, as well as at campus events. A student assures us, "The Student Bar Association spends a lot of time planning activities to students. There are many active students groups as well." According to another, "Students get along well and the ones that choose to socialize together have a great time."

Still, many students choose to maintain a life outside of school, living off-campus with their friends or spouses. Getting to campus is easy since "The train runs literally out the front door of the law school." One student advises, "There is a bar that students usually hang out at which can be fun, but sometimes after seeing these people all day and every day, it's good to do something away from the law school crowd." Luckily, that is easy to accomplish at Villanova thanks to the school's "amazing" location. One student enthuses, "It is twenty-five minutes from Philadelphia, as well as a short drive to New York City, Washington, D.C., Baltimore, the beaches, and skiing!"

Most students say that they get along with their classmates, though some say the student body is pretty "homogenous" and "not exactly diverse." However, "Villanova has openly stated that they feel that diversity is a compelling interest at the institution" and many believe that "in time, Villanova will be one of the more diverse legal institutions."

Getting In

For the admitted class, students in the 25th percentile had an average LSAT score of 159 and a 3.27 GPA. Admitted students in the 75th percentile had an average LSAT score of 163 and a 3.62 GPA. However, Villanova may consider students with a lower GPA if they offer other important qualities, such as commitment to service, volunteer work, or unique professional experience. The majority of students who enter do so within a year or two of college, and the average age of a Villanova student in their first year is twenty-five.

Clinical program required	No
Legal writing course requirement	Yes
Legal methods course requirement	No
Legal research course requirement	Yes
Moot court requirement	Yes
Public interest law requirement	No

ADMISSIONS

Selectivity Rating	84
# applications received	3,739
% applicants accepted	44
% acceptees attending	15
Median LSAT	160
LSAT Range (25th to 75th percentile)	159–163
Median undergrad GPA	3.33
Application fee	$75
Regular application deadline	4/1
Transfer students accepted	Yes
Evening division offered	No
Part-time accepted	No
CAS accepted	Yes

FINANCIAL FACTS

Annual tuition	$36,690
Books and supplies	$4,845
Fees	$390
Room & Board	$15,975
Financial aid application deadline	4/1
% first-year students receiving some sort of aid	83
% all students receiving some sort of aid	83
% of aid that is merit based	6
% receiving scholarships	26
Average grant	$16,361
Average loan	$40,639
Average total aid package	$43,407
Average debt	$116,878

EMPLOYMENT INFORMATION

Career Rating	**85**
% grads employed nine months out	86
State for bar exam	PA, NJ, NY, DE
Pass rate for first-time bar	91

Prominent Alumni
Hon. Edward G. Rendell, Governor, State of Pennsylvania; Hon. Marjorie O. Rendell, Judge, U.S. Court of Appeals for the Third Circuit; Jeffrey S. Moorad, General Partner, Arizona Diamondbacks.

Grads Employed by Field (%)
Academic (2)
Business/Industry (12)
Government (5)
Judicial Clerkship (14)
Military (1)
Private Practice (44)
Public Interest (4)

WAKE FOREST UNIVERSITY
SCHOOL OF LAW

Academics

Wake Forest provides a topnotch legal education to aspiring lawyers who are prepared to work extremely hard. Classes "are incredibly difficult" and "the curriculum [has a greater number of requirements] than your average law school." While that might cause a few students to complain, most readily acknowledge that this "makes you much more prepared for the bar and practice." Additionally, Wake's relatively small size certainly comes with some advantages and disadvantages. As a knowledgeable third-year explains, "Class selection can be somewhat limited. Some classes are only offered every other year, and so a 2L will need to plan ahead for two years, in some instances, in order to ensure he gets a specific course. On the other hand, the small size contributes to a familial setting that I have always found to be one of the school's strongest points."

Students at Wake also agree that professor accessibility is a boon to their education. Indeed, the faculty makes a concerted effort to "actually know your name and get to know you outside the classroom setting, which makes an exceptional academic experience." Moreover, their "doors are always open" and they frequently "welcome students...[into] their office to discuss course material or career advice." It's truly evident that professors at Wake genuinely "care about your education and want you to understand the material." A thrilled third-year eagerly adds, "All [faculty] members have a true love of teaching (as opposed to research) and their passion shows. I am not exaggerating when I say that most professors are accessible the entire week and most weekends. They will literally bend over backwards to help a student."

Perhaps not surprisingly, this openness and accessibility extends to the "very friendly and personable" administration as well. As an impressed second-year tells us, "A few of the deans know all of the students by name, which makes the school feel like a big family." Students also appreciate that they "don't dodge tough questions when it comes to policy decisions." Or, as one happy second-year simply sums up, "The administration at Wake Forest is run like a well-oiled machine."

R. Jay Shively, Assistant Dean of Admissions and Financial Aid
Box 7206, Winston-Salem, NC 27109
Tel: 336-758-5437 Fax: 336-758-3930
E-Mail: admissions@law.wfu.edu • Website: www.law.wfu.edu

Life

Students are generally at ease the moment they step onto Wake's campus. As a second-year shares, "I noticed from my first visit and it still holds true that the quality of people here are second to none. There will always be a spectrum, but on the whole the administrators, professors, and students really do strive for a family atmosphere. All schools pitch this, but Wake really delivers."

Moreover, there's a lot of learning to be done outside of the classroom at Wake as well. For example, "Respected practicing attorneys, renowned authors, and public figures often speak at on-campus events, and stick around to talk privately with smaller groups of students as well." Impressively, Wake has also managed to lure United States Supreme Court Justices to campus. Indeed, one ecstatic student brags that a justice "visited an entire day with students during my second year and another… is a regular contributor to the study abroad program in the summer." This helps to ensure that the court is not seen as" simply some mythical creature students discuss in class, but a tangible entity filled with real people."

While hometown Winston-Salem might not have the bustling night-life of other, more urban areas, it certainly has "an abundance of great restaurants" of which students are quick to take advantage. Moreover, "nearby outdoor activities make it a great place to spend three years. If you are into hiking or mountain biking you will have ample opportunities to exploit the great locations all over the area, just within a 30 minute drive."

Getting In

Securing admission to Wake Forest Law is no simple feat. The median GPA of successful applicants is 3.6 and the median LSAT score is 163. Therefore, you'll need a strong undergraduate record if you hope to be a competitive candidate.

Clinical program required	No
Legal writing course requirement	Yes
Legal methods course requirement	No
Legal research course requirement	Yes
Moot court requirement	No
Public interest law requirement	No

ADMISSIONS

Selectivity Rating	84
# applications received	3,410
% applicants accepted	42
% acceptees attending	9
Average LSAT	162
Median LSAT	163
LSAT Range (25th to 75th percentile)	159–165
Average undergrad GPA	3.54
Median undergrad GPA	3.6
Application fee	$65
Regular application deadline	3/15
Regular notification	5/1
Transfer students accepted	Yes
Evening division offered	No
Part-time accepted	No
CAS accepted	Yes

FINANCIAL FACTS

Annual tuition	$39,190
Books and supplies	$1,400
Fees	$500
Room & Board	$20,085
Financial aid application deadline	3/15
% first-year students receiving some sort of aid	92
% all students receiving some sort of aid	94
% of aid that is merit based	26
% receiving scholarships	61
Average grant	$23,780
Average loan	$39,020
Average total aid package	$59,775
Average debt	$120,000

EMPLOYMENT INFORMATION

Career Rating	85	State for bar exam	NC, VA, GA, NY, FL
Total 2012 JD Grads	156	Pass rate for first-time bar	95
% for whom you have useable information	100	**Grads Employed by Field (%)**	
% grads employed nine months out	88	Academic (1)	
# employed full-time	132	Business/Industry (12)	
# employed part-time	4	Government (13)	
# employed bar required	121	Judicial Clerkship (8)	
# employed JD preferred	13	Military (1)	
# employed professional/other	3	Private Practice (49)	
# employed non-professional	0	Public Interest (4)	
# pursuing advanced degree	5		
# unemployed and seeking employment	13		
# not seeking employment	1		

WASHBURN UNIVERSITY
SCHOOL OF LAW

INSTITUTIONAL INFORMATION

Public/private	Public
Affiliation	No Affiliation
% faculty female	39
% faculty underrepresented minority	17
Total faculty	36

SURVEY SAYS...

Diverse opinions accepted in classrooms, Great research resources, Great library staff, Abundant externship/internship/clerkship opportunities

STUDENTS

Enrollment of law school	385
% male/female	61/39
% from out-of-state	37
% part-time	0
% underrepresented minority	15
% international	2
# of countries represented	6
Average age of entering class	25

ACADEMICS

Academic Experience Rating	**83**
Profs interesting rating	85
Profs accessible rating	94
Hours of study per day	3.83

Academic Specialties

Advocacy, Business and Transactional Law, Estate Planning, Family Law, Government Services, International and Comparative Law, Law and Government, Oil & Gas law, Natural Resources Law and Taxation

Advanced Degrees Offered

JD degree, 90 credit hours, 3 years

Combined Degrees Offered

JD/MBA; JD/MSW

Academics

Washburn University is a school with a "hometown" feel and "great community spirit" that offers terrific "bang for the buck." Students describe their academic experience as "simply fantastic," and the school as "familial, warm, and comfortable!" If there is a downside to Washburn, it is its location in Topeka, Kansas. "'The law school is great, Topeka is really terrible.' Is a thought that goes through my mind regularly," a 1L says. However, Topeka, the capital of Kansas, does help the school offer "wonderful networking opportunities," and "the local alumni... are very involved with the school and student events." Topeka also "has the benefit of being the center of politics in Kansas," a 1L notes before adding "but that is about it." Some highlights of Washburn's School of Law are "the Center of Excellence and Certificate Programs" which "are highly practical and well respected in the industry."

Students say "the administration and professors are great" at Washburn, and everyone is "very approachable, friendly, and willing to help." "The deans treat us as colleagues and not as mere students,'" a happy 1L says. "They solicit and welcome our views and input on everything we can be part of." The "highly intellectual, experienced, [and] energetic" professors "are very easy to talk to both in and out of class" and "have an open-door policy." A few students do grumble about the "grading policies," wondering "could we get rid of the curve?!" Still, "class sizes are wonderful" and the faculty and staff "are willing to do whatever it takes for their students to succeed." "Every professor has practical experience from all over the country and many of which are still highly regarded in their respected fields," one 3L says. Another student states: "I love that the curriculum is taught in a way that you can see the application of the material to real life work experience."

The law school's facility "was constructed in the 1960s" and is in desperate need of "a cosmetic makeover." Luckily, the school is "building a new law school soon" after getting "approval of funding for a brand new, $140 million law school." The current building still houses the "largest research library in the region" and "electronic resources and IT department [that] are second to none." "The library and study areas are very good," "the classrooms are all of great size," and "the resources available are more than adequate." Classes contain "ample room for books, laptop, and legal pad." However, students have nothing kind to say about the "terrible" and "nonexistent" parking situation. "If you aren't there at 8, expect to be parking half a mile away," a 3L explains. Still, the "excitement is very high with the announcement of a new building" and students are high on Washburn. "Washburn approaches learning from a community perspective," a 1L says, explaining what makes Washburn unique. "If we support one another they whole community will flourish, rather than making it a race to the top."

YOLANDA INGRAM, DIRECTOR OF ADMISSIONS
1700 COLLEGE AVENUE, TOPEKA, KS 66621-1140
TEL: 785-670-1185 FAX: 785-670-1120
E-MAIL: ADMISSIONS@WASHBURNLAW.EDU • WEBSITE: WASHBURNLAW.EDU

Life

The environment at Washburn is "very collaborative," and the students "all more or less tend to get along and look out for each other." The school lacks "cutthroat competition" found at some law schools. Instead, "everyone is so friendly and genuinely wants you to succeed!" "From the academic atmosphere to the social atmosphere every facet of the school has been welcoming and accommodating," a 1L says of their first semester. Students have little positive to say about Topeka." The town is described as "a dump with nothing to do" as well as "a mecca" for "crime and poverty." Other students contend, "Topeka is not really terrible." There are "a lot of wonderful attributes such as the low cost of living" and many "family friendly activities." The city is "located very close to Lawrence (20 miles) and Kansas City (45) both of which offer anything you could think of needing." As one student sums it up, "it's not a pleasant place to live, but definitely a pleasant place to study the law!"

Getting In

The average GPA and LSAT scores for the 2012 class were 3.18 and 153 respectively. In addition to these scores, letters of recommendation, and personal statement, Washburn looks at factors such as work experience and a history of community service when judging applicants. The admissions committee also recognizes the benefits of a diverse student body.

Clinical program required	No
Legal writing	
course requirement	Yes
Legal methods	
course requirement	Yes
Legal research	
course requirement	Yes
Moot court requirement	No
Public interest	
law requirement	No

ADMISSIONS

Selectivity Rating	77
# applications received	604
% applicants accepted	59
% acceptees attending	37
Average LSAT	153
Median LSAT	153
LSAT Range	
(25th to 75th percentile)	150–156
Average undergrad GPA	3.18
Median undergrad GPA	3.18
Application fee	$40
Regular application deadline	4/1
Early application deadline	4/1
Transfer students accepted	Yes
Evening division offered	No
Part-time accepted	No
CAS accepted	Yes

FINANCIAL FACTS

Annual tuition (in-state	
out-of-state)	$17,910/$27,960
Books and supplies	$1,800
Fees	$70
Room & Board	$9,261
Financial aid application	
deadline	7/1
% first-year students receiving	
some sort of aid	89
% all students receiving	
some sort of aid	91
% of aid that is merit based	21
% receiving scholarships	43
Average grant	$13,150
Average loan	$25,901
Average total aid package	$28,621
Average debt	$78,106

EMPLOYMENT INFORMATION

Career Rating	**81**	**Prominent Alumni**
Total 2012 JD Grads	156	Lillian A. Apodaca, Past President Hispanic
% grads employed nine months out	80	Bar Association; Robert J. Dole, Former
Median starting salary	$48,999	U.S. Senator; Bill Kurtis, Journalist/
# employed full-time	122	American Justice.
# employed part-time	4	**Grads Employed by Field (%)**
# employed bar required	100	Academic (1)
# employed JD preferred	20	Business/Industry (12)
# employed professional/other	1	Government (14)
# employed non-professional	4	Judicial Clerkship (5)
# pursuing advanced degree	9	Military (1)
# unemployed and seeking employment	12	Private Practice (44)
# not seeking employment	5	Public Interest (2)
% grads employed by school	0	
State for bar exam	KS, MO	
Pass rate for first-time bar	89.3	

WASHINGTON AND LEE UNIVERSITY
SCHOOL OF LAW

INSTITUTIONAL INFORMATION

Public/private	Private
Student-faculty ratio	10:1
% faculty part-time	38
% faculty female	24
% faculty underrepresented minority	3
Total faculty	66

SURVEY SAYS...

Great research resources, Abundant externship/internship/clerkship opportunities

STUDENTS

Enrollment of law school	457
% male/female	55/45
% from out-of-state	80
% part-time	0
% underrepresented minority	15
% international	1
# of countries represented	10
Average age of entering class	23

ACADEMICS

Academic Experience Rating	**95**
Profs interesting rating	97
Profs accessible rating	99
Hours of study per day	4.72

Advanced Degrees Offered
Master of Laws (LLM) in United States Law, 1 year

Combined Degrees Offered
JD/MHA, 6 years

Academics

Washington and Lee may be "small in size, but [it] has the resources of a large tier-one law school." W&L small size means "tiny class sizes" with great "faculty to student ratio[s]." It also fosters a friendly atmosphere where everyone "genuinely care[s] about you and your success." Other benefits include a "strong alumni presence," "challenging, but fulfilling" academics, and "the slow atmosphere of Lexington, VA" that "leaves fewer distractions from school." By far the most raved about aspect of W&L's School of Law is that it has the "best 3L program in the country" that "has revolutionized legal teaching." The third year program "focuses heavily on practice preparation and client interaction" and students are "put through an 'immersion' course at the beginning of each semester, which is an intense practice-based scenario in litigation (fall semester) and transaction work (spring semester)." This is a great improvement "over the traditional law school curriculum where 3L is basically just a year of spending money and killing time."

"The facilities themselves are good, especially for such a small school," and "classrooms are equipped with up-to-date technology." While it's not in the most attractive or state of the art building...the campus as a whole is quite beautiful and homey," one student observes. Another says "Sydney Lewis Hall is a 1970s monstrosity," but "the administration is making a concerted effort to renovate the building." One benefit of Washington and Lee's facilities is that every student has "their own study carrel" in the "amazing" library. Like the building itself, these carrels may be "a bit old (and cold)," but are still a luxury that not every law school affords. As a 1L explains, "Law school is not a walk in the park but W & L makes it as nice as it can be, in a lot of ways."

Students give high ratings to the staff, saying "everyone from the cafeteria employees to the dean of the school is phenomenal." "The administration is extremely caring and helpful," but "the faculty are head and shoulders above the administration." Students say the biggest strength of the school is the "teachers, teachers, and teachers." The "brilliant" professors at W&L are "extremely accessible" with a "strict open-door policy that gives the entire school a community feel." There could be more "diversity among professors" though, and the administration "[sells] more parking passes than there are parking spots." On the downside, "The Office of Career Planning is widely regarded as an unhelpful place." Professors use "the Socratic method, and classes have always been an environment of tolerance." "If you want to stay anywhere near sane during law school, this is the place to go," a 1L concludes.

Life

Washington and Lee's School of Law has something of a party reputation, and "law school sports and cocktail parties are frequent." The school itself actually "fund[s] weekend parties throughout the month of February that we host at our homes (but don't pay for alcohol or cleanup the next day.)" Because of the school's small size, "the students all get to know each other very well well, and the professors/administrators also get to know each of us on an individual basis." The student body is not very diverse, but "the administration is consciously making an effort to bring in students from all backgrounds." The city of Lexington is "a very slow moving place with not a lot to do other than study," although "it's close enough to Roanoke and Richmond" if students desire something only a "real city" can provide. "The Indian food in Roanoke (less than an hour away) is great," one student reports. The area is "very rural," but some students like the "natural" surroundings which allow for "tubing down the Maury River, hiking House Mountain," and many other outdoor activities.

Getting In

For the 2012 class, the range (25th to 75th percentiles) for GPA and LSAT scores were 3.40 to 3.73 and 159 to 165, respectively. In addition to these scores, Washington and Lee requires letters of recommendation and a personal statement. Interviews and work experience are optional, but are considered important factors by the admissions committee.

Clinical program required	No
Legal writing course requirement	Yes
Legal methods course requirement	No
Legal research course requirement	Yes
Moot court requirement	No
Public interest law requirement	No

ADMISSIONS

Selectivity Rating	**89**
# applications received	3,408
% applicants accepted	30
% acceptees attending	18
Average LSAT	161
Median LSAT	164
LSAT Range (25th to 75th percentile)	159–165
Average undergrad GPA	3.56
Median undergrad GPA	3.62
Application fee	$0
Regular application deadline	3/1
Regular notification	4/6
Transfer students accepted	Yes
Evening division offered	No
Part-time accepted	No
CAS accepted	Yes

FINANCIAL FACTS

Annual tuition	$42,425
Books and supplies	$2,500
Fees	$1,127
Room & Board	$16,123
Financial aid application deadline	2/15
% first-year students receiving some sort of aid	95
% all students receiving some sort of aid	91
% of aid that is merit based	95
% receiving scholarships	68
Average grant	$23,209
Average loan	$42,083
Average total aid package	$51,767
Average debt	$120,642

EMPLOYMENT INFORMATION

Career Rating	**77**	State for bar exam	VA, NY, CA, MD, PA
Total 2012 JD Grads	130	Pass rate for first-time bar	91.9
% grads employed nine months out	67	**Prominent Alumni**	
Median starting salary	$57,404	Bob Goodlatte, Congressman and Chair of	
# employed full-time	80	the House Judiciary Committee; Lisanne	
# employed part-time	7	Thomas, Managing Partner, Jones Day;	
# employed bar required	68	Lewis Powell, U.S. Supreme Court Justice.	
# employed JD preferred	13	**Grads Employed by Field (%)**	
# employed professional/other	3	Academic (2)	
# employed non-professional	3	Business/Industry (9)	
# pursuing advanced degree	6	Government (13)	
# unemployed and seeking employment	25	Judicial Clerkship (14)	
# not seeking employment	7	Private Practice (25)	
% grads employed by school	2	Public Interest (3)	

WASHINGTON UNIVERSITY
SCHOOL OF LAW

INSTITUTIONAL INFORMATION

Public/private	Private
Student-faculty ratio	11:1
% faculty part-time	53
% faculty female	38
% faculty underrepresented minority	13
Total faculty	144

SURVEY SAYS...

Diverse opinions accepted in classrooms, Great research resources, Beautiful campus

STUDENTS

Enrollment of law school	852
% male/female	60/40
% part-time	1
% underrepresented minority	26
% international	9
Average age of entering class	24

ACADEMICS

Academic Experience Rating	94
Profs interesting rating	87
Profs accessible rating	86
Hours of study per day	3.59

Academic Specialties

Civil Procedure, Commercial, Constitutional, Corporation Securities, Criminal, Environmental, Government Services, Human Rights, International, Labor, Legal History, Legal Philosophy, Property, Taxation, Intellectual Property

Advanced Degrees Offered

JD, 3 years; JSD; LLM for Foreign Lawyers; LLM in Taxation; LLM in Intellectual Property and Technology Law; MJS

Combined Degrees Offered

JD/MA in Biology; JD/MA in East Asian Studies; JD/MBA Business Administration; JD/MSW Social Work; JD/MA International Affairs; JD/MA Islamic and Near Eastern Studies; JD/MA Jewish Studies; JD/MA Political Economy and Public Policy

Academics

The once hidden gem of Washington University School of Law has now become a highly visible gem. The excellent academics, "generous" scholarships, and "great course selections" have made this a law school on the rise, and as firms in national metropolitan centers recognize this, WUSL Law's reputation only grows. This excellent reputation "has been priceless in the current job market" for recent graduates, and together, "the student body and administration create a fantastic environment which helps to lessen the inevitable stress of law school."

The "expert" professors are "as accessible as you can possibly find," and they "are very good at what they do, especially the adjuncts," keeping the material "interesting" while "really challenging you to critically think." They also "care a whole lot about your career after school is over if you take time to reach out." Experience is not difficult to come by here, as "it is relatively easy to get into a clinic or practical course."

One student in particular agrees: "Washington University has provided me the opportunity to gain practical experience while obtaining my JD. Since I've started last year, I've had internships with the New Jersey Attorney General, Federal Public Defender's Office and the New York Attorney General." These individuals are "not short on theoretical understanding, either."

The Career Services Office is "top notch" and serves as a huge draw to students in choosing WU as their law school; it is "extremely engaged" and "goes out of their way to connect you with employers, alumni, and other resources to aid you in your job search." "The CSO here is absolutely incredible and I wouldn't be at a different school for anything right now," says one student. If you want to take an extra semester to do an internship, the office "will work with you to make sure you are getting the educational experience you want, while still completing the requirements for graduation." One student was able to spend a semester in New York City working full time doing securities regulation while obtaining a full semester's worth of credits. Another claims, "When I was accepted to the school, they asked what city I wanted to work in when I graduated and what practice areas I was interested in. Soon after I provided this information, they began connecting me with countless attorneys doing exactly what I hope[d] to do in the same city that I want[ed] to do it."

Though many students agree that there is "not enough support for public interest careers" (particularly after your 1L summer), it is clear to anyone who attends WUSL Law that the school truly "looks out for its students," and administrators "are SUPER helpful and bend over backwards to accommodate individual situations." The schools also host "a medley of workshops every day in order to foster students' employment prospects in what is a very bad legal market." Hard work sees a direct result here, and unlike some schools that allow any student to interview at any given firm, at WUSL the "employers turn in a list of who they would like to interview that generally includes those with the highest grades and then it tapers downwards."

JANET BOLIN, ASSOCIATE DEAN OF ADMISSIONS AND STUDENT SERVICES
1 BROOKINGS DRIVE, CAMPUS BOX 1120, ST. LOUIS, MO 63130-4899
TEL: 314-935-4525 FAX: 314-935-8778
E-MAIL: ADMISS@WULAW.WUSTL.EDU • WEBSITE: LAW.WUSTL.EDU

Life

Students at WUSL are "very friendly and social," as well as "relatively laid-back." People are "competitive, but friendly"; if you miss class, "your friends will be more than happy to give you their notes." The school does an excellent job of maintaining a culture of hard work and general sociability. "My classmates are extremely bright and I know they will be excellent connections to have throughout my career," says a student. Student life is "amazing," and everyone is "very happy…well-adjusted," and "have a lot going on outside of the classroom, including good groups of friends." "We are a very social school, I go out with my classmates frequently," says one student.

The law school building is "beautiful," particularly the 24-hour library reading room ("like something out of Harry Potter") and the central courtyard where "students gather during the day and at weekly Happy Hour each Friday." "I feel like just being in the building makes me smarter," says one student. Aside from the Friday Happy Hour, the SBA organizes a "well-attended" bar review every Thursday, which features drink specials and more socializing. St. Louis is "a great place to spend three years," as "there's plenty of things to do, the housing is cheap, and the city has lots of personality," according to one student. The student body is a mix of recent grads and older students, and though the older students with spouses and families are "less involved in the traditional social scene," they do not feel "lost and alone amongst the 22-year-olds." Most people here are more liberal-minded, and there is a consensus that this "type of homogeny could use a little breaking up," if only for the sake of discourse.

Getting In

Now that Washington University's reputation for quality is quite well known, the school receives over 3,800 applications for approximately 240 spots in the entering class, so admission is highly competitive. A two to three page personal statement and two letters or recommendation are required, and these play a very important part in the school's decision. The median LSAT score for the entering class of 2011 was 168, and the median GPA was 3.66.

Clinical program required	No
Legal writing course requirement	Yes
Legal methods course requirement	Yes
Legal research course requirement	Yes
Moot court requirement	No
Public interest law requirement	No

ADMISSIONS

Selectivity Rating	**93**
# applications received	3,847
% applicants accepted	25
% acceptees attending	25
Median LSAT	168
LSAT Range (25th to 75th percentile)	162–169
Median undergrad GPA	3.66
Application fee	$70
Regular application deadline	3/1
Regular notification	4/15
Transfer students accepted	Yes
Evening division offered	No
Part-time accepted	No
CAS accepted	Yes

FINANCIAL FACTS

Annual tuition	$45,320
Books and supplies	$2,000
Fees	$692
Room & Board	$16,600
Financial aid application deadline	3/1
% first-year students receiving some sort of aid	86
% all students receiving some sort of aid	85
% of aid that is merit based	100
% receiving scholarships	70
Average grant	$20,000
Average loan	$42,900
Average total aid package	$51,830
Average debt	$117,000

EMPLOYMENT INFORMATION

Career Rating	**60***
State for bar exam	MO, IL, CA, NY

WAYNE STATE UNIVERSITY
LAW SCHOOL

INSTITUTIONAL INFORMATION

Public/private	Public
Affiliation	No Affiliation
Student-faculty ratio	13:1
% faculty part-time	40
% faculty female	30
% faculty underrepresented minority	6
Total faculty	80

SURVEY SAYS...

Diverse opinions accepted in classrooms, Great research resources, Abundant externship/internship/ clerkship opportunities

STUDENTS

Enrollment of law school	542
% male/female	59/41
% from out-of-state	12
% part-time	23
% underrepresented minority	14
% international	4
# of countries represented	3
Average age of entering class	25

ACADEMICS

Academic Experience Rating	82
Profs interesting rating	83
Profs accessible rating	78
Hours of study per day	2.86

Advanced Degrees Offered
JD, 3 years full-time; LLM, 1 year full-time

Combined Degrees Offered
JD/MBA; JD/MA in Economics, History, Political Science, and Dispute Resolution; JD/MS in Criminal Justice, 4 years each

Academics

A proudly local institution, Wayne State University Law School maintains deep ties in the city of Detroit and with an active alumni network throughout Michigan. Thanks to the school's "very strong connections with Detroit law firms," students feel integrated into the city's legal community before they even graduate from law school. Moreover, "many political leaders and judges around Detroit are Wayne graduates, and often lend a helping hand to fellow Wayne students." As a result of these associations, Wayne Law affords ample "opportunities for federal and state judicial internships," in addition to prestigious clerkships at local law offices. For those who want to give back, the school also operates numerous clinical programs and extracurricular activities within the city. A student elaborates, "There are a lot of great programs and activities for the students to get involved in at school that directly impact Detroit and other areas, like the Keith Center for Civil Rights, Environmental Law Society, and even more!"

Wayne State further demonstrates its commitment to educating Detroit lawyers through its "very reasonable tuition costs" and openness to nontraditional students. Operating a traditional full-time JD program, as well as an evening program, the school "keeps costs down and maintains accessibility to part-time students who otherwise would not have access to a law degree." For both full- and part-time students, the JD curriculum begins with a set of core courses in contracts, civil procedure, torts, and other key areas; thereafter, there are "very few required upper-level courses," and "you can really be independent in planning your own schedule." Of particular note, "the business law classes, especially the tax classes, are second to none," spearheaded by a team of "highly respected professors who not only have in-depth knowledge of the law but significant experience practicing." On the other hand, "the course offerings are not the most diverse," so "it is always a race to get into the desired courses." Fortunately, most classes are excellent. Wayne State's "outstanding" professors all "come from great law schools and have a real passion for teaching." Whenever students reach out for additional guidance, professors "answer emails promptly and are always available for personal meetings when needed." In addition to the academic curriculum, Wayne State students appreciate the "practical skills offerings, including a very strong national mock trial team," in addition to the clinics; citing their strength, many would like to see the school offer "more practical skills credits" for these activities.

The academic programs are a great return in terms of the cost of tuition, but not everything is state-of-the-art at Wayne Law. "Classroom buildings could use an update," as well as new technology. At the same time, "the new Damon Keith Center for Civil Rights is fantastic," and "the library is run extremely well and the librarians are very helpful." When it comes to the nuts and bolts, the "administration is wonderful. Both by appointment and walk in there is always someone who is not only there to help you but who is genuinely happy to help you." Unlike students at many law schools, Wayne State students specifically praise the school's career services department. A current student details, "When I was trying to apply to internships with federal judges, career services edited and checked my resume, and cover letter several times for me. Then, when I got an interview, career services did a mock interview with me and provided me with the names of several WSU students who had internships with the judge in the past, as well as alumni who had clerked for him." Another adds, "They blew me away not only with their sincere and genuine interest in helping all students obtain employment, but also the creative and innovative ways they go about doing so in this difficult legal market." Again, those local connections come in handy when it comes to the job hunt: "If you

ERICKA M. JACKSON, ASSISTANT DEAN OF ADMISSIONS
471 W. PALMER, DETROIT, MI 48202
TEL: 313-577-3937 FAX: 313-993-8129
E-MAIL: LAWINQUIRE@WAYNE.EDU • WEBSITE: WWW.LAW.WAYNE.EDU

want to work at a large firm in Detroit or southeastern Michigan, Wayne State gives you the best opportunity to do so."

Life

With its dual daytime and evening JD programs, as well as its strong local ties, Wayne State attracts students who are "diverse in ethnicity, as well as in life experience." Students share a sense of purpose and are "committed to becoming quality attorneys." Despite their common drive towards excellence, "competitiveness among students is generally low," and there is an ever increasing "camaraderie among the law students at Wayne Law." From student clubs to speakers, "there always seems to be something going on" around campus, so it's easy for interested students to get involved outside the classroom.

The law school is located on Wayne State's urban campus in midtown Detroit. Many Wayne students live in the suburbs and commute to the city for classes, while others "love and enjoy living in Detroit proper." Despite tough times, students insist that Detroit is "an amazing city to bicycle around, be it to bars, art museums, concerts, Belle Isle or the Detroit Riverfront." They also express that "there are a lot of social outlets within Detroit and its suburbs that are frequented by the law students." For example, "people who are into the arts will be especially enthralled by the exploding population of young artists, lending to endless art shows and guerilla art installations."

Getting In

Wayne Law enrolls one class per year, with the semester starting in August. The admissions committee reviews each application individually, evaluating a student's academic record, LSAT scores, personal qualities, and leadership or volunteer experience, among other factors. Students in the 50th percentile had an average LSAT score of 156 and an average GPA of 3.32. The acceptance rate fluctuates every year but hovers around 40 percent.

Clinical program required	No
Legal writing course requirement	Yes
Legal methods course requirement	No
Legal research course requirement	Yes
Moot court requirement	No
Public interest law requirement	No

ADMISSIONS

Selectivity Rating	79
# applications received	748
% applicants accepted	54
% acceptees attending	32
Average LSAT	156
Median LSAT	156
LSAT Range	
(25th to 75th percentile)	153–159
Average undergrad GPA	3.32
Median undergrad GPA	3.37
Application fee	$0
Regular application deadline	5/15
Transfer students accepted	Yes
Evening division offered	Yes
Part-time accepted	Yes
CAS accepted	Yes

FINANCIAL FACTS

Annual tuition (in-state out-of-state)	$25,530/$28,055
Books and supplies	$1,632
Fees	$1,605
Room & Board (on/off campus)	$9,026/$12,447
Financial aid application deadline	6/30
% first-year students receiving some sort of aid	90
% all students receiving some sort of aid	93
% of aid that is merit based	23
% receiving scholarships	50
Average grant	$17,629
Average loan	$29,716
Average total aid package	$32,270
Average debt	$80,482

EMPLOYMENT INFORMATION

Career Rating	92	% grads employed by school	1
Total 2012 JD Grads	168	State for bar exam	MI
% for whom you have useable information	99	Pass rate for first-time bar	78
% grads employed nine months out	87	**Prominent Alumni**	
Median starting salary	$82,000	Eugene Driker, Business Law; Hon. Nancy	
% job accepting grads providing		G. Edmunds, Judge, U.S. District Court;	
useable salary information	28	Tyrone C. Fahner, Antitrust.	
# employed full-time	125	**Grads Employed by Field (%)**	
# employed part-time	15	Academic (5)	
# employed bar required	90	Business/Industry (16)	
# employed JD preferred	30	Government (8)	
# employed professional/other	19	Judicial Clerkship (2)	
# employed non-professional	1	Private Practice (66)	
# pursuing advanced degree	4	Public Interest (5)	
# unemployed and seeking employment	18		
# not seeking employment	0		

WEST VIRGINIA UNIVERSITY
COLLEGE OF LAW

INSTITUTIONAL INFORMATION

Public/private	Public
Affiliation	No Affiliation
Student-faculty ratio	11:1
% faculty part-time	42
% faculty female	34
% faculty underrepresented minority	9
Total faculty	59

SURVEY SAYS...
Great research resources, Great library staff

STUDENTS

Enrollment of law school	404
% male/female	64/36
% from out-of-state	32
% part-time	2
% underrepresented minority	12
% international	1
# of countries represented	3
Average age of entering class	25

ACADEMICS

Academic Experience Rating	65
Profs interesting rating	74
Profs accessible rating	70
Hours of study per day	3.71

Academic Specialties
Civil Procedure, Commercial, Constitutional, Corporation Securities, Criminal, Environmental, Government Services, Human Rights, International, Labor, Legal History, Legal Philosophy, Property, Taxation

Advanced Degrees Offered
JD, 3 years

Combined Degrees Offered
JD/MPA, 3 years; JD/EMBA, 3 years

Academics

West Virginia University's College of Law provides students with a "personal, yet professional, atmosphere," where the "emphasis [is] on being a functional lawyer." The dirt-cheap tuition (for in-state residents, who comprise the overwhelming majority of students here) and "passionate, intelligent, and helpful" people that make up the faculty, staff, and student body, all converge to offer a "great value" to the happy students that go here.

As one might expect from the only law school in the state, the school has "a great relationship with the state and state bar." This you-rub-my-back-and-I'll-rub yours relationship leads one second-year student to comment, "If you plan to practice law in West Virginia, the College of Law is a brilliant choice—who better to learn from than the justices and lobbyists who wrote the law?" Indeed, much of the curriculum is designed to groom students into local West Virginia lawyers, with many classes devoted to property law, especially coal, oil, gas, and mineral rights law. Most students do choose to practice within the state after graduation, which helps the school focus both its curriculum and its alumni network with stellar results. Career Services is "particularly strong" in placing students in jobs throughout West Virginia, attributable in part to "an active on-campus interview program and in part to WVU's intimate connection with the West Virginia legal community."

The College of Law enjoys faculty members who are a combination of "inspirational, well-published, and leading state authorities in their subjects." Professors "care about students as individuals" and "encourage...and help them to achieve whatever types of goals that individual has." All teachers "know material well and convey the information in an easy-to-understand way." People are torn as to the efficacy of the Legal Research and Writing Program, which has undergone a recent revamping, but the Academic Excellence Program is available to "provide an essential foundation for struggling students."

The administration at West Virginia University's College of Law is "very laid-back" and follows the same open-door policy as the faculty. Although there are around 450 students, the administration "seemingly knows everyone's names," and it's not unusual to see "both faculty and administrators lounging with students during lunch hours." Students share some grievances regarding the rather clunky and inflexible registration system, as courses for first-year students are pretty much set in stone, and "you get the classes at the times they pick, no exceptions." Fortunately, the diversity of classes expands in the second year of law school, but even then, the online registration process can feel like a "gladiatorial battle to get into the classes you like." Moral of the story: get there first. "I know many students who routinely have 'unusual' schedules made up of whatever was left over after twenty minutes of registration," says a 2L.

Though the law school building is "outdated," the recently renovated classrooms within are "fantastic," which is also how students describe WVU Law's staff—particularly the "very friendly and helpful" library staff, which includes" a librarian that will literally help you at any hour of the night (she'll even be your Facebook friend)."

Life

The camaraderie among WVU Law students lends to an atmosphere that is "like one big family." "West Virginia has a small bar and we will all be practicing together after graduation, so everyone treats each other with respect," says a 2L. Students "form study groups, help each other out, and much more." "We do not see one another as competition, but as colleagues," says a student. The student body (and the faculty) is "not very racially diverse," "not too competitive," and there are "excellent relations amongst students."

The school provides a good deal of social events for students to take part in. And take part they do: Students "work during the week, and cut loose on the weekends." WVU football is the fulcrum of many social activities, and there is a fair amount of alcohol involved in the ample tailgating and extracurricular activities on offer here. Luckily, Morgantown is a "social city," providing "ample opportunities to explore your social life to any extent to which you desire," though students note it does help to have a car.

Getting In

For a recently admitted class, accepted students at the 25th percentile had an average LSAT score of 152 and an average GPA of 3.15. Applicants are required to submit three letters of recommendation from people who have personal knowledge of their character, skills, and aptitude for law study and practice. At least one recommendation must be from a former professor.

Clinical program required	No
Legal writing course requirement	Yes
Legal methods course requirement	No
Legal research course requirement	Yes
Moot court requirement	No
Public interest law requirement	No

ADMISSIONS

Selectivity Rating	78
# applications received	984
% applicants accepted	54
% acceptees attending	27
Average LSAT	155
Median LSAT	154
LSAT Range (25th to 75th percentile)	152–158
Average undergrad GPA	3.36
Median undergrad GPA	3.36
Application fee	$50
Regular application deadline	3/1
Transfer students accepted	Yes
Evening division offered	No
Part-time accepted	Yes
CAS accepted	Yes

FINANCIAL FACTS

Annual tuition (in-state out-of-state)	$5,152/$17,252
Books and supplies	$2,400
Fees	$14,115
Room & Board	$10,270
Financial aid application deadline	3/1
% first-year students receiving some sort of aid	86
% all students receiving some sort of aid	86
% of aid that is merit based	28
% receiving scholarships	28
Average grant	$8,063
Average loan	$25,819
Average total aid package	$21,984
Average debt	$72,000

EMPLOYMENT INFORMATION

Career Rating	84
Total 2012 JD Grads	142
% grads employed nine months out	87
Median starting salary	$58,675
# employed full-time	124
# employed part-time	4
# employed bar required	108
# employed JD preferred	9
# employed professional/other	6
# employed non-professional	0
# pursuing advanced degree	5
# unemployed and seeking employment	8
# not seeking employment	2
% grads employed by school	0
State for bar exam	WV, PA, VA
Pass rate for first-time bar	78.3

Prominent Alumni
Judge Robert King, U.S. Court of Appeals for the Fourth Circuit; Paul Virtue, Partner with Baker & McKenzie; Charlotte Lane, former Commissioner on the International Trade Commission.

Grads Employed by Field (%)
Academic (2)
Business/Industry (11)
Government (7)
Judicial Clerkship (17)
Private Practice (58)
Public Interest (4)

WHITTIER COLLEGE
LAW SCHOOL

INSTITUTIONAL INFORMATION

Public/private	Private
Affiliation	No Affiliation
% faculty part-time	45
% faculty female	69
% faculty underrepresented minority	13
Total faculty	68

SURVEY SAYS...

Diverse opinions accepted in classrooms, Students love Costa Mesa, CA

STUDENTS

Enrollment of law school	275
% male/female	52/48
% from out-of-state	17
% part-time	19
% underrepresented minority	41
# of countries represented	8
Average age of entering class	27

ACADEMICS

Academic Experience Rating	**75**
Profs interesting rating	89
Profs accessible rating	76
Hours of study per day	4.07

Academic Specialties

Criminal, Environmental, International, Intellectual Property

Advanced Degrees Offered

JD, 3 years full-time, 4 years part-time [day only]; LLM American Legal Studies, 24 credits, 1 year

Academics

Classes are small at Whittier Law School. "This is important because it personalizes the classroom experience," explains a 2L. "The quality of teaching is extremely high" as well. The "amazing" professors at Whittier are "dedicated, smart, funny," and they are "there to teach you the law, not to hide the ball or play games." Faculty members are accessible, too, even though many adjuncts practice as real attorneys at least part time. "They are always available and attend many of our student events," beams a 2L. Students are split in their views concerning the administration. Enthusiasts note that "everyone who counts knows your name and says hello." They say that the "very responsive" top brass tries to accommodate all types of students. Critics charge that the indifferent management is "a dysfunctional nightmare." "They might find it good to start caring about their students," suggests a disgruntled 3L.

Academic bells and whistles here include a "ridiculously comprehensive legal writing program." There's a specialized certificate in Children's Rights, Environmental Law, Intellectual Property, International and Comparative Law, Trial and Appellate Practice and additional concentrations in business law and criminal law. There are five clinics. There are summer study abroad opportunities in China, France, Israel, Mexico, and Spain. Whittier is also "a school that is serious about helping with bar prep." "The grading system is particularly harsh," though. The "vicious" curve allows "A" grades for no more than 10 percent of the students in any first-year course. Some 20 percent of all the students in every 1L course will get a "D" or an "F." Students at the bottom of the heap end up getting kicked out after the first year.

Career Development Office offers a Career Law Day, as well as private externship placements, and Whittier also has more than 5,000 alumni.The immediate region is pretty rich with law firms. It also happens to be the tenth largest economy on the planet. The school recently restructured their career services office, hiring four new staff members to help provide more extensive career counseling and on-campus networking opportunities.

Whittier Law School is located in "a very office building-heavy section" in the heart of suburban Orange County, "ten minutes from the Orange County and U.S. district courthouses." The library and research facilities are reportedly "excellent," but "The classrooms have no windows," observes a 2L. "There's nothing aesthetically pleasing about it at all."

Life

The student population at Whittier is pretty diverse. "Many ethnic groups and nationalities" are represented. "There also seems to be socioeconomic diversity," notes a 1L. "There are many stereotypical Orange Countians filling the parking lot with cars that cost more than houses. However, there are also many students getting by on loans and part-time jobs." Students describe themselves as "extremely intelligent." Politics vary widely. "There's a decidedly conservative bent among students who've been out in the world," though, and, on the whole, it's probably safe to say that "the students are more conservative than the teachers."

Some students warn that the academic environment is really intense. "Sabotage" does happen, they claim. First-year students are "crazy competitive and not always nice to each other." Others tell us that a "friendly, familial atmosphere" and a great sense of camaraderie" pervade the campus. "We are silently competitive against each other

Thomas McColl, Assistant Dean for Admissions and Financial Aid
3333 Harbor Boulevard, Costa Mesa, CA 92626
Tel: 714-444-4141 Fax: 714-444-0250
E-Mail: info@law.whittier.edu • Website: www.law.whittier.edu

academically. In general, we are like a big law school family," says a 3L. "Most students are very friendly and helpful." Either way, there seems to be some consensus that full-time day students are "more competitive" while the "older, working" nontraditional students who attend at night "are more willing to help each other."

The quality of life outside the classroom is pretty high. The quality of life outside the classroom is pretty high, with a friendly atmosphere across campus and plenty of open green spaces for studying and socializing. The cost of living is "reasonable," at least compared to the much higher rents and costs in nearby Los Angeles. Sunshine is constant, and the weather is nice pretty much all the time. Students enjoy "close proximity to Southern California beaches such as Huntington, Newport, and Laguna." "There is an active organization on campus for just about anything a student could think of." "Students who live near the campus are exceedingly social." "There are some cliques and an in crowd." "There are many groups of people who strike me as being very tight," observes a 2L.

Getting In

Whittier has a perennially generous acceptance rate. At the same time, the raw numbers for admitted applicants are pretty high. Admitted students at the 25th percentile have LSAT scores around 150 and GPAs in the B–/C+ range. Admitted students at the 75th percentile have LSAT scores of 155 or so, and their undergraduate GPA is a tad over 3.3.

Clinical program required	No
Legal writing course requirement	Yes
Legal methods course requirement	Yes
Legal research course requirement	Yes
Moot court requirement	Yes
Public interest law requirement	No

ADMISSIONS

Selectivity Rating	72
# applications received	2,245
% applicants accepted	56
% acceptees attending	22
Average LSAT	152
Median LSAT	152
LSAT Range (25th to 75th percentile)	141–167
Average undergrad GPA	2.92
Median undergrad GPA	2.95
Application fee	$60
Regular application deadline	
Early application deadline	3/15
Transfer students accepted	Yes
Evening division offered	No
Part-time accepted	Yes
CAS accepted	Yes

FINANCIAL FACTS

Annual tuition	$39,090
Books and supplies	$1,656
Fees	$50
Room & Board	$14,986
Financial aid application deadline	5/1
% first-year students receiving some sort of aid	95
% all students receiving some sort of aid	94
% of aid that is merit based	80
% receiving scholarships	49
Average grant	$10,849
Average loan	$51,262
Average total aid package	$58,366
Average debt	$140,911

EMPLOYMENT INFORMATION

Career Rating	71
Total 2012 JD Grads	123
% grads employed nine months out	55
Median starting salary	$55,000
# employed full-time	38
# employed part-time	13
# employed bar required	32
# employed JD preferred	16
# employed professional/other	10
# employed non-professional	6
# pursuing advanced degree	0
# unemployed and seeking employment	48
# not seeking employment	4
% grads employed by school	2
State for bar exam	CA, NV, AZ, NY, TX
Pass rate for first-time bar	57

Prominent Alumni
Paul Kiesel, Kiesel, Boucher & Larson; Paul Irving, U.S. Sergeant of Arms, former head of Secret Service and Homeland Security, Washington DC; Hon. Florence-Marie Cooper, United States District Court, Central District of California.

Grads Employed by Field (%)
Academic (1)
Business/Industry (22)
Government (1)
Private Practice (28)
Public Interest (2)

WIDENER UNIVERSITY
SCHOOL OF LAW—DELAWARE CAMPUS

INSTITUTIONAL INFORMATION

Public/private	Private
% faculty part-time	41
% faculty female	38
% faculty underrepresented minority	11
Total faculty	93

SURVEY SAYS...

Diverse opinions accepted in classrooms, Great research resources

STUDENTS

Enrollment of law school	817
% male/female	57/43
% from out-of-state	81
% part-time	35
% underrepresented minority	19
# of countries represented	4
Average age of entering class	23

ACADEMICS

Academic Experience Rating	69
Profs interesting rating	78
Profs accessible rating	78
Hours of study per day	4.04

Academic Specialties

Civil Procedure, Commercial, Constitutional, Corporation Securities, Criminal, Environmental, International, Health, Trial Advocacy

Advanced Degrees Offered

Master of Laws in Corporate Law and Finance (LLM), 24 credits; Master of Laws in Health Law (LLM), 24 credits; Master of Jurisprudence (MJ), 30 credits; Doctor of Juridical Science in Health Law (SJD), 8 credits; Doctor of Laws in Health Law (DL), 8 credits

Combined Degrees Offered

JD/PsyD (JD/Doctorate of Psychology), 6 years; JD/MBA (JD/Masters of Business Administration), 4 years; JD/MMP (JD/Master of Marine Policy); JD/MPH (JD/Master of Public Health), 4 years

Clinical program required	No

Academics

Widener University is "the only law school in Delaware", and in this privileged position, offers unique "access to the Delaware legal community" and opportunities "to network with the corporate capital of the United States" or, some argue, "the world." Widener builds its curricula in order to prepare students to maximize business law opportunities: "The greatest strengths this school offers are its encouragement of practical skills courses, such as judicial and clinical externships, its emphasis on legal research and writing, and its focus on business contracts drafting."

In fact, the university's location near Wilmington offers portals to extracurriculars, internships, and jobs in "the Philadelphia, Delaware, NJ region" as well. Many non-traditional students are attracted by Widener's "availability of an evening program" and "relatively humane tuition", in addition to the fact that "most of the professors aren't the 'Ivory Tower' type and try to keep things interesting." Student opinions of the faculty, while mostly positive, are somewhat mixed overall: "It mostly has wonderful professors that are interesting and engaging," but "The faculty varies from wildly overqualified to merely a heartbeat in the front of the room." Despite the critics, many report that "Professors are willing to help and do anything they can to help you succeed," and one student argues, "I have a graduate degree from an Ivy League university and the quality of my professors at Widener Law meet or exceed those at my prior institution."

"As for how the school is run, this place is a nightmare. Nothing is organized in an efficient way. The staff have been rude and not helpful to students." Aspiring lawyers looking to compete are eager for Widener to improve job placement—" the career development office sucks"—by doing more to raise its national ranking. "Administration of the school overall needs to improve, and to improve our school's reputation especially." "It's pretty damaging in interviews to say you go to Widener when they're also interviewing grads from Penn, Villanova, etc." That said, Dean Ammons gets positive mentions, despite "being somewhat of lightning rod", for "positioning the school as a real regional option for those desiring a quality legal education." Students name "availability [of] internships and externships" as a strength of the university, and tout the strong reputation of the school in the local area along with the convenient nearby corporate centers that provide a wider breadth of experiences. Facilities are very unpopular, with students calling them "terrible" and "sub-par for the amount of tuition we pay", though "all classrooms are equipped with a smartboard, computer, etc." Though student feedback about some facets is mixed, many students express the belief that, "Our administration really works with the students in order to promote a healthy educational environment."

BARBARA AYARS, ASSISTANT DEAN FOR ADMISSIONS
P.O. BOX 7474, 4601 CONCORD PIKE, WILMINGTON, DE 19803-0474
TEL: 302-477-2703 FAX: 302-477-2224
E-MAIL: LAWADMISSIONS@WIDENER.EDU • WEBSITE: LAW.WIDENER.EDU

Life

Widener's social culture, while present, is diminished by the prevalence of commuting and/or evening students. The Student Bar Association hosts some "social events." "The administration is hit and miss, the Office of Student Affairs has a wonderful staff. They work hard for the students, are easily accessible, and helpful 100% of the way."

Students find Widener's library unpleasant and too limited in access. The "Library is dirty, cold, and has a mold problem on the third floor. There is a shortage of outlets even though everyone has laptops and not enough study rooms for group study." Many students contend that Widener should retool the library to be "open 24/7 while classes are in session."

Getting In

The admissions committee at Widener gives the most weight to undergraduate GPA and LSAT scores, but they do consider other factors as well, including work experience, other graduate study, extracurricular activities and community involvement. Personal statements are required and letters of recommendation are highly encouraged as Widener takes a holistic approach to file review and looks beyond numerical indicators. Candidates are encouraged to apply early; however, applications are accepted on a rolling basis. If candidates choose to apply to both the Harrisburg and Delaware campuses, they may waive their right to choose which campus they will attend

Legal writing	
course requirement	Yes
Legal methods	
course requirement	Yes
Legal research	
course requirement	Yes
Moot court requirement	No
Public interest	
law requirement	No

ADMISSIONS

Selectivity Rating	**70**
# applications received	1,541
% applicants accepted	58
% acceptees attending	17
Average LSAT	151
Median LSAT	150
LSAT Range	
(25th to 75th percentile)	148–153
Average undergrad GPA	3.03
Median undergrad GPA	3.09
Application fee	$60
Regular application deadline	5/15
Transfer students accepted	Yes
Evening division offered	Yes
Part-time accepted	Yes
CAS accepted	Yes

FINANCIAL FACTS

Annual tuition (in-state	
out-of-state)	$38,160
Books and supplies	$1,550
Fees	$150
Room & Board	$10,521
Financial aid application	
deadline	4/1
% first-year students receiving	
some sort of aid	92
% all students receiving	
some sort of aid	92
% of aid that is merit based	11
% receiving scholarships	32
Average grant	$10,680
Average loan	$39,348
Average total aid package	$42,337
Average debt	$121,422

EMPLOYMENT INFORMATION

Career Rating	**75**	
Total 2012 JD Grads	269	
% for whom you have useable		
information	94	
% grads employed nine months out	80	
Median starting salary	$50,000	
% job accepting grads providing		
useable salary information	32	
# employed full-time	181	
# employed part-time	35	
# employed bar required	118	
# employed JD preferred	50	
# employed professional/other	37	
# employed non-professional	10	
# pursuing advanced degree	3	
# unemployed and seeking employment	24	
# not seeking employment	10	
% grads employed by school	0	
State for bar exam	PA, MD	
Pass rate for first-time bar	78	

Prominent Alumni

Carl W. Battle, Class of '82, Senior Vice President and Chief Patent Counsel Glaxo Smith Kline; Cynthia Rhoades Ryan, Class of '79, Chief Counsel, Nat'l Geospatial Intell Agency; Marc R. Abrams Class of '78, Partner, Wilkie Farr & Gallagher LLP.

Grads Employed by Field (%)

Academic (1)
Business/Industry (22)
Government (10)
Judicial Clerkship (11)
Private Practice (33)
Public Interest (3)

WIDENER UNIVERSITY
SCHOOL OF LAW—HARRISBURG CAMPUS

INSTITUTIONAL INFORMATION

Public/private	Private
Affiliation	No Affiliation
Student-faculty ratio	17:1
% faculty part-time	14
% faculty female	48
% faculty underrepresented minority	17
Total faculty	23

SURVEY SAYS...

Diverse opinions accepted in classrooms, Great research resources, Great library staff

STUDENTS

Enrollment of law school	364
% male/female	47/53
% from out-of-state	26
% part-time	22
% underrepresented minority	13
# of countries represented	0
Average age of entering class	23

ACADEMICS

Academic Experience Rating	78
Profs interesting rating	85
Profs accessible rating	86
Hours of study per day	4.39

Academic Specialties

Constitutional, Environmental, Government Services

Advanced Degrees Offered

Commercial law

Combined Degrees Offered

JD/MSLS (JD/Master of Science in Library Sciences) (in conjunction with Clarion University of PA), 4 years

Academics

Some two hours away from the nearest major urban center, Widener may feel far removed from the region's major centers of education, but you'd never know it from the curriculum. Coursework can be challenging but rewarding, such as the "aggressive legal methods curriculum," which is "designed to work in tandem with the core classes to help set the theory in a practical context." When it comes to grading, "the curve at Widener is unusually strict and is a major cause for concern among new students," even if "the material itself is entirely fair." However, if the "numerous tools and resources" provided to students and the "extremely knowledgeable and very accessible" professors don't help them overcome these obstacles, mentoring programs with upper level students and "practicing attorneys who have graduated from this school" will.

In addition, the faculty here "seems to genuinely care about the welfare of the students," led by professors who "truly make sure that students have every opportunity to excel. " Indeed, the "passionate" professors at Widener are "the school's greatest asset," a group who "strive to ensure that the students succeed both academically and professionally." This is helped out by the tools provided to students. Technology is embraced on campus. "Every classroom is equipped with smart boards, dry erase boards, and chalkboards, as well as overhead flat screen televisions to enable easier viewing for those sitting in the rear of the room." The "exceptional" resources that are at your fingertips are a sign that "every avenue is used as a learning tool at Widener."

Students feel they have a voice in their education because the "very accessible and helpful" administration "welcomes new ideas" and "works hard to ensure that the ideas are heard," making it "eminently clear how much the faculty cares about the academic and professional success of their students." If there is a gripe, it is that the administration "seems to be oblivious to the state of the job market." While educators do a good job of preparing students for job opportunities, "career services is not every helpful or good with informing students of opportunities for internships or for on campus groups." "With such huge emphasis placed on trying to find internships and legal experience," one student complains, "I feel as though the Career Development Office could use some work." That said, "a lot of the frustration stems from a practicality beyond the CDO's control; there are many law students and not very many openings for them."

Life

The "small feel" of Widener makes it a place "where everyone knows each other." Students can display "high competition," but because it's not cut-throat competition it "raises everyone's drive to achieve." A few feel there is too much closeness among students, with "people knowing too much of each other's business" and suggesting that perhaps "there's not much that can be done about this at such a small school." Still, though the small campus results in an intimacy not found in larger schools, "you can stay out of other people's business fairly easily."

BARBARA AYARS, ASSISTANT DEAN OF ADMISSIONS
3800 VARTAN WAY, P.O. BOX 69380, HARRISBURG, PA 17106-9380
TEL: 717-541-3903 FAX: 717-541-3999
E-MAIL: LAWADMISSIONS@WIDENER.EDU • WEBSITE: LAW.WIDENER.EDU

Harrisburg is a short hop from plenty of diversions from coursework, including multiple state parks and the popular Hershey amusement park. It is also less than two hours from Philadelphia, making the city's lively culture, thriving nightlife and historic interest a popular day or weekend trip. For those seeking good times in town, however, the nature of social interaction can be one-dimensional. There are minor league baseball and hockey teams, but "if you don't like bars, don't count on having a social life, because all people like to do is drink." In addition, those juggling school with full-time work and family may find that their road is an uphill one, since students in the extended division complain it is run "just like the day division," which shows "no regard to the fact that all extended division students work and most have families."

Getting In

The admissions committee at Widener gives the most weight to undergraduate GPA and LSAT scores, but they do consider other factors as well, including work experience, other graduate study, extracurricular activities and community involvement. Personal statements are required and letters of recommendation are highly encouraged as Widener takes a holistic approach to file review and looks beyond numerical indicators. Candidates are encouraged to apply early; however, applications are accepted on a rolling basis. If candidates choose to apply to both the Harrisburg and Delaware campuses, they may waive their right to choose which campus they will attend.

Clinical program required	No
Legal writing course requirement	Yes
Legal methods course requirement	Yes
Legal research course requirement	Yes
Moot court requirement	No
Public interest law requirement	No

ADMISSIONS

Selectivity Rating	72
# applications received	1,043
% applicants accepted	53
% acceptees attending	15
Average LSAT	149
Median LSAT	149
LSAT Range (25th to 75th percentile)	147–152
Average undergrad GPA	3.13
Median undergrad GPA	3.16
Application fee	$60
Regular application deadline	5/15
Transfer students accepted	Yes
Evening division offered	Yes
Part-time accepted	Yes
CAS accepted	Yes

FINANCIAL FACTS

Annual tuition	$38,160
Books and supplies	$1,550
Fees	$150
Room & Board	$10,521
Financial aid application deadline	4/1
% first-year students receiving some sort of aid	91
% all students receiving some sort of aid	98
% of aid that is merit based	9
% receiving scholarships	24
Average grant	$10,037
Average loan	$42,549
Average total aid package	$45,370
Average debt	$126,515

EMPLOYMENT INFORMATION

Career Rating	80	
Total 2012 JD Grads	122	
% for whom you have useable information	89	
% grads employed nine months out	73	
Median starting salary	$62,250	
% job accepting grads providing useable salary information	20	
# employed full-time	79	
# employed part-time	12	
# employed bar required	58	
# employed JD preferred	12	
# employed non-professional	0	
# pursuing advanced degree	0	
# unemployed and seeking employment	0	
State for bar exam	PA, MD, DE	
Pass rate for first-time bar	81	

Prominent Alumni
Eugene DePasquale, Class of '02, Pennsylvania Auditor General; Michael J. Aiello, Class of '94, Partner, Weil, Gotshal & Manges; Megan Totino Consedine, Class of '94, Pennsylvania State Senate Secretary and Parliamentarian.

Grads Employed by Field (%)
Academic (2)
Business/Industry (15)
Government (12)
Judicial Clerkship (7)
Military (2)
Private Practice (34)
Public Interest (2)

WILLAMETTE UNIVERSITY
COLLEGE OF LAW

INSTITUTIONAL INFORMATION

Public/private	Private
Affiliation	Methodist
Student-faculty ratio	13:1
% faculty part-time	33
% faculty female	31
% faculty underrepresented minority	13
Total faculty	52

SURVEY SAYS...

Great research resources, Great library staff

STUDENTS

Enrollment of law school	390
% male/female	64/36
% from out-of-state	63
% part-time	0
% underrepresented minority	18
# of countries represented	1
Average age of entering class	26

ACADEMICS

Academic Experience Rating	**86**
Profs interesting rating	88
Profs accessible rating	84
Hours of study per day	4.38

Academic Specialties

Government Services, Dispute Resolution, Law & Business, International and Comparative Law, Sustainability Law

Advanced Degrees Offered

LLM in Transnational Law, 1 year; LLM in Dispute Resolution, 1 year

Combined Degrees Offered

Joint degree with Willamette University Atkinson Graduate School of Management (4 year JD/MBA)

Academics

Willamette University College of Law is "a smaller school in the Pacific Northwest," "in the state capital city" of Salem, Oregon. Highlights here include an exemplary legal research and writing program. A JD/MBA program allows students to earn both degrees in four years. There are three journals, six specialized clinics, and a broad externship program. Certificates are available in dispute resolution, business law, international and comparative law (reportedly "wonderful"), law and government, and sustainability law. Study abroad programs in Hamburg, Germany; Quito, Ecuador; and Shanghai, China are another big hit. Students also laud their surroundings. "The facilities at Willamette are, by far, among the best," they say. The "beautiful building" is located on the peaceful and collegiate-looking campus of the larger university. Classrooms are recently renovated and modern. "You have access to the library 24/7," too, which can be an invaluable perk when finals roll around each semester.

Classes are definitely on the smaller side, and they're generally "entertaining." "The greatest strength of Willamette Law has to be the faculty," relates a 2L. "The faculty is knowledgeable, accessible, and seems to generally enjoy teaching students—an extremely valuable trifecta." The "very helpful" top brass gets a lot of love as well. "The school's administration works as effectively as possible," says a 3L. "They are very focused on getting us to pass the bar," agrees a happy 1L, "and very focused on getting us a job post graduation."

Course scheduling is probably the biggest single source of frustration among students. After the first year, it can be hard to get into the classes you want (and occasionally need). The fairly strict grading curve comes in for some grief as well. "Grade deflation" is alive and well, and a handful of 1Ls at the bottom of the class at Willamette are inevitably asked to leave each year. On one hand, it's an intimidating situation. On the other hand, it "will really help motivate."

When the time comes to get a job as an actual attorney, there's good news and bad news for newly minted Willamette alums. On the minus side, the generally mild climate and the culture of Oregon are both professionally appealing for many people. Competition for jobs (especially in Portland) is fierce because the legal market is not huge and a lot of transplant lawyers want to work in the state. On the plus side, the law school here is "down the street from" the Capitol building and various courts. Consequently, students have "fantastic access" to state legislative bodies, state courts, and state agencies. "Great networking opportunities" and prospects for practical experience outside of school abound. Students can "cooperate with the judicial process" in ways that students at the other two law schools in the state cannot.

Life

Students tell us that ethnic diversity is "increasing" at Willamette. More than 20 percent of the population here represents some minority group. "No longer can you count the number of minority students on one hand." Diversity shows itself in other ways, too. There's a decent-sized contingent of older students who are looking to transition into another, more lucrative career, for example. Also, just more than half the students come from a state other than Oregon. Some students are "very competitive" when it comes to grades. At the same time, "Willamette is a tight-knit community." "People generally hang out with the same group of friends they made in their first year of law school, but everyone still remains friendly to others."

CAROLYN DENNIS, DIRECTOR OF ADMISSION
245 WINTER STREET SE, SALEM, OR 97301-3922
TEL: 503-370-6282 FAX: 503-370-6087
E-MAIL: LAW-ADMISSION@WILLAMETTE.EDU • WEBSITE: WWW.WILLAMETTE.EDU/WUCL

Views about life outside the classroom vary. Some students consider the "small" surrounding burg of Salem "an inexpensive and livable town in a pleasant state." They call the immediate location "great for serious students." They point out that "Salem is less than an hour's drive from Portland and is in the heart of wine country." They also note that temperatures are mild all year, and the surrounding area is a paradise for lovers of the outdoors. Opportunities for hiking, skiing, and frolicking at the beach are all within relatively easy reach. Closer to home, students also have access to a fabulous campus recreation center.

Getting In

The acceptance rate is high, but Willamette is a small school and the candidates competing for spots tend to have solid credentials. Admitted students at the 25th percentile have LSAT scores that hover in the low 150s and GPAs around 3.0. Admitted students at the 75th percentile have LSAT scores of 158 or so; their GPAs are about 3.5.

Clinical program required	No
Legal writing course requirement	Yes
Legal methods course requirement	No
Legal research course requirement	Yes
Moot court requirement	Yes
Public interest law requirement	No

ADMISSIONS
Selectivity Rating	85
# applications received	1,092
% applicants accepted	49
% acceptees attending	26
Average LSAT	153
LSAT Range (25th to 75th percentile)	151–156
Average undergrad GPA	3.18
Application fee	$50
Regular application deadline	3/1
Transfer students accepted	Yes
Evening division offered	No
Part-time accepted	No
CAS accepted	Yes

FINANCIAL FACTS
Annual tuition	$36,210
Books and supplies	$1,534
Fees	$180
Room & Board (off-campus)	$15,300
Financial aid application deadline	3/1
% first-year students receiving some sort of aid	100
% all students receiving some sort of aid	97
% of aid that is merit based	16
% receiving scholarships	69
Average grant	$11,000
Average loan	$43,515
Average total aid package	$48,081
Average debt	$119,468

EMPLOYMENT INFORMATION

Career Rating	92
% grads employed nine months out	86
Median starting salary	$54,500
State for bar exam	OR, WA, AK, ID, CA
Pass rate for first-time bar	89

Prominent Alumni
Jay Inslee, Governor, State of Washington; Virginia Linder, Justice, State of Oregon Supreme Court; Mark Prater, Chief Tax Counsel, US Senate Committee on Finance; Amanda Marshall, US Attorney for the District of Oregon.

Grads Employed by Field (%)
Academic (4)
Business/Industry (15)
Government (16)
Judicial Clerkship (2)
Private Practice (60)
Public Interest (2)

WILLIAM MITCHELL COLLEGE OF LAW

Academics

"Unlike some of the other top law schools, William Mitchell College of Law prepares its students to actually practice law upon graduation and not five years down the road." At William Mitchell, a private institution in St. Paul, most students acknowledge this as fact; they feel competent and ready. The legal writing, research, moot courts, and other competitions prepare students for the real world, as well as bolster confidence. One student had an externship "with a judge and worked fifteen-plus hours a week as a law clerk." The school places "a huge emphasis on getting involved in clinics, becoming research assistants, and networking with other lawyers and judges." This is all made possible by the "Mitchell Mafia," an alumni network comprising more than 11,000 graduates, which is "one of the greatest strengths of William Mitchell." "The alumni are constantly working to ensure that students have the best opportunities available to them." "If you want practical experience to set your resume apart, such as clinics, externships, internships, moot court, journal, volunteer work, etc., you will get it, if you apply." William Mitchell also offers courses in which students practice law in a simulated environment, such as Legal Practicum and Advanced Advocacy. Don't worry—there's theory thrown in as well, but it all seems to work together to instill a confidence in the graduating class that's seen in few other law schools.

Most full-time faculty members maintain a practice outside of academia. Students say this enhances the classroom experience. "They have pushed me to think outside the box analytically and to view the assigned readings with a critical eye." The professors "care deeply about sharing their knowledge." "They are teachers at heart first, academics second." In addition to full-time professors, there are "a plethora of wonderful adjunct faculty, who are willing to teach specialized courses." For one student who was called to duty and another studying abroad, the professors remained accessible through prompt e-mails and lecture podcasts. "These are people who love to teach." Also, "There is a good balance in age and experience of faculty members, and new adjunct faculty are constantly being recruited." They're "some of the best professors I have experienced in any educational setting." "The intellectual property courses and faculty were amazing and have prepared me for a successful career in entertainment law."

"William Mitchell seems to go out of its way to assist students." Both part- and full-time students think the administration is "helpful, friendly, and accessible." They're "willing to bend over backwards to make things happen." They "learn the students' names and often engage them in casual conversation." The "library is beautiful," "definitely one of the best in the country." The technology, accessibility, materials, and study space are much better than at other schools. Classrooms are aesthetically pleasing, as well as "very modern, and equipped with the newest technology." "The reference librarians are very accommodating and patient." "I cannot emphasize how smoothly things are done."

Life

"The environment fostered here is incredibly welcoming and supportive, yet challenging at the same time." "I don't think we are a competitive school at all. We support each other; no one wants others to do poorly, so they can do better." One student mentions feeling "comfortable here from day one." Students are on the fence about the degree of diversity at William Mitchell, but one student says, "I happened to be incredibly intrigued by the diversity within the institution. It is not every day that I have an opportunity to argue the pros and cons of affirmative action with an African American

Julie Ekkers, Asst. Dean and Director of Admissions
875 Summit Avenue, St. Paul, MN 55105
Tel: 651-290-6476 Fax: 651-290-6414
E-Mail: admissions@wmitchell.edu • Website: www.wmitchell.edu

biochemist from Illinois and a former Soviet refugee from the Ukraine." More than a few described the school's desire for students to maintain "life balance" while in law school. "Many have made long-lasting friendships" and "found a great social culture at Mitchell," regardless of whether they're part- or full-time students. "The school does a nice job of catering to working professionals." "Late-night happy hours after class are routine." However, if you don't drink, you'll "still find a great social culture at Mitchell."

Students like that William Mitchell "is only a law school." Administratively and otherwise, there are no undergraduates and no other professionals working toward degrees. The "beautiful" campus is in a "perfect" location, "one block over from St. Paul's popular Grand Avenue." There are "plenty of bars and restaurants along with an eclectic mix of retail stores." It's "one of the most beautiful neighborhoods in any major American city." Although some admit the campus is slightly remote, "There are two bus lines within blocks of the school that run to downtown St. Paul and Minneapolis, and from there you can go anywhere."

Getting In

William Mitchell has a high acceptance rate. LSAT scores, undergraduate GPAs, a personal essay, and letters of recommendation are all considered important by the admissions committee. Admitted students in the 25th percentile have GPAs close to 3.15 and LSAT scores of 152. Admitted students in the 75th percentile have LSAT scores close to 159 and GPAs of 3.6.

Clinical program required	No
Legal writing course requirement	Yes
Legal methods course requirement	Yes
Legal research course requirement	Yes
Moot court requirement	No
Public interest law requirement	No

ADMISSIONS

Selectivity Rating	70
# applications received	1,032
% applicants accepted	76
% acceptees attending	33
Average LSAT	154
Median LSAT	154
LSAT Range (25th to 75th percentile)	150–158
Average undergrad GPA	3.33
Median undergrad GPA	3.38
Application fee	$0
Regular application deadline	8/1
Transfer students accepted	Yes
Evening division offered	Yes
Part-time accepted	Yes
CAS accepted	Yes

FINANCIAL FACTS

Annual tuition	$36,020
Books and supplies	$1,550
Fees	$220
Room & Board (on/off campus)	$0/$17,800
Financial aid application deadline	3/15
% first-year students receiving some sort of aid	94
% all students receiving some sort of aid	96
% of aid that is merit based	100
% receiving scholarships	66
Average grant	$17,517
Average loan	$29,019
Average total aid package	$35,068
Average debt	$116,575

EMPLOYMENT INFORMATION

Career Rating	86	
Total 2012 JD Grads	303	**Prominent Alumni**
% for whom you have useable information	99	Warren E. Burger, Chief Justice, U.S. Supreme Court (1969-1986); Rosalie Wahl, Justice, Minnesota Supreme Court (retired); Douglas Amdahl, Chief Justice, Minnesota Supreme Court (retired).
% grads employed nine months out	85	
Median starting salary	$52,000	
% job accepting grads providing useable salary information	68	**Grads Employed by Field (%)**
# employed full-time	235	Academic (2)
# employed part-time	24	Business/Industry (26)
# employed bar required	172	Government (8)
# employed JD preferred	64	Judicial Clerkship (10)
# employed professional/other	19	Military (1)
# employed non-professional	4	Private Practice (34)
# pursuing advanced degree	2	Public Interest (3)
# unemployed and seeking employment	32	
# not seeking employment	7	
% grads employed by school	0	
State for bar exam	MN, WI	
Pass rate for first-time bar	93.5	

YALE UNIVERSITY
LAW SCHOOL

Academics

It's hard to beat Yale Law School, where the atmosphere is "highly intellectual" and classes are mostly "small" (first-year classes vary in size from fifteen to ninety students). One of the many uniquely cool things about Yale is that "there aren't very many required courses." All 1Ls must complete course work in constitutional law, contracts, procedure, and torts. There's also a small, seminar-style legal research and writing course, and that's pretty much it. Best of all, there are "no grades." First semester classes are graded pass/fail. After first semester, there is some semblance of grades but, since Yale doesn't keep track of class rank, it's not a big deal.

Academically, "This is the best place in the world." "It's easy to learn about whatever you're interested in, from medieval European law to helping immigrants in the modern-day United States," says one student. Yale is home to cutting-edge centers and programs galore. Clinical opportunities are vast and available "in your first year," which is a rarity. You can represent family members in juvenile neglect cases, provide legal services for nonprofit organizations, or participate in complicated federal civil rights cases. It's also "easy" to obtain joint-degrees or simply "cross-register for other classes" at Yale. A particularly unique program allows students to get a joint-degree at the Woodrow Wilson School of Public and International Affairs at Princeton.

Student report that the administration is "generally friendly." Word on the faculty is mixed. "I love all my professors," beams a 2L. "They will help me with anything." Nearly all agree that "most professors are delighted to help you." When jobs and clerkships are on the line, it's not uncommon for professors to personally make calls on behalf of students "to high-profile firms or government officials." Other students, however, tell us the faculty isn't all it's cracked up to be. "Quality teaching is not valued enough," gripes a critic. "Professors are hired based on their scholarship rather than their ability to teach or their interest in interacting with students."

Employment prospects are simply awesome. A degree from Yale virtually guarantees "an easy time finding a good job" and a lifetime of financial security. There is "very solid career support" (including "lots of free wine" at recruiting events). But did you know that Yale prolifically produces public interest attorneys? It's true. Every one of Yale's graduates could immediately take the big firm route but, each year, hordes of them don't. Yale "encourages diverse career paths" and "nontraditional routes" ("especially in academia and public interest") and annually awards dozens of public interest fellowships to current students and newly minted grads. There's a "great" loan forgiveness program too.

Facilities are phenomenal. Yale boasts wireless Internet access throughout the Law School, wireless common areas, and perhaps the greatest law library in the history of humanity. "The research facilities are spectacular." Aesthetically, "Everything is beautiful," especially if you are into "wood paneling, stained glass windows, and hand-carved moldings." "If you care about architecture and Ivy League ambiance, come to Yale."

Life

Though the student population "is a bit Ivy heavy," it doesn't necessarily follow that everyone is wealthy. Approximately 80 percent of the lucky souls here receive financial assistance of some kind. It does follow, however, that students are pretty conceited about their intelligence and their privileged educational status. "If egos were light, an astronaut

Asha Rangappa, Associate Dean
P.O. Box 208215, New Haven, CT 06520-8215
Tel: 203-432-4995
E-Mail: admissions.law@yale.edu • Website: www.law.yale.edu

on the moon would have to shade his eyes from the glare of New Haven," analogizes one student. "I'm not sure there's a cure for that, but it might not be wise to tell us in the first week of torts that many of us will wind up on the federal bench."

"There are parties," swears a 1L. However, for many students, the social scene at Yale is simply an extension of academic life. Lectures and cultural events of all kinds are, of course, never-ending. The surrounding city of New Haven is lively in its own way and New York City and Boston are both easily accessible by train. On campus, Yale offers an "encouraging environment" and a "wonderful community." "Because of the small size of each class and the enormous number of activities, it is incredibly easy to get involved with journals (even the *Journal*) and any other student group you might want to try." "Students are very engaged and motivated, but not generally in a way that stresses everyone else out," explains one student. "The no-grades policy for first semester completely eliminates the competition I expect exists at other schools." "People ask me what law school is like, and I can honestly say, 'I work pretty hard, but it's fun,'" says a satisfied student. "Then those people stare at me oddly, and maybe they're right that 'fun' isn't exactly the right word. But I've found it enriching and enjoyable and the people I've met here have been great."

Getting In

Let's not sugarcoat the situation: It's ridiculously hard to get into Yale Law School. With a stellar grade point average of 3.75 and a near-perfect LSAT score of, say, 176, you have about a 40 percent chance of getting accepted. With a perfectly good GPA of 3.4 and a perfectly good LSAT score of 168, your shot at getting into Yale is a little more than 1 percent. The folks in admissions at Yale say that they don't use any kind of formula or index. They consider many factors including grades; LSAT scores (including multiple LSAT scores), extracurricular activities, ethnic and socioeconomic diversity, and letters of recommendation.

Clinical program required	No
Legal writing course requirement	No
Legal methods course requirement	No
Legal research course requirement	No
Moot court requirement	No
Public interest law requirement	No

ADMISSIONS

Selectivity Rating	99
# applications received	2,943
% applicants accepted	8
% acceptees attending	83
Average LSAT	173
Median LSAT	173
LSAT Range (25th to 75th percentile)	170–176
Average undergrad GPA	3.90
Median undergrad GPA	3.9
Application fee	$60
Regular application deadline	2/28
Transfer students accepted	Yes
Evening division offered	No
Part-time accepted	No
CAS accepted	Yes

FINANCIAL FACTS

Annual tuition	$51,350
Books and supplies	$1,100
Fees	$2,250
Room & Board	$17,000
Financial aid application deadline	3/15
% first-year students receiving some sort of aid	73
% all students receiving some sort of aid	73
% of aid that is merit based	0
% receiving scholarships	56
Average grant	$22,734
Average loan	$44,077
Average total aid package	$58,093
Average debt	$110,741

EMPLOYMENT INFORMATION

Career Rating	95	Grads Employed by Field (%)
Total 2012 JD Grads	222	Academic (4)
% grads employed nine months out	95	Business/Industry (4)
Median starting salary	$64,724	Government (3)
# employed full-time	209	Judicial Clerkship (41)
# employed part-time	2	Private Practice (36)
# employed bar required	183	Public Interest (11)
# employed JD preferred	21	
# employed professional/other	7	
# employed non-professional	0	
# pursuing advanced degree	5	
# unemployed and seeking employment	0	
# not seeking employment	1	
State for bar exam	NY, CA	
Pass rate for first-time bar	97.6	

LAW SCHOOL DATA LISTINGS

In this section you will find data listings of the ABA-approved schools not appearing in the "Law School Descriptive Profiles" section of the book. Here you will also find listings of the California Bar Accredited, but not ABA-approved law schools, as well as listings of Canadian law schools. Explanations of what each field of data signifies in the listings may be found in the "How to Use This Book" section.

ATLANTA'S JOHN MARSHALL LAW SCHOOL

1422 W. Peachtree St. NW, Atlanta, GA 30309
Admissions Phone: *404-872-3593* • **Admissions Fax:** *404-873-3802*
Admissions E-Mail: *admissions@johnmarshall.edu*
Website: *www.johnmarshall.edu*

INSTITUTIONAL INFORMATION
Public/private: Private
Religious affiliation: No Affiliation
Student-faculty ratio: 13:1
% faculty part-time: 40
% faculty female: 48
% faculty underrepresented minority: 28
Total faculty: 79

STUDENTS
Enrollment of law school: 182
% male/female: 53/47
% from out-of-state: 19
% part-time: 35
% underrepresented minority: 30
# of countries represented: 3
Average age of entering class: 30

ACADEMICS
Academic Specialties:
Criminal
Advanced Degrees Offered:
JD, 88 credit hour program; full-time, 4 years, part-time, 3 years. JD Honors Program in Criminal Justice (JD HPCJ), 88 credit hour program. Master of Laws (LLM) degree in American Legal Studies, residential or online, 24 credit hour program. LLM in Employment Law, online, 24 credit hour program.
Clinical program required: No
Legal writing course requirement: Yes
Legal methods course requirement: No
Legal research court requirement: Yes
Moot court requirement: Yes
Public interest law requirement: No

ADMISSIONS
Selectivity Rating: 71
 # applications received: 1,444
% applicants accepted: 52
% acceptees attending: 16
Average LSAT: 150
Median LSAT: 150
LSAT Range (25th to 75th percentile): 148–153
Average undergrad GPA: 2.92
Median undergrad GPA: 2.99
Application fee: $50
Early application deadline: 11/15
Early application notification: 2/1
Transfer students accepted: Yes

Evening division offered: Yes
Part-time accepted: Yes
CAS accepted: Yes

FINANCIAL FACTS
Annual tuition: $36,000
Books and supplies: $2,520
Fees: $183
Room & Board (on/off campus): $21,652
Financial aid application deadline: 7/14
% first-year students receiving aid: 85
% all students receiving aid: 92
% of aid that is merit based: 3
% receiving scholarships: 16
Average grant: $15,166
Average loan: $50,905
Average total aid package: $46,598
Average debt: $142,515

EMPLOYMENT INFORMATION
Total 2012 JD Grads: 177
% grads employed nine months out: 88
Median starting salary: $55,000
% job accepting grads providing useable salary information: 22
 # employed bar required: 52
% grads employed by school: 0
State for bar exam: GA, TN, FL, VA, NY
Pass rate for first-time bar: 66
Employers Who Frequently Hire Grads: Georgia Public Interest Organizations, Georgia District Attorneys, Georgia Public Defenders, Georgia Solicitor Generals, small and medium firms. Many John Marshall grads start their own practice or business.
Prominent Alumni: Honorable Alan Blackburn, Former Judge, Court of Appeals/ Balch & Bingham; Honorable Alvin T. Wong, Judge, State Court of DeKalb County; Honorable James Bodiford, Chief Judge, Cobb Superior Court; Honorable Albert Rahn III, Senior Judge, Superior Court; Adam Malone, Attorney, Malone Law Office.
Grads Employed by Field (%)
Academic: (2)
Business/Industry: (21)
Government: (9)
Judicial Clerkship: (3)
Military: (0)
Private Practice: (61)
Public Interest: (4)

BARRY UNIVERSITY

School of Law

6441 E. Colonial Drive, Orlando, FL 32807
Admissions Phone: 321-206-5656 • *Admissions Fax:* 321-206-5620
Admissions E-Mail: bpierpont@mail.barry.edu • *Website:* www.barry.edu/law

INSTITUTIONAL INFORMATION
Public/private: Private
Religious affiliation: Roman Catholic
% faculty part-time: 36
% faculty female: 33
% faculty underrepresented minority: 18
Total faculty: 66

STUDENTS
Enrollment of law school: 293
% male/female: 42/58
% from out-of-state: 32
% part-time: 21
% underrepresented minority: 41
% international: 1
# of countries represented: 7
Average age of entering class: 27

ACADEMICS
Academic Specialties:
Environmental
Clinical program required: No
Legal writing course requirement: Yes
Legal methods course requirement: No
Legal research court requirement: Yes
Moot court requirement: No
Public interest law requirement: Yes

ADMISSIONS
Selectivity Rating: 66
applications received: 1,974
% applicants accepted: 74
% acceptees attending: 20
Average LSAT: 148
Median LSAT: 147
LSAT Range (25th to 75th percentile): 145–152
Average undergrad GPA: 2.92
Median undergrad GPA: 2.92
Application fee: $0
Regular application deadline: 5/1
Transfer students accepted: Yes
Evening division offered: Yes
Part-time accepted: Yes
CAS accepted: Yes

FINANCIAL FACTS
Annual tuition: $34,300
Books and supplies: $2,000
Room & Board: $13,650
Financial aid application deadline: 6/30
% first-year students receiving aid: 100
Average debt: $148,191

EMPLOYMENT INFORMATION
Total 2012 JD Grads: 200
% grads employed nine months out: 67
Median starting salary: $42,125
employed full-time: 118
employed part-time: 15
employed bar required: 104
employed JD preferred: 11
employed professional/other: 8
employed non-professional: 7
pursuing advanced degree: 8
unemployed and seeking employment: 39
not seeking employment: 4
% grads employed by school: 0
State for bar exam: FL
Pass rate for first-time bar: 81.7
Employers Who Frequently Hire Grads: Public Sector Employers including state, county, and local government; Private Sector Employers.
Grads Employed by Field (%)
Academic: (1)
Business/Industry: (9)
Government: (9)
Judicial Clerkship: (2)
Military: (1)
Private Practice: (41)
Public Interest: (5)

CALIFORNIA WESTERN

School of Law

225 Cedar Street, San Diego, CA 92101
Admissions Phone: 619-525-1401 • *Admissions Fax:* 619-615-1401
Admissions E-Mail: admissions@cwsl.edu
Website: www.californiawestern.edu

INSTITUTIONAL INFORMATION
Public/private: Private
Religious affiliation: No Affiliation
Student-faculty ratio: 17:1
% faculty part-time: 22
% faculty female: 35
% faculty underrepresented minority: 11
Total faculty: 118

STUDENTS
Enrollment of law school: 905
% male/female: 47/53
% from out-of-state: 45
% part-time: 10
% underrepresented minority: 34
% international: 1
# of countries represented: 15
Average age of entering class: 25

ACADEMICS
Academic Specialties:
Constitutional, Criminal, Human Rights, International, Labor, Taxation, Intellectual Property

Advanced Degrees Offered:
JD, 2–3 years; MCL/LLM, 9 months; LLM Trial Advocacy, 1 year.
Combined Degrees Offered:
 JD/MSW, 4 years; JD/MBA, 4 years; JD/PhD, 5 years; Master's in Health Law.
Clinical program required: No
Legal writing course requirement: Yes
Legal methods course requirement: Yes
Legal research court requirement: Yes
Moot court requirement: No
Public interest law requirement: No

ADMISSIONS
Selectivity Rating: 76
applications received: 2,433
% applicants accepted: 54
% acceptees attending: 26
Average LSAT: 153
LSAT Range (25th to 75th percentile): 150–155
Average undergrad GPA: 3.25
Application fee: $55
Regular application deadline: 4/1
Transfer students accepted: Yes
Evening division offered: No
Part-time accepted: Yes
CAS accepted: Yes

FINANCIAL FACTS
Annual tuition: $38,400
Books and supplies: $1,300
Fees: $100
Room & Board: $11,600
Financial aid application deadline: 4/1
% first-year students receiving aid: 87
% all students receiving aid: 87
% receiving scholarships: 29
Average grant: $20,918
Average loan: $51,750
Average total aid package: $59,612
Average debt: $96,502

EMPLOYMENT INFORMATION
% grads employed nine months out: 86
Median starting salary: $73,999
State for bar exam: CA, NV, AZ, NY
Pass rate for first-time bar: 86
Employers Who Frequently Hire Grads: Multiple national private, public, and non-profit employers of all sizes.
Prominent Alumni: Lisa Haile, Partner at DLA Piper, Rudnick, Gray, Cary; Garland Burrell, US District Court Judge; Duane Layton, Partner at Mayer, Brown, Rowe and Maw; David Roger, D.A., Clark County, Nevada; James Lorenz, US District Court Judge.
Grads Employed by Field (%)
Academic: (1)
Business/Industry: (13)
Government: (12)
Judicial Clerkship: (5)
Military: (2)
Private Practice: (60)
Public Interest: (7)

DUQUESNE UNIVERSITY
School of Law

900 Locust Street, Pittsburgh, PA 15282
Admissions Phone: 412-396-6296 • **Admissions Fax:** 412-396-1073
Admissions E-Mail: lawadmissions@duq.edu • **Website:** www.law.duq.edu

INSTITUTIONAL INFORMATION
Public/private: Private
Student-faculty ratio: 23:1
% faculty female: 21
% faculty underrepresented minority: 16
Total faculty: 26

STUDENTS
Enrollment of law school: 630
% male/female: 50/50
% from out-of-state: 38
% part-time: 35
% underrepresented minority: 7
% international: 0
Average age of entering class: 23

ACADEMICS
Combined Degrees Offered:
JD/MBA, 4 years; JD/MDiv, 5 years; JD/M Environmental Science and Management, 4 years; JD/MS Taxation, 4 years
Clinical program required: No
Legal writing course requirement: Yes
Legal methods course requirement: Yes
Legal research court requirement: Yes
Moot court requirement: No
Public interest law requirement: No

ADMISSIONS
Selectivity Rating: 85
Average LSAT: 154
Average undergrad GPA: 3.40
Application fee: $60
Regular application deadline: 3/1
Regular notification: 4/1
Early application deadline: 12/1
Early application notification: 12/31
Transfer students accepted: Yes
Evening division offered: Yes
Part-time accepted: Yes
CAS accepted: Yes

FINANCIAL FACTS
Annual tuition (in-state/out-of-state): $34,634
Books and supplies: $1,500
Fees (in-state/out-of-state): $720
Room & Board: $10,930
Financial aid application deadline: 5/1

EMPLOYMENT INFORMATION
Median starting salary: $59,693
State for bar exam: PA
Pass rate for first-time bar: 71
Employers Who Frequently Hire Grads: Reed Smith, Kirkpatrick & Lockhart, Buchanon Ingersoll, Eckert, Seamans.

Grads Employed by Field (%)
Academic: (1)
Business/Industry: (25)
Government: (4)
Judicial Clerkship: (6)
Private Practice: (61)
Public Interest: (3)

ELON UNIVERSITY

School of Law

201 N. Greene Street, Greensboro, NC 27401
Admissions Phone: 336-279-9200 • **Admissions Fax:** 336-279-8199
Admissions E-Mail: law@elon.edu • **Website:** law.elon.edu

INSTITUTIONAL INFORMATION
Public/private: Private
Religious affiliation: No Affiliation
Student-faculty ratio: 15:1
% faculty part-time: 28
% faculty female: 31
% faculty underrepresented minority: 10
Total faculty: 39

STUDENTS
Enrollment of law school: 327
% male/female: 57/43
% part-time: 0
% underrepresented minority: 13
% international: 0
Average age of entering class: 23

ACADEMICS
Advanced Degrees Offered:
JD; 3-year full-time program
Clinical program required: No
Legal writing course requirement: Yes
Legal methods course requirement: Yes
Legal research court requirement: Yes
Moot court requirement: No
Public interest law requirement: Yes

ADMISSIONS
Selectivity Rating: 75
applications received: 888
% applicants accepted: 56
% acceptees attending: 20
Median LSAT: 155
LSAT Range (25th to 75th percentile): 150–158
Median undergrad GPA: 3.16
Application fee: $50
Regular application deadline: 6/30
Early application deadline: 11/15
Early application notification: 12/30
Transfer students accepted: Yes
Evening division offered: No
Part-time accepted: No
CAS accepted: Yes

FINANCIAL FACTS
Annual tuition: $36,100
Books and supplies: $12,225
Room & Board (on/off campus): N/A/$12,000
Financial aid application deadline: 7/1
% first-year students receiving aid: 72
% all students receiving aid: 94
% of aid that is merit based: 25
% receiving scholarships: 80
Average grant: $15,995
Average loan: $42,921
Average total aid package: $48,876
Average debt: $94,823

EMPLOYMENT INFORMATION
Total 2012 JD Grads: 112
% grads employed nine months out: 76
Median starting salary: $45,000
% job accepting grads providing useable salary information: 29
# employed full-time: 75
# employed part-time: 10
# employed bar required: 70
# employed JD preferred: 11
# employed professional/other: 4
# pursuing advanced degree: 1
# unemployed and seeking employment: 24
# not seeking employment: 0
% grads employed by school: 0
State for bar exam: NC
Pass rate for first-time bar: 76
Grads Employed by Field (%)
Academic: (5)
Business/Industry: (20)
Government: (5)
Judicial Clerkship: (4)
Military: (0)
Private Practice: (38)
Public Interest: (3)

FLORIDA A&M UNIVERSITY

College of Law

P.O. Box 3113, Orlando, FL 32802
Admissions Phone: 407-254-3268 • **Admissions Fax:** 407-254-3213
Admissions E-Mail: famulaw.admissions@famu.edu
Website: www.famu.edu/law

INSTITUTIONAL INFORMATION
Public/private: Public
Student-faculty ratio: 13:1
Total faculty: 40

STUDENTS
Enrollment of law school: 293
% male/female: 40/60

% part-time: 31
% underrepresented minority: 53
Average age of entering class: 33

ACADEMICS

Advanced Degrees Offered:
JD (3-year full-time student; 4-year part-time student)
Clinical program required: Yes
Legal writing course requirement: No
Legal methods course requirement: Yes
Legal research court requirement: No
Moot court requirement: No
Public interest law requirement: Yes

ADMISSIONS

Selectivity Rating: 86
applications received: 540
% applicants accepted: 36
% acceptees attending: 62
Average LSAT: 148
LSAT Range (25th to 75th percentile): 143–150
Average undergrad GPA: 3.10
Application fee: $20
Regular application deadline: 5/1
Transfer students accepted: No
Evening division offered: Yes
Part-time accepted: Yes
CAS accepted: Yes

FINANCIAL FACTS

Annual tuition (in-state/out-of-state): $7,140/$26,580
Books and supplies: $13,591
Financial aid application deadline: 4/1
% first-year students receiving aid: 88
% all students receiving aid: 92
% receiving scholarships: 16
Average grant: $1,800
Average loan: $18,500

FLORIDA COASTAL SCHOOL OF LAW

8787 Baypine Road, Jacksonville, FL 32256
Admissions Phone: *904-680-7710 •* ***Admissions Fax:*** *904-680-7692*
Admissions E-Mail: admissions@fcsl.edu *•* ***Website:*** www.fcsl.edu

INSTITUTIONAL INFORMATION

Public/private: Private
Religious affiliation: No Affiliation
% faculty part-time: 31
% faculty female: 49
% faculty underrepresented minority: 13
Total faculty: 137

STUDENTS

Enrollment of law school: 1,308
% male/female: 54/46
% from out-of-state: 60

% part-time: 11
% underrepresented minority: 24
% international: 1
# of countries represented: 8
Average age of entering class: 25

ACADEMICS

Academic Specialties:
Commercial, Constitutional, Criminal, Environmental, International, Labor, Property, Taxation
Advanced Degrees Offered:
JD 2 1/2–3 years full-time, 3 1/2–4 years part-time
Combined Degrees Offered:
JD/MBA: The Davis College of Business at Jacksonville University (JU) and Florida Coastal School of Law (Coastal Law) have created a joint degree program through which qualified individuals may enroll in the Coastal Law JD and the Davis MBA programs simultaneously.
Clinical program required: Yes
Legal writing course requirement: Yes
Legal methods course requirement: Yes
Legal research court requirement: Yes
Moot court requirement: No
Public interest law requirement: No

ADMISSIONS

Selectivity Rating: 69
applications received: 6,331
% applicants accepted: 62
% acceptees attending: 16
Average LSAT: 150
LSAT Range (25th to 75th percentile): 147–153
Average undergrad GPA: 3.21
Application fee: $0
Transfer students accepted: Yes
Evening division offered: No
Part-time accepted: Yes
CAS accepted: Yes

FINANCIAL FACTS

Annual tuition (in-state/out-of-state): $31,124/$31,124
Books and supplies: $1,200
Fees (in-state/out-of-state): $1,468/$1,468
Room & Board (on/off campus): n/a/$19,570
Financial aid application deadline: 8/1
% first-year students receiving aid: 85
% all students receiving aid: 85
% of aid that is merit based: 10
% receiving scholarships: 25
Average grant: $6,200
Average loan: $18,500
Average total aid package: $23,000
Average debt: $60,000

EMPLOYMENT INFORMATION

% grads employed nine months out: 97
Median starting salary: $48,525
State for bar exam: FL, GA, SC, NC
Pass rate for first-time bar: 85
Employers Who Frequently Hire Grads: Small to mid-sized Florida firms, Florida prosecutors' and public defenders' offices.

Grads Employed by Field (%)
Academic: (2)
Business/Industry: (17)
Government: (15)
Judicial Clerkship: (3)
Private Practice: (50)
Public Interest: (14)

GOLDEN GATE UNIVERSITY
School of Law

Law Admissions Office, 536 Mission Street, San Francisco, CA 94105
Admissions Phone: 415-442-6630 • **Admissions Fax:** 415-442-6631
Admissions E-Mail: lawadmit@ggu.edu • **Website:** www.law.ggu.edu

INSTITUTIONAL INFORMATION
Public/private: Private
Religious affiliation: No Affiliation
Student-faculty ratio: 19:1
% faculty part-time: 62
% faculty female: 43
% faculty underrepresented minority: 17
Total faculty: 108

STUDENTS
Enrollment of law school: 227
% male/female: 46/54
% from out-of-state: 37
% part-time: 42
% underrepresented minority: 44
% international: 1
# of countries represented: 20
Average age of entering class: 27

ACADEMICS
Academic Specialties:
Criminal, Environmental, International, Labor, Property, Taxation, Intellectual Property
Advanced Degrees Offered:
JD full-time (3 years), JD part-time evening (4 years), LLM (1 year), SJD (1 year), JD/LLM in Taxation (3.5 years)
Combined Degrees Offered:
JD/MBA, 3.5–4 years, JD/PhD, 7 years
Clinical program required: No
Legal writing course requirement: Yes
Legal methods course requirement: No
Legal research court requirement: Yes
Moot court requirement: Yes
Public interest law requirement: No

ADMISSIONS
Selectivity Rating: 67
applications received: 1,793
% applicants accepted: 73
% acceptees attending: 14
Average LSAT: 151
Median LSAT: 151

LSAT Range (25th to 75th percentile): 148–154
Average undergrad GPA: 3.27
Median undergrad GPA: 3.12
Application fee: $60
Regular application deadline: 4/1
Early application deadline: 12/31
Early application notification: 2/15
Transfer students accepted: Yes
Evening division offered: Yes
Part-time accepted: Yes
CAS accepted: Yes

FINANCIAL FACTS
Annual tuition (in-state/out-of-state): $41,700
Books and supplies: $1,400
Fees (in-state/out-of-state): $290
Room & Board: $14,850
Financial aid application deadline:
% first-year students receiving aid: 96
% all students receiving aid: 89
% of aid that is merit based: 90
% receiving scholarships: 50
Average grant: $12,000
Average loan: $30,000
Average total aid package: $69,340
Average debt: $137,484

EMPLOYMENT INFORMATION
Total 2012 JD Grads: 186
% grads employed nine months out: 68
# employed full-time: 83
# employed part-time: 43
# employed bar required: 74
# employed JD preferred: 25
# employed professional/other: 20
# employed non-professional: 7
# pursuing advanced degree: 9
# unemployed and seeking employment: 38
# not seeking employment: 6
% grads employed by school: 13
State for bar exam: CA
Pass rate for first-time bar: 70
Employers Who Frequently Hire Grads: Small, medium, and large law firms, government agencies, public interest organizations, businesses and corporations.
Prominent Alumni: Justice Jesse Carter (deceased), California Supreme Court Justice; Morgan Christen, Circuit Judge of the United States Court of Appeals for the Ninth Circuit; Karen Hawkins, Director of Professional Responsibility, IRS; Mark S. Anderson, Vice President and General Counsel, Dolby Labs.; Marjorie Randolph, Senior VP for HR and Admin., Walt Disney Studios.
Grads Employed by Field (%)
Academic: (3)
Business/Industry: (16)
Government: (9)
Judicial Clerkship: (3)
Military: (1)
Private Practice: (24)
Public Interest: (17)

HOWARD UNIVERSITY
School of Law

2900 Van Ness Street, NW, Suite 219, Washington, DC 20008
Admissions Phone: 202-806-8008 • **Admissions Fax:** 202-806-8162
Admissions E-Mail: admissions@law.howard.edu
Website: www.law.howard.edu

INSTITUTIONAL INFORMATION
Public/private: Private
Student-faculty ratio: 13:1
% faculty part-time: 45
% faculty female: 40
% faculty underrepresented minority: 78
Total faculty: 67

STUDENTS
Enrollment of law school: 402
% male/female: 40/60
% underrepresented minority: 94

ACADEMICS
Academic Specialties:
Commercial, Constitutional, Corporation Securities, Criminal, Environmental, Human Rights, International, Labor, Property, Taxation, Intellectual Property
Advanced Degrees Offered:
LLM (foreign lawyers only) 1–2 years
Combined Degrees Offered:
JD/MBA, 4 years
Clinical program required: No
Legal writing course requirement: Yes
Legal methods course requirement: Yes
Legal research court requirement: No
Moot court requirement: No
Public interest law requirement: No

ADMISSIONS
Selectivity Rating: 93
applications received: 2,550
% applicants accepted: 17
% acceptees attending: 37
Average LSAT: 153
LSAT Range (25th to 75th percentile): 148–158
Average undergrad GPA: 25.00
Application fee: $60
Regular application deadline: 3/31
Transfer students accepted: Yes
Evening division offered: No
Part-time accepted: No
CAS accepted: Yes

FINANCIAL FACTS
Annual tuition (in-state/out-of-state): $15,990
Books and supplies: $1,103
Fees (in-state/out-of-state): $655
Room & Board (on/off campus): $98,698/$10,169
Financial aid application deadline: 3/1

% first-year students receiving aid: 90
% all students receiving aid: 95
% of aid that is merit based: 58
Average grant: $13,000
Average loan: $18,500
Average total aid package: $29,000
Average debt: $60,000

EMPLOYMENT INFORMATION
% grads employed nine months out: 96
Median starting salary: $72,465
Employers Who Frequently Hire Grads: Law Firms; Judicial Clerkships; Government Agencies
Grads Employed by Field (%)
Academic: (3)
Business/Industry: (13)
Government: (18)
Judicial Clerkship: (15)
Military: (1)
Private Practice: (43)
Public Interest: (7)

LIBERTY UNIVERSITY
School of Law

1971 University Blvd., Lynchburg, VA 24502
Admissions Phone: (434) 592-5300 • **Admissions Fax:** (434) 592-5400
Admissions E-Mail: lawadmissions@liberty.edu • **Website:** law.liberty.edu

INSTITUTIONAL INFORMATION
Public/private: Private
Religious affiliation: Baptist
Student-faculty ratio: 13:1
% faculty part-time: 24
% faculty female: 32
% faculty underrepresented minority: 27
Total faculty: 41

STUDENTS
Enrollment of law school: 245
% male/female: 63/37
% from out-of-state: 37
% part-time: 0
% underrepresented minority: 17
% international: 1
# of countries represented: 4
Average age of entering class: 23

ACADEMICS
Academic Specialties:
Commercial, Constitutional, Criminal, International, Legal Philosophy, Property
Advanced Degrees Offered:
JD, 3 years; Other degrees are in development
Combined Degrees Offered:
JD/MBA; JD/MEd; JD/EdS; JD/EdD; JD/MAR; JD/MDiv; JD/MA History; JD/MA Public Policy; JD/MA Human Services
Clinical program required: No
Legal writing course requirement: Yes

Legal methods course requirement: Yes
Legal research court requirement: Yes
Moot court requirement: Yes
Public interest law requirement: No

ADMISSIONS
Selectivity Rating: 82
applications received: 380
% applicants accepted: 48
% acceptees attending: 45
Average LSAT: 150
Median LSAT: 150
LSAT Range (25th to 75th percentile): 148–155
Average undergrad GPA: 3.32
Median undergrad GPA: 3.32
Application fee: $50
Regular application deadline: 6/1
Transfer students accepted: Yes
Evening division offered: No
Part-time accepted: No
CAS accepted: Yes

FINANCIAL FACTS
Annual tuition (in-state/out-of-state): $30,396/$30,396
Books and supplies: $3,264
Fees (in-state/out-of-state): $1,606/$1,606
Room & Board: $10,115
Financial aid application deadline: 6/1
% first-year students receiving aid: 99
% all students receiving aid: 99
% of aid that is merit based: 44
% receiving scholarships: 98
Average grant: $16,977
Average loan: $25,617
Average total aid package: $38,241
Average debt: $66,829

EMPLOYMENT INFORMATION
Total 2012 JD Grads: 90
% grads employed nine months out: 72
Median starting salary: $50,000
% job accepting grads providing useable salary information: 73
# employed full-time: 60
# employed part-time: 5
# employed bar required: 50
# employed JD preferred: 10
# employed professional/other: 2
# employed non-professional: 1
# pursuing advanced degree: 2
# unemployed and seeking employment: 18
# not seeking employment: 1
% grads employed by school: 1
State for bar exam: VA, NC, NY, TX, FL
Pass rate for first-time bar: 72
Employers Who Frequently Hire Grads: Delta Star
Alabama Supreme Court
Lynchburg Public Defenders Office
Liberty Counsel
Internal Revenue Service
Office of the Attorney Generàl (Virginia)
Supreme Court of Virginia
Court of Appeals of Virginia
Special Counsel
Prominent Alumni: Matthew Krause, Texas State House Representative, Texas

State House; Sarah Seitz, Legislative Director and Counsel, The United States House of Representatives; Brian Bosche, Reporter, The Blaze TV; Jeremy White, General Counsel, National Rifle Association; Paul Brodersen, Deputy General Counsel, Samaritan Ministries International.
Grads Employed by Field (%)
Academic: (2)
Business/Industry: (16)
Government: (12)
Judicial Clerkship: (4)
Military: (0)
Private Practice: (8)
Public Interest: (4)

NORTHERN KENTUCKY UNIVERSITY
Salmon P. Chase College of Law

Nunn Hall, Room 101, Highland Heights, KY 41099
Admissions Phone: 859-572-5490 • Admissions Fax: 859-572-6081
Admissions E-Mail: chaselaw.nku.edu/admissions
Website: chaselaw.nku.edu

INSTITUTIONAL INFORMATION
Public/private: Public
Religious affiliation: No Affiliation
% faculty part-time: 25
% faculty female: 28
% faculty underrepresented minority: 6
Total faculty: 61

STUDENTS
Enrollment of law school: 515
% male/female: 74/26
% from out-of-state: 37
% part-time: 33
% underrepresented minority: 6
% international: 0
# of countries represented: 1
Average age of entering class: 27

ACADEMICS
Academic Specialties:
Labor, Taxation
Combined Degrees Offered:
JD/MBA: 3.5–4 years full-time
Clinical program required: No
Legal writing course requirement: Yes
Legal methods course requirement: Yes
Legal research court requirement: Yes
Moot court requirement: No
Public interest law requirement: Yes

ADMISSIONS
Selectivity Rating: 70
applications received: 733

% applicants accepted: 68
% acceptees attending: 36
Average LSAT: 152
Median LSAT: 152
LSAT Range (25th to 75th percentile): 149–155
Average undergrad GPA: 3.17
Median undergrad GPA: 3.17
Application fee: $40
Regular application deadline: 4/1
Early application deadline: 2/1
Transfer students accepted: Yes
Evening division offered: Yes
Part-time accepted: Yes
CAS accepted: Yes
International Students
 TOEFL recommended of international students

FINANCIAL FACTS
Annual tuition (in-state/out-of-state): $15,782/$33,540
Books and supplies: $1,200
Fees (in-state/out-of-state): $192/$192
Room & Board (on/off campus): $17,989/$20,989
Financial aid application deadline: 2/1
% first-year students receiving aid: 88
% all students receiving aid: 89
% of aid that is merit based: 18
% receiving scholarships: 44
Average grant: $12,119
Average loan: $26,792
Average total aid package: $29,550
Average debt: $85,711

EMPLOYMENT INFORMATION
Total 2012 JD Grads: 162
% grads employed nine months out: 87
Median starting salary: $50,000
% job accepting grads providing useable salary information: 67
# employed full-time: 122
# employed part-time: 7
# employed bar required: 72
# employed JD preferred: 35
# employed professional/other: 18
# employed non-professional: 4
# pursuing advanced degree: 1
# unemployed and seeking employment: 19
# not seeking employment: 3
% grads employed by school: 1
State for bar exam: KY, OH
Pass rate for first-time bar: 81
Employers Who Frequently Hire Grads: Procter & Gamble; Dinsmore & Shohl; U.S. Department of Labor; Kentucky Department of Public Advocacy; Taft, Stettinius & Hollister; Freund, Freeze & Arnold; Adams, Stepner, Woltermann & Dusing; Keating Muething & Klekamp; Frost Brown Todd; Kentucky Office of Commonwealth's Attorney; Deters, Benzinger & LaVelle; and Fidelity Investments.
Prominent Alumni: Steve J. Chabot, United States Congressman; Patricia L. Herbold, Former United States Ambassador to Singapore; Dustin E. McCoy, Chair & CEO, Brunswick Corp.; W. Bruce Lunsford, Chair & CEO, Lunsford Capital, LLC; Katie Kratz Stine, Senator & President Pro Tempore, Ky. State Senate.

Grads Employed by Field (%)
Academic: (2)
Business/Industry: (19)
Government: (10)
Judicial Clerkship: (1)
Military: (0)
Private Practice: (40)
Public Interest: (7)

OHIO NORTHERN UNIVERSITY
Pettit College of Law

Ohio Northern University, Pettit College of Law, 119 Tilton Hall of Law, Ada, OH 45810-1599
Admissions Phone: 877-452-9668 • **Admissions Fax:** 419-772-3042
Admissions E-Mail: lawadmissions@onu.edu • **Website:** www.law.onu.edu

INSTITUTIONAL INFORMATION
Public/private: Private
Religious affiliation: Methodist
Student-faculty ratio: 12:1
% faculty part-time: 26
% faculty female: 38
% faculty underrepresented minority: 12
Total faculty: 34

STUDENTS
Enrollment of law school: 274
% male/female: 56/44
% from out-of-state: 68
% part-time: 0
% underrepresented minority: 17
% international: 1
# of countries represented: 8
Average age of entering class: 24

ACADEMICS
Academic Specialties:
Civil Procedure, Commercial, Constitutional, Corporation Securities, Criminal, Environmental, Government Services, Human Rights, International, Labor, Legal History, Property, Taxation, Intellectual Property
Advanced Degrees Offered:
JD, 3 years
Combined Degrees Offered:
JD/LLM in Democratic Governance and Rule of Law, 3 years; JD/MPPA (Masters of Professional Practice in Accounting), 3 years
Clinical program required: No
Legal writing course requirement: Yes
Legal methods course requirement: Yes
Legal research court requirement: Yes
Moot court requirement: No
Public interest law requirement: No

ADMISSIONS

Selectivity Rating: 73
applications received: 843
% applicants accepted: 57
% acceptees attending: 17
Median LSAT: 152
LSAT Range (25th to 75th percentile): 145–154
Median undergrad GPA: 3.18
Application fee: $0
Regular application deadline: 8/15
Transfer students accepted: Yes
Evening division offered: No
Part-time accepted: No
CAS accepted: Yes

FINANCIAL FACTS

Annual tuition (in-state/out-of-state): $33,684
Books and supplies: $1,500
Fees (in-state/out-of-state): $250
Room & Board (on/off campus): $11,320/$11,320
Financial aid application deadline: 6/1
% first-year students receiving aid: 84
% all students receiving aid: 95
% of aid that is merit based: 26
% receiving scholarships: 61
Average grant: $21,097
Average loan: $34,226
Average total aid package: $45,587
Average debt: $94,824

EMPLOYMENT INFORMATION

Total 2012 JD Grads: 95
% grads employed nine months out: 81
Median starting salary: $50,000
employed full-time: 71
employed part-time: 2
employed bar required: 62
employed JD preferred: 8
employed professional/other: 3
pursuing advanced degree: 2
unemployed and seeking employment: 14
not seeking employment: 1
% grads employed by school: 0
State for bar exam: OH, FL, PA, NC, IN
Pass rate for first-time bar: 91
Prominent Alumni: Michael DeWine, Ohio Attorney General; Gregory Frost, U.S. District Judge Southern Ohio; Benjamin Brafman, Senior Partner at Brafman & Ross, New York City; Greg Miller, U.S. Attorney for Northwest Florida; Jessica Price Smith, U.S. Bankruptcy Court Northern District of Ohio.
Grads Employed by Field (%)
Academic: (0)
Business/Industry: (18)
Government: (29)
Judicial Clerkship: (3)
Military: (5)
Private Practice: (48)
Public Interest: (3)

THE PENNSYLVANIA STATE UNIVERSITY
The Dickinson School of Law

Lewis Katz Building, University Park, PA 16802
Admissions Phone: 814-867-1251 • *Admissions Fax:* 814-863-7274
Admissions E-Mail: admissions@law.psu.edu • *Website:* www.law.psu.edu

INSTITUTIONAL INFORMATION

Public/private: Public
Religious affiliation: No Affiliation
% faculty part-time: 21
% faculty female: 43
% faculty underrepresented minority: 13
Total faculty: 89

STUDENTS

Enrollment of law school: 617
% male/female: 58/42
% underrepresented minority: 14
% international: 2
Average age of entering class: 24

ACADEMICS

Academic Specialties:
Civil Procedure, Commercial, Constitutional, Corporation Securities, Criminal, Environmental, Government Services, Human Rights, International, Labor, Legal History, Legal Philosophy, Property, Taxation, Intellectual Property
Advanced Degrees Offered:
JD 3 years, LLM in Comparative Law 1 year
Combined Degrees Offered:
JD/Master of International Affairs; JD/Masters of Business Administration; JD/Master of Public Administration; JD/Masters of Environmental Pollution Control; JD/Master of Science in Information Systems; JD/MS or PhD - Forest Resources; JD/MA or PhD, Educational Theory & Policy; JD/ M.Ed. or - Educational Leadership; JD/M.Ed. or D.Ed. or Ph.D., Higher Education; JD/ Master of Science in Human Resources & Employment Relations.
Clinical program required: No
Legal writing course requirement: Yes
Legal methods course requirement: Yes
Legal research court requirement: Yes
Moot court requirement: No
Public interest law requirement: No

ADMISSIONS

Selectivity Rating: 89
applications received: 5,326
% applicants accepted: 29
% acceptees attending: 15
Median LSAT: 159
LSAT Range (25th to 75th percentile): 151–172
Median undergrad GPA: 3.6
Application fee: $60
Regular application deadline: 3/1
Transfer students accepted: Yes
Evening division offered: No
Part-time accepted: No
CAS accepted: Yes

FINANCIAL FACTS
Annual tuition (in-state/out-of-state): $35,928/$35,928
Books and supplies: $1,456
Fees (in-state/out-of-state): $888/$888
Room & Board (on/off campus): $22,300/$22,300
Financial aid application deadline: 3/1
% first-year students receiving aid: 95
% all students receiving aid: 92
% of aid that is merit based: 83
% receiving scholarships: 60
Average grant: $12,172
Average loan: $38,987
Average total aid package: $45,672
Average debt: $117,988

EMPLOYMENT INFORMATION
% grads employed nine months out: 78
State for bar exam: PA
Pass rate for first-time bar: 89
Employers Who Frequently Hire Grads: Dickinson graduates are hired by a variety of employers each year including national law firms, small firms, federal and state judges, government agencies, public interest organizations, and other entities.
Prominent Alumni: Hon. Thomas Ridge, Secretary of Homeland Security and PA Governor; Hon. Pedro Cortes, PA Secretary of the Commonwealth; Hon. D. Brooks Smith, Third Circuit Court of Appeals; Hon. Thomas Vanaskie, Third Circuit Court of Appeals; Hon. J. Michael Eakin, PA Supreme Court.
Grads Employed by Field (%)
Academic: (4)
Business/Industry: (23)
Government: (14)
Judicial Clerkship: (19)
Military: (1)
Private Practice: (31)
Public Interest: (3)

SAINT LOUIS UNIVERSITY
School of Law

100 North Tucker Blvd (as of August 1, 2013), St. Louis, MO 63101
Admissions Phone: 314-977-2800 • Admissions Fax: 314-977-1464
Admissions E-Mail: admissions@law.slu.edu • Website: law.slu.edu

INSTITUTIONAL INFORMATION
Public/private: Private
Religious affiliation: Roman Catholic
% faculty part-time: 0
% faculty female: 51
% faculty underrepresented minority: 13
Total faculty: 69

STUDENTS
Enrollment of law school: 205
% male/female: 48/52
% from out-of-state: 34
% part-time: 9
% underrepresented minority: 15

# of countries represented: 3
Average age of entering class: 25

ACADEMICS
Academic Specialties:
Criminal, Environmental, International, Labor, Property, Taxation, Intellectual Property
Advanced Degrees Offered:
LLM Health Law, 1 year full-time, 2 years part-time; LLM for Foreign Lawyers, 1 year full-time
Combined Degrees Offered:
JD/MBA, 3.5 years; JD/MA in Public Administration, 4 years; JD/MHA, 4 years; JD/MPH, 4 years, JD/PhD in Health Care Ethics, 4–6 years; JD/MSW, 4 years; JD/MA in Sociology in Criminal Justice, 4 years; JD/MA in Public Health/Health Policy, 4 years; JD/MA Accounting 4 years; JD/MS in Health Outcomes Research & Evaluation Sciences, 4 years
Clinical program required: No
Legal writing course requirement: Yes
Legal methods course requirement: Yes
Legal research court requirement: Yes
Moot court requirement: No
Public interest law requirement: No

ADMISSIONS
Selectivity Rating: 75
applications received: 1,237
% applicants accepted: 60
% acceptees attending: 28
Average LSAT: 155
Median LSAT: 156
LSAT Range (25th to 75th percentile): 151–159
Average undergrad GPA: 3.44
Median undergrad GPA: 3.45
Application fee: $55
Regular application deadline: 5/1
Transfer students accepted: Yes
Evening division offered: Yes
Part-time accepted: Yes
CAS accepted: Yes

FINANCIAL FACTS
Annual tuition (in-state/out-of-state): $36,440/$36,440
Books and supplies: $1,500
Fees (in-state/out-of-state): $445/$445
Room & Board (on/off campus): n/a/$10,380
Financial aid application deadline:
% first-year students receiving aid: 90
% all students receiving aid: 87
% receiving scholarships: 47
Average grant: $18,227
Average loan: $39,197
Average total aid package: $44,516
Average debt: $121,742

EMPLOYMENT INFORMATION
Total 2012 JD Grads: 276
% grads employed nine months out: 86
# employed full-time: 226
# employed part-time: 11
# employed bar required: 195
# employed JD preferred: 35
# employed professional/other: 6
# employed non-professional: 1
# pursuing advanced degree: 5
# unemployed and seeking employment: 14

not seeking employment: 20
% grads employed by school: 2
State for bar exam: MO
Pass rate for first-time bar: 93.6
Employers Who Frequently Hire Grads: Brown & James; Bryan Cave; Lewis, Rice & Fingersh; Thompson Coburn; Armstrong Teasdale, LLP; Greensfelder, Hemker & Gale; Evans & Dixon; Husch & Eppenberger; King & Spalding; Proskauer Rose; Missouri Attorney General; Missouri State Public Defender; Health and Human Services; Land of Lincoln Legal Assistance Foundation; Missouri Court of Appeals for the Eastern District; United States District Court, Eastern District of Missouri.
Prominent Alumni: Gary Rutledge, Vice President, Secretary and General Counsel of Anheuser-Busch Companies Inc.; Malcolm Harkins, Partner, Proskauer Rose; Ben Dogra, Co-Head, Creative Artists Agency (CAA) Football
Grads Employed by Field (%)
Academic: (1)
Business/Industry: (24)
Government: (14)
Judicial Clerkship: (5)
Private Practice: (46)
Public Interest: (10)

ST. MARY'S UNIVERSITY
School of Law

One Camino Santa Maria, San Antonio, TX 78228-8601
Admissions Phone: 866-639-5831 • ***Admissions Fax:***
Admissions E-Mail: lawadmissions@stmarytx.edu
Website: www.stmarytx.edu/law

INSTITUTIONAL INFORMATION
Public/private: Private
Religious affiliation: Roman Catholic
Student-faculty ratio: 22:1
% faculty part-time: 63
% faculty female: 39
% faculty underrepresented minority: 15
Total faculty: 82

STUDENTS
Enrollment of law school: 817
% male/female: 56/44
% from out-of-state: 10
% part-time: 24
% underrepresented minority: 35
% international: 1
Average age of entering class: 24

ACADEMICS
Academic Specialties:
Constitutional, Criminal, Human Rights, International
Advanced Degrees Offered:
LLM in International and Comparative Law for U.S. educated graduates; LLM in American Legal Studies for foreign educated graduates. (Each 1 year)

Combined Degrees Offered:
JD/MA International Relations; JD/MPA Public Administration; JD/MA English Language and Literature; JD/MA Theology; JD/MS Computer Science; JD/MS Engineering; JD/MBA Business Administration; JD/MA Communication Studies (all 3.5–4 years total)
Clinical program required: No
Legal writing course requirement: Yes
Legal methods course requirement: Yes
Legal research court requirement: Yes
Moot court requirement: Yes
Public interest law requirement: No

ADMISSIONS
Selectivity Rating: 78
applications received: 1,691
% applicants accepted: 53
% acceptees attending: 28
Median LSAT: 153
LSAT Range (25th to 75th percentile): 151–155
Median undergrad GPA: 3.10
Application fee: $55
Regular application deadline: 3/1
Regular notification: 4/1
Transfer students accepted: Yes
Evening division offered: Yes
Part-time accepted: Yes
CAS accepted: Yes

FINANCIAL FACTS
Annual tuition (in-state/out-of-state): $29,940/$29,940
Books and supplies: $1,500
Fees (in-state/out-of-state): $626/$626
Room & Board (on/off campus): $10,994/$10,994
Financial aid application deadline: 3/31
% first-year students receiving aid: 88
% all students receiving aid: 85
% of aid that is merit based: 7
% receiving scholarships: 27
Average grant: $6,728
Average loan: $20,859
Average total aid package: $33,388
Average debt: $111,758

EMPLOYMENT INFORMATION
Total 2012 JD Grads: 268
% grads employed nine months out: 86
Median starting salary: $56,000
employed full-time: 215
employed part-time: 15
employed bar required: 188
employed JD preferred: 28
employed professional/other: 14
pursuing advanced degree: 2
unemployed and seeking employment: 32
not seeking employment: 3
% grads employed by school: 1
State for bar exam: TX, FL, MO, OK, NM
Pass rate for first-time bar: 83
Employers Who Frequently Hire Grads: Bexar County District Attorney's Office; Fourth Court of Appeals; Cox Smith Matthew LLP; Texas Office of the Attorney General.

Prominent Alumni: John Cornyn, United States Senator from Texas; Charles Gonzalez, Congressman; Alma L. Lopez, Former Chief Justice of the Texas Court of Appeals; Thomas Mummert, U.S. Magistrate Judge; Nelson Wolff, Former Mayor of San Antonio.

Grads Employed by Field (%)
Academic: (1)
Business/Industry: (14)
Government: (13)
Judicial Clerkship: (3)
Military: (1)
Private Practice: (65)
Public Interest: (3)

FINANCIAL FACTS
Annual tuition (in-state/out-of-state): $4,466/$7,562
Books and supplies: $700
Room & Board: $6,000
Financial aid application deadline:
Average grant: $1
Average loan: $1

EMPLOYMENT INFORMATION
State for bar exam: TX
Pass rate for first-time bar: 68
Grads Employed by Field (%)
Government: (2)
Judicial Clerkship: (4)
Private Practice: (87)
Public Interest: (5)

TEXAS SOUTHERN UNIVERSITY
Thurgood Marshall School of Law

3100 Cleburne Avenue, Houston, TX 77004
Admissions Phone: 713-313-7114 • **Admissions Fax:**
Admissions E-Mail: lawadmit@tsulaw.edu • **Website:** www.tsulaw.edu

INSTITUTIONAL INFORMATION
Public/private: Public
Student-faculty ratio: 17:1
% faculty female: 20
% faculty underrepresented minority: 83
Total faculty: 35

STUDENTS
Enrollment of law school: 541
% male/female: 57/43
% underrepresented minority: 77

ACADEMICS
Academic Specialties:
 Commercial, Corporation Securities
Clinical program required: No
Legal writing course requirement: No
Legal methods course requirement: No
Legal research court requirement:
Moot court requirement:
Public interest law requirement:

ADMISSIONS
Selectivity Rating: 80
applications received: 1,460
% applicants accepted: 37
% acceptees attending: 49
Average LSAT: 141
LSAT Range (25th to 75th percentile): 138–144
Average undergrad GPA: 2.80
Application fee: $50
Regular application deadline: 4/1
Transfer students accepted: Yes
Evening division offered: No
Part-time accepted: No
CAS accepted: No

TEXAS WESLEYAN UNIVERSITY
School of Law

1515 Commerce Street, Office of Admissions, Fort Worth, TX 76102
Admissions Phone: 817-212-4040 • **Admissions Fax:** 817-212-4141
Admissions E-Mail: lawadmissions@law.txwes.edu • **Website:** law.txwes.edu

INSTITUTIONAL INFORMATION
Public/private: Private
Religious affiliation: Methodist
% faculty part-time: 39
% faculty female: 45
% faculty underrepresented minority: 18
Total faculty: 56

STUDENTS
Enrollment of law school: 236
% male/female: 59/41
% from out-of-state: 8
% part-time: 31
% underrepresented minority: 24
% international: 1
# of countries represented: 7
Average age of entering class: 25

ACADEMICS
Advanced Degrees Offered:
JD, 3 years, full-time; 4 years part-time.
Clinical program required: No
Legal writing course requirement: Yes
Legal methods course requirement: Yes
Legal research court requirement: Yes
Moot court requirement: Yes
Public interest law requirement: Yes

ADMISSIONS
Selectivity Rating: 81
applications received: 1,506
% applicants accepted: 43

% acceptees attending: 25
Average LSAT: 153
Median LSAT: 153
LSAT Range (25th to 75th percentile): 151–156
Average undergrad GPA: 3.21
Median undergrad GPA: 3.21
Application fee: $55
Regular application deadline: 3/31
Transfer students accepted: Yes
Evening division offered: Yes
Part-time accepted: Yes
CAS accepted: Yes

FINANCIAL FACTS
Annual tuition (in-state/out-of-state): $28,000/$28,000
Books and supplies: $1,800
Fees (in-state/out-of-state): $790/$790
Room & Board: $10,845
Financial aid application deadline:
% first-year students receiving aid: 90
% all students receiving aid: 89
% of aid that is merit based: 0
% receiving scholarships: 70
Average grant: $7,124
Average loan: $29,405
Average total aid package: $36,529
Average debt: $96,387

EMPLOYMENT INFORMATION
State for bar exam: TX, OK, NY, CA, NM
Pass rate for first-time bar: 87.8
Employers Who Frequently Hire Grads: Mid to small size private practice firms, district attorney's offices, government agencies, various corporations and businesses.
Prominent Alumni: Craig Watkins, Dallas County District Attorney; Carlos Cortez, Judge, 44th District of Dallas County; Susan Hawk, Judge, 291st Criminal District Court; Nancy Berger, Judge, 322nd District Family Court of Tarrant County; Phil King, State Representative, 61st District.

THOMAS JEFFERSON SCHOOL OF LAW
School of Law

1155 Island Avenue, San Diego, CA 92101
Admissions Phone: 619-297-9700 • **Admissions Fax:** 619-961-1300
Admissions E-Mail: admissions@tjsl.edu • **Website:** www.tjsl.edu

INSTITUTIONAL INFORMATION
Public/private: Private
Student-faculty ratio: 19:1
% faculty part-time: 49
% faculty female: 37
% faculty underrepresented minority: 7
Total faculty: 84

STUDENTS
Enrollment of law school: 440
% male/female: 63/37
% from out-of-state: 31
% part-time: 23
% underrepresented minority: 25
% international: 2
# of countries represented: 1
Average age of entering class: 26

ACADEMICS
Academic Specialties:
Civil Procedure, Commercial, Constitutional, Corporation Securities, Criminal, Environmental, Government Services, Human Rights, International, Labor, Property, Taxation, Intellectual Property
Advanced Degrees Offered:
 JD 3 years full-time; JD 4 years part-time
Combined Degrees Offered:
 JD/MBA with San Diego State University, 4 years
Clinical program required: No
Legal writing course requirement: Yes
Legal methods course requirement: No
Legal research court requirement: No
Moot court requirement: No
Public interest law requirement: No

ADMISSIONS
Selectivity Rating: 73
applications received: 2,697
% applicants accepted: 55
% acceptees attending: 30
Average LSAT: 150
Median LSAT: 151
LSAT Range (25th to 75th percentile): 139–167
Average undergrad GPA: 3.00
Median undergrad GPA: 3.00
Application fee: $50
                         Early application deadline: 12/1
Transfer students accepted: Yes
Evening division offered: Yes
Part-time accepted: Yes
CAS accepted: Yes

FINANCIAL FACTS
Annual tuition (in-state/out-of-state): $41,000
Books and supplies: $1,900
Fees (in-state/out-of-state): $1,730
Room & Board (on/off campus): $17,280/$17,280
Financial aid application deadline: 4/15
% first-year students receiving aid: 93
% all students receiving aid: 93
% of aid that is merit based: 9
% receiving scholarships: 49
Average grant: $15,047
Average loan: $51,533
Average total aid package: $57,480
Average debt: $153,000

EMPLOYMENT INFORMATION
Total 2012 JD Grads: 236
% grads employed nine months out: 61
Median starting salary: $60,000
employed full-time: 98
employed part-time: 39

employed bar required: 96
employed JD preferred: 18
employed professional/other: 17
employed non-professional: 6
pursuing advanced degree: 6
unemployed and seeking employment: 74
not seeking employment: 10
% grads employed by school: 0
State for bar exam: CA, NY, AZ, NJ, NV
Pass rate for first-time bar: 72.9
Employers Who Frequently Hire Grads: Various private law firms, corporations, government agencies, nonprofits and courts.
Prominent Alumni: Bonnie Dumanis, San Diego District Attorney; Duncan Hunter, Member of U.S. Congress; Roger Benitez, U.S. District Court, Southern District, CA; Mattias Luukkonen, DLA Piper US LLP; Dan Vrechek, Qualcomm.
Grads Employed by Field (%)
Academic: (1)
Business/Industry: (27)
Government: (9)
Judicial Clerkship: (7)
Military: (0)
Private Practice: (54)
Public Interest: (2)

UNIVERSITY OF BALTIMORE
School of Law

1420 North Charles Street, Baltimore, MD 21201
Admissions Phone: 410-837-5809 • *Admissions Fax:* 410-837-4450
Admissions E-Mail: lwadmiss@ubmail.ubalt.edu • *Website:* law.ubalt.edu

INSTITUTIONAL INFORMATION
Public/private: Public
% faculty part-time: 60
% faculty female: 37
% faculty underrepresented minority: 11
Total faculty: 190

STUDENTS
Enrollment of law school: 1,098
% male/female: 50/50
% from out-of-state: 15
% part-time: 33
% underrepresented minority: 16
% international: 1
# of countries represented: 3
Average age of entering class: 25

ACADEMICS
Academic Specialties:
Criminal, Government Services, International, Property, Intellectual Property
Advanced Degrees Offered:
LLM in Taxation; LLM in Law of the United States
Combined Degrees Offered:
JD/MBA, JD/MS in Criminal Justice, JD/MPA, JD/PhD in Policy Science in conjuction with the Univ. of Maryland at Baltimore, JD/LLM in Taxation, JD/MS in Negotiation and Conflict Management. Most combined degrees add 1 year of study.
Clinical program required: No

Legal writing course requirement: Yes
Legal methods course requirement: Yes
Legal research court requirement: Yes
Moot court requirement: No
Public interest law requirement: No

ADMISSIONS
Selectivity Rating: 83
applications received: 1,619
% applicants accepted: 44
% acceptees attending: 33
Average LSAT: 156
Median LSAT: 156
LSAT Range (25th to 75th percentile): 152–159
Average undergrad GPA: 3.24
Median undergrad GPA: 3.31
Application fee: $60
Regular application deadline: 7/30
Transfer students accepted: Yes
Evening division offered: Yes
Part-time accepted: Yes
CAS accepted: Yes
International Students
  TOEFL recommended of international students

FINANCIAL FACTS
Annual tuition (in-state/out-of-state): $23,928/$36,030
Books and supplies: $1,600
Fees (in-state/out-of-state): $1,870/$1,870
Room & Board: $12,000
Financial aid application deadline: 4/1
% first-year students receiving aid: 88
% all students receiving aid: 86
% receiving scholarships: 20
Average grant: $16,000
Average loan: $17,062
Average total aid package: $36,842
Average debt: $105,028

EMPLOYMENT INFORMATION
Total 2012 JD Grads: 298
% grads employed nine months out: 91
Median starting salary: $45,000
employed full-time: 207
employed part-time: 46
employed bar required: 150
employed JD preferred: 81
employed professional/other: 28
employed non-professional: 7
pursuing advanced degree: 7
unemployed and seeking employment: 16
not seeking employment: 2
% grads employed by school: 0
State for bar exam: MD
Pass rate for first-time bar: 88
Employers Who Frequently Hire Grads: Non-profit Organizations; DLA Piper, Venable LLP, Miles & Stockbridge, Ober Kaler, Gordon Feinblatt, Ballard Spahr, Whiteford Taylor, Saul Ewing, Office of the Public Defender, Office of the State's Attorney, Department of Justice, McGuire Woods, Public Interest Organizations.
Prominent Alumni: William Donald Schaefer, Former Governor of Maryland; Catherine O'Malley, Judge, First Lady of Maryland; C.A. Dutch Ruppersberger, US Congress, House of Representatives; Joseph Curran, Former Attorney General of Maryland; Peter Angelos, Owner, Baltimore Orioles.

Grads Employed by Field (%)
Academic: (3)
Business/Industry: (17)
Government: (1509)
Judicial Clerkship: (20)
Military: (1)
Private Practice: (37)
Public Interest: (3)

UNIVERSITY OF DETROIT MERCY

School of Law

651 East Jefferson Avenue, Detroit, MI 48226
Admissions Phone: 313-596-0264 • *Admissions Fax:* 313-596-0280
Admissions E-Mail: udmlawao@udmercy.edu
Website: www.law.udmercy.edu

INSTITUTIONAL INFORMATION
Public/private: Private
Religious affiliation: Roman Catholic
% faculty part-time: 47
% faculty female: 33
% faculty underrepresented minority: 1
Total faculty: 77

STUDENTS
Enrollment of law school: 616
% male/female: 54/46
% from out-of-state: 42
% part-time: 18
% underrepresented minority: 11
% international: 33
# of countries represented: 2
Average age of entering class: 25

ACADEMICS
Academic Specialties:
 Commercial, Human Rights, International, Labor, Taxation, Intellectual Property
Advanced Degrees Offered:
JD, 3 years full-time; JD/MBA, 4 years full-time; Canadian & American Dual
JD, 3 years full-time
Combined Degrees Offered:
JD/MBA, 4 years full-time;Canadian & American Dual JD, 3 years full-time; JD/
LED 4-5 years full-time
Clinical program required: Yes
Legal writing course requirement: Yes
Legal methods course requirement: Yes
Legal research court requirement: Yes
Moot court requirement: Yes
Public interest law requirement: Yes

ADMISSIONS
Selectivity Rating: 81
applications received: 1,250
% applicants accepted: 48
% acceptees attending: 32

Median LSAT: 150
LSAT Range (25th to 75th percentile): 146–157
Median undergrad GPA: 3.09
Application fee: $50
Regular application deadline: 4/15
Transfer students accepted: Yes
Evening division offered: Yes
Part-time accepted: Yes
CAS accepted: Yes

FINANCIAL FACTS
Annual tuition (in-state/out-of-state): $38,100/$38,100
Books and supplies: $10,684
Fees (in-state/out-of-state): $80/$80
Room & Board: $11,853
Financial aid application deadline: 4/1
% of aid that is merit based: 100
% receiving scholarships: 26
Average debt: $130,166

EMPLOYMENT INFORMATION
State for bar exam: MI
Pass rate for first-time bar: 67.1
Employers Who Frequently Hire Grads: Private sector employers, including
local firms (Dykema Gossett PLLC; Butzel Long, Plunkett Cooney PC). Public
sector employers, including state and federal judges and county prosecutors
offices.

UNIVERSITY OF LA VERNE

College of Law

320 East D Street, Ontario, CA 91764
Admissions Phone: (877) 858-4529 • *Admissions Fax:* (909) 460-2082
Admissions E-Mail: lawadm@laverne.edu • *Website:* law.laverne.edu

INSTITUTIONAL INFORMATION
Public/private: Private
Student-faculty ratio: 16:1
% faculty part-time: 46
% faculty female: 39
% faculty underrepresented minority: 27
Total faculty: 41

STUDENTS
Enrollment of law school: 425
% male/female: 55/45
% part-time: 27
% underrepresented minority: 40
% international: 3
Average age of entering class: 27

ACADEMICS
Advanced Degrees Offered:
JD, 3 years, full-time, 4 years part-time
Combined Degrees Offered:
JD/MBA, JD/MPA, 4 years
Clinical program required: No
Legal writing course requirement: Yes
Legal methods course requirement: Yes

Legal research court requirement: Yes
Moot court requirement: No
Public interest law requirement: No

ADMISSIONS
Selectivity Rating: 79
applications received: 1,231
% applicants accepted: 45
% acceptees attending: 24
Average LSAT: 153
Median LSAT: 153
LSAT Range (25th to 75th percentile): 150–155
Average undergrad GPA: 3.06
Median undergrad GPA: 3.07
Application fee: $50
Transfer students accepted: Yes
Evening division offered: Yes
Part-time accepted: Yes
CAS accepted: Yes
International Students
 TOEFL recommended of international students

FINANCIAL FACTS
Annual tuition (in-state/out-of-state): $39,900
Books and supplies: $1,656
Fees (in-state/out-of-state): $862
Room & Board (on/off campus): $18,225/$18,225
Financial aid application deadline: 3/2

EMPLOYMENT INFORMATION
% grads employed nine months out: 60
Median starting salary: $61,002
State for bar exam: CA, TX, AZ, UT, MT
Pass rate for first-time bar: 53
Employers Who Frequently Hire Grads: Private law firms, businesses, government agencies, public interest organizations.
Prominent Alumni: Thomas M. Finn, HSC Regional Director (S.Region), Dublin, Ireland; The Honorable Dennis Aichroth, Judge, Superior Court, Los Angeles, CA; The Honorable Jean Pfeiffer Leonard, Judge, Juvenile Court, Riverside, CA; Eileen M. Teichert, City Attorney for the City of Sacramento, CA; James J. Manning, Jr., Senior Attorney, Reid & Hellyer, Riverside, CA.
Grads Employed by Field (%)
Academic: (3)
Business/Industry: (26)
Government: (7)
Judicial Clerkship: (2)
Military: (0)
Private Practice: (62)
Public Interest: (0)

UNIVERSITY OF LOUISVILLE
Louis D. Brandeis School of Law

University of Louisville, Wyatt Hall - Room 108, Louisville, KY 40292
Admissions Phone: 502-852-6364 • **Admissions Fax:** 502-852-8971
Admissions E-Mail: lawadmissions@louisville.edu
Website: www.law.louisville.edu

INSTITUTIONAL INFORMATION
Public/private: Public
Student-faculty ratio: 13:1
% faculty part-time: 0
% faculty female: 40
% faculty underrepresented minority: 8
Total faculty: 35

STUDENTS
Enrollment of law school: 400
% male/female: 59/41
% from out-of-state: 21
% part-time: 7
% underrepresented minority: 5
% international: 1
# of countries represented: 2
Average age of entering class: 26

ACADEMICS
Academic Specialties:
Civil Procedure, Commercial, Constitutional, Corporation Securities, Criminal, Environmental, International, Labor, Legal Philosophy, Property, Taxation, Intellectual Property
Advanced Degrees Offered:
 JD, 3 years, full-time, 4–5 years part-time
Combined Degrees Offered:
Dual Degree Programs: JD/MBA, JD/MSSW, JD/MDiv, JD/MA in Humanities, JD/MA in Poli Sci, JD/MA in Urban Planning; JD/MA Bioethics (4–5 years)
Clinical program required: Yes
Legal writing course requirement: Yes
Legal methods course requirement: Yes
Legal research court requirement: Yes
Moot court requirement: Yes
Public interest law requirement: Yes

ADMISSIONS
Selectivity Rating: 87
applications received: 1,495
% applicants accepted: 31
% acceptees attending: 28
Median LSAT: 156
LSAT Range (25th to 75th percentile): 152–158
Median undergrad GPA: 3,42
Application fee: $50
Regular application deadline: 3/15
Early application deadline: 3/15
Transfer students accepted: Yes
Evening division offered: No
Part-time accepted: Yes
CAS accepted: Yes

FINANCIAL FACTS

Annual tuition (in-state/out-of-state): $16,536/$31,948
Books and supplies: $1,000
Room & Board (on/off campus): $8,370/$8,370
Financial aid application deadline: 3/15
% first-year students receiving aid: 85
% all students receiving aid: 85
% of aid that is merit based: 100
% receiving scholarships: 75
Average grant: $10,000
Average loan: $25,488
Average total aid package: $35,488

EMPLOYMENT INFORMATION

% grads employed nine months out: 98
Median starting salary: $63,000
State for bar exam: KY, IN, TN, OH
Pass rate for first-time bar: 89
Employers Who Frequently Hire Grads: Frost, Brown & Todd; Dinsmore & Shohl; Greenebaum, Doll & McDonald; Wyatt, Tarrant & Combs; Stites & Harbison
Prominent Alumni: Chris Dodd, US Senator; Ron Mazzoli, Former US Congressman; Joseph Lambert, Chief Justice of Kentucky; Stanley Chauvin, Former ABA President; Ernie Allen, Director, National Center for Missing & Exploited.
Grads Employed by Field (%)
Academic: (5)
Business/Industry: (17)
Government: (17)
Judicial Clerkship: (7)
Military: (0)
Private Practice: (54)
Public Interest: (7)

UNIVERSITY OF MONTANA
School of Law

University of Montana School of Law, Room 181, Missoula, MT 59812
Admissions Phone: 406-243-2698 • **Admissions Fax:** 406-243-6601
Admissions E-Mail: lori.freeman@umontana.edu
Website: www.umt.edu/law

INSTITUTIONAL INFORMATION

Public/private: Public
% faculty female: 40
% faculty underrepresented minority: 12
Total faculty: 25

STUDENTS

Enrollment of law school: 247
% male/female: 57/43
% part-time: 0
% underrepresented minority: 10
% international: 1
# of countries represented: 3
Average age of entering class: 28

ACADEMICS

Academic Specialties:
Environmental, Taxation
Advanced Degrees Offered:
JD, 3 years
Combined Degrees Offered:
JD/MPA, 4 years; JD/MBA, 4 years; JD/MS-EVST, 4 years
Clinical program required: Yes
Legal writing course requirement: Yes
Legal methods course requirement: Yes
Legal research court requirement: Yes
Moot court requirement: No
Public interest law requirement: Yes

ADMISSIONS

Selectivity Rating: 78
applications received: 325
% applicants accepted: 58
% acceptees attending: 43
Average LSAT: 155
Median LSAT: 154
LSAT Range (25th to 75th percentile): 152–158
Average undergrad GPA: 3.34
Median undergrad GPA: 3.49
Application fee: $60
Regular application deadline: 3/15
Early application deadline: 2/15
Transfer students accepted: Yes
Evening division offered: No
Part-time accepted: No
CAS accepted: Yes

FINANCIAL FACTS

Annual tuition (in-state/out-of-state): $11,250/$27,917
Books and supplies: $1,200
Room & Board (on/off campus): $13,590/$13,590
Financial aid application deadline: 3/1
% first-year students receiving aid: 36
% all students receiving aid: 43
% of aid that is merit based: 89
% receiving scholarships: 43
Average grant: $2,500
Average loan: $4,077
Average total aid package: $3,485
Average debt: $64,539

EMPLOYMENT INFORMATION

Total 2012 JD Grads: 82
% grads employed nine months out: 78
Median starting salary: $50,000
% job accepting grads providing useable salary information: 84
# employed full-time: 60
# employed part-time: 4
# employed bar required: 53
# employed JD preferred: 4
# employed professional/other: 5
# employed non-professional: 2
# pursuing advanced degree: 6
# unemployed and seeking employment: 9
# not seeking employment: 2
% grads employed by school: 0
State for bar exam: MT, AK, CO, ID, WA
Pass rate for first-time bar: 88

Employers Who Frequently Hire Grads: Church, Harris, Johnson & Williams; Garlington, Lohn & Robinson; Milodragovich, Dale, Steinbrenner & Nygren; Moulton, Bellingham, Longo and Mather; Holland & Hart; Crowley Fleck; Smith, Walsh, Clark and Gregoire; MT Sup. Ct.; MT Dist. Cts.; MT Fed. Dist. Cts.

Prominent Alumni: Hon. Justin Miller, U. S. Court of Appeals for the District of Columbia Cir; Dean USC School of Law & Duke Law School; Hon. James R. Browning, U. S. Court of Appeals for the 9th Cir.; Clerk of U. S. Supreme Court; Hon. William J. Jameson, U. S. District Court, Montana Div.; Past President of the American Bar Association; Gov. Marc F. Racicot, Governor for State of Montana; Attorney General for State of Montana; Denise Juneau, 1st Native American state-wide elected official, Montana Superintendent of Public Instruction.

Grads Employed by Field (%)
Academic: (0)
Business/Industry: (9)
Government: (10)
Judicial Clerkship: (20)
Military: (2)
Private Practice: (35)
Public Interest: (5)

VALPARAISO UNIVERSITY
School of Law

Wesemann Hall, Valparaiso, IN 46383
Admissions Phone: 888-825-7652 • **Admissions Fax:** 219-465-7808
Admissions E-Mail: valpolaw@valpo.edu • **Website:** www.valpo.edu/law

INSTITUTIONAL INFORMATION
Public/private: Private
Religious affiliation: Lutheran
Student-faculty ratio: 17:1
% faculty part-time: 50
% faculty female: 42
% faculty underrepresented minority: 6
Total faculty: 50

STUDENTS
Enrollment of law school: 523
% male/female: 55/45
% from out-of-state: 68
% part-time: 8
% underrepresented minority: 12
% international: 2
# of countries represented: 4
Average age of entering class: 24

ACADEMICS
Academic Specialties:
Civil Procedure, Commercial, Constitutional, Corporation Securities, Criminal, Environmental, Government Services, Human Rights, International, Labor, Legal History, Legal Philosophy, Property, Intellectual Property

Advanced Degrees Offered:
JD, 3 years, full-time, 5 years part-time; LLM, 1 year, full-time

Combined Degrees Offered:
All Dual Degree programs take 4 years; JD/MBA, JD/CMHC, JD/PSY, JD/MA International Commerce and Policy, JD/MA Sports Administration, JD/MALS-Create your own program

Clinical program required: No
Legal writing course requirement: Yes
Legal methods course requirement: Yes
Legal research court requirement: Yes
Moot court requirement: No
Public interest law requirement: Yes

ADMISSIONS
Selectivity Rating: 86
 # applications received: 2,589
% applicants accepted: 30
% acceptees attending: 22
Average LSAT: 151
LSAT Range (25th to 75th percentile): 144–162
Average undergrad GPA: 3.31
Application fee: $60
Regular application deadline: 6/1
Transfer students accepted: Yes
Evening division offered: No
Part-time accepted: Yes
CAS accepted: Yes

FINANCIAL FACTS
Annual tuition (in-state/out-of-state): $28,250
Books and supplies: $2,000
Fees (in-state/out-of-state): $612
Room & Board (on/off campus): $7,300/$7,300
Financial aid application deadline: 4/1
% first-year students receiving aid: 90
% all students receiving aid: 95
% of aid that is merit based: 35
% receiving scholarships: 34
Average grant: $15,214
Average loan: $18,500
Average total aid package: $39,850
Average debt: $56,000

EMPLOYMENT INFORMATION
Median starting salary: $56,000
State for bar exam: IN, IL, MI, WI, GA
Pass rate for first-time bar: 84
Employers Who Frequently Hire Grads: These statistics may be reviewed on www.valpo.edu/law or you may contact our Career Planning Office at 219-465-7814.

Prominent Alumni: Stephan Todd, VP Law & Environment US Steel Corporation; Cornell Boggs, VP & General Counsel, Tyco Plastics & Adhesives; Honorable Nancy Vaidik, Justice, Indiana Court of Appeals; Koreen Ryan, Senior Council, South Asia McDonald's Corporation; Honorable Robert Rucker, Justice, Supreme Court of Indiana.

Grads Employed by Field (%)
Academic: (1)
Business/Industry: (16)
Government: (12)
Judicial Clerkship: (4)
Military: (1)
Private Practice: (63)
Public Interest: (2)

WESTERN NEW ENGLAND UNIVERSITY

School of Law

1215 Wilbraham Road, Springfield, MA 01119
Admissions Phone: 413-782-1406 • **Admissions Fax:** 413-796-2067
Admissions E-Mail: admissions@law.wne.edu • **Website:** www.law.wne.edu

INSTITUTIONAL INFORMATION

Public/private: Private
% faculty part-time: 14
% faculty female: 38
% faculty underrepresented minority: 10
Total faculty: 48

STUDENTS

Enrollment of law school: 365
% male/female: 52/48
% from out-of-state: 67
% part-time: 29
% underrepresented minority: 19
# of countries represented: 2
Average age of entering class: 26

ACADEMICS

Academic Specialties:
Criminal, International
Advanced Degrees Offered:
Western New England University School of Law offers classes towards an LLM in Estate Planning and Elder Law. The programs can be completed over 1, 2 or 3 years. The School of Law also offers classes toward an LLM in Closely Held Business. The program can be completed in 2 or 3 years. Both programs are offered entirely online.
Combined Degrees Offered:
JD/Master of Regional Planning with University of Masssachusetts, 4 years total; JD/Masters of Social Work with Springfield College, 4 years total; JD/Masters of Business Administration with Western New England University, as short as 3 years or as long as 4 years; JD/Masters of Accounting with Western New England College, 4 years total.
Clinical program required: No
Legal writing course requirement: Yes
Legal methods course requirement: No
Legal research court requirement: Yes
Moot court requirement: Yes
Public interest law requirement: No

ADMISSIONS

Selectivity Rating: 68
 # applications received: 863
% applicants accepted: 76
% acceptees attending: 12
Average LSAT: 151
Median LSAT: 150
LSAT Range (25th to 75th percentile): 147–152
Average undergrad GPA: 3.11
Median undergrad GPA: 3.14
Application fee: $50
Transfer students accepted: Yes
Evening division offered: Yes

Part-time accepted: Yes
CAS accepted: Yes

FINANCIAL FACTS

Annual tuition (in-state/out-of-state): $38,116
Books and supplies: $1,600
Fees (in-state/out-of-state): $1,458
Room & Board (on/off campus): $14,070/$14,070
Financial aid application deadline:
% first-year students receiving aid: 99
% all students receiving aid: 97
% receiving scholarships: 72
Average grant: $15,994
Average loan: $39,137
Average total aid package: $51,938
Average debt: $118,900

EMPLOYMENT INFORMATION

Total 2012 JD Grads: 160
 # employed full-time: 102
 # employed part-time: 21
 # employed bar required: 57
 # employed JD preferred: 43
 # employed professional/other: 13
 # employed non-professional: 10
 # pursuing advanced degree: 5
 # unemployed and seeking employment: 25
 # not seeking employment: 2
% grads employed by school: 0
State for bar exam: CT, MA, NY, NJ, MD
Pass rate for first-time bar: 72.2
Employers Who Frequently Hire Grads: Law firms (e.g. Shatz, Schwartz & Fentin, Halloran & Sage; Murtha Cullina; Shipman & Goodwin, Bacon & Wilson) Local District Attorney offices and Public Defender offices.
Prominent Alumni: Lois Lerner, Director, IRS; Timothy Murray, Lt. Governor, Massachusetts.
Grads Employed by Field (%)
Academic: (0)
Business/Industry: (20)
Government: (16)
Judicial Clerkship: (6)
Military: (0)
Private Practice: (31)
Public Interest: (4)

WESTERN STATE COLLEGE OF LAW AT ARGOSY UNIVERSITY

1111 North State College Boulevard, Fullerton, CA 92831
Admissions Phone: 714-459-1101 • **Admissions Fax:** 714-441-1748
Admissions E-Mail: adm@wsulaw.edu • **Website:** www.wsulaw.edu

INSTITUTIONAL INFORMATION
Public/private: Private
% faculty part-time: 44
% faculty female: 44
% faculty underrepresented minority: 31
Total faculty: 36

STUDENTS
Enrollment of law school: 470
% male/female: 51/49
% from out-of-state: 4
% part-time: 32
% underrepresented minority: 40
% international: 2
# of countries represented: 4
Average age of entering class: 27

ACADEMICS
Academic Specialties:
Criminal
Advanced Degrees Offered:
JD, 3 years, full-time, 4 years, part-time
Clinical program required: No
Legal writing course requirement: Yes
Legal methods course requirement: Yes
Legal research court requirement: Yes
Moot court requirement: Yes
Public interest law requirement: No

ADMISSIONS
Selectivity Rating: 73
applications received: 1,408
% applicants accepted: 54
% acceptees attending: 19
Average LSAT: 152
Median LSAT: 151
LSAT Range (25th to 75th percentile): 149–155
Average undergrad GPA: 3.09
Median undergrad GPA: 3.13
Application fee: $60
Early application deadline: 4/1
Early application notification: 4/1
Transfer students accepted: Yes
Evening division offered: Yes
Part-time accepted: Yes
CAS accepted: Yes

FINANCIAL FACTS
Annual tuition (in-state/out-of-state): $39,200/$39,200
Books and supplies: $2,400
Fees (in-state/out-of-state): $400/$400
Room & Board: $10,669

Financial aid application deadline:
% first-year students receiving aid: 98
% all students receiving aid: 93
% of aid that is merit based: 23
% receiving scholarships: 60
Average grant: $14,733
Average loan: $37,185
Average total aid package: $41,247
Average debt: $98,968

EMPLOYMENT INFORMATION
Total 2012 JD Grads: 83
% grads employed nine months out: 63
Median starting salary: $55,000
% job accepting grads providing useable salary information: 69
# employed full-time: 41
# employed part-time: 7
# employed bar required: 31
# employed JD preferred: 9
# employed professional/other: 2
# employed non-professional: 5
# pursuing advanced degree: 0
# unemployed and seeking employment: 23
# not seeking employment: 4
% grads employed by school: 0
State for bar exam: CA, AZ, NY, VA, UT
Pass rate for first-time bar: 79
Employers Who Frequently Hire Grads: Small-sized law firms, district attorneys, public defenders, corporations, state governments, federal governments.
Prominent Alumni: Lucetta Dunn, CEO, Orange County Business Council; George Gascon, District Attorney of San Francisco County; Kevin Calcagnie, Partner, Robinson, Calagnie, Robinson, Shapiro & Davis; Craig Robison, Supervising Judge, Orange County Sup. Court; John Montevideo, President, Consumer Attorneys of California.
Grads Employed by Field (%)
Business/Industry: (21)
Government: (4)
Judicial Clerkship: (0)
Military: (2)
Private Practice: (71)
Public Interest: (2)

CAL NORTHERN
School of Law

1395 Ridgewood Drive, Suite 100, Chico, CA 95973
Admissions Phone: *530-891-6900* • **Admissions Fax:** *530-891-3429*
Admissions E-Mail: *info@calnorthern.edu* • **Website:** *www.calnorthern.edu*

INSTITUTIONAL INFORMATION
Public/private: Private
Student-faculty ratio: 4:1
% faculty part-time: 100
% faculty female: 28
Total faculty: 18

STUDENTS
Enrollment of law school: 60
% part-time: 100
Average age of entering class: 32

ACADEMICS
Advanced Degrees Offered:
JD only, 4 year program
Clinical program required: No
Legal writing course requirement: Yes
Legal methods course requirement: Yes
Legal research court requirement: Yes
Moot court requirement: Yes
Public interest law requirement: No

ADMISSIONS
Selectivity Rating: 74
 # applications received: 29
% applicants accepted: 72
% acceptees attending: 100
Average LSAT: 145
Average undergrad GPA: 3.03
Application fee: $50
Regular application deadline: 6/1
Regular notification: 7/3
Transfer students accepted: Yes
Evening division offered: Yes
Part-time accepted: Yes
CAS accepted: No

FINANCIAL FACTS
Annual tuition (in-state/out-of-state): $7,920
Books and supplies: $800
Fees (in-state/out-of-state): $115
Average grant: $250
Average loan: $8,000

EMPLOYMENT INFORMATION
% grads employed nine months out: 100
State for bar exam: CA
Pass rate for first-time bar: 67
Prominent Alumni: Rick Keene, California State Assemblyman.

EMPIRE COLLEGE
School of Law

3035 Cleveland Avenue, Santa Rosa, CA 95403
Admissions Phone: *707-546-4000* • **Admissions Fax:** *707-284-2814*
Admissions E-Mail: *spatel@empirecollege.com* • **Website:** *www.empcol.edu*

INSTITUTIONAL INFORMATION
Public/private: Private
Religious affiliation: No Affiliation
Student-faculty ratio: 3:1
% faculty part-time: 100
% faculty female: 22
Total faculty: 59

STUDENTS
Enrollment of law school: 128
% part-time: 100
Average age of entering class: 38

ACADEMICS
Academic Specialties:
Civil Procedure, Constitutional, Criminal, Environmental, Legal History, Property, Intellectual Property
Clinical program required: No
Legal writing course requirement: Yes
Legal methods course requirement: No
Legal research court requirement: Yes
Moot court requirement: Yes
Public interest law requirement: No

ADMISSIONS
Selectivity Rating: 60*
 # applications received: 79
Average LSAT: 25
LSAT Range (25th to 75th percentile): 20–96
Average undergrad GPA: 2.95
Application fee: $50
Transfer students accepted: Yes
Evening division offered: Yes
Part-time accepted: Yes
CAS accepted: No

FINANCIAL FACTS
Annual tuition (in-state/out-of-state): $12,255
Books and supplies: $400
Fees (in-state/out-of-state): $223

EMPLOYMENT INFORMATION
State for bar exam: CA
Pass rate for first-time bar: 44
Employers Who Frequently Hire Grads:
Office of the District Attorney, Public Defender's office, Private, Business
Prominent Alumni: Jeanne Buckley, Superior Court Commissioner (ret.); Raima Ballinger, Judge, Sonoma Co. Superior Court; Francisca Tisher, Judge, Napa Co. Superior Court; Lawrence E. Ornell, Juvenile Superior Court Commissioner; Ron Brown, Judge, Mendocino Co. Superior Court.

Grads Employed by Field (%)
Business/Industry: (12)
Government: (22)
Private Practice: (58)

GLENDALE UNIVERSITY
College of Law

220 North Glendale Avenue, Glendale, CA 91206
Admissions Phone: 818-247-0770 • **Admissions Fax:** 818-247-0872
Admissions E-Mail: admissions@glendalelaw.edu
Website: www.glendalelaw.edu

INSTITUTIONAL INFORMATION
Public/private: Private
Religious affiliation: No Affiliation
Student-faculty ratio: 25:1

STUDENTS
Enrollment of law school: 130
% part-time: 100
Average age of entering class: 32

ACADEMICS
Advanced Degrees Offered:
Juris Doctor, 4 years
Clinical program required: No
Legal writing course requirement: Yes
Legal methods course requirement: Yes
Legal research court requirement: Yes
Moot court requirement: Yes
Public interest law requirement: No

ADMISSIONS
Selectivity Rating: 81
applications received: 140
% applicants accepted: 49
% acceptees attending: 71
Average LSAT: 145
Average undergrad GPA: 3.0
Application fee: $65
Transfer students accepted: Yes
Evening division offered: Yes
Part-time accepted: Yes
CAS accepted: Yes

EMPLOYMENT INFORMATION
State for bar exam: CA
Pass rate for first-time bar: 50

HUMPHREYS COLLEGE
School of Law

6650 Inglewood Avenue, Stockton, CA 95207
Admissions Phone: 209-478-0800 • **Admissions Fax:** 209-478-8721
Admissions E-Mail: selopez@humphreys.edu
Website: www.humphreys.edu/law

INSTITUTIONAL INFORMATION
Public/private: Private
Student-faculty ratio: 6:1
% faculty part-time: 83
% faculty female: 17
% faculty underrepresented minority: 0
Total faculty: 12

STUDENTS
Enrollment of law school: 60
% from out-of-state: 0
% part-time: 100
% international: 0
Average age of entering class: 33

ACADEMICS
Clinical program required: No
Legal writing course requirement: No
Legal methods course requirement: Yes

ADMISSIONS
Selectivity Rating: 73
applications received: 52
% applicants accepted: 62
% acceptees attending: 59
Average LSAT: 149
Average undergrad GPA: 2.8
Application fee: $20
Regular application deadline: 6/1
Transfer students accepted: Yes
Evening division offered: Yes
Part-time accepted: Yes
CAS accepted: No

FINANCIAL FACTS
Annual tuition (in-state/out-of-state): $7,062
Books and supplies: $650
Fees (in-state/out-of-state): $0
% first-year students receiving aid: 21
% all students receiving aid: 66
% receiving scholarships: 0
Average grant: $0
Average loan: $14,658
Average total aid package: $14,658
Average debt: $48,000

EMPLOYMENT INFORMATION
State for bar exam: CA
Pass rate for first-time bar: 54
Employers Who Frequently Hire Grads:
D.A. offices; Police Departments

Grads Employed by Field (%)
Academic: (5)
Business/Industry: (5)
Government: (30)
Private Practice: (60)

JOHN F. KENNEDY UNIVERSITY

School of Law

100 Ellinwood Way, Pleasant Hill, CA 94523
Admissions Phone: 925-969-3330 • *Admissions Fax:* 925-969-3331
Admissions E-Mail: law@jfku.edu • *Website:* www.jfku.edu/law

INSTITUTIONAL INFORMATION
Public/private: Private
Student-faculty ratio: 30:1
% faculty part-time: 94
% faculty female: 54
Total faculty: 54

STUDENTS
Enrollment of law school: 154
% male/female: 43/57
% part-time: 6
# of countries represented: 1
Average age of entering class: 37

ACADEMICS
Clinical program required: No
Legal writing course requirement: Yes
Legal methods course requirement: Yes
Legal research court requirement: Yes
Moot court requirement: No
Public interest law requirement: No

ADMISSIONS
Selectivity Rating: 81
applications received: 122
% applicants accepted: 43
% acceptees attending: 43
Average LSAT: 148
Average undergrad GPA: 3.03
Application fee: $75
Regular application deadline: 7/1
Transfer students accepted: Yes
Evening division offered: Yes
Part-time accepted: Yes
CAS accepted: Yes

FINANCIAL FACTS
Annual tuition (in-state/out-of-state): $9,920
Books and supplies: $1,540
Fees (in-state/out-of-state): $198
% first-year students receiving aid: 70
% all students receiving aid: 70

% of aid that is merit based: 1
% receiving scholarships: 0
Average grant: $0
Average loan: $18,500
Average total aid package: $18,500
Average debt: $70,000

EMPLOYMENT INFORMATION
State for bar exam: CA
Pass rate for first-time bar: 45

LINCOLN LAW SCHOOL OF SACRAMENTO

3140 J Street, Sacramento, CA 95816
Admissions Phone: 916-446-1275 • *Admissions Fax:* 916-446-5641
Admissions E-Mail: info@lincolnlaw.edu • *Website:* www.lincolnlaw.edu

INSTITUTIONAL INFORMATION
Public/private: Private
Student-faculty ratio: 40:1
% faculty part-time: 100
% faculty female: 20
% faculty underrepresented minority: 10
Total faculty: 25

STUDENTS
Enrollment of law school: 275
% from out-of-state: 0
% part-time: 100
% international: 0
Average age of entering class: 35

ACADEMICS
Academic Specialties:
Civil Procedure, Commercial, Constitutional, Corporation Securities, Criminal, Environmental, Government Services, Labor, Legal History, Legal Philosophy, Property, Taxation, Intellectual Property
Advanced Degrees Offered:
JD, 4 year
Clinical program required: No
Legal writing course requirement: Yes
Legal methods course requirement: Yes
Legal research court requirement: Yes
Moot court requirement: Yes
Public interest law requirement: No

ADMISSIONS
Selectivity Rating: 72
applications received: 150
% applicants accepted: 70
% acceptees attending: 90
Average LSAT: 145
LSAT Range (25th to 75th percentile): 8–86
Average undergrad GPA: 2.8
Application fee: $30
Transfer students accepted: Yes

Evening division offered: Yes
Part-time accepted: Yes
CAS accepted: Yes

FINANCIAL FACTS
Annual tuition (in-state/out-of-state): $7,000
Books and supplies: $500
Room & Board(on/off campus): $6,000
Financial aid application deadline: 6/1
% first-year students receiving aid: 10
% all students receiving aid: 20
% of aid that is merit based: 2
% receiving scholarships: 20
Average grant: $500
Average loan: $10,000
Average total aid package: $7,000
Average debt: $10,500

EMPLOYMENT INFORMATION
Median starting salary: $40,000
State for bar exam: CA, OR, NV, AZ, CO
Pass rate for first-time bar: 60
Employers Who Frequently Hire Grads:
District Attorney's Office; Attorney Generals Office; Public Defender's Office; local private firms.
Prominent Alumni: Jan Scully, Sacramento County District Attorney; Brad Fenocchio, Placer County District Attorney; Robert Holzapfel, Glenn County District Attorney; Hon. Gerald Bakarich, Sacramento County Superior Court Judge; Hon. Sue Harlan, Amador County Superior Court Judge.
Grads Employed by Field (%)
Business/Industry: (10)
Government: (30)
Judicial Clerkship: (5)
Private Practice: (50)
Public Interest: (5)

LINCOLN LAW SCHOOL OF SAN JOSE

One North First Street, San Jose, CA 95113
Admissions Phone: 408-977-7227 • Admissions Fax: 408-977-7228
Admissions E-Mail: admissions@lincolnlawsj.edu
Website: www.lincolnlawsj.edu

INSTITUTIONAL INFORMATION
Public/private: Private
Student-faculty ratio: 1:1

ACADEMICS
Clinical program required: No
Legal writing course requirement: No
Legal methods course requirement: No

ADMISSIONS
Selectivity Rating: 60*
Application fee: $45
Transfer students accepted: Yes

Evening division offered: Yes
Part-time accepted: Yes
CAS accepted: Yes

FINANCIAL FACTS
Fees (in-state/out-of-state): $130

MONTEREY COLLEGE OF LAW

100 Col. Durham St., Seaside, CA 93955
Admissions Phone: 831-582-4000 • Admissions Fax: 831-582-4095
Admissions E-Mail: wlariviere@montereylaw.edu
Website: www.montereylaw.edu

INSTITUTIONAL INFORMATION
Public/private: Private
Student-faculty ratio: 25:1
% faculty part-time: 100
% faculty female: 23
% faculty underrepresented minority: 2
Total faculty: 44

STUDENTS
Enrollment of law school: 100
% part-time: 100
# of countries represented: 3
Average age of entering class: 30

ACADEMICS
Academic Specialties:
Civil Procedure, Commerciäl, Constitutional, Corporation Securities, Criminal, Environmental, Government Services, Human Rights, International, Labor, Property, Taxation, Intellectual Property
Advanced Degrees Offered:
JD, 4 year evening program; Master of Legal Studies, 2 year evening program.
Clinical program required: Yes
Legal writing course requirement: Yes
Legal methods course requirement: Yes
Legal research court requirement: Yes
Moot court requirement: Yes
Public interest law requirement: No

ADMISSIONS
Selectivity Rating: 90
applications received: 120
% applicants accepted: 44
% acceptees attending: 102
Average LSAT: 153
LSAT Range (25th to 75th percentile): 141–169
Average undergrad GPA: 3.17
Application fee: $75
Regular application deadline: 5/1
Early application deadline: 2/15
Early application notification: 3/1
Transfer students accepted: Yes
Evening division offered: Yes

Part-time accepted: Yes
CAS accepted: No

FINANCIAL FACTS
Annual tuition (in-state/out-of-state): $0
Books and supplies: $1,000
Fees (in-state/out-of-state): $0
Room & Board (on/off campus): $0
% first-year students receiving aid: 26
% all students receiving aid: 55
% of aid that is merit based: 30
% receiving scholarships: 25
Average grant: $750
Average loan: $5,000

EMPLOYMENT INFORMATION
% grads employed nine months out: 90
Median starting salary: $35,000
State for bar exam: CA
Pass rate for first-time bar: 40
Employers Who Frequently Hire Grads:
Governmental Offices, Public Agencies, Private Law Firms, Public Defender's Office, District Attorney's Office.
Prominent Alumni: Hon. John Salazar, Judge; Hon. Kim Baskett, Judicial Commissioner; Hon. Denine Guy, Judge; Hon. Russel Scott, Judge; Hon. Sam Lavarato, Jr., Judge.
Grads Employed by Field (%)
Business/Industry: (35)
Government: (5)
Private Practice: (40)
Public Interest: (20)

SAN FRANCISCO LAW SCHOOL

20 Haight Street, San Francisco, CA 94102
Admissions Phone: 415-626-5550 • Admissions Fax: 415-626-5584
Admissions E-Mail: admin@sfls.edu • Website: www.sfls.edu

INSTITUTIONAL INFORMATION
Public/private: Private
Student-faculty ratio: 25:1
% faculty part-time: 100
% faculty female: 13
% faculty underrepresented minority: 1
Total faculty: 32

STUDENTS
Enrollment of law school: 115
% from out-of-state: 0
% part-time: 100
% international: 0
Average age of entering class: 38

ACADEMICS
Advanced Degrees Offered:
JD, 4 year program beginning in August, 4.5 year program beginning in January.

Clinical program required: No
Legal writing course requirement: Yes
Legal methods course requirement: No
Legal research court requirement: Yes
Moot court requirement: Yes
Public interest law requirement: No

ADMISSIONS
Selectivity Rating: 60*
applications received: 150
% applicants accepted: 58
Average LSAT: 1
Average undergrad GPA: 2.80
Application fee: $50
Regular application deadline: 6/5
Transfer students accepted: Yes
Evening division offered: Yes
Part-time accepted: Yes
CAS accepted: No
International Students

FINANCIAL FACTS
Annual tuition (in-state/out-of-state): $6,700
Books and supplies: $350
Fees (in-state/out-of-state): $170
Room & Board (on/off campus): $25,000
% first-year students receiving aid: 0
% all students receiving aid: 0
% of aid that is merit based: 40

EMPLOYMENT INFORMATION
State for bar exam: CA
Pass rate for first-time bar: 30
Employers Who Frequently Hire Grads:
SF Public Defender, SFDA, Private Sector.
Prominent Alumni: Edmund G. Brown (late), Governor of California; Milton Marks, Jr. (late), California State Senator; Leo T. McCarthy, Lt. Governor of California; Hon. Lynn O'Malley Taylor, Judge of the Superior Court; Hon. Henry Needham, Judge of the Superior Court.
Grads Employed by Field (%)
Academic: (5)
Business/Industry: (5)
Government: (20)
Judicial Clerkship: (5)
Private Practice: (60)
Public Interest: (5)

SAN JOAQUIN COLLEGE OF LAW

901 Fifth Street, Clovis, CA 93612-1312
Admissions Phone: 559-323-2100 • Admissions Fax: 559-323-5566
Admissions E-Mail: jcanalin@sjcl.org • Website: www.sjcl.edu

INSTITUTIONAL INFORMATION
Public/private: Private
Student-faculty ratio: 16:1
% faculty part-time: 83

% faculty female: 45
% faculty underrepresented minority: 14
Total faculty: 36

STUDENTS
Enrollment of law school: 185
% male/female: 54/46
% part-time: 87
% underrepresented minority: 26
Average age of entering class: 33

ACADEMICS
Academic Specialties:
Commercial, Corporation Securities, Criminal, Environmental, International, Labor, Taxation
Advanced Degrees Offered:
JD, 3–5 years; MS Taxation, 2 years
Clinical program required: Yes
Legal writing course requirement: No
Legal methods course requirement: Yes

ADMISSIONS
Selectivity Rating: 71
applications received: 135
% applicants accepted: 80
% acceptees attending: 84
Average LSAT: 148
LSAT Range (25th to 75th percentile): 139–174
Average undergrad GPA: 2.9
Application fee: $40
Early application notification: 6/30
Transfer students accepted: Yes
Evening division offered: Yes
Part-time accepted: Yes
CAS accepted: No

FINANCIAL FACTS
Annual tuition (in-state/out-of-state): $10,212
Books and supplies: $550
Fees (in-state/out-of-state): $125
% first-year students receiving aid: 75
% all students receiving aid: 75
% of aid that is merit based: 12
% receiving scholarships: 14
Average grant: $1,600
Average loan: $14,500
Average total aid package: $18,500
Average debt: $62,500

EMPLOYMENT INFORMATION
State for bar exam: CA
Pass rate for first-time bar: 56
Employers Who Frequently Hire Grads:
Local DA and DD; various small firms
Grads Employed by Field (%)
Government: (23)
Private Practice: (70)
Public Interest: (5)

SANTA BARBARA AND VENTURA COLLEGES OF LAW

20 East Victoria Street, Santa Barbara, CA 93101
Admissions Phone: 805-966-0010 • Admissions Fax: 805-966-7181
Admissions E-Mail: admit@venturalaw.edu
Website: www.santabarbaralaw.edu

INSTITUTIONAL INFORMATION
Public/private: Private
Student-faculty ratio: 11:1
% faculty part-time: 100
% faculty female: 26
% faculty underrepresented minority: 5
Total faculty: 19

STUDENTS
Enrollment of law school: 917
% male/female: 51/49

ACADEMICS
Advanced Degrees Offered:
None
Clinical program required: Yes
Legal writing course requirement: Yes
Legal methods course requirement: No
Legal research court requirement: Yes
Moot court requirement: No
Public interest law requirement: No

ADMISSIONS
Selectivity Rating: 78
applications received: 2,528
% applicants accepted: 50
% acceptees attending: 23
Average LSAT: 156
LSAT Range (25th to 75th percentile): 153–158
Average undergrad GPA: 3.2
Application fee: $40
Early application deadline: 3/1
Transfer students accepted: No
Evening division offered: Yes
Part-time accepted: Yes
CAS accepted: No

FINANCIAL FACTS
Annual tuition: $22,000
Books and supplies: $903
Fees (in-state/out-of-state): $0
Room & Board: $9,787
% first-year students receiving aid: 77
% all students receiving aid: 85
% of aid that is merit based: 7
% receiving scholarships: 31
Average grant: $8,071
Average debt: $60,379

EMPLOYMENT INFORMATION

Median starting salary: $58,000
State for bar exam: CA
Pass rate for first-time bar: 71
Grads Employed by Field (%)
Academic: (2)
Business/Industry: (24)
Government: (8)
Judicial Clerkship: (4)
Military: (1)
Private Practice: (58)
Public Interest: (3)

SOUTHERN CALIFORNIA INSTITUTE OF LAW

College of Law

877 South Victoria Avenue, Ventura, CA 93003
***Admissions Phone:** 805-644-2327 • **Admissions Fax:** 805-644-2367*
***Admissions E-Mail:** 1973 scil@msn.com • **Website:** www.lawdegree.com*

INSTITUTIONAL INFORMATION

Public/private: Private
Student-faculty ratio: 5:1
% faculty part-time: 75
% faculty female: 50
% faculty underrepresented minority: 10

STUDENTS

Enrollment of law school: 50
% male/female: 60/40
% from out-of-state: 0
% part-time: 100
% underrepresented minority: 15
% international: 0
Average age of entering class: 32

ACADEMICS

Clinical program required: No
Legal writing course requirement: No
Legal methods course requirement: Yes

ADMISSIONS

Selectivity Rating: 60*
applications received: 50
Average LSAT:
Average undergrad GPA:
Application fee:
Transfer students accepted: No
Evening division offered: No
Part-time accepted: No
CAS accepted: No

FINANCIAL FACTS

Annual tuition (in-state/out-of-state): $6,480
Books and supplies: $500
% of aid that is merit based: 100

EMPLOYMENT INFORMATION

Median starting salary: $30,000
State for bar exam: CA
Pass rate for first-time bar: 50
Employers Who Frequently Hire Grads:
local law firms, government & state agencies.

UNIVERSITY OF WEST LOS ANGELES

School of Law

9920 S. La Cienega Blvd. #404, Inglewood, CA 90301
***Admissions Phone:** 310-342-5210 • **Admissions Fax:** 310-342-5295*
***Admissions E-Mail:** tsmith@uwla.edu • **Website:** www.uwla.edu*

INSTITUTIONAL INFORMATION

Public/private: Private
Religious affiliation: No Affiliation
Student-faculty ratio: 30:1
% faculty part-time: 81
% faculty female: 19
% faculty underrepresented minority: 17
Total faculty: 36

STUDENTS

Enrollment of law school: 262
% male/female: 45/55
% part-time: 87
% underrepresented minority: 24
Average age of entering class:

ACADEMICS

Advanced Degrees Offered:
JD, 3 years, full-time, 4 years, part-time
Clinical program required: No
Legal writing course requirement: Yes
Legal methods course requirement: Yes
Legal research court requirement: Yes
Moot court requirement: No
Public interest law requirement: No

ADMISSIONS

Selectivity Rating: 82
applications received: 59
% applicants accepted: 47
% acceptees attending: 61
Average LSAT: 148
Average undergrad GPA: 3.1
Application fee: $55
Transfer students accepted: Yes
Evening division offered: Yes

Part-time accepted: Yes
CAS accepted: Yes

FINANCIAL FACTS
Annual tuition (in-state/out-of-state): $19,488
Books and supplies: $900
Fees (in-state/out-of-state): $1,600
% first-year students receiving aid: 0
% all students receiving aid: 0
% receiving scholarships: 5
Average total aid package: $0
Average debt: $0

EMPLOYMENT INFORMATION
State for bar exam: CA
Pass rate for first-time bar: 35
Prominent Alumni: Paula Zinneman, California Real Estate Commissioner; Gail Margolis, Director, Mental Health Services, State of CA; Hon. Ron Skyers, LA Superior Court Judge; Lael Rubin, District Attorney's Office.

DALHOUSIE
Law School

Dalhousie Law School, 6061 University Avenue, Halifax, NS B3H 4H9
Admissions Phone: 902-494-2068 • Admissions Fax: 902-494-1316
Admissions E-Mail: law.admissions@dal.ca • Website: www.dal.ca/law/

INSTITUTIONAL INFORMATION
Public/private: Public
Student-faculty ratio: 13:1
% faculty female: 45
% faculty underrepresented minority: 6
Total faculty: 35
Average age of entering class: 25

ACADEMICS
Academic Specialties:
Commercial, Corporation Securities, Environmental, International
Advanced Degrees Offered:
LLM, JSD
Combined Degrees Offered:
LLB/MBA, LLB/MLIS, LLB/MPA, LLB/MHSA, 4 years
Clinical program required: No
Legal writing course requirement: Yes
Legal methods course requirement: No
Legal research court requirement: Yes
Moot court requirement: Yes
Public interest law requirement: No

ADMISSIONS
Selectivity Rating: 92
applications received: 1,285
% applicants accepted: 30
% acceptees attending: 42
Average LSAT: 161
Application fee: $70
Regular application deadline: 2/28
Early application deadline: 11/30
Transfer students accepted: Yes
Evening division offered: No
Part-time accepted: Yes
CAS accepted: No

FINANCIAL FACTS
Annual tuition: $12,475
Books and supplies: $1,200
Room & Board (on/off campus): $3,500
Financial aid application deadline: 10/31
% of aid that is merit based: 43
Average grant: $4,212
Average loan: $8,000
Average total aid package: $2,500

EMPLOYMENT INFORMATION
Employers Who Frequently Hire Grads: Law firms, government agencies, courts.
Grads Employed by Field (%)
Business/Industry: (1)
Government: (1)
Judicial Clerkship: (1)
Private Practice: (97)

MCGILL UNIVERSITY
Faculty of Law

3644 Peel Street, Room #406, , Montreal, QC H3A 1W9
Admissions Phone: (514) 398-6646 • Admissions Fax: (514) 398-8453
Admissions E-Mail: gradadmissions.law@mcgill.ca
Website: www.law.mcgill.ca/graduate/

INSTITUTIONAL INFORMATION
Public/private: Public
Average age of entering class: 35

ACADEMICS
Clinical program required: No
Legal writing course requirement: No
Legal methods course requirement: No

ADMISSIONS
Selectivity Rating: 60*
applications received: 248
% applicants accepted: 49
% acceptees attending: 25
Average undergrad GPA: 3.0
Application fee: $80
Regular application deadline: 2/1
Regular notification: 1/30
Early application deadline: 9/15
Early application notification: 1/30
Transfer students accepted: No
Evening division offered: No
Part-time accepted: No
CAS accepted: No

FINANCIAL FACTS
Annual tuition (in-state/out-of-state): $9,876/$19,698
Books and supplies: $800
Fees (in-state/out-of-state): $3,211/$11,919
Room & Board (on/off campus): $9,600

QUEEN'S UNIVERSITY

Faculty of Law

Macdonald Hall, Rm 200, 128 Union St., Queen's University, Kingston, ON K7L 3N6

Admissions Phone: 613-533-2220 • Admissions Fax: 613-533-6611
Admissions E-Mail: jd@queensu.ca • Website: law.queensu.ca

INSTITUTIONAL INFORMATION
Public/private: Public
Religious affiliation: No Affiliation
Student-faculty ratio: 17:1
Total faculty: 77

STUDENTS
Enrollment of law school: 165
% male/female: 50/50
% part-time: 2
Average age of entering class: 23

ACADEMICS
Academic Specialties:
Civil Procedure, Commercial, Constitutional, Corporation Securities, Criminal, Environmental, Human Rights, International, Labor, Legal Philosophy, Property, Taxation, Intellectual Property
Advanced Degrees Offered:
The Master of Laws (LLM) Program, administered jointly by the Faculty of Law and the School of Graduate Studies and Research, is designed to enable students of high academic merit to pursue advanced study independent research and coursework. Faculty and library resources enable the Faculty of Law to provide intensive supervision for about twelve full-time resident graduate students each year. Students enrolled in the LLM program are required to be in full-time residence in Kingston for two academic terms, normally from September to August, and are expected to complete all requirements for the degree during that period. However, the School of Graduate Studies allows up to 5 years for the completion of the thesis. For information about the Ph.D. program, please see http://law.queensu.ca/graduateStudies/phdProgram.html Application for admission to the Ph.D. and LLM programs must be made online at http://www.queensu.ca/sgsr. Email address is: lawgrad@queensu.ca.
Clinical program required: No
Legal writing course requirement: Yes
Legal methods course requirement: Yes
Legal research court requirement: Yes
Moot court requirement: Yes
Public interest law requirement: Yes

ADMISSIONS
Selectivity Rating: 97
applications received: 2,690
% applicants accepted: 20
% acceptees attending: 30
Average LSAT: 162
Median LSAT: 162
LSAT Range (25th to 75th percentile): 160–164
Average undergrad GPA: 3.8
Application fee: $185
Regular application deadline: 11/1
Transfer students accepted: Yes
Evening division offered: No

Part-time accepted: Yes
CAS accepted: No

FINANCIAL FACTS
Annual tuition (in-state/out-of-state): $15,357/$29,575 intl
Books and supplies: $2,830
Fees (in-state/out-of-state): $1,153/$1,836 intl
Room & Board (on/off campus): 6,930
Financial aid application deadline: 10/31
% all students receiving aid: 85
% of aid that is merit based: 25
% receiving scholarships: 25
Average grant: $2,828
Average loan: $12,225
Average total aid package: $11,985

EMPLOYMENT INFORMATION
% grads employed nine months out: 98
Median starting salary: $60,000
State for bar exam: NY, MA
Pass rate for first-time bar: 100
Prominent Alumni: David R.Allgood (Artsci '70, Law '74, Executive Vice President & General Counsel, Royal Bank of Canada; The Honourable Annemarie Bonkalo, (Artsci '71), Law '76, Chief Justice, Ontario Court of Justice; The Honourable Thomas A. Cromwell, (Mus'73),Law '76, Justice, Supreme Court of Canada; The Right Honourable David Johnston Law '66, LLD'91, Governor General of Canada; The Honourable David Stratas, Law '84, Justice, Federal Court of Appeal.
Grads Employed by Field (%)
Academic: (0)
Government: (10)
Judicial Clerkship: (7)
Military: (0)
Private Practice: (83)
Public Interest: (0)

THE UNIVERSITY OF WESTERN ONTARIO

Faculty of Law

Administrative Wing, Faculty of Law, London, ON N5X 3T5

Admissions Phone: (519) 661-3347 • Admissions Fax: (519) 661-2063
Admissions E-Mail: lawapp@uwo.ca • Website: www.law.uwo.ca

INSTITUTIONAL INFORMATION
Public/private: Public
Religious affiliation: No Affiliation
Student-faculty ratio: 7:1
% faculty part-time: 33
% faculty female: 27
% faculty underrepresented minority: 0
Total faculty: 33

STUDENTS
Enrollment of law school: 161
% male/female: 52/48

% from out-of-state: 15
% part-time: 2
# of countries represented: 5
Average age of entering class: 25

ACADEMICS
Academic Specialties:
Criminal, Taxation, Intellectual Property
Advanced Degrees Offered:
LLB, 3 years; LLM, 1 year (research based)
Combined Degrees Offered:
HBA/LLB; BESc/LLB (four degree programs in Engineering; BSc (Computer Science); LLB Honors BA (History); LLB BA (Kin); LLB Honors BA (MIT); LLB Honors BA (Political Science); LLB LLB/MBA Ph.D. Philosophy
Clinical program required: No
Legal writing course requirement: Yes
Legal methods course requirement: Yes
Legal research court requirement: Yes
Moot court requirement: Yes
Public interest law requirement: No

ADMISSIONS
Selectivity Rating: 96
applications received: 2,374
% applicants accepted: 21
% acceptees attending: 32
Average LSAT: 160
LSAT Range (25th to 75th percentile): 155–173
Average undergrad GPA: 3.72
Application fee: $75
Regular application deadline: 11/1
Transfer students accepted: Yes
Evening division offered: No
Part-time accepted: Yes
CAS accepted: No

FINANCIAL FACTS
Annual tuition (in-state/out-of-state): $11,372/
Books and supplies: $1,400
Fees (in-state/out-of-state): $890/
Room & Board: $8,000
Financial aid application deadline: 10/7
% first-year students receiving aid: 60
% all students receiving aid: 50
% of aid that is merit based: 80
% receiving scholarships: 50
Average grant: $5,000
Average loan: $0
Average total aid package: $3,000
Average debt: $0

EMPLOYMENT INFORMATION
% grads employed nine months out: 99
Median starting salary: $50,000
State for bar exam: NY
Pass rate for first-time bar: 100
Grads Employed by Field (%)
Business/Industry: (2)
Government: (3)
Judicial Clerkship: (3)
Private Practice: (91)

UNIVERSITÉ DE MONCTON
Facute' de droit

Faculte' de droit, Université de Moncton, Moncton, NB E1A 3E9
Admissions Phone: 506-858-4564 • **Admissions Fax:** 506-858-4534
Admissions E-Mail: edr@umoncton.ca • **Website:** www.umoncton.ca/droit

INSTITUTIONAL INFORMATION
Public/private: Public

STUDENTS
Enrollment of law school: 50

ACADEMICS
Clinical program required: No
Legal writing course requirement: No
Legal methods course requirement: No

ADMISSIONS
Selectivity Rating: 60*
Application fee: $39
Regular application deadline: 3/31

UNIVERSITY OF ALBERTA
Faculty of Law

University of Alberta, Law Centre, Edmonton, AB T6G 2H5
Admissions Phone: (780) 492-3115 • **Admissions Fax:** (780) 492-4924
Admissions E-Mail: sgarskey@law.ualberta.ca
Website: www.law.ualberta.ca/

INSTITUTIONAL INFORMATION
Public/private: Public
% faculty part-time: 62
% faculty female: 33
Total faculty: 42

STUDENTS
Enrollment of law school: 518
% male/female: 47/53
% from out-of-state: 27
% part-time: 0
% underrepresented minority: 3
# of countries represented: 2
Average age of entering class: 25

ACADEMICS
Academic Specialties:
Civil Procedure, Commercial, Constitutional, Corporation Securities, Criminal, Environmental, Government Services, Human Rights, International, Labor, Legal History, Legal Philosophy, Property, Taxation, Intellectual Property

Advanced Degrees Offered:
LLM, can be completed in one year, some will take longer; PhD program, newly approved in 2007
Combined Degrees Offered:
LLB/MBA program, 4 years
Clinical program required: No
Legal writing course requirement: Yes
Legal methods course requirement: No
Legal research court requirement: Yes
Moot court requirement: Yes
Public interest law requirement: No

ADMISSIONS

Selectivity Rating: 94
 # applications received: 1,232
% applicants accepted: 30
% acceptees attending: 48
Average LSAT: 161
LSAT Range (25th to 75th percentile): 149–178
Average undergrad GPA: 3.7
Application fee: $100
Regular application deadline: 11/1
Transfer students accepted: Yes
Evening division offered: No
Part-time accepted: Yes
CAS accepted: No
International Students
 TOEFL required of international students

FINANCIAL FACTS

Annual tuition (in-state/out-of-state): $4,686/$4,686
Books and supplies: $1,500
Fees (in-state/out-of-state): $4,773/$4,773
Room & Board (on/off campus): $6,500/$10,000
Financial aid application deadline: 6/1
% first-year students receiving aid: 44
% all students receiving aid: 42
% of aid that is merit based: 30
% receiving scholarships: 23
Average grant: $5,000
Average total aid package: $3,159

EMPLOYMENT INFORMATION

Prominent Alumni: Hon. Beverley McLachlin, Chief Justice Supreme Court of Canada; Hon. E. Peter Lougheed, Former Premier of the Province of Alberta; Frank MacInnis, CEO/President of EMCOR; David McLean, Chairman of CN Railway; Clarence Campbell, Former National Hockey League Pres/Rhodes Scholar.
Grads Employed by Field (%)
Government: (6)
Judicial Clerkship: (7)
Private Practice: (85)
Public Interest: (2)

UNIVERSITY OF BRITISH COLUMBIA
Faculty of Law

1822 East Mall, Vancouver, BC V6T 1Z1
Admissions Phone: *604-822-6303* • **Admissions Fax:** *604-822-9486*
Admissions E-Mail: *admissions@law.ubc.ca* • **Website:** *www.law.ubc.ca*

INSTITUTIONAL INFORMATION

Public/private: Public
Student-faculty ratio: 8:1
% faculty part-time: 69
% faculty female: 32
% faculty underrepresented minority: 7
Total faculty: 143

STUDENTS

Enrollment of law school: 609
% male/female: 52/48
% from out-of-state: 35
% part-time: 2
% underrepresented minority: 8
% international: 4
# of countries represented: 10
Average age of entering class: 25

ACADEMICS

Academic Specialties:
Corporation Securities, Criminal, Environmental, Human Rights, International, Legal History, Taxation
Advanced Degrees Offered:
The Juris Doctor (JD) Degree is a 3 year program full-time. The Master of Laws (LLM) Degree is a 12 month program. The LLM (Master of Laws) and the LLMCL (Master of Law in Common Law) are 1 year programs. The Doctorate (PhD Degree is a 2–4 year program.
Combined Degrees Offered:
The combined JD/MBA Program is 4 years in length and is administered jointly by the Faculty of Commerce and the Faculty of Law. Students are required to complete 86 credits in law and 45 credits in the MBA program. The combined JD/MA (MAPPS) permits students to obtain the degrees of JD and MA in Asia Pacific Policy Studies (MAPPS) through combined enrollment in the Faculty of Law and the Institute of Asian Research. The program is 3 years in length and requires students to take 86 Law credits (excluding IAR 500) and 30 MAPPS credits. The University of British Columbia (UBC) Faculty of Law and the University of Hawai'i (UH) at Manoa William S. Richardson School of Law Joint Legal Education Program allows students who complete the 4 year program to receive a JD degree from UBC and a JD degree from UH. The University of British Columbia (UBC) and the University of Hong Kong (HKU) Joint Legal Education Program allows students who complete the 4 year program to receive a JD degree from UBC and a Postgraduate Certificate in Laws (PCLL program) from HKU.
Clinical program required: No
Legal writing course requirement: Yes
Legal methods course requirement: No
Legal research court requirement: Yes
Moot court requirement: Yes
Public interest law requirement: No

ADMISSIONS

Selectivity Rating: 97
applications received: 2,149
% applicants accepted: 18
% acceptees attending: 49
Average LSAT: 166
Median LSAT: 167
LSAT Range (25th to 75th percentile): 161–168
Average undergrad GPA: 3.85
Median undergrad GPA: 3.85
Application fee: $80
Regular application deadline: 12/1
Early application deadline: 9/30
Transfer students accepted: Yes
Evening division offered: No
Part-time accepted: Yes
CAS accepted: No

FINANCIAL FACTS
Annual tuition (in-state/out-of-state): $10,545/$22,458
Books and supplies: $2,293
Fees (in-state/out-of-state): $967/$967
Room & Board (on/off campus): $9,200/$10,400
% first-year students receiving aid: 67
% all students receiving aid: 69
% of aid that is merit based: 9
% receiving scholarships: 56
Average grant: $5,378
Average loan: $9,840
Average total aid package: $13,037
Average debt: $26,533

EMPLOYMENT INFORMATION
Total 2012 JD Grads: 180
% grads employed nine months out: 96
# employed full-time: 156
# pursuing advanced degree: 4
# unemployed and seeking employment: 6
# not seeking employment: 7
State for bar exam: BC, AB, ON, NY,
Pass rate for first-time bar: 99
Employers Who Frequently Hire Grads: British Columbia Law Firms and Government Agencies (including Lower Mainland, Vancouver Island and Interior); Ontario Law Firms and Government Agencies; Alberta Law Firms and Government Agencies; Yukon/Northwest Territories Law Firms; New York Law Firms; Canadian Public Interest Organizations; Canadian Courts (both Federal and Provincial); Corporate Legal Departments; Canadian Crown Corporations.
Prominent Alumni: Frank Iacobucci, Former Justice Supreme Court of Canada; Lance Finch, Chief Justice of British Columbia; Kim Campbell, Former Prime Minister of Canada; Don Brenner, Chief Justice of British Columbia Supreme Court; Ujjal Dosanjh, Former Premier of British Columbia & Attorney Gen.
Grads Employed by Field (%)
Business/Industry: (1)
Government: (7)
Judicial Clerkship: (9)
Private Practice: (76)
Public Interest: (1)

UNIVERSITY OF CALGARY
Faculty of Law

Murray Fraser Hall, 2500 University Drive NW, Calgary, AB T2N 1N4
Admissions Phone: 403-220-4155 • Admissions Fax: 403-210-9662
Admissions E-Mail: law@ucalgary.ca • Website: www.law.ucalgary.ca/

INSTITUTIONAL INFORMATION
Public/private: Public
Religious affiliation: No Affiliation
Student-faculty ratio: 12:1
% faculty female: 50
Total faculty: 21

STUDENTS
Enrollment of law school: 325
% male/female: 48/52
% from out-of-state: 53
% part-time: 0
% underrepresented minority: 0
# of countries represented: 2
Average age of entering class: 25

ACADEMICS
Academic Specialties:
Environmental
Advanced Degrees Offered:
JD, 3 years; LLM, 15–18 months
Combined Degrees Offered:
JD/MBA, 4 years Law and Masters of Business Administration; JD/MEDes Law and Masters of Environmental Design
Clinical program required: No
Legal writing course requirement: Yes
Legal methods course requirement: Yes
Legal research court requirement: Yes
Moot court requirement: Yes

ADMISSIONS
Selectivity Rating: 97
applications received: 1,243
% applicants accepted: 19
% acceptees attending: 48
Average LSAT: 160
LSAT Range (25th to 75th percentile): 40–99
Average undergrad GPA: 3.57
Application fee: $100
Regular application deadline: 11/1
Transfer students accepted: Yes
Evening division offered: No
Part-time accepted: Yes
CAS accepted: No
International Students
 TOEFL required of international students

FINANCIAL FACTS
Annual tuition (in-state/out-of-state): $13,000/$12,500
Books and supplies: $1,800
Fees (in-state/out-of-state): $581/$581
Room & Board (on/off campus): $8,000/$12,000

University of Manitoba

Robson Hall, Faculty of Law

201 Robson Hall, 224 Dysart Road, University of Manitoba, Winnipeg, MB R3T 2N2

Admissions Phone: *(204) 480-1485* • **Admissions Fax:** *(204) 474-7580*

Admissions E-Mail: *lawadmissions@umanitoba.ca*

Website: *www.umanitoba.ca/law*

INSTITUTIONAL INFORMATION
Public/private: Public
Religious affiliation: No Affiliation
Student-faculty ratio: 15:1
% faculty part-time: 43
% faculty female: 30
Total faculty: 23

STUDENTS
Enrollment of law school: 106
% male/female: 49/51
% from out-of-state: 30
% part-time: 3
% international: 1
Average age of entering class: 24

ACADEMICS
Academic Specialties:
Civil Procedure, Commercial, Constitutional, Corporation Securities, Criminal, Environmental, Government Services, Human Rights, International, Labor, Legal History, Legal Philosophy, Property, Taxation, Intellectual Property
Advanced Degrees Offered:
LLM, 1 year
Clinical program required: No
Legal writing course requirement: Yes
Legal methods course requirement: Yes
Legal research court requirement: Yes
Moot court requirement: Yes
Public interest law requirement: No

ADMISSIONS
Selectivity Rating: 96
applications received: 1,109
% applicants accepted: 26
% acceptees attending: 37
Average LSAT: 162
Median LSAT: 162
LSAT Range (25th to 75th percentile): 153–172
Average undergrad GPA: 3.89
Median undergrad GPA: 3.90
Application fee: $125
Regular application deadline: 11/1
Early application deadline: 11/1
Transfer students accepted: Yes
Evening division offered: No
Part-time accepted: Yes
CAS accepted: No

FINANCIAL FACTS
Annual tuition (in-state/out-of-state): $8,949/
Books and supplies: $3,000
Fees (in-state/out-of-state): $880/
Room & Board (on/off campus): $10,000/$20,000
Financial aid application deadline: 10/1
% of aid that is merit based: 0
Average loan: $11,900
Average debt: $20,000

EMPLOYMENT INFORMATION
% grads employed nine months out: 97
Median starting salary: $45,000
Pass rate for first-time bar: 100

University of New Brunswick

Faculty of Law

Law Admissions Office, Faculty of Law, P.O. Box 44271, University of New Brunswick, Fredericton, NB E3B 6C2

Admissions Phone: *(506) 453-4693* • **Admissions Fax:** *(506) 458-7722*

Admissions E-Mail: *lawadmit@unb.ca* • **Website:** *law.unb.ca*

INSTITUTIONAL INFORMATION
Public/private: Public
Student-faculty ratio: 13:1
% faculty part-time: 9
% faculty female: 33
Total faculty: 20

STUDENTS
% part-time: 0
Average age of entering class: 26

ACADEMICS
Academic Specialties:
Civil Procedure, Commercial, Constitutional, Criminal, Environmental, Human Rights, International, Labor, Legal History, Legal Philosophy, Taxation, Intellectual Property
Advanced Degrees Offered:
LLB (Bachelor of Law), 3 year degree program
Combined Degrees Offered:
LLB/MBA, 4 year degree program
Clinical program required: No
Legal writing course requirement: Yes
Legal methods course requirement: Yes
Legal research court requirement: No
Moot court requirement: Yes
Public interest law requirement: No

ADMISSIONS

Selectivity Rating: 97
applications received: 992
% applicants accepted: 22
% acceptees attending: 39
Average LSAT: 159
LSAT Range (25th to 75th percentile): 151–173
Average undergrad GPA: 3.8
Application fee: $50
Regular application deadline: 3/1
Regular notification: 3/2
Transfer students accepted: Yes
Evening division offered: No
Part-time accepted: No
CAS accepted: No

FINANCIAL FACTS

Annual tuition (in-state/out-of-state): $9,032/$9,032
Books and supplies: $1,500
Fees (in-state/out-of-state): $663/$663
Room & Board (on/off campus): $6,000/
Financial aid application deadline: 11/15
% first-year students receiving aid: 51
% of aid that is merit based: 82
% receiving scholarships: 44
Average total aid package: $1,000

EMPLOYMENT INFORMATION

% grads employed nine months out: 80
State for bar exam: NB, NS, NL, PE, ON
Grads Employed by Field (%)
Government: (6)
Private Practice: (72)

UNIVERSITY OF OTTAWA
Faculty of Law

P.O. Box 450, Stn. A, 57 Louis Pasteur St., Ottawa, ON K1N 6N5
Admissions Phone: *613-562-5800* • **Admissions Fax:** *613-562-5124*
Admissions E-Mail: *comlaw@uottawa.ca*
Website: *www.commonlaw.uottawa.ca*

INSTITUTIONAL INFORMATION

Public/private: Public
Student-faculty ratio: 17:1
% faculty part-time: 100
% faculty female: 51
% faculty underrepresented minority: 15
Total faculty: 53

STUDENTS

Enrollment of law school: 219
% male/female: 42/58
% part-time: 6
Average age of entering class: 26

ACADEMICS

Academic Specialties:
Environmental, Human Rights, International, Intellectual Property
Combined Degrees Offered:
LLB/JD (4 years), LLB /MBA (4 years), LLB/MA (4 years), LLB/LLL (4 years)
Clinical program required: No
Legal writing course requirement: No
Legal methods course requirement: No
Legal research court requirement: No
Moot court requirement: Yes
Public interest law requirement: Yes

ADMISSIONS

Selectivity Rating: 60*
applications received: 3,391
% applicants accepted: 18
% acceptees attending: 35
Average undergrad GPA: 3.53
Application fee: $75
Regular application deadline: 11/1
Transfer students accepted: Yes
Evening division offered: No
CAS accepted: No

FINANCIAL FACTS

Annual tuition: $9,180
Books and supplies: $1,100
Fees (in-state/out-of-state): $439
Room & Board (on/off campus): $10,000
Financial aid application deadline: 3/15
% first-year students receiving aid: 65
% all students receiving aid: 65
% of aid that is merit based: 67
% receiving scholarships: 16
Average grant: $1,815
Average loan: $1,159
Average total aid package: $10,440

EMPLOYMENT INFORMATION

% grads employed nine months out: 60
State for bar exam: NY, MA
Pass rate for first-time bar: 95
Grads Employed by Field (%)
Government: (1)
Judicial Clerkship: (1)
Private Practice: (57)
Public Interest: (1)

UNIVERSITY OF SASKATCHEWAN
College of Law

College of Law University of Saskatchewan, 15 Campus Drive,
Saskatoon, SK S7N 5A6
Admissions Phone: 306-966-5045 • **Admissions Fax:** 306-966-5900
Admissions E-Mail: law_admissions@usask.ca
Website: www.usask.ca/law/

INSTITUTIONAL INFORMATION
Public/private: Public
% faculty part-time: 10
% faculty female: 12
Total faculty: 31

STUDENTS
Enrollment of law school: 300
% male/female: /
% from out-of-state:
% part-time:
% underrepresented minority:
% international:
# of countries represented:
Average age of entering class: 27

ACADEMICS
Clinical program required: No
Legal writing course requirement: Yes
Legal methods course requirement: No
Legal research court requirement: Yes

ADMISSIONS
Selectivity Rating: 93
applications received: 1,082
% applicants accepted: 25
% acceptees attending: 47
Average LSAT: 160
LSAT Range (25th to 75th percentile): 151–172
Average undergrad GPA: 3.32
Application fee: $125
Regular application deadline: 2/1
Transfer students accepted: Yes
Evening division offered: No
Part-time accepted: Yes
CAS accepted: No

FINANCIAL FACTS
Annual tuition (in-state/out-of-state): $8,490/$8,490
Books and supplies: $2,200
Fees (in-state/out-of-state): $729/$729

UNIVERSITY OF VICTORIA
Faculty of Law

P.O. Box 2400, STN CSC, Victoria, BC V8W 3H7
Admissions Phone: 250-721-8151 • **Admissions Fax:** 250-721-6390
Admissions E-Mail: lawadmss@uvic.ca • **Website:** www.law.uvic.ca

INSTITUTIONAL INFORMATION
Public/private: Public
Religious affiliation: No Affiliation
Student-faculty ratio: 7:1
% faculty part-time: 43
% faculty female: 30
% faculty underrepresented minority: 9
Total faculty: 60

STUDENTS
Enrollment of law school: 360
% male/female: 40/60
% from out-of-state:
% part-time: 2
% underrepresented minority: 25
% international:
# of countries represented: 6
Average age of entering class: 26

ACADEMICS
Academic Specialties:
Environmental, International, Intellectual Property
Advanced Degrees Offered:
LLM, 1 year; Ph.D., 3 years
Combined Degrees Offered:
Bachelor of Laws/Master's of Public Administration (LLB/MPA), 4 years; Bachelor of Laws/Master's of Business Administration (LLB/MBA), 4 years; Bachelor of Common Law/Bachelor of Civil Law (LLB/BCL), 4.5 years
Clinical program required: No
Legal writing course requirement: Yes
Legal methods course requirement: Yes
Legal research court requirement: Yes
Moot court requirement: Yes
Public interest law requirement: No

ADMISSIONS
Selectivity Rating: 94
applications received: 1,018
% applicants accepted: 30
% acceptees attending: 35
Average LSAT: 162
LSAT Range (25th to 75th percentile): 157–172
Average undergrad GPA: 3.84
Application fee: $75
Regular application deadline: 2/1
Regular notification: 2/1
Early application deadline: 11/30
Transfer students accepted: Yes
Evening division offered: No
Part-time accepted: Yes
CAS accepted: No

FINANCIAL FACTS
Annual tuition (in-state/out-of-state): $8,178/$21,748
Books and supplies: $2,000
Fees (in-state/out-of-state): $1,009/$1,009
Room & Board (on/off campus): $7,000/$10,000
Financial aid application deadline: 6/1
% of aid that is merit based: 35
Average loan: $12,000
Average debt: $30,000

EMPLOYMENT INFORMATION
% grads employed nine months out: 95
Employers Who Frequently Hire Grads: Local, provincial and national law firms; federal and provincial government; judicial clerkships; and non-profit organizations.
Prominent Alumni: Laura Lynch (1988), International Correspondent, Canadian Broadcasting Corporation; Thomas Crabtree (1983), Chief Judge, BC Provincial Court; Gary Lunn (1995), Federal Minister of State for Sport; Carla Qualtrough (1997), President, Canadian Paralympic Committee; Allan Seckel (1983), Deputy Minister to the Premier of British Columbia and Head of the BC Public Service.
Grads Employed by Field (%)
Academic: (3)
Government: (10)
Judicial Clerkship: (11)
Private Practice: (55)
Public Interest: (2)

UNIVERSITY OF WINDSOR
Faculty of Law

Faculty of Law, 401 Sunset Avenue, Windsor, ON N9B 3P4
Admissions Phone: 519-253-3000 • Admissions Fax: 519-973-7064
Admissions E-Mail: lawadmit@uwindsor.ca • Website: www.uwindsor.ca/law

INSTITUTIONAL INFORMATION
Public/private: Public
Student-faculty ratio: 7:1
% faculty part-time: 63
% faculty female: 17
% faculty underrepresented minority: 6

STUDENTS
Enrollment of law school: 619
% male/female: 50/50
% from out-of-state:
% part-time: 1
% international: 1

ACADEMICS
Academic Specialties:
Civil Procedure, Commercial, Constitutional, Corporation Securities, Criminal, Environmental, Human Rights, International, Labor, Legal History, Legal Philosophy, Property, Taxation, Intellectual Property
Combined Degrees Offered:
Canadian & American Dual JD Program, 3 years; MSW/JD Program, 3–4 years; MBA/JD Program, 3 years
Clinical program required: No

Legal writing course requirement: Yes
Legal methods course requirement: Yes
Legal research court requirement: Yes
Moot court requirement: Yes
Public interest law requirement: No

ADMISSIONS
Selectivity Rating: 60*
applications received: 2,731
% applicants accepted: 18
% acceptees attending: 44
Application fee: $195
Regular application deadline: 1/11
Transfer students accepted: Yes
Evening division offered: No
Part-time accepted: Yes
CAS accepted: No

FINANCIAL FACTS
Annual tuition (in-state/out-of-state): $15,855/$27,487
Books and supplies: $2,000
Fees (in-state/out-of-state): incl/incl
Room & Board (on/off campus): $9,225
% of aid that is merit based: 25
% receiving scholarships: 62
Average grant: $5,130
Average loan: $12,900
Average total aid package: $1,687,849

EMPLOYMENT INFORMATION
State for bar exam: ON, AB, BC, NS, NF
Pass rate for first-time bar: 99
Employers Who Frequently Hire Grads: Law Firms
Prominent Alumni:
Grads Employed by Field (%)
Government: (9)
Judicial Clerkship: (5)
Private Practice: (76)
Public Interest: (2)

YORK UNIVERSITY
Osgoode Hall Law School

1012 Ignat Kaneff Bldg., 4700 Keele Street, Toronto, ON M3J 1P3
Admissions Phone: 416-736-5712 • Admissions Fax: 416-736-5618
Admissions E-Mail: admissions@osgoode.yorku.ca
Website: www.osgoode.yorku.ca

INSTITUTIONAL INFORMATION
Public/private: Public
% faculty female: 44
Total faculty: 160

STUDENTS
Enrollment of law school: 890

ACADEMICS

Advanced Degrees Offered:
JD, 3 years; LLM
Combined Degrees Offered:
JD/MBA, 3 and 4 years; JD/MES, 4 years; JD/MA (Philosophy), 4 years
Clinical program required: No
Legal writing course requirement: No
Legal methods course requirement: No
Public interest law requirement: Yes

ADMISSIONS

Selectivity Rating: 60*
 # applications received: 3,138
Application fee: $90
Regular application deadline: 11/1
Transfer students accepted: Yes
Evening division offered: No
Part-time accepted: No
CAS accepted: No

FINANCIAL FACTS

Annual tuition (in-state/out-of-state): $20,564/$20,564
Books and supplies: $1,500
Fees (in-state/out-of-state): $850/$850
Room & Board (on/off campus): $10,000/$10,000
Financial aid application deadline: 11/1

SCHOOL SAYS . . .

In this section, you'll find schools with extended listings describing admissions, curriculum, internships, and much more. This is your chance to get in-depth information on programs that interest you. The Princeton Review charges each school a small fee to be listed, and the editorial responsibility is solely that of the university.

CHAPMAN UNIVERSITY

AT A GLANCE

Chapman University School of Law offers a collaborative, personalized and rigorous legal education. Graduates develop the skills to provide passionate, ethical and helpful service to their clients and to society.

CAMPUS AND LOCATION

The law school is located on the beautiful 42-acre Chapman University campus, in the heart of charming and historic Old Towne in Orange, California. The Old Towne shopping district, located just one block from campus, has been featured in numerous film productions due to its historic architecture and mix of upscale restaurants and antique shops. The campus setting presents many opportunities to develop interdisciplinary courses and degree programs with other schools of the university, including popular joint programs with the business and film schools. Chapman University was founded in 1861 and the law school was established in 1995. The university is located 15 miles east of Newport Beach, 35 miles south of Los Angeles and 90 miles north of San Diego.

For visitor information, see http://www.chapman.edu/law/about/visiting-school.

DEGREES OFFERED

Chapman offers a traditional Juris Doctor and joint JD/MBA and JD/MFA in Film & Television Producing. LLM programs are offered in Business and Economics, Entertainment and Media Law, International & Comparative Law, Taxation and Trial Advocacy.

PROGRAMS AND CURRICULUM

The School of Law requires 88 academic credits for graduation. First-year courses are required and cover traditional subjects: Contracts, Torts, Civil Procedure, Property, Criminal Law, and Legal Research and Writing. Upper-level courses are also required in the following areas: Constitutional Law, Corporations, Evidence, Federal Income Taxation and Professional Responsibility. Law students may choose from a wide range of non-required electives, and may opt to earn an emphasis certificate in Advocacy and Dispute Resolution, Business Law, Entertainment Law, Environmental, Land Use, and Real Estate (ENLURE), International Law or Tax Law.

FACILITIES

The four-story Kennedy Hall law school building offers an efficient and comfortable learning environment for law students. The structure incorporates modern technology in an architecturally stunning design that utilizes brickwork and structural elements from a preexisting historic school building on the law school site. Classrooms and seminar rooms are equipped with state-of-the-art technology for enhanced teaching and learning, and are capable of accommodating future changes in electronic, visual and on-site learning. The award winning, three-story library occupies one full wing of the building. Two courtrooms, one designed for trials and the other for appellate hearings, provide fully equipped facilities for trial advocacy exercises, mock court competitions and formal hearings by visiting courts. Key student organizations and publications have private offices. The school provides a spacious student lounge with a television, kitchen, vending machines, game room and comfortable couches and tables to ensure that the law school experience at Chapman is both productive and pleasant. The law school is located directly across the street from the Chapman University campus, with multiple eateries and cafes, a spacious fitness center, an aquatic center, lighted tennis courts, indoor basketball courts and an outdoor track.

EXPENSES AND FINANCIAL AID

Chapman offers a generous scholarship program, awarding over 8 million dollars to JD students for the 2012–2013 academic term. Most scholarships are merit-based (LSAT and GPA), with some need-based and special emphasis funds available as well. In addition, Chapman participates in all federal loan programs, so most students can meet all expenses while completing their JD or LLM degree. Tuition and fees for 2013–2014 are $44,830 for full time JD students. There is no additional charge for out-of-state students. The total cost of living expense budget for an off-campus full time JD student for 2013–14, is $27,894 (includes books and supplies).

FACULTY

Chapman law professors include four former U.S. Supreme Court clerks, a former member of the United States Congress, a Nobel laureate and a host of distinguished scholars as well as noted visiting professors and practice-savvy adjunct professors. Students have easy access to the faculty and frequent opportunities to engage them in both formal and informal settings. Faculty papers have been published in prestigious law journals at Harvard, Stanford, UC—Berkeley and numerous other highly regarded law schools.

STUDENTS

Chapman provides a comfortable environment for the rigorous study of law. The school has earned a unique reputation for its friendly, collegial and collaborative students, who enjoy significant opportunities to work closely with faculty, administrators and staff. As a result, every year since 2005, Chapman has been ranked in the top 10 of the nation's law schools for "Best Quality of Life" by The Princeton Review. Chapman has more than 40 student law organizations, providing valuable networking opportunities, special events and guest speakers in a variety of legal specializations. Each spring, students attend the Barrister's Ball, a popular dance party hosted by the Student Bar Association.

ADMISSIONS

The School of Law at Chapman University has a rolling admissions policy. Chapman enrolls approximately 150 students in each first year class. Though substantial weight is placed on traditional measures of academic ability, the law school also recognizes that other factors and attributes contribute greatly to a person's ability to succeed as a law student and lawyer. Thus, in the review process, factors such as grade trends, graduate degrees, overcoming obstacles, work experience, leadership positions, extracurricular activities and community service are also considered.

Applicants are required to submit a formal application, personal statement, resume, two letters of recommendation, a non-refundable application fee of $75, and the CAS report from the Law School Admission Council (LSAC). The CAS report generally includes the LSAT score(s), official transcript(s) and letters of recommendation. Applicants should be advised that the law school averages LSAT scores and does not accept LSAT scores prior to February 2009 for the 2014 entering class. The application deadline is April 15 of each year.

SPECIAL PROGRAMS

Chapman University School of Law has a thriving clinical program. Clinics provide pro bono services to individuals in a diverse range of legal subject areas, including tax, entertainment, elder law, family violence/immigration, constitutional law and mediation. Each clinical program is directed by a faculty member with significant clinical experience. Students participate in classroom and hands-on field work that may include client contact, research projects, document preparation, brief writing and court appearances. Chapman also offers a supplemental bar preparation program designed to provide intensive bar examination practice beyond the existing bar-tested curriculum. The program allows students to maximize their preparation for all three tested elements of the bar examination during their second and third years of law study, contributing to Chapman's impressive overall pass rates.

CAREER SERVICES AND PLACEMENT

Chapman's Career Services Office offers comprehensive career services to aid law students and alumni in selecting their career paths and achieving their employment goals. The attorney counselors help match students' education, skill sets and interests with both traditional and non-traditional employment opportunities. In keeping with Chapman's mission of personalized education, the Career Services Office staff meet personally and often with individual students and alumni to review resumes and cover letters, to aid in self-assessment and goal orientation, to discuss specific opportunities unique to the student's needs, to provide training and support, to give encouragement in exploring career options and to assist in building professional networks.

PACE UNIVERSITY

AT A GLANCE

Pace Law School, founded in 1976, has over 7,000 alumni throughout the country and the world, and its environmental law program is consistently ranked among the top three in the nation. The Law School is recognized for excellence in other areas as well, including but not limited to its international, criminal justice, public interest law, and clinical training and skills programs. The Law School offers full-time and part-time day JD programs, as well as a January Accelerated Program that provides students the opportunity to complete law school in two and a half years instead of three. Also offered are the Master of Laws degrees in Comparative Legal Studies and Environmental Law, including the nation's first graduate-level programs in Climate Change and Land Use and Sustainable Development, and a Doctor of Laws degree in Environmental Law. The Law School is part of Pace University, a comprehensive, independent, and diversified university with campuses in New York City and Westchester County.

CAREER SERVICES AND PLACEMENT

The Law School's White Plains campus houses its academic facilities, student activities center, and residence hall. Just 20 miles from Manhattan, the campus provides a suburban feel in an urban setting. With convenient access to New York City, as well as nearby Connecticut and New Jersey, White Plains is headquarters to some of the nation's largest corporations, a large legal community, and local, county, state, and federal courts. This concentration of resources enables the Law School to attract dynamic professors and speakers and to offer excellent opportunities for internships and post-graduation employment.

DEGREES OFFERED

The Law School offers: JD, LLM in Comparative Legal Studies, JD/LLM and SJD in Environmental Law, JD/MBA and JD/MPA with Pace University, JD/M.E.M. with Yale University School of Forestry and Environmental Studies, JD/M.S. with Bard College, Center for Environmental Policy, JD/M.A. with Sarah Lawrence College in Women's Studies.

PROGRAMS AND CURRICULUM

Students can explore a range of subject areas or pursue a concentrated curriculum. The academic program prepares students to practice in any jurisdiction in the United States. The Law School's accomplished faculty—comprised of dedicated scholars, researchers, and practitioners—brings extensive experience and innovative teaching techniques to the classroom. Many classes have fewer than 25 students, facilitating close faculty-student relationships. Beyond the rich curricular programs, students have access to many extracurricular activities, such as student-run organizations and law reviews, prominent on-campus lecture series, and research in highly regarded Centers.

FACILITIES

The library is an airy, modern facility with wireless access, two computer labs, and six public terminals. Housing over 403,000 volumes, the library also provides access through interlibrary loan to materials held in libraries throughout the United States. It is a member of several library consortia, through which students can use academic libraries located in the New York metropolitan region. The library subscribes to many online databases, including Lexis, Westlaw, HeinOnline, and BNA.

EXPENSES AND FINANCIAL AID

Tuition for the 2013–2014 academic year is $43,630 for full-time students and $32,724 for part-time students. The on-campus residence hall houses 109 full-time students and features single rooms with internet access, telephones, voice mail, and cable television. The Admissions Office also assists students in securing off-campus housing.

A comprehensive aid program includes scholarships, need-based grants, employment loans, and a loan forgiveness program for graduates who choose a public interest career. In 2013, the average scholarship award totaled $18,000/year. Criteria for funds may include financial need, academic merit, education costs, or credit considerations.

FACULTY

The Law School includes 46 full-time and 95 adjunct professors. Faculty scholarship covers diverse areas of law such as Civil Litigation, Civil Procedure, Constitutional Law, Contracts, Evidence, Family Law, Federalism and Separation of Powers, Federal Jurisdiction, Federal Law and Procedure, Property, Torts, Animal Law, Gender Law, Prisoner's Rights, Feminist Legal Theory, Americans with Disabilities Act, Children's Legal Representation, Sexual Orientation and Gender Identity, Environmental, International Commercial Law, Land Use, and Prosecutorial and Judicial Ethics. Many faculty members author widely circulated, influential legal publications and have drafted groundbreaking legislation.

STUDENTS

The diverse 2012 entering class represented 19 states, several countries, and over 105 undergraduate schools. The average age is 25 and the age range is 21–61. The diversity population is 27 percent. The new January-entering class, now in its third year, has 27 students.

SPECIAL PROGRAMS

The Law School offers many clinics, simulation courses, and externships through on-campus centers, institutes, and lawyering skills programs. Students represent clients through the Pace Women's Justice Center's Family Court Externship, preserve individual liberties through the John Jay Legal Services Immigration Justice Clinic, and prosecute criminal cases with Assistant District Attorneys through a prosecution externship. Environmental students work on conservation and development through the Land Use Law Center and accelerate the transition to clean, efficient, and renewable energy alternatives through the Pace Energy and Climate Center.

The international programs allow students to spend a summer abroad at a United Nations War Crimes Tribunal, or intern abroad with law firms and corporate legal departments handling international trade matters. Through judicial externship programs, students hone legal writing skills in the chambers of a state or federal judge.

ADDITIONAL INFORMATION

Address: 78 North Broadway, White Plains, NY 10603 Admissions Phone: 914-422-4210; Admissions E-mail: admissions@law.pace.edu, Web Address: www.law.pace.edu

CAREER SERVICES AND PLACEMENT

Through a variety of outreach activities, the Law School's Center for Career and Professional Development (CCPD) and Public Interest Law Center actively work to foster and maintain relationships with the legal community. The CCPD maintains a website for job postings and recruitment programs and hosts an annual career fair. In addition, the CCPD provides direct, personal career counseling to students and arranges panels, networking events, and presentations to enable students to learn about legal fields and meet members of the bench and bar. The Public Interest Law Center (PILC) provides individual career counseling and a range of events and support for students focused on public interest careers. The PILC also sponsors a Pro Bono Justice Program, offering over ten programs through which law students gain hands-on legal skills while providing needed legal services, and facilitates funding for students working in public interest summer internships.

SOUTHERN ILLINOIS UNIVERSITY

AT A GLANCE

SIU Law is an outstanding public law school that provides an optimal mix of theoretical and experiential educational opportunities in a student-centered environment. Students learn from faculty members who are nationally recognized in their fields and are engaged with the legal community on local, state, national, and international levels. An excellent student/faculty ratio (13:1) allows students to benefit from individualized attention from professors and administrators who genuinely care about their success.

CAMPUS AND LOCATION

SIU Law is located on the Carbondale campus of Southern Illinois University, a Carnegie-classified high research public university offering thirty-four doctoral and professional degree programs, seventy-three programs at the master's level, and more than eighty undergraduate fields of study. SIUC is a 143-year-old university with a diverse, multicultural student body of approximately 20,000. Carbondale is in one of the most scenic areas of Illinois. A national forest, state parks, festivals, and cultural events, combined with a relatively low cost of living, make Carbondale's quality of life among the highest in small cities in Illinois.

DEGREES OFFERED

In addition to the Juris Doctor, SIU offers concurrent JD/Master's degree programs in accountancy, business administration, education, electrical and computer engineering, public administration, and social work. A six-year program offered in cooperation with the School of Medicine permits students to concurrently obtain JD and MD degrees. SIU also offers a Master of Legal Studies (MLS) degree, and a Master of Laws (LLM) degree. The LLM is offered in two forms: a general LLM providing customizable specialization, and a highly specialized LLM in Health Law and Policy.

PROGRAMS AND CURRICULUM

Students receive a strong grounding in legal theory and excellent training in professional skills. In addition to a nationally recognized Lawyering Skills Program and an award-winning professionalism program, SIU provides skills training through clinical and externship programs, a semester-in-practice program, a comprehensive trial and appellate moot court program, and pro bono opportunities including work with the Illinois Innocence Project and the Immigration Detention Center.

The Lawyering Skills Program offers an integrated approach to research, writing, and analysis. This instruction is supplemented by a Writing Across the Curriculum program in the doctrinal courses as well as a comprehensive Academic Success Program.

Beyond the required coursework, students can individualize their learning through a wide variety of elective courses as well as experiential learning opportunities.

The Center for Health Law and Policy advances education, research, and policy dealing with critical issues in health law, public policy and medical ethics.

Students interested in international study can participate in the Ireland Summer Study Abroad Program and a legal globalization course in which they travel abroad for in-depth study of the impact of globalization on culture and legal and political structures in other regions of the world.

FACILITIES

SIU Law's primary facility is the Lesar Law Building. The clinics are located directly across from the main building. All together, the facilities offer over 100,000 square feet of space. Students enjoy 24-hour access to the law library and wireless access to a wide array of electronic legal materials.

EXPENSES AND FINANCIAL AID

2012–2013 full-time, annual tuition: Illinois resident - $13,642; *non-resident - $35,214

*The University permits non-residents to change their residency status to in-state after residing in Illinois for six months.

Financial support from the State of Illinois, combined with a generous program of scholarships, allow SIU Law graduates to enjoy an average debt load that is below the national average. Admissions scholarships are awarded on a competitive basis. Continuing students may apply for additional scholarships and awards. A completed FAFSA is the only required form.

FACULTY

SIU Law faculty are drawn from distinguished practice and academic settings. They are recognized for their legal research and scholarship, as well as for their ability and commitment to teaching. Students have the opportunity to study with professors who are leaders in the legal profession, and to work with them in their service to local, state, and national legal organizations.

STUDENTS

Students come to SIU from all across the country. Although a majority enter law school upon completion of their undergraduate programs, many are returning to school mid-career, after military service, or after completing post-baccalaureate degrees. During law school, students find a welcoming community of peers with whom to study, work, socialize and collaborate on activities ranging from scholarship and skills building to pro bono and public service projects.

ADMISSIONS

Full-time students are admitted each fall. Applicants are required to register with the Credential Assembly Service (CAS), and all undergraduate and graduate transcripts and letters of recommendation must be sent directly to LSAC. The Admissions Committee conducts a holistic review of every file including non-numeric factors. Therefore, all applicants are required to submit a personal statement and a resume in addition to the application for admission.

SPECIAL PROGRAMS

A new and expanding Semester-in-Practice Program allows upper-level students the opportunity to spend a semester studying and working in law placements both in and away from Carbondale. Current programs include "Law and Government" in the state capital, "Criminal Trial Practice" in Chicago and Missouri, and "Health Law and Policy" in the capital or Carbondale.

CAREER SERVICES AND PLACEMENT

Graduates find employment nationwide, with alumni in 49 states and several countries. The Office of Career Services provides services for students and alumni, including individual career counseling, on-campus interviews, career workshops, and access to the online Symplicity system. Students also have the opportunity to participate in regional and national job fairs and career conferences.

ST. THOMAS UNIVERSITY

AT A GLANCE

St. Thomas University School of Law is a highly-regarded student-centered law school where diversity is cherished, a commitment to human rights and international law flourishes, and the Catholic heritage of social justice enhances the education of all faiths.

One of the greatest strengths of our law school is the profound sense of community shared by students, faculty, and administration. St. Thomas Law is a leader in diversity, boasting one of the most culturally diverse student bodies in the country. This global diversity, within such a close-knit community, facilitates a cosmopolitan learning environment where intellectual discovery thrives.

A hallmark of St. Thomas Law is our emphasis on practical training, student engagement, social justice, and ethical behavior. Our students and alumni have a deep sense of justice and charity, and fully utilize their education and experience to lead the way in making our legal system one that truly champions the rights of the powerless.

CAMPUS AND LOCATION

St. Thomas University School of Law's location in Miami, Florida, provides an ideal setting for the study of law. Miami is a vibrant, thriving international community. As a hub of domestic and international trade, an innovative center for fine arts and one of the world's most popular vacation spots, Miami is a dynamic place to live and study. Miami enjoys a rapidly expanding multinational legal community and is home to federal and state trial and appellate courts.

DEGREES OFFERED

St. Thomas University School of Law offers the traditional JD degree, several joint degrees, an LLM and J.S.D. degree and an LL.M in Environmental Sustainability. Our joint degree program includes:

JD/MBA or M.S. in Sports Administration;

JD/MBA in International Business;

JD/MBA in Accounting; and,

JD/M.S. in Marriage and Family Counseling.

St. Thomas University School of Law also offers advanced degrees: the LLM and the J.S.D. in Intercultural Human Rights and the LLM in Environmental Sustainability.

JD students are able to enroll in the classes offered through the LLM programs and can earn Certificates in Human Rights and Environmental Sustainability.

SPECIAL PROGRAMS

St. Thomas University School of Law is committed to student success both in law school and beyond. Using an interactive and cooperative approach to learning, the Academic Support and Legal Research and Writing Programs emphasize the practical skills required for the successful practice of law.

Additionally, St. Thomas Law has a national reputation for its Appellate and Trial Advocacy Programs.

FACILITIES

The law school is designed to provide our students with an outstanding environment for learning the law. Computers and printers are in abundant supply throughout the law library. The law library offers Internet access to online databases and has been a leader in applying technology to legal education. Our wireless network allows students to conduct Internet-based research from anywhere on the law school's campus. Our classrooms and Moot Court Room have all been recently renovated.

EXPENSES AND FINANCIAL AID

Tuition and fees for the JD degree for 2011–2012 are $34,618 per year.

St. Thomas University School of Law offers merit-based scholarships to qualified students. St. Thomas also offers financial assistance apart from scholarships to eligible students in the form of loans. Many St. Thomas Law students receive some form of financial assistance. In addition St. Thomas Law covers the expense for a national BAR prep course for all graduates.

FACULTY

The faculty at St. Thomas is committed to teaching, research and service. Our exceptional faculty members have earned law degrees from some of the nation's most prestigious institutions, including Harvard, Yale, Columbia, Michigan, Pennsylvania, Georgetown, and New York University and many hold advance degrees. They are leaders in their fields with impressive records of publication in top law reviews and extensive practical experience.

A hallmark of the St. Thomas experience is the genuinely close relationship between faculty and students. Because of this relationship St. Thomas Law ranked 4th in the country for "Best Quality of Life" in the 2011 Princeton Reviews' Best 172 Law Schools (2011 edition).

STUDENT LIFE

St. Thomas University School of Law offers a rich student life. With more than twenty student organizations to choose from, students easily find activities that appeal to their interests. Students also enjoy the wealth of activities, cultural and sporting events, and nightlife offered in Miami and Fort Lauderdale.

ADMISSIONS

The Law School Admissions Committee evaluates each applicant's potential for excellence in the study of law. The Law School Admission Test (LSAT) score and undergraduate grade point average are factors; the committee also considers course of study, graduate degrees, work experience, community service, and so forth.

St. Thomas also offers an alternative process for admission for a select group of candidates through our Summer Conditional Admit Program. The Program targets candidates who demonstrate excellent qualitative credentials but lack certain quantitative measurements. Successful candidates are offered admission to the law school for that year's fall entering class.

CAREER SERVICES AND PLACEMENT

St. Thomas Law provides first-rate career services that result in successful and rewarding employment for our graduates, whether their goals are to enter into private law practice, government, business and industry, or public interest areas of law. St. Thomas Law graduates are partners in major national law firms.

STETSON UNIVERSITY

AT A GLANCE

Stetson University College of Law, Florida's first law school, offers full- and part-time JD and LLM programs in Tampa Bay. Stetson is nationally ranked first for advocacy and fifth for legal writing.

CAMPUS AND LOCATION

Stetson's main law campus is located in Gulfport, a suburb of St. Petersburg. A satellite campus in downtown Tampa hosts some classes, conferences, and the Tampa branch of Florida's Second District Court of Appeal.

DEGREES OFFERED

In addition to the Juris Doctor degree, Stetson offers dual-degree programs for the JD/MBA, JD/Grado (Spain), JD/M.I.C.L. (master's in France) and JD/MPH Stetson also offers an on-campus LLM in International Law and online LLM programs in Advocacy and Elder Law.

PROGRAMS AND CURRICULUM

Stetson's curriculum combines a strong foundation of legal doctrine and theory with a nationally ranked program in the practical advocacy, legal research and writing skills required to become a successful attorney.

Stetson allows students the opportunity to specialize their legal education through a variety of programs. JD students may earn certificates of concentration in advocacy, elder law, environmental law, international law and social justice advocacy. High-achieving students may be invited to participate in Stetson's Honors Program based on several factors including excellent performance in the required curriculum. Each year, a limited number of students interested in intellectual property may participate in Stetson's semester exchange program with the University of New Hampshire School of Law.

Stetson's extensive international offerings include a fall semester in London, exchange programs with law schools in France, Australia and Spain, summer programs in Argentina, China, the Netherlands, Spain and Switzerland, as well as a winter break course in the Cayman Islands.

Stetson also has centers for excellence and institutes in the fields of advocacy, biodiversity law, Caribbean law, elder law, higher education law, international law and veterans law. Stetson is home to the Stetson Law Review, the Journal for International Aging Law and Policy, the Journal for International Wildlife Law and Policy, and the new Stetson Journal of Advocacy and the Law.

FACILITIES

Stetson's main law campus features technologically advanced classrooms, five courtrooms, recreational facilities and the Dolly and Homer Hand library, culminating in an idyllic environment for the study of law. The Tampa Law Center includes two courtrooms, fully equipped classrooms and seminar rooms, study rooms, and a satellite law library. The law libraries contain more than 419,000 volumes, 750,000 titles and 48 group study rooms. There is a laptop requirement for all students, and high-speed wireless access is available throughout both campuses.

EXPENSES AND FINANCIAL AID

2013–2014 full-time tuition (fall/spring): $37,462

2013–2014 part-time tuition (fall/spring/summer): $32,592

Scholarships are offered on a competitive basis, and need and merit scholarships are offered for continuing students. There is no financial aid deadline, and a completed FAFSA is the only required form.

FACULTY

Stetson's full-time regular faculty of 48 professors engage in projects of regional, national, and international prominence, and they make teaching and working with students their top priority. More than 50 practicing attorneys and judges serve as adjunct professors each semester.

STUDENTS

Stetson offers cultural programs, experiential education trips, community service opportunities, leadership workshops, and around 45 active student organizations. The ABA Law Student Division has recognized Stetson with numerous regional and national awards, and Stetson's Student Leadership Development Program was awarded the ABA's prestigious E. Smythe Gambrell Award for excellence in professionalism. Stetson students donate more than 24,000 hours of pro bono service annually to more than 150 organizations.

ADMISSIONS

Stetson University College of Law admits full-time and part-time students each fall. As a prerequisite to enrollment, applicants are required to have earned a baccalaureate degree from a college or university that is accredited by an accrediting agency recognized by the U.S. Department of Education. A final, official transcript evidencing the conferral of the degree must be submitted before enrollment. All applicants are required to take the LSAT and register with the JDCAS. One letter of recommendation is required, and a maximum of three letters will be accepted. The personal statement is also required. More details are available at www.law.stetson.edu/admissions. An equal opportunity education institution, Stetson is fully accredited by the American Bar Association and has been an Association of American Law Schools member since 1931.

SPECIAL PROGRAMS

Recognized by U.S. News as No. 1 for advocacy and No. 5 for legal writing, Stetson routinely wins international, national, regional and state competitions for alternative dispute resolution, mock trial and moot court.

Stetson offers upper-level students a wide variety of opportunities to work closely with attorneys and judges, and, in some cases, actually represent clients and try cases. Hundreds of students are placed annually into 36 different clinical, internship and externship programs, including competitive opportunities to intern with the Florida and Georgia Supreme Courts, the U.S. Court of Appeals for Veterans Claims, and organizations in Washington, D.C.

CAREER SERVICES AND PLACEMENT

Stetson's commitment to helping students achieve their goals is reflected in its strong career development program. An accessible career development staff supports students' professional choices through individual coaching sessions and group workshops on subjects ranging from interviewing techniques to résumé writing. Stetson also offers a comprehensive program of bar preparation services, including custom study plans, individual counseling, bar-prep seminars, and sample exam grading by a former grader for the Florida Board of Bar Examiners. Stetson Law alumni reside in 48 states and 22 countries, and approximately 90 percent of recent graduates practice in Florida.

TOURO LAW CENTER

AT A GLANCE

Touro Law Center is committed to providing the best in legal education. Touro Law students are encouraged to examine the moral goals of the law while promoting social justice and community service. Touro Law, accredited by the American Bar Association (ABA) and a member of the Association of American Law Schools (AALS), offers students full-time and part-time JD programs as well as dual degree and LLM programs.

AT A GLANCE (SHORT FORM)

Touro Law Center is committed to providing the best in legal education. Touro Law students are encouraged to examine the moral goals of the law while promoting social justice and community service.

CAMPUS AND LOCATION

Touro Law occupies a 185,000 sq. ft state-of-the-art building in Central Islip on the south shore of Long Island, New York. Touro Law is at the center of what is arguably the nation's first integrated "law campus," comprised of a U.S. courthouse and New York State court center. More than mere physical proximity, students interact with legal professionals daily through classroom instruction, court visits, clinics, externships and other academic and social forums.

DEGREES OFFERED

Touro Law offers full-time and part-time (4 year part-time day, 4 year part-time evening and 5 year part-time evening) Juris Doctor programs as well as JD/MBA, JD/MPA and JD/M.S.W. dual degrees. Touro also offers an LLM degree in General Studies to graduates of U.S. law schools and an LLM degree in U.S. Legal Studies for foreign law graduates.

PROGRAMS AND CURRICULUM

The cornerstone of Touro Law's curriculum is the Collaborative Court Program - a new, integrative three-year curricular option for students. This comprehensive learning method has been designed to prepare students for the successful practice of law. The Program is comprised of three separate components: Court Observation, Court Integration and Court Specialization. Touro Law also offers several clinics: Civil Rights Litigation, Elder Law, Family Law, Mortgage Foreclosure and Bankruptcy, Not-for-Profit Corporation Law and Veterans' and Servicemembers' Rights.

Touro students also have the opportunity to participate in a variety of externships including Business, Law & Technology Externship, Civil Practice Externship, Criminal Law Externship, Judicial Clerkship, and the US Attorney's Office Externship. In addition, Touro Law also offers vibrant study abroad opportunities in Croatia, India, Germany, Israel and Vietnam as well as summer internships in law firms, courts, and government offices in Europe and Israel.

FACILITIES

Touro Law Center's facility was designed to be a student-centered learning center. The building houses a clinical wing, a state-of-the-art auditorium, a public advocacy center, mock trial classrooms, computer labs, meeting spaces, cafeteria, bookstore, the Gould Law Library and more. The infrastructure is high-tech, supporting wireless access, smart classrooms and new technology.

EXPENSES AND FINANCIAL AID

Generous institutional scholarship aid is available to entering and continuing students. Awards include dean's fellowships, merit scholarship, and incentive awards. Touro Law also offers stipends for Public Interest Law Fellowships, judicial clerkships, and summer federal work-study placements. Touro provides access to federal loans and work study, New York State loan and assistance programs, and need-based Touro Grants. Most students receive some form of financial aid, and 60 percent of entering students receive scholarships.

FACULTY

Touro Law's faculty is comprised of 50 full-time faculty members. Every entering student is assigned a faculty advisor, matched by background or interest area, for discussions on any aspect of the law school experience including study strategy, course selection, career goals, etc. With an open-door policy and a student faculty ratio of 16:1, Touro Law students benefit from a personal and dynamic educational experience.

STUDENTS

The Law Center's students, coming from diverse backgrounds and experiences, represent over 112 undergraduate institutions and a broad mix of majors. Women comprise approximately 48 percent of the total enrollment; minorities, 29 percent.

ADMISSIONS

Touro Law Center seeks to identify applicants who show an ability to pursue the study of law successfully and to make an important contribution to the Law Center's educational program, to the legal profession and to society. While significant weight is attached to a student's undergraduate cumulative grade point average and Law School Admission Test (LSAT) score(s), the selection process is not strictly mathematical and includes an evaluation of several other factors including professional experiences and achievement, writing ability, rigor of undergraduate institution, letters of recommendation, and more.

SPECIAL PROGRAMS

Touro Law Center is home to the William Randolph Hearst Public Advocacy Center, the first of its kind in the nation. Touro Law provides furnished offices at no cost to 15 non-profit legal advocacy agencies while providing hands-on working opportunities for students.

ADDITIONAL INFORMATION

Touro Law Center provides a unique program of outside-the-classroom assistance. Teaching assistants (TAs) review material covered in class and conduct small-group sessions on effective study methods and test-taking techniques. The Writing Resources Center offers workshops and tutorials to assist students in producing a professional work product. The Legal Education Access Program (LEAP) enhances the experience of students of color through a four-week summer program for new students with additional mentoring during the academic year. The Honors Program, beginning in the second year, allows outstanding opportunities for students who receive additional scholarship assistance and access to academic enrichment initiatives.

CAREER SERVICES AND PLACEMENT

The Career Services staff assists students and graduates in securing part-time, full-time and summer employment. In addition to placing students with national, regional and local law firms, there are opportunities in federal, state, and local courts and government agencies, and in the legal departments of corporations and municipalities.

THE UNIVERSITY OF THE DISTRICT OF COLUMBIA
David A. Clarke School of Law

AT A GLANCE

The University of the District of Columbia David A. Clarke School of Law (UDC-DCSL) is the only public law school in the Nation's Capital. The School of Law is unique among law schools, with a mission to recruit and enroll students from under-represented communities. The School of Law is also one of the most diverse student bodies in the country, with the most extensive clinical requirements of any law school in the country.

CAMPUS AND LOCATION

UDC-DCSL is located on the campus of the University of the District of Columbia, the country's only urban public land grant Historically Black University. The University and School of Law are located in the upper Northwest section of the District on Connecticut Avenue, one of the city's major thoroughfares. The Van Ness/UDC Metro station is located directly in front of the University, making the campus easily accessible. The campus, which is undergoing a major "greening" with over 100,000 square feet of green roofs and other amenities, is surrounded by a quiet tree-lined residential community, Rock Creek Park, the National Zoo, embassies and small businesses. The University sits on several acres of land on Connecticut Avenue, NW.

DEGREES OFFERED

The School of Law offers the Juris Doctor (JD) degree and full-time day and part-time evening divisions, and the LLM degree in Clinical Legal Education, Social Justice and Systems Change.

PROGRAMS AND CURRICULUM

The School of Law offers the best of both worlds for the study of law – a traditional legal education supplemented by hands-on clinical training. Students are required to complete 90 credits to graduate, 14 of which are earned in two semesters of clinical work. The Clinics include Legislation, Juvenile & Special Education, Community Development, Low-Income Tax, HIV/AIDS, Immigration & International Human Rights, and Whistleblower Protection (at the Government Accountability Project.) Students are also required to complete 40 hours of community service, and may participate in a ten- or four-credit internship elective.

FACILITIES

In August 2011, the School of Law moved to a new spacious five-story facility, located about one block from the main University campus.

Every seat in the $1.6 million recently-renovated Mason Law Library is wired and WIFI access is available everywhere in the library. The classrooms and lecture halls are wired and high-tech.

EXPENSES AND FINANCIAL AID

The School of Law offers its students an affordable legal education and a comprehensive financial aid program. Tuition for District of Columbia resident full-time students is $10,620 per year (2013–2014). Tuition for non-DC resident full-time students is $21,240 per year (2013–2014). Tuition for DC resident part-time students is $7560 per year (2013–2014), and $15,120 per year for non-DC resident part-time students. Non-DC resident students may be eligible for resident tuition after residing in the District for one year. Students may be eligible as well for the following financial assistance: Federal loans, merit scholarships, need-based grants, work-study, Dean's Fellowships, Continuing Student Scholarships, and the full-tuition three-year Advocate for Justice Scholarship. For more information on the law school's financial aid program, you may visit www.law.udc.edu.

ADMISSION

The School of Law considers the entire applicant profile when rendering an admission decision. While the candidate's LSAT and grades play an important role in the admission process, other factors are also considered, e.g., the applicant's range of life experiences, the content and mechanics of the candidate's application essays, community involvement, family background, and letters of recommendations.

The average LSAT for the 2012 entering class is 152.

The Committee on Admission requests TOEFL on a case-by-case basis.

SPECIAL PROGRAMS

Other programs for students include the Summer Public Interest Fellowship Program, for which all 1L's are eligible to receive $4,000 grants for full-time, lawyer-supervised, law-related work at a non-profit, government agency, or judge's chambers anywhere in the world; the for-credit Internship Program; and federal work-study opportunities.

ADDITIONAL INFORMATION

Students enjoy a 12-to-1 student-faculty ratio and individualized attention from and access to faculty and administration, The School of Law also affords students a spirited, committed and collegial setting and community in which to study law.

CAREER SERVICES AND PROFESSIONAL DEVELOPMENT

For more information on career services and professional development, you may visit the school website at www.law.udc.edu or contact Career Services Director Dena Bauman at dbauman@udc.edu. The School of Law has over 3,000 alumni, the majority of whom are connected to the School of Law via email. Alumni provide invaluable resources to both students and other alumni. For information, contact Alumni Director Joseph Libertelli at jfl@udc.edu.

DEAN INTERVIEWS

In this section, deans from several schools provide detailed answers to our questions about their law schools' resources, academic programs, and financial aid, as well as questions about students, graduates, and applicants. The Princeton Review charges each school a small fee to appear in this section.

SOUTHERN ILLINOIS UNIVERSITY

Q. Are there particular strengths of your school associated with your parent university, such as key centers / institutes of research, facilities, joint degree programs with other schools on campus, or other synergies?

Dean Fountaine

A. Southern Illinois University Carbondale is a Carnegie-classified high research public university offering thirty-four doctoral and professional degree programs, seventy-three programs at the master's level, and more than eighty undergraduate fields of study. Being part of this system allows the law school the opportunity to work in collaboration with a wide variety of academic partners. Our longest standing and most developed partnership is with the School of Medicine. This partnership, which started in the early 1980s, allowed SIU to offer one of the first JD/MD programs in the nation. It also allows us to operate the Center for Health Law & Policy which gives students opportunities to attend annual programs such as a lecture series, Bioethicist-in-Residence, and Health Policy Institute, as well as experiential learning opportunities through the Elder Law Clinic, the Law & Health Project, and the Health Law & Policy Semester-in-Practice Program. We are also the host of the annual National Health Law Moot Court Competition.

Q. Students who are interested in law and policy have the advantage of attending events and programs organized by the Paul Simon Public Policy Institute whose guests have included individuals such as Coretta Scott King, Ted Sorenson, Walter Cronkite, Maya Angelou, Morris Dees, and Barbara Bush.

A. An increasing number of our students are opting to distinguish themselves in the evolving legal employment market by earning a joint degree. Students can couple a JD with a Masters of Accountancy, Masters of Business Administration, Masters of Science in Education, Masters of Public Administration, Masters of Social Work, Masters of Electrical & Computer Engineering, or Doctor of Medicine.

Q. Describe the faculty at your school. What areas of academics / research have become the "hallmarks" of your faculty? What level of interaction do professors have with their students? (High vs. moderate, in-class only vs. outside of class, one-on-one mentoring or not)

A. Our faculty members are drawn from distinguished practice and academic settings. They are known not only for their legal research and scholarship, but also for their ability and commitment to teaching. We have nationally recognized scholars who are active with local, state, and national bar associations where they serve as leaders on committees that help shape policy, educate the bench and bar, draft and pass legislation, etc.

Q. We currently offer Specializations in four areas in which our faculty have developed particularly robust academic and experiential opportunities: Health Law & Policy, International & Comparative Law, Business & Transactional Law, and Intellectual Property.

A. Our nationally recognized Lawyering Skills Program and the ABA Gambrell Award- winning Professionalism Series bridge the gap between theory and practice and prepare graduates to function effectively as professionals. One component of the professionalism program is the Induction Ceremony during which first-year students recite the "Declaration of Professional Commitment" that they drafted as a class, with guidance from practicing attorneys and judges. Most years a member of the Illinois Supreme Court presides over the ceremony. SIU was the first law school in Illinois, and among the first in the country, to have a program like this for first-year students.

Q. With a total student body of less than 400 students, faculty are able to provide a highly personalized learning environment. Students can expect faculty to maintain an open-door policy, and serve as mentors throughout their time as students, and sometimes throughout their careers as attorneys.

A. Please describe extracurricular academic programs at your school (e.g., Clinics, Study Abroad, Journals)

Q. We have three, live-client Clinics that allow our students the opportunity for hands-on training, under the close supervision of expert attorneys. In the Civil Practice/Elder Law Clinic, students work under attorney supervision to provide civil legal representation to individuals who are 60 years or older and live in one of the 13 southern most counties in Illinois. Students practice legal skills such as case management, legal drafting, client interviewing, presenting cases in court, etc. In the Domestic Violence Clinic, students work under the supervision of an attorney to represent victims of domestic violence. Students learn about the Illinois Domestic Violence Act and its enforcement, and practice legal skills such as client interviewing, court representation, legal drafting, etc. In the Juvenile Justice Clinic, students work under the supervision of an attorney to perform legal services and duties to minors for whom the clinic attorney has been appointed guardian ad litem. The guardian ad litem represents the best interests of these minors for whom neglect, abuse or dependency petitions have been filed.

A. Our Academic Success Program provides opportunities for first-year students to master the skills of legal analysis that they need to succeed in law school. All 1L students are placed in a small study group in their first semester. The study group is led by an upper class student (Taylor Mattis Fellow) who helps the 1Ls learn about law school classes, grading, exam protocol, etc., and also offers feedback on briefing, outlining and other skills. Students have the chance to join optional second-semester study groups that focus on reviewing material and preparing for exams. The Program also offers preparation for bar admission and the bar exam.

Q. We offer three Semester-in-Practice programs. The Law & Government Semester-in-Practice offers second- and third-year law students the opportunity to learn about State and Local Government while living and working in the capital, Springfield, Illinois. Residence in Springfield, allows students to work in externship placements under the supervision of government or quasi-government lawyers, while still earning a full semester (15 credit hours) of academic credit. The Criminal Trial Semester-in-Practice Program combines an externship at the Missouri Public Defender's Office in Jackson, Missouri, or in State's Attorney offices in the Chicago area, with criminal law courses. In the Health Law and Policy Semester Away Program students are able to spend a semester in Springfield, IL, where they earn academic credit working at externship sites such as hospital and health care systems, health-related government agencies, and the SIU School of Medicine.

A. Qualifying students have the opportunity to write for the Southern Illinois University Law Journal or the Journal of Legal Medicine. The SIU Law Journal, published since 1976, is staffed and administered by students with the assistance of a faculty advisor. The Journal publishes articles of general scholarly interest, and devotes one issue each year to a survey of significant legal developments in Illinois during the previous year. The Journal of Legal Medicine is the official quarterly publication of the American College of Legal Medicine. It is regarded as one of the prominent publications in the nation in the area of health law. It offers in-depth discussion of topics related to legal medicine, health law and policy, professional liability, hospital law, food and drug law, medical legal research and education, and a broad range of related topics. In each issue a "Commentary" section features articles written by SIU law students.

Q. We have an active and respected program for students interested in moot court. Early in the fall semester, second-year students may participate in the SIU Intramural Moot Court Competition. In teams of two, the students write a brief and argue a challenging problem of federal law. Most years, the Intramural Competition will use the problem written for the National Health Law Moot Court Competition, which SIU hosts in November. After the first year, students may compete for selection to the Appellate Advocacy Division of the Moot Court Board. Students interested in appellate advocacy participate in a multi-round Intramural Moot Court Competition during the fall of their second year. From these students, several are selected to represent the school in national moot court competitions. Teams from the SIU School of Law have had much success in national competitions for more than twenty years. Students who are interested in trial rather than appellate advocacy may try out in their second year for membership in the Trial Advocacy Division of the Moot Court Board.

A. In partnership with the University of Missouri - Kansas City School of Law we offer an annual Ireland Summer Study Abroad Program. This program provides students both an opportunity to travel and earn up to 7.0 hours of ABA-approved credit. The Program takes place at four premier institutions: the Diseart Cultural Centre in Dingle, National University of Ireland-Galway, University College University-Dublin and Prifysgol Bangor University, School of Law in Wales. The program is designed to provide students with an understanding of the legal structure, institutions, and social history of both Irish political entities and the laws applicable to the conduct of commerce by foreign (including U.S.) companies in Ireland and through Ireland to the European continent.

Q. We also offer a Legal Globalization and Comparative Law course which introduces students to the phenomenon of globalization and its impact on cultures and legal systems using different countries and topics of examination as case studies. Students will learn about a particular country and a specific legal topic. This might include examination of a country's history, legal systems, culture, and languages. Students will travel to the country of examination with their instructor, typically for a period of one week, to continue their studies. Activities in the country of destination might include service learning and other experiential learning opportunities, lectures from foreign academics, business leaders, governmental officials, and attorneys, and visits to legal institutions.

Career / Internship Placement

Q. Describe the typical internships among your students, and the full-time career placement mix (in terms of types of employers and jobs). What is the geographic diversity of your graduates (across states and countries)?

A. Through our Public Interest Externship Program, students work in publicly funded law offices, non-profit agencies or corporations. Common placements include prosecutors' or defenders' offices, legal services offices, government offices with legal departments, etc. Although many of our placements are in Illinois (including Chicago and Springfield), we have approved sites all across the country. Over summers, many students return to their home states or visit states where they hope to work, and that has allowed us to develop a long list of approved sites based on these experiences. In addition to the states surrounding Illinois, students have also worked as far away as Alaska, New York, Washington state, and Canada. Because of our health law program, agency placements have included sites like the Centers for Disease Control and the National Institute of Health. Students who participate in the Law and Government Semester-in-Practice Program in the state capital can choose from a long list of State and Local Government Externship sites, e.g., the Opinions Division of the Illinois Attorney General's Office; Legal Counsel for the Illinois Speaker of the House; Legal Counsel for the Illinois Joint Legislative Committee on Administrative Rules; Legal Counsel for the Illinois Senate President; the Illinois Legislative Reference Bureau; the Illinois Department of Aging; Legal Counsel for the Illinois Governor; etc.

Q. Students may also participate in the Judicial Externship Program where they can serve as student law clerks for judges in locations approved by the supervising professor. Student clerks observe court proceedings, do research and writing and take part in all or most activities in Judge's chambers.

A. Our alumni enjoy success in many different areas, both in the public and private sectors. Alumni practice law in 49 of the 50 states and internationally in over 10 countries. More than 80 alumni have or are currently filling federal and state judgeships.

Q. Speaking to the qualified students comparing your school to your top peer schools, what are the key advantages of your school?

A. SIU School of Law provides an excellent and accessible legal education that creates life-changing opportunities for our students. We offer a distinctive value as a small, student-centered law school at a major research university. SIU Law is a vibrant learning community where students work closely with their professors, who are dedicated teachers, devoted mentors, and expert scholars with significant practice experience. An SIU legal education combines innovative teaching, practical hands-on training, and collaboration among students and faculty on groundbreaking legal research and meaningful public service projects. We inspire students to realize their full potential and to embrace new perspectives through pro bono work, clinics, externships, and global educational opportunities. The SIU School of Law empowers students with the transformative experiences and skills they need to realize their dreams and to make a difference now and throughout their careers.

As one of only three law schools in Illinois that receive financial support from the state of Illinois, we are able to offer this level of quality for one of the lowest tuition rates in the country. This means that our graduates benefit from an average debt load below the national average, which gives them the freedom to consider a much wider range of career choices, including public interest work.

INDEX

ALPHABETICAL INDEX

INDEX BY LOCATION

$30,000–$40,000

NOTES

NOTES

NOTES

NOTES